DISCOVER
BRITAIN

THE ILLUSTRATED WALKING AND EXPLORING GUIDE

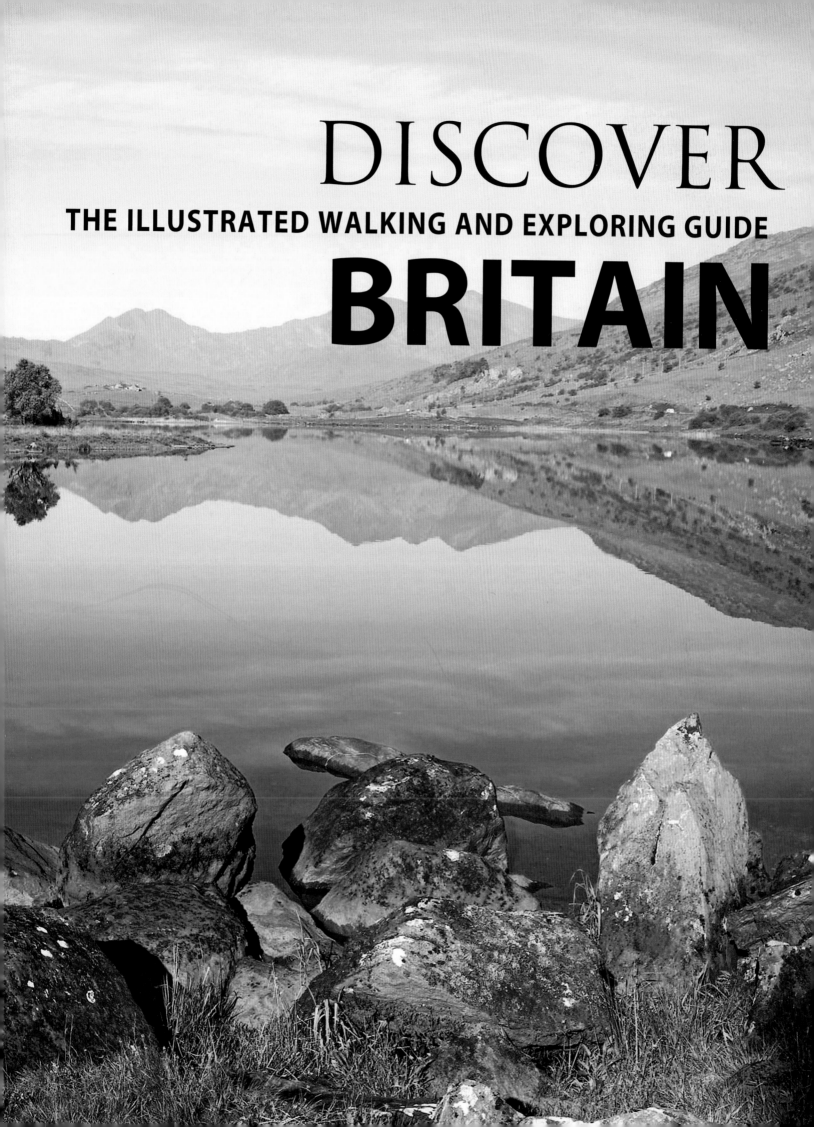

DISCOVER

THE ILLUSTRATED WALKING AND EXPLORING GUIDE

BRITAIN

Produced by AA Publishing
© AA Media Limited 2010

First published 2001
Reprinted 2002
Revised and updated 2009

Published by AA Publishing (a trading name of AA Media Limited, whose registered office is Fanum House, Basing View, Basingstoke, Hampshire RG21 4EA; registered number 06112600).

This product includes mapping data licensed from the Ordnance Survey® with the permission of the Controller of Her Majesty's Stationery Office. © Crown Copyright 2010. All rights reserved. Licence number 100021153.

978-0-7495-6453-7
978-0-7495-6508-4 (SS)

A CIP catalogue record for this book is available from the British Library.

The contents of this book are believed correct at the time of printing. Nevertheless, the publishers cannot be held responsible for any errors or omissions or for changes in the details given in this book or for the consequences of any reliance on the information it provides. This does not affect your statutory rights. We have tried to ensure accuracy in this book, but things do change and we would be grateful if readers would advise us of any inaccuracies they may encounter.

We have taken all reasonable steps to ensure that these walks are safe and achievable by walkers with a realistic level of fitness. However, all outdoor activities involve a degree of risk and the publishers accept no responsibility for any injuries caused to readers whilst following these walks. For more advice on using this book and walking safely see page 8.

Visit AA Publishing at theAA.com/shop

Some of these routes may appear in other AA walks books.

Prepared for AA Publishing by Starfish Design, Editorial and Project Management Ltd

Cover created by Tracey Butler Design

For AA Publishing:
Editor: David Popey
Picture Research: Lesley Grayson
Image Manipulation and Internal Repro: Sarah Montgomery and James Tims
Cartography provided by the Mapping Services Department of AA Publishing

Original contributors: Tony Aldous, Chris Bagshaw, Juliet Barker, Nick Channer, Christine Collins, Paddy Dillon, Martin Dunning, Rebecca Ford, John Gilham, David Hancock, Des Hannigan, Christopher Knowles, Alison Layland, Laurence Main, Guy Mansell, Terry Marsh, Julie Meech, John Morrison, Paul Murphy, Brian Pearce, Richard Sale, Hamish Scott, Roly Smith, Christopher Somerville, Hugh Taylor & Moira McCrossan, Hilary Weston, Stephen Whitehorn, Angela Wigglesworth, Nia Williams, David Winpenny.

Printed and bound by Oriental Press

A04141

Pages 2–3: Snowdon reflected in Llynau Mymbyr near Capel Curig
Pages 10–11: Cattle Grazing at Uley Bury, Gloucestershire

CONTENTS

Regional Contents with Key Map   6–7

About this Book   8–9

Discover Britain   10–11

THE WEST COUNTRY

Regional Map   15

Literary Settings: Writers in the West Country   28–29

Church and Home: Buildings in the Landscape   42–43

West Country Walks   54–69

SOUTHERN ENGLAND

Regional Map   73

Customs and Festivals   82–83

The New Forest   94–95

Steam Railways   104–105

London   114–129

Cosmopolitan London   116–117

Pomp and Circumstance   118–119

London Buildings, Old and New   120–121

The Green Lungs of London   122–123

Crossing the Thames   124–125

Off-centre London   126–127

Southern England Walks   128–141

THE HEART OF ENGLAND

Regional Map   144

Waterways of Central England   154–155

Rare Breeds and Traditional Crops   168–169

New Towns and Old Cities   176–177

The Heart of England Walks   184–197

WALES & THE BORDERS

Regional Map   201

The Welsh Marches – A Frontier Land   212–213

The National Parks of Wales   224–225

Wales & the Borders Walks   230–245

NORTHERN ENGLAND

Regional Map   249

The Peak District   256–257

The Abbeys of the North   262–263

The North York Moors   272–273

Northern England Walks   284–297

SCOTLAND

Regional Map   301

The Wildlife of Scotland   312–313

Scotland's Strongholds   322–323

Highlands and Islands   330–333

Scotland Walks   334–347

Index   348–355

Acknowledgements   356

REGIONAL CONTENTS

In this book mainland Britain has been divided into six regions as shown on the colour-coded map, opposite. A map of each individual region appears at the beginning of the appropriate section, indicating the location of the walks within the region.

The numbers listed below and shown opposite correspond to the major town, city or landscape feature around which each road map extract is based.

THE WEST COUNTRY

1	Land's End	14–15
2	Truro	16–17
3	St Austell	18–19
4	Plymouth	20–21
5	Tintagel	22–23
6	Barnstaple	24–25
7	Exeter	28–29
8	Lyme Regis	30–31
9	Dorchester	32–33
10	Bournemouth	34–35
11	Glastonbury	36–37
12	Yeovil	38–39
13	Salisbury	42–43
14	Bath	44–45
15	Marlborough	46–47
16	Gloucester	48–49
17	Forest of Dean	50–51
	West Country Walks	52–69

SOUTHERN ENGLAND

1	Isle of Wight	72–73
2	Portsmouth	74–75
3	Chichester	76–77
4	Brighton	78–79
5	Eastbourne	82–83
6	Hastings	84–85
7	Tunbridge Wells	86–87
8	Dover	88–89
9	Canterbury	90–91
10	Winchester	94–95
11	Basingstoke	96–97
12	Guildford	98–99
13	Richmond	100–101
14	Newbury	104–105
15	Windsor	106–107
16	Oxford	108–109
17	St Albans	110–111
18	London	112–127
	Southern England Walks	128–141

THE HEART OF ENGLAND

1	Stratford-upon-Avon	144–145
2	Coventry	146–147
3	Birmingham	148–149
4	Northampton	150–151
5	Cambridge	152–153
6	Lavenham	156–157
7	Colchester	158–159
8	Ipswich	160–161
9	Bury St Edmunds	162–163
10	King's Lynn	164–165
11	Norwich	166–167
12	Leicester	170–171
13	Stamford	172–173
14	Lincoln	174–175
15	Stoke-on-Trent	178–179
16	Nottingham	180–181
	The Heart of England Walks	182–193

WALES & THE BORDERS

1	Pembroke	196–197
2	Swansea	198–199
3	Cardiff	200–201
4	Cardigan	202–203
5	Hereford	204–205
6	Aberystwyth	208–209
7	Ludlow	210–211
8	Worcester	212–213
9	Shewsbury	214–215
10	Anglesey	216–217
11	Llandudno	220–221
12	Chester	222–223
	Wales & the Borders Walks	224–243

NORTHERN ENGLAND

1	Liverpool	246–247
2	Manchester	248–249
3	Sheffield	250–251
4	Blackpool	254–255
5	Leeds	256–257
6	Lancaster	260–261
7	Malham	262–263
8	Ripon	264–265
9	York	266–267
10	Isle of Man	270–271
11	Windermere	272–273
12	Carlisle	274–275
13	Durham	276–277
14	Alnwick	278–279
	Northern England Walks	280–299

SCOTLAND

1	Dumfries	302–303
2	Arran	304–305
3	Ayr	306–307
4	Glasgow	308–309
5	Edinburgh	310–311
6	Stirling	314–315
7	Perth	316–317
8	Dundee	318–319
9	Pitlochry	320–321
10	Fort William	324–325
11	Aberdeen	326–327
12	Inverness	328–329
	Scotland Walks	334–351

Inverness
12

11 Aberdeen

Fort William
10

9

Dundee
7   8

6

Edinburgh
Glasgow   5
4

2

3

14

1

Newcastle upon Tyne
12
Carlisle   13

11

8

6   7   9

4   5   Hull
Leeds

Liverpool   Manchester
1   2   3   14
Chester
12

Nottingham
15   16

10   11

Shrewsbury   10   Norwich   11
9
12   13
7   Leicester
3   Birmingham   4

2   5
8   Cambridge
1   9
5   8
7

17   16   Oxford   17
16
Swansea   LONDON
2   Bristol   18
3   15   14   15   13
Cardiff   14
15
11   12
11   13   7   9   8
6   13   10
12   Southampton   6
2   3   Brighton
Exeter   8 Bournemouth   4   5
7   9   10   1

5

4   Plymouth
3

2

1

ABOUT THIS BOOK

Discover Britain is divided into six regional sections, each of which opens with an introduction and a regional map showing the extent of the total area covered by that chapter. Within the regional chapters, each featured area occupies a double-page spread, with the appropriate mapping extract, generally at a scale of 1:200,000 (for an explanation of symbols used on the area maps, see opposite). The text highlights places of interest around the main location – selected towns, cities and landscape features – which are arranged in alphabetical order. The margins of these pages provide information about additional points of interest, which can include some historical background, or special attractions. Contact details for the local tourist information offices are included; these can provide further information, tell you what's on locally and perhaps help with finding accommodation in the area.

Interspersed between these pages about key places are features which explore topics that are linked to the region, from literary associations to wildlife. The pages in the London sub-section consist entirely of special features about particular aspects of the nation's capital.

The Walks

At the end of each regional chapter is a section containing recommended walks in the area. The route of each walk, cross-referenced where appropriate, is shown on a map, and clear directions help you follow the walk.

A panel with each walk details the total distance, terrain, conditions underfoot, parking, public toilets and any special conditions that apply, such as restricted access or level of dog friendliness. The minimum time suggested for the walk is for reasonably fit walkers and doesn't allow for stops. An indication of the gradients you will encounter is shown by the rating ▲▲▲ (no steep slopes) to ▲▲▲ (several very steep slopes). Walks are also rated for their difficulty – those rated +++ or +++ are usually shorter and easier with little total ascent. The hardest walks are marked +++.

Many of the car parks suggested are public, but occasionally you may find you have to park on the roadside or in a lay-by. Please be considerate when you leave your car, ensuring that access roads or gates are not blocked and that other vehicles can pass safely. The start of each walk is given as a six-figure grid reference prefixed by two letters indicating the 100-km square of the National Grid to which it refers. Each walk has a suggested Ordnance Survey Explorer map where you'll find more information on using grid references.

Walking in Safety

All these walks are suitable for any reasonably fit person, but less experienced walkers should try the easier walks first. Although each walk here has been researched with a view to minimising the risks to the walkers who follow its route, no walk in the countryside can be considered to be completely free from risk. Walking will always require a degree of common sense and judgement to ensure that it is as safe as possible.

- Be particularly careful on cliff paths and in upland terrain, where the consequences of a slip can be very serious.
- Remember always to check tidal conditions before walking along the seashore.
- Some sections of route are by, or cross, busy roads. Take care and remember traffic is a danger even on minor country lanes.
- Be careful around farmyard machinery and livestock, especially if you have children with you.
- Be aware of the consequences of changes in the weather and check the forecast before you set out. Carry spare clothing and a torch if you are walking in the winter months. Remember that the weather can change very quickly at any time of the year, and in moorland and heathland areas, mist and fog can make route finding much harder. Don't set out in these conditions unless you are confident of your navigation skills in poor visibility. In summer, remember to take account of the heat and sun; wear a hat and sunscreen, and carry spare water.
- On walks away from centres of population, you should carry a whistle and survival bag. If you do have an accident requiring the emergency services, make a note of your position as accurately as possible and dial 999.

MAP SYMBOLS

MOTORING INFORMATION

M4	Motorway with number
11	Motorway junction with and without number
3	Restricted motorway junctions
S Fleet	Motorway service area
	Motorway and junction under construction
A3	Primary route single/dual carriageway
11	Primary route junction with and without number
3	Restricted primary route junctions
S Grantham North	Primary route service area
BATH	Primary route destination
A1123	Other A road single/dual carriageway
B2070	B road single/dual carriageway
	Minor road more than 4 metres wide, less than 4 metres wide
	Roundabout
	Interchange/junction
	Narrow primary/other A/B road with passing places (Scotland)
	Road under construction
	Road tunnel
Toll	Road toll, steep gradient (arrows point downhill)

MOTORING INFORMATION

5	Distance in miles between symbols
or V	Vehicle ferry
	Fast vehicle ferry or catamaran
	Railway line, in tunnel
	Railway station and level crossing
	Tourist railway
✈ H F	Airport, heliport, international freight terminal
H	24-hour Accident & Emergency hospital
C	Crematorium
50	Speed camera site (fixed location) with speed limit in mph
40	Section of road with two or more fixed speed cameras, with speed limit in mph
60 60	Average speed (SPECS™) camera system with speed limit in mph
V	Fixed speed camera site with variable speed limit
P+R	Park and Ride (at least 6 days per week)
	City, town, village or other built-up area
628 637 ▲ Lecht Summit	Height in metres, mountain pass
	Sandy beach
	National boundary
	County, administrative boundary

TOURING INFORMATION

	Scenic Route
i	Tourist Information Centre
i	Tourist Information Centre (seasonal)
V	Visitor or heritage centre
	Abbey, cathedral or priory
	Ruined abbey, cathedral or priory
	Castle
	Historic house or building
M	Museum or art gallery
	Industrial interest
	Aqueduct or viaduct
	Garden
	Arboretum
	Vineyard
	Country park
	Agricultural showground
	Theme park
	Farm or animal centre
	Zoological or wildlife collection
	Bird collection
	Aquarium
RSPB	RSPB site
	National Nature Reserve (England, Scotland, Wales)
	Local nature reserve
	Forest drive
	National trail
	Viewpoint
	Picnic site
	Hill-fort
	Roman antiquity

TOURING INFORMATION

	Prehistoric monument
1066	Battle site with year
	Steam railway centre
	Cave
	Windmill
	Monument
	Golf course
	County cricket ground
	Rugby Union national stadium
	International athletics stadium
	Horse racing
	Show jumping
	Motor-racing circuit
	Air show venue
	Ski slope – natural
	Ski slope – artificial
	National Trust property
	National Trust for Scotland property
	English Heritage site
	Historic Scotland site
	Cadw (Welsh heritage) site
★	Other place of interest
	Boxed symbols indicate attractions within urban areas
	World Heritage Site (UNESCO)
	National Park
	National Scenic Area (Scotland)
	Forest Park
	Heritage coast
	Major shopping centre

DISCOVER BRITAIN

Visitors to Britain from abroad, particularly those from much larger countries, are usually amazed by the diversity contained within a relatively small area. Landscape, architecture, customs, accents and even that indistinct quality we call 'atmosphere' can all vary enormously within the space of a half-day on the road. And because of the lay of the land, many of these variations pop up suddenly to surprise you as you round a corner or crest a hill. Some of the most lonely and remote ranges of hills and moorland areas are, in fact, very close to our most vibrant cities, and in the middle of huge conurbations there are vast green areas of parkland.

Discover Britain brings together all the elements that make up the best of Britain, combining the famous places that absolutely should not be missed with lots of lesser-known delights, chosen and written about by writers who have a specialised knowledge and affinity with particular areas. Britain is well worth exploring, and the words and pictures you will find within the following pages offer the incentive and inspiration to set off – on wheels or on foot – and enjoy this wonderful island.

THE WEST
COUNTRY

THE WEST COUNTRY

The scene at Fowey epitomises the seafaring flavour of the West Country

The West Country, with its dwindling peninsula reaching out into the Atlantic, inspires a greater sense of 'Island Britain' than anywhere else in England. It is a land of diverse, yet complementary landscapes that retain strong elements of the ancient civilisations that were overtaken, but never submerged by successive conquests.

The farmed landscape of the West Country includes Dorset's serene and rolling acres and the unremitting flatness of the Somerset Levels. It embraces Devon's lush pastures, the tiny prehistoric fields of Cornwall's rugged Land's End Peninsula and the Mediterranean flower meadows of the Isles of Scilly. Within the farmed lowland are islands of high ground such as the slight, smooth Polden Hills and the Blackdown Hills of Somerset, the bulky Mendips, breached by craggy ravines, the tawny Quantocks, and the high, wild acres of Dartmoor, Exmoor and Bodmin Moor.

The West Country is defined by its villages and country towns rather than by great cities or industrial conurbations. Even the metropolitan centres of the west reflect the culture of rural and maritime England. Exeter is identified with its glorious cathedral in a wide green space; Taunton's urban image is mellowed by county cricket and cider apples; Plymouth, with its powerful seagoing traditions, turns its face towards the great gulf of Plymouth Sound and the open sea. In a thousand villages, centuries of complex history have created unique communities. Yet between the thatched serenity of wooded Selworthy in Somerset and the cobbled streets of Cornish St Ives lies unity within diversity.

There is always a sense of escape in the West Country, of there being enough land to go round, of an ancient landscape not yet overpowered by technology. Most strikingly there is the sea, the great element that makes the West Country so emphatically the heart of maritime England. From Devon and Cornish shores came the great adventurers of Elizabethan England – the Raleighs, the Drakes and the Grenvilles. Today, the colourful fishing boats and fishermen of numerous West Country ports retain a flavour of the old-time buccaneering spirit.

Above all there is that sense of detachment that attracts all those who want to escape the rigours of an increasingly stressful urban Britain. Discover the marvellous contrasts of this favoured region, its beautiful and varied countryside, its outstanding beaches and resorts, its ancient market towns and secluded villages, and its friendly and accomplished people.

Previous page: Tintagel, north Cornwall

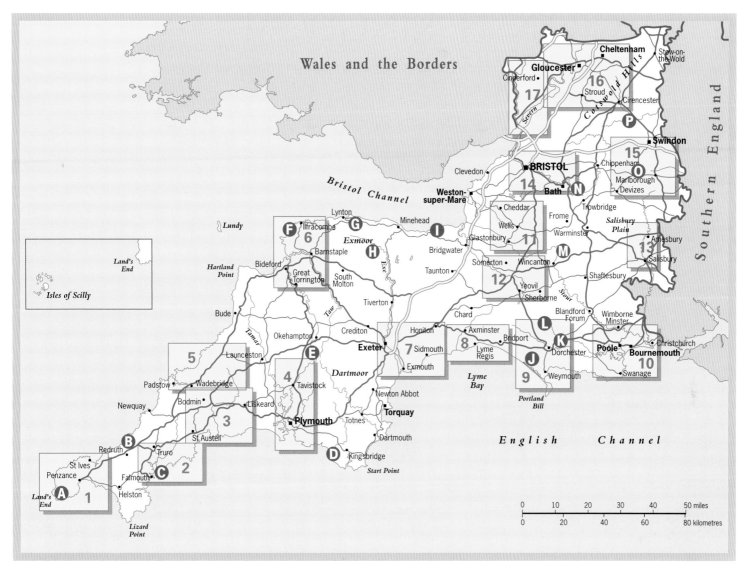

Section Contents

1	A Granite Kingdom	16–17
2	Hidden Cornwall	18–19
3	Clay Country and Ancient Ports	20–21
4	A Great River in the Shadow of Dartmoor	22–23
5	A Land of Legends and Wilderness	24–25
6	Historic Ports and Famous Resorts	26–27
7	Regency Resorts and a Great Cathedral	30–31
8	Dorset's Heritage Coast	32–33
9	Golden Beaches, Golden Villages	34–35
10	From Bournemouth Rock to Purbeck Stone	36–37
11	Caverns and Cathedrals, Cheese and Wine	38–39
12	Camelot Country	40–41
13	Standing Stones and a Soaring Spire	44–45
14	A Tale of Two Cities	46–47
15	Mysterious Sites of Marlborough Country	48–49
16	The Gloucester Cotswolds	50–51
17	The Forest of Dean	52–53

Features

Literary Settings: Writers in the West Country	28–29
Church and Home: Buildings in the Landscape	42–43

Walks

A	Golden Beaches and Cliffs at Porthcurno	54
B	Cliffs and Deep Woods at Portreath and Tehidy	55
C	St Anthony's Guns and Guiding Lights	56
D	Burgh Island Paradise	57
E	Dartmoor's Highest Tors	58
F	North Devon Coast Classic	59
G	Down the Doone Valley	60
H	A Visit to the Tarr Steps	61
I	An Amble in the Quantocks	62
J	Dorset's Other Hardy	63
K	By Hardy's Cottage and 'Egdon Heath'	64
L	Giant Steps to Cerne Abbas	65
M	More Borders at Three County Corner	66
N	A Canal and a Church at Bradford-on-Avon	67
O	Avebury – Pagan Pastures	68
P	The Infant Thames at Cricklade	69

A GRANITE KINGDOM

Magnificent sea cliffs, golden beaches, tawny moorland and flower-filled lanes are the themes of the Land's End peninsula and the Isles of Scilly. This is an ancient landscape with a concentration of prehistoric remains which is unrivalled in Britain. The mainland towns of Penzance and St Ives have more than a hint of Mediterranean Europe about them, and the Isles of Scilly are known, deservedly, as the Fortunate Islands.

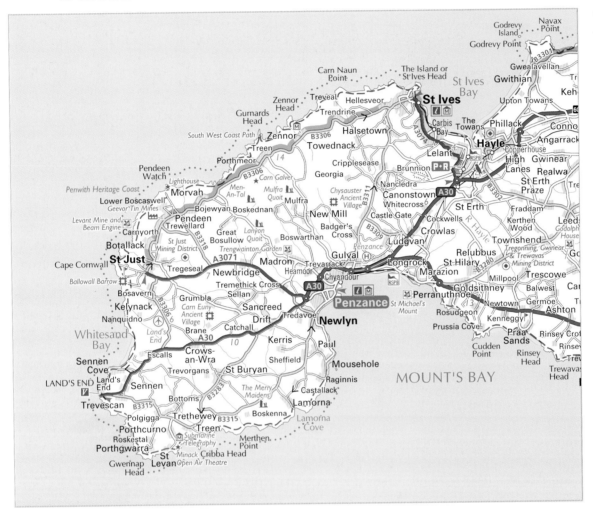

Tin Mining

The north coast of the Land's End peninsula is Cornwall's tin-mining coast, a landscape which is spectacular by nature, yet in places devastated by industry. Mining for copper, tin and other minerals in Cornwall began in pre-Roman times, when early 'tinners' dug out surface deposits and extracted mineral-rich silt from moorland streams. Deep mining developed by the 17th and 18th centuries and reached its peak during the latter half of the 19th century. The ups and downs of the industry saw thousands of Cornish miners emigrating to Australia, South Africa and the Americas. Below ground, from St Just to St Ives, is a stygian maze of old workings, some running beneath the sea, and most now flooded. The enduring emblems of the industry are the granite mine stacks and treatment works that invest the raw landscape of the coast and moorlands with a haunting beauty. The last working coastal mine of Geevor, at Pendeen near St Just, closed in 1990. It is still called Geevor Tin Mine, but now has a fascinating visitor centre complete with an interactive 'Hard Rock' museum and tours of parts of the mine.

The coastline at Land's End appears almost to have been thrust up from the seabed

Cape Cornwall

Cape Cornwall lies on the rugged north coast of the Land's End peninsula. It is the only 'Cape' in England and is so by nature of its position at the meeting of the English Channel and St George's Channel. Most of the coastline to north and south of the Cape is in the care of the National Trust, which is promoting a fruitful programme of conservation of the area's Victorian tin-mining relics. Just inland from the Cape is the sturdy little town of St Just, where tin mining and Methodism defined the heart of 19th-century Cornwall. It is also the most westerly town in England, and has a fine Norman church.

The Isles of Scilly

The Isles of Scilly lie 28 miles (17.5 km) southwest of Land's End and are reached by ferry or helicopter from Penzance. The five inhabited islands are St Mary's, St Agnes, St Martin's, Bryher and Tresco, each one uniquely different from the other. Travel by inter-island boats and aboard numerous pleasure launches is the best way of enjoying this beautiful mosaic of islands and dragon-backed reefs within their setting of blue sea and golden sands. The main island of St Mary's is the busy hub of island life, but all enjoy an extraordinary atmosphere of tranquillity, especially the smaller islands.

The dramatic cliffs at Land's End: the headland may sometimes be fraught with danger but it will always be an attraction for tourists

Land's End

Land's End is the most westerly point in England. The top of the headland is broad and rather featureless except for the cluster of buildings that make up the modern 'Land's End Experience'. It is the flanking cliffs that make Land's End so astounding. They rise in enormous pinnacles and crumbling buttresses, which enclose boulder-strewn coves and echoing ravines called 'zawns'. Access on foot to the top of the headland is time-honoured and free; there is a charge for car parking and for entrance to the Land's End exhibitions, which offer diversions in plenty. The real diversion, in wild weather especially, is the head-on collision between the mighty Atlantic and the great cliffs.

Penzance

The friendly, bustling town of Penzance enjoys a sunny outlook across the broad waters of Mount's Bay, and the palm trees and brilliantly coloured shrubs of its parks and gardens enhance the 'Cornish Riviera' theme. At the top end of Market Jew Street stands a statue of Humphry Davy, chemist, scientist and inventor of the miners' safety lamp. Chapel Street, with its mix of Georgian and Regency houses, pubs, antiques shops and art galleries, leads down to the busy harbour, an important focus for the midsummer festival of Golowan, two weeks of lively events that focus on Celtic traditions. Behind the town, lush fields and woods rise steadily to the ancient hills of Celtic Cornwall, where stone circles and standing stones of the Bronze Age pepper the moors and where substantial remnants of Iron-Age villages are preserved at sites such as Chysauster and Carn Euny.

Porthcurno

Porthcurno Bay is flanked to the east by the rugged promontory of Treryn Dinas, with its remnants of Iron-Age defensive embankments and its massive Logan Rock, or 'rocking stone'. To the southeast is the astonishing open-air Minack Theatre, carved out of the cliffs in classical style and famous for its summer performances against the biggest backdrop the Atlantic can offer. Between both headlands is a glorious natural amphitheatre of granite pinnacles and towers, grassy cliffs and beaches of golden shell sand.

St Ives

The harbour area of St Ives draws you in through narrow alleyways and cobbled lanes that have intriguing names such as Salubrious Terrace, Teetotal Street, The Digey; they weave with random charm, dappled with sun and shade, amidst tightly packed granite cottages and houses, art galleries, craft markets, good pubs and restaurants.

The town's beaches are world class. Once it was pilchard fishing that ruled the St Ives harbour area of 'Downlong', but late 19th-century tourism coincided with the arrival of the group of talented English painters, who brought to St Ives the custom of painting outdoors that they had learned in French painting schools. Today the importance of this artistic tradition is validated in the shape of the acclaimed St Ives Tate Gallery, a specially designed building above the magnificent Porthmeor Beach, which focuses on the mainly abstract work of the St Ives School of painters.

Small fishing boats and Cornish cottages in Mousehole on the Land's End peninsula

See Walk A, page 54
Golden Beaches and Cliffs at Porthcurno

See Walk B, page 55
Cliffs and Deep Woods at Porthreath and Tehidy

Tourist Information
Penzance: Station Road
(tel: 01736 362207)
St Ives: The Guildhall,
Street-an-Pol
(tel: 01736 796297)

The Modernist St Ives Tate Gallery features a distinct rotunda providing good views of the town beach

Mousehole

The village of Mousehole lies on the western edge of Mount's Bay. Clustered houses and cottages are linked by narrow, sinuous alleyways crouch above a high-walled little harbour; the village has robust Cornish identity which is still intact. The name is pronounced 'Mouzel' and its meaning is obscure. One hundred years ago Mousehole had such a large pilchard-fishing fleet that people walked across the harbour from boat to boat.

HIDDEN CORNWALL

Between Truro and Falmouth lies a hidden Cornwall of tidal rivers and creeks that merge into the great natural harbour of Falmouth Estuary. It is a country of mellow woods and lush fields. To the east is the beautiful Roseland Peninsula with its secluded coastline of sandy bays and quiet coves. While Truro maintains its position as the commercial and administrative centre of the county, Falmouth is the main port.

A dinghy moored just off the leafy banks of the Helford Estuary

Mevagissey's huge pilchard fleet is no more, but working boats can still be found here

The Dodman

South of Mevagissey is mighty Dodman Point, a high blunt-headed promontory with a formidable Iron-Age earthwork lying across its broad neck. It encloses the headland's seaward area, which may have been used as a commercial and ceremonial centre in pre-Roman times. The earth banks are over 20ft (6m) high and are 2,000ft (609m) in length.

Falmouth

The estuary of the River Fal is one of the finest natural harbours in the world. Falmouth has seen hard times throughout its history, but vessels of all types and sizes still ply to and fro, and shipbuilding and repairs, cargo handling, and the fuelling and supply of ships still flourish. Falmouth prospered during the late 17th century, when it became the packet station from where small, fast-sailing brigantines took mail to British colonies worldwide. The busy streets and narrow alleyways, known as 'Opes', retain a flavour of those salty times and the National Maritime Museum

Cornwall in Discovery Quay outlines the port's maritime history. To the east of Falmouth is the 16th-century Pendennis Castle, while along the town's southern seafront are some fine hotels, and there are several pleasant beaches. Visitors can make sea and river trips on pleasure launches from Falmouth's piers.

Mevagissey

Mevagissey is the archetypal Cornish fishing port, and pilchard fishing and processing was its main industry from Tudor times until the middle of the 20th century. At one time pilchards were known universally as 'Mevagissey Ducks'. Today, the village still has a busy fishing fleet, although tourism is now its main industry. The timeless charm of its narrow streets, old houses and harbour attracts large numbers of visitors during the busy summer months. A few miles inland from Mevagissey are the Heligan Gardens, remarkable Victorian gardens rescued during the early 1990s after being totally overgrown for 80 years.

Mylor

Mylor lies on the west bank of the Upper Fal estuary, its boundaries defined by tidal creeks. Mylor Bridge is the gateway to twin peninsulas that have a serenity that is far removed from the unpredictability of the sea. North of Mylor Bridge, the famous Pandora Inn stands at the old ferry crossing of Restronguet Passage.

St Mawes and the Roseland Peninsula

The Roseland Peninsula makes up the eastern arm of the Fal estuary. At its southern point is St Anthony Head and Zone Point, and further north is the yachting haven of St Mawes, with the 16th-century St Mawes Castle close by. Access to The Roseland by road can be north from Truro along a circuitous route or, more directly, south across the River

Helford and The Lizard

South of Falmouth lies The Lizard Peninsula, a broad, flat landscape with large areas of heathland and coastal cliffs that support rare plants of international importance. Between Falmouth and The Lizard is the Helford Estuary, presenting a more serene face of maritime Cornwall than that of the exposed craggy Atlantic coasts of the west. The tree-lined muddy creeks of Helford are wonderfully reclusive; Daphne du Maurier based her romantic novel *Frenchman's Creek* on a quiet corner of the Helford. On the north bank of the river is the National Trust's exquisite Glendurgan Garden, and the equally ravishing privately owned Trebah Garden. Both are open to the public.

Fishing

Pilchards once shoaled through Cornish waters in their millions, and ports such as Mevagissey, Polperro, Mousehole, St Ives and Port Isaac owed their survival to the annual bounty. But the pilchard shoals decreased by the early decades of the 20th century and Cornwall's fishermen were forced to diversify. They did so with great success, although the pressures of modern bureaucracy and of international competition are eroding the Cornish trade. Today, fishing of all types is carried out by Cornish vessels from the major port of Newlyn, and from smaller harbours such as Mevagissey and Padstow, and even from slipways and beaches at Penberth in Mount's Bay and Cadgwith on The Lizard. Methods used include baiting pots for crabs and lobsters, gill-netting for hake and dogfish, trawling for mackerel or for Dover sole, haddock and cod, and even 'ripping' for squid using multi-hooked weights. Cornish-caught fish are famous for their quality and variety.

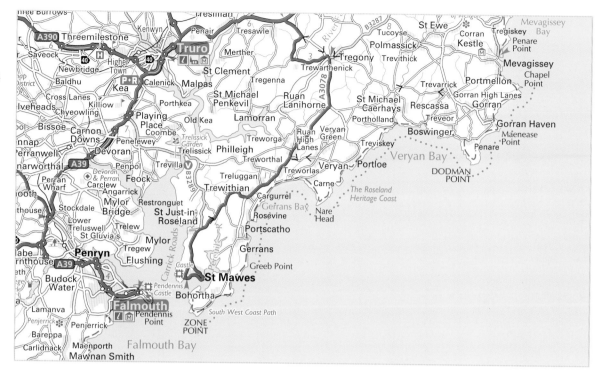

Fal via the King Harry vehicle ferry. There is a charming little church at St Just-in-Roseland, which stands above a narrow creek and is surrounded by exotic shrubs and palm trees.

Trelissick

The National Trust's Trelissick estate comprises 370 acres (150ha) of parkland on the shores of the River Fal, and its great glory lies in the superb ornamental gardens. There are various species of rhododendrons, camellias, magnolias and hydrangeas and many South American shrubs of fragile and colourful beauty. The surrounding parkland has been laid out with delightful walks. Facilities for visitors here include a restaurant, a National Trust shop, and an art and craft gallery.

Truro

Cornwall's cathedral city has a reassuring small-town atmosphere that enhances rather than diminishes its stature. It is a busy place, the commercial and administrative centre of the county, and the main shopping centre. Truro's Victorian cathedral has given a powerful focus to the city, its tall spires unchallenged by any of the surrounding domestic buildings, its pale stone reflecting the light. By the late 18th century Truro had become the political and cultural centre of Georgian Cornwall. The legacy includes such splendid features as Lemon Street, worthy of Bath and one of the most

complete Georgian streets to survive in the country. The Royal Cornwall Museum is in River Street and has an important mineral collection, an art gallery, and displays on Cornish archaeology and mining. The deeply wooded countryside of the Truro and Tresillian rivers is quickly reached from the city at the charming villages of St Clement and Malpas.

Veryan

The small village of Veryan lies just inland from the lofty Nare Head and the secluded beaches of Gerrans Bay. Veryan's Church of St Symphorian is darkly impressive, its churchyard dense with trees and shrubs. The village is famous for its unique round houses, five in number, with thatched roofs reminiscent of village huts in Africa, each crowned with a cross. They date from the early 19th century and may have been built as curiosities, although local legend claims that their circular design was planned so that the devil couldn't hide in corners.

See Walk C, page 56
St Anthony's Guns and Guiding Lights

Tourist Information
Falmouth: 11 Market Strand, Prince of Wales Pier (tel: 01326 312300)
Truro: Municipal Buildings, Boscawen Street (tel: 01872 274555)

The pretty church at St-Just-in-Roseland is reflected in the calm waters of the tidal creek

CLAY COUNTRY AND ANCIENT PORTS

The southeast coast of Cornwall has none of the raw grandeur of the north and west of the county. Here is a softer beauty of rounded headlands and wooded estuaries. Yet the coastal communities of Looe and Fowey are bustling places with a strong maritime heritage. Inland, at St Austell, and on the fringes of Bodmin Moor, the historic Cornish industries of coppermining, quarrying and china clay have left their sometimes surreal marks on the landscape.

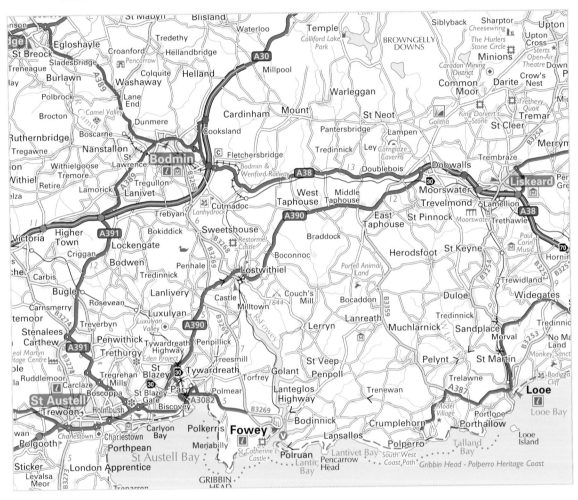

A ferry boat with passengers plies the waters of the River Fowey

Bodmin

Bodmin was once the county town of Cornwall and, although it has lost that status to Truro, it retains a strong Cornish identity. In the 10th century a monastery was founded here, and the enshrining of relics of St Petroc, Cornwall's most important Celtic saint, turned Bodmin into the major religious site in medieval times. Bodmin Riding and Heritage Day, on the first weekend of July, mixes this religious history with local hunting traditions. The town's Helliers (huntsmen) track the costumed 'Beast of Bodmin' around the streets, while a musical band

of Ragadaziow (local worthies) guard the bones of the saint. The beast is captured, caged and paraded through the streets, together with the religious relics. Local children take the side of the underdog, waving placards and chanting 'Free the Beast'.

Fowey

Fowey (pronounced 'Foy') seems more of a riverside town than a seaport. Its jostling houses look out across the sheltered estuary of the River Fowey to the hazy beauty of Polruan on the opposite shore.

Clay Country

Around St Austell are the famous clay 'Alps', the white moonscape of ever-changing spoil heaps of the china clay industry. Visitors can explore a number of scenic clay trails that have been opened up around the town.

China clay is granite in which the feldspar crystals have decomposed into kaolin. It is found at various locations around Cornwall, but especially on Hensbarrow, the high plateau north of St Austell. Kaolin was used in China for the making of porcelain as early as AD700. The pure kaolin is separated from quartz-sand and mica, and transformed into flat-topped buttes and escarpments.

Clay was exported through the port of Par and from a custom-built dock at Charlestown to the south of St Austell. Today the modern industry produces more than two million tonnes of clay annually.

But ocean-going ships glide upstream to the clay-loading wharves at Golant and the estuary is full of yachts and pleasure boats in summer. Trafalgar Square, at the heart of the town, has a museum and aquarium, and the dark solidity of St Fimbarrus's Church, with its fine decorated tower, stands here in withdrawn seclusion. Beyond lies the busy Town Quay and the narrow Fore Street, which leads on through the attractive streets. High above Fore Street the intriguing Gothic building of Place, home of the Treffry family since the 14th century, overlooks the town.

Looe

The East and West Looe Rivers merge at Looe and divide the town into two parts that are connected by a graceful bridge. The sea unites both communities in the business of fishing and a busy fish market brings colour and liveliness to the quay.

East Looe is the larger of the two communities. Behind the harbour front, a maze of streets with connecting alleyways lies between tall colour-washed buildings, busy shops and good pubs and restaurants. A bathing machine for discreet undressing is said to have been sited at Looe Beach as early as 1800, when the Napoleonic Wars made rich British patrons seek home-grown 'Rivieras' as an alternative to the French original.

On the west bank of the West Looe River, Kilminorth Wood is a nature reserve with pleasant woodland walks.

Lostwithiel

Lostwithiel was a flourishing port until the upper reaches of the River Fowey became silted during the 14th century. A fine medieval bridge still spans the river, and another striking feature of the town is the elegant spire of the Church of St Bartholomew. To the north are the ruins of Restormel Castle, the best-preserved military building in Cornwall.

Minions

Minions, on the southeastern edge of Bodmin Moor, was a mining village from the mid-19th century until well into the 20th. Nearby is the Cheesewring Quarry, from which granite was sent nationwide to build docks, breakwaters and public works such as the Thames Embankment. On the lip of the quarry is The Cheesewring, a rock formation named after its resemblance to a cider press (cheese is the name given to apple pulp).

Polperro

Polperro lies at the seaward end of a steep, narrow valley, which is crammed with pixie-like houses and an enchanting tangle of narrow lanes, leading down to a boat-bobbing harbour. A stream tumbles through the village and into the harbour by an intriguing building known as the House on Props.

St Austell

In medieval times St Austell was just a village, but it was even then a commercial and industrial centre. The handsome Church of the Holy Trinity is a token of early prosperity and opposite the church is the grand Town Hall with its monumental Italianate façade, behind which is the old Market Hall, still intact and with massive wooden roof trusses. The heart of modern St Austell has been sensibly pedestrianised and is a convenient shopping centre for the area.

An orange tree in the Eden Project's warm temperate biome, which re-creates the Mediterranean climate

The Eden Project

The Eden Project is a spectacular 'global garden' that was opened in March 2001 in what was once an old clay pit near St Austell. It is made up of a series of enormous geodesic domes called 'biomes', in which the environments of the world's major climate zones are re-created, complete with a huge collection of exotic plants and trees. Eden also features exhibitions, music and theatre events, arts projects and educational facilities.

Tourist Information

Bodmin: Shire House, Mount Folly Square (tel: 01208 76616)
Fowey: 5 South Street (tel: 01726 833616)
Looe: The Guildhall, Fore Street, East Looe (tel: 01503 262072)
Lostwithiel: Community Centre, Liddicoat Road (tel: 01208 872207)

In the 18th century, brandy, gin, tea and tobacco smuggled from Guernsey found their way to the sheltered cove of Polperro

A GREAT RIVER IN THE SHADOW OF DARTMOOR

The River Tamar is one of the great natural boundaries of the West Country. It provides an emphatic border between Devon and Cornwall, finally merging with Dartmoor's River Tavy to flow into the great gulf of Plymouth Sound. The historic town of Plymouth dominates the region, yet within a few miles of the city boundaries lies Dartmoor's magnificent wilderness, and to either side of Plymouth Sound are remote and beautiful coastlines.

The Postbridge Clapper Bridge in Dartmoor is made of flat slabs that are thought to have spanned the East Dart River since the 14th century

Calstock

Cornish Calstock faces the fields of Devon across the slow, muddy glide of the River Tamar, spanned here by a tall railway viaduct which dates from 1909 and has a surprising elegance. Calstock was a port, a railway town and an industrial and agricultural centre for hundreds of years. Its commercial stature has declined, but the village has survived and is now a delightful focus of river cruises and more leisurely rail journeys on the picturesque Tamar Valley Line. A short way upstream, and still on the Cornish side, is the National Trust's Cotehele, a well-preserved Elizabethan house of great charm.

Lydford

The village of Lydford lies on the wooded western fringes of Dartmoor. The ruins of Lydford's modest, yet prominent castle makes a pleasing group with the little Church of St Petroc on one side and the village pub on the other. A mile (1.6km) beyond the village is the National Trust's Lydford Gorge. Walkways, requiring some agility in places, lead into the atmospheric Devil's Cauldron, a series of fissures and

hollows in the rock through which pours the River Lyd. A mile (1.6km) downstream is the elegant ribbon of the White Lady Waterfall, which can be viewed by following more amenable pathways.

Noss Mayo

The River Yealm (pronounced 'Yam') reaches the sea between tree-muffled banks at Noss Mayo, an exquisite contrast to the great gaping mouth of Plymouth Sound only a mile (1.6km) or so to the west. The village lies on the south side of the subsidiary Newton Creek, while its larger counterpart, Newton Ferrers, occupies the north bank. Noss Mayo has the advantage of greater seclusion; at its heart is an even smaller creek, around which cottages and houses cluster and where two creekside pubs further enhance the peaceful well-being of it all.

Plymouth

Plymouth is Devon's largest urban area, and the modern city extends inland far beyond its historic waterfront. The original port of Sutton was insignificant until it became the base from which many of the great maritime adventures of the 16th century began. Since that time, Plymouth's naval dockyards have been its life, though they are now in decline. The famous Hoe stands above the breathtaking vista of Plymouth Sound and Drake's Island, while to the north, on the west side of Sutton harbour, is the Barbican area of the old town. It is an intriguing tangle of narrow old streets and alleys such as the cobbled New Street, an Elizabethan survival. The Barbican is further enhanced by its busy fishing harbour, yacht marina, National Marine Aquarium and variety of eateries. Beyond the Barbican and The Hoe, the rebuilding of war-devastated central Plymouth has produced a spacious, modern city centre.

Dartmoor

Dartmoor's status as a National Park indicates its importance as a substantial area of wild land. The moor is remote yet accessible, wild and rugged, yet with peaceful, wooded valleys and sheltered corners – an absorbing landscape of fascinating extremes. The National Park covers an area of 368sq miles (954sq km). The northern half, south of Okehampton and east of Tavistock, is the highest and wildest part, where the great hills of Yes Tor, High Willhays and Hangingstone Hill dominate a rolling wilderness of lonely moorland and granite outcrops. Here the endearing Dartmoor ponies graze amidst a landscape rich in prehistoric remains.

Southern Dartmoor has fewer well-defined summits but is just as wild and remote. It runs south from the bleak village of Princetown, with its grim-walled prison, across the marshy levels of typical *Hound of the Baskervilles* country, and then through the lonely wilderness of Erme Plains to Ivybridge.

Eastern Dartmoor is a fascinating landscape where knuckly masses of granite protrude from grassy moorland at Haytor and Fox Tor and where the raw edge of the open moorland is blurred by green valleys. Nestling here are the lovely villages of Chagford, Buckland in the Moor, Widecombe in the Moor and Bovey Tracey.

The Rame Peninsula

The Rame Peninsula is the Cornish western arm of Plymouth Sound. On its eastern side, directly opposite Plymouth, is Mount Edgcumbe, a fine 18th-century house which was restored after it was bombed during the Plymouth blitz of 1941. The formal gardens are magnificent, and most of the large estate has been turned into a country park, with scenic walks along miles of beautiful coastline. To the south is Rame Head, crowned by the ruin of a small chapel. The headland was fortified during the Iron Age and its protective embankments are well preserved. Between Rame Head and Mount Edgcumbe are the linked villages of Cawsand and Kingsand, once great centres of both pilchard fishing and the famous 'free trade' of smuggling.

Shaugh Prior

The valley of the River Plym on Dartmoor's southwestern edge is a ragged palimpsest of ancient remains, old tin mines and still active clay workings. The village of Shaugh Prior lies just south of the river and has a proud little church of granite and a good Devon pub. Just west of the village is Shaugh Bridge, at the junction of the rivers Meavy and Plym, and the broad swathe of woodland that lies upstream from the bridge has a network of pathways. It is owned by the National Trust and includes the towering granite cliffs of The Dewerstone.

Tavistock

Tin, wool and copper brought prosperity to Tavistock over the years. Today, it is a busy market town of great charm, the western gateway to Dartmoor. At the heart of Tavistock is Bedford Square, flanked by some of the finest Victorian town buildings in the West Country, including the Town Hall and the Lloyds TSB Bank and HSBC Bank buildings. On the south side of the square is the Church of St Eustace, dating mainly from the early 16th century, on the site of a 10th-century Benedictine abbey. Fragments of the abbey still survive – within the churchyard, in a nearby gatehouse now known as Betsy Grimbal's Tower, and in the restored medieval gatehouse adjacent to the Town Hall. Behind the Town Hall is an attractive Pannier Market and there are good shops in the busy streets off Bedford Square. At the southwestern end of Plymouth Road is a statue of Sir Francis Drake, who was born at nearby Crowndale.

See Walk D, page 57
Burgh Island Paradise

See Walk E, page 58
Dartmoor's Highest Tors

Tourist Information
Plymouth: 3–5 The Barbican (tel: 01752 306330)
Tavistock: Town Hall, Bedford Square (seasonal) (tel: 01822 612938)

Spectacular Rame Head forms the most southerly point at Mount Edgcumbe County Park

A LAND OF LEGENDS AND WILDERNESS

The granite wilderness of Bodmin Moor contrasts with spectacular coastal cliffs of dark slate in this dramatic corner of North Cornwall. It is a land that claims King Arthur for its own, and that inspired such poets as Hardy, Tennyson and Betjeman with its mix of wild countryside, wooded valleys and stormy seas.

Dozmary Pool on Bodmin Moor, where, according to local Arthurian legend, Sir Bedivere returned Excalibur to the Lady of the Lake

Tourist Information

Camelford: North Cornwall Museum, The Cleake (seasonal) (tel: 01840 212954)
Launceston: Market House Arcade, Market Street (tel: 01566 772321)
Padstow: Red Brick Building, North Quay (seasonal) (tel: 01841 533449)

Bodmin Moor

Bodmin Moor is dissected by the busy ribbon of the A30. To the east is lower ground and the wooded folds of the valley of the River Fowey. To the west is true moorland, a surviving wilderness that culminates in the rock-crested hills of Rough Tor (pronounced 'Row Tor') and Brown Willy, both worthy of mountain status, though they are below 2,000ft (609.6m) in height. This is the granite roof of Cornwall, exhilarating country where smooth, whale-backed boulders, silvery white in the sun, protrude from the moorland grass and heather.

Brown Willy is the highest point, less dragon-backed than Rough Tor, but more remote. On the slopes of Rough Tor are numerous remains of ancient field boundaries and Bronze-Age hut circles.

Boscastle

At Boscastle harbour the sea fights to get in between high jagged cliffs, and when it does the narrow entrance to the channel reverberates with the crashing of the waves. It is the only natural harbour along 50 miles (80.5km) of savage coastline,

but is not an easy one. In Victorian times, when Boscastle was a thriving port, ships were brought in safely by teams of men manipulating ropes that were strung from the vessel to stone bollards on either side of the harbour quays. Today, Boscastle is a popular visitor destination. To the south, Willapark is a high rounded headland, site of an Iron-Age fort. The Valency Valley runs inland from the harbour, its deep woods and singing river, hazy bluebells and dense greenery contrasting with the raw, rugged coast. A little way inland is the peaceful church of St Juliot, where Thomas Hardy met his future wife, Emma.

Launceston

Launceston (pronounced 'Lanson') was once a walled town, a frontier stronghold of the Normans, and the impressive ruins of its Norman motte and bailey castle dominate the surrounding countryside. The sturdy South Gate is a reminder of its former status. There are handsome Georgian buildings round the central area of The Square and there is a good museum in Castle Street. The Church of St Mary Magdalene is distinguished by the wealth of carving on its granite exterior.

Padstow

Padstow stands sheltered deep within the Camel Estuary. It has been a fair refuge for shipping for centuries, though reaching the port across the notorious sandbank, Doom Bar, has caused countless harrowing wrecks and loss of life. Padstow is still a busy fishing port of great character. The tightly packed houses, in exposed stone or in bright colour-wash, rise in tiers towards the dignified Church of St Petroc. Above the church is Prideaux Place, a fine Tudor building that is still occupied, but is open to the public on certain days. Padstow is famous for its May Day celebration, the wild processional dance of the 'Obby Oss' that takes place from dawn to dusk to welcome in the summer.

Pentire and The Rumps

The great promontory that makes up the northern arm of the Camel Estuary, and that culminates in Pentire Point and The Rumps, is in the care of the National Trust. The smaller promontory of The Rumps, with its eponymous twin hills, juts into the sea from the larger headland. The Rumps was the site of a substantial fortified settlement of the Iron Age and its earth embankments are visible across the narrow neck of the headland. The great pillow lava cliffs of Pentire are steep and spectacular. In spring and summer the cliffs are a glorious mass of pink thrift, saffron-coloured kidney vetch and the powder-blue squill.

Arthurian enthusiasm. The area has seen much more daring enterprise than the King Arthur industry – when slate was quarried from the cliffs, men worked the sheer faces suspended on ropes. Tintagel is busy during the holiday season, when tolerance of crowds is needed if the undoubted attractions are to be enjoyed. The National Trust's Old Post Office in the main street is a delightfully eccentric building, originally a small manor house of the 14th or 15th century.

Port Isaac harbour was a thriving port until the 19th century when it began to suffer from both road and rail competition for the transportation of goods

Padstow's unique 'Obby Oss' celebration is a fertility ritual dating back to the 14th century that attracts thousands of visitors

Port Isaac

Port Isaac is a compact little fishing village which, though hugely popular with visitors, has been spared the worst impact of traffic because of sensible parking arrangements. Port Isaac developed as a pilchard fishing port, and slate from the nearby Delabole Quarry was shipped out from the little beach. Narrow alleyways wriggle between the jostling houses.

Tintagel

The skeletal ruins of Tintagel Castle on the awesome headland known as The Island is attraction enough, but Tintagel also has the legendary King Arthur grafted on to its image and is awash with

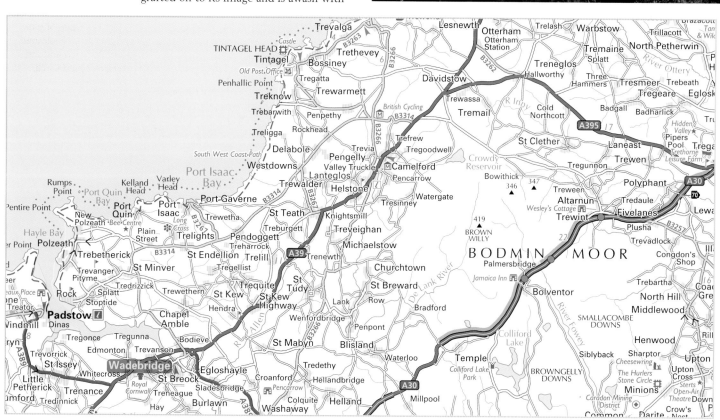

HISTORIC PORTS AND FAMOUS RESORTS

The great maritime past of North Devon is still evident today in the historic river ports of Barnstaple and Bideford and throughout the fascinating landscape of the estuary of the rivers Taw and Torridge. Eastwards along the coast are the famous resorts of Ilfracombe and Combe Martin, within easy distance of the great rolling hills of Exmoor. It is an area of remarkable contrasts that never ceases to surprise and fascinate.

Ilfracombe's centuries-old harbour is the largest on the North Devon coast and the starting point of many scenic boat trips

Appledore

Appledore, with its terraces of stone and colour-washed houses along narrow alleys, has a long quay on the broad estuary of the rivers Taw and Torridge. The background to Appledore's great maritime traditions can be found at the excellent North Devon Maritime Museum in Odun Road.

Barnstaple

North Devon's principal market town lies on a crook of land between the rivers Yeo and Taw. These waterways, and the low-lying marshes south of the Taw, made the task of defence easier for the Saxon founders of the settlement. Barnstaple's High Street is partly pedestrianised and at its heart is the splendid Town Hall, behind which lies the Pannier Market with its great canopied roof and its arched side entrances facing the row of arcaded shops known as Butcher's Row. Nearby, in a quiet leafy square, is the Church of St Peter and Mary Magdalene, with a wonderfully crooked spire. The Heritage Centre in the ornate Queen Anne's Building, and the North Devon Museum, relate local history.

Bideford

Bideford once rivalled London as a port and eclipsed Barnstaple at various times throughout centuries of rivalry. The Long Bridge over the Torridge is impressive, and the size of the still active 17th-century quay reflects its importance in the days when Bideford ships sailed far and wide. One, the *Kathleen & May*, has been restored and makes trips around the country.

Behind the tall buildings that line Quay Road is a network of narrow back streets. Bideford is a bustling little town, with regular pannier markets, and the Burton Art Gallery and Museum is worth a visit. The town is one of the access points for the scenic Tarka Trail, recalling the area's link with Henry Williamson's *Tarka the Otter*.

Combe Martin

Combe Martin's main 'street', 1.5 miles (2.4km) long, with five name changes, runs down a narrow valley to a pleasant beach between wings of slabby rock. This is a popular traditional seaside resort, and the adjoining coastline is magnificent, especially to the east.

Croyde

Croyde has a real flavour of rural Devon by the sea. A small stream runs alongside the main street, with small bridges to the

Marram grass acts as a natural stabiliser on the shifting sands of Croyde's pretty beach

Exmoor and The Quantocks

Exmoor is an area of windswept high ground pierced by deep river valleys and dimpled with wooded combes. It is an invigoratingly open landscape of wild yet fragile beauty that is also a thriving working environment. Most of Exmoor is contained within the 267sq miles (693sq km) of the Exmoor National Park. To the east, beyond the Brendon Hills, lie the Quantocks, a reprise of Exmoor's landscape within a single range of hills. The high ground rises dramatically from the smooth-browed coast, through the lonely heights of The Chains, Dunkery Beacon and Wills Neck, and its turbulent rivers rush to the coast down steep, wooded valleys.

To the south the wild moorland merges imperceptibly with the wooded and cultivated countryside of Devon and Somerset and sends down, from its waterlogged heights, the rivers Exe and Barle. Embedded in this remarkable landscape is an ancient pattern of prehistoric settlement, of small towns and villages, tiny hamlets and farmsteads. The high moorland is the domain of the red deer and the tough little Exmoor pony, the piping skylark and the circling buzzard. It is the country of the mythical robber barons, the Doones of Badgworthy Water, who inspired R. D. Blackmore's novel *Lorna Doone*, to which the real Exmoor provides an authentic background.

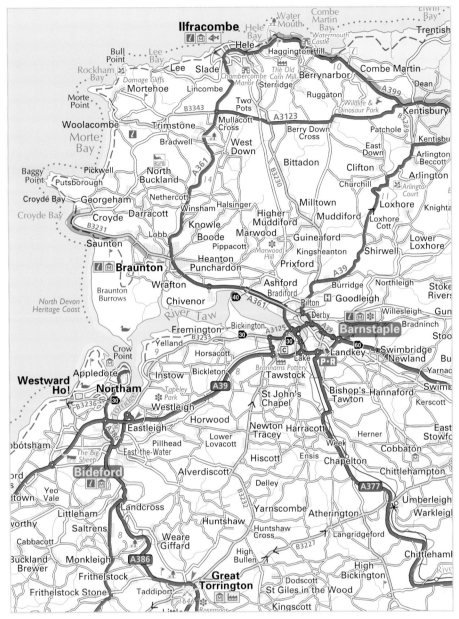

👣 **See Walk F, page 59**
North Devon Coast Classic

👣 **See Walk G, page 60**
Down the Doone Valley

Tourist Information

Barnstaple: The Square (tel: 01271 375000)
Bideford: Victoria Park (tel: 01237 477676/471455)
Combe Martin: Cross Street (seasonal) (tel: 01271 883319)
Ilfracombe: The Seafront (tel: 01271 863001)

thatched cottages, and to seaward is the wide Croyde Bay. To the south is the dune country of Braunton Burrows and Saunton Sands; north lies the protective arm of Baggy Point, where steep cliffs rise dramatically from the sea and the clamour of sea birds fills the air above a glittering sea.

Great Torrington

Great Torrington stands high above the Torridge, and the view of riverside fields and woods from the rim of the soaring escarpment is breathtaking. The town centre has the satisfying character of a market square, with a Georgian Town Hall and other fine old buildings. 'Torrington 1646' recalls the last major conflict of the Civil War, encapsulating 17th-century life, and Dartington Crystal offers factory tours, a shop and a restaurant. Just outside the town are the wonderful Rosemoor Gardens.

Ilfracombe

High Victorian architecture reached ultimate expression in Ilfracombe's seafront hotels and the grand houses of Torrs Walk. The town is built round a number of distinctive hills, one of which – Lantern Hill – is topped by the tiny lighthouse chapel of St Nicholas. The heart of town is sheltered by Capstone Point, criss-crossed with pleasant walkways and overlooking a fine flower-filled promenade. Here is the aptly named modern Landmark Theatre complex.

Old Ilfracombe is gathered round the harbour, the steep, narrow Fore Street and the busy High Street. The hilly nature of the coast denies Ilfracombe the advantages of wide beaches or panoramic views, but the intriguing Tunnels Beach is reached through tunnels in the cliff, and there are more beaches north of the harbour. Coastal cruises take visitors to nearby Lundy island and on wildlife watching trips.

The River Torridge had a key role in the development of Bideford, with much of the silk and wool from its thriving textile industry being shipped out from here

LITERARY SETTINGS: WRITERS IN THE WEST COUNTRY

The poet John Heath-Stubbs captured, grudgingly it seems, both the inspiration and the awe of the wildest parts of the west of England, when he spoke of a hideous and wicked country/Sloping to hateful sunsets and the end of time. Most writers have been more happily captivated than that. For Heath-Stubbs, it seems, too much raw nature was unnerving. The poet's uneasy words were inspired by the powerful Atlantic coast of Gurnards Head near Land's End, itself the Belerium, the 'Seat of Storms', of the Roman writer Tacitus, an early commentator within the literary setting.

Samuel Taylor Coleridge

Thomas Hardy

R. D. Blackmore

From those Roman times until the present day, the West Country has continued to attract poets and writers. From the beautiful countryside of Dorset, Thomas Hardy created his own landscape of 'Wessex', at the gates of the West Country, yet Hardy too was drawn further west, to the spectacular coastline of North Cornwall. Here he met his wife Emma at the exquisite little church of St Juliot, near Boscastle, and much bitter-sweet romance ensued. The pair strolled out at Beeny Cliff just north of Boscastle and above 'the opal and the sapphire of that wandering western sea' – lines in which Hardy captured the essence of the Cornish coast better, perhaps, than generations of writers since. But before Hardy, the north coast of Devon gave inspiration to Charles Kingsley, who grew up at the exquisite village of Clovelly, lived later at Bideford, and gave the breezy name of *Westward Ho!* to his most famous novel – and subsequently to a seaside village.

Evocative Landscapes

The coast of North Cornwall more recently inspired John Betjeman, whose lifelong association with Padstow, further south from Hardy's Beeny Cliff, added a richer, more robust tone to the poetry of suburbia. South of Padstow, the rugged tin-mining coast of St Agnes and Perranporth inspired Winston Graham's marvellous *Poldark* saga, epic narrative of life in 18th- and 19th-century Cornwall from the pen of a modern master.

The Atlantic coast of the west was ever inspirational, but so too were the high moors of Exmoor and the Quantocks. Amidst the wooded combes and soft rolling heaths of the Quantocks, the poet Samuel Taylor Coleridge and his friends, William and Dorothy Wordsworth, found the intensely pastoral inspiration for their great Romantic poems, even before the Lake District claimed them for its own.

Between Exmoor and the sea, Coleridge wrote his fevered, flawed masterpiece 'Kubla Khan', its opium-induced fantasies rudely interrupted by the unannounced visit of 'a person from Porlock', who was thus immortalised as perhaps the most notorious full stop in literary history. Directly inland from Porlock, amidst the heathland wastes of Badgworthy Water, is 'Doone Country', the inspiration for R. D. Blackmore's famously romantic novel *Lorna Doone*. The legend of the robber Doones of Badgworthy, said to originate from an exiled and disaffected Scottish noble family, was part of Exmoor lore long before Blackmore's masterly embellishment, but with all its lonely, compelling beauty, the moorland wilderness cried out for just such a rattling good tale. Blackmore's novel merged romance with reality and turned into shrines of literary pilgrimage such places as the little church at Oare where Lorna was shot and wounded by Carver Doone during her wedding to John Ridd.

Coleridge Cottage in Nether Stowey was where the great poet wrote some of his most famous poems, including The Rime of the Ancient Mariner

Romance and mystery

R. D. Blackmore's 20th-century counterpart was undoubtedly Daphne du Maurier, whose grasp of the romantic and the picturesque gave rise to such popular novels as *Jamaica Inn* and *Frenchman's Creek*. The former borrowed some of its imagery from the forlorn heights of Cornwall's Bodmin Moor; the latter focused on the tree-shrouded creeks of the Helford River on the county's southwest coast. But du Maurier's true literary setting was the lovely landscape of the River Fowey. Here, amidst the wooded parkland of Menabilly House, were shaped the novels *My Cousin Rachel* and *Rebecca*, who woke and 'dreamt of Manderley'. It was here too that du Maurier was inspired to write the short story about predatory seabirds – subsequently filmed by Alfred Hitchcock as *The Birds* – after watching a cloud of screaming gulls foraging in the wake of a tractor as it drew its plough through the rich earth of the Cornish fields. Similar inspiration for one of the greatest detective stories ever written, *The Hound of the Baskervilles*, was drawn from Dartmoor by Sir Arthur Conan Doyle. The novelist had stayed on the southeastern edge of the moor, at Manaton, and had been gripped by the changing moods of its great waste, and by the Gothic atmosphere of the lonely granite tors that rise eerily like castles above the marshy low ground.

While R. D. Blackmore and Hardy gave us such enduring romantic novels as *Lorna Doone* and *Tess of the D'Urbervilles*, the 20th-century writer John Fowles has established Lyme Regis as the setting for his powerful novel *The French Lieutenant's Woman*, with its more complex literary romanticism. The novel is now immortalised on film, most dramatically by the image of the tragic heroine, Sarah Woodruff, precarious in body and soul, on the storm-battered harbour wall of The Cobb at Lyme. Here also, the more formal romance of Jane Austen's *Persuasion* depicts Louisa Musgrove falling from the Higher Cobb, intent on landing in Captain Wentworth's arms, but knocking herself unconscious instead.

Continuing inspiration

The literary inspiration of the West Country continues today, its dramatic landscapes inspiring even those writers whose themes may not necessarily reflect a West Country setting. Near Land's End lives the novelist John Le Carré, whose books range the cosmopolitan world of Europe and Asia, yet whose hard work of writing is often carried out against the background of the restless Atlantic. A near neighbour of Le Carré's was Derek Tangye, author of a gently sentimental series of autobiographical novels about his beloved West Cornwall, who died in 1996. The novelist Mary Wesley lived in Totnes and wrote more sophisticated novels than perhaps Daphne du Maurier would ever have dared. Wesley based her scintillating *Camomile Lawn* on Cornwall's Roseland Peninsula.

The popular novelist Rosamunde Pilcher has strong connections with the north coast of West Cornwall near St Ives, and the film version of her novel *The Shell Seekers* was filmed in the town.

Earlier literary figures connected with the St Ives area included Virginia Woolf, who based her novel *To the Lighthouse* on the nearby Godrevy lighthouse. D. H. Lawrence lived at Zennor for a period during the First World War, hounded by the authorities because of his pacifist stance and his wife Frieda's German nationality. Lawrence described vividly his Cornish experiences in the nightmare sequence in his novel *Kangaroo*. Locations in the West Country have inspired some of the most seminal works of English poetry and prose. Near Yeovil is East Coker, ancestral home of T. S. Eliot, whose ashes are buried here, and who attached the name of this archetypal English village to the second poem of his *Four Quartets*. Coleridge was born at Ottery St Mary. John Galsworthy lived for 18 years at Manaton in East Dartmoor, where he worked on *The Forsyte Saga*. At the unlikely setting of nearby Chagford, Evelyn Waugh wrote *Brideshead Revisited*, whose characters would have felt positively uneasy amidst Dartmoor's ruggedness. Torquay was the birthplace of Agatha Christie, who also lived on the inspiring Dart Estuary and wrote several of her famous crime novels on the nearby Burgh Island off Salcombe. And in the delightful valleys of the rivers Taw and Torridge in North Devon Henry Williamson wrote *Tarka The Otter* and *Salar The Salmon*.

Malmsmead, with its charming packhorse bridge, is the location of Lorna Doone Farm, which featured in R. D. Blackmore's tragic tale

Hardy's Cottage in Higher Brockhampton was the novelist's home as a young man and where he wrote Under the Greenwood Tree

REGENCY RESORTS AND A GREAT CATHEDRAL

The southeast coast of Devon lies within the sheltering arm of Lyme Bay. The climate is benign, and there is a fascinating variety of coastal landscape, from the dazzling white of Beer's chalk cliffs to the long shingle beaches of Sidmouth and Budleigh Salterton, framed between great red cliffs. Inland are quiet, meandering lanes, sleepy villages and busy country towns. The focus of the region is the county town of Exeter, with its magnificent 14th-century cathedral and historic quayside.

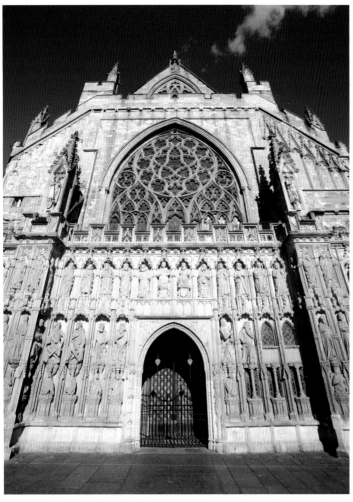

Sculpted figures, including King Alfred, William the Conqueror and Richard I adorn Exeter Cathedral's west front

Oystercatchers make the most of low tide on the River Exe Estuary in Dawlish Warren

Exeter

Exeter was the Roman headquarters of the southwest, and the heart of the modern city lies within a surviving framework of its much-restored Roman walls. The focus of Exeter is the cathedral, an outstanding building within a splendid Close. The powerful 12th-century towers survive, and the interior is a feast of 13th-century Gothic design – overall a masterpiece of English architecture. The city's civic buildings complement the cathedral with their mix of period styles. The remodelling of the bomb-damaged city centre has, in the main, been a happy one. The many attractions include the Historic Quayside, with its waterside paths, boat trips and visitor centre, the Royal Albert Memorial Museum and the underground passages.

Budleigh Salterton

Budleigh Salterton developed as a Victorian resort along the same lines as Torquay and Sidmouth, though on a less grand scale. Today it has a detached, genteel air, less commercialised than its Torbay neighbours. The long gentle curve of the shingle beach runs from the mouth of the River Otter to the slopes of the wooded West Down. Budleigh has handsome Victorian villas, and several Regency period *cottages ornés*, mock-rustic buildings with surprising thatch crowning Gothic-style façades.

Exmouth

Exmouth, at the broad, sandy mouth of the Exe Estuary, has an open, airy feel to its beaches and promenade. Above the seafront are dignified Georgian houses, while the eastern end of the town is a tight network of small streets around the harbour and dock area. Just outside the

Dawlish Warren

The resort of Dawlish closes down in winter, but on the great sand spit that projects for 1.5 miles (2.4km) into the Exe Estuary there is wildlife in profusion all year round. The area was used as a rabbit warren in the 18th century, hence the name. Today the 500 acres (200ha) of mudflats, dunes and saltmarshes is a major nature reserve where huge numbers of birds – grey plovers, dunlin, black-tailed godwits, curlews, Brent geese, sandpipers and more congregate. The Warren is also noted for its plant life and its rare butterflies.

Tourist Information

Budleigh Salterton:
Fore Street (tel: 01395 445275)

Exeter: Civic Centre, Paris Street (tel: 01392 265700)

Exmouth: Alexandra Terrace (tel: 01395 222299)

Honiton: Lace Walk Car Park (tel: 01404 43716)

Ottery St Mary: 10a Broad Street (tel: 01404 813964)

Sidmouth: Office Ham Lane (tel: 01395 516441)

The English Riviera

To be called 'The English Riviera' is giving more than a degree of latitude to publicity. But Torquay – or more precisely Torbay, of which Torquay is emphatically the focus – is a triumph of robust self-confidence. The originally modest 'Tor Quay' developed from being a Navy supply depot during the Napoleonic Wars to being a rest centre for officers and their families. Victorian fashion confirmed Torquay's future as a resort. Modern Torquay is perhaps too over-powering for some, but a healthy prosperity has saved it and its neighbour, Paignton, from becoming too brash. There are wide promenades, palm-fringed gardens and parks, and handsome 19th-century Italianate villas to take the edge off the more brutal modern buildings that have elbowed their way in. Torbay as a whole caters for all tastes in holidaymaking.

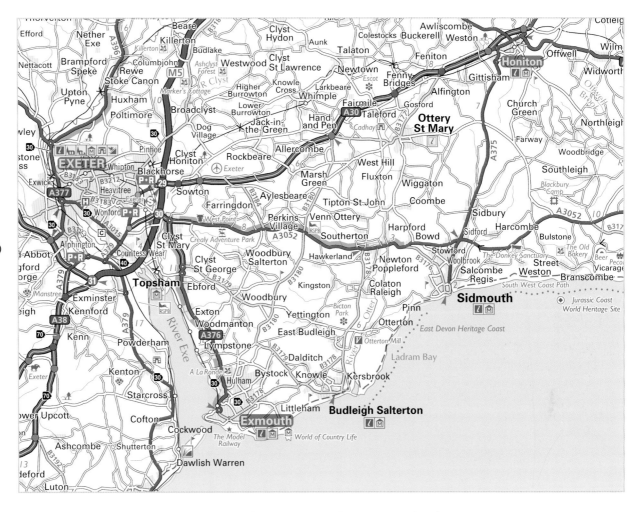

town is the National Trust's A La Ronde, a delightfully eccentric building, with interior feather friezes and shell gallery.

Honiton

Honiton, with its wide High Street, presents the face of a Georgian town, fires having destroyed the medieval original. Old coaching yards provide attractive adjuncts, and there is a lively pannier market twice a week. Honiton is famed for its elegant lace, a cottage industry that reached its zenith with the making of Queen Victoria's wedding veil, and the Allhallows Museum in High Street has excellent displays of lacemaking. The town has latterly become a centre for antiques and antiquarian books, with more than 30 shops and regular auctions.

Ottery St Mary

Ottery St Mary's handsome church replicates, in a minor way, the great cathedral of Exeter. It is a stately focus for Ottery's attractive townscape, with its sloping square in the setting of Silver Street and Gold Street, the 18th-century Paternoster Ro, and Mill Street, leading to

the River Otter. The poet Samuel Taylor Coleridge was born in Ottery amidst these evocative surroundings. The annual Tar Barrel Rolling event on 5 November is a popular attraction. To the northwest is Cadhay (occasionally open), a small Tudor manor house with a charming inner courtyard.

Sidmouth

Sidmouth is beautifully framed between high cliffs of red marl. The delightful esplanade is a mile (1.6km) long, and fishing boats are still launched from the beach. Sidmouth was a Regency resort of great style and the modern town retains the self-assurance and gentility of those days. The town has been carefully and imaginatively preserved. Handsome Victorian architecture has helped to maintain the image, expressed by the restrained, balconied hotels and the fine Georgian houses that line the seafront. A recurring motif of Sidmouth is the *cottage orné*, an affectation of the Regency period. Sidmouth Folk Week has pride of place in the town's calendar, with music, dance and storytelling events in early August.

Exmouth is a popular windsurfing spot and attracts an increasing number of kitesurfers

DORSET'S HERITAGE COAST

The shores of Lyme Bay are a fascinating mix of fossil-bearing rocks, land-slipped cliffs and chalk headlands. To the east lies Bridport; further west is Lyme Regis, a famous resort of great character; and on the far western edge of the bay, just within the Devon border, is the charming little town of Beer, in the shelter of the most westerly chalk cliffs in England.

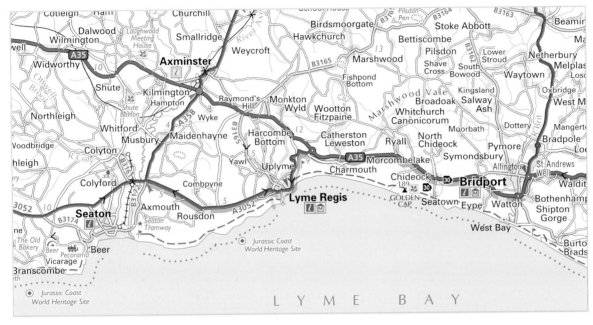

Axminster

The sheltered waters of Beer's bay mean fishermen can go out in all weathers and regularly bring in huge hauls of delicious fresh crab

Axminster was destroyed by fire during the Civil War and its oldest surviving houses are from the 18th and 19th centuries; they make a surprisingly serene townscape in spite of the busy flow of traffic on the main through road. The dignified Church of St Mary on its churchyard green dominates Trinity Square at the centre of the town.

Axminster's fame rests on carpet-making. The industry began in 1755 in Thomas Whitty House, Silver Street, the narrow street running south from Trinity Square. The building, where the world-famous carpets were once made, is to be turned into a heritage centre.

Beer

The rather lip-smacking name of Beer, sheltered by the high chalk cliffs of Beer Head to the west, comes from the Anglo-Saxon word *beare*, meaning 'grove'. Mosaic-walled cottages of flint and stone line the long ramble of Fore Street, down which a small stream tumbles through stone conduits. Common Lane rises from the seaward end of Fore Street past a terrace of delightful cottages, also faced with flint, but with brick trim. Beer beach is a wide apron of shingle upon which fishing boats with broad, undercut sterns are hauled up by a capstan engine. The Jubilee Gardens are cut into the cliff face behind the beach. Close to the town are the Beer Quarry Caves, worked since Roman times, from which the distinctive local stone was taken for such eminent buildings as Exeter Cathedral.

The Free Traders

A romantic image of smuggling has been especially associated with the West Country for generations. Proximity to France, coupled with the skills of West Country seamen made this coast the ideal arena for 'free trade'. Smuggling flourished during the 18th and early 19th centuries as a reaction to punitive taxes on imported goods. It had a sheen of respectability because so many of the goods were luxury items, and the wealthy had no qualms about buying smuggled goods. Smuggling still goes on around these shores, but drug trafficking has cast a disturbing light on the romance of 'free trade'.

Keen fossil collectors flock to the coast around Lyme Regis, where ammonites, with their distinctive spiral forms, can be found

Fossils

Fossils are the remnants of ancient animals and plants preserved within sediments that were subsequently transformed into rock, and the cliffs between Lyme Regis and Charmouth are well known for their fossils. These rocks are of the Jurassic period of 190 million years ago, and are composed of shale with alternate bands of limestone, laid down by the ancient sea that once covered most of England and Wales. Most of the fossils here are of ammonites – shell-dwelling creatures – and of primitive fish and marine reptiles. Some discoveries have been spectacular. A local woman, Mary Anning, became one of the most accomplished amateur collectors and was held in great regard by the leading palaeontologists of the day. She discovered a rare fossil of a winged lizard in 1828. Good collections of fossils are displayed in Lyme Regis at the museum in Bridge Street and at Dinosaurland in Coombe Street.

Bridport

Big, broad streets characterise Bridport, Hardy's 'Port Bredy' in his short story *Fellow Townsmen*. It is a town with a sturdy tradition of making nets and rope – considered the best in England – that dates from at least the 11th century and continues to this day. The modern town tends to merge with suburbs and fast main roads, but the flavour of an older Bridport is still captured in side streets and alleyways, and the local museum tells its history dating back to its Saxon origins.

Bridport Harbour, rewritten as West Bay by the hand of Victorian tourism, is a lively link that ties what is essentially a country town to the sea. It found fame as the location of the BBC series *Harbour Lights* in the 1990s.

Colyton

Colyton, a few miles inland from Seaton, has busy sawmills, corn mills and a tannery, and is surrounded by modern housing. And yet it has one of the loveliest town centres in all of Devon and an outer hinterland of wooded hills, lush fields and wandering lanes. A sloping site adds to the individuality of the Market Place, where the façade of the 17th-century Church House strikes a satisfying note. Behind Church House stands the Church of St Andrew, the octagonal top storey of its crossing tower adding a Continental touch. The tower is crowned by a remarkably confident weathercock.

Lyme Regis

Stylish Lyme Regis has a genteel, subdued atmosphere even when its Marine Parade is crowded with people. Its best buildings are Georgian, such as those in Broad Street, although their handsome façades hide older houses. The great arm of Lyme's harbour-cum-breakwater, the Cobb, protects the town from the worst of the prevailing southwesterly winds, famously depicted framing the cloaked and forlorn figure of Meryl Streep as Sarah Woodruff in the film of John Fowles's *The French Lieutenant's Woman*. Jane Austen based part of *Persuasion* on Lyme Regis, having stayed in the town in 1803–04.

Lyme's early prosperity was built on worldwide trade that merged at times with lucrative smuggling. Both enterprises declined, but the town thrived on the early development of tourism, coupled with

an influx of palaeontologists, attracted by Lyme's fossil sites in Black Ven Cliff.

Gun Cliff Walk, a ruggedly attractive promenade, built to disguise the town's state-of-the-art resewerage works – which have also brought the local bathing waters up to EC standards – is overlooked by the popular Marine Theatre. West of Lyme is the Undercliff, a green jungle of land-slipped woods; to the east is the shining summit of Golden Cap, towering above the sea.

Seaton

Seaton's seemingly endless pebble beach, backed by a rather featureless seafront, is well-framed between the slumped cliffs of the Undercliff National Nature Reserve to the east and Beer Head to the west. Old Seaton survives at the western end of the esplanade, where the narrow Fore Street winds down to Marine Place and to a refreshing open space above the sea. At the east end of the beach the River Axe flows quietly into the sea through the old harbour, and the enduringly popular Seaton Tramway operates open-topped and enclosed trams on a 3-mile (5km) route along the lovely Axe Valley to Colyton. Other attractions include a traditional cider-maker and the Sea Discovery Centre, featuring the marine life of Lyme Bay.

The Cobb in Lyme Regis dates back to the time of Edward I

Tourist Information
Axminster: The Old Court House, Church Street (seasonal) (tel: 01297 34386)
Bridport: 32 South Street (tel: 01308 24901)
Lyme Regis: Guildhall Cottage, Church Street (tel: 01297 442138)
Seaton: The Underfleet (tel: 01297 21660)

Beer's distinctive white chalk cliffs rise for 130m (3,600ft) above the sea, forming a scenic backdrop to its pretty pebble beach

GOLDEN BEACHES, GOLDEN VILLAGES

From the glorious golden stone of Abbotsbury to bleak grey Portland, from buckets and spades at Weymouth to Dorchester's Roman digs, this popular slice of South Dorset offers some colourful contrasts. There are surprises, too: a unique swannery; a mysterious ancient giant; a castle that is not a castle; and the pebble beach to end all pebble beaches.

Chesil Beach lies at the heart of the Jurassic Coast, a UNESCO World Heritage Site

Abbotsbury

Abbotsbury is a lovely thatched, golden ironstone village in a valley of outstanding natural beauty. Its abbey is now a ruin and only the mighty 15th-century thatched Tithe Barn, housing a museum of agricultural and rural bygones, still stands tall.

By the sea, on a lagoon protected by Chesil Beach (see below), is the Abbotsbury Swannery, once a fresh food larder for the abbots, and now a unique visitor attraction. Swans have been kept here for 600 years and the setting is as tranquil and delightful as the birds are graceful. A flower-lined path alongside a stream leads to the lagoon where up to 600 swans gather, and there are walkways through the reedbed. On the edge of the village the Abbotsbury Sub-Tropical Gardens have evolved from an 18th-century walled garden into an award-winning collection of rare and exotic plants.

Cerne Abbas

The picturesque village of Cerne Abbas hosts a glorious collection of architectural styles; from golden ironstone houses to colour-washed cottages, the old chequered flint and sandstone courthouse and the beamed and jettied Pitchmarket on Abbey Street. At the top of this street is a splendidly restored house, built around the 15th-century gateway of the old abbey. The adjacent Abbot's Porch and the Abbey Guest House are open to visitors.

Just outside the village is the viewing point for the famous Cerne Giant, a 180ft (54.8m) tall chalk figure of a naked man with a large erect phallus, brandishing a 120ft (36.6m) long club. The style of the figure suggests that the giant may be of Romano-British origin.

Chesil Beach

In Old English *chesil* means 'shingle', but this is no ordinary shingle beach. It comprises an 18-mile (28.8km) bank of pebbles up to 40ft (12.2m) high and 150–200 yards (137–183m) wide, enclosing the Fleet Lagoon (where an oyster farm can be visited). The stones are naturally graded by powerful currents – swimming is not advised here – and decrease from cannonball-sized in the east to pea-sized in the west. The best view is from Portland.

Dorchester

The 'Casterbridge' of Thomas Hardy's novels is stamped with his signature: the statue at the top of the town; his study, reconstructed in the museum; St Peter's Church, which he helped to restore; Max Gate, the house he designed and occupied until his death in 1928; and any number of references along the High Street. But Dorchester is much more. The Dorset County Museum introduces the Roman town (*Durnovaria*), with excellent mosaics, and the Roman boundaries can be followed along traffic-free avenues to the remains of a Roman town house. The dark side of Dorchester's history is in its unsavoury judicial role. In the Old Crown Court the six Tolpuddle Martyrs were sentenced to deportation in 1834 for forming a trade union (court and cells are open to the public) and opposite, in

Historic and Literary Houses

Dorchester is ringed by a number of inviting houses. Athelhampton (5 miles/8km northeast) is probably the finest, a romantic 15th-century manor with a magnificent medieval hall. Thomas Hardy described 16th-century Wolfeton (1.5 miles/2.4km north) as an 'ivied manor house flanked by battlemented towers'. Hardy's Cottage, his birthplace, is at Higher Bockhampton (3 miles/4.8km northeast).

been colonised by a profusion of wild flowers and butterflies, and one has become an imaginative sculpture park. Many areas are designated Sites of Special Scientific Interest and there are excellent opportunities for birdwatching, fossil-hunting, rock-climbing and walking. Down on the coast, the former Naval Air Station has become a world-class diving and water-sports centre.

From Weymouth's harbour, boat trips head to Portland and the World Heritage coast, both for fishing and sightseeing

Weymouth's attractions include a traditional funfair, complete with carousel, on the sands

what is now Judge Jeffreys Restaurant, is where the infamous judge lodged while conducting the Bloody Assizes in 1685, meting out vicious retribution (74 deaths and 175 deportations) on the supporters of the unsuccessful bid for the throne by the Duke of Monmouth.

Portland

Portland, linked to the mainland only by a causeway, is famous for its stone, which was used in such diverse buildings as St Paul's Cathedral in London and the UN Building in New York. Some quarries are still working, others have

Weymouth

George III first popularised sea bathing at Weymouth in 1798 and he is honoured by a jolly statue on the Esplanade. Weymouth is a lively seaside resort with up-to-the-minute attractions and events, a long golden beach and a picturesque harbour busy with small fishing boats. Nothe Fort is now a Museum of Coastal Defence, while Brewer's Quay, a handsomely redeveloped Victorian brewery, houses shops, the Weymouth Museum, a multi-media Timewalk and other attractions. At the east end of the beach Weymouth Sea Life Park is within Lodmore Country Park.

See Walk J, page 63
Dorset's Other Hardy

See Walk K, page 64
By Hardy's Cottage and 'Egdon Heath'

See Walk L, page 65
Giant Steps to Cerne Abbas

Tourist Information

Dorchester: Unit 11, Antelope Walk (tel: 01305 267992)
Portland: Portland Bill Lighthouse (seasonal) (tel: 01305 861233)
Weymouth: King's Statue, The Esplanade (tel: 01305 785747)

Maiden Castle

Maiden Castle is not actually a castle at all, it is the finest earthworks (i.e. a fortification made of earth) in Britain. When built, largely in the first century BC, this hilltop retreat was fortified with ramparts and complex chicane-style entrances, easily defended against primitive attackers, though not against the technically advanced Roman legions, who in AD43 slaughtered its inhabitants. All structures have long gone but its series of concentric rings, covering 115 acres (47ha), are still impressive. Try to view the hillfort in the early morning or early evening light, when the shadows accentuate the rings.

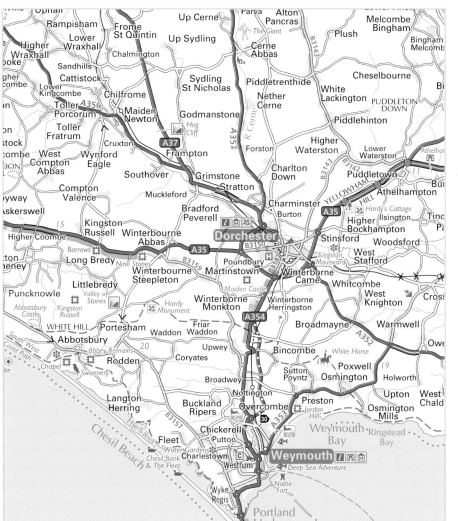

FROM BOURNEMOUTH ROCK TO PURBECK STONE

The contrasting faces of the British seaside lie along this short stretch of coast; from Bournemouth's lively beaches and genteel gardens, to unspoilt Studland and the natural wild haven of Brownsea Island. Poole offers a maritime flavour, while inland the picturesque market towns of East Dorset and the Isle of Purbeck boast ancient churches and ruined castles.

Bournemouth's pier began life as a wooden construction, built in 1861, but was replaced by an iron pier in 1880

12th-century Corfe Castle rises high above the Isle of Purbeck

Bournemouth

Popular since the early 19th century (Queen Victoria once recommended it to Disraeli), Bournemouth has shaken off its one-time image as a refuge for the elderly and is now a lively, year-round resort for all ages. Its natural features – 7 miles (11km) of glorious sands backed by steep 'chines' – remain the focus of the town, and beautiful gardens, illuminated by candles after dark, snake their way up the hillside. The town itself has excellent shopping and a huge variety of restaurants. The area around the pier has a fairground atmosphere in summer, with its merry-go-round, street performers and Friday-night fireworks. Nearby are the Oceanarium and the Waterfront Complex. The cultural counterpoint to all this is the excellent Russell-Cotes Art Gallery and Museum.

Christchurch

Christchurch takes its name from its priory, the longest parish church in England, and also one of the most impressive. Its Norman origins are clearly visible. Next to the priory are other reminders of the Conquest: the keep of the Norman castle and the 'Norman House', both in picturesque ruins.

From here, follow the shady Convent Walk beside the peaceful old mill stream to the Town Quay, a charming pastoral scene where lawns and gardens meet slow-flowing waters, dotted with small pleasure craft, ducks and swans. The Edwardian power station now houses the Museum of Electricity, with nostalgic exhibits and interactive experiments. Water-powered Place Mill has milling objects, arts and crafts, and the Red House Museum and Gardens can be found on Quay Road.

Corfe Castle

Corfe Castle (National Trust) is one of the most dramatic and picturesque spots in the whole southwest. Built high on a hill in 1080–1105, it dominated this region until it was slighted after the Civil War. Now it is a romantic ruin, offering marvellous views and dark, distant memories – the tragic boy-king Edward (the Martyr) was murdered here in AD978. The village below is an attractive collection of low stone houses, many of which date from the 16th to 18th centuries. There is a model village, a small museum in the tiny Town Hall and steam train rides on the reopened Swanage–Wareham Railway.

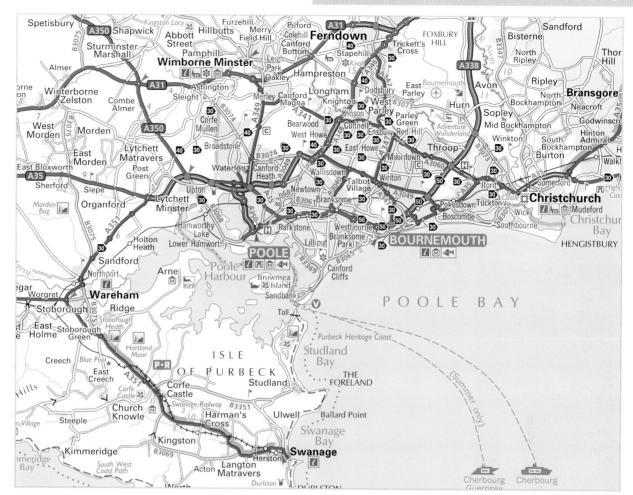

Natural Beauty

Just west of Corfe Castle lies Lulworth Cove, a perfect circle of beach and one of southern England's most photographed spots. The cliff archway of adjacent Durdle Door is the most spectacular of the many sea- and wind-eroded rock formations to be found here.

The natural beauty of Poole Harbour and its islands is remarkable for a very different reason; over 100 million barrels of oil have been taken from here in recent years, making it the largest on-shore oilfield in Western Europe, and yet its exploitation has been rendered almost invisible by painstaking environmental management.

Poole

Poole Harbour is the second largest natural harbour in the world (after Sydney) and the jewel in its crown is Brownsea Island, a 500-acre (200ha) nature reserve, home to deer, rare red squirrel and waterfowl. Poole Quay, still a working harbour, has undergone development to provide a smart marina for the local fishing fleet and pleasure craft. The Waterfront Museum relates the town's colourful maritime history, while its adjunct, 15th-century Scaplen's Court, is also dedicated to local history. Poole Pottery offers an interesting factory tour and there is an Aquarium and Serpentarium. One of Europe's finest gardens is Compton Acres, where a number of gardens have been reproduced in colourful and magnificent detail. Of the five main gardens – all classically themed – the Italian, Japanese and Wooded Valley Garden stand out.

Wareham

The Quay at Wareham features on countless calendars. Across the languorous River Frome, plied by pleasure craft, is the picture-perfect square, with its old granary house backed by the Anglo-Saxon church and priory of Lady St Mary. The church holds a stone coffin that is popularly

supposed to be that of Edward the Martyr (see Corfe Castle opposite). St Martin's, at the north end of the High Street also dates from Saxon times and has an impressive memorial to T. E. Lawrence (of Arabia), who also features in the town's museum.

Wimborne Minster

Narrow Georgian streets and hidden courtyards distinguish this charming market town, and at its heart stands the sturdy and attractive Minster Church of St Cuthburga, founded in AD705. Seek out its astronomical clock, its chained library and, on the outside, the colourful Quarter Jack figure which strikes the church bell every 15 minutes. Opposite the church is the excellent Priest's House Museum, portraying 400 years of East Dorset history.

Tourist Information

Bournemouth:
Westover Road
(tel: 0845 051 1701)
Christchurch:
49 High Street
(tel: 01202 471780)
Poole: Enefco House,
Poole Quay (tel: 01202 253253)
Wareham: Holy Trinity Church, South Street
(tel: 01929 552740)
Wimborne Minster:
29 High Street,
(tel: 01202 886116)

Durdle Door near Lulworth is a geological marvel of weathered limestone

CAVERNS AND CATHEDRALS; CHEESE AND WINE

The Mendip Hills are a welcome contrast to the flatness of the Somerset Levels. The craggy valleys of Cheddar and Burrington Combe slice deeply into their smooth flanks and, on the lush, southern slopes, strawberries, apples and grapes flourish. To the south lies Wells, site of a magnificent cathedral. Further south again is Glastonbury, with its ruined abbey and the mysterious Glastonbury Tor, focus of both Christian and Arthurian legends.

An array of 350 oak panels, each different from the other, forms the glorious waggon-head roof (c1450) in the church of St Peter and St Paul, at Shepton Mallet

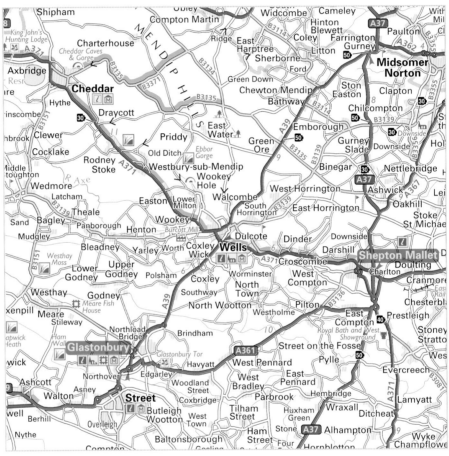

The Mendip Hills

The Mendips, rising to about 1,000ft (300m), were once islands in a vast prehistoric lake. The limestone flanks of the hills are pierced by great ravines – Cheddar Gorge, Ebbor Gorge, Burrington Combe – and are riddled with the serpentine cave systems which make these hills so popular with cavers. Villages such as Priddy stand at the heart of grassy sheep country, where Bronze Age burial mounds and old lead workings, dating from Roman to Victorian times, lie amidst the lonely fields. Along the south-facing slopes of the Mendips, strawberries are grown and Mendip vineyards produce good English wines to match Somerset's famous cider.

Axbridge

Axbridge lies between the Mendips and the motorway. The Square, at the heart of the village, draws in the converging streets to a happy centre of medieval design. It is overlooked by the Church of St John the Baptist, and two ancient open wells lie beneath arches in the churchyard wall. The most striking building is King John's Hunting Lodge (National Trust) at the corner of High Street and The Square. Timber-framed and beautifully preserved, it now houses a good museum. The name is rather misleading, though – King John predated the building by 300 years, but it was certainly once an inn, coincidentally called the King's Head.

Cheddar

To give a name to a world-famous cheese is recognition enough for any place, but Cheddar is also noted for the spectacular scenery of the great gorge that slices into the flanks of the gentle Mendip Hills. The vast limestone bluffs that rise from the roadside are marble-white where the rock is exposed, but in places are draped with ivy and with precariously rooted trees. The showcaves of the lower gorge are an enduring tourist attraction, and these have been joined by other places to visit, including cheese-makers. There are several footpaths around and above the gorge and some spectacular views, notably from the top of Jacob's Ladder.

The 17th-century nave in the Grade I listed St John the Baptist church, Axbridge

Wookey Hole

Wookey Hole is a system of three underground chambers through which the River Axe flows into a lake from the heart of the Mendip Hills. There is strong evidence of Iron-Age, and possibly earlier Stone-Age occupation. The attractions of the Wookey Hole complex are delightfully bizarre. They include the essential guided tour of the floodlit caves along walkways and past fanciful silhouettes and colourful features. At the surface there is a Victorian papermill, a fairground exhibition with several rides from around the turn of the century, an old Penny Arcade and the Magical Mirror Maze.

Glastonbury

Christian symbolism vies with Arthurian legend and 'new age' culture in the shadow of the enigmatic Glastonbury Tor. Joseph of Arimathea is said to have brought the Holy Grail to Glastonbury, and from his staff is said to have sprung the original Glastonbury Thorn. The great abbey was founded by King Ine in AD700. In 1191, after a destructive fire, the monks claimed to have discovered the bones of Arthur and Guinevere in the abbey grounds, thus boosting its fading appeal as a place of pilgrimage. Outstanding town buildings include the Elizabethan George and Pilgrim Hotel, the Tribunal, with its Somerset Rural Life Museum, and the Peat Moors Centre. Traditional shops are interspersed with those giving off the smell of incense and the sounds of meditation music.

Shepton Mallet

Shepton Mallet's marketplace has lost some of its character, but retains a number of listed buildings, including the 15th-century Shambles, an open-sided market

stall. From here streets and alleyways run to the River Sheppey. The market cross, with its three-stage pinnacle and arcaded base, is of 15th-century design, and was partly rebuilt in the 19th century. Wealth from the medieval wool industry paid for the splendid Church of St Peter and St Paul.

Street

Street and feet go together. The town's modern development came through the family of Cyrus Clark, which for generations dominated the footwear market in Britain. The family's strange mixture of austere Quakerism and generous paternalism has left Street with few pubs, but with an excellent library, swimming pools and a theatre among its 'improving' facilities. There is a shoe museum in High Street, and Clark's Village of factory outlet shops is a great attraction.

Wells

The glory of Wells is its magnificent cathedral and attendant ecclesiastical buildings – the merging of solid dignity with elegance in stone. The city, England's smallest, complements all this with unpretentious charm. The spacious Market Place has the style of a piazza, and gives access to the exhilarating expanse of the cathedral green through a narrow archway known as Penniless Porch. From the green, the splendour of the cathedral's west front is overwhelming. North of the cathedral is Vicar's Close, a glorious time capsule from the Middle Ages, though remodelled and restored in part. To the south the Bishop's Palace sits graciously within its moat.

In legend, the holy hill of Glastonbury Tor is home to Gwyn ap Nudd, King of the Fairies

See Walk M, page 66
More Borders at Three County Corner

See Walk N, page 67
A Canal and a Church at Bradford-on-Avon

Tourist Information

Cheddar: The Gorge (seasonal) (tel: 01934 744071)
Glastonbury: The Tribunal, 9 High Street (tel: 01458 832954)
Sedgemoor Services: Somerset Visitor Centre, M5 South, near Axbridge (tel: 01934 750833)
Shepton Mallet: 70 High Street (tel: 01749 345258)
Taunton: Paul Street (tel: 01823 336344)
Wells: Town Hall, Market Place (tel: 01749 672552)

Gough's Cave, Cheddar, where a Victorian archaeologist discovered Britain's oldest complete skeleton, dating from 7150BC

CAMELOT COUNTRY

The border between Somerset and Dorset passes through a serene and beautiful landscape which is famous for its associations with the legendary King Arthur and his court of Camelot. It is a land of great houses such as Montacute, of splendid abbeys and churches at Sherborne and North Cadbury, and of villages of lovely cottages in honey-coloured stone from Ham Hill.

Elizabethan-era Montacute House, seen through the trees, with the church of St Catherine (left), which holds the tombs of those who built the mansion

The Cadburys

The Cadburys, North and South, are just over a mile (1.6 km) apart, and both are distinguished by great works. North Cadbury has its Church of St Michael the Archangel, an ambitious early 15th-century building of strong character, matched by the adjacent late Elizabethan house of Cadbury Court. South Cadbury has its more modest Church of St Thomas à Becket, but on the high hill above are the spectacular outlines of Cadbury Castle, a fortified prehistoric encampment of 18 acres (7ha). It is one of the largest of its kind in Britain and is claimed, inevitably, as the one true 'Camelot', the royal court of the legendary King Arthur. Today, the sheep-grazed hilltop is as green as felt. In places the surviving defensive banks rise to over 40ft (12.2m) from the external ditch.

Montacute

Montacute provides a veritable feast of fine buildings, displaying the glowing stone of Ham Hill at its best. The honey-coloured walls and tiled roofs are mellow with age and are mottled with lichen. The heart of the village is The Borough, a proper village square flanked by delightful houses. At one corner is the entrance to Montacute House (National Trust), one of the most grandly self-conscious Elizabethan buildings in England. Inside are exquisite rooms that rise elegantly to the final flourish of the Long Gallery, 189ft (57.7m) long, which is hung with a National Gallery collection of portraits of the period.

Muchelney

The name 'Muchelney' means 'Great Island', the site of this serene little community being on a raised area of land amidst watery levels. The Church of St Peter and St Paul, dominating the scene, has some startling features inside, not least the enchantingly overpainted wagon roof of the nave, upon which bosomy angels swirl amidst stars and billowing clouds. Across the road from the church is the National Trust's Priest's House, of medieval date and remarkably authentic inside. But Muchelney's greatest treasure is the Abbot's Lodging (English Heritage), a welcome survival amidst the ruins of Muchelney Abbey. Deceptively small from outside, the interior is breathtaking, full of golden light and with some glorious features.

Sherborne

Sherborne's main thoroughfare is called Cheap Street, though there is nothing undersold about this most self-confident of Dorset towns, where Georgian and Victorian buildings adhere to the medieval framework. Sherborne Abbey is a powerful building and, though it has a rather stolid exterior, the interior is splendid. It has all the dignity of a cathedral, and the exquisite fan-vaulting and extravagant decoration of the choir give density and richness to the constrained space. Sherborne has two castles – the ruined Norman castle east of the town and Sir Walter Raleigh's 16th-century extravagance nearby, lavishly furnished and standing in beautiful grounds.

High Fliers

The modest tower of the pleasant little church at Yeovilton rises above the cluster of neighbouring houses. But Yeovilton's fame rises much higher than that, on the wings of the powerful aircraft of the adjoining Royal Naval Air Station. The station houses the Fleet Air Arm Museum where the development of Naval flying is detailed from the early days of the Royal Naval Air Service. There are more than 40 aircraft on display, covering 100 years of naval flying, as well as exciting high-tech exhibits, including a flight simulator and the 'Ultimate Aircraft Carrier Experience' – all the sights, smells, sounds and activity of the flight deck of a carrier. Here, too, is the British prototype of *Concorde*, which visitors can climb aboard.

Tourist Information

Sherborne: 3 Tilton Court, Digby Road (tel: 01935 815341)
Somerton: The Parish Rooms, Market Place (tel: 01458 274070)
Yeovil: Hendford (tel: 01935 845946)

A modern-day bronze of St Matthew, in the Church of St Michael the Archangel, North Cadbury

Golden Stone

Five miles (8km) to the west of Yeovil, above Montacute and Tintinhull, stands Ham Hill, site of a vast fortified settlement that rivals Cadbury Castle in size and that was used from Stone-Age times to the Roman period. Over the years the hilltop was farmed intensively and parts were used as rabbit warrens, but in the main it was quarried for its building stone. The rock of Ham Hill was deposited 170 million years ago as sediments of shell and sand on the bed of a warm and shallow sea, subsequently compressed and cemented, with iron compounds seeping through the mix to give the golden hue that has made 'Hamstone' so aesthetically pleasing. See local examples in the villages of Stoke-sub-Hamden, Tintinhull and Montacute, including the splendid Montacute House.

Somerton

Somerton's enduring appeal is the beauty of its Market Square and adjacent streets. The blurred greyness of Blue Lias stone enhances the buildings that line the Square, and at its heart is the market cross, octagonal and open-arched, with central tiers of shelves for produce. The inside angles of the pillars have little stone seats that are surprisingly comfortable.

From every angle good buildings catch the eye. The Church of St Michael, with an octagonal tower, fills the space to the north without overshadowing the Square. Broad Street leads from the Square and continues the theme of utterly charming buildings.

Yeovil

Yeovil has lost its old market town status and is now a thriving commercial and industrial centre, its traditional glove-making now diversified. Today its name is associated with the construction of helicopters. As elsewhere, modernisation has transformed the town, but there is interest still in the centre. Yeovil's Church of St John rather sternly occupies a central eminence between Princes Street and Silver Street. It is built of limestone that has weathered to give the exterior a satsifyingly rugged appearance, although dressings of Ham Hill stone have suffered from erosion.

High Street retains the style of a marketplace at its eastern end, where it merges with the pedestrianised Middle Street. Off High Street, to the south, is King George Street, where handsome neo-Georgian buildings, now mainly finance houses, create a pleasingly classical enclave. Just south of the town centre is the Ninesprings Country Park, a green space extending to 40 acres (16ha).

Behind the high altar at Sherborne Abbey is an 1884 reredos, designed by R. H. Carpenter

CHURCH AND HOME: BUILDINGS IN THE LANDSCAPE

For many people, the West Country means the picture-postcard thatched cottages of Dorset, Somerset and Devon, the cobbled streets of the famous coastal villages of Clovelly and St Ives, and the elaborate façades of seaside hotels in Torquay and Ilfracombe. But, memorable images apart, it is the building materials that characterise the different parts of a region, as represented by cottages and castles, churches and cathedrals. Above all else, the best buildings appear to have grown from the very landscape that they adorn.

Founded in 1141 as a Cistercian Monastery, Forde Abbey was a seat of religious learning until King Henry VIII dissolved the monasteries in 1539

The vaulted interior of 19th-century Truro Cathedral, built of local granite and stone

Local stone

In the border country of Somerset and Dorset some of the finest building stone is found. The exquisite golden stone of Somerset's Ham Hill was transported across the county border to give such splendid buildings as Sherborne Abbey its mellow hue. Hamstone has been lavished on great Somerset houses too, as much as on the charming vernacular buildings of so many of the county's villages. In the immediate hinterland of Ham Hill are the Tudor and Jacobean piles of Montacute House, Tintinhull and the restored Barrington Court, the latter further enhanced by the 20th-century development of its gardens. All three are in the care of the National Trust and are open to the public.

In Cornwall the availability of durable granite has produced the solid four-square certainty of church tower and farmhouse alike, the roughness and earthy colour of the unadorned stone merging with the knuckly landscape of Dartmoor and the Atlantic coast of Cornwall. But in the non-granite country of Devon cottages were often built of 'cob', unbaked mud that was remarkably durable. In Cornwall and Devon too, the use of less attractive slates and shales has resulted in darker, more sombre buildings that still merge satisfyingly with the landscape from which they emerged.

Granite is a rock that is often at its best when low to the ground, absorbed by the landscape rather than set monumentally upon it. Yet types of Cornish granite have produced such great buildings

as Lanhydrock, near Bodmin, and the magnificent Antony House, on the banks of the River Lynher opposite Plymouth.

Church architecture

An enduring motif of West Country architecture is the local church, with its stately tower rising fortress-like from surrounding woods, or dominating the lower roof-line of numerous towns and villages. Somerset is particularly noted for its elegant church towers. Spires were few in Somerset; instead the tall, square tower, with its characteristic Somerset tracery and its elegant lace-like pinnacles and statue niches, big windows and ornamental string courses, has been the glory of the West Country for centuries. There are especially fine church buildings at Wells, Taunton, Glastonbury, Shepton Mallet, Huish Episcopi and Yeovil.

There was less church-building during the 17th and 18th centuries. That period saw the development of nonconformist chapels and meeting places, and it was not until the 19th century that a new religious self-confidence produced such fine Regency churches as Teignmouth's St James's and the Norman-influenced St Paul's at Honiton. Large numbers of nonconformist churches were built throughout the West Country during the 19th century. They were simple preaching places, although neoclassical and Gothic themes emerged. In Cornwall, stern-faced Methodist chapels still dominate the rural landscape, their main façades seemingly always to face the unsmiling north, as if to deny even the sun its elevated place.

Changing styles

The Romans left few traces of their presence west of Exeter, the Anglo-Saxons likewise. But Norman influence was substantial in churches and castles and there are numerous West Country churches that have some element of Norman work that has survived the repeated restorations and extensions of the ensuing centuries.

It is the 15th and 16th centuries, however, that have bequeathed us fairly complete buildings. Rural buildings of the period were still vulnerable to structural erosion and decay from the impact of the heavy work that went on around them, but in Devon, good examples of larger farmhouses still exist. These include Sir Walter Raleigh's birthplace of Hayes Barton near Budleigh Salterton, constructed of cob and with a fine Devon thatch.

Good stone buildings of the period include the outstanding George Inn at Norton St Philip, between Bath and Frome. The George is pure medieval, its ground floor of stone with a fine entrance archway, the upper storeys timber-framed. In Glastonbury High Street is another famous Inn – The George and Pilgrim – this time in three storeys of ornamented stone. A few yards further along is the 15th-century Gothic building known as the Tribunal.

The great buildings of the late 16th century are well represented in the West Country by beautiful houses such as Montacute and by town buildings such as the Guildhall at Exeter. Later developments of the Stuart period produced Somerset's Forde Abbey, an example of how buildings evolve from earlier forms. Forde lies on the site of a 12th-century Cistercian abbey and parts of the abbey are incorporated into the 17th-century house. Tintinhull near Yeovil is another example of incorporation, the mainly 17th-century building having absorbed parts of a 16th-century farmhouse.

The last 200 years

By the 18th century urban architecture was becoming increasingly sophisticated, as the burgeoning merchant class expressed its aspirations. Great country houses also reflected this. Devon's Saltram House, the county's finest country mansion, is an outstanding early Georgian building with fine interiors, the whole maintained by the National Trust. But it was urban building that became the focus for fashionable

Hundreds of statues, many of which were originally painted and gilded, adorn the 13th-century west front of Wells Cathedral

architecture. The legacy of the Georgian and Regency periods, so evident in our great cities and in such places as Bath, can be seen in most West Country towns of any size. Even as far west as Truro the stylish neoclassicism of entire terraces, such as those of Lemon Street, matched the sophistication of those of Bath, and the red-brick elegance of Taunton's Hammet Street and The Crescent match the crescents and terraces of Exeter.

During the late 18th century and well into the Victorian period, the 'seaside' architecture peculiar to holiday resorts produced some outstanding buildings in towns such as Sidmouth, Ilfracombe and Torquay. Sidmouth still has some very fine Regency buildings, including the fascinating *cottage orné*, a mock-rustic style incorporating Gothic façades topped with lavish thatch. At Ilfracombe, the use of polychromatic brickwork resulted in some outstanding Victorian Gothic buildings.

It was a stylishness soon to be overtaken by the bland and brutal convenience architecture of the 20th century, as technology and commercial enterprise ensured the triumph of function over style. Yet good modern architecture is still given breathing space, even in the featureless world of supermarkets and tower blocks. Award-winning buildings include Truro's Crown Court, designed by the same architects who were responsible for the Tate Gallery at St Ives, and in 1995 Sainsbury's superstore at Plymouth won an award for

its bold design that features a white canopy made of overlapping sail-like armatures.

But it is in the surviving older buildings of Dorset, Somerset, Devon and Cornwall that the great legacy of good West Country architecture is enshrined – the Hamstone villages, the thatched houses of quiet hamlets, and the lichened and mossy cottages of fishing villages. Above all, the marvellous churches and cathedrals and the great country houses of the west remain as priceless jewels within the landscape.

The spectacular fan vaulted roof of Sherborne Abbey is one of England's earliest and finest

STANDING STONES AND A SOARING SPIRE

The great sarsen stones of Stonehenge tower 21ft (6.4m) high and weigh up to 50 tonnes; the majestic spire of Salisbury soars to over 400ft (121.9m) and is visible for many miles around. They were around some 3,000 years apart, perhaps even to different deities, but one commonality is clear – both inspire awe and turn thoughts from worldly to spiritual matters.

One of the best known of all prehistoric monuments, Stonehenge together with Avebury was made a World Heritage Site in 1986

Amesbury

According to legend, Amesbury Abbey was founded in Saxon times by an uncle of King Arthur and it was here that Queen Guinevere retreated and died. The abbey was refounded by Henry II and became one of England's most important religious houses until its dissolution in 1539–40. Today all that remains of the abbey is the atmospheric low flint Church of St Mary.

Heale Garden

Charles II sheltered in Heale House after the Battle of Worcester in 1651, and a very restful spot it is too. The house is not open to the public but the charming gardens by the side of the peaceful River Avon evoke the quiet of a bygone age. Notable features include great pergola tunnels of apples and Japanese water gardens which criss-cross tiny streams.

Old Sarum

It is not easy to visualise today, but this now deserted 56-acre (23ha) hilltop site was the forerunner of modern Salisbury – a town complete with a royal castle and cathedral built by the Normans.

Old Sarum (English Heritage) had been occupied since the Iron Age, but by the early 13th century, friction between clerics and troops, and the parched and very uncomfortable windswept nature of the site, prompted a move. This was done quite literally, taking cathedral and castle stones down to New Sarum (Salisbury) for use in the new Cathedral Close. Substantial parts of the lower castle remain; elsewhere are only fragments, but the views and ambience alone make the trip worthwhile.

Salisbury

At 404ft (123.1m) high, the spire of Salisbury Cathedral is not only the tallest in England but is still the mighty landmark it was intended to be when erected in the 14th century. The cathedral is an architectural masterpiece, built in just 38 years (excluding the spire) during the 13th century, and is unique for its harmony. Although the interior may not quite live up to the promise of the superb exterior, it holds many fine monuments. The cathedral's fine cloisters, among the country's largest, lead to the the library, home to one of the four copies of Magna Carta, and to the very fine chapter house.

The Cathedral Close, originally designed to house the clerics, now forms a glorious precinct to the cathedral. Most of the houses have been altered over the centuries, so their appearance is now 16th to 18th century, and four of these are open to the public as museums. Mompesson House (National Trust), built in 1701, boasts superb plasterwork, a collection of glassware and a charming garden where tea can be taken. The award-winning Salisbury and South Wiltshire Museum, home of the Stonehenge Gallery and an archaeological collection

Woodhenge (English Heritage) is an even older circle than Stonehenge and, like its illustrious neighbour, is aligned to indicate where the sun would rise and set on the solstices. The wooden staves that made up the circular arrangements have long gone and their positions are marked by rather unflattering concrete posts. In the middle of these is what is presumed to be an altar stone. Near here the remains of a child with a deliberately fractured skull were found, leading to suppositions of human sacrifice. There are interpretive boards next to the site, but for more information visit the Wiltshire Heritage Museum, Devizes.

The ruins of Old Sarum reveal settlements spanning four millennia of human history

Salisbury's beautiful cathedral has provided both spiritual and artistic inspiration since it was built in the 13th century

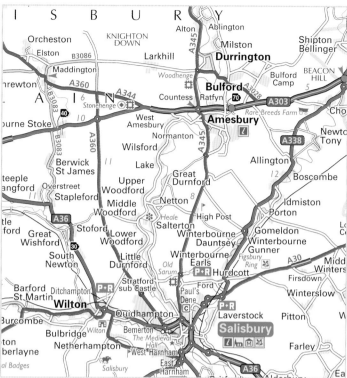

of national importance, resides in the late 14th-century King's House, while there is a military museum in the 13th-century Wardrobe.

A good introduction to the city can be found in the magnificent 13th-century Medieval Hall, where a large-screen presentation runs continuously. Other notable historic buildings include the Guildhall and the 13th-century Poultry Cross. Queen Elizabeth's Gardens, alongside the River Avon, enjoy a bucolic water-meadow setting and a classic view of the cathedral.

Stonehenge

Europe's most famous and most easily recognisable ancient site continues to impress and to intrigue. The origins of Stonehenge (English Heritage/National Trust) go back around 5,000 years to 3000BC, when the first bank and ditch was constructed, possibly with a wooden building at its centre. A thousand years later the first stone circle was raised, but left unfinished. The present stone circle, *c*1500BC, is possibly the remains of a temple and is famous for its trilithons, the large door-frame-shaped stone arrangements, which are actually slotted together with mortise and tenon joints. These are arranged so that when the sun rises and sets on the solstices it shines straight through the circle along The Avenue on to the Heel Stone. However, despite this solar alignment, evidence that Stonehenge was some sort of observatory or lunar calendar is still slight and the purpose of the design remains a mystery.

In 2000, access at the Summer Solstice was granted for the first time in 16 years and the event has passed off peacefully ever since, marking a new atmosphere of cooperation. Plans to build a new visitor centre are currently being developed.

Wilton

The pretty village of Wilton is famous for carpets and for Wilton House, home to the Earls of Pembroke and one of the great country houses of England. The present

house (1649–52) was built by Inigo Jones and is notable for its art treasures and sumptuous interiors, including the Cube Room (30ft/9.1m long, wide and high) and the Double Cube Room. The latter is full of Van Dycks, and there are other Old Masters around the house. The focal point of the grounds is the Palladian Bridge, based on the Rialto Bridge in Venice.

In the village centre is a ruined Saxon church, and off handsome West Street is a rather incongruous mid-19th-century Italianate basilica. The Royal Wilton Carpet Factory began weaving in the early 18th century, continuing an age-old local tradition. It remains on its original site, and offers factory tours and demonstrations of hand-weaving. Wilton's museum is in the courtyard, and some old factory buildings now form Wilton Shopping Village, with a variety of factory outlets in a pleasant riverside setting.

Tourist Information
Amesbury: The Library,
Smithfield Street
(tel: 01980 622833)
Salisbury: Fish Row
(tel: 01722 334956)

The Palladian south front of Wilton House, its severe lines softened by climbing shrubs

A TALE OF TWO CITIES

When John Betjeman referred to one of the two great western cities as 'the most beautiful, interesting and distinguished in England', the only surprise was that he was referring not to Bath but to Bristol. Bath can console itself with the fact that it is one of only a handful of World Heritage Cities, and is probably the finest 18th-century city in the world.

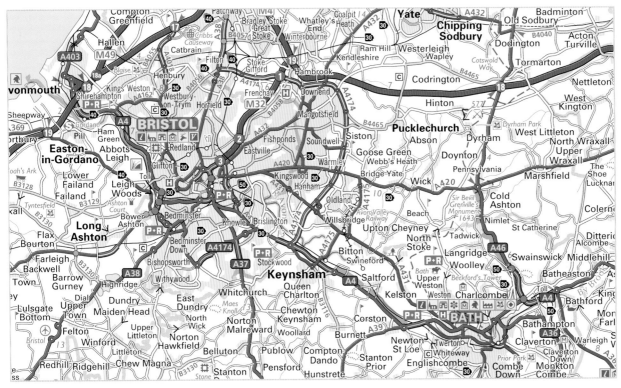

Man of Manners

Richard 'Beau' Nash (1674–1762) was first attracted to Bath as a gambler. Recognising its potential as a resort he organised balls and social functions on an opulent scale and opened the Pump Room to accommodate many of these events. He became the arbiter of fashion, laid down social rules and made the city a safer and cleaner place. He forbade the wearing of swords in the city and even smoking in certain public places (the latter being a particularly strong measure in those days). Bath became the most fashionable place in England, and Nash, for his foresight, became an extremely wealthy man.

The magnificant sweep of Bath's Royal Crescent once included some of the city's finest residences

Bath

Bath is a World Heritage Site, but its history and superb architecture have not set it in a time warp – it is also a lively centre for the arts, with good restaurants and excellent shopping. It owes its importance to its hot springs, which are unique in Britain. The Romans built a great bathing complex here, and the site comprises the most impressive Roman remains in Britain, superbly preserved and presented. Just around the corner is Thermae Bath Spa, a 21st-century leisure complex that has revived the tradition of hot-spring bathing in the city.

During the 18th century the city bloomed, made fashionable by Richard 'Beau' Nash and made beautiful by the two John Woods (father and son), working with the honey-coloured Bath stone. One of the city's most famous landmarks is the 18th-century Pulteney Bridge, lined with tiny shops and dubbed 'Florence on Avon' for its Italianate appearance. A short walk due north leads to the Assembly Rooms, an architectural masterpiece, which, along with the Pump Room, was the hub of 18th-century social life. The highly acclaimed and extensive Fashion Museum now resides in the basement. Close by, the Circus is a perfect appetiser for the Royal Crescent, the tour de force of John Wood the younger. Built in 1767, it is a majestic curved terrace of 30 houses, and No. 1 has been splendidly restored to show visitors

Originally covered by a 40m-high (130ft) vaulted ceiling, the Great Bath is today the centrepiece of the Roman bathing complex in the city of Bath

The magnificent Clifton suspension bridge was designed by Isambard Kingdom Brunel and completed in 1864

Man of Iron

Isambard Kingdom Brunel (1806–59) was the greatest designer and wrought-iron architect of early Victorian England. Moving on from his triumphs with the Great Western Railway (which included the design of Bristol Temple Meads station), he built the famous transatlantic paddle steamer, the *Great Western*, launched from Bristol in 1837, then superseded this with the SS *Great Britain*. This was the first ever iron ocean-going propeller-driven ship and when launched was also the world's biggest ship. Brunel's pièce de résistance was the Clifton Suspension Bridge, which, sadly, he did not live to see completed.

Bristol

The city of Bristol celebrated the Millennium by spending £97 million on its harbourside area, an impressive redevelopment that combines up-to-the-minute attractions – science and nature discovery centres, IMAX cinema – with trendy nightspots and restaurants and boat services that explore the historic waterways.

The history of the city is inextricably linked to the harbour. It was from here that John Cabot set sail in the 15th century on a voyage that resulted in the discovery of Newfoundland; from here that Brunel launched his famous ships; from here that countless pioneers set sail for the New World. Brunel's SS *Great Britain* is back at the Great Western Dock, restored and open to the public, beside the Maritime Heritage Centre and a replica of the *Matthew* in which Cabot made his voyage of discovery to Newfoundland. The Bristol Industrial Museum is on Princes Wharf.

A short walk away is Bristol's finest church, St Mary Redcliffe, a magnificent 14th-century building described by Elizabeth I as the 'the fairest parish church in England'. Historic harbourside King Street is picturesque and lively, featuring the outstanding 17th-century Landoger

Trow inn, and the Theatre Royal, the oldest continuously working theatre in Britain, established in 1776 (ask to look inside).

Bristol Cathedral is a handsome uniform 'hall church', blending a 19th-century nave with early medieval work. Nearby, off Park Street, the Georgian House, built 1787–91, is well worth a visit. Park Street is where you will find the excellent City Museum and Art Gallery, while other attractions include the British Empire and Commonwealth Museum, housed in Brunel's historic railway station. The city is also a buzzing centre for nightlife, culture and artistic events and has interesting little shops along narrow lanes as well as big modern shopping malls.

Chew Magna

Wool brought prosperity to this pretty red sandstone village in the Middle Ages and many of its fine buildings are a reminder of that period. Look for the Old School Room, formerly a church brewery, and the Old Bakehouse, as well as the stone cottages and fine 18th-century mansions that line the High Street. The Church of St Andrews is part Norman and has a rare wooden monument to a knight.

Clifton

Clifton is a suburb of Bristol but, for sightseeing interest, merits a day in its own right. Foremost is the majestic Clifton Suspension Bridge, spanning the Avon Gorge, 702ft (214m) long, with the muddy Avon 245ft (74.7m) below. Alongside is Clifton Village, a delightful Georgian area. Nearby, the gloriously landscaped Bristol Zoo showcases around 300 species of wildlife.

Dyrham

Dyrham is a pretty village with many 17th- and 18th-century stone houses and a fine 15th-century church. Dyrham Park is a beautiful William-and-Mary house (National Trust), built 1691–1710 and little altered over the centuries. *Dyrham* means 'deer park', and a herd of fallow deer grace the 263-acre (107ha) grounds that lie beyond the elegant formal gardens.

Tourist Information
Bath: Abbey Chambers, Abbey Church Yard (tel: 0906 711 2000 premium rate)
Bristol: The Annexe, Wildscreen Walk, Harbourside (tel: 0333 321 0101)

A replica of John Cabot's historic ship, the Matthew, *in Bristol's docks; the original reached Newfoundland in 1497*

Bath paragraph (left column continuation)

how it would have looked back then. For another glimpse of 18th-century life, visit the Jane Austen Centre.

The Pump Room, directly above the Roman Baths, offers a taste of old Bath, both literally and metaphorically. Here you can drink the spa water, or take tea to the strains of the Pump Room Trio. Adjacent Bath Abbey is where, in AD973, Edgar was crowned first king of all England. The present building was begun in the late 1490s and is famous for its fan-vaulting and monuments. A two-minute walk south takes you to Bath's oldest dwelling, Sally Lunn's House, built *c*1622 and now delightful tea rooms serving the delicious Sally Lunn Buns. Bath's many attractions include the fascinating Building of Bath Collection, with spectacular models and full-size reconstructions.

MYSTERIOUS SITES OF MARLBOROUGH COUNTRY

The rolling scenery around the Marlborough Downs, cut through by the ancient Ridgeway, is home to many strange shapes and sights – impenetrable Silbury Hill, the 60-tonne sarsen stones of Avebury, a veritable herd of white horses cut into the chalk downland and Merlin's Mound. What do they all mean? Help may be at hand in the Wiltshire Heritage Museum, Devizes and you can learn about the coming of the Iron Horse in modern-day Swindon.

Unlike its smaller neighbour, Stonehenge, the Avebury stone circle is completely accessible, including the West Kennett Long Barrow (above)

Avebury

In 1633 the antiquary and author John Aubrey wrote to King Charles II recommending him to visit Avebury because [it] does as much exceed in greatness the renowned Stonehenge as a cathedral doeth a parish church'. These days Avebury, the largest stone circle in the world, is even more attractive, with an excellent National Trust interpretation centre.

Avebury comprises a total of 200 standing stones, which were arranged into circles and 'avenues', surrounded by huge circular earthworks, c2500–2200BC. These patterns were destroyed over the ages and only partly restored in the 1930s, thanks largely to Alexander Keiller (of marmalade fame), who founded a museum in the village. Visit the museum before seeing the stones, as their layout is not easy to understand from ground level.

The Great Barn Rural Life Museum, in a huge 17th-century thatched barn, illustrates pre-war rural life in Wiltshire, and 16th-century Avebury Manor (National Trust) can also be visited.

Devizes

Devizes is the main market town of Wiltshire, and its large marketplace has a fine 19th-century market cross and fountain. The square is lined with 18th-century houses and is the location of both the Devizes Visitor Centre and the Town Hall. The adjacent Shambles has been a lively covered market since 1835, and at the north end of the marketplace is the imposing Victorian façade at the Wadworth Brewery; the stables are open to the public. In Long Street is the excellent Wiltshire Heritage Museum, which includes important finds from many of the county's famous sites, including Stonehenge, Woodhenge and West Long Barrow.

The Kennett and Avon Canal, with its colourful narrowboats, runs almost through the town centre, with a famous staircase of locks nearby. A small museum here interprets the history of the canal and boat trips are available at weekends.

Marlborough

It is often claimed that Marlborough has the broadest High Street in England, possibly in Europe. Whether or not this is so, it is certainly one of the most handsome and individualistic streets in the country, with charming colonnaded and tile-hung houses and shops, splendid old inns, a classical-style Victorian Town Hall and a fine church at each end. One of the oldest buildings is the Merchant's House, dating from 1656, which is now a museum of 17th-century town life. Just beyond the south end of the High Street is the famous public school of Marlborough College. In the grounds (open to the public) is the College Chapel and The Mound, legendary burial place of Merlin.

An Ancient Route

The Ridgeway is one of the oldest existing pathways in Europe. Evidence suggests that feet may have tramped along it for up to 5,000 years, and until around 200 years ago this broad track was used as a main highway for driving sheep and cattle. It runs from Ivinghoe Beacon (near Dunstable) to Overton Hill (West Kennett), and the southwestern section, a broad track which runs along the top of the chalk downland ridge, is particularly pleasant and has far-reaching views. You can cycle, ride a horse or travel the Ridgeway by Shanks's pony, while recreational motorists can access three sections of the route in summer, and a short fourth section all year round.

White Horses

Six giant white chalk horses inhabit this area – the Marlborough Horse, carved by boys from the public school in 1804; the Alton Barnes Horse, cut in 1812; the Cherhill Horse of 1780; the Broad Town Horse of 1864; the Hackpen Horse (commemorating Queen Victoria's Diamond Jubilee in 1897); and the Devizes Millennium White Horse, cut in 1999. All were inspired by such ancient chalk figures as the Uffington Horse (see page 111). Wiltshire has two more white nags, the oldest and largest being the Westbury Horse, carved at Bratton Down in 1778 (on top of a much older figure); the other is near Pewsey.

Near Devizes, a flight of 16 locks ferries canal boats up and down Caen Hill

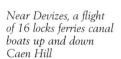

Silbury Hill/West Kennett Long Barrow

Another mystery roughly contemporary with Avebury and Stonehenge is posed by the cone of Silbury Hill. This is the largest man-made mound in Europe, constructed in three definite stages *c*2800BC. To put the monumental nature of this 130ft (40m) tall project into some context, it is estimated that the third stage alone took some 4 million man hours! Its purpose, however, continues to elude – no clue, in fact nothing at all, has ever been found within. As this is a Site of Special Scientific Interest, visitors are requested not to climb the hill.

More straightforward is the West Kennett Long Barrow, south of the hill and reached by footpath from the road. One of Britain's largest Neolithic burial tombs, it measures 330ft (100m) long by 75ft (22.9m) wide, was constructed *c*3000BC and was in use for 1,000 years after that.

Swindon

Swindon is a thoroughly modern city which owes its importance to the Great Western Railway. From 1842 to 1948 jobs and prosperity came from the locomotive workshops. That heyday can be traced at STEAM – Museum of the Great Western Railway, which has some splendid old locomotives, a reconstructed station platform, lots of hands-on exhibits and nostalgic film footage.

There is more rail memorabilia on the outskirts of town, in the Swindon and Cricklade Railway, a preserved steam line. Swindon's Museum and Art Gallery, in the older part of the town, has a good collection of 20th-century art.

See Walk O, page 68
Avebury – Pagan Pastures

Tourist Information
Avebury: Chapel Centre, Green Street (seasonal) (tel: 01672 539179)
Devizes: Cromwell House, Market Place (tel: 01380 734669)
Marlborough: The Library, High Street (tel: 01672 512663)
Swindon: 37 Regent Street (tel: 01793 530328/466454)

THE GLOUCESTER COTSWOLDS

While Cirencester is the self-styled 'Capital of the Cotswolds' and Cheltenham claims to be the 'Centre for the Cotswolds', it is Painswick, once the 'Queen of the Cotswolds', which conforms best to the popular idyllic image. Gloucester has one of England's great cathedrals and excellent museums; elsewhere are charming gardens, bird collections and castles to explore.

The acclaimed Corinium Museum in Cirencester is home to one of the largest collections of Roman antiquities in Britain

Cheltenham

Cheltenham began its transformation into Cheltenham Spa in 1738, with the discovery of Old Well (the famous Cheltenham Ladies' College now occupies the site). In 1788 King George III came to take the waters, stayed for five weeks, and soon Cheltenham was Britain's most important spa. Other wells were discovered, the most famous being at Pittville, and the beautiful domed Pittville Pump Room, built in 1825–30, is still open to visitors. You can taste the salty alkaline water here.

At the heart of town lies the Promenade, dominated by a massive golden terrace and lined with elegant shops, statues, trees and flower beds. It encapsulates the genteel image and complements the superb 18th-century architecture of Britain's most complete Regency town.

The Cheltenham Art Gallery and Museum has a lively, varied local collection with outstanding Arts and Crafts exhibits. Nearby, in Clarence Road, Cheltenham's most famous son, Gustav Holst, was born in 1874; it is now the Holst Birthplace Museum. Cheltenham hosts a full programme of festivals and events, including the international music festival every July, and the famous National Hunt Festival at the racecourse every March.

Cirencester

Corinium, as the town was known by the Romans, was for a time second only in importance to *Londinium*, and the outline of an 8,000-seat Roman amphitheatre can still be seen to the west. All other Roman interest appears in the incongruously high-tech Corinium Museum, which includes some impressive mosaics.

The heart of modern Cirencester is the Market Place, an attractive medley of Cotswold-stone and Victorian buildings, watched over by the outstanding 15th-century church of St John Baptist. Adjacent are the Abbey Grounds, where the outline of the former Norman Abbey is marked out and a small part of the Roman city wall can be seen. Cirencester Park,

Berkeley Castle

This compact classic fortress, complete with circular Norman keep and inner bailey, has been home to the famous Berkeley family for nearly 850 years and has two main claims to historical fame. In 1215, in the splendid Great Hall, the Barons met before proceeding to Runnymede to force the Magna Carta upon King John, while in 1327, in the dungeon of its keep, King Edward II was horribly murdered. The other highlights of an entertaining guided castle tour are the picture gallery, the dining room, the medieval buttery and kitchens, and the State Apartments.

Sudeley Castle

Enjoying a glorious Cotswolds setting, Sudeley Castle is an impressive sight. Originally built in the 15th century, it was slighted after the Civil War, leaving the romantic ruins of the banqueting house, and only rebuilt in the 19th century. The apartments are royally appointed and hung with Old Masters.

Sudeley was favoured by the Tudor monarchs, and became home to Katherine Parr, the only one of Henry VIII's wives to outlive him, when she married Lord Seymour.

The Gothic arched windows of Gloucester's Sudeley Castle ruins and tall sycamores both watch over a formal garden

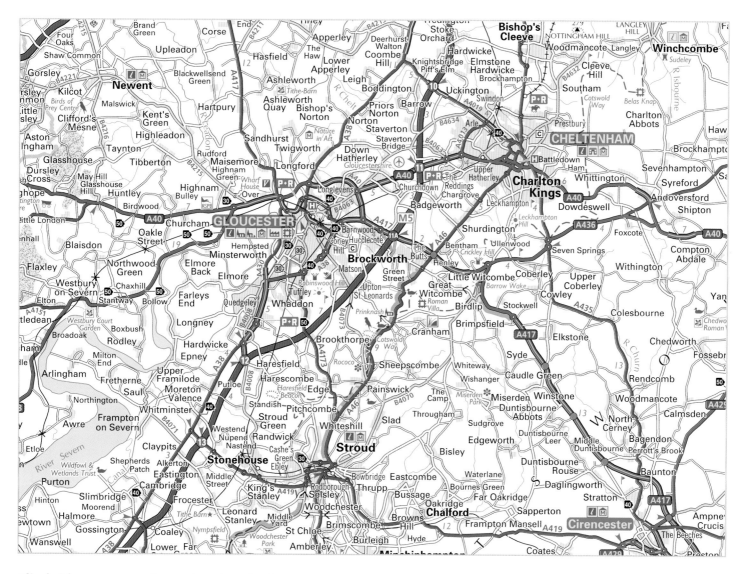

Slimbridge

Founded in 1946 by the renowned naturalist Sir Peter Scott, the Slimbridge Wildfowl and Wetlands Trust hosts the world's largest collection of wildfowl, with more than 180 different kinds of swan, geese and ducks. Many of the birds are very tame and delight children by feeding at close quarters. Serious 'twitchers' can be found in the hides with binoculars (available for hire), seeking out more elusive species. There is also a pink flamingo colony and other exotic varieties can be found in the Tropical House.

famous for polo, makes for a pleasant stroll, and other attractions include New Brewery Arts, with craft workshops and exhibitions.

Gloucester

The glory of Gloucester is its magnificent cathedral, and the great medieval East Window, dating from c1352, is the largest example in Britain – best seen from the Choir, itself a masterpiece. Among many fine monuments, the tombs of Edward II and Robert of Normandy (son of William the Conqueror) are both remarkable. The charming College Court contains the House of The Tailor of Gloucester, housing a Beatrix Potter exhibition. At Westgate a range of Tudor houses contains the splendid Folk Museum.

Gloucester is the most inland port in Britain, important to canal trade for some 200 years. The docks have been developed as a tourist attraction, with the highly acclaimed National Waterways Museum as its centrepiece. Nearby are the collections of the Soldiers of Gloucestershire Museum.

Painswick

Painswick is the quintessential Gloucestershire Cotswold village, a collection of old stone cottages around a web of narrow streets. The churchyard has 99 yew trees, trimmed into giant lollipops and tunnels, amid several 18th-century table-tombs. Close by, Painswick Rococo Garden is a restoration of a mid-18th-century garden.

Prinknash

Set on a hillside, Prinknash (pronounced 'Prinnersh') Abbey will disappoint visitors in search of antiquity. Its controversial 1930s buildings (not open to the public) find few admirers. Within its spacious and pleasant grounds, however, the Bird and Deer Park is charmingly informal, where pheasants and waterfowl roam around a wooded valley.

Sculpted yews show the way to Grade 1-listed St Mary's church in Painswick

Tourist Information

Cheltenham: 77 Promenade (tel: 01242 522878)
Cirencester: Corn Hall, Market Place (tel: 01285 654180)
Gloucester: 28 Southgate Street (tel: 01452 396572)
Painswick: The Library, Stroud Road (seasonal) (tel: 01452 813552)

THE FOREST OF DEAN

The oak, beech, ash and birch trees of the Royal Forest of Dean (35sq-miles/90sq-km) are an echo of medieval England, when the area between the Severn and the Wye was a royal hunting preserve. But the trees hide evidence of 2,000 years of industry in iron and coal. Further south, the elegantly ridged estuary of the Severn opens the way to the Atlantic.

Bluebells carpet the woodland floor beneath a great oak in woodland near Soudley

Coleford

Coleford, 'capital' of the Forest of Dean, holds an important place in the history of iron and steel. It was here in 1810 that David Mushet settled, and his son Robert invented self-hardening steel; Whitecliff Furnace, an early coke blast furnace, can still be seen in Newland Street. There is a railway museum in the old station.

Half a mile (0.8km) away on the Chepstow Road is Puzzle Wood, which contains open ironworkings dating back to pre-Roman times, with a network of paths that wind maze-like through lovely woodland. Further down the same road are Clearwell Caves and the Hopewell Colliery Museum with tours led by one of the few remaining Forest Freeminers.

Tourist Information

Coleford: High Street (tel: 01594 812388)
Monmouth: Shire Hall, Agincourt Square (tel: 01600 713899)

Goodrich Castle

This great red sandstone castle seems to grow naturally from the rocky bluff overlooking the River Wye where, as recorded in the Domesday Book, Godric Mapplestone first built a fortress to guard an ancient river crossing. Most of what we see today dates from the early 14th century, when it was the principal residence of the Talbot family, Earls of Shrewsbury.

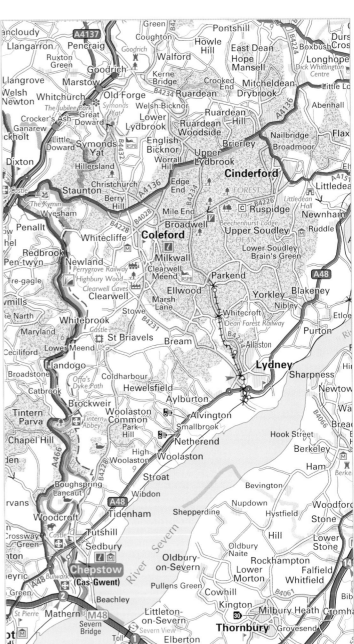

Lydney

Lydney is perhaps best known as the terminus of the Dean Forest Railway, which links with the main line between Birmingham and South Wales. The line runs between here and Parkend, with heritage steam and diesel trains. Just outside the town is Lydney Park, home

The River Wye loops around the foot of the 473ft (144m) Yat Rock, famous for its population of peregrine falcons

Symonds Yat

The Wye executes a great sweeping horseshoe meander, cutting a wooded gorge around Huntsham Hill, on the edge of the Forest of Dean at this justly famous viewpoint. *Yat* means 'gate' and the view from Yat Rock up- or down-river is one of the finest in Britain.

Symonds Yat has become famous in ornithological circles in recent years as the nesting place for peregrine falcons in the nearby limestone cliffs. Binoculars are provided for visitors to observe these powerful raptors swooping down from the rocks on to unfortunate passing pigeons.

Nearby at Symonds Yat West is the Jubilee Park with its Silver Jubilee Maze, Museum of Mazes and Splendour of the Orient attraction.

Tintern Abbey

One of Britain's most beautiful abbey ruins, Tintern, in its lovely setting in the wooded valley of the Wye, has attracted the attention of poets and painters over the centuries. Its stately roofless walls still rise gracefully from the valley, and the rose window in the east end is almost intact. The Abbey was founded by the Cistercians in 1131, and the white-robed monks were involved in the Forest of Dean's iron industry. Tintern Abbey was suppressed by Henry VIII in 1536.

The Queen of Forests

The Queen of Forests all that west of Severn lie, Her broad and bushy top Dean holdeth up so high

The 17th-century poet, Michael Drayton, was the first to praise the beauty of the Royal Forest of Dean and, despite the fact that it is now a commercial forest producing around 55,000cu m of timber each year, it retains its ancient, timeless atmosphere. The remains of coal-mining and ironworking show that the forest has always earned its keep.

Nearly half the forest is planted with broadleaved trees, and it has one of the largest areas of ancient oaks in Britain. It is the home of a wide range of wildlife, most notably pied flycatchers, which have taken advantage of a special nestbox scheme in the forest.

of Lord Bledisloe, which has the remains of a Roman temple in the beautiful grounds.

Speech House

Standing in the centre of the forest near Cannop Pond, this house, dating from 1680, is the site of the Verderer's Court for the Forest of Dean.

The Speech House picnic site is one of the places where you can join the circular Forest of Dean Sculpture Trail, a series of permanent sculptures by modern artists, strategically placed to blend harmoniously into the forest scene.

Soudley

Soudley is the site of the award-winning Dean Heritage Centre. Housed in an old mill, it features a waterwheel, beam engine and a reconstructed forester's cottage, complete with Gloucester Old Spot pig. This is one of the few places in Britain where you can witness charcoal being produced by the traditional method of open-air burning. A series of nature trails lead off from here, venturing deep into the forest.

Tintern Abbey was the first Cistercian monastery in Wales, its rustic setting on the River Wye inspiring evocative works by Turner and Wordsworth

GOLDEN BEACHES AND CLIFFS AT PORTHCURNO

Along interlocking footpaths between sandy coves and granite cliffs on the Land's End peninsula.

The open-air Minack Theatre

Distance: 3.5 miles (5.7km)
Minimum time: 2hrs 30min
Ascent/Gradient: 164ft (50m) ▲▲▲
Level of difficulty: +++
Paths: Coastal footpath
Landscape: Granite sea cliffs and inland fields and heath
Suggested map: OS Explorer 102 Land's End
Start/finish: Grid reference: SW 384224
Dog friendliness: Dogs should be kept under control on beach and fields
Parking: Porthcurno, St Levan and Porthgwarra
Public toilets: Porthgwarra and Porthcurno

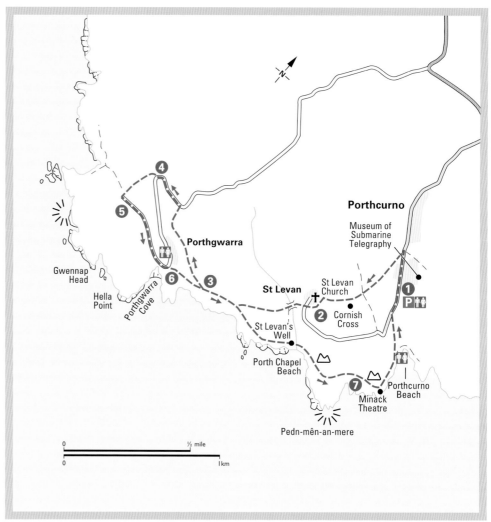

❶ From Porthcurno car park, walk back up the approach road, then just before Sea View House, turn sharply left along a track and follow it to reach cottages. Pass to the right of the cottages and turn right through a gap. Follow a field path past the granite Cornish Cross and go through a wooden gate.

❷ Enter St Levan churchyard by a granite stile. Go round the far side of the church to the entrance gate and on to a surfaced lane. Cross the lane and follow the path opposite, signed to Porthgwarra Cove. Cross a footbridge, then in about 55 yards (50m), at a junction, take the right fork and follow the path to merge with the main coast path and keep ahead.

❸ Where the path begins to descend towards Porthgwarra Cove, branch off right up some wooden steps. Reach a surfaced track by a house and turn up right, then at a road turn left.

❹ Go round a sharp left-hand bend, then at a footpath signpost, go right down a grassy path and cross a stone footbridge. Continue uphill to reach a bend on a track, just up from large granite houses.

❺ Turn left, go over a stile beside a gate, then continue down a surfaced lane to Porthgwarra Cove. Just past the shop and café, and opposite a red telephone box, go right down a track, signposted 'Coast Path', then follow the path round left. Just past a house, go sharp right at a junction and climb up the steps.

❻ Continue along the coast path, partly reversing the previous route past Point ❸. Keep right at a junction, and eventually descend past St Levan's Well to just above Porth Chapel Beach. (Dogs should be on a lead.) Follow the coast path steeply over Pedn-mên-an-mere, and continue to the Minack Theatre (see p.15) car park.

❼ For the surefooted, cross the car park and go down the track to the left of the Minack complex, then descend the steep cliff steps, with great care. When the path levels off, continue to a junction. The right fork takes you to Porthcurno Beach and back to the car park. The continuation leads to the road opposite the Beach Café, where a right turn leads to the car park. A less challenging alternative to the cliff steps is to turn left out of the Minack car park. Follow the approach road to a T-junction with a public road. Turn right, watching out for traffic.

CLIFFS AND DEEP WOODS AT PORTREATH AND TEHIDY

A route along spectacular cliffs followed by a contrasting stroll through woods.

Distance: 4 miles (6.4km)
Minimum time: 3hrs
Ascent/Gradient: 459ft (140m) ▲▲▲
Level of difficulty: +++
Paths: Good coastal path, woodland path, farm tracks
Landscape: Precipitous sea cliffs and deep woodland
Suggested map: OS Explorer 104 Redruth & St Agnes
Start/finish: Grid reference: SW 654453
Dog friendliness: Dogs on lead through grazed areas
Parking: Portreath Beach, Basset's Cove, Tehidy Country Park and East Lodge
Public toilets: Portreath and East Lodge Car Park

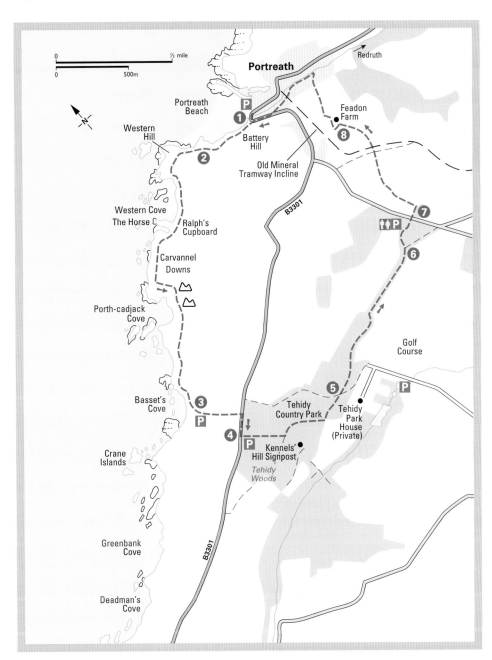

❶ Cross the bridge opposite Portreath Beach car park and turn right up Battery Hill, signposted 'Coast Path'. Follow the lane uphill and on to where it ends at houses above the beach. Go left in front of garages, signposted 'Coast Path Gwithian'.

❷ Follow the path through a gate and then keep straight uphill to the cliff top. Don't go too close to the cliff edge. Turn left and follow the path round the cliff edge above Ralph's Cupboard. Continue by steep paths into and out of Porth-cadjack Cove.

❸ Reach a car parking area above Basset's Cove. Follow the broad track inland, then at the public road cross over and turn right for a short distance.

❹ Turn left into a car park. Go through the car park and down a tree-lined track. Turn left at a T-junction and follow a track to another T-junction. There are private houses on the other side of the junction. Turn left along another broad track.

❺ Reach a junction and four-way signpost beside two seats. (A café can be reached in 0.25 mile/400m down the right-hand signposted track.) On the main route, keep straight on, signposted 'East Lodge'. Reach a junction by a seat. Keep right and go through a wooden kissing gate. Eyes left here before crossing to check for keen golfers about to tee-off. Go through a kissing gate and continue to follow the track alongside the golf course.

❻ About 40 yards (37m) beyond the end of the golf course section, at a junction, bear off left into woods. Stay on the main path, ignoring side paths, then bear round right to East Lodge car park and to a public road.

❼ Cross the road diagonally right and then go left between wooden posts with red marks. Keep to the good track ahead. Pass holiday chalets and reach a T-junction above farm buildings at Feadon Farm and the Duchy College.

❽ Turn left, then in a few paces turn right down a concrete track. At a farmyard go sharp left by a public footpath sign and follow a path down through woods keeping to the main path, to reach a surfaced road. Just past 'Glenfeadon Castle', turn left along Glenfeadon Terrace, pass beneath a bridge, then at a junction keep ahead along Tregea Terrace and back to Portreath Beach car park.

Walk C

ST ANTHONY'S GUNS AND GUIDING LIGHTS

A walk on the beautiful Roseland Peninsula, visiting an ancient church, a lighthouse and an old gun battery.

The lighthouse at St Anthony Head has been protecting Falmouth's shipping since 1835

Distance: 6.5 miles (10.4km)

Minimum time: 4hrs

Ascent/Gradient: 230ft (70m) ▲▲▲

Level of difficulty: +++

Paths: Excellent coastal and creekside footpaths. May be muddy in places during wet weather, 12 stiles

Landscape: Picturesque headland with open coast on one side and sheltered tidal creek and estuary on the other

Suggested map: OS Explorer 105 Falmouth & Mevagissey

Start/finish: Grid reference: SW 848313

Dog friendliness: Dogs on lead through grazed areas

Parking: National Trust St Anthony Head car park. Can be busy in summer. There is alternative parking on the route at Porth Farm (SW 868329)

Public toilets: St Anthony Head car park and Porth Farm car park

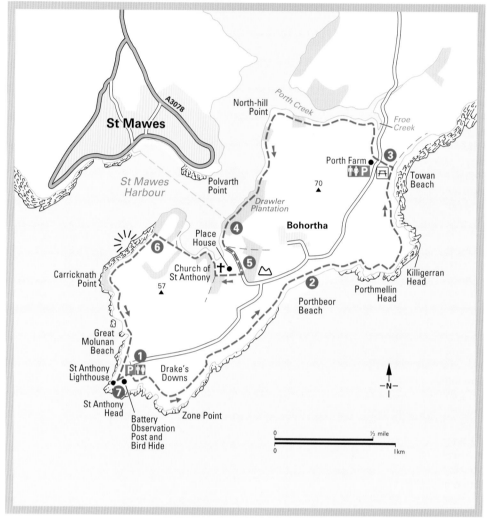

❶ Leave the St Anthony Head car park at its far end and keep straight ahead along a surfaced lane past a row of holiday cottages on the left. Follow the coast path, running parallel with the old military road alongside Drake's Downs, to where it passes above Porthbeor Beach at a junction with the beach access path.

❷ Follow the coast path round Porthmellin Head and Killigerran Head to reach Towan Beach. At the junction with the beach access path, turn left and inland. Bear off left before a gate and go through a roofed passageway (there are toilets on the left), to reach a road.

❸ Go straight across the road and through a gapway, signed 'Porth Farm', then go down a surfaced drive. Turn into the entrance to the National Trust car park, then bear off left along a path signposted 'Place via Percuil River'. Soon

cross a footbridge, then turn right. Follow the edge of Froe Creek and then follow a path alongside Porth Creek and through Drawler Plantation, ignoring side paths to 'Bohortha'.

❹ Pass a small jetty where the St Mawes ferry picks up passengers. Continue to a kissing gate and on to the road end in front of Place House. Go left along the road and uphill for 160 yards (150m).

❺ Turn right and cross a stile, signposted 'Church of St Anthony and St Anthony Head'. Follow the path past the gravestones to the church. Keep dogs under control here. Go up the steps opposite the church door and follow a shady path uphill. Keep right at a junction, and then, at the next junction with a broad track, turn left. Soon, go through a gate on the left, then follow the edge of the field uphill.

Cross over a stile (there's a seat to your left) or go through a gate and head downhill to the water's edge.

❻ Turn left and follow the coast path around Carricknath Point. Just past Great Molunan Beach, cross a causewayed dam above a small quay, then, at a junction, keep right and follow the coast path signs. At a junction with a surfaced track coming down from the left, keep straight ahead to St Anthony Lighthouse.

❼ Return to the junction and climb the steep, surfaced track to reach the car park. Halfway up, another track leads off right to the preserved Battery Observation Post and to the bird hide above Zone Point. Just past this turn, at another junction, keep right and go up steps to reach the car park.

BURGH ISLAND PARADISE

A chance to mingle with the stars in an art deco dream and have a drink in Devon's oldest inn.

Distance: 4 miles (6.4km)
Minimum time: 1hr 45min
Ascent/Gradient: 246ft (75m) ▲▲▲
Level of difficulty: +++
Paths: Fields, tracks (muddy in winter) and coast path, 3 stiles
Landscape: Rolling coastal farmland and cliff top
Suggested map: OS Explorer OL20 South Devon
Start/finish: Grid reference: SX 652442
Dog friendliness: Keep under control at all times; on lead through fields
Parking: Huge car park at Bigbury-on-Sea
Public toilets: At Bigbury-on-Sea car park; also in car park at Bantham

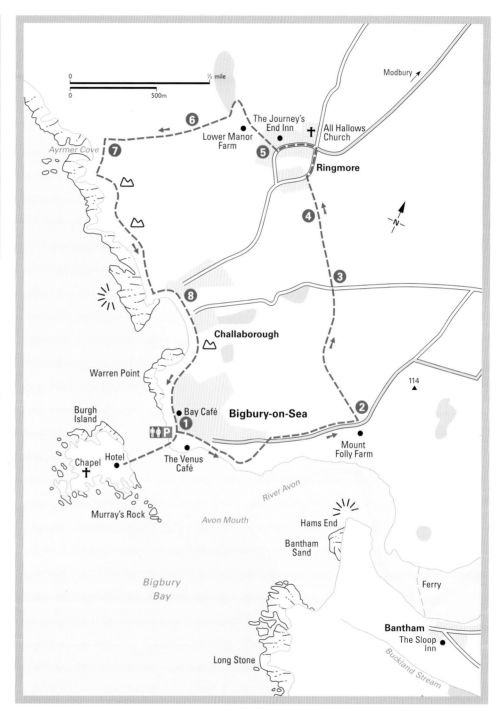

❶ Leave the car park through the entrance. Follow coast path signs right (low tide route along beach to the seasonal ferry to Bantham), then left towards the road and right on to cliffs. Turn left before bungalows, then left to the road. Cross over, go through a kissing gate and turn right uphill, passing through two big gates, to reach a path junction near Mount Folly Farm.

❷ Turn left along a gritty track (signed 'Ringmore'). At the field top is a path junction; go through the kissing gate and keep ahead downhill, still signed 'Ringmore', with a fence right. Pass through a metal gate, drop through a kissing gate, keep ahead to another on a farm track; walk up the next field, crossing a stile on to a lane.

❸ Cross over, following signs for Ringmore, through a metal gate. Walk down into the next combe, keeping the hedgebank right. Cross the stream at the bottom on a concrete walkway, and over a stile. Ignore the path left, but go straight ahead, uphill, through a plantation and gate on to a narrow path between a fence and hedge.

❹ Pass through a kissing gate, bear right then turn immediately left uphill to a path junction; pass through the kissing gate and follow the path to Ringmore. Turn right at the lane, then left at the church to find The Journey's End Inn on the right.

❺ From the pub, turn right down the narrow lane which gives way to a footpath. It winds round gardens to meet a tarmac lane. Turn left downhill. Walk straight on down the track, eventually passing Lower Manor Farm, and keep going down past the 'National Trust Ayrmer Cove' notice. After a small gate and stream crossing, keep straight on at a path junction.

❻ Pass through a kissing gate and walk towards the cove on a grassy path above the combe (left). Pass through gates and over a stile to gain the beach.

❼ Follow coast path signs ('Challaborough') left over a small footbridge, then climb very steeply uphill to the cliff top and great views over Burgh Island. The cliffs are unstable here so take care. The path leads to Challaborough which is basically one huge holiday park.

❽ Turn right along the beach road and pick up the track uphill along the coast towards Bigbury-on-Sea. Go straight on to meet the tarmac road, then bear right on the coast path to the car park.

Walk E

DARTMOOR'S HIGHEST TORS

A view of Yes Tor and High Willhays – without having to climb them – and an ancient oak woodland.

Grassy banks slope down gently to the West Okement River

Distance: 4.5 miles (7.2km)
Minimum time: 2hrs
Ascent/Gradient: 722ft (220m) ▲▲▲
Level of difficulty: +++
Paths: Grassy tracks and open moorland, some boggy patches
Landscape: Reservoir, ancient oak woodland and open moorland
Suggested map: OS Outdoor Leisure 28 Dartmoor
Start/finish: Grid reference: SX 562918
Dog friendliness: Keep dogs under control, watch for sheep
Parking: Car park at Meldon Reservoir (voluntary contributions)
Public toilets: At car park

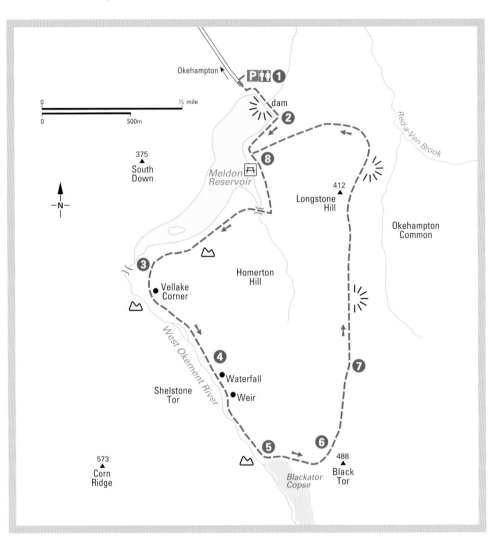

❶ Walk up the stone steps by the toilets, through the gate and go left on a tarmac way towards the dam, signposted 'Bridleway to Moor'. Cross over the dam.

❷ Turn right along a stony track. You will soon see a gate (right) leading to a waterside picnic area. Don't go over the stile, but leave the track here to go straight on, following the edge of the reservoir through a side valley and over a small footbridge. The narrow path undulates to a steepish descent at the end of the reservoir to meet the broad marshy valley of the West Okement River; the swell of Corn Ridge, 1,762ft (537m), lies ahead.

❸ Pass the small wooden footbridge and take the narrow path along the left edge of the valley, keeping to the bottom of the steep slope that rises on your left. The path broadens uphill and becomes grassy as it rounds Vellake Corner above the tumbling river below to the right.

❹ At the top of the hill the track levels and Blackator Copse can be glimpsed ahead. Follow the river upstream past a waterfall and weir, go left of a granite enclosure, and along the left bank through open moorland to enter Blackator Copse – a wonderful picnic spot.

❺ Retrace your steps out of the trees and bear right around the copse edge, uphill aiming for the left outcrop of Black Tor on the ridge above. Pick your way through the bracken to gain the left edge of the left outcrop. The right outcrop rises to 1,647ft (502m).

❻ Climb to the top of the tor if you wish; if not, keep ahead in the same direction, away from Blackator Copse, aiming for a fairly obvious track visible ahead over Longstone Hill. To find it, go slightly downhill from the tor to cross two small streams, then pass between granite blocks marking the track.

❼ The intermittent track runs straight across open moor. Where the Red-a-Ven Brook Valley appears below to the right, enjoy the view of (left to right) Row Tor, West Mill Tor and Yes Tor. High Willhays, Dartmoor's highest point, lies just out of sight to the right. The track bears left around the end of the hill, with good views towards the quarry and viaduct, and drops back to the reservoir.

❽ Bear right on the track, then left over the dam and back to the car park.

NORTH DEVON COAST CLASSIC

A walk of contrasts: Lee Bay – the 'fuchsia valley' – and craggy Morte Point.

Distance: 7 miles (11.3km)
Minimum time: 4hrs
Ascent/Gradient: 426ft (130m) ▲▲▲
Level of difficulty: +++
Paths: Fields, tracks and coast path, 15 stiles
Landscape: Coastal farmland, wooded valleys and cliff tops
Suggested map: OS Explorer 139 Bideford, Ilfracombe & Barnstaple
Start/finish: Grid reference: SS 457452
Dog friendliness: Dogs under control at all times; some difficult stiles
Parking: Car park at Mortehoe
Public toilets: Lee Bay and car park at Mortehoe

❶ Take the lane opposite the car park to 'Lighthouse & Lee'. Pass North Morte Farm Campsite to reach the lane end at the private road to Bull Point lighthouse.

❷ Follow footpath signs past the gate (right) across Easewell Farm Campsite and through the campsite complex on the signed footpath to Lee. Leave the buildings over a stile (with a pond right) and cross the field to Yarde Farm via a gate. Turn left immediately along a grassy track slightly uphill to a gate/stile into a field. Keep the hedge on the left, descend through a gate/stile; keep along the left edge of the next field, and through a gate/stile on to a tarmac drive.

❸ Turn left, following signs through Damage Barton Farm, bearing right as signed at the end of the buildings. After a few steps a footpath sign on the building ahead directs you left. Soon after, another sign points right, then left through a gate. Walk uphill through gorse to reach a footpath post. Go right towards another signpost, fork right up the track, then follow odd wooden posts through a gate. Follow footpath signs up the field to the next signpost, which is atop a small hill. Turn left through a gate, then bear half right across the field to reach a lane via a stile.

❹ Cross the lane and over a stile into an 'Open Access Area'. Follow faded signs to Lee across the meadow. Cross over a stile and go steeply downhill into the wooded Borough Valley. At the bottom, turn left.

❺ Cross a stile and follow the valley down to emerge from the woods and turn right over a bridge and stile. Cross the field then a stile and turn right up the lane to The Grampus Inn.

❻ Retrace your steps down the path past toilets to the rocky cove at Lee Bay. Turn left steeply uphill and join the coast path through a gate. Follow coast path signs to reach a stile/

footbridge/stile in a deep combe, then a steep climb up and over a stile into another combe and rocky cove. Cross the footbridge/stile and walk up above Bull Point.

❼ Follow coast path signs left of the lighthouse towards Morte Point. Go through a gate into a combe – 91 steps lead up the other side. Cross Windy Lag and then

a stile to Rockham Bay, where steps lead to the beach. Cross two stiles and walk on to reach Morte Point.

❽ Follow the coast path signs past Windy Cove. Go through a gate, walk past Grunta Beach, then follow signs left, steeply uphill, to join the road just below Mortehoe via a gate. Proceed uphill, bearing right to the start.

Walk G
DOWN THE DOONE VALLEY

Fact and fiction intertwine in this moorland valley walk which visits the tiny church celebrated in R. D. Blackmore's classic novel Lorna Doone.

Weir Water is spanned by Robbers Bridge in an area once notorious for bandits and vagabonds.

Distance: 8.75 miles (14.1km)
Minimum time: 4hrs 30min
Ascent/Gradient: 1,250ft (380m) ▲▲▲
Level of difficulty: +++
Paths: Some steep ground, pathless open moor
Landscape: Bleak, grassy moor, then a charming enclosed valley
Suggested map: OS Explorer OL 9 Exmoor
Start/finish: Grid reference: SS 820464
Dog friendliness: Well-controlled – livestock throughout, horse riders in Doone Valley
Parking: Car park (free) at Robbers Bridge
Public toilets: None en route; toilets at County Gate on A39

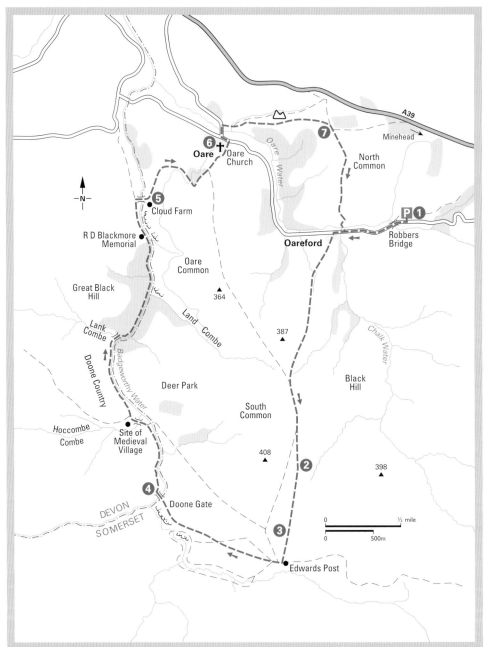

❶ Cross Robbers Bridge and follow the road to Oareford. Turn left up the bridleway track signed 'Larkbarrow'. After a mile (1.6km), the now faint track runs straight up across two grassy fields to a signposted gate where a bridleway from Oare Church joins the route. Keep ahead up this third field over its rounded crest, and bear slightly left to a gate at its back left corner.

❷ Go through a gate on the left, and then a narrow gate on the right to rougher moorland. Take a faint path ahead for 140 yards (128m). Here bear slightly right on a smaller path to go through a shallow col or gap. Now a wider path arrives from the right. Bear left on it to large and small wooden gates.

❸ The path ahead leads down, with a bank on its left, to Edwards Post. Turn right ('Badgworthy Valley') on a clear path that gradually climbs to a gate. It then drops towards the Badgworthy Valley, rises again, then drops to cross the railed footbridge at Doone Gate.

❹ Straight up to a wide path and turn right. Continue down the main valley, through woods, to a large footbridge to Cloud Farm.

❺ Pass to the left of Cloud Farm, on to a track that passes through a farm shed, then climbs out of the valley. Where it ends, follow the lower side of a field to the edge of a wooded combe. Turn right for 70 yards (64m) to a gate on the left. A track passes above the combe and turns down beyond it. Where the track bends right, keep downhill through waymarked gates, to turn left on the valley road below beside Oare Church.

❻ Turn right, signposted 'Porlock', and follow the road for 130 yards (118m) to cross Oare Water. Turn right along the riverside to ford a small stream. A few paces further on, turn up left to a small summer house and then turn right between gorse bushes. A grass path leads straight up a sharp spur. It continues beside a fence to a gate; keep ahead, across heather, to the right-hand corner of a plantation.

❼ Turn right on a small track ('Oareford'). This bends left near a field corner; here keep ahead, past a blue-topped post on a path towards some tall trees. Pass to the right of these trees, which mark ancient field-edges, to a small gate. A path leads steeply down to a footbridge into Oareford. Turn left to return to your car.

A VISIT TO THE TARR STEPS

Visit one of the 'oldest' bridges in the world, set in a quiet valley clothed in ancient woodland.

The 17-span medieval clapper bridge, known as the Tarr Steps

Distance: 5.25 miles (8.4km)
Minimum time: 2hrs 30min
Ascent/Gradient: 700ft (213m) ▲▲▲
Level of difficulty: +++
Paths: Riverside paths and field tracks, some open moor, may be muddy, no stiles
Landscape: Wooded river valley and pasture slopes above
Suggested map: OS Explorer OL 9 Exmoor
Start/finish: Grid reference: SS 872323
Dog friendliness: Dogs can run off-lead along the River Barle
Parking: Just over 0.25 mile (400m) east of Tarr Steps – can be full in summer. (Parking at Tarr Steps for disabled people only.)
Public toilets: At car park

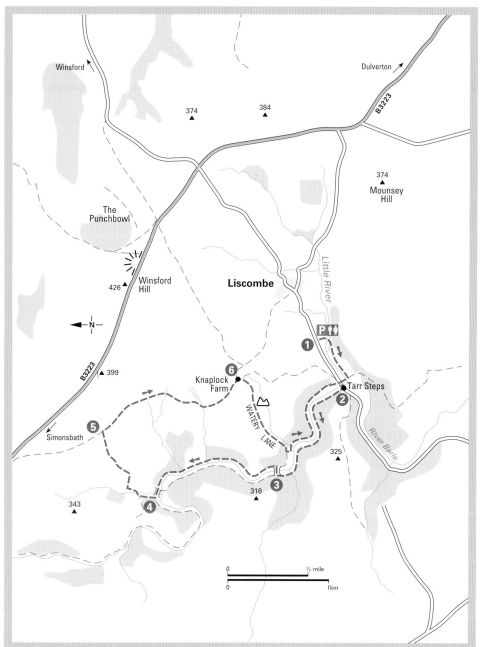

❶ Leave the bottom of the car park by the left-hand junction, signposted 'Scenic Path'. This takes you down to the left of the road to the Little River, crossing two footbridges on its way to Tarr Steps, over the River Barle, ahead.

❷ Cross the Steps, turning upstream at the far side (signed 'North Barton Wood'). Follow a wide riverbank path past what looks like a wire footbridge but is, in fact, a device for intercepting floating trees in times of flood. After 0.75 mile (1.2km), cross a sidestream on a stone bridge (mini Tarr Steps), and immediately afterwards a long footbridge over the River Barle.

❸ Cross, and continue upstream, with the river now on the left. After 0.75 mile (1.2km) the path crosses a small wooden footbridge, and then divides at a signpost.

❹ Turn right, uphill, signed 'Winsford Hill'. A wide path goes up through the woods with a stream on its right. Where it meets a track turn briefly right to ford the stream, then continue uphill on a narrower signed path. At a low bank with beech trees, turn right to a gate and follow the foot of a field to a tarred lane. Go up this to

a cattle grid on to open moor. Here, bear right on a faint track that heads up between gorse bushes. After 250 yards (229m) it reaches a four-way signpost.

❺ Turn right ('Knaplock') and slant down to a hedge corner. The route follows the foot of the open moor, but is about to divert up left to avoid some bog. After 170 yards (155m) a sign points back down to the moor-foot banking. A beech bank crosses ahead: aim for a gate at the lower end of this, where a soft track leads forward, with occasional blue paint-spots. After 0.25 mile (400m) the track turns downhill, then back to the left. It becomes firmer and drier as it reaches Knaplock Farm.

❻ Among the farm buildings turn downhill signed 'Tarr Steps', to exit on a muddy farm track. This develops into a steep, narrow and stony track, Watery Lane. After its initial descent it becomes a smooth path down to the River Barle. Turn left, downstream. When the path rises a little above the river, look out for a fork on the right, signed 'Footpath'. This re-joins the river to pass through an open field that's just right for a more comfortable sunbathe than the busy Tarr Steps. Cross the road and a small footbridge, then turn left up the path to your car.

Walk 1

AN AMBLE IN THE QUANTOCKS

An up-and-down walk in the glorious Quantock combes.

Wildlife, walkers and farm animals share the land around the Quantock Hills

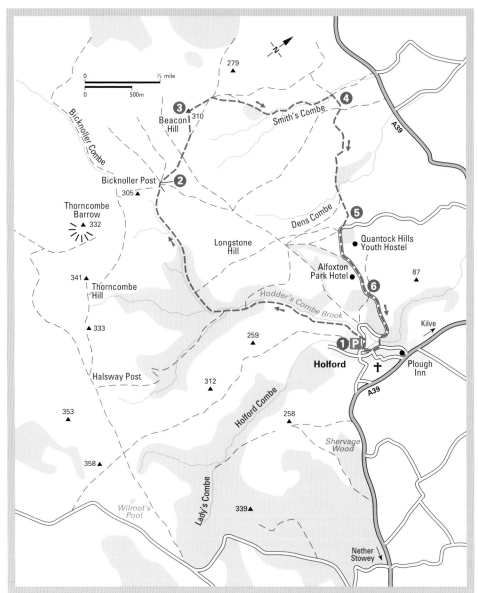

Distance: 5.5 miles (8.8km)

Minimum time: 2hrs 40min

Ascent/Gradient: 1,000ft (305m) ▲▲▲

Level of difficulty: +++

Paths: Wide, smooth paths, with one slightly rough descent, some streams to cross, no stiles

Landscape: Deep, wooded hollows and rolling hilltops

Suggested map: OS Explorer 140 Quantock Hills & Bridgwater

Start/finish: Grid reference: ST 154410

Dog friendliness: Keep dogs on lead throughout, due to livestock

Parking: At back of Holford (free)

Public toilets: None en route

❶ Two tracks leave the road beside the car park. Take the right-hand one, which is marked with a bridleway sign. It becomes an earth track through woods, with Hodder's Combe Brook on its right. After 0.75 mile (1.2km) the small track fords the stream and forks. Take the right-hand option, entering a side valley. The path runs up the valley floor, crossing to the right-hand side of the stream – ignore a further side valley and path forking left. Go up gently through oakwoods floored with bilberry (locally known as 'whortleberry'), then mixed heather and bracken, to reach the Quantock ridge. As the ground eases, keep ahead over two cross-tracks to Bicknoller Post.

❷ Just behind the oak post, turn right, then keep slightly left and uphill on the widest of the tracks. This track becomes a double one, almost a 'dual carriageway'. Bear left off it to the trig point on Beacon Hill.

❸ At the trig point, bend half-right to another marker post on the 'dual carriageway' track. A smaller path goes down directly ahead, into Smith's Combe. The path weaves around, crossing the stream several times.

❹ At the foot of the valley, with green fields below, is a four-way 'Quantock Greenway' signpost: turn right ('Holford'), uphill at first. The path runs around the base of the hills, with a belt of trees below and then the green fields. At the first spur crest is another signpost: keep ahead for Holford. The path runs around the base of the hills, with a belt of trees below and then the green fields. It drops to cross a stream, Dens Combe. After 0.25 mile (400m), reach a junction with a wide gate leading out on tarmac.

❺ Don't go through the gate, but strike uphill to another 'Quantock Greenway' signpost. Keep left to pass above a pink house on to a tarred lane. Follow it ahead below a couple of houses. The lane runs out past Alfoxton, with the walled garden of the grand house (once Wordsworth's, now a hotel) on the left and the stable block with its clock on the right. At the foot of the hotel driveway is a small parking area.

❻ Follow the lane for 650 yards (594m), then, as it bends right, look out for a waymarker and railings a little way down in the trees. Below is a spectacular footbridge leading across into Holford. Turn right, and at the first junction turn right again, to the car park.

DORSET'S OTHER HARDY

A long walk over rolling farmland from a high vantage point above Abbotsbury, where Nelson's fighting companion is remembered.

Hundreds of swans gather to be fed at the swannery near Abbotsbury

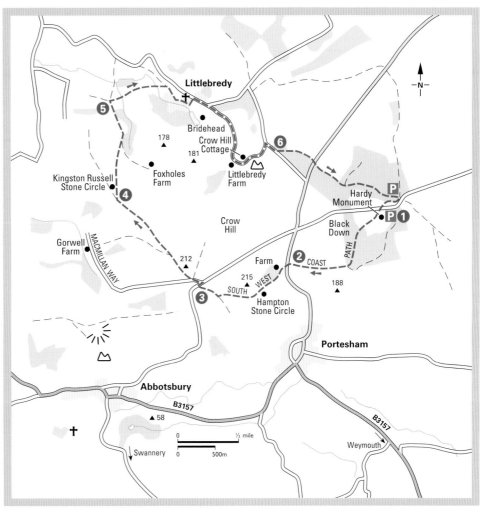

Distance: 7 miles (11.3km)
Minimum time: 3hrs 30min
Ascent/Gradient: 784ft (228m) ▲▲▲
Level of difficulty: +++
Paths: Field tracks, quiet roads, woodland tracks, 15 stiles
Landscape: Rolling hills and escarpments above Abbotsbury
Suggested map: OS Explorer OL15 Purbeck & South Dorset
Start/finish: Grid reference: SY 613876
Dog friendliness: Some unfriendly stiles and electric fences
Parking: By Hardy Monument, signed off road between Portesham and Winterbourne Abbas; additional parking by barrier
Public toilets: None en route; nearest in Back Street, Abbotsbury

❶ Facing the road, turn left down a path by the entrance to the monument, signposted 'Inland Route'. Follow the broad track down through the woods. At the bottom, fork right, then turn right opposite a ruin, and immediately bear left, over a stile. Walk up the edge of two fields. At the corner go over a stone stile and immediately cross the right-hand of two stiles. Walk alongside the fence to the hedge.

❷ Turn left on to the road and right towards a farm, where you take a gate on the left and go up a track, then through another gate and bear right. Pass Hampton Stone Circle and keep straight on. Cross a stile and bear along the fence, signposted 'West Bexington'. Follow the path along the hillside and up through a gate to a road.

❸ Turn right and take the first road left. Soon, at a cattlegrid, bear right along a track. Go through a gate (blue marker) and walk ahead down the hedge. Keep straight on through three fields.

❹ Go through a gate to a junction of tracks. Bear right across the field, passing Kingston Russell Stone Circle. Go through a gate and bear slightly left over the hill, passing grassy earthworks (remains of prehistoric round huts) on the left. At the bottom, go straight on down to a gate. Go through and bear left, then go through a gate to your right and down the hill.

❺ In the middle of the field turn right. Cross a footbridge to go through a gate. Cross a stream and walk straight ahead up the field. Bear left along the hedge. Cross a double stile and head diagonally left. Cross another footbridge over a stream. Turn right, bear left up through some trees, then go up to the right, to a stile. Cross and go over the hill towards Littlebredy. Cross a stile by a fingerpost and go straight on. Pass the church, go left through a gate and turn right on to the road. Bear right at the junction, at the cycle route sign. Continue past Crow Hill Cottage and up a long hill. At the junction turn right.

❻ Just after a bridleway signpost, turn left on a track which leads beside some woods and past a barn. Cross the road and go straight ahead. Descend through the woods and, where the track divides, turn up to the right. After 0.5 mile (800m), turn right and at the road take a rising path on the right to reach the road opposite the Hardy Monument.

BY HARDY'S COTTAGE AND 'EGDON HEATH'

A circuit across wooded heath and farmland to the place where the author Thomas Hardy, quite literally, left his heart.

Hardy's Cottage, where the author lived until he was 34 years old

Distance: 5 miles (8km)
Minimum time: 2hrs
Ascent/Gradient: 328ft (100m) ▲▲▲
Level of difficulty: +++
Paths: Woodland and heathland tracks, muddy field paths and bridleways, firm paths, road, 13 stiles
Landscape: Woodland, tree-clad heath, open meadows, waterway, rolling farmland
Suggested map: OS Explorer 117 Cerne Abbas & Bere Regis or OL15 Purbeck & South Dorset
Start/finish: Grid reference: SY 725921
Dog friendliness: Not allowed in Hardy's garden or cottage; deer shooting year-round in woods – keep dogs close
Parking: Thorncombe Wood (donations) below Hardy's Cottage
Public toilets: None en route; nearest northwest on A35

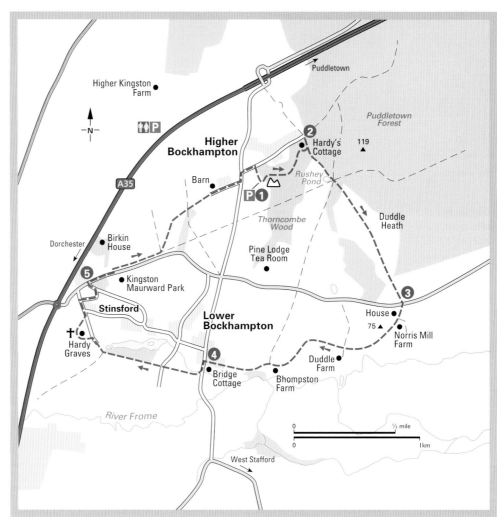

❶ Take the steep woodland path to the right of the display boards, signposted 'Hardy's Cottage'. Turn left at the fingerpost and follow the winding route down to a crossroads of tracks, marked by a monument. Turn left for Hardy's Cottage.

❷ Retrace your route up behind the cottage and bear left, signed 'Rushey Pond' on a path that bears right. At a crossroads by the pond, take the path ahead signed 'Norris Mill'. Immediately fork right; the path heads down between fences, soon passing through heathland, then between rhododendrons. Cross a stile and bear right. Enter a field by a stile and turn left up the field, towards a house.

❸ Cross the road on to a farm track which keeps to the right of some barns. Where the track ends, bear right over a field. Cross a pair of stiles in the hedge, then go straight ahead across the fields and a drive, passing Duddle Farm (left). Cross a bridge and stile down into a field. Go straight on and bear left, following the track round the hill. Cross a stile by a converted barn and walk up the drive. At the fingerpost keep straight on through a gate. Bear left to a stile and walk along the field edge to a gate, then walk down the field to a gate at the far corner. Go through and straight on, with the river away to your left. Go through the farmyard and along a road.

❹ Turn left by Bridge Cottage. Cross the river and immediately turn right, on to a causeway. After 0.5 mile (800m) turn right, signed 'Stinsford'. Walk up and turn left into the churchyard, just below the church. Pass the church to your left, and the Hardy family graves to your right. Leave by the top gate and walk up the road. Pass Casterbridge training centre and turn right along the road. Take the next turn left to the main road by a lodge.

❺ Turn right, up the road. After the entrance to Birkin House, bear left through a gate and immediately turn right on to a path through woodland, parallel with the road. Descend, cross a stile and bear left, signposted 'Higher Bockhampton', and inside the field bear diagonally right uphill. At the top corner keep straight on through a gate and follow the fence up towards a barn. Pass this and take a gate on the left and bear right on a track to the road. Turn left, then right by the postbox, and right again to return to the car park.

GIANT STEPS TO CERNE ABBAS

A valley walk from Minterne Magna to see a famous chalk hill carving.

The prehistoric Cerne Abbas Giant

Distance: 5.5 miles (8.8km)
Minimum time: 2hrs 30min
Ascent/Gradient: 591ft (180m) ▲▲▲
Level of difficulty: +++
Paths: Country paths and tracks, minor road, main road, 5 stiles
Landscape: Head of Cerne Valley, scattered with old settlements
Suggested map: OS Explorer 117 Cerne Abbas & Bere Regis
Start/finish: Grid reference: ST 659043
Dog friendliness: Lead essential on road stretches
Parking: Car park (free) opposite church in Minterne Magna and in Cerne Abbas
Public toilets: Cerne Abbas

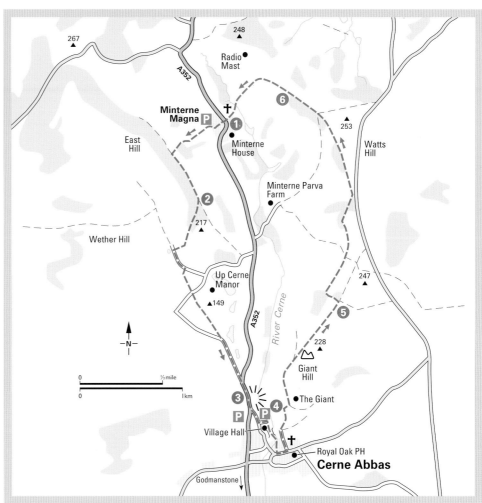

❶ With the road behind you, take the bridleway on the left side of the car park, which soon bends right and then left round some trees, and left again on the other side. Follow the track, keeping right at a fork, uphill, and where the hedge begins pass round to the right side of it. At the top, turn left on a track inside the woods.

❷ Fork right down through the woods. At the bottom, turn left along the road. After a bend take the footpath right, across the field. After a line of trees veer diagonally left, towards the right-hand of two white gates. Cross a road, pass to the right of this gate, and continue straight on down the field, with Up Cerne Manor in view to the left. Pass another white gate to the right of a pond, then turn left on the road. At the end bear right on to the A352.

❸ Soon cross to the car park for the best view of the Giant. Fork left on the road down to the village and turn left, signposted 'Village Hall'. Turn right by the stream, signposted 'Village Centre'. Continue to the high street. Turn left, and left again in front of the New Inn, and left by the Royal Oak, to the church. Walk past the Old Pitchmarket to the Abbey. Turn right into the churchyard and bear left. Go through a gate and head left.

❹ Cross a stile, then turn right up some steps. Now follow the path to the left, round the contour of the hill and past a National Trust sign for the Cerne Abbas Giant, below a fence. After 0.25 mile (400m), as the path divides, keep right, up the hill, to the top. Bear left along the ridge, cross a stile by a fingerpost and head diagonally right, to another fingerpost.

❺ At the fingerpost turn left, signed 'Wessex Ridgeway', and go down through a gate. Soon turn right and follow the bridleway along the hillside. Keep straight ahead at a junction of tracks (signed 'Barne's Lane'), then dip down through a gateway and go straight on inside the top edge of some woods. Keep straight on to go through a gate near the road. Turn left away from the road (signed 'Minterne Magna') along the left edge of a large field. At a gateway turn left on to a gravel lane.

❻ Directly above Minterne House, turn left through a small gate and signed 'Minterne Magna', towards the mast and follow fingerposts to the village, down through several gates and then along a broad track past the church to return to the car park.

Walk M

MORE BORDERS AT THREE COUNTY CORNER

An expedition through parts of Somerset, Dorset and Wiltshire, to Stourhead and Alfred's Tower.

The monumental Alfred's Tower, a banker's folly from the 18th century

Distance: 8.5 miles (13.7km)

Minimum time: 4hrs

Ascent/Gradient: 750ft (229m) ▲▲▲

Level of difficulty: +++

Paths: Some tracks and some small paths and field-edges, 17 stiles

Landscape: Tree-covered ridge

Suggested map: OS Explorer 142 Shepton Mallet

Start/finish: Grid reference: ST 755314

Dog friendliness: Moderate freedom on tracks and in woodland

Parking: Pen Selwood church; some verge parking at Bleak Farm

Public toilets: Near Spread Eagle Inn – from Point ❺ continue through arch for a quarter of a mile (400m)

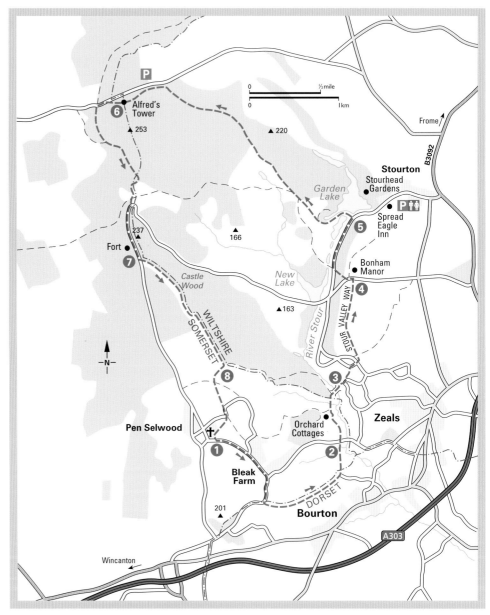

❶ Go to the right through the churchyard to join a road beyond. Turn left through Bleak Farm village, bear right ('Bourton'), then left into an inconspicuous sunken track. This ends at the top of a tarred lane; here turn left through a white gate, signed 'Pen Mill Hill'. The path on the right heads diagonally down a field to to a kissing gate in a dip. Follow a green track past a pond to a road.

❷ From here to Point ❹ is marked 'Stour Valley Way'. Cross on to a path waymarked 'Coombe Street'. Pass below Orchard Cottages, then turn up left over a stile, and right over another. Cross a stream in a dip to a stile below a thatched cottage. A woodland path bends to the right to a footbridge over the tiny River Stour.

❸ Go up on a tarred lane and turn left briefly. Keep ahead into a hedged way for 30 yards (27m) to a stile on the right. Go up and round left to another stile. The lane beyond leads to a T-junction; go across and turn left on to a bridleway track. Go through a gate to follow the left edge of a field into a hedged track to emerge opposite Bonham Manor.

❹ Turn left, and at the second signpost bear right to a road below. Follow this to the right, to a rustic rock arch. A track on the left is signposted 'Alfred's Tower'.

❺ The main track (blue arrows) heads into a wooded valley with Alfred's Tower visible ahead. At a fork take the track ahead, along the foot of the wood, then into it. Finally it reaches open ground at the hilltop, with a road ahead. Turn left, in a grassy avenue, to Alfred's Tower.

❻ Join the road ahead for 220 yards (201m), down to a sunken path on the left signed 'Penselwood'. Follow this, ignoring paths on both sides, on to a track descending to a major junction. Here bear right to a lane. Bear right again, on a tarmac road signed 'Penselwood'.

This leads over a hilltop containing a Roman fort. At the road's highest point, open ground appears on the left.

❼ Cross a stile to go forward 40 yards (37m), then bend to the right down a grassy glade. This gives way to field-edges with stiles, the mature trees of Castle Wood still on your left. After several fields, a gate on the left would lead into the wood.

❽ Don't go through the gate; instead turn right around the foot of the field to two gates on the left, keep right over two stiles, then bear left down two fields to a road bend. Keep ahead to a sharp right-hand bend, where the right-hand of two gates starts a field path to Pen Selwood church.

A CANAL AND A CHURCH AT BRADFORD-ON-AVON

Combine a visit to this enchanting riverside town and its surprising Saxon church, with a canalside stroll.

The 13th-century bridge at Bradford-on-Avon

Distance: 3.25 miles (5.3km)
Minimum time: 1hr 45min
Ascent/Gradient: 164ft (50m) ▲▲▲
Level of difficulty: +++
Paths: Towpath, field and woodland paths, metalled lanes
Landscape: Canal, river valley, wooded hillsides, town streets
Suggested map: OS Explorer156 Chippenham & Bradford-on-Avon
Start/finish: Grid reference: ST 824606
Dog friendliness: On lead through town
Parking: Bradford-on-Avon station car park (charge), Avoncliff station
Public toilets: Station car park

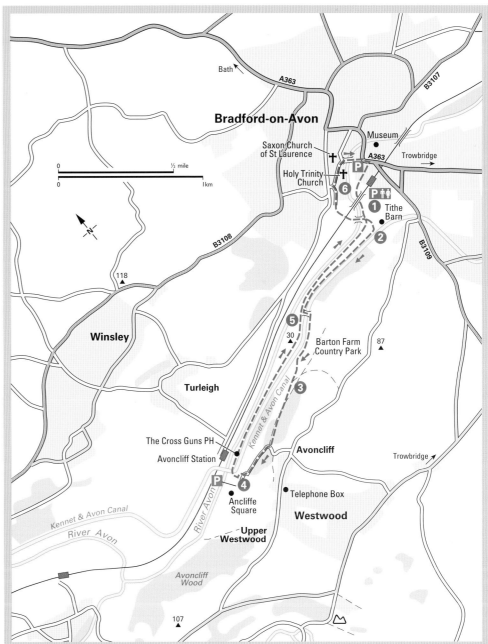

❶ Walk to the end of the car park, away from the station, and follow the path left beneath the railway and beside the River Avon. Enter Barton Farm Country Park and keep to the path across a grassy area to a junction of paths. With the packhorse bridge right, bear right, then left to pass to the right of the tithe barn to reach the Kennett and Avon Canal.

❷ Turn right along the towpath, signed to Avoncliff. Cross the bridge over the canal in 0.5 mile (800m) and follow the path right to a footbridge and gate. Proceed along the right-hand field-edge to a further gate, then bear diagonally left uphill away from the canal to a kissing gate.

❸ Follow the path along the edge of woodland. Keep to this path as it bears left uphill through the trees to reach a metalled lane. Turn right and walk steeply downhill to the canal at Avoncliff.

❹ Don't cross the aqueduct; instead pass the Mad Hatter Café, descend the steps on your right and pass beneath the canal. Keep right by The Cross Guns and join the towpath towards Bradford-on-Avon. Continue for 0.75 mile (1.2km) to the bridge passed on your outward route.

❺ Bear off left downhill along a metalled track and follow it beside the River Avon back into Barton Farm Country Park. Cross the packhorse bridge and the railway and follow

the walled path uphill and right into Barton Orchard. Bear right at the end down the alleyway to Church Street.

❻ Continue ahead past the Holy Trinity Church and the Church of St Laurence. Cross the footbridge and go through St Margaret's car park to the road. Turn right, then right again to the station car park.

**Walk
0**

AVEBURY – PAGAN PASTURES

Explore the famous stone circle and some fine prehistoric monuments.

The Avebury stone circle allows visitors close access

Distance: 5 miles (8km)
Minimum time: 2hrs 30min
Ascent/Gradient: 262ft (80m) ▲▲▲
Level of difficulty: +++
Paths: Tracks, field paths, some road walking, 4 stiles
Landscape: Downland pasture, water-meadows, woodland and village
Suggested map: OS Explorer 157 Marlborough & Savernake Forest
Start/finish: Grid reference: SU 099696
Dog friendliness: Keep dogs under control across pasture and National Trust property
Parking: Large National Trust car park in Avebury
Public toilets: Avebury

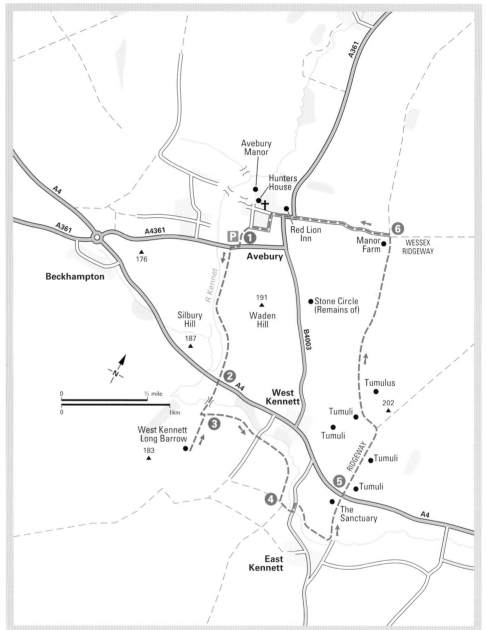

❶ From the car park, walk to the main road and turn right. In 50 yards (46m), cross and go through a gate with a blue bridleway sign. Pass through another gate and follow the path alongside the river. Go through two more gates and cross two stiles, passing Silbury Hill.

❷ Beyond a gate, walk down the right-hand field-edge to a gate and the A4. Cross over and turn left, then almost immediately right through a gate. Walk down the gravel track and cross a bridge over a stream. The track soon narrows to a footpath. Go through a kissing gate and turn sharp left.

❸ To visit West Long Barrow, shortly turn right. Otherwise go straight on around the left-hand field-edge to a stile and continue along a track. At a staggered junction, keep ahead across a stile and walk along the right-hand field boundary. Keep to the right in the corner by a redundant stile and cross the stile on your right in the next corner and proceed up a narrow footpath.

❹ At a T-junction, go left and descend to the road. Turn left, then just beyond the bridge, take the bridle path sharp right. Follow the

right-hand field-edge to a gap in the corner and turn sharp left following a track uphill. At the top you'll see tumuli on the right and the Sanctuary on the left. Continue to the A4.

❺ Cross the A4 and head up the Ridgeway. After 500 yards (457m), turn left off the Ridgeway on to a byway. Bear half right by the clump of trees on a tumulus and keep to the established track, eventually reaching a T-junction by a series of farm buildings, Manor Farm.

❻ Turn left, signed 'Avebury', and follow the metalled track through the earthwork and straight over the staggered crossroads by the Red Lion Inn. Turn left opposite the National Trust signpost and walk back to the car park.

On the walk to Avebury, Silbury Hill dominates the horizon

THE INFANT THAMES AT CRICKLADE

An easy ramble across water-meadows beside the Thames and disused canals.

Quarrying at Cotswold Water Park has produced a watery reed-bed haven for 20,000 birds

Distance: 5.5 miles (8.8km)

Minimum time: 2hrs 30min

Ascent/Gradient: Negligible ▲▲▲

Level of difficulty: +++

Paths: Field paths and bridle paths, disused railway, town streets, 6 stiles

Landscape: Flat river valley

Suggested map: OS Explorer 169 Cirencester & Swindon

Start/finish: Grid reference: SU 100934

Dog friendliness: Dogs can be off-lead along old railway line

Parking: Cricklade Town Hall car park (free)

Public toilets: Cricklade High Street

❶ Turn right out of the car park, keep ahead at the roundabout and walk along the High Street. Pass St Mary's Church, then turn left along North Wall before the river bridge. Shortly, bear right to a gate and join the attractive Thames Path. Continue on this route, walking along the field-edge to reach houses.

❷ Go through the kissing gate on your right and bear left across the field to a gate. Follow the fenced footpath, cross a plank bridge and pass through the gate immediately on your right-hand side. Cross the river bridge and turn left through a gate. Walk beside the infant River Thames, crossing two gates to enter North Meadow.

❸ Continue and cross a stile by a bridge. Go through the gate immediately right and keep straight ahead, ignoring the Thames Path, left. Follow the path beside the disused canal. Cross

a footbridge and a stile, then, at a fence, bear right to cross a footbridge close to a house named The Basin. Bear right along the drive.

❹ Cross a bridge and turn left through the gateway. Shortly, bear right to join the path along the left side of the old canal. Keep to the path for 0.5 mile (800m) to the road. Turn left into Cerney Wick to reach a T-junction.

❺ Cross the stone stile opposite and keep ahead through the paddock to a stone stile and lane. Cross the lane and go through the gate opposite, continuing ahead to a kissing gate and stile. Follow the path ahead. Bear right, then left and bear off left (yellow arrow) into trees.

❻ Cross a footbridge and proceed ahead along the field-edge to a stile. Turn left along the old railway, signed 'Cricklade'. Cross the River

Thames in a mile (1.6km) and keep to the path along the former trackbed to reach a bridge.

❼ Follow the gravel path to the Leisure Centre. Bear left on to the road, following it right, then turn left opposite the entrance to the Leisure Centre car park. Turn right, then next left and follow the road to the church (St Sampsons).

❽ Walk beside the barrier and turn right in front of the Gatehouse into the churchyard. Bear left to the main gates and follow the lane to a T-junction. Turn right to make your way back to the car park.

SOUTHERN ENGLAND

SOUTHERN ENGLAND

Knebworth House, once the home of Victorian novelist Edward Bulwer Lytton, who wrote 'The pen is mightier than the sword'

The character of Southern England has been moulded by three main factors. Firstly, it is predominantly lowland with a relatively gentle climate, its highest point being not mountains but ranges of rolling chalk downland. Secondly, it is Britain's nearest point to continental Europe and over the centuries routes to and from the Channel ports have been forged, first for trade and for the passage of Christian missionaries, archbishops, kings and ambassadors, and later for recreational travellers. The third element is the pole position of London, the nation's centre of commerce and government. This is an exceptionally prosperous region, but, because 19th-century industrialisation focused on the Midlands and the North, it has remained free of big industrial towns. Expansion has instead been recent, and largely in the form of commerce and technology-related developments.

Two of the region's biggest attractions are its landscape and its history. Thanks to more than 60 years of green belt and other planning policies to protect the countryside, much of this landscape is remarkably tranquil. The Thames and most of the region's coastline have generally been spared the spread of obtrusive development. There are many pleasant seaside resorts, but long stretches of coastline are designated 'Heritage Coast', or have been acquired and conserved by the National Trust.

As for history, the great set pieces include prehistoric monuments such as the great Iron-Age fortress of Danebury in Hampshire, the extensive and well-preserved Roman villa at Fishbourne and Norman castles such as Rochester, Bodiam and, of course, Windsor. There is a wealth of stately homes, from the enormous Blenheim Palace in Oxfordshire to more modest but elegant country houses, all with landscaped grounds and gardens which, in the 18th and 19th centuries, made 'the English Garden' renowned throughout Europe. English Heritage and the National Trust have played leading roles in preserving these treasures, as have many private owners who have striven, often against financial odds, to maintain their family homes.

The region's treasures also include great historic cities like Winchester, Canterbury and Oxford, and countless country towns and villages where the conservation of attractive old buildings and townscapes has been reconciled with the demands of everyday living. Places like Southampton, Portsmouth, Brighton and the Medway Towns may have suffered from urban sprawl, but they too have their historic cores and have done much to preserve and promote their individual character. And often – outstandingly in Oxford, thanks to the patronage of university and colleges – excellent new buildings sit amicably alongside the medieval, the Jacobean and the Georgian, demonstrating that our architectural 'heritage' is still in the making.

Previous page: Beachy Head, East Sussex

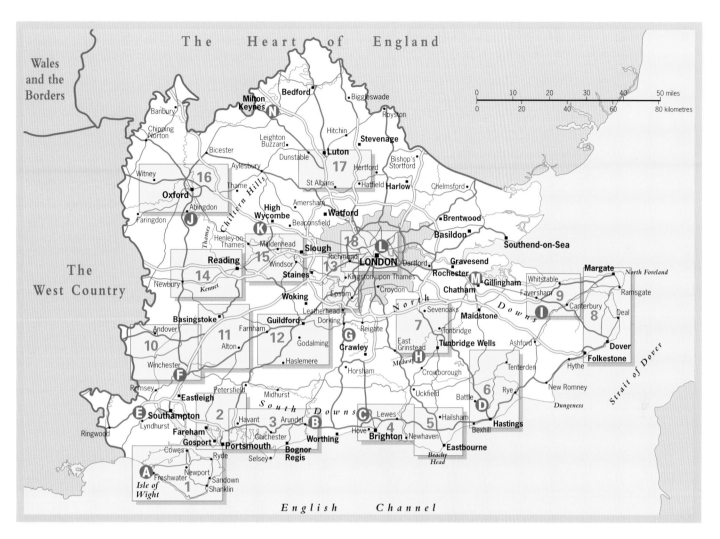

Section Contents

1	The Isle of Wight	74–75
2	Hampshire's Naval Heritage	76–77
3	Creeks and Harbours below the Downs	78–79
4	Sussex by the Sea	80–81
5	Downland Villages and a Stately Resort	84–85
6	The Coast and Countryside of the Norman Conquest	86–87
7	Castles and Mansions in Peaceful Seclusion	88–89
8	Historic Ports of the Gateway to England	90–91
9	Kentish Towns and a Great Cathedral	92–93
10	The Heart of Hampshire	96–97
11	Ancient and Modern in Northeast Hampshire	98–99
12	Surrey Towns and Military Heritage	100–101
13	Palaces and Gardens on the Thames	102–103
14	Valleys of the Thames and Kennet	106–107
15	The Royal County	108–109
16	Thames-side Towns and a Great Seat of Learning	110–111
17	New Towns, Old Palaces	112–113

Features

Customs and Festivals	82–83
The New Forest	94–95
Steam Railways	104–105
London	114–127

Walks

A	Tennyson's Freshwater	128
B	Standing Guard Over Arundel	129
C	Devil's Dyke and the World's Grandest View	130
D	Battle – Britain's Most Famous Battlefield	131
E	Trails of the New Forest	132
F	Alfred's Ancient Capital	133
G	A Pilgrimage to Waverley	134
H	Pooh's Ashdown Forest	135
I	Mr Darcy's Chilham	136
J	Abingdon's Architecture	137
K	Turville on TV	138
L	Guts and Garters in the Ripper's East End	139
M	A Dickens of a Walk at Rochester	140
N	A Tour of Milton Keynes, City of the Future	141

THE ISLE OF WIGHT

'Cowes you cannot milk; Freshwater you cannot drink; Needles you cannot thread'. The Isle of Wight can too easily be written off as old-fashioned and open to witticisms. But being an island has given it a certain tranquillity, which helps visitors to enjoy the fine views, unspoiled villages, and relaxed little towns that attracted Queen Victoria and Prince Albert.

The noticeable gap in the Needles is where the 36m-high (120ft) shaft of rock known as 'Lot's Wife' stood until it collapsed into the sea in 1764

Brading

Brading's past intertwines with that of the Oglander family, of nearby Nunwell House. Part Georgian, part Jacobean, the house was where Charles I spent his last night of freedom. There are fine gardens, channel views, and a museum of the Home Guard of World War II. To the west is the island's finest Roman villa, with mosaic floors, and Morton Manor, which has gardens and a vineyard.

Carisbrooke

Standing on a spur of chalk downland, Carisbrooke Castle was for centuries the residence of the island's governor, and is Wight's only medieval castle. A perennial attraction are the donkeys which raise water from the well in the middle

courtyard. The keep, gatehouse and curtain wall are 12th century, and the outer bastions were built in the 16th century.

Cowes

To many people Cowes means yachting – particularly Cowes Week, its international yachting festival. West Cowes became a place of consequence when Henry VIII built a fort there; this is now the head-quarters of the Royal Yacht Squadron, and the focus of Cowes Week. Prince's Green on the waterside is a good viewpoint. East Cowes is the terminus of the car ferry from Southampton, and beyond it is Osborne House (see right).

The Needles and Alum Bay

The line of chalk which runs through the island from east to west emerges in the west in the spectacular chalk stacks of The Needles. On the north side of the headland lies Alum Bay, famous for its coloured sands. Some of the many acres of the island owned by the National Trust are here, including Needles Old Battery, a Victorian defence, complete with guns, that sits 250ft (76m) above sea level, with views of the Needles, the lighthouse and the coastline.

Newport

The geographical and administrative centre of the island, Newport is a pleasant market town with Georgian and Jacobean buildings among those of later times. It centres on St James's Square, from which runs the High Street with a fine pedimented Guildhall. Quays and warehouses on the River Medina are reminders that the 'port' in the name was a real one.

Sandown and Shanklin

These twin resorts on Sandown Bay are popular for family holidays, with beautiful sandy beaches and plenty of

Victoria and Osborne

Queen Victoria and Prince Albert bought the 1,000-acre (405ha) Osborne estate in 1845 as (to use the Queen's own words) 'a place of one's own, quiet and retired'. Prince Albert, who much admired Thomas Cubitt's Italianate London terraces, set about designing and building Osborne House (with Cubitt advising) in the style of an Italian villa, with terraced gardens overlooking Osborne Bay and the Solent. 'It is impossible', wrote Victoria, 'to imagine a prettier spot. We can walk anywhere without being followed or mobbed.' She could even swim from her private beach, conveyed into the water by a wheeled bathing machine, which English Heritage exhibits there today. The state and private apartments are largely untouched since Victoria's death and offer a fascinating insight into the lives of the royal family.

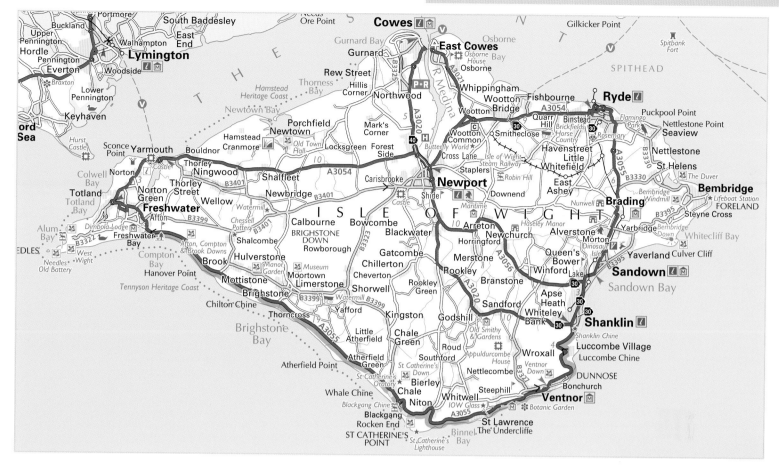

Tennyson and The Isle of Wight

As a young poet, Tennyson suffered from adverse criticism and meagre earnings, but in 1850 publication of his great poem 'In Memoriam' set the seal on his growing reputation, leading to his succeeding Wordsworth as Poet Laureate. To escape from the public eye, he rented Farringford at Freshwater, which he later purchased with the proceeds of his best-selling poem, 'Maud'. Here he entertained such eminent fellow Victorians as Benjamin Jowett, Master of Balliol, and Sir James Knowles, editor of the *Contemporary Review*. Poems he wrote there include 'Maud' and 'Idylls of the King'. His granite monument stands on Tennyson Down.

entertainments and attractions. Fine Victorian and Edwardian façades line the seafront, reflecting the days when the likes of Darwin, Lewis Carroll and Henry Longfellow were among the visitors. A pterodactyl-shaped building in Sandown houses Dinosaur Isle, with reconstructed dinosaurs, special effects and hands-on exhibits alongside the laboratories where experts study this aspect of the island's distant past.

Wroxall and Appuldurcombe

Hidden among the downs, Wroxall is an excellent centre for walks. Just west of the village stands the still-impressive shell of what was the island's grandest mansion, the 18th-century baroque Appuldurcombe House, its architect unknown.

Yarmouth

Yarmouth owes its importance to its harbour, and a strategic position which led Henry VIII to build the castle. A short walk away is Fort Victoria, also designed to defend the Needles Channel, complete with a planetarium, a marine aquarium, model railway and a country park.

The entrance gatehouse to Carisbrooke Castle

Tennyson's monument on the crest of Tennyson Down was erected in 1897

See Walk A, page 128
Tennyson's Freshwater

Tourist Information

All telephone enquiries to 01983 313818
Personal callers:
Cowes: Fountain Quay
Newport: The Guildhall, High Street
Ryde: Union Street
Sandown: 8 High Street
Shanklin: 67 High Street
Ventnor: 34 High Street (seasonal)
Yarmouth: The Quay

HAMPSHIRE'S NAVAL HERITAGE

This is Navy country, with Portsmouth's great dockyard and Gosport's naval victualling and ordnance yards; the walls of Old Portsmouth and the great forts of the Napoleonic era on (and off) the coast; the Georgian houses for navy officers at Fareham and Alverstoke. Its impact extended upcountry with hilltop signal stations that connected Portsmouth to the Admiralty.

Powered by steam and sail, Portsmouth's HMS Warrior was the Royal Navy's first ocean-going armoured battleship

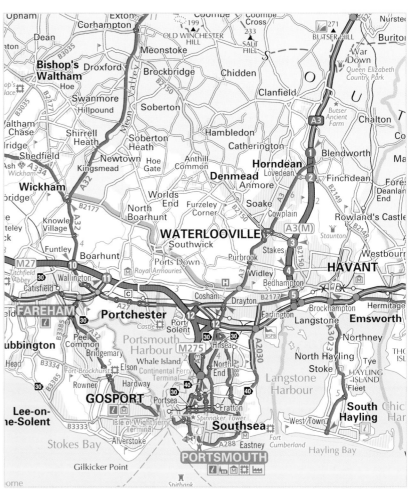

Bishop's Waltham

This was the medieval seat of the Bishops of Winchester, and the remains of their palace are still impressive. They include the great hall, kitchen, three-storey tower, and the moat which surrounded it all. English Heritage has furnished the ground floor of the dower house as a 19th-century farmhouse. The first floor has an exhibition on Winchester's mighty bishops, one of whom laid out this charming little town.

Tourist Information
Fareham: Westbury Manor, West Street (tel: 01329 221342) Gosport: Bus Station complex (tel: 023 9252 2944) Portsmouth: The Hard (tel: 023 9282 6722) Southsea: Clarence Esplanade (seasonal) (tel: 023 9282 6722)

Fareham

From the bypass or the M27, Fareham looks like a thoroughly modern commuter town for Portsmouth. In fact, Georgian naval officers also preferred to live here and commute to the docks. Today's modern shopping centre is in West Street, which has probably been the salvation of its fine High Street, where many naval families lived.

Fareham was once a brick-producing centre, turning out the richly coloured 'Fareham Reds'. These fine 'sale-glazed' blue-grey bricks and the later 'whites' (which are actually yellow), together with mathematical tiles and Georgian features such as doorcases, windows and porches, all make for a harmonious townscape.

View through a quoin at Fort Nelson, Fareham

The lofty Spinnaker Tower reflects Portsmouth's seafaring past with its mast-and-sail-like design

Queen Elizabeth Country Park

The London–Portsmouth road past Hampshire's windy Butser Hill has long been busy – in the stagecoach era, a prodigious two coaches an hour passed Cannonball Corner. The present dual carriageway carries rather more traffic, considerably faster, but should not blind travellers to the very rewarding Queen Elizabeth Country Park, which straddles the road. There is beech forest to the east with deer, a wildlife trail and waymarked walks, and open downland to the west, with a demonstration Iron-Age farm, bracing walks and wonderful views. An underpass links them, and there is an excellent park centre with exhibitions, audiovisual displays and a café.

Gosport

Across the harbour mouth from Portsmouth, Gosport, too, has been dominated by the Navy, who built the Royal Clarence Victualling Yard in the 18th and 19th centuries to feed its sailors, and the Haslar Royal Naval Hospital to care for them. Barracks were built for the Marines, and an ordnance depot at Priddy's Hard, and ramparts were constructed. In the 19th century several monumental forts were built, part of a chain of 'Palmerston Forts' which guarded Portsmouth Harbour from a landward attack, should the threatened French invasion occur. The main attractions here are the Royal Navy Submarine Museum, with guided tours of HMS *Alliance*, and Explosion! at Priddy's Hard.

Second World War bombs and post-war redevelopment have left relatively few of the Georgian and Victorian buildings intact. Three worth viewing are Holy Trinity Church with its landmark campanile, the splendid colonnaded ghost of the town's dead 1840s railway station and, to the west at Alverstoke, the gently curving, classical colonnaded Anglesea Crescent.

Hambledon

This pretty village is, as a granite monument opposite the Bat & Ball Inn at nearby Broadhalfpenny Down proclaims, traditionally the birthplace of the game of cricket. The Hambledon Cricket Club was founded in 1750, when the rules of the game were regularised, and in 1777 a Hambledon village team beat their All-England competitors.

Portchester

The face Portchester presents to the A27 belies its historic importance. Persist, follow Castle Street to its end, and you come to an unspoiled 18th-century village centre round a green. One fork leads past Portchester House to a shingle shore with views of Portsmouth Harbour; the other leads to the castle. This has a history going back nearly 2,000 years. The walls are those of a Roman fort, around 600ft (183m) square, and the most complete in Europe. Within, and rising above them, is a medieval castle and palace, used by Henry I when commuting to and from Normandy. An English Heritage exhibition tells the story. Also within the walls is a remarkably complete 12th-century church.

Portsmouth

Portsmouth is packed on to a little island, with sea or harbour on three sides, linked to the rest of Hampshire by four bridges and a causeway. For centuries it has been dominated by the Navy, which has powerfully affected its social, economic and political life. Old Portsmouth clusters picturesquely round the original harbour and the Camber, guarded to seaward by Henry VIII's town walls; Portsea, north of the old town, developed in the 18th century; the Landport is the modern city's commercial heart; to the east is the elegant seaside resort of Southsea.

In the waterfront area, the Millennium Promenade is a 4-mile (6.4km) trail around the most historic landmarks, marked by distinctive chain-link paving. Gunwharf Quays, with its outlet shopping, entertainments and restaurants, is overlooked by the Spinnaker Tower. This symbol of the waterfront's redevelopment stands 170m (558ft) high, affording breathtaking views of the coast from its viewing platform. From Ide Hill, visitors can see far over the Weald towards Bough Beech Reservoir, where there are fly-fishing and sailing facilities.

The Historic Dockyard itself remains one of Britain's foremost attractions, containing three of the greatest ships ever built – HMS *Victory*, the 1860 ironclad HMS *Warrior* and the Tudor warship *Mary Rose*, salvaged after 400 years on the seabed. Georgian dockyard buildings contain the exciting Dockyard Apprentice Exhibition, Action Stations and the Royal Naval Museum, and there are harbour cruises.

Southsea Castle, built by Henry VIII, is now open to the public, and nearby attractions include the D-Day Museum, containing the impressive Overlord Embroidery depicting the D-Day Landings, the Royal Marines Museum and a Sea Life Centre. In 19th-century Landport is Charles Dickens' Birthplace Museum, and on Portsdown Hill Fort Nelson has artillery displays – as well as demonstrations.

HMS Victory, *the flagship of Admiral Horatio Nelson and the veteran of five battles, is preserved in Portsmouth and open for guided tours*

Buildings of Defence

The Ministry of Defence, with around 500 listed buildings and ancient monuments, is one of Britain's biggest owners of historic buildings. Hampshire, with defence estates ranging from Aldershot's barrack blocks to the Palmerston Forts around Portsmouth, has probably the biggest share. But just as their historic and architectural importance was increasingly being recognised, many became surplus to MOD requirements. Hampshire's Historic Buildings Bureau has played a key role in finding appropriate, viable new uses – such as the development of Portsmouth's Naval Dockyard as a heritage attraction, and the conservation of Winchester's once-threatened Peninsular Barracks as very special luxury flats.

CREEKS AND HARBOURS BELOW THE DOWNS

The countryside around Chichester is varied and interesting, with flat coastal land to the east culminating in a string of traditional seaside resorts, complete with piers and bandstands. To the south and west is a landscape broken by meandering rivers and the long, marshy arms of Chichester Harbour. Inland are the Downs, and the woodlands and villages of the Weald.

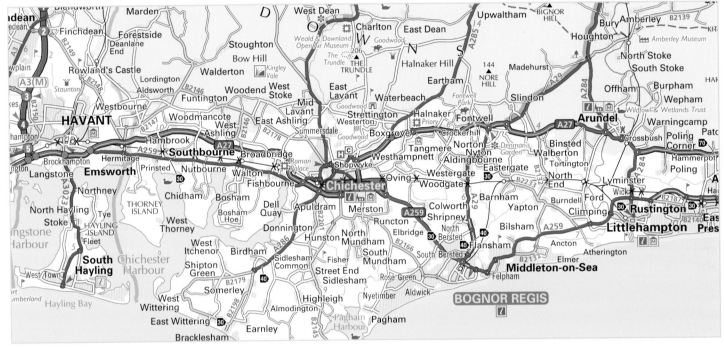

Arundel Castle towers over the town and the River Arun which gave both its name

Amberley

A charming, tranquil village in the Arun Valley, Amberley has a history going back to medieval times and was the summer residence of the Bishops of Chichester. Amberley Wildbrooks are noted for their landscape and ecological qualities. Amberley Museum, imaginatively created from 36 acres (15ha) of depleted chalk pits, brings to life the industrial heritage of the area with craft workshops: a blacksmith, potter, printer and boat-builder; and a narrow-gauge railway and vintage buses.

Arundel

This hilltop town rises dramatically out of the flood plain of the Arun with its silhouette of castle, parish church and Roman Catholic cathedral. From a distance it looks older than it is. The 11th-century castle was rebuilt in Georgian times in fashionable Gothic style and the cathedral is an 1890s celebration of the liberation of English catholicism by the Dukes of Norfolk. The Church of St Nicholas, dating from 1380, houses both Anglican and Roman Catholic worship under one roof. The town, largely Georgian and Victorian, is pleasing, with lots of antiques

Amberley is notable for its profusion of thatched cottages and community of skilled local craftspeople

The Weald and Downland Museum

Established in 1971 on the West Dean Estate near the village of Singleton, the Weald and Downland Open Air Museum is a collection of more than 40 traditional, mostly timber-framed buildings from the Weald and Downland area – rescued and re-erected here when they faced destruction on their previous sites. They include a medieval farmhouse, 18th-century barns, a granary, a Tudor market hall, carpenter's and plumber's workshops, a blacksmith's forge and a village school. The watermill, still grinding flour, is a great attraction. The Weald and Downland is far from being a dead museum.

Demonstrations of building crafts and hands-on displays make it all come vividly alive, and the buildings have been skilfully positioned to look as if they have always been here.

and other specialist shops, art galleries and the Arundel Museum and Heritage Centre. The Wildfowl and Wetlands Trust reserve here is a sanctuary for thousands of waterfowl, including some rare species.

Chichester

Chichester's glory is its cathedral, still dominating the surrounding flat coastal lands and, despite later changes, still recognisably 12th century. The town goes back much further – as its 'chester' suffix suggest, it was a Roman settlement. The four main streets, which meet at the 16th-century market cross, have many fine old buildings and the circular Walls Walk offers fine views. The lanes repay exploration, particularly to the southeast, where 18th-century Pallant House, a Queen Anne town house furnished in period style, is now an art gallery. In parkland to the north is the Chichester Festival Theatre and the smaller Minerva Theatre.

Denman's Garden

John Brookes, leading garden writer and designer, created this modern garden and his skilfully planned vistas provide colour, shape and texture all the year round. There are also rare species under glass, and the Georgian stables now house Brooks'

When officers of the Sussex Militia had nowhere to race their horses, the Duke of Richmond came to their rescue and Goodwood was born in 1801

studio and school of garden design. Nearby Slindon is a delightful village largely owned by the National Trust.

Emsworth

Emsworth is an old port at the head of one of the channels of Chichester Harbour. The original town (now bypassed) is an agreeable jumble of streets, lanes and alleys on a peninsula between two creeks. The large sea-filled basin to the south-west corner was created to power a tide mill.

Goodwood

'Glorious Goodwood' evokes visions of blue skies and fluffy clouds over the Downs as crowds throng the famous racecourse. It has other attractions and is full of history. Trundle Hill was a major Neolithic encampment, and owes its name to a later wheel-shaped Iron-Age fort. The 18th-century Goodwood House, home of the Dukes of Richmond, endorses the importance of the horse hereabouts – the stables are as grand as the house. Both house and grounds are open to visitors.

Stansted Park

The present house here dates from the early 20th century, replacing a 17th-century house by Talman which was largely destroyed by fire. The grounds are the main attraction, with a long beech avenue, woodlands and fine gardens. There is also a theatre museum. Talman's buildings would seem to be fire-prone – he also designed Uppark to the north, which was all but destroyed in the same way in 1989, but has since been splendidly restored.

Fishbourne

The Romans sailed their ships up Chichester Harbour's Fishbourne Channel in the first century AD, and Fishbourne Roman Palace – discovered only in 1960 and excavated by Professor Barry Cunliffe – is one of Britain's most important and splendid Roman sites. Built on a lavish scale, it was designed to show the conquered Britons just what Roman civilisation could achieve. After a fire, the remains were used in the building of the Roman settlement of *Noviomagus* – the original Chichester.

 See Walk B, page 129
Standing Guard Over Arundel

Tourist Information
Arundel: 1–3 Crown Yard Mews, River Road (tel: 01903 882268)
Bognor Regis: Belmont Street (tel: 01243 823140)
Chichester: 29a South Street (tel: 01243 775888)

SUSSEX BY THE SEA

It is easy to see why this part of Sussex has been popular for so long. The sea, setting a limit to the landscape, provides a destination and brings a stimulating whiff of salt to the air; the South Downs offer the traveller from London a sense of arriving in a brighter, cleaner and somehow freer world. And between hills and sea is Brighton – big, bustling and colourful.

Brighton

Brighton has been called 'London by the sea', and there is a lot of London about it. Not just its racy reputation and hyperactive club scene, but also stuccoed terraces that might be in Belgravia and a sophistication that comes from having a commuting population of actors, lawyers, medical specialists and other professionals. It has a superb arts diary, with an annual arts festival featuring theatre, exhibitions and concerts. Its two universities and college of technology also add to the buzz of human activity.

The best-known architectural set piece is the Royal Pavilion, rebuilt by John Nash in Indian style between 1815 and 1822 for the Prince Regent. If its exotic skyline extends the imagination, some of the interiors are positively mind-boggling. Some of Brighton's liveliest areas are in humble streets behind the seafront – the maze of The Lanes has long been a tourist attraction, but the once run-down North

The Lanes in Brighton attract a busy shopping and tourist trade

Laine area between the Pavilion and the station has developed a lively craft-and-café scene.

Other attractions include the Marina, with moorings for 2,000 boats, overlooked by harbourside bars and restaurants, outlet shopping, leisure facilities and apartments. The 100-year-old Volks electric railway still runs along the seashore and there are two piers, though the West Pier, in spite of its Grade I listing, is nothing more than a collapsed, burnt-out shell. A 5,000-seat conference and exhibition centre draws the largest trade union and political party conferences.

Ditchling

This picture-postcard village has for many years attracted artists and craftsmen – notably sculptor and designer Eric Gill, who made his home here in the 1920s. The 13th-century church, though

Hove

The boundary between Hove and Brighton has long been obscure, even to locals, but Hove does have a distinctive character. It is sedate rather than breezy, and stylish in a more reserved way. Its chief glory is its procession of early and mid-19th-century seafront terraces punctuated by squares and crescents. At Hove Park, high up above the seafront, stands a large Victorian pumping station where, in 1866, great steam-powered beam engines began pumping up water to send it down into the baths and basins of Brighton and Hove. In the late 1940s, smaller but more powerful electric pumps took on the task, and in 1971 it was proposed to demolish the building and break up its engines for scrap. Happily, conservationist protests saved them, and the building became the British Engineerium, a temple to the age of steam and Britain's engineers – with one of the preserved beam engines 'in steam' from time to time.

Brighton Pier, with its funfair, arcades and fast food stalls, aims to draw a family crowd

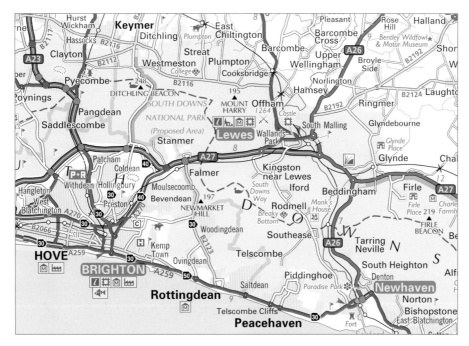

somewhat over-restored, is still beautiful and there are some fine timber-framed houses. Half an hour's uphill walk to the south is the National Trust-owned Ditchling Beacon, at 813ft (247.7m) one of the high points of the Sussex Downs.

Glynde

Set at the foot of the Downs, Glynde is a village rich in visual and other delights. It is full of typical Sussex cottages, and Glynde Place is a particularly fine Elizabethan manor house, built in 1579 from Sussex flint and stone from Caen in Normandy. It also has an unusual parish church, built in 1763 in Palladian style. On Mount Caburn to the west of the village is an Iron-Age hill fort, and a mile (1.6km) north is Glyndebourne Opera House, founded by John Christie in the 1930s and later enhanced by the completion of an award-winning auditorium by architect Sir Michael Hopkins.

Lewes

Castle-crowned, with a lovely curving High Street full of idiosyncratic, mature old buildings, the county town of East Sussex is one of those places that even the most enlightened town planning could never have achieved. Centuries of serendipitous development and adequate means have made it what it is. Access to stone from the ruins of the great Cluniac priory of St Pancras was a good start.

Off the High Street run innumerable lanes and alleys, where houses are of warm brick, timber and sometimes the local

speciality – mathematical tiles. While there are some fine timber-framed houses, most is Georgian. Despite its comfortable image, Lewes has traditionally been radical and nonconformist. Thomas Paine, author of *The Rights of Man*, lived here, and in the more distant past of Mary's reign, this strongly Puritan town produced 17 Protestant martyrs, who are remembered each Guy Fawkes Day with torch-lit processions and elaborate firework displays (see page 83).

Ditchling Beacon affords views over the suburbs of Brighton to the south and the Lower Weald (seen above) to the north

👣 **See Walk C, page 130**
Devil's Dyke and the
World's Grandest View

Tourist Information
Brighton: Royal Pavilion
(tel: 0906 711 2255
premium rate)
Lewes: 187 High Street
(tel: 01273 483448)

Steep cobbled streets in Lewes, which gets its name from a Saxon word meaning 'slopes'

CUSTOMS AND FESTIVALS

Traditional customs and festivals in southern England are many and varied. Some, like 'first-footing' on New Year's Eve, pancakes on Shrove Tuesday, and bonfires and fireworks on Guy Fawkes Day, are nationwide, but sometimes may have peculiar local variants. Many go back to pagan times, though the early Christian Church took them over. The variety of traditional festivals celebrated is, moreover, being interestingly extended and enriched as schools and communities respond to an increasingly multicultural population.

Thus primary school children in Kent or Oxfordshire are quite likely to know about Holi (when Hindus celebrate the end of winter), Id-ul-Fitr (the end of the Ramadan fast for Muslims), Vesak (when Buddhists leave gifts on the doorsteps of the poor), Shavuot (when Jews celebrate the first fruits of the harvest), or the Chinese New Year marked with firecrackers and (as in London's Chinatown) dragon dancers. But in these two pages we look at some of the more traditional customs and festivals of the south and southeast.

Choir boys at the May Day celebrations in Oxford

The First Quarter

One curious New Year custom is Queen's College, Oxford's Needle and Thread Gaudy (feast), when the college bursar presents each guest at table with a needle threaded with silk, and says: 'Take this and be thrifty.' Sound advice, no doubt, but all a bit of a joke, in arcane Oxford style. 'Needle' and 'thread' in Norman French are *aiguille* and *fil* – a pun on the college's 14th-century founder, Robert de Eglesfield.

Solemnity and fun are mixed in a different way in London in February, with the annual Clowns' Service at Holy Trinity Church, Dalston. Clowns attend in full costume and make-up and end with a prayer thanking God 'for causing me to share with others

your precious gift of laughter'. It began relatively recently, in 1946, as a tribute to the great 19th-century clown Joseph Grimaldi.

In March people at Stockbridge in Hampshire elect jurors to the Courts Leet and Baron, which traditionally resolved disputes over the local commons. These now belong to the National Trust, but the revived ceremony is fun and provides a useful forum for discussion of local matters.

Rites of Spring

Easter and the period preceding it are rich in colourful customs, starting with Shrove Tuesday – traditionally associated with pancakes. This, it seems, is because pancake-making used up perishable foodstuffs before the 40 days of Lent. A well-known variant is the pancake race at Olney, Buckinghamshire. Contrary to general belief, dropping the pancake does not disqualify, though it may dull the appetite.

On Maundy Thursday the sovereign distributes Maundy Money – specially minted silver coins – at Westminster Abbey and various cathedrals. In London Easter Sunday sees the Easter Parade in Battersea Park, followed on Easter Monday by the Harness Horse Parade in Regent's Park. On Dunstable Down in Bedfordshire they roll oranges down the hill to waiting children.

May Day ceremonies are perhaps most spectacular in Oxford, where at 6am choristers climb the 144ft (44m) tower of Magdalen College to sing a Latin hymn to the (surprisingly large) assembled crowd. The tower's bells ring out, and a day of

celebrations begins with morris dancing, punting parties and picnics.

Towards the end of May at Rye, Sussex, the inauguration of the new mayor is strangely celebrated by the new incumbent throwing of hot pennies to children from the town hall. Along the coast, the Vicar of Hastings blesses the sea, presumably to enhance the catch (these days his pulpit is a lifeboat). Also in May, the charter trustees of High Wycombe, Buckinghamshire, choose a mayor, who is then weighed by the mayoress, out-going mayor and various others, the presiding weights-and-measures official pronouncing either 'Some more' (meaning 'You've put on weight since last year') or 'No more' (meaning 'You haven't').

Summer Celebrations

On a June Saturday in each leap year, Great Dunmow in Essex is the scene of the well-known Dunmow Flitch, a 900-year-old custom in which married couples seek to convince a local jury of 'six maids and six bachelors' that they have never been unfaithful nor had cross words. National celebrities dressed in wig and gown act as prosecuting and defending counsel; the prize for successful defendants is the flitch – a whole side of bacon.

On the second Wednesday in July the new Master of the Vintners' Company (a City of London livery company) processes from Vintners' Hall in Upper Thames Street to the Church of St James Garlickhithe, he and his entourage carrying nosegays against noxious fumes or infection, and preceded by their Wine Porter, who sweeps a clean path with his broom. Later in the month the Vintners are concerned with Swan Upping on the Thames – the nicking of beaks of each swan to show whether it belongs to the Queen, the Vintners or the Dyers.

In August the Thames is the scene of the Doggett's Coat and Badge Race, when recently qualified Thames Watermen compete in a sculling race from London Bridge to Chelsea's Cadogan Pier. Thomas Doggett, an Irish actor-manager who died in 1721, inaugurated the race to show his support for George I and his new Hanoverian dynasty – the prizes being £5, a scarlet coat, breeches and shoes, and a huge silver badge.

Winter Customs

The first day of October sees the Lord Chancellor processing from a service in Westminster Abbey to the House of Lords where he greets his guests and gives them 'Breakfast' (a reception for lawyers and others); and on the first Sunday London's Costermongers congregate for their service in St Martin-in-the-Fields, many of them kitted out in the dressy manner of 19th-century street traders, including 'Pearly Kings and Queens', their clothes studded with innumerable pearl buttons.

Following Guy Fawkes' unsuccessful attempt to blow up King and Parliament in 1605, bonfires and fireworks in England are mostly not at the New Year but on 5 November. Nowhere is this festival so thoroughly celebrated as in Lewes, Sussex, where the memory of 17 Protestant martyrs in the

Lewes is the setting for several of the country's biggest and most spectacular Guy Fawkes fireworks displays

reign of Queen Mary led to a (these days not serious) anti-Papist tradition. Lewes has a number of bonfire societies in different parts of the town, who dress up, go in procession and burn effigies of currently hated politicians and others on giant bonfires. In London, the second Saturday in November sees the City's new Lord Mayor ride in his state coach to be sworn in at the Royal Courts of Justice. The procession accompanying him consists of mobile floats on various aspects of a theme chosen by the incoming Lord Mayor.

On Christmas Day the Serpentine in Hyde Park is the scene of a swimming race for the Peter Pan Cup, originally presented in 1864 by Peter Pan's creator Sir James Barrie. The swimmers meet at 9am, and may need to break ice first.

Daily Events

Finally, some customs and ceremonies take place every day of the year. At the ancient Hospital of St Cross in Winchester, the first 32 people to arrive can claim, with no questions asked, a slice of bread (presented on a wooden platter) and a drink of ale from a horn cup. And each evening at the Tower of London the approaching Chief Yeoman Warder and his escort are challenged by a sentry, leading to the following exchange: 'Halt, who goes there?' 'The Keys.' 'Whose keys?' 'Queen Elizabeth's keys.' The sentry then presents arms, the Chief Warder removes his hat and proclaims, 'God preserve Queen Elizabeth,' and the whole guard responds 'Amen!'

Swan Upping, in July, is a long-standing custom on the River Thames

DOWNLAND VILLAGES AND A STATELY RESORT

A high, grass-covered stretch of the South Downs dominates this area, which is broken by the Cuckmere Valley, with flatter arable farmlands to its north. The stylish Victorian seaside resort of Eastbourne is to the east, with the Pevensey Levels beyond and the great chalk cliffs of Beachy Head and the Seven Sisters standing guard before the English Channel.

From the village of Alfriston, a footpath leads to glorious views over the South Downs

Alfriston

Where the little Cuckmere River breaks through the South Downs on its way to pebbly Cuckmere Haven stands the ancient village of Alfriston. Its heart is at the market cross, a triangular space where North Street and West Street converge into High Street, and inns and other old buildings line the thoroughfare. The village's second centre is a green called the Tye, which is near the river. Here stands the ancient and ample parish church of St Andrew's, known as 'the Cathedral of the South Downs'. Here also you will find the 14th-century Clergy House, the first building ever to be acquired by the National Trust. The South Downs Way drops down into the village before climbing again on the other side. Over the river is Litlington (with a shady tea garden), and to the north is the Long Man of Wilmington, a huge figure cut in the chalk of Windover Hill.

Bloomsbury in Sussex

The Bloomsbury Group of the 1910s and 1920s did not spend all their time in London WC2. Several of them had a foot in Sussex. The Monks House at Rodmell, part 16th century, was bought in 1919 by Leonard and Virginia Woolf as a country retreat. Now owned by the National Trust, it contains Woolf memorabilia and furniture painted by Vanessa and Clive Bell and Duncan Grant. These three lived at Charleston Farmhouse, off the A27 east of Lewes, where they were visited by (among others) Lytton Strachey and John Maynard Keynes. The house and garden, preserved and restored by a trust, are full of work by Grant and the Bells, and nearby Berwick Church has wall paintings by the trio.

Beachy Head and the Seven Sisters

Eastwards between Cuckmere Haven and Eastbourne runs a spectacular switchback of chalk cliffs, the Seven Sisters, culminating in Beachy Head. Derived from the Norman French, *beau chef* (beautiful headland), its name is tautological, but the views are spectacular. Over the years the National Trust has gradually acquired most of this coast and its hinterland, preserving it and restoring old farming patterns. As you walk the Sisters, each seems bigger and more exhausting than the last – but the views repay the exertion.

Charleston Farmhouse, near Westdean, with its fireplace painted by Duncan Grant

Eastbourne

After Brighton, the largest of Sussex's seaside resorts is Eastbourne, which developed very differently. The first entrepreneurial stirrings here were in the 18th century, but Eastbourne is a Victorian creation – well planned and generous in quality thanks to two dominant land-owners, the 7th Duke of Devonshire and Carew Davis Gilbert. Compton Place, west of the town centre, was the Duke of Devonshire's seat. Eastbourne has a pier, spacious esplanades, stately seafront hotels, and four theatres. Its location is enviable, with sea to the east and Downs to the west.

The town's origins are much earlier. A Roman boat was discovered here, and St Mary's Church, with its green sandstone tower, has some 13th-century interior features. Historic buildings in the town include the 16th-century Old Parsonage and the timber-framed Lamb Inn. The Redoubt, another feature of the area, is a Martello Tower built as part of the coastal defences against Napoleon.

Tourist Information
Eastbourne: 3 Cornfield Road (tel: 0871 663 0031)

Herstmonceux

Herstmonceux Castle dates from the 14th century and was built in the fashionable brick of those times. According to Sir Nikolaus Pevsner, it shows the advent of all-round architectural symmetry in England three generations before the Renaissance. It was restored in the 1930s and a decade later became home to the Royal Greenwich Observatory, which had been forced out of London by atmospheric pollution. A new observatory complex was built here. In 1990 the observatory moved to Cambridge, and the complex became the Observatory Science Centre, with lots of interactive displays and experiments. In Herstmonceux village, a mile (1.6km) north, the 12th-century All Saints Church has monuments to members of the Fiennes family, who were owners of the castle.

Geometric flower bed arrangements (a Victorian technique known as 'carpet bedding') gives Eastbourne's Carpet Gardens their name

Ghost stories and smuggler tales add to the allure of Beachy Head

Pevensey

Straddling the old highway from Eastbourne to Hastings across the levels, Pevensey has seen plenty of history. The Romans landed here and built a huge ten-acre (4ha) fort, *Anderida*. William the Conqueror also landed here, and the Normans built a more compact stone castle within the Roman defences. Several centuries later the town joined the Cinque Ports federation. Pevensey was once on the coast (its final 'ey' indicates that it was an island between two creeks), but the river silted up and the sea receded, leaving it high and dry. The sea is now half a mile (0.8km) away at modern Pevensey Bay.

The little town is full of attractive old houses that speak eloquently of the past, including the Mint House, recalling the time when Pevensey had a royal mint, the Court House, which was the equivalent of a town hall when the town had its own corporation, and several old and very atmospheric inns.

Westdean

Westdean is a tiny village hidden in a secluded valley among woodlands just north of the A259 at Exceat Bridge. The best way to discover it is on foot via a scenic footpath that starts at the car park at Seven Sisters Country Park. The path takes you sharply uphill through woodlands, then just as sharply down again by steps to the village. There are good walks from here through Friston Forest to Jevington, or by woodland and downland to Alfriston, passing Charleston Manor, part 13th century and with fine barns and dovecote. Pevsner calls it 'a perfect house in a perfect setting'.

The South Downs Way

One of the Countryside Commission's National Trails, this is a 100-mile (161km) long-distance path running along the downs from Eastbourne to Winchester (see page 133). On rolling chalk downland, the path offers bracing walking and splendid views, and is generally dry underfoot. Few people walk it all in one go. There is easy access from a number of towns and railway stations, lateral bus services, and a network of cross paths, which, when combined with village car parks, mean that you can sample it a stretch at a time.

THE COAST AND COUNTRYSIDE OF THE NORMAN CONQUEST

Here you will find three diverse kinds of country. The western sea coast has three contiguous but distinctive resorts – Hastings, St Leonards and Bexhill. The well-wooded hills behind them merge into the Kentish Weald. The flat marshlands round the ancient towns of Winchelsea and Rye extend inland along the River Rother and the Royal Military Canal to the Isle of Oxney.

Fishermen relied on Hastings' 'net shops' to keep their equipment dry. Lack of space meant the sheds had to be vertically stacked

clean lines and pioneering use of concrete, steel and glass must have had quite an impact in 1934. Today it is an arts centre. Bexhill was the birthplace of British motor racing, remembered in the Motoring Heritage Centre, the Cooden Beach Heritage Gallery and the annual Festival of Motoring.

Battle

It was here, and not 7 miles (11.2km) away at Hastings, that William the Conqueror defeated the Saxon King Harold and changed the course of English history. There was no town here then, only open land, but William built a church, an abbey soon followed, and the town grew up around it. Most of the battlefield is still open sheep pasture, which enhances the Abbey's setting, but the momentous battle is brought to life by an audio-tour and a video introduction. There is also a museum devoted to abbey life. Several other museums interpreting aspects of its history can be seen in the town.

Bexhill

Originally a fishing village, vestiges of which can be seen round the parish church, Bexhill was developed as a resort in the 1880s by the Earls de la Warr, who gave their name to the US state of Delaware as well as to the seafront De La Warr Pavilion. Designed by the leading modern movement architect Erich Mendelsohn, in Britain as a refugee from Nazi Germany, its

Legend has it that the altar in Battle Abbey was built on the spot where King Harold was killed

Hastings

Unlike most of its sister Cinque Ports, Hastings still gains a living from the sea. Fishing boats put out from the beach, where curious, tall wooden sheds, known as the net shops, are a distinctive landmark, and in their midst is the Fishermen's Museum housing the *Enterprise*, the last sailing lugger built in Hastings. This museum is at Hastings' eastern end, where the Old Town nestles picturesquely in the Bourne Valley under the shadow of Hastings Castle. The Castle now houses the 1066 Story, and St Mary in the Castle Arts Centre. Nearby are St Clements Caves, where interactive displays take you into the world of smuggling. Two cliff railways make it easy to explore this end of the town.

West of the Old Town – compulsive territory for exploring on foot – is the town centre seaside resort and with lots of family attractions, including the shingle (and, at low tide, sandy) beach. But beyond all this comes the still recognisably Georgian and Victorian Hastings, with marina and grand but faded architectural set pieces like Wellington and Warrior squares, interspersed with streets of terraced houses.

Here Hastings merges into St Leonards, the creation of a successful Georgian builder, James Burton, and his better-known architect son, Decimus. To promote their new watering place, they persuaded the young Princess Victoria and her mama to visit. St Leonards is a planned resort with style, with villas laid out round a landscaped quarry and its own centre, with a market and public buildings in classical stucco.

Rye

A walled town and port on the River Rother, Rye joined the Cinque Ports federation as an 'Antient Town', and it certainly deserves that title. Its twisting streets and lanes contain a wealth of old buildings – St Mary's Church, with golden 'quarter boys' who seldom fail to draw a crowd when they march out to strike the hour, the Mermaid Inn ('restored in 1420') in cobbled Mermaid Street, and the timber-framed houses of tranquil Church Square. The early 18th-century Lamb House in West Street was the home of author Henry James and a meeting place of the Edwardian literary establishment. Though much photographed and visited, Rye is still a busy working town, and also, once you get away from the honeypot tourist attractions, has many tranquil corners and hidden delights. Rye Heritage Centre is the ideal place to start.

Tenterden

Tenterden, one of a whole series of characteristic Wealden towns and villages in this part of Kent, is full of white weather boarding and warm, weathered brick and tile. It is dominated by St Mildred's Church, whose grey four-stage buttressed tower has been described as 'magnificent ... the finest of any parish church in Kent'. A hundred feet (30m) high, on a fine day it gives glimpses of the French coast. Station Road is where you will find the town museum and the Kent and East Sussex Railway (see page 105) offering steam-hauled rides through the Rother Valley. The town grew rich on iron-founding and wool, and was a 'limb' of the Cinque Ports, with quays at Smallhythe, 2 miles (3.2km) to the south, linking it to the sea. There the National Trust owns the 16th-century Smallhythe Place, once home of actress Ellen Terry and containing much theatrical memorabilia. The Chapel Down Winery's vineyard and herb garden are open to visitors.

Winchelsea

Like Rye, Winchelsea joined the Cinque Ports, but its character is very different from its bustling, prosperous neighbour. When 13th-century storms all but destroyed the original town, Edward I planned a new Winchelsea along the lines of the French *bastides*. But the sea receded, the harbour silted up, trade stagnated, buildings fell empty and the ambitious grid of streets was never completed. What remains, though, is a delightful and tranquil fragment.

A stained-glass window from the Mermaid Inn, Rye; notorious 18th-century smugglers, the Hawkhurst Gang, were regulars at the inn

 **See Walk D, page 131**
Battle – Britain's Most Famous Battlefield

Tourist Information

Battle: Battle Abbey, Gatehouse (tel: 01424 773721)
Hastings: Queens Square, Priory Meadow (tel: 0845 274 1001)
Rye: Heritage Centre, Strand Quay (tel: 01797 226696)

In the 16th century, steeply cobbled Mermaid Street was Rye's main thoroughfare; many of its buildings have survived to this day

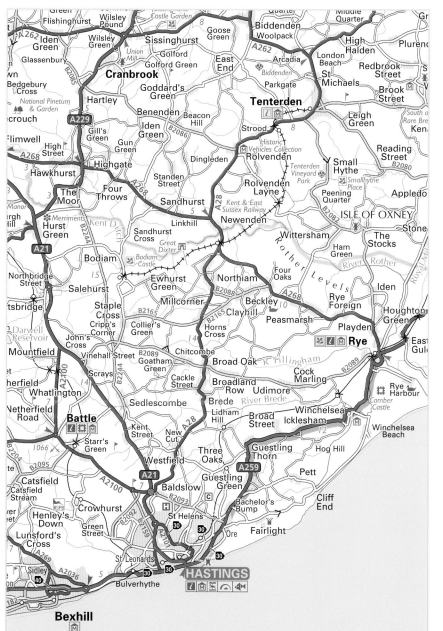

CASTLES AND MANSIONS IN PEACEFUL SECLUSION

Motorists on the M25, M20 and A21 may well pass by, completely unaware of the tranquil landscapes and delightful country towns hidden away beyond the slip roads. It is an area rich in historic houses, not, for the most part, the classical 18th-century stately home, but medieval manor houses and great mansions of an earlier era.

An annual jousting tournament, garden tours and a boating lake make Hever Castle a popular summer attraction

Chartwell

This was Sir Winston Churchill's home from 1922 to 1964. When he lost the 1945 election, Sir Winston considered selling Chartwell, but friends bought it and presented it to the National Trust, who allowed him to live there undisturbed for his lifetime. It is a Victorian house, remodelled in the 1920s, which is unremarkable, though superbly situated, and is full of reminders of the great statesman.

Edenbridge

Edenbridge is a sleepy little town tucked away in the Kentish Weald close to the Sussex border, away from main commuter routes. Its core lies around a narrow High Street with half-timbered houses and the Crown Inn, whose sign spectacularly bridges the street. Mill buildings on the little River Eden indicate the town's role as an agricultural centre.

Hever

A fortified manor house rather than a serious fortress, Hever Castle stands romantically in its moat with what looks like a medieval village alongside. Built in the 13th century, it was the childhood home of Henry VIII's second wife, Anne Boleyn. The interior seems never to have been very grand until a rich American, William Waldorf Astor, bought Hever in 1903 and spent much time and money restoring and transforming it with the finest Edwardian craftsmanship, and filling it with furniture, tapestries and works of art. He also transformed the grounds, which include an Italian garden with statuary, a maze, topiary, a lake and a walled rose garden.

Ide Hill and Toy's Hill

The wooded uplands of the Greensand Ridge, west of Sevenoaks and south of the M25, are marvellous walking country – thanks in no small measure to the National Trust's acquisition of 320 acres (130ha) at Toy's Hill and neighbouring Ide Hill, with its village green, pubs and hilltop church. From Ide Hill, visitors can look south over the Weald towards Bough Beech Resevoir with its fly-fishing and sailing facilities.

Leeds Castle

Leeds Castle, off the M20 just east of Maidstone, is a world and several centuries away from the roar of the motorway. Described by Lord Conway as 'the loveliest castle in the world', it stands on the site of the manor of the Saxon royal family. It, too, was a royal palace for three centuries, and it stands romantically silhouetted on two small islands in a lake, which is itself islanded in 500 acres (200ha) of tranquil gardens and landscaped parkland. It is Norman in origin and its oldest part is the Gloriette, on the smaller island, with rooms that include Henry VIII's fine banqueting hall. This is joined by a bridge to the main castle, battlemented Jacobean on Norman foundations. The grounds contain a vineyard, maze and grotto, as well as woodland and water gardens, where a variety of waterfowl, as well as peacocks, roam freely. The Culpeper Garden is full of herbs, roses and lupins, and you can visit the greenhouses. There is also a museum of medieval dog collars.

The colonnaded promenade of the Pantiles was the place to be seen in 18th-century Tunbridge Wells; today lined with pavement cafés and shops, it is still a pleasant place for a stroll

A decorative pale blue door of a whitewashed house in Westerham village

Ightham and Ightham Mote

Ightham is one of those Kentish villages which, despite its proximity to London, maintains a robustly independent existence. It is picturesque, with half-timbered houses and inns, and a 12th- to 15th-century church with notable monuments. About 3 miles (4.8km) to the south lies Ightham Mote, a magical manor house, islanded in a moat, with fortified gateway, gardens, lakes, fountains and dovecote. C. H. Robinson, an American, having first seen it as a young man on a cycling tour, returned a rich man, bought and rescued it, then bequeathed it to the National Trust, who have steadily carried out its restoration.

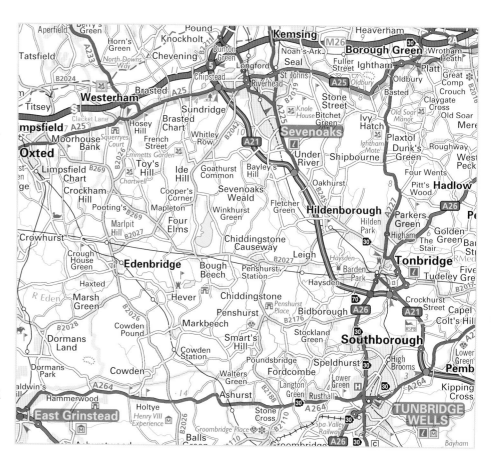

Sissinghurst Castle Gardens

Never a real castle, Sissinghurst was the mansion built by the son of a Tudor courtier. It had suffered several centuries of neglect when Vita Sackville-West and her husband Harold Nicolson bought it in 1930 and created, among the walls of ruined buildings, a unique and intimate series of gardens and landscapes – 'outdoor rooms', protected by the high brick walls, including the famous White Garden which has so influenced garden design. The surviving buildings which they made their home include the red-brick Tudor entrance range and four-storey Elizabethan Tower, with fine views and the book-lined study where Vita did her writing.

Penshurst

Sir John de Pulteney, a rich London merchant who was four times Lord Mayor, began Penshurst Place in 1340. Although extended in Tudor and Elizabethan times, it is among the finest and most complete of medieval manor houses. Featuring a lofty Baron's Hall, it gives a vivid impression of how the rich and powerful would have lived. Not least of its delights is the way courtyards, galleries, walled gardens and house interconnect. It stands in, but not aloof from, the charming village of Penshurst.

Sevenoaks and Knole

Though a commuter town, Sevenoaks has retained its character and identity and is well worth a leisurely browse. But its glory is Knole House, whose gates open out of the high street into its 1,000-acre (405ha) park. Traditionally said to have a courtyard for each month of the year, a staircase for each week and a room for each day, it is more a palace than a house. Begun in the mid-15th century by Thomas Bourchier, Archbishop of Canterbury, its scale was almost that of a little town, with brewhouse, bakehouse and other supporting facilities. Henry VIII confiscated and enlarged Knole, then in the 17th century it passed to the Sackville family, who gave it some of its finest interior features.

Tunbridge Wells

Royal Tunbridge Wells' beginnings as a spa date from 1606, when Lord North discovered a medicinal spring while trying to find his way along muddy Kentish roads. Royal patronage followed, and Beau Nash came in 1735 to preside over the social life of the town as master of ceremonies. The heart of the original town is The Pantiles, a tree-lined promenade, paved with these curved roofing tiles and with tall 17th- and 18th-century houses. Here an interpretive display, 'A Day at the Wells', tells the story of the spa's development. Its appeal today rests on a combination of attractive old buildings and streets and, starting right in the centre of the town, the rising parkland of Tunbridge Wells Common.

Westerham

Only half a mile (0.8km) from the M25, but not directly accessible from it, Westerham is another world – a prosperous country town astride the old main road, with the Greensand Hills rising to the south. It has picturesque buildings and a triangular green with a statue of James Wolfe, victor of Quebec, who was born here. His home is now a museum.

Winston Churchill gazes at the people of Westerham, near Chartwell, his former home. The wartime Prime Minister was a favourite subject of sculptor Oscar Nemon

See Walk H, page 135
Pooh's Ashdown Forest

Tourist Information
Sevenoaks: Buckhurst Lane (tel: 01732 450305)
Tonbridge: Tonbridge Castle, Castle Street (tel: 01732 770929)
Tunbridge Wells: Old Fish Market, The Pantiles (tel: 01892 515675)

HISTORIC PORTS OF THE GATEWAY TO ENGLAND

East Kent is England's front door to continental Europe and it was for thousands of years the obvious way in for invaders. It also witnessed the more peaceful passage of kings and queens, churchmen and ambassadors. The white cliffs of both Dover and Calais remind us that Britain and France were once joined – a link which the Channel Tunnel has now restored.

Dover Castle, one of the largest in Britain, was strategically located at the shortest crossing point to Europe. An underground hospital and the command centre for the Dunkirk evacuation are legacies from the Second World War

More than 130 ferries dock each day at Dover's cross-channel ferry terminal; Dover Castle can be seen nearby

Deal

Deal, a fishing port and seaside resort, is a delightful jumble of narrow lanes, which make dog-legs to divert the driving winds from the Channel. It is a 17th- to 19th-century townscape that, overall, amounts to more than the sum of its individual buildings. These include St Leonard's Church, which is part Norman, but with a cupola maintained by Trinity House as a landmark for shipping, the stately Royal Marine barracks towards Walmer, and three castles built by Henry VIII, namely Deal, Sandown and Walmer.

Dover

Modern Dover is a pleasant seaside town enlivened by the presence of Britain's busiest ferry port. Boat trips from De Bradelei Wharf explore the harbour, with views of visiting ships, the famous white cliffs and a townscape dominated by its great fortress. And you can board the beautifully restored *Sorceress*, a 120-year-old 'gentleman's yacht' with royal connections.

Described by a medieval historian as 'the key to the kingdom', Dover has borne the brunt of onslaught by invading forces for more than 2,000 years. The castle dates back to 1066, but most of what we see today is 12th century. When Napoleon threatened, an elaborate set of fortifications was added – a network of tunnels that stretches back from the cliff face, where an additional tier of well-protected guns were installed above the shore-level batteries.

The tunnels were not needed against Napoleon, but came into their own during the Second World War, when, under constant artillery bombardment, they became known as 'Hellfire Corner'. Here the evacuation of 330,000 troops from Dunkirk was organised, and a tunnel extensions housed a Combined Services Headquarters for the defence of southeast England.

The Dover Museum has fascinating exhibits, notably its award-winning Bronze Age Boat Gallery housing the remains of a vessel that is about 3,600 years old. Loan items from the British Museum, and a re-created dwelling give a broad picture of life in Bronze-Age Britain. The town also has the remarkably well-preserved Roman Painted House, a Transport Museum and the Women's Land Army Museum.

Folkestone

Eight miles (13km) southwest of Dover, beyond the great white cliffs and the downland behind them, lies this traditional seaside resort with a wide and sweeping promenade, turn-of-the-20th-century terraces and crescents, and superb sea views. A zigzag path leads down to the Lower Leas coastal park with wooded area, children's adventure playground and a 250-seat amphitheatre. A pededstrianised shopping area leads down to the harbour and Quarterhouse, an entertainment venue with bars and restaurants.

The Cinque Ports

The Cinque Ports (pronounced 'Sink') were the forerunners of the Royal Navy. The name 'Cinque' comes from the fact that there were originally five – Dover, Hastings, Hythe, New Romney and Sandwich – all prosperous Kent and Sussex ports that could provide the king with ships and men to defend the coast and fight sea battles. By 1278 they were supplying 57 ships, fully manned, for 15 days a year, in return for valuable privileges such as freedom from taxes and customs duties and the right to hold their own courts. The five were soon joined by two 'Antient Towns', Rye and Winchelsea, and by subsidiary ports known as 'limbs'. The Cinque Ports confederation still exists, but only as a focus for pageantry. Its ceremonial head is the Lord Warden, an office held by, among others, the Duke of Wellington, Sir Winston Churchill and Her Majesty, Queen Elizabeth the Queen Mother.

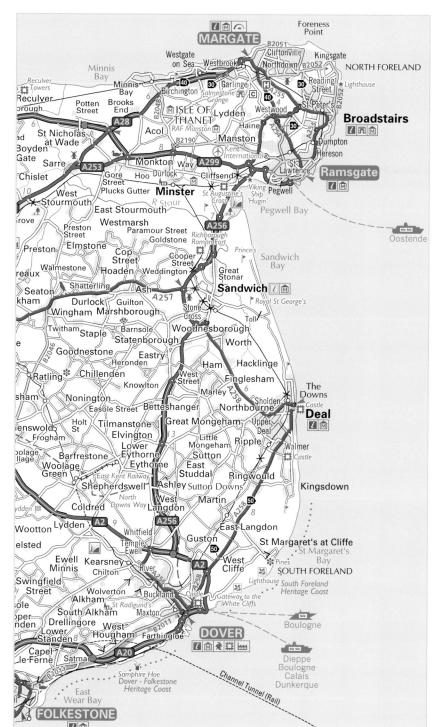

People buying ice cream from an ice-cream stall on the beach at Margate

The Thanet Resorts

The Isle of Thanet is no longer physically an island, and yet it retains a certain insular independence. Inland is a broad agricultural hinterland, while on its coastline is an almost unbroken string of seaside resorts. The biggest and brashest of these is Margate to the north, which has been not unfairly described as 'never smart but always jolly'.

Ramsgate, on Thanet's east coast, has more style, with its splendid Royal Harbour, Regency cliff-top terraces and bustling ferry port. The area is benefiting from a joint regeneration programme by the County Council, the District Council and the Civic Trust, who are conserving buildings and streetscapes and encouraging new initiatives, such as the development of sailing facilities along the coast.

Broadstairs, which adjoins Ramsgate, is the archetypal Victorian seaside resort, with aspirations to become a place of consequence and style which have never quite been achieved. But Broadstairs is likeable, with a High Street that charges downhill, then suddenly swerves left because of a cliff, below which lies the sheltered, popular beach of Viking Bay. Dickens was fond of Broadstairs, and in various houses in the town wrote all or part of *David Copperfield*, *Pickwick Papers* and *Nicholas Nickleby*.

Tourist Information
Broadstairs: Town Clerk's Office, Pierremont Hall (tel: 01843 868718)
Deal: High Street (tel: 01304 369576)
Dover: Townwall Street (tel: 01304 205108)
Folkestone: Harbour Street (tel: 01303 258594)
Margate: 22 High Street (tel: 0870 264 6111)
Ramsgate: 17 Albert Court, York Street (tel: 0870 264 6111)
Sandwich: The Guildhall, Cattle Market (seasonal) (tel: 01304 613565)

A small fishing port until it cottoned on to the Georgian craze for 'sea bathing', Margate is now the archetypal English beach resort

Sandwich

While old Deal is hidden among suburban sprawl, Sandwich has been preserved as a walled town in a largely green setting. This is a town perfect to walk in, whether on the ramparts or through the narrow twisting streets, with their overhanging timber-framed buildings. The Elizabethan Guildhall houses the town museum. In the 13th century, Sandwich was England's chief port for wool exports, but in the 15th century the river silted up and that trade moved to Deal, leaving Sandwich tranquil and unspoiled.

KENTISH TOWNS AND A GREAT CATHEDRAL

Many visitors race through this part of Kent, completely missing out on its treasures – historic Canterbury, with its great cathedral and atmospheric old streets, delightful small towns and villages; and a countryside that is amazingly tranquil and beautiful. Among the downland and woodland are lovely old farms, manor houses, churches and pubs.

The Tudor Christchurch Gate at Canterbury Cathedral displays the heraldic symbols of Henry VII, while the statue of Christ, centre, replaces one destroyed during the Puritan Revolution

Along the coast from Faversham, Rochester Castle is a 12th-century stronghold from which rebel noblemen launched attacks on London

Canterbury

The glory of Canterbury is its great cathedral, which, together with St Augustine's Abbey and St Martin's Church forms a World Heritage Site. Whether viewed from the London approach, where each first glimpse of its magnificent west front surprises anew, or from the high ground of the university campus to the north, this cradle of English Christianity gains from being surrounded still by a huddle of domestic-scale buildings and streets with few modern intrusions. The cathedral, founded in the eighth century but destroyed by fire, was rebuilt by Archbishop Lanfranc in the 1070s. In

1178 it was the scene of Thomas à Becket's murder and his canonisation swelled the flow of pilgrims.

Exploring the city, with its traffic-free High Street, walks on the medieval walls, and summer boat trips on the River Stour, is highly rewarding. The West Gate, one of the finest medieval fortified gatehouses in England, contains a small museum and offers panoramic views of the city from its battlements. Though the tower itself is only open on Saturdays, just below are the 11 acres (4.5ha) of the public Westgate Gardens, a popular spot for summer picnics and outdoor events.

The Museum of Canterbury reveals the city's 2,000-year history through interactive exhibits, while on the same site the Rupert Bear Museum has themed games and workshops for children. High-street stores and restaurants dominate the open-air and pedestrianised Whitefriars shopping centre.

Chilham

Set on the hillside above the Stour southwest of Canterbury, Chilham may be regarded as the perfect Kentish village, with its mellow brick and stone cottages and their luxuriant gardens, its church, rectory, pub and village square. As if all this were not perfection enough, through

The Pilgrims' Way

The Pilgrims' Way can be traced as a track running along the ridge of the North Downs in Surrey and Kent, and in popular imagination was the route by which pilgrims to the tomb of Thomas à Becket arrived on foot in Canterbury. In reality it is something of a misnomer. As a dry, high-level route across the chalk uplands, it dates from prehistoric times and, though some pilgrims from London or Winchester used it, most of them probably followed the Roman Watling Street. Today's walkers following the Countryside Commission's waymarked North Downs Way towards Canterbury may well derive added pleasure from seeing themselves as modern pilgrims, particularly if they call in at the Chaucer Centre and the Canterbury Tales visitor attraction on arrival in the city.

The Medway Towns

The best approach to Rochester is from the London direction by the A2 (the Roman Watling Street). On the approach to the bridge across the Medway, the four square stone keep of its Norman Castle looms ahead, guarding the river crossing, with the cathedral close behind. The Charles Dickens Centre celebrates the writer's many associations with the area, and two annual Dickens festivals are held here.

Chatham, further downriver, once had a major naval dockyard, partly redeveloped to provide offices and housing, but the most historic part, begun under Henry VIII, and nobly redeveloped in Georgian times, has been conserved as a fascinating living museum.

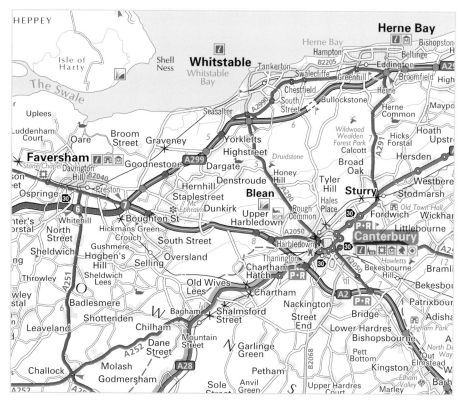

👣 **See Walk I, page 136**
Mr Darcy's Chilham

👣 **See Walk M, page 140**
A Dickens of a Walk at Rochester

Tourist Information

Canterbury: 12 Sun Street (tel: 01227 378100)
Faversham: 11 Preston Street (tel: 01795 534542)
Rochester: 95 High Street (tel: 01634 843666)
Whitstable: 57 Harbour Street (tel: 01227 378100)

a gateway on one side of the square is the unexpected bonus of Chilham Castle. The building is Jacobean, with battlements for show rather than defence, marking the status of its 17th-century owner, Master of the Rolls Sir Dudley Digges. Popularity has not spoiled Chilham, which seems to slow visitors down to its own tranquil pace.

Faversham

This market town has a port, a brewery and streets of quirky but comfortable old houses, and is well worth a visit. Faversham has no great architectural set piece, though it has nearly 500 listed buildings, including a Guildhall with Georgian upper storeys set on the open timber arches of the 16th-century original. A good starting point for any visit is the 15th-century Fleur de Lis Centre, which provides a lively outline of the town's history and attractions. At Iron Wharf sailing barges may still be seen, and the Chart Gunpowder Mills have been restored to show the early days of an explosives industry that periodically shattered the peace of the Swale marshes. At nearby Ospringe is the 16th-century Maison Dieu, founded in medieval times as a leper hospital.

Thomas Arden, sometime mayor of the town who lived at 80 Abbey Street, is the leading character in a 16th-century play, *Arden of Faversham*, which tells of his murder in 1551 by his wife and her lover.

Every autumn there is a colourful Hop Festival in the town centre. Faversham has, like other small towns, needed ingenuity to conserve its past while still providing for modern life.

Whitstable

A Victorian seaside resort was grafted on to the existing fishing village after the railway arrived in 1830, but Whitstable's chief fame comes from its oyster beds. Oysters, mussels and a variety of fresh sea fish, are available at several establishments in the town – including Wheelers Oyster Bar in the High Street and the Crab and Winkle on the harbour. This takes its name from the old railway line that linked the town with Canterbury, now the basis of a cycle route. The town and seafront feature historic alleyways, boutique-style shops and a pebble beach.

An oyster boat rests on Whitstable's pebble beach. The Whitstable Oyster Fishery Company was created by an act of Parliament in 1896, but its origins go back to 1574, when Elizabeth I signed a document to protect the local oyster beds from theft and accidental damage

THE NEW FOREST

The thatched hamlet of Swan Green

The name, it has been observed, is doubly misleading. The New Forest was 'new' only in 1097, when William the Conqueror declared it a royal hunting preserve, and 'forest' then meant not a large area of woodland, as we think of today, but an area of land reserved for hunting. Then, as now, trees occupied less space than the heathland and the often rather marshy fields, but today, though 130sq miles (336sq km) of New Forest are still 'preserved', it is for public enjoyment and for conservation as an ecological and landscape asset, rather than for a monarch's days out in the saddle.

The Living and Working Forest

Occupying a large part of southwest Hampshire, the New Forest is both a major tourist attraction and a conservation area. A wide-ranging and detailed New Forest Heritage Area Management Strategy seeks to reconcile these conflicting functions, together with a third element – commercial timber production. The New Forest became a National Park in 2005, after much consultation due to the number of land owners and other interested parties involved. It is England's eighth National Park, and the first to be created in over 50 years. The park area covers mostly southwest Hampshire, and a rich variety of ancient landscapes from pretty heathland and woodland to huge swathes of atmospheric coastal salt marsh and mudflats.

The Forest encompasses not just beautiful scenery, flora and fauna, but towns and villages, and people who make a living from the land. The Forest's 1,500 deer belong to the Crown and are managed by the Commission, but the 3,000 or so New Forest ponies belong to the Commoners – locals whose 11th-century predecessors secured grazing and other rights when the savage Forest Law deprived them of the right to hunt.

The 'capital' of the Forest is Lyndhurst, seat of the Commission's local administration, of the ancient but still important Court of Verderers, and the New Forest District Council. A town of a few thousand people, it is idyllically set with great forestry 'inclosures' to north and south, and open heathlands to east and west, its church spire a distinctive landmark. The New Forest

Highland Water runs through a dense thicket at Queen Bower, near Brockenhurst in the New Forest National Park

Museum and Visitor Centre adjoining the main car park at Lyndhurst provides both general tourist information and audiovisual and other displays on how the Forest came into existence, its way of life and its customs and traditions.

Forest Attractions

As well as the obvious attractions of the landscape and wildlife, the Forest has a number of places of interest to visit. The thrill of seeing native species in the wild is always an uncertainty, but visitors can be sure of seeing some of the animals at close hand at a number of attractions: New Forest

Owl, Otter and Wildlife Park, at Longdown, houses one of Britain's largest native wildlife collections, including otter observation pools, wild boar, a walk-through deer enclosure, all in a lovely woodland setting; there is a Deer Sanctuary at Bolderwood (west of Lyndhurst); while an owl, raptor and reptile centre near Ringwood, dedicated to putting birds back into the wild, has more than 100 spacious aviaries. The Longdown Activity Farm near Ashurst offers close encounters with farm animals and plenty of play areas.

The Forest's days as a Norman hunting preserve are recalled at the Rufus Stone,

Around 3,000 New Forest ponies roam freely in and around the forest, much as they have done for the past 1,000 years

from the past remains. South of the modern shopping centre, Above Bar is a surviving gateway of the medieval town, the fortified Bargate.

To right and left of Bargate run the impressive remains of the town walls with defensive towers, including the picturesquely named Catchcold Tower and Blue Anchor Postern. The Tudor House, a fine example of a rich merchant's town house of around 1500, is now a museum, its finest exhibit arguably its handsome banqueting hall. Other medieval and Tudor buildings now house museums, including the Museum of Archaeology in God's House Tower on the old Town Quay, and the Maritime Museum, housed in the early 15th-century Wool House.

More recent history is celebrated in the Hall of Aviation, which tells the story of aviation – particularly flying boats and seaplanes – in and around the Solent. The name 'Supermarine' attaches not only to the *Spitfire*, first built in Southampton, but also to the racing seaplanes that took part in the Schneider Trophy races here in 1929 and 1931. The modern helicopter was also created in Southampton, and several are on show.

Southampton is very green, with a series of six parks right in the heart of the city, while to the north the 368 acres (149ha) of Southampton Common drive a green wedge between the adjacent suburbs. The waterfront is also a pleasant public amenity, with Mayflower Park looking out over the Test Estuary between Town Quay and the Western Docks and the Ocean Village focusing on the 'festival market' concept, with shops, bars and restaurants.

commemorating the allegedly accidental shooting of the unpopular King William II (Rufus) while he was hunting.

A good way to appreciate the best of the woodland is on the magnificent Rhinefield and Bolderwood ornamental drives, and there are horse-drawn wagon rides as well as many waymarked woodland walks, all with skilfully sited car parks.

Of the Forest's half-dozen villages, Minstead is among the most visited, with its thatched cottages and largely 18th-century All Saints Church, notable for its three-decker pulpit, box pews and two galleries, one above the other. Furzey Gardens at Minstead consists of 8 acres (3ha) of flowering trees and shrubs. More famous are the Exbury Gardens, which are spectacularly colourful during the rhododendron season, and Spinners at Boldre, near Lymington, is another lovely garden to visit. Burley in the southeast of the Forest, set amidst bracing open heathland, is a good centre for walkers. Castle Hill, 1.25 miles (2km) north, is an Iron-Age camp and one of the best vantage points to view the Forest.

In the southeast of the Forest stands Beaulieu Abbey, founded by King John for the Cistercians, but home of the Montagu family since 1538. Its battlemented Palace House was once the abbey's gatehouse, though its present appearance owes much to an 1870s 'restoration'. Understanding of the medieval remains is greatly helped by an exhibition about monastic life. Alongside the

Abbey is the third Lord Montagu's pride and joy, his splendid National Motor Museum, with more than 250 exhibits, including a fascinating range of cars, commercial vehicles and motorcycles. Another popular attraction is 'Wheels', described as 'a futuristic ride on space-age pods through 100 years of motoring', as well as a monorail and veteran bus rides.

Buckler's Hard, 2.5 miles (4km) down the Beaulieu River, is a remnant of an early 18th-century plan to build Montagu Town, a port to rival Southampton. Two rows of attractive brick cottages were as far as the project got, but the little settlement was important for 80 years as a shipyard – Nelson's *Agamemnon* was built here, using 2,000 New Forest oaks. Buckler's Hard's Maritime Museum vividly evokes that era. On the next little river to the west stands Lymington, a lively yachting and ferry port and the New Forest's main market town. Its mellow streetscape and roofscape, mixed with masts and the steeple of St Michael's Church, are as lively as the Saturday high-street market.

A City on the Forest Fringe

A large, modern city, port, and regional shopping and commercial centre, Southampton nonetheless has a long history. There was a Roman town on the east bank of the Itchen at Bitterne, and on the west bank the Saxons had a town called Hamwic. Despite Second World War bombs and post-war development, a great deal

Fallow deer are one of the five species found in the New Forest. Although shy, there are plenty of them, so they can be spotted without too much difficulty

THE HEART OF HAMPSHIRE

Amidst glorious chalk downland, this area is far enough from London in one direction, and Southampton and Portsmouth in the other, to keep its independence and more sensible pace of life. It focuses chiefly on Winchester, the historic capital of Wessex; the famous trout waters of the Rivers Test and Itchen meander gently through the area.

King John's House in Romsey, where medieval graffiti and a floor made of sheep's bones await the visitor

Andover

As one of the towns which expanded to take 'overspill' from London in the 1960s, the comfortable market town of Andover grew from a population of 10,000 to around 40,000, somewhat obscuring the fact that it has a history going back to Saxon times. The High Street has attractive buildings, including the alluringly Grecian Town Hall of 1824. St Mary's Church, standing dramatically on a hill above the town, is one of Hampshire's best Victorian churches, the gift of a Winchester headmaster who retired to Andover, but died just before its completion in 1845. Andover's excellent Museum of the Iron Age has a good interpretive display on Danebury Hillfort.

Hillier Gardens and Arboretum

The Sir Harold Hillier Gardens and Arboretum, at Ampfield on the A31 between Winchester and Romsey, were begun by the famous nurseryman in 1953. Sir Harold gave the gardens in trust to Hampshire County Council in 1977. Now extending to 180 acres (73ha), they contain a unique collection of 42,000 plants and trees, including the British Isles' largest collection of hardy plants. Its sheer diversity ensures interest in all seasons – even winter has its subtle wonders, from fragrant witch hazels to beautiful bark. Guided tours are offered, and workshops take place regularly throughout the year.

Red-hot poker plant, Hillier Gardens

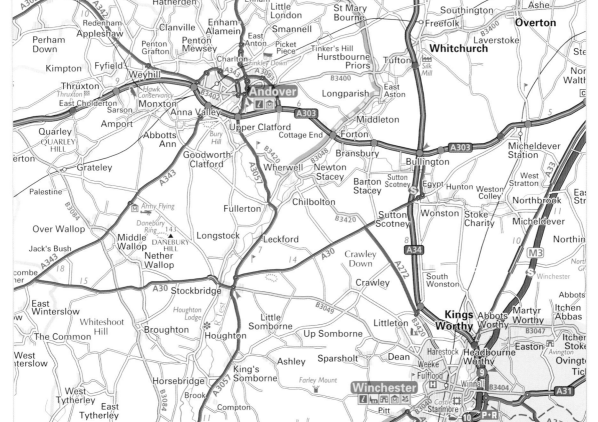

Romsey

Of all Hampshire's market towns, Romsey has one of the best townscapes. The town's chief glory is Romsey Abbey, which owes its survival to the 16th-century civic leaders. After the Dissolution, there was wholesale demolition of monastic buildings, but Romsey's representatives bought the abbey church and thus preserved it. Largely built in 1120–30 on the site of two earlier Saxon churches, it has, with its round Romanesque arches, an impressive simple grandeur. Of many old and beautiful houses in the town, the finest is King John's Hunting Lodge, a hall house of 1230. It is now a heritage centre, and provides town trails to guide your explorations. On the edge of the town, on the banks of the River Test, is Broadlands, an elegant Palladian mansion, once home to Lord Palmerston, but better known as the home of Lord Mountbatten until his untimely death. It is now occupied by his grandson, Lord Romsey, and is an interesting house to visit.

Danebury and the Wallops

Danebury Hillfort is an impressive, oval-shaped 13-acre (5ha) Iron-Age fortress with three lines of ditches and ramparts, increasing in strength and height towards the centre; the innermost is 16ft (4.9m) high and a prodigious 60ft (18.2m) broad. It existed from the sixth century BC until around 100BC, when even improved defences and an elaborately fortified eastern entrance did not prevent it from being overrun. Danebury Hill is southwest of Andover, near the picturesque village of Nether Wallop.

At Middle Wallop is the award-winning Museum of Army Flying, with its historic aircraft, including the largest collection of gliders in Europe.

Headbourne Worthy

St Swithun's Church here is a Saxon church with one treasure which is regarded as internationally important – a Saxon rood, or representation of Christ on the Cross, the Virgin and St John the Baptist. Religious fanatics damaged the figures, but it is still powerful. The church is delightfully situated, with a tributary of the River Itchen flowing round it.

Mottisfont

An Augustinian priory founded in 1201, Mottisfont Abbey was, at the Dissolution, handed to Lord Sandys, who turned it into a house. It was remodelled and extended in Georgian times; the living rooms are in the nave of what was the priory church. The overall picture is harmonious and tranquil; a little river runs through the garden with its trees and lawns, and the well or 'font' which gave it its name. Come in the early summer for the magnificent display provided here by the National Collection of old-fashioned roses. In the house, the Whistler Room (which has trompe l'oeil decorations by Whistler) and the Cellarium have been restored.

Winchester

Winchester is probably less appreciated as a historic town than, say, York or Canterbury. Yet it was capital of England under Saxon kings, joint capital for the Normans, with treasury and Domesday Book kept here. Its greatest glory is the cathedral, at 556ft (169.4m) the longest in Europe. It was begun by the Normans, but the magnificent nave is 13th to 14th century, in part the work of William de Wynford, master mason of Windsor Castle. Wynford was borrowed from the king by Winchester's most famous bishop, William of Wykeham, who founded Winchester College.

The cathedral does not provide many dramatic distant views. The drama is, on entering the Close through a narrow gate or lane, to find this immense building, set among green lawns with mature trees and a delicious mixture of domestic-scale architecture as its backdrop. This tranquil oasis connects with two other areas worth exploring: north is the High Street; south is a second walled precinct, that of Winchester College – one of England's oldest public schools. Some of its oldest parts are again by de Wynford, with additions and alterations from the 15th century right up to the 19th and 20th, yet somehow it forms a harmonious whole.

In the Broadway is a statue of King Alfred, whose burial place was discovered in 1999 at Hyde Abbey. From here to the fortified West Gate runs the High Street, largely pedestrianised and showing that the city is alive and well and adapting with the times. Thanks to narrowings and projecting buildings, the High Street does not reveal itself all at once and, though its overall flavour is Georgian, it has a pleasing variety of styles, not to mention an excellent variety of shops.

Other delights include waterside walks in the Abbey Grounds, the 18th-century City Mill, Henry III's splendid medieval Great Hall of the Castle, and, to the south, the 12th-century Hospital of St Cross and the still peaceful water meadows beyond.

See Walk F, page 133
Alfred's Ancient Capital

Tourist Information
Andover: 6 Church Close
(tel: 01264 324320)
Romsey: 13 Church Street
(tel: 01794 512987)
Winchester: Guildhall,
High Street
(tel: 01962 840500)

Winchester Cathedral is famous for its chantry chapels, where daily Masses were said for the bishops buried beneath them

ANCIENT AND MODERN IN NORTHEAST HAMPSHIRE

The broad, rolling expanses of the central Hampshire plain lie between the North Wessex Downs and those of east Hampshire. This is prosperous farming country, which is dotted with pretty villages and well-preserved market towns of a previous era. Amidst all this rural tranquillity, Basingstoke is a potent symbol of London's influence.

Above the waters of the River Arle, the Fulling Mill at Alresford has stood since the 13th century. 'Fulling' is the process of using water to cleanse and thicken cloth, usually wool

Alresford

This delightful place actually consists of Old Alresford and New Alresford, though 'Old' and 'New' are relative terms. New Alresford was 'new' in 1200, when Bishop de Lucy of Winchester laid it out as one of his planned new towns, alongside the existing village of Alresford to the north. He dammed the little River Arle, creating a 200-acre (81ha) reservoir with the aim of making the Itchen (which it joins downstream) navigable to Southampton. Old Alresford is tiny, with an 18th-century church and two substantial Georgian houses. The route from the north past watercress beds is a delight. Crossing de Lucy's dam, you come to New Alresford's Broad Street, a sumptuous Georgian townscape. A major attraction here is the restored steam railway known as the 'Watercress Line', from the days when this local harvest was its main cargo.

Alton

Traditionally a brewing centre, Alton dates back to Roman times, though the straight main thoroughfare is part of a much older route – a Bronze-Age track, later the Pilgrims' Way. The High Street is rich in

18th-century buildings. The oldest parts of the church of St Lawrence are Norman, with a second 15th-century nave and chancel alongside. The beautiful 17th-century pulpit was where Royalist colonel Richard Boles died, refusing to surrender though outnumbered and outgunned by the Parliamentarians. Its main doorway still has their musket balls embedded in it.

Basingstoke

As the 21st century got under way, the oft-maligned town of Basingstoke was getting a much-needed facelift. Prior to the mid-1960s, it was a pleasant, small market town, until the demands of London overspill development largely flattened the old town centre and ringed it with vast housing and industrial estates. In spite of this, the town prospered, and piecemeal improvements were made over the intervening decades, notably the provision of the superb Anvil concert hall, the refurbishment of the Haymarket Theatre and the building of a leisure park.

The excellent Milestones Museum provides the best reason yet for visiting the town, its labyrinth of street scenes depicting Hampshire's history using state-of-the-art technology. The town's original museum, the Willis in the old Town Hall, is also very interesting, and determined explorers can find some attractive parts of the old town, including the Holy Ghost Chapel ruins near the station, St Michael's Church and some attractive old almshouses at the 'top of town'. There is a pleasant footpath to Basing House along the course of the old Basingstoke Canal.

Northington Grange

William Wilkins, architect of the National Gallery, designed the Grange at Northington in 1809 for London banker Henry Drummond. Encasing an earlier house, he created a stunning Greek temple

Gilbert White and Selborne

The writings and reputation of Gilbert White have brought countless visitors to the little Hampshire village of Selborne for over two centuries. White was born there in 1720, went to Oxford and, after ordination, returned to serve as curate to neighbouring parishes. His passion for natural history led him to observe the area's flora and fauna in great detail, and in 1789 he published his *Natural History and Antiquities of Selborne*. White's house, The Wakes, is now a museum devoted to him; it also has displays on two members of the Oates family – Captain Lawrence Oates, the Antarctic explorer; and Frank Oates, a widely travelled naturalist. White's garden has been restored to its 18th-century form, and the church has a memorial window featuring many species of birds he observed.

Only the Great Barn still remains of the huge palace castle that was Basing House

The gardens that inspired the writings of 18th-century naturalist Gilbert White, at his home in Selborne

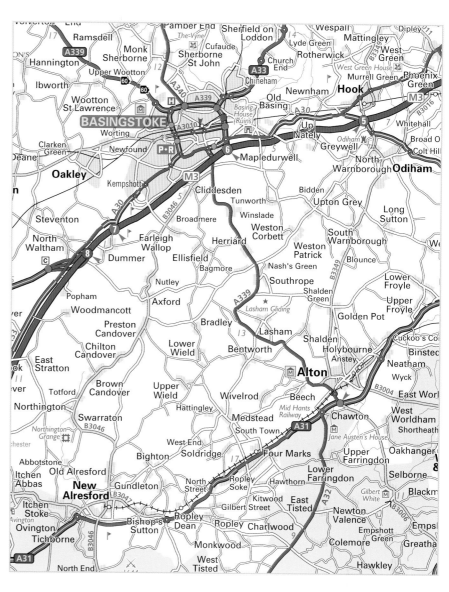

Jane Austen and Hampshire

Though readers of Jane Austen's *Persuasion* or *Northanger Abbey* may associate her with the fashionable world of Bath – and she did indeed live there for five years – she was born at Steventon in Hampshire. This village near Basingstoke is where she lived for her first 25 years and she died at Winchester, but in between she lived at two other Hampshire addresses – in Southampton and, more famously, at Chawton near Alton. She was at her most creative during the eight years (1809–17) she lived at Chawton, and her modest brick house is now a Jane Austen museum, providing many insights into her life and writings.

with a Parthenon-like portico supported by two rows of giant Doric columns. Its decay by the 1960s was such that its owner wished to demolish it. There was a national outcry and the Environment Secretary intervened. English Heritage rescued the mansion, stabilised the structure and carried out some restoration works.

Odiham

This is among the most attractive of Hampshire's small towns. Notable buildings include the church and The Priory, part Queen Anne, part Tudor; but the High Street, lined with mellow brick Georgian houses and older timber-framed buildings, deserves exploration. It used to groan under the weight of through-traffic, until it won its fight for a bypass. The Basingstoke Canal has been restored and boat trips are available in summer.

Old Basing

Here once stood Basing House, England's largest private home. It belonged to William Paulet, First Marquess of Winchester, and Lord Treasurer to three Tudor monarchs. In the Civil War, the house was defended by the Royalists but after a 2½-year siege fell to an assault led

by Cromwell. What we see today includes Norman earthworks, the remains of Tudor kitchens, cellars, towers and a tunnel 300ft (91.4m) long. The Civil War defences were designed by Inigo Jones, who was there during the siege, and there is a re-created 17th-century garden.

The Vyne

A fascinating and harmonious mixture of periods and styles, The Vyne includes the original Tudor House, built in the early 1500s by William Sandys, courtier to Henry VIII. The classical portico was added in the 1650s for Chaloner Chute, barrister and Speaker of the House of Commons, while the dramatic classical staircase was installed in the 1770s by his grandson, John. Outside are peaceful gardens, a lake and woodland walks.

The Jacobean garden at Basing House, painstakingly re-created to the original plan

Tourist Information
Petersfield: County Library, 27 The Square (tel: 01730 268829)

SURREY TOWNS AND MILITARY HERITAGE

The countryside here includes upland Surrey, with its prosperous market towns, a great sweep of chalk downland with a patchwork of woodland and villages beyond, and the open commons and heathlands around Hindhead. Historic Guildford is the main town, while to the northwest are the military towns of Aldershot and Farnborough.

Minutes from High Street stands the tower keep of Guildford Castle. A favourite residence of Henry III, the castle was later neglected, but the keep has benefited from 21st-century restoration work

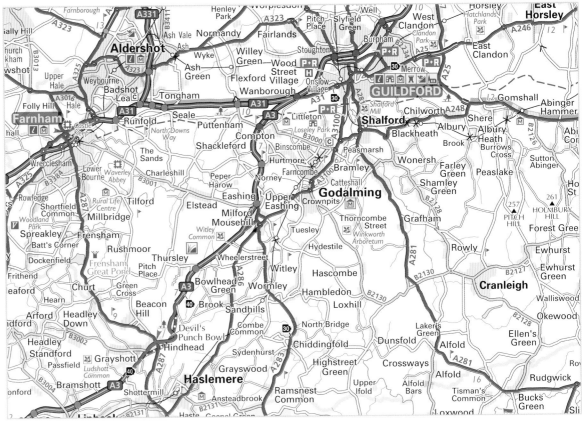

👣 **See Walk G, page 134**
A Pilgrimage to Waverley

Tourist Information
Aldershot: 2a High Street
(tel: 01252 320968)
Guildford: 14 Tunsgate
(tel: 01483 444333)
Haslemere: 78 High
Street (tel: 01428
645425)

Abinger Hammer

Few of those who pass Abinger Hammer's picturesque clockhouse, with its gilded weather vane and brightly painted figure of a sturdy blacksmith poised to strike the hour, realise that this pretty little village has an industrial past. Iron was worked here in Tudor times, and later the Tillingbourne was dammed to power mechanical hammers. The village still has its working smithy. At Abinger Common to the southwest is Goddards, a country house by Sir Edwin Lutyens with gardens by Gertrude Jekyll, which is open by appointment.

Aldershot

Until the Crimean War Aldershot was a small village, but from 1854 onwards the Army developed it with a dreary grid

of 'short-back-and-sides' architecture. Maturing trees and, landscaping have softened this image, and though the main attractions are not architectural, the town has won Britain in Bloom awards. Britain's military heritage is celebrated here – outstandingly in the Aldershot Military Museum, the Airborne Forces Museum and the Red Church. The nearby bronze equestrian statue of the Duke of Wellington originally stood atop Constitution Arch at London's Hyde Park Corner.

Farnham

Part of this attractive town was originally laid out in the 12th century by the Bishop of Winchester, and the castle was the

Though a thriving modern town, Farnham has preserved its narrow cobbled streets, mellow red-brick buildings and 12th-century church

with some interesting hillside buildings. There are some attractive walks along the River Wey.

Haslemere

This was little more than a village until the railway came in 1859, but the Victorian commuter cottages fit well into the delicious wooded, hilly landscape. In the centre are some older buildings, notably the Town Hall, rebuilt in 1814 but looking much older, and the Haslemere Educational Museum, which has some rare collections and a delightful garden. One big influence on the town was Arnold Dolmetsch, instrument maker and pioneer of early music, who made Haslemere his home. He set up workshops for making authentic instruments for the performance of early music, and established the annual music festival (July) which bears his name.

Hindhead

William Cobbett, reaching Hindhead in his Rural Rides, called it 'the most villainous spot that God ever made'. Today this certainly seems a severe judgement, but Cobbett's concern with agricultural potential – Hindhead is on heathland 850ft (259m) above sea level – and the fact that it was the haunt of highwaymen, were some justification. The later Victorians and Edwardians saw things differently – the air was pure, the landscape well-wooded and the views agreeable, and they built spacious brick and tile-hung houses among the pine trees. Notable residents included George Bernard Shaw, Sir Arthur Conan Doyle and Dr Marie Stopes, celebrated botanist and advocate of family planning.

Hindhead Commons, now owned by the National Trust, include the dramatic Devil's Punch Bowl, formed by springs cutting down and back from their sources, and Gibbet Hill, where three footpads were hanged after murdering a sailor.

bishop's palace. In the early 18th century the town prospered as a corn market and hop-growing centre, and this financed the fine Georgian buildings which give it its character, particularly in Castle Street and West Street. The early 19th-century Maltings were saved from demolition by a local trust and now form a lively arts and community centre.

Guildford

For centuries a prosperous market town, sited where the River Wey breaks through the North Downs, Guildford today is testimony to the compromises that often need to be made between conserving the past and ensuring continued prosperity. Bulky, unsympathetic 1960s and 1970s buildings and insensitive road building did violence to the townscape, and yet the town is very much alive, and there is much to see. Sightseeing 'musts' include the castle with 12th-century tower keep, and the Guildhall, with its superb 17th-century front, resembling the decorated poop of a sailing ship. When exploring the attractive High Street, don't miss The Angel, the last survivor of a whole string of coaching inns along here, and the delightful Quarry Street which runs off it below the castle. Pedestrianisation of many streets and lanes around High Street makes exploration on foot a more enjoyable experience. By the riverside is the 1960s Yvonne Arnaud Theatre, and on Stag Hill to the west stands the imposing brick-built cathedral, also completed in the 1960s; to its north on a sloping site lies the University of Surrey campus,

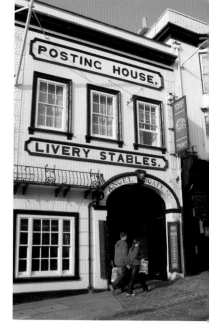

The old Posting House and Livery Stables in Guildford's High Street

Gibbet Hill, the second highest point in Surrey near the natural amphitheatre of Devil's Punch Bowl near Hindhead

PALACES AND GARDENS ON THE THAMES

The southwestern suburbs of London which border the Thames are among its environmentally most favoured, with several large green open spaces – the parks of Richmond, Bushey and Hampton Court and the Royal Botanical Gardens at Kew. A string of historic houses and palaces lines the Thames, while Richmond is one of London's liveliest town centres.

Ham House was constructed in 1610 for Sir Thomas Vavasour; the interior of the house was remodelled substantially during the 17th century

Claremont and Painshill

The A3 out of London is not the most beautiful of landscapes, but as it heads into Surrey it offers access to two outstanding 18th-century landscape gardens. Claremont is one of the earliest surviving examples of the English landscape art, and has been carefully restored by the National Trust. It dates from 1708, when architect Sir John Vanbrugh bought the site, which he thought 'romantick'. He later sold it to Thomas Pelham, Duke of Newcastle, who employed both Vanbrugh and William Kent. Kent provided a lake and grotto; Vanbrugh, a striking hilltop Belvedere.

Painshill Park, 3 miles (4.8km) further along the A3, was created between 1738 and 1773 by the Honourable Charles Hamilton, plantsman, painter and gifted designer, who transformed barren heathland into ornamental pleasure grounds of dramatic and often exotic beauty. Painshill is dominated by a meandering 14-acre (6ha) lake fed from the River Mole by a giant waterwheel. Other features include a grotto, Gothic-style temple, ruined abbey, Chinese bridge, castellated tower, Turkish tent and working vineyard. After 1948 the landscape sank

into dereliction, but, during the 1980s and 1990s the Painshill Park Trust peeled back the jungle to reveal and restore what Hamilton created.

Ham House, Marble Hill and Orleans House

Upstream from Richmond is a string of splendid 18th-century riverside buildings. First, on the north bank, is Marble Hill House, a magnificent Palladian villa built in the 1720s for Henrietta Howard, Countess of Suffolk, and set in 66 acres (27ha) of parkland. A few hundred yards upstream is Ham House, a large 17th-century house of exceptional interest, restored by the National Trust, together with its gardens. Finally, back across the river is the baroque Octagon Room of the Orleans House Gallery, built around 1720 by James Gibbs for William III's Secretary of State for Scotland; an adjoining wing is now an art gallery. A ferryman (seasonal) will row you swiftly and inexpensively from the Ham side to Marble Hill Park.

Among the many statues in the 60 acres (26ha) of formal gardens at Hampton Court, a recurring theme is the lion and the unicorn, supporters of the shield in the Royal Coat of Arms

Hampton Court

Hampton Court Palace was not originally a royal palace, but built by Cardinal Wolsey, Henry VIII's most powerful minister. Such a tangible display of power and wealth was not to the King's liking, and, though Wolsey decided to give the palace to his monarch, his doom was already sealed. The great Tudor brick gatehouse dominates the main approach to the palace, and beyond the huge Base Court lies the Clock Court with its 16th-century astronomical clock and Henry VIII's Great Hall. Wren extended and remodelled the palace for William and Mary, adding the great East Front and the arcaded Fountain Court. Particular attractions include the Tudor kitchens, Orangery, the Hampton Court vine and the maze.

Kew

Kew is synonymous with the Royal Botanic Gardens, 300 acres (121ha) of landscaped gardens devoted to the propagation, study and display of plant species. It all began with a small garden started in 1759 by Princess Augusta, widowed daughter-in-law of George II. Botanically, Kew is a world leader; architecturally it contains some spectacular buildings, including Decimus Burton's Palm House and Temperate House, the Pagoda by William Chambers and the elegant Princess of Wales Conservatory. But Kew is not just the gardens. Kew Palace, which is sometimes known as the Dutch House, is the modest house dating from 1631 where George III and his family lived for a time. Kew Village is centred on its green, and has a Georgian parish church, old houses and a riverside path.

Kingston upon Thames

Saxon kings were crowned here, and this is where the Normans built the first Thames bridge above London Bridge. Today, though there are attractive old streets, Kingston is primarily a busy shopping and commercial centre, where John Lewis and the Bentall shopping centre are most prominent.

Richmond

Richmond combines a wealth of historic buildings and splendid Thames views with a bustling commercial centre and lively arts and restaurant scene. Architectural gems include its two greens and the adjacent lanes. Richmond Hill has 18th-century houses, a fine view upriver, and a fine riverside group by Richmond Bridge. Most of it is not as old as it looks, a 1980s neoclassical stage-set by architect Quinlan Terry, with functional modern offices behind it. The design is immensely popular, providing a dramatic backdrop to the lively riverside area. The Richmond Theatre on The Green is the best-preserved London theatre. Richmond Park, at 2,469 acres (1,000ha), is the largest of London's Royal Parks.

When it was first built in 1762, many people thought the 10-storey pagoda at the Royal Botanical Gardens was an eyesore

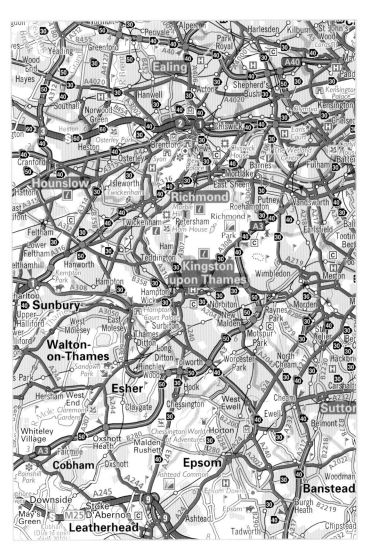

Tourist Information
Kingston upon Thames:
The Market House,
Market Place
(tel: 020 8547 5592)
Richmond upon Thames:
Old Town Hall, Whittaker Avenue
(tel: 020 8940 9125)
Twickenham: Civic Centre, 44 York Street
(tel: 020 8891 7272)

Richmond, with its mix of urban and bucolic riverside, is a great starting point for a boat trip on the Thames

STEAM RAILWAYS

In the 1940s and 1950s, southern England was still criss-crossed by dozens of branch railway lines, mostly operated with steam-hauled trains. Typically built at the height of railway optimism in the late 19th century, they had for several decades been starved of money for either maintenance or modernisation, and were increasingly suffering from road transport competition.

Even before Dr Richard (later Lord) Beeching began wielding his notorious axe in 1963, many lines were struggling. But in those rationalising days there grew up a body of men and women who were unwilling to let these well-loved railways die. And, paradoxically, the fact that there had been no money available to modernise them added to their attraction.

Enthusiasts have restored this signal box to its former gleaming glory at the Bluebell Railway, Sheffield Park, in East Sussex. Visitors to the Kent and Sussex line can learn the ropes of being a signalman

The Fight for Survival

The fight to save the branch lines was tough. From the nationalised railway's point of view, the sensible course was to take up track, which might be reused or sold as scrap, and then to sell the land section by section for the best price obtainable. Buyers were there – property developers in towns and around stations; farmers in the open countryside, though the prices they were prepared to pay for overgrown cuttings and embankments were limited.

From the rail preservationists' point of view, piecemeal sales posed a dire threat. Even the smallest bite out of a proposed route prevented through running, and some ambitious plans had to be restricted to short stretches of line or sidings. Fortunately, this was not always the case. With surprisingly enthusiastic public backing and some support from the local authorities, a number of preservation societies succeeded in securing viable routes, acquiring and restoring track, locomotives, rolling stock and buildings, and running respectable services.

Then a strange thing happened. As the realities of grimy, gritty, smoke-invaded commuting receded, so the steam railway as a tourist attraction gained romantic appeal.

And it has a powerful appeal, not just to the retired railwaymen and the amateur (but knowledgeable) volunteer, but also to visitors who would not know a gland from a piston rod.

Kent Railways

In southeast England, the preserved lines cluster most closely in the south coast counties of Kent and Sussex. On the border between the two is the Spa Valley Railway.

The line runs through the bucolic Kentish Weald, between the town of Royal Tunbridge Wells and the village of Groombridge. The original line dates back to the railway races of the Victorian era, when companies competed to build more direct and quicker routes. Tunbridge Wells West opened in 1866 and became the starting point for faster journeys to Brighton and London Victoria. Its death knell was sounded in 1985, but campaigners fought back. A new station house was built, and half a mile (0.8km) of track opened in 1996. Within two years, they had reached Groombridge, 3.5 miles (5.6km) away, and built at new station along the route at High Rocks. Today, the railway's revitalised locomotive stock consists of 12 steam engines and 10 diesels, with on-board dining options including the 'Fish and Chip Special' and 'Wine-and-Dine' curry evenings. The popular 'Real Ale Special' features guest ales from local breweries.

On Kent's east coast is one of the best known of all steam railways, the 15-inch gauge 13.5 mile (22km) Romney, Hythe and Dymchurch. Financed by railway enthusiast Captain J. E. P. Howey in the late 1920s and built by Henry Greenly, it was threatened with closure after Howey's death, but saved by a consortium in 1972. It runs from Hythe, near Folkestone, along the coast to Dymchurch, St Mary's Bay, New Romney and Dungeness, and operates an intensive

Preserving the railways is not just about trains – stations are cared for, too

daily service between Easter and the end of September, plus weekends in March and October.

The Kent and East Sussex Railway is, by contrast, full size and standard gauge. The first line to be built under the 1896 Light Railways Act, it opened in 1900, closed in 1961 and – as a result of the 'sheer dogged persistence and enthusiasm' of the preservationists – reopened in 1974, 20 years after British Rail ran its last passenger train. One of England's classic rural railways, with sharp curves, steep gradients and short trains calling at tiny country stations, it originally ran around 21 miles (33.8km) from Robertsbridge to Headcorn.

From just under 2 miles (3km) initially reopened, the line was extended to about 10.5 miles (17km), with trains running from Tenterden in Kent via Rolvenden and Wittersham Road through Northiam in East Sussex, and finally to Bodiam, depositing passengers just a short distance from the famous castle.

The popular Kent and East Sussex line also entices travellers with various specials – journeys which include a six-course meal, served in traditional style aboard the Wealden Pullman, the luxurious 1926 Pullman Bar Car 'Barbara' among them, and there are also pre-Christmas Santa Specials and 'railway experiences' where visitors can try their hand at driving a steam locomotive and operating a signal box.

Steaming Through Sussex

The Bluebell Railway and the Lavender Line are two preserved steam railways in Sussex. The Bluebell, saved for posterity in 1960, runs for around 9 miles (14km) from

Sheffield Park Station, just off the A275 East Grinstead–Lewes road, via Horsted Keynes and West Hoathly Tunnel to Kingscote. Its name comes from the beautiful woodland en route that is a mass of bluebells in the spring. Not only does the Bluebell Line run a Pullman for Saturday dinner and Sunday lunch, but there is also a restaurant at Sheffield Park and a real-ale bar, the Bessemer Arms, named after the local resident who initially saved the line from closure.

The Lavender Line has nothing to do with flowers, but is named after the coal merchants A. E. Lavender & Sons, who operated out of the station yard. The railway began life in 1858 as part of the former Lewes–Uckfield Railway, but closed in 1969. It operates from the carefully restored station at Isfield, south of Uckfield.

Hampshire and Isle of Wight Tracks

The Mid Hants Railway runs for 10.5 miles (16.9km) from the main line station at Alton through beautiful Hampshire countryside to Alresford, with intermediate stops at Medstead & Four Marks and Ropley. It is still known as the 'Watercress Line', from the days when Hampshire watercress growers would transport their harvest to London markets by rail. The line ceased operation in 1973, 108 years after it opened. It was saved by dedicated enthusiasts, and now runs at weekends

between October and March, then most days between April and September, with an hourly frequency of trains.

On the Isle of Wight main-line services have shrunk from half a dozen lines, covering virtually every corner of the island in the late 1940s, to just one electrified line from Ryde to Sandown and Shanklin. But the days of steam are kept alive by the Isle of Wight Steam Railway running for 5 miles (8km) from Havenstreet and linking with the main line at Smallbrook Junction.

Other steam railways in the southeast include the Colne Valley Railway (a restored stretch of Edwardian branch line at Castle Hedingham, Essex) and the Great Cockcrow miniature steam railway at Lyne near Chertsey, Surrey. Steam enthusiasts also head for the Great Western Society's Didcot Railway Centre in Oxfordshire. The Harpenden Railway Museum in Hertfordshire is a collection of railwayana assembled in their own garden by Geoff and Sue Woodward – it is open to the public on selected days.

Most of the railways featured here operate special themed attractions, including Santa Specials, Thomas the Tank Engine Weekends, Wartime Weekends and Vintage and Classic Vehicle and Bus events, with participants in full period costume.

A magnificent steam engine, saved from the scrapyard for the 'Watercress Line' in Hampshire

VALLEYS OF THE THAMES AND KENNET

Two features dominate this countryside – the Thames, meandering northwest to southeast towards Reading, and a belt of uplands crossing it diagonally: Chilterns to the northeast; Berkshire Down to the south-west. All converge at Goring Gap. Below the Downs, the Kennet and Avon Canal drops gently down from Newbury to join the Thames at Reading.

A Dutch barge on the Kennet and Avon Canal; many such barges are old working boats converted to leisure use

Highclere Castle, stately home of the Earls of Carnarvon

The Kennet and Avon Canal

The Kennet and Avon Canal, built by the great engineer John Rennie, opened in 1810, linking the Thames to the Bristol Channel. It went the way of all canals, its prosperity killed off by the coming of the railway, and by the 1950s it was sliding into dereliction. Canal enthusiasts successfully fought against the plans too close it, and mobilised a voluntary effort to help restore it. Parts of the canal had been in use for leisure purposes for some time, but in 1990, with the whole 57 miles (92km) again navigable, Her Majesty the Queen formally reopened the canal at Devizes (see page 48). A Heritage Lottery Fund grant was secured to carry out a complete restoration, successfully accomplished in 2003. As well as boating, and walking and cycling along its towpaths, the wildlife and industrial interest is immense. At Crofton the oldest working beam engine in the world is still doing its original job.

Basildon Park

Basildon Park is the most splendid Georgian mansion in Berkshire. In golden Bath stone, it is on a grand scale – the central building, with double-storey portico, Ionic columns and pediment, is flanked by twin two-storey pavilions. Inside, the focal point is the unusual Octagon Room, but all around is fine plasterwork, paintings and furniture. The garden and woodland walks are also delightful.

Goring and Streatley

Goring and Streatley face each other across the Thames, one in Oxfordshire, the other in Berkshire, linked by a bridge with lock and weirs. This is also a key link in the 85-mile (137km) Ridgeway path from Avebury to Ivinghoe Beacon in Buckinghamshire. There is splendid walking in both directions and Goring is particularly attractive, with a 12th-century church, a 17th-century vicarage and 18th-century almshouses.

Highclere Castle

Highclere Castle is actually a magnificent early Victorian mansion, designed by Sir Charles Barry (architect of the Houses of Parliament). It is a great square building, with towers and pinnacles, and the façades have a lovely golden glow. This is the home of the Earls of Carnarvon. The Fifth Earl was famous as one of the discoverers of the tomb of Tutankhamen and the castle contains many of his Egyptian relics. There is also a horseracing exhibition, and the castle hosts special events, including concerts, craft fairs and country shows.

Mapledurham

This small village, on the Oxfordshire side of the Thames beyond Reading's western sprawl, has traditionally been dominated by its manor house. Built in 1585 by Sir Richard Blount, Mapledurham House is one of England's largest Elizabethan houses. With its patterned brickwork, battlemented parapets and tall chimneys, it stands in riverside grounds – evoking literary connections with *The Wind in the Willows* and *The Forsyte Saga*. A working 15th-century watermill here still produces flour.

Newbury

Newbury's controversial bypass has eased the appalling traffic congestion that once blighted the town, and its main shopping street, where signs of its long history peep out above the modern shopfronts, is now partially pedestrianised. The Kennet and Avon Canal cuts through the town, providing pleasant towpath walks and narrowboat trips. The town's prosperity was originally founded on the cloth trade, which peaked in the 18th century, when both the turnpike road and the canal reached the town. Later, the railway detoured north, hitting the town's prosperity, but probably saving some attractive areas that may not have survived a 19th-century boom. These include the delightfully crooked 17th-century weavers' cottages and the 1626 Cloth Hall, which now houses the West Berkshire Museum.

Ruined Donnington Castle, on the edge of town, has twin-towered gatehouse and earth ramparts, which featured prominently during the Civil War.

Reading

From the M4 or the railway, Reading appears to be a thoroughly modern town, prospering on computers, insurance and similar new industries. The town centre has been revitalised with one of Britain's finest shopping centres – the Oracle – which incorporates an attractive riverside area. But the town has a long history, with a 12th-century Cluniac abbey and a borough charter of 1542, but you have to search for visible signs of it. The lively Museum of Reading in the Town Hall is a good place to start. Reading University has a fascinating Museum of English Rural Life.

Silchester

The best-preserved Roman walls in Britain, almost 1.5 miles (2.4km) round, defended the regional capital of *Calleva Atrebatum*, which was laid out by Hadrian. Settlement on the site goes back even further – a smaller pre-Roman ring of defences lies under the remains of the third-century Roman town. Also within the site is an impressive and restored Roman amphitheatre. The site is notable for being one of the few Roman towns that was abandoned, although noone really knows why.

At the Mapledurham Estate, a historic watermill is still producing high-quality stone-ground flour

Tourist Information
Newbury: The Granary, Wharf Street (tel: 01635 30267)

Stratfield Saye

Stratfield Saye was the gift of a grateful nation to Arthur Wellesley, first Duke of Wellington, victor of Waterloo and later Prime Minister. He chose it for its rich farmlands rather than for the house, which he later extended and remodelled, and its contents provide the main interest. They tell of the life and times of the great Duke and include his maps, weapons and personal effects. Wellington Country Park, 3 miles (4.8km) east, includes a National Dairy Museum tracing dairy farming's development from the time of Waterloo to the present day.

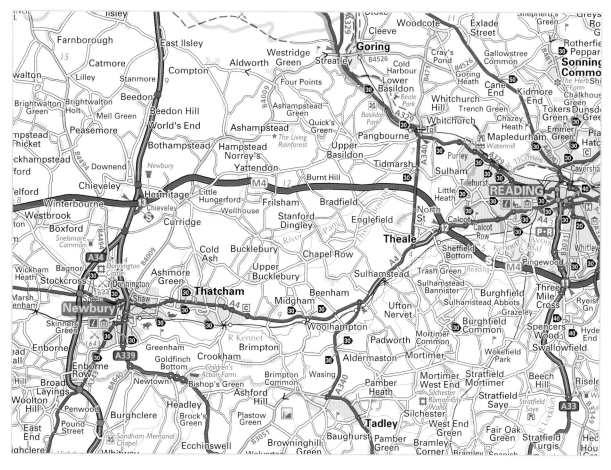

THE ROYAL COUNTY

The 'Royal' County of Berkshire has numerous connections with the crown – Windsor, royal residence from the 12th century right to the present day, the annual Royal Ascot race meeting and Henley Royal Regatta. At Runnymede in adjoining Surrey, the Magna Carta is traditionally held to have laid the foundation of English civil liberties; on Eton's playing fields, Waterloo is (more questionably) said to have been won.

St Mary's Church, Henley, watches over single scullers training on the Thames

Ascot

Everyone has heard of Royal Ascot, but few realise it was Queen Anne who built the first racecourse there in 1711. It was revived by the Duke of Cumberland, who established a stud in nearby Windsor Great Park. Traditionally the sovereign opens Royal Ascot each June, driving round the course in an open carriage.

Cookham and Cliveden

Cookham is famous as the birthplace of artist Stanley Spencer, whose religious paintings include *Christ Preaching at Cookham Regatta*. A former Methodist chapel now houses the Stanley Spencer Gallery. The riverside, delicate cast-iron bridge, green and old houses all add to the charm of the village. Across the river is Cliveden, the great mansion designed by Sir Charles Barry in 1849 and made famous in the 1930s by Nancy, Lady Astor and her influential 'Cliveden Set'. Now owned by the National Trust, the house is let as a luxury hotel, but three rooms and the riverside grounds are open to visitors.

Eton

The little town of Eton, hemmed in tightly between the Thames and the riverside meadows, represents a small point of repose between the two great monuments of Windsor Castle and Eton College. Across Telford's fine Windsor Bridge (thankfully traffic-free) you enter a High Street full of pleasingly idiosyncratic buildings, with a wealth of Georgian façades and 19th-century shopfronts, many with old timber-framed structures behind them.

Eton College, founded in 1440 by Henry VI, starts at the north end. It was originally a religious community with a school for poor boys, but present-day pupils are not noticeably impoverished and have included 20 British prime ministers and countless other public figures. Notable buildings include the chapel, with its fan-vaulted roof and fine east window, and Lupton's Range with its twin-towered gatehouse leading to Cloister Court.

Henley-on-Thames

Henley is boating. It has two regattas, Henley Royal and the less well-known Town Regatta, and the River and Rowing Museum in Mill Meadows. The best approach is across the bridge from Berkshire, where two 18th-century inns, the Angel and the Red Lion, frame the tower of St Mary's Church. Around the marketplace and Hart Street there are some pleasant streets to explore.

As a functioning school, all visits to Eton College are guided

Burnham Beeches

In 1880 the City of London Corporation bought nearly 200 acres (80ha) of ancient commons and woodland in Buckinghamshire, between Burnham and Beaconsfield, including extensive beech woods with 300-year-old trees. The Corporation still maintains them as a public open space.

Boats for rent await custom below the iron bridge at Cookham

The Thames Path

At Goring Gap two of the Countryside Commission's 'national trails' (long-distance footpaths) cross: the 85-mile (136km) ancient track of the Ridgeway (see page 48), and the Thames Path. Starting at the river's source near Cirencester, it runs for 213 miles (340km) all the way to the Thames Barrier on the tideway below Greenwich. Much of the route is through a lush countryside of woods and waterside meadows, but it also passes many historic places – including Oxford, Windsor, Hampton Court, Westminster and the Tower of London. For centuries, travelling on the Thames was much easier than any overland route, and the river was the great royal thoroughfare and strategic highway of southeast England.

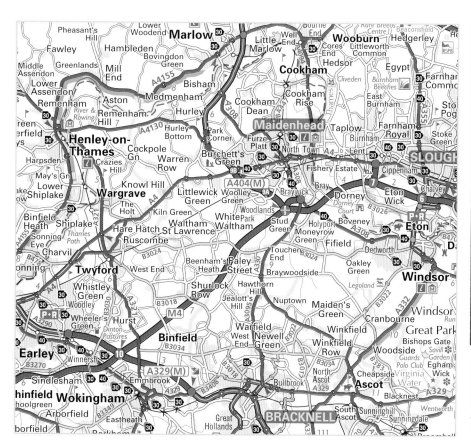

When plague engulfed London, it was to Windsor Castle that Elizabeth I fled, a safe distance upstream on the Thames

Windsor

Windsor Castle is England's largest, with 13 acres (5ha) inside its curtain wall, and it stands on a cliff above the Thames, dominating both river and town centre. William the Conqueror built the first castle here, but the earliest stone buildings we see today date from the 1160s. Not only a fortress, the castle has also been a royal residence for 900 years. The massive round keep is the heart of its defences, but transition from fortress to royal palace was celebrated in the late 18th and early 19th century by additions and remodelling in a romantic Gothick style by James Wyatt and his nephew Jeffry Wyattville. After a disastrous fire that gutted many of the state apartments in 1992, architects were commissioned to design interiors in a style akin to theirs. Architecturally, the castle's prime glory must be the 15th- to 16th- century St George's Chapel, with its tall, slender columns and marvellous vaulted ceiling, an outstanding example of Perpendicular church architecture.

To the south and east of the castle lies the Home Park, in which stands the recently restored 17th-century Frogmore House, the least known of the royal residences, now furnished with contents reflecting the taste of former royal residents, including Queen Victoria's mother. South of the town is the immense, 4,800-acre (1944ha) Windsor Great Park, with the vista of its Long Walk stretching towards Virginia Water. It incorporates houses, woodlands, monuments, lakes and its own estate village. The Savill Garden and Valley Gardens are well worth a visit.

The town is utterly dominated by the castle, and this lends a particular atmosphere to the little streets that radiate out from its huge stone walls. There are many interesting old buildings, particularly in the cobbled streets of Guildhall Island – look for the curious Market Cross House, which slants precariously next door to the more upright Guildhall. The Town and Crown Exhibition charts Windsor's history. Apart from its history, Windsor is a very stylish town, with excellent restaurants and shopping, notably in the Windsor Royal Station development, a pleasant concourse beneath the original Victorian arches and glass roof. The River Thames is another attraction, and boat trips run from the Promenade.

Old Windsor, beyond the Home Park, has a 13th-century flint church with shingled spire and agreeable riverside setting. To the southeast lie the historic Runnymede meadows where King John sealed Magna Carta in 1215.

Tourist Information

Henley-on-Thames:
Town Hall, Market Place
(tel: 01491 578034)
Windsor: Old Booking Hall, Thames Street
(tel: 01753 743900)

THAMES-SIDE TOWNS AND A GREAT SEAT OF LEARNING

Oxford, on the Thames (here called the Isis) and the River Cherwell, is a unique architectural treasure-house which can be no more than sampled in a brief visit. To its north lies Blenheim, a palace outshining any royal residence of its day, but built not for a king but for a victorious general. Around them, you will find pleasant countryside and delightful towns and villages.

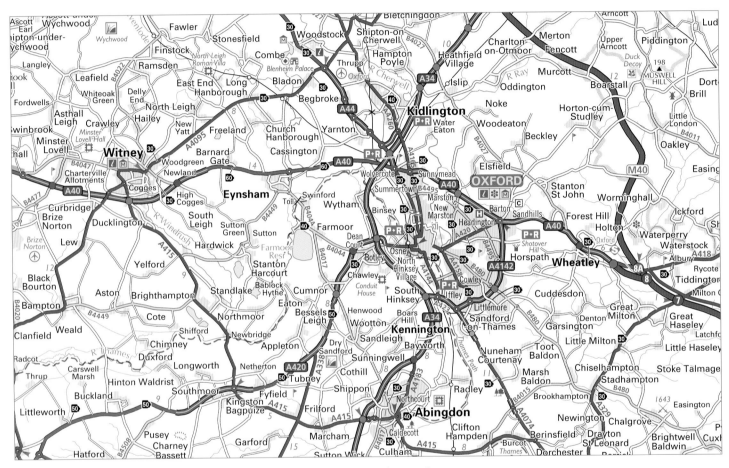

Queen Anne's gift of 1705, to fund the construction of Blenheim Palace, would be worth over £3 million today

Abingdon

The abbey of Abingdon has all but disappeared, its impressive 15th-century Gateway and Long Gallery being the chief reminders of the religious house, founded in AD675, in whose shadow the town began. It was once the county town of Berkshire, but it lost that distinction to Reading, and then boundary changes placed it in Oxfordshire. Its heart is the beautifully repaved marketplace, with its many splendid buildings; the most outstanding is the 17th-century County Hall. East St Helen's Street leads to St Helen's Church, with its splendid 13th-century steeple. Near the Thames bridge, Abingdon's Old Gaol of 1811 has been skilfully converted into an arts and sports centre, and there are lovely riverside walks.

Rousham House

Rousham stands as a monument to the great 18th-century architect and garden designer, William Kent, who remodelled the house and, more importantly, the gardens for General James Dormer. The garden, in hanging woods above the Cherwell, is one of the earliest and least altered 'Picturesque' landscapes, with cascades, temples, ponds and statues, artfully contrived vistas and visual surprises.

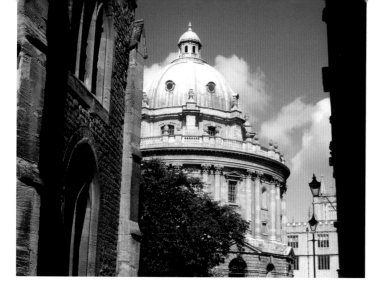

The Sheldonian Theatre, Oxford, with its 19th-century rooftop lantern was Christopher Wren's first work when it was built in the 1660s

👣 **See Walk J, page 137**
Abingdon's Architecture

👣 **See Walk K, page 138**
Turville on TV

Tourist Information
Abingdon: Abbey Close
(tel: 01235 522711)
Faringdon: 5 Market
Place (tel: 01367
242191)
Oxford: 15–16 Broad
Street (tel: 01865
252200)
Wantage: Vale and
Downland Centre,
19 Church Street
(tel: 01235 760176)
Woodstock: Oxfordshire
Museum, Part Street
(tel: 01993 813276)

Blenheim and Woodstock

As a token of the nation's gratitude for his victory over the French at Blenheim in 1704, Queen Anne presented John Churchill, 1st Duke of Marlborough, with the wherewithall to build Blenheim Palace, Britain's most magnificent stately home and a World Heritage Site. This vast baroque edifice, with its fantastic skyline, was the work of Sir John Vanbrugh, at that time better known as a dramatist than an architect, and it is indeed a dramatic tour de force. Blenheim's 2,000-acre (810ha) park was landscaped by 'Capability' Brown; it can be reached on foot from the little town of Woodstock, in itself charming. Note especially the market place with the Star and the Bear hotels, and 16th- and 17th-century houses in Park Street.

Minster Lovell

A romantic ruin by the peaceful River Windrush, Minster Lovell Hall was built in the 15th century by the 7th Lord Lovell and its handsome remains are now cared for by English Heritage. Note the medieval dovecote with nesting boxes.

Oxford

Oxford presents many different faces to the world, some of them delicious and memorable – distant views of its 'dreaming spires', close-ups of numerous college quadrangles, halls and chapels, looking down from Folly Bridge on punts full of lively undergraduates. Oxford is, of course, dominated by its university, though the town was large and prosperous in Saxon times, long before licensed teachers had begun to gather in halls and colleges. Having grown up thus, Oxford University remains a federation of self-governing colleges. There are university buildings, some of them historic and superb, such as the 16th-century Bodleian Library, the adjoining medieval Divinity School, and

Wren's Sheldonian Theatre. But if a visitor in the High asks, 'Where's the university?', the answer must be, 'All around you.' There are about 40 colleges, some very ancient, others surprisingly modern.

Among the most spectacular colleges is Christ Church, with its huge Tom Quad and Tom Tower by Wren housing its massive bell, Great Tom; its chapel also serves as Oxford's cathedral. Riverside Magdalen (pronounced 'maudlin') also has a great bell tower, a sequence of quadrangles and a walled deer park. Merton is the oldest in foundation and perhaps the most medieval in atmosphere. Outstanding among the dozen or so 20th-century foundations is St Catherine's, which was designed by the great Danish architect Arne Jacobsen and recently extended.

You can visit some of the colleges at certain times, and Oxford has many excellent museums and galleries, including the Ashmolean Museum, which is the oldest museum in Britain, and the Museum of Oxford. Situated in the historic Town Hall building, it tells the story of the city's past with artefacts, film and audio guides. Fresh-air attractions include the country's oldest botanic garden and the excellent walking tours led by the city's official guides.

Stanton St John

This attractive village lies a couple of miles from Oxford's northeast boundary, close to the edge of the remarkable Otmoor. This is a low-lying saucer-shaped basin, crossed by a Roman road, and is divided up by drainage dykes which inspired the chessboard landscape featured in Lewis Carroll's *Through the Looking Glass*. It was threatened by the M40 extension, but powerful protests got it diverted to loop round to the east. In the Church of St John the Baptist, the 13th-century chancel demands a long appreciative look.

Waterperry

Waterperry is known for its Horticultural Centre, comprising a college and 83 acres (34ha) of gardens and nurseries, most open to the public, beside the River Thame. Waterperry House is classical 18th and 19th century with a 17th-century wing. St Mary's Church is small and charming, with Saxon and Norman parts remaining.

An aerial view of the most artistic of the British white horses

The Vale of The White Horse

The Vale of the White Horse runs eastwards from near Swindon to follow the little River Ock down to meet the Thames at Abingdon. It is bounded on the north by the Berkshire Downs on which, cut in the chalk at Uffington, is the white horse which gives it its name. It was once thought that the horse was carved in AD871 to celebrate King Alfred's victory over the Danes, but it is now considered to be at least 2,000 years old. On the hilltop above the horse is Uffington Castle, an Iron-Age fort covering 8 acres (3.25ha) and standing on the route of the ancient Ridgeway (now a long-distance footpath). About half a mile (0.8km) west along the track is Wayland's Smithy, a megalithic long barrow which has lost part of its earth mound, so its chambers are open to view. An excellent introduction to the Vale, its pretty villages and historic sites is provided by the Vale and Downland Centre in Wantage.

NEW TOWNS, OLD PALACES

This is where Ebenezer Howard's dream of garden cities for overcrowded Londoners first took shape, most extensively at Welwyn. Yet just across the railway from its twin new town, Hatfield, is the great Jacobean palace of Hatfield House. Just as close to modern Luton, the mansion of Luton Hoo provides a showcase for an outstanding, historic art collection.

The gargoyles and dragons of Knebworth House were put to good effect when it became Wayne Manor for Tim Burton's Batman *movie*

The east wing and gardens of Hatfield House; Robert Cecil's gardener returned from Europe with plants that had never been seen before in England

Ayot St Lawrence

A pleasant if unexciting village among wooded hills northwest of Welwyn Garden City, Ayot St Lawrence has two points of distinction: its churches (one 14th century and in ruins, the other 18th century with Greek portico and colonnades) and the fact that George Bernard Shaw came to live here at the age of 50 and remained until his death 44 years later. His house, Shaw's Corner (National Trust), is undistinguished, but the downstairs rooms remain as they were during his lifetime, and in the garden is the summerhouse where he did much of his writing.

Hatfield

The original town of Hatfield grew up round the gateway to the palace of the Bishops of Ely. Its remains are to be found in the grounds of Hatfield House, home of the Marquesses of Salisbury and among the most spectacular Jacobean houses in England. It was built by Robert Cecil, First Earl of Salisbury, James I's chief minister,

and has been the Cecil family's home ever since. Elizabeth I spent much of her girlhood here, and appointed William Cecil, Lord Burghley, as her chief minister.

The old town has some fine Georgian houses and inns, including the Eight Bells, which Dickens knew and featured in *Oliver Twist*. In contrast is the new town, mostly across the railway to the west, which was designated a new town in 1948 and developed in tandem with the existing Welwyn Garden City.

Luton

This Bedfordshire town is most widely known for its football team and Vauxhall car factory, but it also has London's fourth (and independent) international airport, a very new university and, just to the south, Luton Hoo. Though only just over a mile (1.6km) from the town's suburban southern edge, this great house in its 'Capability' Brown landscape is another world. The mansion itself, restyled in the 20th century by Ritz Hotel architects Mewès and Davis, provides a sumptuous

Knebworth

Knebworth House has been the home of the Lytton family since 1490, but the High Gothic exterior we see today is a Victorian transformation carried out by the novelist and statesman Sir Edward Bulwer-Lytton. Behind this façade, the original Tudor-great-hall-turned-Jacobean-banqueting-hall remains. The gardens were laid out by Lutyens (who also designed part of St Martin's Church) and include a herb garden by Gertrude Jekyll. The house stands in a 200-acre (80ha) country park.

Whipsnade Zoo

Opened in 1931 on a spacious site on the edge of the Downs south of Dunstable, Whipsnade was a pioneer of humane treatment of zoo animals. Its 600 acres (243ha) provide the space for animals to roam in natural breeding groups – hence its considerable success in the captive breeding of rare and endangered species. You can explore the park on foot, by car or on the free Trailbreaker Roadtrain (seasonal), which lets you hop on and off at various points and enables you to concentrate on the animals, not the road. There is also the Great Whipsnade Railway (seasonal) and many other attractions and special events.

setting for a unique collection of works of art, acquired by diamond merchant Sir Julius Wernher and his son Harold. They include Gobelin tapestries, Dutch and Italian masters, ceramics, Fabergé jewellery, and mementos of the Russian imperial family.

St Albans

St Albans is a historic place, with a great cathedral standing high above the River Ver. The medieval street pattern is discernible and some medieval buildings remain. The Fighting Cocks Inn and Kingsbury Watermill are worth visiting. Below the town, across the Ver, is a blissfully green and open landscape in which are the extensive remains of the Roman city of *Verulamium*, with the excellent Roman Museum housing excavated finds, mosaics and recreated Roman rooms. The Roman Theatre, unique in having a stage, is the only one in Britain that is open to the public. Both the cathedral and town take their name from Alban, a Roman who in the third-century became Britain's first Christian martyr.

The Museum of St Albans has various collections and reconstructed workshops, and the town boasts an Organ Museum, which includes great theatre organs and other instruments. In early summer a visit to the Gardens of the Rose at Chiswell Green is a must. Here over 30,000 colourful and fragrant plants are on display.

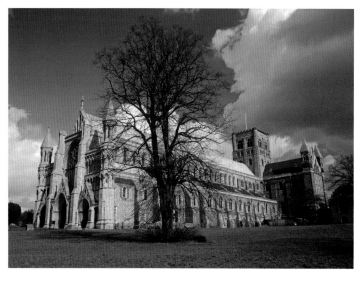

Welwyn Garden City

This was, after Letchworth, the flagship of Ebenezer Howard's Garden City Movement, which aimed to create an attractive, healthy living and working environment as an alternative to the crowded, unhealthy conditions in London. It provided houses with gardens, industry which was separate but within easy reach and access to countryside. Building started in 1919 and the original garden city neighbourhoods have a distinctive style and maturity. Welwyn expanded greatly as a post-war new town. Stevenage to the north, another 1940s new town, was built round an existing settlement following similar principles.

Baron Grimthorpe (1816–1905) is responsible for the 1883 west frontage of St Albans Cathedral, a design that was derided at the time

See Walk N, page 141
A Tour of Milton Keynes, City of the Future

Tourist Information
Hertford: 10 Market Place (tel: 01992 584322)
Luton: The Library, St George's Square (tel: 01582 401579)
St Albans: Town Hall, Market Place (tel: 01727 864511)

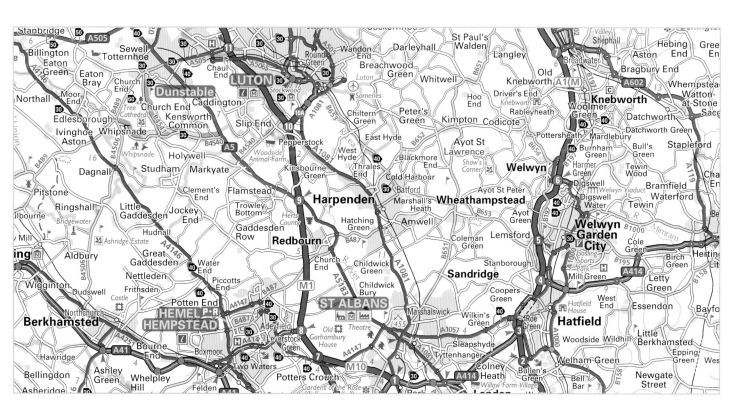

LONDON

The 19th-century Albert Bridge, one of many, and one of the most elegant, spanning the Thames in London

It is impossible to sum up London in a few pages, such is the diversity of this most vibrant of cities. Instead, these pages concentrate on a small selection of its many features – some familiar to residents and visitors alike, but others perhaps a little surprising. Think of London and we usually think of ceremony and tradition, entertainment and business. These pages touch on a few of these topics in an attempt to show the contrasting faces of modern London.

Today's London is a sprawling metropolis, teeming with energy and seemingly swallowing up all in its path, stretching from Surrey to Kent and Essex and receiving around 26 million visitors annually – over three times its own population. But, despite its traffic, crowds and somewhat eccentric public transport system, London can be a charming and subtle place. Cosmopolitan London shows the rich diversity of cultures and traditions which have become an integral part of the capital's life over the decades, with different communities stamping their own character on various parts of the city. Then follow the traditions and ceremonies familiar to millions around the world, from the State Opening of Parliament to the Promenade Concerts, and from Trooping the Colour to the Lord Mayor's Show – traditions which give London its unique character.

That London is a progressive city is shown in its buildings, ancient and modern, from the famous dome of St Paul's Cathedral to the spectacular Gherkin that has become just as familiar. The capital also has its genteel side, reflected in its profusion of green spaces – its great parks, heaths, commons and elegant squares, each offering its own particular respite from the bustle of the city. Then there is the Thames itself, spanned by some 30 diverse bridges, including the awesome Tower Bridge, the elegant arches of the Westminster crossing and the Millennium Bridge. We end our brief tour with a trip out of the city to the surrounding historic houses, royal palaces and gardens further afield.

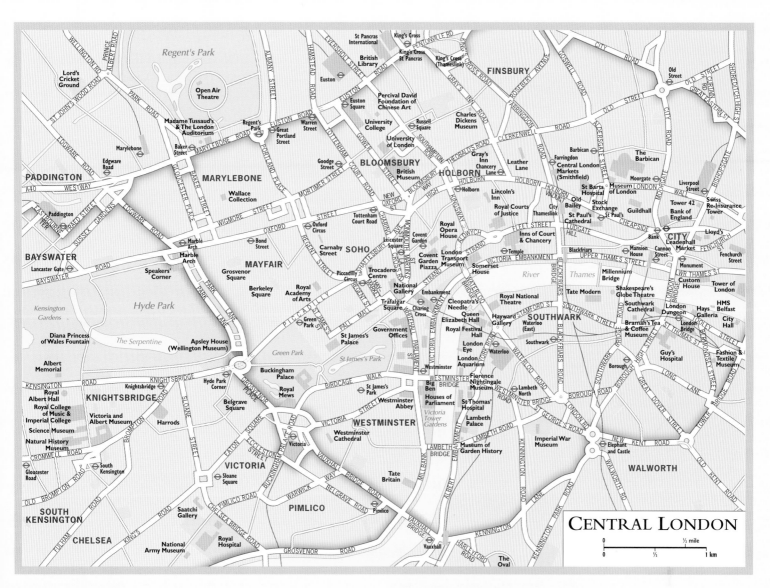

CENTRAL LONDON

0 ——————— ½ mile
0 —— ½ —— 1 km

Section Contents

Cosmopolitan London   116–117
Pomp and Circumstance   118–119
London Buildings, Old and New   120–121
The Green Lungs of London   122–123
Crossing the Thames   124–125
Off-Centre London   126–127

The clock tower of the Houses of Parliament may be known around the world as Big Ben, but only the bell within the tower can truly lay claim to the name

Planned to stand for just five years from the Millennium, the London Eye continues to bring in the crowds

The Doc Marten boot came to symbolise the punk spirit of late 1970s London

COSMOPOLITAN LONDON

Travel by bus or ride the London Underground and you will be surrounded by the buzz of half a dozen languages and a group of fellow passengers who reflect the ever-changing population of the city. Like any big city, London has always attracted immigrants (notably from Ireland), but after the Second World War London needed workers in large numbers and scoured the Commonwealth for them. Indians, Pakistanis, Bangladeshis and Jamaicans came to the capital, their critical mass allowing culture, language and cuisine to survive and thrive. As global barriers have broken down, newer influences have come to London, with the removal of EU barriers on worker movement adding more to the mix.

London's skyline, too, is rapidly changing. There are new mosques, Hindu temples and a plethora of foreign architects working in London. Iraqi-born Zaha Hadid has designed the acclaimed Aquatics Centre for the 2012 Olympics, while Italy's Renzo Piano is responsible for the skyscraping 'Shard of Glass' at London Bridge. Today's London is intensely multicultural, a place where all languages are spoken, where nothing is off the menu and anything is possible – the only limits are your time and your imagination.

Ethnic Villages

A cultural mix is not altogether new to London. Spitalfields, barely 10 minutes' walk from the Bank of England, is these days the home or workplace for several thousand Bangladeshis – the shops and colourful street market in Brick Lane might almost be in Dacca or Calcutta, were it not for the climate. Yet Spitalfields has been an immigrant quarter for three centuries. First came French Huguenots, fleeing religious persecution, then in the 1880s, similarly impelled, Jews came from Eastern Europe. The Bangladeshis, arriving in the 1970s, were just the latest wave of incomers seeking shelter and a better life. A direct reflection of the development of this area can be seen in the plain 18th-century building on the corner of Brick Lane and Fournier Street – it was built as a Huguenot chapel, became a synagogue, and is now the local mosque.

One of the longer-established communities is London's Chinatown, which was originally established in Limehouse in the 1890s, after several hundred Chinese seamen from ships in West India Docks decided to stay. Those who were ships' cooks opened restaurants. After the heavy bombing of the docks during the Second World War, this community mostly moved to Soho, and by the 1970s the area round Gerrard Street had become Chinatown, with not only Chinese restaurants but Chinese accountants, supermarkets, bookmakers and the like. Other 'ethnic villages' in London have included Little Italy, established in the 19th century in Clerkenwell, strong Caribbean communities in Brixton and Notting Hill, Greek Cypriots in Kentish Town and Turkish Cypriots around New Cross.

A New Skyline

It is estimated that one in three architects working in London is foreign, but buildings that reflect the city's cultural diversity are only now beginning to be seen. Places of worship are one field in which new, consciously exotic buildings have appeared. Best known perhaps is the London Central Mosque at Hanover Gate, Regent's Park by Frederick Gibberd. The mosque's gilded dome and high minaret blend in well with the Regency terraces, themselves rather exotic in places. Casson & Conder's Ismali Centre, built for the Aga Khan, graces the South Kensington cityscape with its Persian roof garden. Both by British architects, these buildings may be called 'modified Islamic' in style.

One of the London's most confident architectural expressions of ethnicity is in Neasden, where the Shri Swaminarayan Mandir temple was funded and built by the local Hindu community, using traditional methods and materials. Holding 2,500 worshippers it rivals Angkor Wat in beauty and size.

More modest, but just as dynamic, are developments at the East London Mosque in Tower Hamlets, with its new Muslim Learning Centre, complete with library, gym and crèche. A few miles away,

Chinatown's authentic restaurants feed thousands every day. Try to catch the Chinese New Year celebrations in January or February

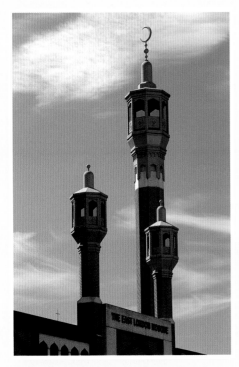

In Tower Hamlets, home to the East London Mosque (above), English is a second language for 80 per cent of young children

developments in north London include a £50 million Jewish Community Centre on Finchley Road. All over the city, as communities grow in size and confidence, the cityscape, and the people who occupy it, are changing – and London is richer for it.

The Food of the Nations

The choice of restaurants in central London is enormous, with areas such as Soho and adjoining Covent Garden long established as melting pots of different cultures.

France is represented by such establishments as Chez Gérard, with restaurants across the West End ('the best steak-frites this side of Paris'), Mon Plaisir, Monmouth Street (50 years in Covent Garden and noted for its pre-theatre fixed-price menus), and Grill St Quentin (Breton oysters and lobsters) in Brompton Road.

Italian restaurants are more numerous. Among the oldest is Bertorelli's which has been serving customers from its first restaurant in Charlotte Street since 1913. Nearly a century later, it has six central London locations. Its dominant flavour is of Tuscany. The family-run Spaghetti House chain still provides good, honest Italian food at Goodge Street, where it started 50 years ago, but now has 10 more London restaurants.

Other European gastronomy is represented by, among others, the Gay Hussar (Hungarian) in Soho and Belgo Centraal in Earlham Street, Covent Garden, for all things Belgian – including an array of beers.

Spanish and Latin American eating places, including tapas bars, have multiplied in recent years. Cafe Pacifico in Covent Garden has the noise, bustle and fiery flavours of a Mexican cantina, while the Gaucho Grill in Swallow Street offers Argentinian beef prepared 'in the refined style of barbecue cooking known as assado'. Salsa! offers Latin food, music and dance in Charing Cross Road and you can sample Hispanic American specialities at Fiesta Havana in Fulham Road.

East London's Brick Lane boasts a plethora of Indian and Bangladeshi restaurants, and a thriving Sunday market to boot

Eastern Mediterranean and Middle East cuisine find expression in countless kebab houses and tavernas. Among the more stylish are Halepi (Cypriot) near Hyde Park, Pasha (Moroccan) in Gloucester Road, South Kensington, and the Maroush chain (Lebanese). The oldest Indian restaurant in

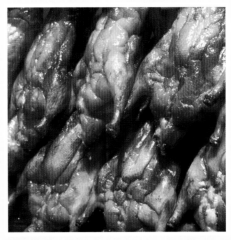

Teriyaki glazed roast chickens, a staple of London's Japanese restaurant scene

London is Veeraswamy in Regent Street, which is good but expensive. The Punjab in Neal Street specialises in dishes from that region, Mandeer in Hanway Place offers excellent vegetarian Indian dishes in an exotic subterranean environment, while Brick Lane cannot be beaten for sheer choice.

For Chinese food, the whole area from Shaftesbury Avenue through Chinatown to Leicester Square is thronged with eating places, including the long-established Gallery Rendezvous in Beak Street and the Ming in Greek Street. In the Isle of Dogs, Lotus is a floating Chinese restaurant, but leader of the pack must be Michelin-starred Hakkasan in Fitzrovia. Asian cuisine has exploded in London within the last two decades with fusion the watchword. Bloomsbury is the birthplace of worldwide chain Wagamama – now there are a couple of dozen throughout London, while Asia de Cuba in St Martin's Lane combines a sumptuous interior with one of London's best fusion menus.

Among the offerings at the sprawling Borough Food Market, London Bridge, are breads from across the world, green and black Mediterranean olives and Middle Eastern pastries

POMP AND CIRCUMSTANCE

London has many odd and colourful ceremonies. Some are public, others private; some vouchsafe passers-by a glimpse of worthy-looking persons in bizarre old-fashioned costume, processing through the public street in the course of honouring some ancient tradition. Often the origins and purpose seem obscure; these are traditions kept alive when the reasons for them have long disappeared. But these colourful ceremonies can be savoured simply because they are colourful. Parliament, the Monarchy, Armed Forces, Law and the City of London are the main focuses of traditional ceremony.

Royal Traditions

Ceremonial relations between Crown and Parliament reflect the struggle of the elected House of Commons in the 17th century to assert its independence from the Stuart kings. Thus, when the Queen opens each new session of Parliament, it is not in the House of Commons – no sovereign has been admitted here since the Civil War and subsequent execution of Charles I – but in the House of Lords.

The State Opening of Parliament usually takes place in late October or early November and begins with a coach carrying the imperial state crown to Parliament, followed some 20 minutes later by the Queen in the splendid Irish state coach. From Buckingham Palace they drive down the Mall, through Horse Guards Arch into Whitehall and thus to Parliament. As the Queen enters the Lords, guns in Hyde Park fire a salute; as she takes her seat on the throne, the Lord Great Chamberlain (a hereditary royal official) raises his wand to summon the Commons. But when Black Rod, a House of Lords official, arrives at the Commons chamber, something odd happens. The Sergeant at Arms, a Commons official, slams the door in his face. This recalls Charles I's attempt to arrest five MPs in 1642, one of the events which led

Blues and Royals 'beating the retreat' on Horse Guards Parade

The Lord Mayor's Show brings colour and pomp to the 'Square Mile'

to the Civil War. However, eventually Black Rod gets to delivers his message, and MPs follow the Speaker of the House of Commons to the Lords to hear the Queen's Speech. In a curious way, this is proof of Parliament's triumph, because the speech is written not by the Queen, but by government ministers and it sets out their policies and legislative programme for the new parliamentary session.

Earlier that day another historic ceremony is performed. The Queen's bodyguard of Yeomen of the Guard, in their picturesque red and black uniforms, search the cellars beneath the Palace of Westminster for gunpowder – recalling the attempt on 5 November 1605 to blow up King James I and Parliament.

The most colourful of the public royal ceremonies is the annual Trooping the Colour, which celebrates the sovereign's

official birthday, usually on the second Saturday of June. The parade's original purpose was to show the men of a particular regiment their 'colour' of flag so that they would recognise it as a rallying point in battle. In today's ceremony, the Queen, dressed in the uniform of the Foot Guards she is reviewing, goes with an escort of Household Cavalry to Horse Guards and inspects the parade; there is then a march past, and finally the Queen leads her Foot Guards back to Buckingham Palace. Until 1987, the Queen rode on horseback; now she rides in a carriage.

Beating the Retreat is another display of military precision involving the marching and drilling bands of the Household Division in their colourful uniforms. It takes place on Horse Guards Parade in late May or early June and involves mounted bands, trumpeters, massed marching bands and pipes and drums. The name has nothing to do with defeat in battle – it goes back to the ancient custom of signalling or 'beating' the retreat of sunlight at nightfall.

For those who miss these annual parades, the Changing of the Guard is a colourful daily ceremony which takes place at four royal palaces in London. Most impressive is that at Buckingham Palace, with one detachment of Foot Guards, in their scarlet tunics and tall bearskin helmets, taking over from another the duty of guarding the Queen's residence. Similar ceremonies also takes place at the Horse Guards in Whitehall, St James's Palace and the Tower of London.

Civic Dignitaries

Over the years London's local authorities have often been reorganised to suit new conditions, but the oldest, the City of London Corporation, which administers only the 'Square Mile' – the tiny area containing London's financial centre – has retained its independence. It combines an efficient (though arguably undemocratic) administration with the pomp and pageantry of 800 years of proud municipal independence.

Its figurehead is the Lord Mayor, elected each year in an unbroken 800-year tradition by the liverymen of the City livery companies, or guilds. When the reigning Lord Mayor and Sheriffs arrive at Guildhall in their traditional robes of office, the Keeper of Guildhall presents them with nosegays of garden flowers. This tradition goes back to the days when they were

Ceremony in Music

A different kind of 'Pomp and Circumstance' exists in Elgar's five marches of that name, redolent of the imperial pride of the Edwardian era. At least one (No. 1), features each year at the festive Last Night of the Proms (the Henry Wood Promenade Concerts) at the Royal Albert Hall. Sung lustily by the Prom audience with the words of 'Land of Hope and Glory', it typifies the way in which Londoners enjoy celebrating the past without necessarily taking too seriously the attitudes that lie behind such traditions.

The imposing Royal Albert Hall

believed to give protection not only against the evil smells of London streets, but against the diseases harboured there.

The election of the Lord Mayor takes place around Michaelmas Day (29 September), followed in November by the Lord Mayor's Procession (or Lord Mayor's Show). This dates back to the Magna Carta in 1215, when King John, under pressure from his barons, sought support from the City in return for giving it a new charter allowing annual elections. His proviso was that each new Lord Mayor took an oath of allegiance before the king or his justices, and so, on a Saturday each November, the new Lord Mayor of London goes in procession to the Royal Courts of Justice in the Strand to swear loyalty to the Crown.

The processional route is along Cheapside, Ludgate Hill and Fleet Street to the Strand. The Lord Mayor's gilded coach, built in 1757 and looking for all the world as if it has come straight out of a fairy tale, has actually come straight out of the Museum of London, harnessed to six magnificent Shire horses; he is attended by a personal

bodyguard of pikemen in armour and musketeers from England's oldest regiment, the Honourable Artillery Company. A huge retinue of mobile floats or tableaux make up the procession, and illustrate various aspects of a theme chosen by the new Lord Mayor for his year of office.

Another highlight of the City calendar is the Lord Mayor's Banquet, held on the Monday following the Show, and the most important in a series of banquets and feasts which each Lord Mayor must enjoy or endure during his year of office. The new Lord Mayor and Sheriffs give this banquet in honour of the outgoing Lord Mayor, and invite some 700 VIPs, the most important of them welcomed with fanfares by splendidly costumed trumpeters. The evening is normally the occasion for a major speech by the Prime Minister.

Foot Guards at the Changing of the Guard (left) and Guildhall (right) where the City's Lord Mayors are installed

LONDON BUILDINGS, OLD AND NEW

London's architectural treasures range from great set pieces such as the Palace of Westminster to tucked-away gems like the Blewcoat School in nearby Caxton Street. Grand sequences include The Mall, with Nash's stuccoed, columned sweep of Carlton House Terrace, his processional route from Regent's Park along Portland Place and Regent Street and Pall Mall with its Italianate 19th-century gentlemen's clubs.

However, the capital does not stand still and is now reaching for the sky. The City of London has been redefined by Norman Foster's acclaimed Gherkin and the less glorious Broadgate Tower, while the 'Shard of Glass' at London Bridge will eclipse them all in terms of height, controversy and, possibly, beauty. With the new Wembley, bold designs for the Olympic facilities and smaller but no-less-innovative projects all over town, architectural London is booming.

The Heart of the Capital

Perhaps the place to start is at Charing Cross in the heart of London, and the hotel which fronts the station (Decimus Burton, 1834) is worth more than a glance. Trafalgar Square has two fine classical buildings. The first, St Martin in the Fields Church (Gibbs, 1726), has a magnificent temple-like portico and steeple. The other is the National Gallery (Wilkins, 1838), with its controversial but likeable 1991 Sainsbury Wing, designed by American architect Robert Venturi.

Whitehall is full of architectural delights, outstandingly the Banqueting House (Inigo Jones), which, in the early 17th century, was shockingly modern. There is also the Horse Guards (1760), the ceremonial gateway to the parade ground and park beyond, and Richmond Terrace.

William Whitfield's attractive Department of Health building, alongside Richmond Terrace, shows how modern infill can have strength and character, yet exist in sympathy with its surroundings. The same can be said of Portcullis House, where MPs have their offices. Its distinctive Gothic-looking 'chimneys' are in fact part of the energy-saving ventilation system – exhausts for fresh air drawn in at street level. Below ground, Parliament Square is served by a spaciously light and airy station that is part of the Jubilee Line extension of the Underground.

The Houses of Parliament and Westminster Abbey are, of course, the great architectural events of this square, but the Queen Elizabeth II Conference Centre (1986) demonstrates how large modern buildings can sit happily in a historic townscape.

Other notable buildings hereabouts include Westminster Cathedral (Bentley, 1903); and Channel 4's television studios and headquarters in Horseferry Road (Rogers, 1994).

The City and Docklands

The City of London has rather different planning policies from neighbouring Westminster, most of which is now a conservation area. Of course, the City does have its historic jewels – Wren's St Paul's Cathedral, his 'wedding cake' St Bride's and a string of other churches, built after the Great Fire of 1666. The tranquil and beautiful Inns of Court are here, along with such monuments to commerce as the Bank of England, Royal Exchange, Custom House and the Mansion House and Guildhall. Just over the City boundary is that great riverside fortress, the Tower of London.

St Paul's Cathedral (left) is an impressive sight from the Millennium Bridge

Looking over Waterloo Bridge (above) towards the City of London, where 30 St Mary Axe, otherwise know as the Gherkin (right), graces the skyline

The London Eye attracts more than three million visitors per year

However, as a moneymaking concern, the City looks favourably on new developments designed to give its patrons the office accommodation they need. This has resulted in many large, dull or ugly buildings, but some bold and beautiful ones too. Richard Rogers' 1986 Lloyds Building broke the mould, its lofty atrium interior free of pipes and ducts, which were instead put outside on the glass façade. The new Broadgate Tower at Liverpool Street Station is not lacking in scale, but is no match for the taller, spiralling form of 30 St Mary Axe – universally known as the Gherkin.

Unquestionably courageous, Foster's 2004 Stirling Prize winner is a delight to behold, close up or at a distance.

To the east of the City, in the Docklands development, is London's other financial powerhouse, Canary Wharf. Over the years, as successive skyscrapers have been erected, this has taken on the appearance of a mini-Manhattan, but with architecture that is typically utilitarian and often pastiche. This looks set to continue with the North Quay development. Canary Wharf is best reached by the elevated Docklands Light Railway, and, at ground level, is pleasant enough with public spaces, waterside restaurants, bars and shops.

South Bank to Tower Bridge

For the moment, everything on the South Bank is dwarfed by the London Eye. Notable stalwarts of the cultural complex here are the Royal National Theatre (1975) and the Royal Festival Hall (1951). They were joined in 2000 by the enormously successful Tate Modern art gallery, where the sleek Millennium Bridge, despite a wobbly start, brings crowds from across the river. The gallery occupies the old Bankside Power Station, built in 1947 and closed in 1981. Just downstream you see the thatched roof of the replica Globe Theatre (1997), close to the site of the original.

Further along this eminently walkable riverside is 13th-century Southwark

Charles I commissioned Dutch artist Rubens to paint the massive ceiling canvases that adorn Whitehall's Banqueting Hall

Cathedral. Close by, some say too close, the European Union's tallest building is slowly taking shape. At 310m (1,017ft), the 'Shard', designed by Renzo Piano, will dwarf everything in central London, but its elegant tapered glass form, rising from London Bridge Station, may follow the Gherkin into the city's heart. At Tower Bridge, the atrium of Hay's Galleria rises from a former dock basin and 19th-century warehouses have been recycled into the Butlers Wharf development, with flats, restaurants, studios and (appropriately) the Design Museum.

Around the Centre

On the north-central fringe of central London are four buildings of particular merit – the British Museum (Smirke, 1847), University College's original Gower Street group (Wilkins, 1829), St Pancras Station and the new British Library. At St Pancras, the restored High Victorian hotel front (G.C. Scott, 1874) faces Barlow's great 1868 train shed, extended and revitalised to accommodate the Channel Tunnel fast rail link. The Library next door, completed in 2007 and designed by Colin St John Wilson, is clad in red brick to match the station.

The 'museums area' of South Kensington also merits a good, long look. Here is the expression of Queen Victoria's and (especially) Prince Albert's belief in the nation's intellectual and cultural advancement, and stylistically reflects that age. Impressively self-confident buildings in brick, terracotta and stone line spacious boulevards. They include the Victoria and Albert, Natural History and Science museums; Imperial College tower; and the Royal Albert Hall.

The Great Court (2000) of the British Museum, where Norman Foster's impressive glass and steel roof has created a new indoor circulation and exhibit space

THE GREEN LUNGS OF LONDON

Left: Deer in Richmond Park
Above: Greenwich's Royal Observatory

Cities, and the people in them, need to breathe, and one feature of London that appeals to visitors and residents alike is the number and richness of green spaces. A recent survey carried out for the Royal Parks Agency showed that in that particular year its parks attracted some 30 million visitors, which put them collectively above such national tourist attractions as St Paul's Cathedral and the Tower of London. Other research among visitors from abroad shows that they are drawn to London by the relaxed, civilised image created by its parks – particularly the Royal Parks.

Central London Parks

Centuries ago these parks were mostly royal hunting forests outside the confines of a much smaller capital. Central London has now engulfed many of them, and the oldest is St James's Park, with its neat lawns, colourful flower beds and shrubberies around a lovely lake. It is hard to imagine this as marshland, as it was until it was drained to provide Henry VIII with a bowling alley, tilt yard and deer nursery.

St James's Park is an oasis of nature among the royal and civic palaces of Westminster

Charles II redesigned it, and by the late 17th century it was already home to many species of wading birds, including two pelicans given to the king by the Russian ambassador. The variety and profusion of birdlife around the lake is one of its attractions; another is the splendid roofscape seen from the bridge.

St James's Park forms the first link in a great green chain, leading past Buckingham Palace into Green Park, then into the wide expanses of Hyde Park and Kensington Gardens. Lush and restful Green Park is the smallest Royal Park, while Hyde Park is the largest of those in central London – quite exhilarating amidst this densely built-up area. Deer-hunting ceased here in the 1750s, and the deer have long gone, but people still ride horses along a sandy track called Rotten Row. The name is a corruption of *Route du Roi* (king's road), because it is on the line of the road which led to Kensington Palace.

Just north of Rotten Row is the Serpentine, which, with the Long Water, forms a long curving lake. In the park's northeast corner are Marble Arch and Speakers' Corner, where various soapbox orators, from anarchists to evangelists to flat-earthers, traditionally harangue passers-by.

Across the Broad Water lie Kensington Gardens, originally the gardens of Kensington Palace and now effectively

Office workers retreat to the peace of Green Park, escaping the bustle of Piccadilly

Grand Georgian homes surround the 18th-century gardens of Berkeley Square

a westward extension of Hyde Park, though it is more intimate and sedate. Features include the Albert Memorial (currently under restoration), the Round Pond, Broad and Flower Walks, the Sunken Garden and the Orangery. Don't miss the intricately carved Elfin Oak, Frampton's statue of J. M. Barrie's eternally youthful hero, Peter Pan, and (near Lancaster Gate) the recently restored Italian Water Gardens with their fountains and ornate statuary.

London's Little Venice, home to a thriving residential narrowboat community

Regent's Park formed part of an inspired 19th-century property development scheme, a collaboration between architect John Nash and the Prince Regent. It was originally to be the grounds of a new palace, which was never built, and consists of landscaped, wooded parkland with a lake; villas lie hidden within it, and the park is ringed by a sequence of grand stucco terraces. It is a magical combination of landscape and water, with a well-preserved architectural backdrop. Other features include the delightful Queen Mary's Rose Garden and the open-air theatre's summer season. On the northern boundary of the park are London Zoo and the Regent's Canal. The adjacent Primrose Hill, once part of the same hunting forest,

retains a more rural atmosphere, and where it rises to 207ft (63m) there are panoramic views over London.

Further Afield

The outer Royal Parks include three huge open spaces near the Thames in west London, all associated with former royal palaces. Richmond Park still has ancient oak trees, a large herd of deer and lots of other wildlife. From Robin Hood Gate a pedestrian link connects with another huge belt of parkland – Wimbledon Common, with its lake and windmill, and adjoining Putney Heath. Bushy Park and Hampton Court Park lie west and north of Hampton Court Palace and are somewhat similar to Richmond's landscaped parkland, except that Hampton Court's gardens have a more urbane, cultivated character, with formal vistas, a canal lined with lime trees, statuary and the famous maze.

Greenwich Park, too, was a royal hunting park, walled in from adjoining Blackheath. Today it forms part of a unique sequence, which starts on the Thames waterside with Sir Christopher Wren's Royal Naval College. It then moves through the National Maritime Museum's grounds, along the twin colonnades flanking Inigo Jones's superb Queen's House and into the park, which contains Wren's charming hilltop Old Observatory, standing at zero degrees longitude. The sequence continues along a broad chestnut-lined avenue to the windswept, kite-flying Blackheath and terminates at the spire of All Saint's Church in Blackheath Village.

Heaths, Commons and Squares

London's unique inheritance of Royal Parks constitutes only the crème de la crème of its green open spaces, but there are many other appealing tracts of land. Hampstead Heath, Kenwood and Parliament Hill to the north are famous for their wonderful views (Guy Fawkes' compatriots intended to watch the result of their conspiracy to blow up Parliament from here). Epping Forest, a huge green wedge stretching from Wanstead out into Essex, is real countryside on London's doorstep, and on the eastern edge are Lee Valley Park and Thames Chase, the latter a new forest, planted by the Countryside Commission.

Clapham, Tooting, Streatham, Wandsworth and Barnes all have their commons, and

London also has a number of big municipal parks, providing relief from urban sprawl and a refuge for wildlife. The Grand Union and Regent canals, forming an arc of waterways with towpaths round north inner London, offer tranquil walking and are an important part of a network of ecological corridors.

There remain many parts of London which are not so fortunate in having a green open space in their vicinity, and their saving grace is the London square. These railing-enclosed gardens with mature trees are sometimes open to the public, sometimes the private reserve of the residents, but are always a green lung among busy streets. There are more than 600 squares in Greater London, with a huge diversity of character. They range from such fashionable and architecturally magnificent ensembles as Belgrave and Eaton squares to unnumbered squares, crescents and circuses with soft green centres all over London. These – like the parks – bring delight and refreshment to Londoners and visitors alike.

Canada Gate, near Buckingham Palace, is Green Park's grandest entrance

Spellbindingly rural yet accessible, Hampstead Heath is twice the size of Hyde Park

CROSSING THE THAMES

The River Thames was once London's greatest thoroughfare – by far the easiest means of travelling in and out of the capital in the days of horses and carriages, rough, muddy tracks, footpads and highwaymen. But the great river always needed to be crossed, and there have been bridges over the Thames for about 1,000 years. Today there are about 30 of them within Greater London – for road, rail and pedestrians – not to mention the tunnels or the towering Queen Elizabeth II suspension bridge downstream, which doubles up with the twin Dartford tunnels to carry the M25 across the river.

Hungerford Bridge, at Charing Cross. On the left is one of the two Jubilee pedestrian walkways

Central London Bridges

When it comes to bridges in London, most people tend to think first of Tower Bridge, London Bridge and Westminster Bridge. Tower Bridge – until 1991 the lowest bridge on the Thames – reflects the Victorian obsession with Gothic architecture. A glass-covered walkway, 142ft (43m) above the water, links the two towers and gives panoramic views along the river. The opening mechanism was electrified in 1976, but the original hydraulic machinery is now the centrepiece of a museum, which uses state-of-the-art effects to tell the story of the bridge in a dramatic and exciting way.

The next bridge upstream is London Bridge, the oldest and most famous, which has its origins in a wooden bridge built to connect Roman *Londinium* via the Kent section of Watling Street to the Roman ports of *Dubris* (Dover) and *Rutupiae* (Richborough). It was broken or burned down several times until, in 1176, Peter de Colechurch erected the first stone bridge, with a chapel on it dedicated to St Thomas à Becket. Soon after, houses were built alongside its roadway, and the gruesome custom developed of displaying the impaled heads of executed rebels and traitors on the bridge.

De Colechurch's bridge was not well designed. It had many narrow arches, and their piers obstructed the river's flow and made navigation hazardous. But it saw service until the 18th century, when the houses were removed and a wider central channel was created. In 1801 Thomas Telford designed a new and revolutionary single-span iron bridge, but it was too innovative for the powers that be. They built instead a five-arched stone bridge, by the Scottish engineer John Rennie, and built by his more famous son who was knighted upon its completion in 1831. That bridge was bought and transported, stone by stone, to the USA, where it now stands incongruously in the Arizona desert. The latest incarnation of London Bridge is a three-span construction, opened in 1972.

Next upstream are Southwark Bridge and the pedestrian-only Millennium Bridge, which opened in 2000. To the great embarrassment of designers Norman Foster and Arup, the bridge swayed under heavy foot traffic, and was shut for two years, while remedial work was undertaken. After the road and railway bridges at Blackfriars is the 1942 Waterloo Bridge, replacing Rennie's stone bridge of 1817. Trains to Charing Cross run over the Hungerford Bridge (1864), which incorporated the piers from Brunel's earlier suspension bridge; the chains were recycled into his Clifton Suspension Bridge in Bristol. The rail bridge is flanked by the twin pedestrian Golden Jubilee bridges (2002), linking the Embankment to the South Bank arts complex. Although attracting a fraction of the publicity of Foster's bridge, its engineers overcame equally challenging obstacles.

The graceful Millennium Bridge allows pedestrians to cross directly from the Tate Modern to St Paul's Cathedral

Left: The Thames Barrier
Below: The elegant Albert Bridge, which joins Chelsea and Battersea

Westminster Bridge, alongside the Houses of Parliament, was the second bridge to be built in what is now central London. The present structure was completed in 1862, but it replaced an earlier bridge, which opened in 1750. That was the bridge on which Wordsworth wrote his famous sonnet ('Earth has not anything to show more fair ...'), but it later suffered – like others – from the notorious scouring action of strong Thames tides.

The idea of a second crossing at Westminster provoked strong opposition from vested interests – the Thames Watermen had to be bought off with £25,000 compensation; the Archbishop of Canterbury, owner of the horse ferry at Lambeth, collected £21,000 – considerable amounts in those days. Later, in 1862, Lambeth Bridge was completed, right where the Archbishop's ferry used to be – on its east side stands Lambeth Palace, the Archbishop's official residence;

its western approach, Horseferry Road, is a lasting reminder of the ferry. The present bridge was built in 1932.

Upstream again are Vauxhall Bridge, Grosvenor railway bridge (carrying the lines out of Victoria), and Chelsea Bridge, a handsome suspension bridge. On the other side of Battersea Park is perhaps the most attractive of them all, Albert Bridge. Opened in 1873, it was designed by R. M. Ordish and may be described as a 'semi-suspension' bridge – the diagonal stays radiating so picturesquely from the towers to support the deck are rigid; the light suspension chains take only the weight of the stays.

Eighteen London bridges lie upstream of this, starting with Battersea (designed by Sir Joseph Bazalgette, who built the Victoria Embankment). They include the monumental Hammersmith Bridge with its rather Empire-style towers and the suspension footbridge at Teddington Weir, ending with Hampton Court Bridge, of which only one side (Hampton Court) is in London; the other is in Surrey.

Tunnels under the river are numerous, and include several carrying Underground lines. Within London there are also three road tunnels: Rotherhithe, with bends definitely for horse-drawn rather than motor vehicles, and the two Blackwall tunnels. Also downstream of Tower Bridge are two pedestrian tunnels: the one at Woolwich, providing an alternative to the free Woolwich Ferry; the other at Greenwich, connecting the Cutty Sark Gardens to Island Gardens on the Isle of Dogs. The latter tunnel runs parallel to the 1999 Dockland Light Railway (DLR) tunnel, taking trains

across the river to Greenwich, Deptford and Lewisham.

Just upstream of the Woolwich Ferry and foot tunnel is something which is neither a bridge nor a tunnel, but is an important link between the north and south banks of the river. The Thames Barrier is a vital part of a flood defence scheme for London, which was completed in 1984. The Barrier has four enormous curving steel gates, each 200ft (61m) long, shaped like barrels sliced longways, and each weighing 3,200 tonnes. These fit into concrete sills on the river bed and only rise if winds and the North Sea surge threaten to cause flooding in the capital. On the south bank immediately downstream is the visitor centre, with landscaped viewing esplanades, a café and an exhibition.

London's Victorian problem-solvers were at their flamboyant best when creating the opening suspension structure of Tower Bridge (above and left)

OFF-CENTRE LONDON

Most visitors to London look at a few famous tourist attractions, perhaps take a bus tour round the centre, and think they have seen what the city has to offer. To do this is to miss out on some real treats, because 'off-centre London' has interesting and attractive places that are well worth visiting. Here we explore some of the more notable of them – moving clockwise, we start at about the four o'clock position at one of the best known of London's outer limits.

Greenwich and the Southeast

On a pleasant day, you cannot beat the boat trip to Greenwich from the city, and there are various embarkation points in the centre. An alternative route is the Docklands Light Railway via Canary Wharf, but visitors may wish to forgo the rail tunnel, and alight instead at Island Gardens. From here, there is a fine view of the great architectural ensemble that is the Royal Naval College and National Maritime Museum, together with a foot tunnel (1902) to take you across the river.

In Greenwich, the restoration of the *Cutty Sark* was delayed by a disastrous fire in 2007, and completion is scheduled for 2011. In the Naval College, as well as the splendid buildings, there is a busy schedule of special events, and a new interpretation centre, Discover Greenwich. The National Maritime Museum is home to the Old Royal Observatory, standing at zero degrees longitude in Greenwich Park, and the restored 17th-century Queen's House, now

Hampton Court Palace, riverside playground of Henry VIII

used as an art gallery. North of the park on the riverfront, the Millennium Dome is now the O_2 Centre, with regular sporting and entertainment events.

Woolwich to the east has the imposing Royal Artillery Barracks, famous for having the longest continuous façade in Britain. Appropriately, this is the chosen venue for the 2012 Olympic shooting events. Within the Barracks is Firepower, the Royal Artillery Museum. Also at Woolwich is the Thames Barrier Visitor Centre, while at nearby

Eltham are impressive ruins of a medieval royal palace.

To the south, near Bromley, are Chislehurst Caves, a mysterious labyrinth hewn out of the chalk over a period of 8,000 years. During the Second World War the caves became a huge air-raid shelter, which even had its own church. Northwest again, Dulwich has a historic 'village' centre, the impressive 19th-century Dulwich College and the Dulwich Picture Gallery, with many old masters.

Along the Thames

Richmond combines historic buildings and splendid Thames views with a bustling commercial centre and lively arts and restaurant scene. Architectural set pieces include its two greens, with delightful old lanes, and Richmond Hill, with 18th-century houses and fine views.

Kew, downstream, is best known for the Royal Botanic Gardens, 300 acres (122ha) of landscaped gardens, with some spectacular buildings. Seventeenth-century Kew Palace is the most modest but charming of the royal residences, and Kew Village is charming too. In nearby Brentford is the Kew Bridge Steam Museum, a Victorian pumping station with enormous beam engines and London's only steam railway.

Upstream from Richmond are a string of splendid 18th-century buildings – Marble Hill House, a magnificent Palladian villa of the 1720s set in lovely parkland; Ham House, a large 17th-century house of exceptional interest; and the early 18th-century Orleans House Octagon, its adjoining wing now an art gallery. A ferryman (seasonal) will row you from the Ham side to Marble Hill Park.

Further upstream is Hampton Court Palace, built by Cardinal Wolsey, Henry VIII's most powerful minister, who gave the palace to his monarch. His great gatehouse in Tudor

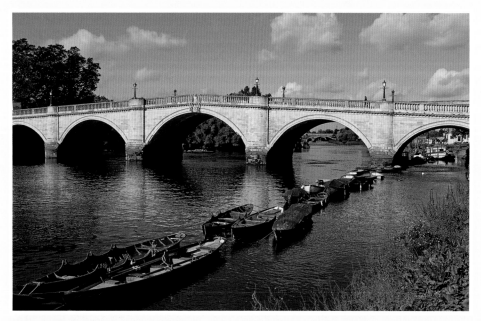

Where Richmond Bridge now stands, two ferries once operated – one for people, and another for horses and carts

The Royal Naval College, designed mainly by Wren and Hawksmoor, on the banks of the River Thames at Greenwich

At Highgate Cemetery, north London, shrub-lined pathways reveal grand old tombs and monuments, including one marking Karl Marx's grave

brick dominates the main approach, and beyond the huge Base Court lies the Clock Court with its 16th-century astronomical clock and Great Hall. Later monarchs all left their mark here, notably the work carried out by Wren for William and Mary, with the arcaded Fountain Court and great East Front, looking out over the formal gardens and lovely parkland.

Downriver, the riverside is studded with attractions – Horace Walpole's 'Gothick castle' at Strawberry Hill, Syon House with its Adam interiors and spacious park, Old Chiswick with its 18th-century Chiswick Mall, and Fulham Palace in Bishop's Park. Chelsea, known for its King's Road boutiques and cafés, also has Wren's Chelsea Hospital (home to the famous pensioners), a maze of streets leading to the river and the Physic Garden, a pioneer botanical garden, founded in 1673.

Further north are two notable historic houses – Lord Burlington's Chiswick House, an essay in Palladian style, and Osterley Park, built in the 16th century by Sir Thomas Gresham, merchant, Lord Mayor of London and founder of the Royal Exchange, and later splendidly remodelled in classical style.

Around North London

Harrow-on-the-Hill is noted for Harrow School, founded in 1572. To the east, at Colindale, is the Royal Air Force Museum, with 95 aircraft and other exhibits, including flight simulators and 'Our Finest Hour', a show which immerses visitors in the Battle of Britain. Hampstead's Fenton

House was built in the late 17th century; it accommodates a collection of musical instruments, and often resounds to the sound of harpsichords or virginals. Keats House is now a museum devoted to the famous poet, and the house once occupied by Sigmund Freud contains his collection of antiquities and displays relating to his work, while Kenwood, in lovely wooded grounds, contains fine art collections. Highgate has the unusual and surprisingly popular attraction of its impressive cemetery, housing the remains of many luminaries, such as George Eliot, Michael Faraday and Karl Marx.

Upriver from central London, the Royal Botanic Gardens at Kew are home to the world's largest collection of living plants

Sporting Museums

Sports fans may choose to visit the MCC Museum at Lord's Cricket Ground in St John's Wood, the Lawn Tennis Museum at the All England Club in Wimbledon, or the popular Wembley Stadium Tour.

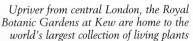

Ham House is a superb riverside mansion, built in 1610

Walk A
TENNYSON'S FRESHWATER

From lofty downland with magnificent coastal views to tranquil estuary scenes, this exhilarating ramble explores the landscape the Romantic poet loved so well.

Distance: 5.75 miles (9.2km)
Minimum time: 3hrs
Ascent/Gradient: 623ft (190m) ▲▲▲
Level of difficulty: +++
Paths: Downland, field and woodland paths, some road walking and stretch of disused railway, 4 stiles
Landscape: Downland, farmland, freshwater marsh and salt marsh
Suggested map: OS Explorer OL29 Isle of Wight
Start/finish: Grid reference: SZ 346857
Dog friendliness: Let off lead on Tennyson Down and along old railway
Parking: Pay-and-display car park at Freshwater Bay
Public toilets: Freshwater Bay and Yarmouth

1 From the car park, turn right along the road, then left before the bus shelter along a metalled track, signed 'Coastal Path'. After 50 yards (46m) bear right through a gate and follow the well-walked path through a gateway and up to the memorial cross at the summit of Tennyson Down.

2 Continue down the wide grassy swathe, which narrows between gorse bushes, to reach the replica of the Old Nodes Beacon. Here, turn very sharp right down a chalk track. At a junction (car park right) keep straight on up the narrow path.

3 The path widens, then descends to a gate into woodland. Proceed close to the woodland fringe before emerging into more open countryside. Just beyond a disused pit on your right, fork left at a waymark post down a narrower path. Cross a stile, then follow the enclosed path as it turns sharp left to a stile. Cross the next field to a stile and turn right along the field-edge to a stile.

4 Cross a farm track, go through a gate and walk along the track (F47) beside Farringford Hotel. Pass beneath a wooden footbridge and continue downhill to a gate and the road. (Turn left if you wish to visit the hotel.) Turn right; then, opposite the thatched church, turn left down Blackbridge Road. Just before Black Bridge, turn left into Afton Marshes Nature Reserve.

5 Join the nature trail, following it across a footbridge and beside the stream to the A3055 (this can be very wet in winter). Turn left and almost immediately cross over to join bridleway (F61) along the course of the old railway. In 0.5 mile (800m) reach the Causeway. Turn left here for the longer loop of Walk 49 or to visit Freshwater church and the Red Lion.

6 On this shorter walk turn right and continue to the B3399. Turn left and shortly cross on to unmetalled Manor Road. In a few paces, bear left, signed 'Freshwater Way', and ascend across grassland towards Afton Down.

7 Keep ahead at a junction of paths beside the golf course, soon to follow the gravel track right to the clubhouse. Go through a gate, pass in front of the building to reach the access track, keeping left to the A3055. Turn right downhill into Freshwater Bay.

Extension
On reaching the Causeway after Point **5**, turn left and follow the lane to All Saints Church and the Red Lion in Freshwater. Take the waymarked path (Freshwater Way) between a cottage and the churchyard wall. Cross a stile and continue along the farm road. At the farmyard entrance cross the double stile on the left and bear right along the field-edge to a stile. Go through a kissing gate at the entrance to Kings Manor Farm, and follow the signposted Freshwater Way along a wide track to a gate and junction of paths. Climb the stile on the right, pass through a copse and bear left, uphill, along the field-edge. Enter the field on your left and walk along the right-hand edge to a stile. Drop down through woodland, and turn left along a track to reach the A3054. Turn right and cross the bridge into Yarmouth, bearing left at the roundabout into the town centre.

From the Square, head for the church and walk along St James Street. Cross the A3054 into Mill Road, then at the sharp left bend, keep ahead towards the old tide mill, built in 1793 to harness the tidal flow of the estuary. Walk by the mudflats and turn right along the old railway line, following it for 1.5 miles (2.4km) to the Causeway. Turn left to re-join the walk at Point **6**.

STANDING GUARD OVER ARUNDEL

Walk

B

A very varied walk following the River Arun to Arundel Park and concluding with a tour of this handsome Sussex town.

Arundel Castle was completely rebuilt in the 19th century

Distance: 3.25 miles (5.3km)
Minimum time: 2hrs
Ascent/Gradient: 197ft (60m) ▲▲▲
Level of difficulty: +++
Paths: Riverside and parkland paths, some road walking, 2 stiles
Landscape: Valley, rolling parkland and town
Suggested map: OS Explorer 121 Arundel & Pulborough
Start/finish: Grid reference: TQ 020071
Dog friendliness: Off lead on tow path. Not permitted in Arundel Park. Final stage of the walk is along busy roads in Arundel
Parking: Mill Road fee-paying car park, Arundel
Public toilets: Arundel town centre and Swanbourne Lake
Note: Arundel Park is closed annually on 24 March

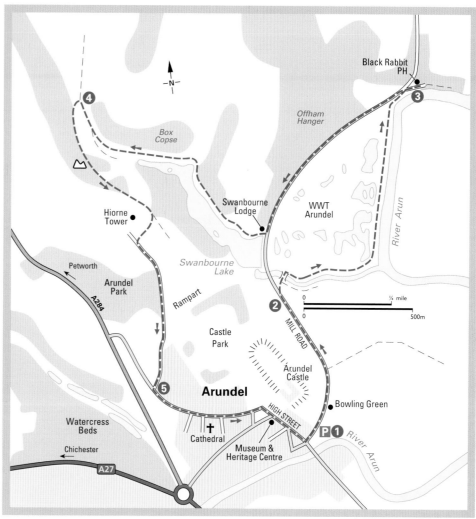

❶ From the car park in Mill Road, turn right and walk along the tree-lined pavement. Pass the bowling green and a glance to your left will reveal a dramatic view of historic Arundel Castle with its imposing battlements.

❷ Follow the road to the elegant stone bridge, avoid the first path on the right and cross over via a footbridge and turn right to join the riverside path, partly shaded by overhanging trees. Emerging from the trees, the path cuts across lush, low-lying ground to reach the western bank of the Arun. Turn left here and walk beside the reed-fringed Arun to the Black Rabbit pub, which can be seen standing out against a curtain of trees.

❸ From the Black Rabbit, turn left on the minor road back towards Arundel, passing the entrance to the WWT Arundel Wetland Centre. Make for the gate leading into Arundel Park and follow the path alongside Swanbourne Lake. Eventually the lake fades from view as the walk reaches deeper into the park. Ignore a turning branching off to the left, just before a gate and stile, and follow the path as it curves gently to the right.

❹ Turn sharply to the left at the next waymarked junction and begin a fairly steep ascent, with the footpath through the park seen curving away down to the left, back towards the lake. This stretch of the walk offers glorious views over elegant Arundel Park. Head for a stile and gate, then bear immediately right up the bank. Cross the grass, following the waymarks and keeping to the left of Hiorne Tower. On reaching a driveway, turn left and walk down to Park Lodge. Keep to the right by the private drive and make for the road.

❺ Turn left, pass Arundel Cathedral and bear left at the road junction by the entrance to Arundel Castle. Go down the hill, back into the centre of Arundel. You'll find Mill Road at the bottom of the High Street.

Walk C

DEVIL'S DYKE AND THE WORLD'S GRANDEST VIEW

A fine walk with glimpses over the most famous of all the dry chalk valleys.

The view from nearby Fulking Escarpment

Distance: 2.75 miles (4.4km)
Minimum time: 1hr 30min
Ascent/Gradient: 656ft (200m) ▲▲▲
Level of difficulty: +++
Paths: Field and woodland paths, 7 stiles
Landscape: Chalk grassland, steep escarpment and woodland
Suggested map: OS Explorer 122 Brighton & Hove
Start/finish: Grid reference: TQ 269112
Dog friendliness: Mostly off lead. On lead on approach to Poynings
Parking: Summer Down free car park
Public toilets: By Devil's Dyke pub

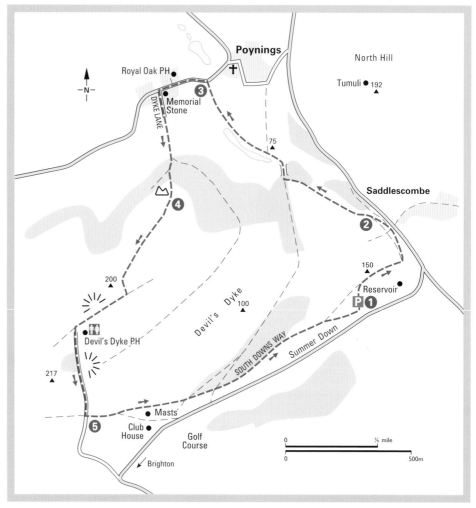

① From the Summer Down car park, go through the kissing gate and then veer right. Join the South Downs Way and follow it alongside lines of trees. Soon the path curves left and drops down to the road. Part company with the South Downs Way at this point, as it crosses over to join the private road to Saddlescombe Farm, and follow the verge for about 75 yards (68m). Bear left at the footpath sign and drop down the bank to a stile.

② Follow the line of the tarmac lane as it curves right to reach a waymark. Leave the lane and walk ahead alongside power lines, keeping the line of trees and bushes on the right. Look for a narrow path disappearing into the vegetation and make for a stile. Drop down some steps into the woods and turn right at a junction with a bridleway. Take the path running off half-left and follow it between fields and a wooded dell. Pass over a stile and continue to a stile in the left boundary. Cross a footbridge to a further stile and now turn right towards Poynings.

③ Head for a gate and footpath sign and turn left at the road. Follow the parallel path along to the Royal Oak and then continue to Dyke Lane on the left. There is a memorial stone here, dedicated to the memory of George Stephen Cave Cuttress, a resident of Poynings for more than 50 years, and erected by his widow. Follow the tarmac bridleway and soon it narrows to a path. On reaching the fork, by a National Trust sign for Devil's Dyke, veer right and begin climbing the steps.

④ Follow the path up to a gate and continue up the stairs. From the higher ground there are breathtaking views to the north and west. Make for a kissing gate and head up the slope towards the inn. Keep the Devil's Dyke pub on your left and take the road round to the left, passing a bridleway on the left. Follow the path parallel to the road and look to the left for a definitive view of Devil's Dyke.

⑤ Head for the South Downs Way and turn left by a National Trust sign for Summer Down to a stile and gate. Follow the trail, keeping Devil's Dyke down to your left, and eventually you reach a stile leading into Summer Down car park.

Devil's Dyke, West Sussex

BATTLE – BRITAIN'S MOST FAMOUS BATTLEFIELD

Take a walk into history and visit the field where two armies battled for the English crown.

Distance: 5 miles (8km)
Minimum time: 2hrs 30min
Ascent/Gradient: 448ft (140m) ▲▲▲
Level of difficulty: +++
Paths: Field and woodland paths, some road walking, 10 stiles
Landscape: Gently undulating farmland and woodland
Suggested map: OS Explorer 124 Hastings & Bexhill
Start/finish: Grid reference: TQ 747156
Dog friendliness: Enclosed woodland paths and stretches of 1066 Country Walk suitable for dogs off lead
Parking: Pay car park at Battle Abbey
Public toilets: Mount Street car park in Battle, Brede Lane in Sedlescombe and Battle Abbey

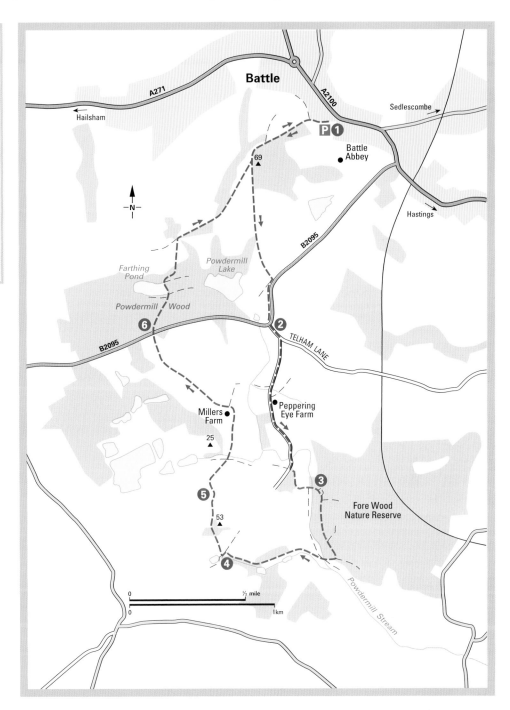

❶ Turn left out of the car park and follow the track to a gate. Keep left along the bridleway beside woodland, the path swinging left to a fingerpost and junction of paths. Bear off left with the 1066 Bexhill Walk marker and walk down the field-edge and through two gates. Join a track and keep ahead, soon to cross a drive via stiles, and follow the fenced path along the field-edge high above the road to a stile.

❷ Cross the B2095 (take care – dangerous bend), walk along Telham Lane and take the Private Road right towards Peppering Eye Farm. Keep to the metalled drive for 0.5 mile (0.8km), passing Stumblet's Barn and crossing a stream to ascend to a junction of paths by Powdermill Cottage. Turn left along a track through the trees, drop downhill and bear off left with the waymarker across the centre of a field to cross a footbridge and enter Fore Wood (RSPB Nature Reserve).

❸ Bear right and follow the yellow-arrowed route through the edge of the wood, ignoring paths left and right, turning right where the path curves left at a bench. Go left at the fingerpost, cross a footbridge and follow the path right through scrub, parallel with the stream. On reaching an open field, keep left around the field-edge, pass a pond and gently climb along a defined path along the top edge of a field. The path becomes a track through trees, passing another larger pond, then soon emerges into a field, keeping ahead along the field-edge to a junction of tracks.

❹ Bear left, then immediately right at a fork, curving left around a pond to reach a waymarker close to pheasant pens. Turn sharp right up the grassy bank, soon enter woodland

and continue to a stile and footbridge. Turn left to another stile, then right along the field-edge passing a pond. Head across the field, pass beneath power cables and through a gate.

❺ Bear diagonally right downhill across the field to a gate and track. Just before some barns, climb the stile on the right to follow the arrowed path around Millers Farm to reach a gate. Re-join the track and follow it out to a road.

❻ Cross the road, pass beside a gate and follow the path through Powdermill Wood. Cross the top end of Farthing Pond, bear sharp right and immediately fork off left, uphill along a narrow path through coppice woodland to a stile. Cross the field aiming to the right of a cottage to reach a stile. Turn right along a track, go through a gate and follow the 1066 Walk uphill through a field and soon retrace your outward route back to the car park.

Walk E

TRAILS OF THE NEW FOREST

Ancient oaks, historic inclosures and exotic towering conifers in the New Forest.

New Forest ponies

Distance: 8 miles (12.9km)

Minimum time: 4hrs

Ascent/Gradient: 318ft (97m) ▲▲▲

Level of difficulty: +++

Paths: Grass and gravel forest tracks, heathland paths, some roads

Landscape: Ornamental Drive, ancient forest inclosures and heathland

Suggested map: OS Explorer OL 22 New Forest

Start/finish: Grid reference: SU 266057

Dog friendliness: Keep dogs under control at all times

Parking: Brock Hill Forestry Commission car park, just off A35

Public toilets: Blackwater car park

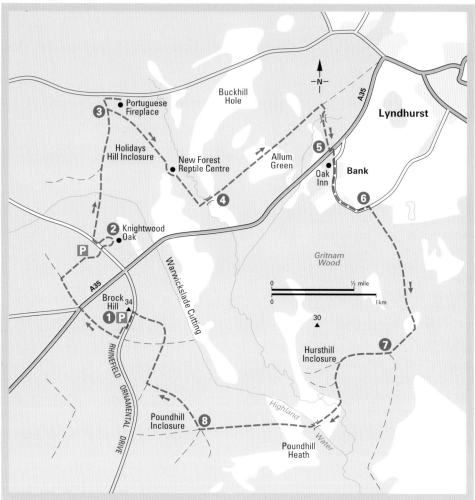

❶ Take the gravel path at the southern end of the car park (beyond the information post), parallel with the road. In 100 yards (91m), turn right just before a bench seat and descend to a gravel track. Cross straight over; then, where the path curves left, keep ahead to reach a gate and the A35. Cross over the A35 (take care), go through a gate and keep to the path, uphill to a junction. Turn right and follow the path to Knightwood Oak car park, then follow the sign to the Knightwood Oak itself.

❷ Return towards the car park and bear right along the road. Turn right again after a few paces, on to a path into mixed woodland. Cross a stream and soon reach a gravel track. Bear right and keep to this trail, passing red marker posts, to a fork. Keep left to reach a gate and road. Turn right to view the Portuguese Fireplace.

❸ Return through Holidays Hill Inclosure to the fork of tracks. Bear left and follow this to the New Forest Reptile Centre. Walk along the access drive past a cottage dated 1811, then, at a barrier on your left, drop down on to a path and follow it across a bridge.

❹ Keep to the main path for 0.75 mile (1.2km), skirting the walls to Allum Green and several clearings, then gently climb through trees to a defined crossing of paths and turn right. Shortly, bear half right across a clearing and concrete footbridge, then continue through the woodland edge to an electricity pole. Bear right for 20 yards (18m), then left through a gate to the A35.

❺ Turn left, then almost immediately right across the road to a gate. Walk ahead to a garden boundary and turn right, the narrow path leading to a lane in Bank. Turn right, pass the Oak Inn and walk through the hamlet.

❻ Just beyond the cattle grid, turn right through a gate on to a gravelled track towards Brockenhurst. Follow this track for nearly a mile (1.4km) to a junction at a small green.

❼ Fork right towards Brockenhurst, and enter Hursthill Inclosure at a gate. Drop down past a turning on the right, then climb again and bear left at a fork. Keep to the waymarked track as it drops past another turning on the right and leaves Hursthill Inclosure at a gate. Walk the long straight track to the bridge over Highland Water, and follow the track round to the right. Soon a gate leads the waymarked trail into Poundhill Inclosure, and another straight section brings you to a five-way junction at waymark post 24.

❽ Turn right here. Ignore all turnings, and follow the track as it turns sharp right and winds its way to a junction with the Ornamental Drive. Turn left for the last 100 yards (91m) back to the car park.

ALFRED'S ANCIENT CAPITAL

Explore Winchester's historic streets, Cathedral Close and the beautiful Itchen Valley.

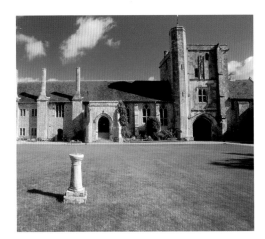

St Cross Hospital, Winchester

Distance: 4 miles (6.4km)
Minimum time: 2hrs
Ascent/Gradient: 499ft (152m) ▲▲▲
Level of difficulty: +++
Paths: Established riverside paths through water-meadows, 3 stiles
Landscape: City streets, riverside, water-meadow and downland
Suggested map: OS Explorer 132 Winchester
Start/finish: Grid reference: SU 485294
Dog friendliness: Under control through water-meadows and by golf course
Parking: Pay-and-display car parks in city centre
Public toilets: The Broadway, Winchester

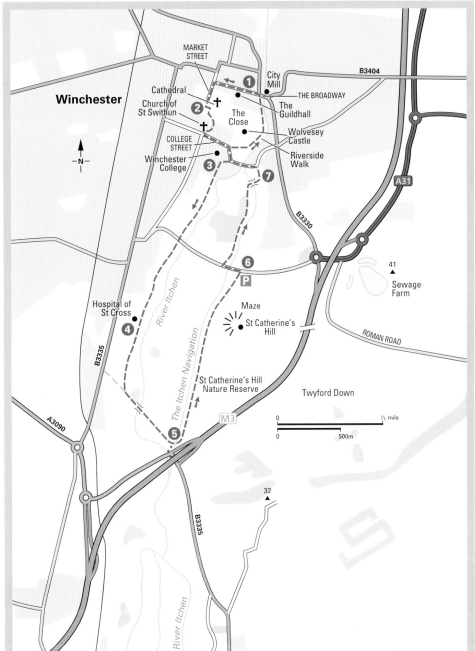

❶ From King Alfred's statue on the Broadway, walk towards the city centre, passing the Guildhall (tourist information centre) on your left. Join the High Street, then in 100 yards (91m), turn left along Market Street. Continue ahead on to Cathedral Green to pass the cathedral's main door.

❷ Turn left down a cloister (signed to Wolvesey Castle), then right through the Close, to Cheyney Court and exit via Prior's Gate. Turn left though Kingsgate, with the tiny Church of St Swithun above, then turn left down College Street and shortly pass the entrance to Winchester College. Beyond the road barrier, turn right along College Walk, then turn right at the end of the wall, along a college access road.

❸ Go left by a private entrance to the college. Follow the path beside the River Itchen for 0.5 mile (800m) to a gate and road bridge. Cross over and follow the riverside gravel path to a gate and cross open meadow towards the Hospital of St Cross.

❹ Keep left alongside the wall and through an avenue of trees to a stile. Keep ahead on the gravel path to two further stiles and join a farm track leading to a traffic-free lane. Turn left and continue across the River Itchen to reach a junction of metalled paths by the M3.

❺ Turn left along a path. Go under an old railway and pass a gate on your right (access to St Catherine's Hill). Keep left at a fork and drop down to follow a narrow path by the Itchen Navigation. Go through the car park to the road.

❻ Turn left across the bridge and take the footpath immediately right. Keep to the path beside the water, disregarding the path left (College Nature Reserve). Soon cross the bridge by rowing sheds to join a metalled track.

❼ Turn left, then left again at the road. Follow it right along College Walk and turn right at the end on to a metalled path. Pass the Old Bishop's Palace (Wolvesey Castle) and follow the path beside the Itchen to Bridge Street, opposite the National Trust's City Mill. Turn left to King Alfred's statue.

A PILGRIMAGE TO WAVERLEY

By the enchanting ruins of Waverley Abbey in the Wey Valley.

The ruins of Waverley Abbey, by the River Wey

Distance: 3 miles (4.8km)
Minimum time: 1hr 30min
Ascent/Gradient: 164ft (50m) ▲▲▲
Level of difficulty: +++
Paths: Sandy and easy to follow, two sections on minor roads
Landscape: Gently rolling, well-wooded countryside
Suggested map: OS Explorer 145 Guildford & Farnham
Start/finish: Grid reference: SU 870455
Dog friendliness: Generally good, but dogs must be on lead along roads
Parking: Waverley Lane between Farnham and Elstead
Public toilets: None en route

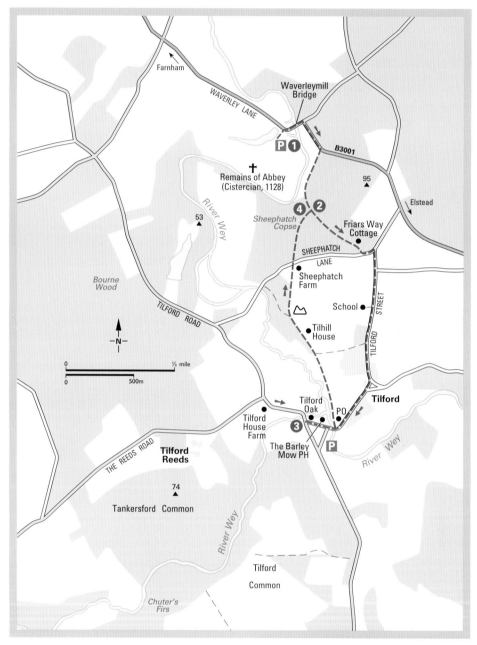

❶ Turn right out of the car park, taking care to watch out for traffic, and follow Waverley Lane (B3001) as it zigzags left and right over Waverleymill Bridge. Continue for 200 yards (182m) until the road bears to the left. Turn right here, on to the public byway, and follow it through to a metal gate and public byway signpost.

❷ Keep straight ahead and follow the path past Friars Way Cottage until you come to Sheephatch Lane. Turn left briefly, then right at the junction with Tilford Street; there's no pavement for the first 400 yards (366m), so go carefully. Now follow the road past the school, over the River Wey bridge and on to Tilford village green, where you'll find the Tilford Oak and The Barley Mow pub.

❸ To continue, retrace your steps across the river bridge. Almost at once, turn left at the public bridleway sign just before the post office. The path climbs gently for 500 yards (457m) and brings you to a tarmac lane. Turn left, pass Tilhill House, and continue up the narrow sandy track straight ahead. At the top of

the short slope, fork right at the public byway waymark for the 400 yards (366m) climb to Sheephatch Farm. Cross Sheephatch Lane, where a public byway sign points your way up the gravelled track opposite. The track leads you confidently through Sheephatch Copse, and soon you'll be dropping down through an ancient sunken way to re-join your outward track at a metal gate and public byway signpost.

❹ Turn left here for the easy walk back to Waverley Lane (B3001). Watch out for the traffic as you turn left, then retrace your outward route over Waverleymill Bridge and back to the car park.

The monks at Waverley Abbey built bridges over the River Wey in the 13th century

POOH'S ASHDOWN FOREST

A spectacular woodland walk exploring the haunts of A. A. Milne's much-loved character, Winnie the Pooh and friends.

Distance: 7 miles (11.3km)
Minimum time: 3hrs
Ascent/Gradient: 170ft (55m) ▲▲▲
Level of difficulty: +++
Paths: Paths and tracks across farmland and woodland, 20 stiles
Landscape: Undulating farmland and dense woodland
Suggested map: OS Explorer 135 Ashdown Forest
Start/finish: Grid reference: TQ 473332
Dog friendliness: Some woodland stretches suitable for dogs off lead. On lead where notices indicate
Parking: Pooh car park (free), off B2026 south of Hartfield
Public toilets: By village hall in Hartfield

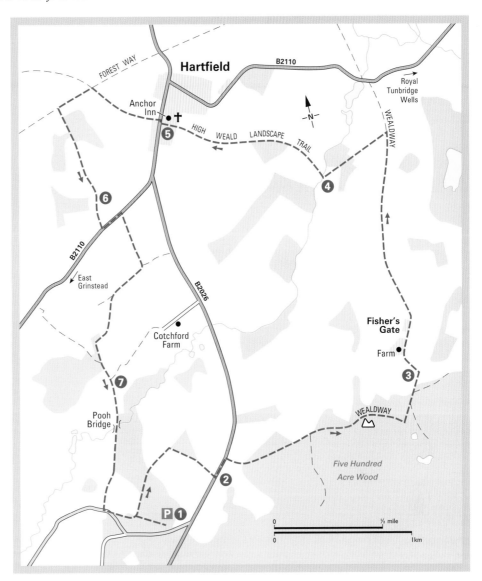

❶ Follow the path signposted 'Pooh Sticks Bridge', take the third turning right and descend to a kissing gate. Cross a tree-ringed field to a kissing gate near the corner, follow the woodland path alongside fencing to a stile and then the left-hand field-edge to a track in the corner; turn right. Cross a drive to a stile and keep ahead, following the path around a paddock to a stile and the road.

❷ Turn left, then bear right opposite The Paddocks and follow the path through Five Hundred Acre Wood to reach the Wealdway. Continue ahead, passing Kovacs Lodge. Climb quite steeply and make a wide sweep to the left. Follow the track round to the right to a fork, veer left and approach a sign for 'Fisher's Gate'.

❸ Take the right-hand path and skirt a farm. Re-join the drive and keep right, following the Wealdway as it cuts across undulating farmland for 0.75 mile (1.2km). Pass a turning to Buckhurst and then bear left over a stile to follow the High Weald Landscape Trail. Cross the field to a gate and stile and cut through the wood to a brick bridge.

❹ Turn right here and follow the fence, passing some paddocks. Veer right through the gateway in the field corner and make for the next field ahead. Head diagonally left across farmland to a stile. Keep to the right edge of the field to a stile, then cross a footbridge and continue by the field-edge. Turn left at a stile and enter the village of Hartfield.

❺ Bear right at the B2026, then left along the left-hand edge of a recreation ground. Cross a stile in the field corner and continue over the next stile to the Forest Way. Turn left and follow the old trackbed until you reach a gate on the left. Cross the pasture to a gate and follow the woodland bridleway. Emerging from the trees, continue to Culvers Farm.

❻ Make for the road. When you reach it, turn left and walk along to the first right-hand footpath, signposted 'Pooh Bridge'. Cross the stile here and follow the clear track ahead to three further stiles before crossing a field. Follow the waymarks and make for a stile in

the corner. Cross a drive to another stile and head diagonally down the field to a stile in the corner. Continue on the path and head for the next stile. Follow the lane south.

❼ When it sweeps left towards Cotchford Farm, go straight on along the public bridleway to Pooh Bridge, then follow the track as it climbs gradually alongside woodland and paddocks. Turn left at the road and, when it bends around to the right, go straight ahead into the trees. Follow the footpath through the wood, back to the Pooh car park.

MR DARCY'S CHILHAM

A lovely walk in countryside close to where Jane Austen wrote Pride and Prejudice.

Black and white timbered buildings, Chilham, Kent

Distance: 6.25 miles (10.1km)
Minimum time: 3hrs
Ascent/Gradient: 591ft (180m) ▲▲▲
Level of difficulty: +++
Paths: Parkland, field paths and woodland tracks, 10 stiles
Landscape: Rolling Kentish countryside with views of Chilham Castle
Suggested map: OS Explorer 149 Sittingbourne & Faversham
Start/finish: Grid reference: TQ 068536
Dog friendliness: Good, though must be kept on lead near grazing animals
Parking: Chilham car park
Public toilets: At car park

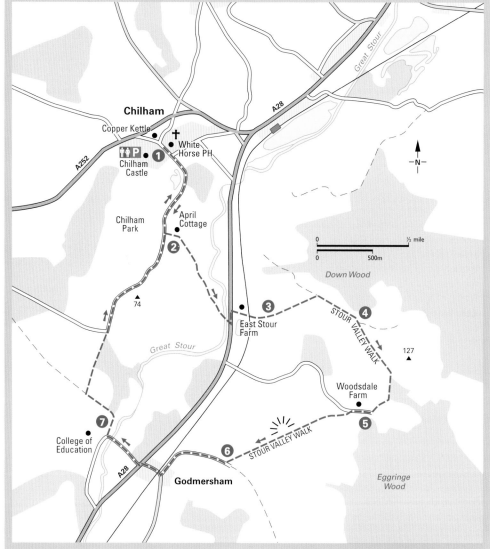

① From the village square, walk down School Hill and follow Mountain Street right for 0.5 mile (800m), skirting Chilham Castle grounds to reach April Cottage. Here you take the waymarked path on the left.

② Pass between the gardens, then fork right across the field to the hedge in the far corner. Cross the stile into the water-meadows beside the Great Stour. Follow the hedge right and through two fields to reach a footbridge over the river. Cross the bridge to reach the busy A28. Turn left here, walk up to East Stour Farm, then turn right and walk through the farmyard, cross a stile and go under the railway bridge.

③ Ignore the stile on your left, cross the stile ahead and bear left through the trees, the path gradually climbing up the valley. Keep an eye out for badger setts in the hedge along here. Continue ahead and follow the Stour Valley Walk as it bears right.

④ At a crossing of paths, keep right with the Stour Valley Walk, go through the wood, and then cross a stile. Continue up a field and into more woodland, where you soon turn right to follow the Stour Valley Walk. Descend and bear right to a stile, crossing a field to another stile and the road.

⑤ Walk right to Woodsdale Farm and climb the stile opposite. Walk diagonally uphill to the top corner, cross another stile and then walk a short distance ahead before forking right along the Stour Valley Walk. Follow this as it takes you diagonally down the fields – look back for great views of Chilham Castle – and through a hedge. Continue in the same direction down to Eggarton Lane.

⑥ Turn right, walk down the lane, and then turn right again under the railway and up to the A28. Cross over and walk along the lane ahead. After crossing the Great Stour, go through the gates of the College of Education and immediately right into the parkland of Godmersham Park.

⑦ Follow the public footpath across a paddock, go through a gate and walk up the track to a crossing of tracks at Deer Lodge. Turn right and continue through two gates to reach the road. Follow this road all the way back into Chilham.

The 15th-century White Horse Inn. St Mary's church is in the background

ABINGDON'S ARCHITECTURE

Explore a former county town and then view it from a classic riverside path.

St Helen's Church, Abingdon

Distance: 7 miles (11.3km)

Minimum time: 2hrs 45min

Ascent/Gradient: Negligible ▲▲▲

Level of difficulty: +++

Paths: Field paths and tracks, stretches of road and Thames Path. Town and village streets (roads can be busy), 4 stiles

Landscape: Flat farmland and meadows south of Abingdon

Suggested map: OS Explorer 170 Abingdon, Wantage

Start/finish: Grid reference: SU503941

Dog friendliness: On lead in Sutton Courtney; not ideal in Abingdon

Parking: Small car park south of the church at Sutton Courtenay

Public toilets: None at start but various in Abingdon, including Old Gaol Leisure Centre and Abbey Meadow Park

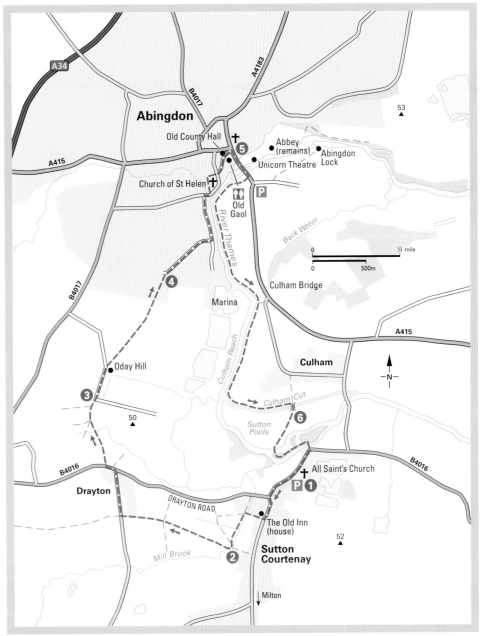

❶ From the car park go across to the B4016 and turn left, joining the adjacent tree-lined path. Take the turning for Milton then, 25 yards (23m) before the recreation ground road, take a narrow fenced path beside a house, The Old Inn. Cross a footbridge to some cottages and swing left to a kissing gate. Keep left at the immediate fork and follow the path alongside the Mill Brook. Cross a double stile and a footbridge and continue to the next stile and footbridge.

❷ Turn right to walk nearly 0.75 mile (1.2km), initially on tarmac but then a broad track, narrowing to a path between hedges. At a road turn right, then left at the next junction, following Drayton Road. Take the second signposted right of way on the right.

❸ Keep ahead when the path joins a tarmac road and, when it curves left by a pair of cottages, look for a stile on the right. Go diagonally across the field, into the next pasture. Keep quite close to the left boundary and aim for some tall trees and houses in the distance. Veer right to the top right-hand corner of the field and find a footbridge with a handrail. Walk ahead with the field margin on your right. At the houses join a tarmac path. This is Overmead.

❹ Follow Overmead, from number 31 counting down all the way to 1, to reach a T-junction. Turn right, passing Lambrick Way, to the next T-junction. Turn left and keep alongside the Thames to The Old Anchor Inn. Soon turn left through an archway by some almshouses. Keep the Church of St Helen on the right and head for the road. Cross over into East St Helen Street and make for the Old County Hall.

❺ Turn right to reach Bridge Street, pass the Broad Face pub and cross the River Thames to the far bank. Go down the steps on the left to the towpath, pass under the road bridge and walk along the riverside path. Pass an illustrated map of Abingdon, go through a gate and cross meadows alongside the Thames, passing the ancient Culham Bridge on the left. Follow the line of Culham Reach and keep beside the water until you reach a sign for Sutton Courtenay.

❻ Once over the cut, follow the path across fields and back to the Thames. Cross several bridges and weirs at Sutton Pools and veer right at the road, passing The Wharf on the right. Follow the village street to the parish church and return to the car park.

TURVILLE ON TV

Climb into glorious woods and enjoy views you may find familiar from
The Vicar of Dibley *and the film* Chitty Chitty Bang Bang.

The Chiltern village of Turville featured in The Vicar of Dibley

Distance: 3 miles (4.8km)
Minimum time: 1hr 30min
Ascent/Gradient: 150ft (45m) ▲▲▲
Level of difficulty: +++
Paths: Field and woodland paths, some road walking, 4 stiles
Landscape: Rolling Chiltern countryside, farmland and woodland
Suggested map: OS Explorer 171 Chiltern Hills West
Start/finish: Grid reference: SU 767911
Dog friendliness: On lead around Turville and Skirmett and across farmland
Parking: Small parking area in centre of Turville
Public toilets: None en route

❶ Take the lane just to the left of the church entrance, with Sleepy Cottage on the corner. Pass Square Close Cottages and the village school before continuing on the Chiltern Way through a tunnel of trees. Climb gently to a gate and keep ahead along the field-edge to a second waymark in the boundary. Branch half-left at this point, heading diagonally down the field to a stile.

❷ Cross the road to a further stile and follow the track through the trees, passing a gas installation on the right. Pass a bench on the left before breaking cover from the trees. Avoid a path branching off to the right and continue up the field slope to the next belt of trees. Turville and its windmill are clearly seen over to the left. Enter the woodland and keep left at the junction. Follow the clear wide path as it contours round the slopes, with the ground, dotted with beech trees, rippling away to the left. Descend the hillside, keeping to the woodland edge. Follow the fence and bear left at the next corner, heading to a stile by Poynatts Farm.

❸ Walk along the drive to the road, bear right and enter Skirmett. On the right is Cobs Cottage and next door to it is the aptly named Ramblers. Pass The Frog Inn and follow the road south to the next junction. An assortment of houses, a telephone box and a postbox line the route. Turn left, pass a stile on the right and walk along to the next left footpath. Go through a gate, follow the field-edge to a bungalow and gate, go through to a drive and make for the road.

❹ Bear right, heading out of the village to the junction with Watery Lane. 'Except for access' signs can be seen here now. Look for the gate and footpath immediately to the right of it. Cross the field to a half-concealed gate in the corner and make for the boundary hedge ahead in the next field. Through the gate, head diagonally right to a hedge by some houses. Through a gate, turn right and follow the lane past a junction to Fingest and visit the church of St Batholomew. Out of same gate bear right at '30mph' sign on to the footpath via a gate. Flint wall gives way to hedge, then field.

❺ Through a gate, cross the road to follow the Chiltern Way between trees, offering teasing glimpses of the Chilterns themselves. Cross a stile and head diagonally down the field towards Turville. Make for a track and follow it to the village green.

The village of Fingest in the Chilterns

GUTS AND GARTERS IN THE RIPPER'S EAST END

Tracing the path of one of the world's most notorious serial killers, Jack the Ripper, in London's East End.

Spitalfields Market, London

Distance: 2.75 miles (4.4km)
Minimum time: 1hr 30min
Ascent/Gradient: Negligible ▲▲▲
Level of difficulty: +++
Paths: Paved streets
Landscape: Plenty of narrow streets and some main roads
Suggested map: AA Street by Street London
Start/finish: Grid reference: SX 652442
Dog friendliness: On lead
Public toilets: None en route

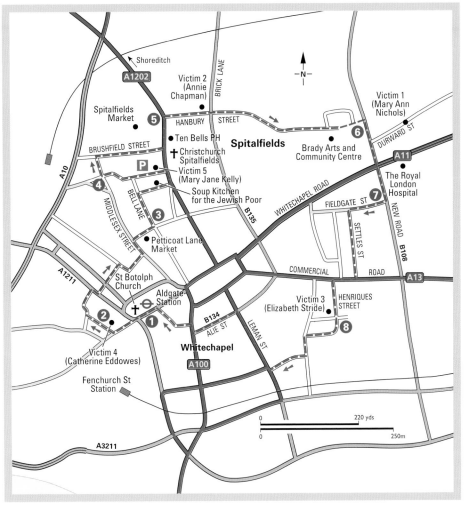

❶ With Aldgate tube station behind you, walk towards St Botolph without Aldgate church on the right. Cross the road at the pedestrian lights and continue ahead, past the school. Turn right along Mitre Street. A few paces further is Mitre Square, where the fourth body, Catherine Eddowes, was discovered by the benches.

❷ Continue ahead, turning right into Creechurch Lane and past some posts marking the boundaries of the City of London. Go across two main roads to reach Stoney Lane. At the end bear right into Gravel Lane and, once past the parade of shops, turn left along Middlesex Street. Take the first right into Wentworth Street, more commonly called Petticoat Lane and host to the famous, thriving market.

❸ Turn left into Bell Lane and right into Brune Street, where you'll see the remains of a Victorian soup kitchen. At the end turn left and left again into White's Row, where the fifth body, that of Mary Jane Kelly, was found (the site is now a car park). Cross Bell Lane and follow Artillery Lane as it narrows to form an alleyway (Artillery Passage).

❹ Turn right into Sandy's Row, past a synagogue, then right and left to reach Brushfield Street. Turn right again past

Spitalfields Market and you'll end up at Hawksmoor's majestic Christ Church Spitalfields, the white building ahead. Bear left to cross at the pedestrian lights and turn left along Commercial Street.

❺ As the road bends, turn right into Hanbury Street, where the Truman's Brewery denotes the murder scene of Annie Chapman, the second victim. Cross Brick Lane and continue along this road for another 500 yards (457m), past the Brady Arts and Community Centre and along an alleyway.

❻ Turn right at the main road and look out for Durward Street on the left, which leads to the site of the first murder (Mary Ann Nichols), although little now remains of the original streets. Instead continue ahead and cross the busy traffic on Whitechapel Road into New Road.

❼ When you get to Fieldgate Street turn right and then take the third left into Settles Street. When you reach the end bear right and cross over at the pedestrian lights, to turn left into Henriques Street. The school here stands on the site of the Ripper's third victim, Elizabeth Stride. Notice the signs 'Cookery' and 'Laundry' above the school's entrance door.

❽ Continue ahead, following the road as it swings to the right. At the end, turn left and then immediately right into Hooper Street and continue ahead, then turn right into Leman Street. Turn right and at the crossroads turn left along Alie Street. At the end cross the road and bear right and then left along Little Somerset Street, which comes out opposite where you began the walk at Aldgate tube.

A DICKENS OF A WALK AT ROCHESTER

Rochester's characterful streets are straight out of a novel by Charles Dickens.

Restoration House, made famous by Charles Dickens' novel Great Expectations

Distance: 6 miles (9.7km)
Minimum time: 3hrs
Ascent/Gradient: 98ft (30m) ▲▲▲
Level of difficulty: +++
Paths: City streets and footpaths/cycleways
Landscape: Historic townscapes and some rundown riverside sections
Suggested map: OS Explorer 163 Gravesend & Rochester
Start/finish: Grid reference: TQ 744685
Dog friendliness: Too busy for most dogs
Parking: Blue Boar car park
Public toilets: At tourist information centre, also at Northgate

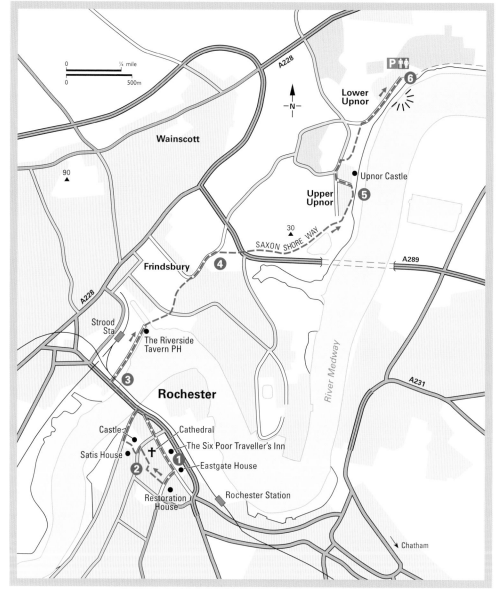

❶ From the Blue Boar car park go left into the pedestrianised part of the High Street. Turn right up Crow Lane, then right by Restoration House into The Vines, a small park. Bear right halfway across the park, then turn right and walk down the hill to the cathedral.

❷ Cross the road, turn left and walk round the castle. Pass Satis House, then turn right and walk by the River Medway until you reach Rochester Bridge. Cross the bridge and, at the traffic lights, go right along Canal Road, which runs under the railway bridge.

❸ Walk along the river, pass The Riverside Tavern and follow the footpath sign. This brings you out to a new estate, where you bear right along a footpath/cycle track, which

is part of the Saxon Shore Way. Keep walking in the same direction along this track, which is intersected by roads at several points. At one point, pass the rusting hull of a ship that could have come from the pages of a Dickens novel.

❹ At a bend in the road the Saxon Shore Way bears right, crosses industrial land and the A289, and then finally takes you close to the riverbank again. At the river continue walking ahead as far as the entrance to Upnor Castle.

❺ Turn left along Upnor's tiny High Street, and then go to the right. Where a road joins from the left, keep walking ahead to join the footpath that runs to the right of the main road. Follow this to Lower Upnor, where you

turn right to reach the quay and enjoy great views of the Medway. For even better views, take a short detour up the hill to your left. Prehistoric wild animals once roamed these slopes, as archaeological evidence shows. One of the most interesting discoveries in the area was made in 1911, when a group of Royal Engineers working near Upnor dug up the remains of a mammoth dating back to the last ice age. It was taken to the Natural History Museum in London.

❻ Retrace your steps back into Rochester. After crossing Rochester Bridge, walk along the High Street, passing sights such as The Six Poor Traveller's Inn and Eastgate House, which is located beside the Blue Boar car park.

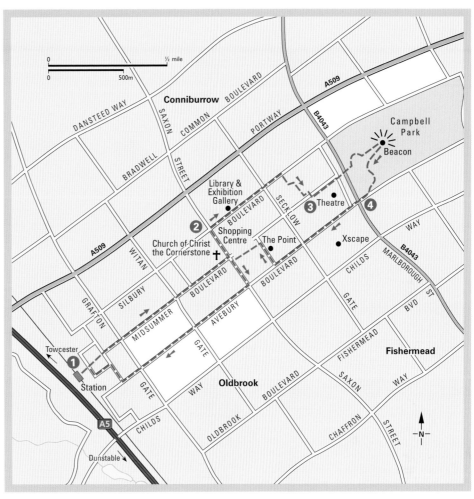

A TOUR OF MILTON KEYNES, CITY OF THE FUTURE

See how a brand-new city has been shaped and styled on this unique walk with a strong architectural theme.

The pyramidial entrance to the Point complex

Distance: 3.5 miles (5.7km)
Minimum time: 2hrs
Ascent/Gradient: Negligble ▲▲▲
Level of difficulty: +++
Paths: Paved walkways, boulevards and park paths
Landscape: City centre and park
Suggested map: OS Explorer 192 Milton Keynes & Buckingham, or street map from tourist information centre
Start/finish: Grid reference: SP 842380
Dog friendliness: Probably not most dogs' idea of fun
Parking: Car park at Milton Keynes station
Public toilets: Milton Keynes station and shopping centres

❶ With your back to the station, aim slightly left, line up with a row of flagpoles and make for two underpasses. Keep ahead along Midsummer Boulevard, passing the sculpture on the left. Make for the next subway and cross Witan Gate and Upper 5th Street. Swing left just before the next subway to visit the domed Church of Christ the Cornerstone. Keep the church on your left and continue to Silbury Boulevard, passing under the subway ahead.

❷ Turn right through a subway and pass Milton Keynes Library and Exhibition Gallery. Pass North 9th Street and a statue of the Lloyds black horse at Lloyds Court. Swing right and pass under the road to approach the shopping

centre at Deer Walk. Don't enter the complex here, but instead turn left and walk along to the next entrance, numbered 11, at Eagle Walk. Go straight through, pass a map of the shopping centre and emerge at Entrance 12, Midsummer Boulevard.

❸ Turn left to Field Walk and turn right here to cross the boulevard. Bear left to reach the tourist information centre, Milton Keynes Theatre and the city's gallery. Continue ahead under the subway and cross the footbridge into Campbell Park. Skirt the round pond and make for the Beacon that represents the highest point in the park. As you approach it, turn sharp right and follow the path as it snakes down through the park. Roughly 30 yards (27m) before a circular seat, bear sharp right to join a grassy path alongside a fence. Make for a second kissing gate and turn right. Walk along

to the next path junction, with a kissing gate on the right. Turn left here, back towards the centre of Milton Keynes. Keep to the left to join a wide concrete ride and follow the waymarked city centre route.

❹ Turn right to cross the road bridge to Bankfield roundabout and go straight ahead along Avebury Boulevard. Cross Secklow Gate and Lower 10th Street, and turn right into Lower 9th Street. Pass The Point and bear left into Midsummer Place Shopping Centre. Cross the concourse and pass the police station. The Church of Christ the Cornerstone can be seen from here. Turn left towards Debenham's and Avebury Boulevard, turning right to the underpass. Walk down to Grafton Gate, veer right just before it and head for Midsummer Boulevard. Go through the underpasses and return to the railway station at the start.

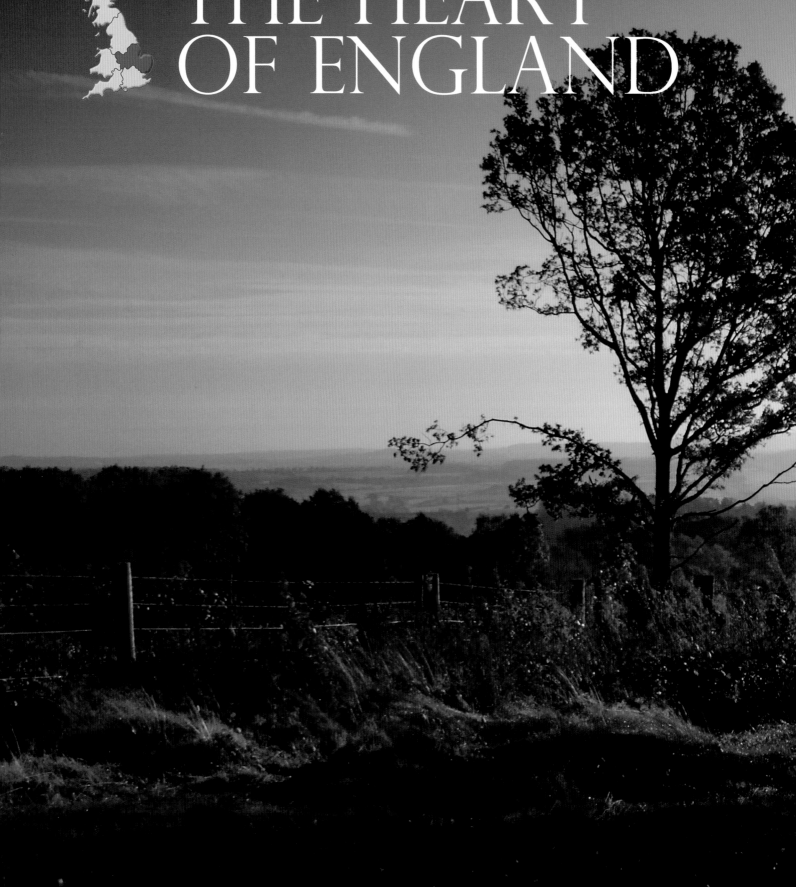

THE HEART OF ENGLAND

THE HEART OF ENGLAND

A view towards Warwick Castle from the River Avon in Warwick

This large area covers two essentially disparate regions linked together only by latitude. East Anglia, which includes Norfolk, Suffolk, Cambridgeshire and Essex, has always been purely rural, its character governed by predominantly flat fertile land and the 'bracing' proximity of the North Sea. The character of central England, which here includes Northamptonshire, Staffordshire, Derbyshire, Nottinghamshire, Lincolnshire and the counties clustering about Birmingham and the Black Country, is entirely different. Here the course of English history has made much more of an impact on the landscape.

In the centuries after the Norman Conquest, the counties of central England were the stage for the great events, the battles and upheavals that gave England its political identity – Bosworth Field, which brought the Tudor dynasty to the throne, and decisive confrontations between Roundheads and Royalists in the Civil War. It was also the heartland of the Industrial Revolution, which, despite the great 17th-century engineering feats of fen drainage, largely passed East Anglia by. In East Anglia, even now, there is little industry. The market towns are still redolent of country life, and villages are just as likely to support a shop specialising in agricultural machinery as they are a greengrocer. For its seclusion alone the east of England, all too often ignored by visitors (with the exception of Cambridge), is worth visiting, but also for its distinctive character, its churches and great houses and its undiscovered countryside.

Middle England, too, has its surprises. Its great cities and towns are usually lively, if lacking in allure, and their industrial heritage has endowed them with some fascinating working museums, notably the Black Country Living Museum at Dudley. There is plenty of railway nostalgia, and restored canals have become attractive leisure facilities which link town and city centres with the most rural landscapes. Between the built-up areas are green belts of charming countryside, which harbour innumerable delights. There are mighty castles, as at Warwick, Kenilworth and Rockingham; Belvoir Castle is more 19th-century fantasy than a castle in the accepted sense, but is a magnificent treasure-house of works of art. There are the great estates of the Dukeries and one of the great Elizabethan palaces – Burghley House. It is barely stretching the truth to say that this area is in some measure awaiting discovery.

Previous page: Looking east from Kinver Edge, Staffordshire

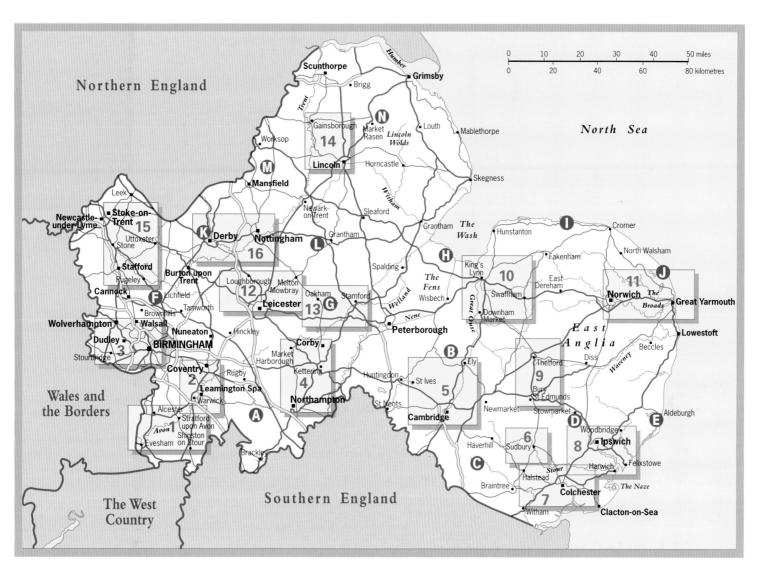

Section Contents

1	Stratford and the Vale of Evesham	146–147
2	Ancient Castles and a Modern Cathedral	148–149
3	England's Industrial Heartland	150–151
4	Churches, Crosses and Resilient Towns	152–153
5	Cambridge and the Fenlands	154–155
6	Medieval Towns and Villages	158–159
7	Romans and Oysters	160–161
8	Ipswich and Constable Country	162–163
9	Ancient Sites and Country Towns	164–165
10	A Secluded Corner of East Anglia	166–167
11	Around Medieval Norwich	168–169
12	Rural Peace and Railway History	172–173
13	England's Smallest County	174–175
14	Lincolnshire's Crowning Glory	176–177
15	The Potteries	180–181
16	Nottingham and Derby	182–183

Features

Waterways of Central England	156–157
Rare Breeds and Traditional Crops	170–171
New Towns and Old Towns	178–179

👣 Walks

Ⓐ	A Village Trail from Badby	184
Ⓑ	Fenland's Big Skies	185
Ⓒ	The Sound of Music at Thaxted	186
Ⓓ	Stowmarket in the Heart of Suffolk	187
Ⓔ	Benjamin Britten's Aldeburgh	188
Ⓕ	Lichfield's Soaring Heaven on Earth	189
Ⓖ	A Rutland Waterside Walk	190
Ⓗ	It all Comes out in the Wash	191
Ⓘ	Blakeney Eye's Magical Marshes	192
Ⓙ	Around the Mysterious Horsey Mere	193
Ⓚ	Mackworth and Markeaton: A Rural Idyll	194
Ⓛ	King of Belvoir Castle	195
Ⓜ	A Merrie Tale of Sherwood Forest	196
Ⓝ	Churches of the Wolds	197

STRATFORD AND THE VALE OF EVESHAM

Between the Cotswold escarpment and the Malvern Hills, the Vale of Evesham bristles with fruit trees and asparagus. Just to its north is what has become known as 'Shakespeare country', which is probably as unfair to the area as it is to the man. As well as the Shakespeare connections, there are lovely old villages, a fine mansion and two of the country's loveliest gardens.

Stratford-upon-Avon

Alcester

This small town has two stately homes – Ragley Hall and Coughton Court. The first, a 17th-century Palladian house set in 400 acres (162ha) of parkland, has remarkable baroque plasterwork by James Gibbs and *The Temptation*, a mural added between 1969 and 1982. In 1409 Coughton Court became the property of the Catholic Throckmorton family, who were thoroughly entangled in a plot in 1583, but only indirectly involved in the more famous 'Gunpowder Plot' of 1605. Protestant rioters destroyed the east wing in 1688, but there remains plenty to see, including the Tudor gatehouse, a fine collection of portraits and lovely gardens.

Descendants of the Lucy family still live in one wing of Charlecote Park, but the house and grounds are open to the public

Charlecote Park

According to legend, the young William Shakespeare was caught poaching deer in the grounds of this Elizabethan mansion by Sir Thomas Lucy, who was to become the model for Justice Shallow in *The Merry Wives of Windsor*. True or not, the house is set in parkland which is still filled with deer and Jacob sheep. The grounds were later landscaped by 'Capability' Brown. The house, built in 1558, was much altered and enlarged in the 19th century, but some of the original buildings, including the gatehouse, stables and brewhouse, remain unaltered. The house, now owned by the National Trust, contains ceramics, lacquerware and furniture, much of it from the collection of William Beckford, the wealthy 18th-century eccentric, traveller and writer.

Hidcote Manor Garden, Gloucestershire, open to the public for walks, tours and open-air theatre, as well as tennis and croquet

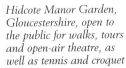

Evesham

Famous for the battle of 1265 in which Simon de Montfort was defeated by royal forces, this pleasant market town used to have an important Benedictine abbey. All that remains today is the bell tower, which was built in 1539 and considered to be the last piece of important monastic construction in the country. The lovely River Avon, which flows through the town, is busy with pleasure boats.

Hidcote Manor Garden

One of the finest gardens in the country, Hidcote (National Trust), close to Mickleton and Chipping Campden, is the result of decades of painstaking nurturing. It consists of a series of small gardens, each with its own character and style, separated by walls and hedges. The gardens are famous for rare shrubs, trees, herbaceous borders and 'old' roses. The modest house (not open to the public) is a mere backdrop to the artistry of the gardens, and, in summer, to productions of period dramas which take place in the open air.

Ilmington

This charming village is Cotswold in flavour, lying at the northern extremity of this magical area. It can best be appreciated by strolling about its streets of pretty cottages and pubs. The Norman church is notable for the wooden furnishings, carved and installed in the 1930s by the craftsman Robert Thompson, the 'mouseman', whose trademark was the little carved mouse that is to be found on each of his pieces of work.

Kiftsgate Court Gardens

A near neighbour of the more famous Hidcote, the gardens of Kiftsgate surround a house of golden Cotswold stone with classical features. The site is dramatic, with a series of gardens tumbling down a steep Cotswold slope, giving panoramic views over the Vale of Evesham and the Malvern Hills beyond. Each area of the garden has its own character and its own plant specialities, and a network of paths links them together, beneath a cliff covered with pine trees. Kiftsgate is especially noted for its roses.

The Royal Shakespeare Company

This world-famous company was founded in 1879 in Stratford-upon-Avon, with the opening of the Shakespeare Memorial Theatre. That theatre was destroyed by fire, and a new one built in 1932. In later decades, the RSC spread its wings far and wide, occupying London's Aldwych theatre in 1960 and a studio theatre (the Warehouse) in 1977. Between 1982 and 2002, it took space in the Barbican and, more recently, the Roundhouse in Camden.

The company expanded at its Stratford home too, opening a studio theatre, The Other Place, in 1974 and the Swan in 1986. Recently the company's Stratford productions moved into the Courtyard Theatre (on the site of The Other Place) while a new 1,000-seat Royal Shakespeare Theatre has been developed in Stratford.

With all this, as well as tours around the world, the RSC consistently manages to present the works of Shakespeare, as well as those of Shakespeare's contemporaries, and modern works. Among the RSC's artistic directors have been Sir Anthony Quayle, Sir Peter Hall and Trevor Nunn.

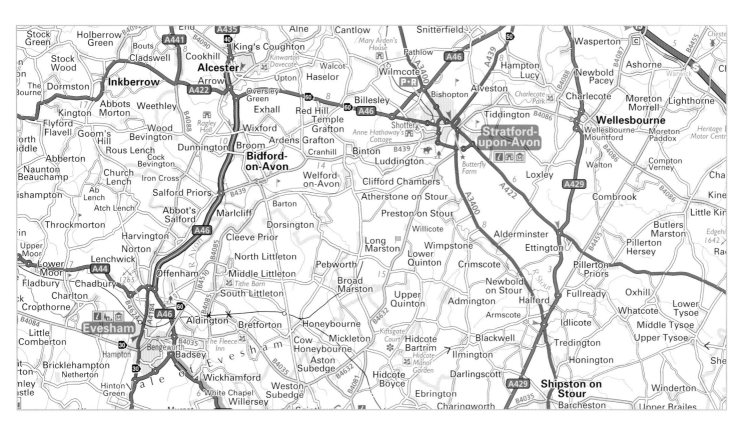

Shipston on Stour

Once an important centre of the wool trade, this small and bustling market town has considerable character, due in part to the interesting variety of houses that date back as far as the 17th century. Its former importance was largely derived from its position on an important coaching route; later it was a beneficiary of a 19th-century endeavour to link Stratford and Moreton by railway. Shipston on Stour is an attractive town for ambling and browsing around (a town trail leaflet is available from some of the local shops) and there are also delightful riverside walks.

Stratford-upon-Avon

This town owes almost everything of its modern prosperity to one man – William Shakespeare, considered by many to be the greatest among all playwrights, who was born here in 1564. In truth, although the town has some attractive features, and although the lure of Shakespeare is apparently irresistible, Stratford has lost its soul to the tourism on which it thrives.

Shakespeare's birthplace is in the town, as are Hall's Croft, where his daughter lived, and New Place where you can see the foundations and garden of his last residence. Ann Hathaway's Cottage and Mary Arden's House are just outside the town. More classically theatrical is the backstage tour of the Royal Shakespeare Company's Courtyard Theatre, with costumes, props, recordings and special displays.

Stratford also has attractions unrelated to Shakespeare, including a butterfly farm and Teddy Bear Museum. The best time to visit Stratford is in the evening, when a stroll along the river can be followed by a visit to one of the RSC theatres. Just to the south of the town is the excellent Shire Horse Centre, popular with families.

Wellesbourne

This is a small and scattered village with a working watermill on the River Dene. The mill, which is open to the public, produces stoneground flour, and there are also demonstrations of other old crafts, such as chair bodging and hurdle making.

Tourist Information

Chipping Campden: Old Police Station, High Street (tel: 01386 841206)
Evesham: The Almonry, Abbey Gate (tel: 01386 446944)
Redditch: Palace Theatre, Alcester Street (tel: 01527 60806)
Stratford-upon-Avon: Bridgefoot (tel: 0870 160 7930)

Kiftsgate Court Garden, Chipping Campden, Gloucestershire

ANCIENT CASTLES AND A MODERN CATHEDRAL

Amidst the Warwickshire countryside are one or two pleasant surprises, including two of the finest castles in the country – one a romantic ruin, the other hardly changed in hundreds of years. Coventry, another place often overlooked as 'industrial', also has a wonderful modern cathedral and Roman remains. Perhaps most unexpected in this area are the pretty villages.

Berkswell

This little village has an imposing Norman church with an unusual Elizabethan porch, its upper part designed as a Priest's room, complete with stove. The Norman crypt is one of the finest in England and may have been the burial place of St Milred, Saxon Bishop of Worcester. Tucked away in a residential area is an old windmill. Something of a curiosity in this part of the world, it is in good condition and is regularly open to the public. Nearby Temple Balsall, founded by the Knights Templar, has some 17th-century almshouses and the 13th-century church and Olde Hall.

The Norman crypt beneath the Church of St John the Baptist, at Berkswell

Coventry

This industrial city, which surpassed Birmingham in importance until the 18th century, is forever associated with Lady Godiva, who rode naked through the city in protest at the heavy taxes imposed by her Saxon husband, Earl Leofric.

Lady Godiva, or at least a statue of her, still presides over the city centre, and nearby are a number of places of interest, including Holy Trinity Church, Whitefriars Carmelite Friary, the Toy Museum in Whitefriars Gate and the 14th-century St Mary Guildhall. But Coventry is best known for its cathedrals. The medieval parish church became a cathedral in 1918, but the Blitz on Coventry in 1940 left only the spire and part of the walls. After the war it was decided to build a new cathedral alongside and linked to the ruins. This ancient/modern combination has the rare distinction among modern buildings of enjoying the general public's approval.

One of the most interesting places to visit is the Coventry Transport Museum, close to the city centre, which contains

A ferocious 10 hours of Luftwaffe attacks on a single night in November 1940 left much of Coventry, including the old cathedral, in ruins

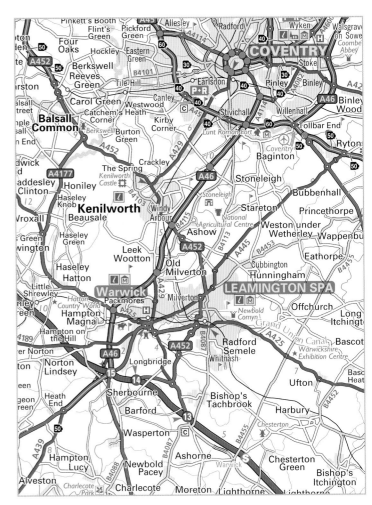

At Kenilworth Castle there has been an impressive restoration of Leicester's Gatehouse, and the painstaking recreation of the Elizabethan garden

more than 400 vehicles. Among these are the great British marques of cars, motorcycles and buses. There is also an impressive model collection and a reconstruction of the Blitz. Air transport is represented at the Midland Air Museum at Coventry Airport in Baginton.

Also in Baginton is Lunt Roman Fort, a reconstruction, based on archaeological evidence, of a Roman fort as it would have been in AD64, just after the Roman invasion. Re-enactments of Roman military manoeuvres take place here and an audio tour is available.

Ufton Fields

There is a fascinating nature reserve on the site of an old limestone quarry here, protecting some of the more vulnerable species of British flora and fauna. According to the season you can see cowslips and orchids, butterflies, dragonflies, grass snakes and toads, all in a natural setting.

Hampton Lucy

This is one of the prettiest villages in Warwickshire and is noted for its church of St Peter ad Vicula (in Chains). The list of rectors goes back to 1279, but the present building is much more recent. In the 1820s a bequest endowed funds for the embellishment of the old church, but it was decided to erect a new one instead. The first architect was Thomas Rickman, but later additions were made by Sir Gilbert Scott and the result is considered an architectural gem.

Kenilworth

Although it is Warwick that tends to receive all the plaudits, the castle at Kenilworth should not be missed. Though looted in the English Civil War, the structure escaped largely unscathed, only to see its keep and battlements torn down shortly afterwards. The nearby Stoneleigh Abbey displays architectural styles spanning 600 years of history.

Leamington Spa

Once a fashionable spa town whose zenith was reached during the late 18th and early 19th centuries, Royal Leamington Spa still exudes something of the elegance of that period, with Regency terraces and crescents. More hints of its genteel past can be found in the pump room, in

Jephson Gardens, laid out in the early 19th century, the Old Town Hall, the Assembly Rooms and in Landsdowne Crescent and Circus. There are a few oddities too, including the Mill Bridge and the Elephant Wash, where travelling circus proprietors brought their animals to be scrubbed.

Warwick

This small town is of great historical importance, noted above all for its magnificent castle, which is in a miraculous state of preservation. Set atop a grassy embankment, with huge towers, ramparts and crenellated walls, it is every child's vision of a medieval castle. Until 1978, when it was sold to Madame Tussauds, it was the seat of the Earls of Warwick.

The ensuing changes (waxwork tableaux, complete with sound effects) are difficult to ignore, as are the crowds, but the castle's aspect and grounds remain extremely impressive.

A short walk brings you to the town centre, an attractive mix of Georgian and medieval architecture. Here you will find the Oken's House and Doll Museum, the church of St Mary, with its glorious Beauchamp Chapel, the well-preserved almshouses of the Lord Leycester Hospital near the city's Westgate, the Warwickshire Museum in the 17th-century market hall and the medieval buildings of Mill Street.

Tourist Information
Coventry: Cathedral Ruins, Priory Street (tel: 02476 225616)
Kenilworth: The Library, 11 Smalley Place (tel: 01926 852595)
Royal Leamington Spa: Royal Pump Room, The Parade (tel: 01926 742762)
Warwick: The Court House, Jury Street (tel: 01926 492212)

Warwick's Lord Leycester Hospital was founded in 1571, by Robert Dudley, First Earl of Leicester. To this day, it fulfils its role as a retirement home for old soldiers

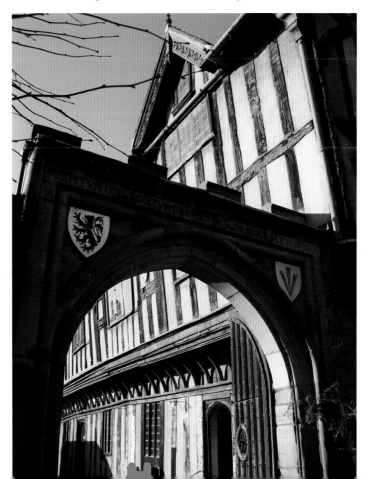

ENGLAND'S INDUSTRIAL HEARTLAND

There is no reason these days to be put off by the word 'industrial'. The major cities and towns of central England have to some extent dusted off their coal-associated reputations and are capitalising on their rich industrial heritage. Birmingham is not alone in become a lively centre of culture and entertainment. The surrounding countryside also has its own allure.

The Bullring has been important in Birmingham since the Middle Ages; it is now a shopping centre

Birmingham

Britain's second largest city is sometimes thought of as an industrial centre with little to offer the visitor. While it is not a city of obvious charm, there is a lot to seek out, and it is a vibrant cultural centre, with exceptionally good nightlife.

The city centres on Victoria Square and Chamberlain Square, which are dominated by the Council House, the Town Hall of 1834 and the excellent Museum and Art Gallery, which houses an excellent collection of Pre-Raphaelite art. The main shopping area runs along New Street to the City Plaza and the Bullring, although the Jewellery Quarter and the wholesale clothing markets are also a magnet to shoppers. The award-winning waterfront complex, Brindleyplace, is full of bustling bars and restaurants, as well as the National Sea Life Centre.

Birmingham's industrial heritage can be explored along it immense canal system, or with a visit to the Thinktank Science Musuem. In addition, there is the Birmingham Railway Museum, with steam train rides, and the National Motorcycle Museum at Bickenhill, with more than 650 machines. For a break from industry, Edgbaston offers the Barber Institute

Cadbury's Victorian founder began Bournville as a purpose-built village to to alleviate the horrors of life for workers in the city centre

of Fine Arts, the Birmingham Botanical Gardens and Canon Hill Park, with its refurbished Midlands Arts Centre (MAC).

Bournville

The most interesting of Birmingham's many suburban towns is a place better known around the world for its chocolate. Bournville is the home of Cadbury's, and owes its very existence to the Quaker Cadbury family who planned the village in 1879 to provide decent working and living conditions for their employees. The main attraction is Cadbury World, attached to the factory, where an exhibition, complete with sounds and smells, relates the history and manufacture of chocolate. Here visitors can sample the product and buy it at reduced prices.

Selly Manor consists of two half-timbered houses that were moved the mile from Bournbrook to Bournville by George Cadbury. Restored and opened to the public, they contain one of the finest displays of crafted furniture in the country.

Clent Hills

This stretch of windswept upland is a wonderful area for walking and offers the finest views in the area. At the summit, just over 1,000ft (305m) high, are four large stones, a curious folly created by landscape gardener and minor poet William Shenstone, who lived 2 miles (3.2km) away at Halesowen. To the northeast of Clent is the small 13th-century chapel marking the site of the martyrdom of St Kenelm, the Mercian prince who was buried at Winchcombe in Gloucestershire and whose shrine became one of the most important medieval places of pilgrimage.

Dudley

Dudley is dominated by castle ruins which look out across seven counties. Part of the castle is Norman, and there is

The City of Birmingham Orchestra

Birmingham has had its orchestra only since 1920, when it was founded by a group of citizens led by Neville Chamberlain. It was the first to receive a municipal grant and its opening concert was conducted by Sir Edward Elgar in the Town Hall. The orchestra soon became internationally respected, but although the principal conductor in 1925, Sir Adrian Boult, was promised a new concert hall, it was not until 1991 that the Symphony Hall finally materialised. Sir Simon Rattle did much to bring international renown to the orchestra, which now performs here more than 75 times a year. The current Music Director is Andris Nelson, and under his stewardship the orchestra tours extensively all over the world and makes regular recordings.

Nanny's rock caves, Kinver Edge

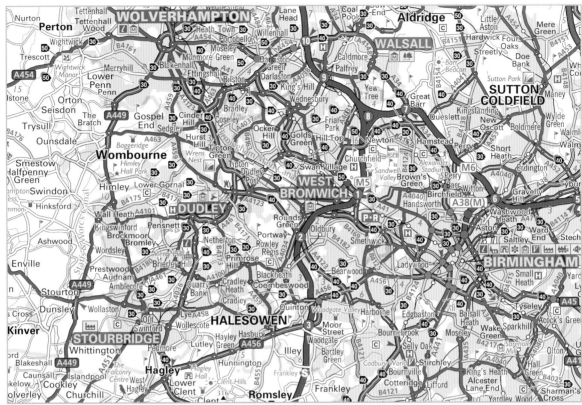

an audiovisual display and visitor centre. Within the 40 acres (16ha) of grounds is Dudley's well-known zoo, which houses one of Britain's largest collections of animals. The Dudley Museum and Art Gallery is also worth a visit, and hosts excellent temporary exhibitions.

A mile (1.6km) from the town centre is the award-winning Black Country Living Museum, a recreation of an industrial village, with shops and a pub, cottages and a chapel. Chain-making demonstrations take place in an authentic workshop, and there is a canal dock with narrowboats and trips into the Dudley Tunnel. Visitors can also go underground in an 1850s mine. Near by is Himley Park, landscaped by 'Capability' Brown, and the Wren's Nest Nature Reserve, widely known for the fossils found here – many of which can now be seen in Dudley's museum.

Kinver Edge

This upland area of sandstone heath and woodland is all that remain of a huge forest that once extended across this area. There are remains of an Iron-Age fort in the north, from where there are fine views, but of greatest interest are the old rock dwellings which were occupied as recently as the 1960s by besom broom makers. Now rather bare, their former occupants made real homes out of them with the addition of bricks and windows.

Stourbridge

Close to Birmingham, Stourbridge is noted for the production of crystal and glass, although it was iron production that originally put Stourbridge on the map – the first steam locomotive to run on rails in America was built here. Visits can be arranged to various glass factories, whilst the Broadfield House Glass Museum at Kingswinford provides a historical background. The Stuart Crystal and Red House Glass Cone Museum features a 100ft (30.5m) high glass cone that was built in 1790.

Wolverhampton

Although not a town that could be described as aesthetically pleasing, Wolverhampton is not entirely devoid of interest. It has an enterprising Art Gallery, and three interesting houses. Moseley Old Hall (National Trust), with 17th-century formal gardens, is the Elizabethan house in which Charles II hid after the Battle of Worcester. Wightwick Manor, also owned by the National Trust, is a 19th-century building in Pre-Raphaelite style. Nearby is Cannock Chase, the largest area of countryside in the county. Edwardian Bantock House is now a museum, surrounded by scenic parkland.

Footpaths, bridleways and trails criss-cross the wildlife-rich Clent Hills, Worcestershire. At Walton Hill there is a wildlife hide

Tourist Information
Birmingham: The Rounda, 150 New Street (tel: 0844 888 3883) Wolverhampton: 18 Queen Square (tel: 01902 556110)

CHURCHES, CROSSES AND RESILIENT TOWNS

Northamptonshire is one of those counties that seems both familiar and remote, not far from everything and yet curiously amorphous. In fact, it is filled with places of interest, including some delightful villages that are very close to the Cotswolds in character, and some particularly fine houses and estates, all reflections of the area's location at the heart of English history.

Kirby Hall dates from 1570. Its west façade is built of the local Weldon stone

Corby

The growth of the steel industry transformed Corby from a village to a large town, but the closure of the steelworks in 1980 had an appalling impact, from which the town is still recovering. Its centre is mostly rather depressing but there are incipient efforts to improve matters. Corby has a pleasant location at the edge of Rockingham Forest, where there are lovely walks at Stoke Wood and Stoke Albany. Rockingham Castle is nearby, impressively overlooking Rockingham village. The town is also well located for Kirby Hall, Deene Park and King's Wood, a nature reserve of ancient woodland.

A blue garden seat, Kelmarsh Hall

Holdenby House

Built by Queen Elizabeth I's Lord Chancellor, Sir Christopher Hatton in the late 16th century, Holdenby was then the largest house in England. Subsequently it became the prison of Charles I, where he was kept under guard for five months after his defeat in the Civil War. Today you can visit Rosemary Verey's Elizabethan Garden and the 17th-century farmstead, which houses rare breeds of animals. There is also a falconry centre and armoury.

Kelmarsh Hall

Designed by James Gibbs, Kelmarsh Hall was built in the 1720s and is one of the finest stately homes in the county, one of only two surviving houses by this talented architect. The south lodge gates, designed in the late 18th century, were made only in the 1960s upon the discovery of the original plans.

Kettering

This town, whose growth has depended upon leather and the quarrying of ironstone, though visually undistinguished, is not without interest. The Alfred East Art Gallery is named after the Royal Academician who bequeathed many of his paintings to the town. Close by is the Manor House Museum, with exhibits ranging from a mummified cat to a car built in Kettering at the turn of the 20th century. Wicksteed Park is a giant playground founded by the industrialist and philanthropist Charles Wicksteed in 1920. It has more than 50 rides, many original.

Lamport Hall

The family home of the Isham baronets between 1560 and 1976, Lamport Hall is essentially Palladian in style and contains a fine art collection. It is set in spacious grounds, complete with alpine garden. A 19th-century Isham is thought to have been the first to import garden gnomes into Britain, from Germany.

Northampton

This is a classic case of a town with a considerable heritage that has suffered, first in a fire (which destroyed most of the medieval buildings) and then at the heavy hands of redevelopment. Despite this, the heart of the city is not without interest. The central market square, one of the largest in Britain, is

Naseby

The Battle of Naseby in 1645 is considered to be the most important engagement of the English Civil War, and perhaps the most crucial for modern Britain. The Royalist forces of Charles I had, until that point, been holding their own, but at Naseby they were beaten decisively by Cromwell's New Army, thus securing the future of parliamentary democracy. The battlefield, 14 miles (22.5km) north of Northampton, is marked with a monument at the point where Cromwell's army gathered to face the Royalists on Dust Hill. The Naseby Battlefield Trail is a 6-mile (10km) self-guided tour that takes in a series of viewing points. Interpretation panels provide information about the historic battle, along with a background to the 17th-century landscape.

*The Eleanor Cross,
Geddington,
Northamptonshire*

Eleanor Crosses

When Queen Eleanor, the wife of Edward I, died in Lincoln in 1290, her body was carried to London for burial. At each stopping place on the journey a stone cross was erected, of which only three others remain, at Geddington, Hardingstone and Waltham Cross. The Hardingstone cross is incomplete, but dramatically sited at the top of the London Road outside Northampton, whilst the cross at Geddington is less time-worn and is picturesquely located in the centre of a charming village.

surrounded by some handsome houses, including Welsh House, which escaped the fire. Nearby is the Guildhall, a Gothic extravaganza decorated with events from Northampton's history. All Saints Church is considered to be the finest 17th-century church outside London, and Northampton has several other religious masterpieces: St Peter's, probably the finest Norman church in the county, and the Church of the Holy Sepulchre, the largest and best preserved of only four round churches in Britain. The Northampton Museum and Art Gallery specialises in footwear, a long-established local industry.

Triangular Lodge

This is close to being a folly, but it is no idle fancy, for it was built by Sir Thomas Tresham in 1593 for serious reasons. It is a stone manifestation of his Catholicism,

an affirmation of his beliefs which were not diminished by his imprisonment for 13 years, charged with being a papist. The building takes its name from the fact that everything about it is triangular; it is constructed according to a factor of three.

Wellingborough

Like Northampton, Wellingborough too had a fire, in 1738, which destroyed much of its medieval heart, but it has escaped some of the worst of modern development. A 15th-century thatched ironstone barn has been restored and there are two handsome old inns in the centre. The Heritage Centre, next to a park that was once the swannery of Crowland Abbey, is dedicated to local history, and also serves light refreshments. The Walks is a relaxing area of promenades, shaded by trees, along the River Nene.

See Walk A, page 184
A Village Trail from Badby

Tourist Information
Corby: One Stop Shop, George Street (tel: 01536 464000)
Kettering: The Coach House, Sheep Street (tel: 01536 410266)
Northampton: Royal and Derngate, Guildhall Road (tel: 01604 622677)

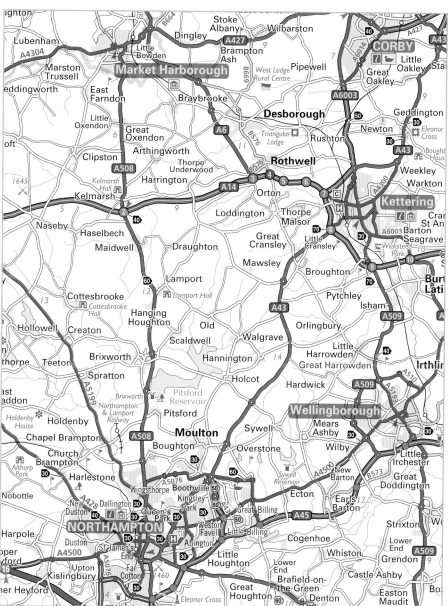

Stone monument to commemorate the Battle of Naseby, Northamptonshire

CAMBRIDGE AND THE FENLANDS

Outside and beyond Cambridge there is a world that is largely unknown to the majority of visitors. This is a pity, for though the county is not blessed with a dramatic landscape, there are plenty of gems to discover in fen and fold. Where hills rise out of the flat land there is usually something special built upon them, most notably at Ely, and the fens have a singular wildness.

Wicken Windmill is one of two windmills in the village

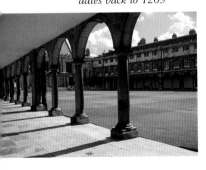

Cambridge University dates back to 1209

Anglesey Abbey

In the village of Lode, east of Cambridge, Anglesey Abbey is part of a former Augustinian foundation that dates back to 1135. After the dispersal of the monks there were a number of owners, including Thomas Hobson who was the inspiration for the notion of 'Hobson's choice', which means having no choice at all. The house contains a marvellously eclectic collection of art and objects that was part of Lord Fairhaven's collection. In the grounds, which belong to the National Trust, 18th-century Lode Watermill is still grinding corn.

Cambridge

Retaining the atmosphere of a rural market town, Cambridge is nevertheless dominated by its university, which grew up along the banks of the River Cam, west of one of the principal shopping areas.

It is possible to visit several of the colleges, although they are subject to restricted opening hours. The most celebrated, because of its chapel, is King's College, though most of its original 15th-century college buildings now house the university administration offices. The chapel is a marvel, however, and certainly inspires the soul to leap to the rafters. The largest of the colleges is Trinity and its Great Court is surrounded by a magnificent collection of Tudor architecture, including the splendid Wren Library.

St John's College has a replica of Venice's Bridge of Sighs, while the university's oldest building is the School of Pythagoras, dating from 1200. Magdalene College has on display the diary of the distinguished former student, Samuel Pepys; the Old Court of Corpus Christi College is where Marlowe wrote *Tamburlaine the Great* and Queen's College boasts a galleried Cloister Court and half-timbered President's Lodge. On Trumpington Street is the Fitzwilliam Museum, which contains a giddy array of exhibits from many of the great civilisations, including European, Chinese and Korean porcelain and paintings from all the great European masters.

The Backs are the water meadows along the Cam, facing the rear of the colleges – a delightful place for strolling and punting, especially in spring or autumn.

Hemingford Grey

This is one of the county's most attractive villages, with some fine houses in the area of the High Street, and the church of St James charmingly located by the river. The Manor House was built in 1150 and is thought to be the oldest continuously inhabited house in the country. Substantial parts of the original Norman house remain, and the garden has been filled with roses and topiary chess pieces.

Madingley

A few miles to the west of Cambridge, Madingley is close to the huge American War Cemetery at Coton, more than 30 acres (12ha) donated by the university, where rows of white marble crosses commemorate the 3,812 Americans who lost their lives while stationed in Britain

Ely

Ely, an island of upland in a sea of fenland, was an outpost of Saxon resistance to the Norman invaders who built a cathedral here to celebrate their eventual victory, complementing the abbey that had stood here since AD673. The cathedral remains the highlight of a visit to Ely, although the city is also home to some of the finest remaining medieval architecture in the country. Work began on the cathedral in 1081 and, among the many additions made over the centuries, perhaps the most impressive are the 14th-century Octagon, an engineering miracle, and the Lady Chapel, with its wonderful stonework.

Among many fine buildings in Ely, Prior Crauden's Chapel and Cromwell House (where Oliver Cromwell lived for many years) are especially interesting, and there are plenty more along the High Street and down on the banks of the Ouse. There are two museums – the Ely Museum and, in the cathedral, the Stained Glass Museum, with examples covering the 14th century to the present day, from all parts of Britain.

Duxford

Duxford is the home of a branch of the Imperial War Museum, housed at an airfield which was an important Spitfire base during the Battle of Britain – events of those days have been simulated in the Operations Room. There are more than 180 historic aircraft here, as well as midget submarines, armoured fighting vehicles and other large exhibits. Duxford Aviation Society's collection of civil aircraft includes the prototype *Concorde 001*, and there is an exhibition on the US 18th Air Force. Major flying displays are held in summer and pleasure flights are available on summer weekends, or visitors can keep their feet almost on the ground in a flight simulator.

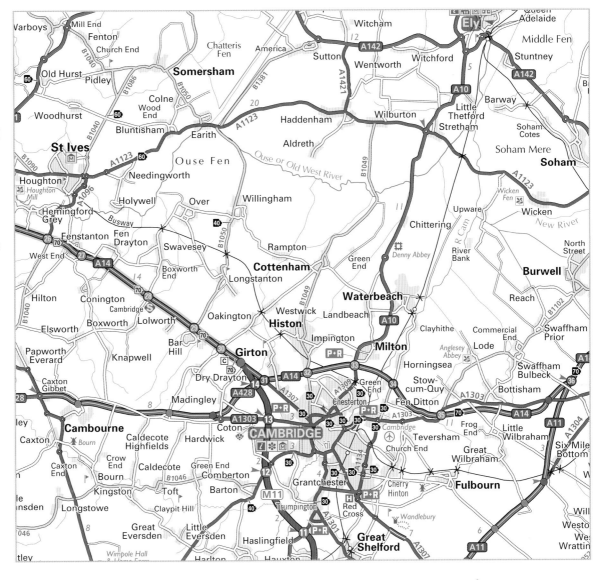

during the Second World War. A long Portland stone wall is inscribed with the names of more than 5,000 of those whose graves are unknown.

The 16th-century Hall, now part of the university, is where Edward VII stayed as an undergraduate.

Wandlebury

The Gog Magog Hills, just southeast of Cambridge, are named after the legendary giants, images of whom were supposed to have been carved into them. The Iron-Age fort crowning the hills was probably built in the fourth century BC and abandoned in the first century AD, when the Romans arrived. A wooded area, with lovely walks, includes a section of Roman road.

Wicken Fen

Near the village of Soham, Wicken Fen is more than 750 acres (304ha) of undrained fenland. Owned by the National Trust,

it gives a splendid insight into how East Anglia would have been before the 17th century. One of the most important 'wetland' reserves in Western Europe, it is also possible to visit a Fenman's cottage and the only complete Fenland windpump. Comprising reed and sedge, an open mere and areas of alder and buckthorn, a nature trail affords the ideal opportunity for discovering the fens.

Looking up to the high domed ceiling in Ely Cathedral

See Walk B, page 185
Fenland's Big Skies

Tourist Information
Cambridge: The Library, Wheeler Street (tel: 0871 226 8006)
Ely: 29 St Mary's Street (tel: 01353 662062)
Huntingdon: The Library, Princes Street (tel: 01480 388588)

WATERWAYS OF CENTRAL ENGLAND

Before the proliferation of the canal system in the late 18th and 19th centuries, the movement of freight across large distances had been a practical impossibility, effectively limited to something like 12 miles (19.3km) by both the cost and the poor state of roads. The only exceptions were those areas lucky enough to be on one of the larger rivers like the Severn and, in the eastern part of the country, the Ouse.

Attempts to find a way of improving on river navigation date back at least to the days of the Romans, who constructed artificial waterways near Lincoln and Cambridge. From the 12th century onwards the idea was resurrected and small-scale navigation allowed the passage of narrow barges here and there. The first pound locks in Britain were introduced in 1566 (having already been in existence in Holland for 200 years), after which the domestication of rivers, such as the Great Ouse, became much easier and their development and use increased throughout the 17th century. These projects were not generally government financed, but were instead in the form of investment by merchants, who were driven by the expectation of eventually being able to make a profit.

The Canal Age

Large-scale construction was nonetheless surprisingly slow to get off the ground considering that most of the technical problems had already been overcome in the 17th century; the first long-distance canal was built only in the 1730s, in Ulster, running between Newry and the Upper Bann. However, it was really with the construction of the Bridgewater Canal, designed by James Brindley, that canals began to proliferate all over the country. Brindley gained his ideas through his experience as a millwright in Leek, Staffordshire – the Bridgewater and the Trent and Mersey were his two greatest achievements.

The success of these canals encouraged the formation of joint stock companies to build others. While this certainly led to a flurry of activity, it also created problems. These companies built their canals as they saw fit and according to local conditions. The lack of coordination meant that some canals were open to just about any size of craft, while others were restricted to narrowboats only. Nonetheless, it became clear that canals were at least of great use locally and construction continued until the 1830s, at which point nearly every town of any importance was within striking distance of a stretch of navigable water.

'Legging' a barge out of the 523m (572 yard) Barnton Tunnel on the Trent and Mersey Canal near Northwich, Cheshire

As England rebuilt after the Second World War, canals provided vital transport links between mines, power stations, factories and their markets

Central England and East Anglia were two of the areas where waterways were particularly important. The Midlands were at the heart of the Industrial Revolution and there are still 130 miles (209.1km) of navigable canal in Birmingham and the Black Country alone. With Wolverhampton and Cannock to the north and Stourbridge to the south, in its great days this area had 212 working locks, with 550 factory side-basins, forming the greatest concentration of industrial canals in the country. In its heyday canal transport carried eight million tonnes a year, and even as late as the 1950s a million tonnes a year were still being transported on the waterways.

The Grand Union Canal, 300 miles (482.8km) long and as important as its name suggests, links London with Birmingham and, had it not been for the outbreak of the Second World War, might have seen wide boats of 66 tonnes pushing along its waters.

A spur breaks away from the Grand Union near Daventry in Northamptonshire and runs for 66 miles (106.3km) to link up with the River Trent. This in turn is linked to the Fossdyke near Lincoln and to the Wash, also served by the River Nene, which is itself linked to the Grand Union via Northampton and Wellingborough.

Decline and Rebirth

Ironically, the canal system, with its network linking large industrial sites, was to become instrumental in its own downfall. Waterways were used to transport the coal that powered the steam locomotives on the railways, which were new, much faster and more efficient. Canals were gradually abandoned, and in some cases drained in order to become railbeds. With one or two major exceptions, commercial traffic has all but died and canals have assumed a new role as leisure amenities. And not only on the water – the old towpaths make excellent walk- and cycle-ways and many tourist offices produce routes and trails to follow.

In Norfolk the greatest navigation is that based on the Great Ouse, one of Britain's greatest rivers. It was first made navigable from the sea upstream to Bedford in the 17th century, when the surrounding land was drained by the Dutchman, Cornelius Vermuyden, creating new waterways. But its commercial usefulness had vanished by the late 19th century, and by the turn of the century much of it lay derelict. Today, after many vicissitudes, it has been reopened through the enthusiasm of the Great Ouse Restoration Society.

The Grand Union Canal at Berkhamstead follows the course of the River Bulbourne

At Foxton Locks, it is possible to watch the narrowboats ascending the 'staircase' of ten locks. There is also a museum and boat trips are available

MEDIEVAL TOWNS AND VILLAGES

These lands on either side of the Stour really do look as if time has passed them by. Lavenham, Sudbury and Clare are full of wonderful old half-timbered houses and, though in 'deep Suffolk', their rich churches and fine houses show they were once leading centres of trade, and castle remains at Clare and Castle Hedingham are evidence of former strategic importance.

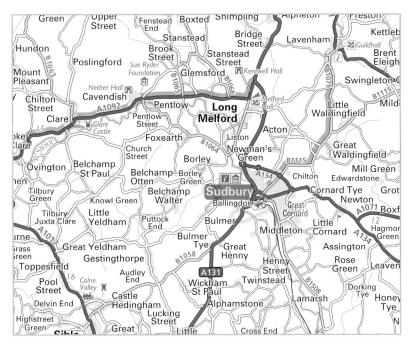

Preserving Suffolk

Not all preservationists are backward-looking, as proved by the Suffolk Preservation Society, based at the delightful 14th-century Little Hall in Lavenham. Founded in 1929, the Society works to conserve the quality of the countryside and buildings of Suffolk, while ensuring that necessary new development is sympathetic and environmentally sustainable. The Society also tries to set a practical example. In the 1970s it turned property developer and used a gift of a piece of land at Wetherden to show how new houses could fit into an existing village. Its sister organisation, the Suffolk Building Preservation Trust, restored the attractive Pakenham Watermill, which is open to visitors, grinds corn and sells the flour.

In the Middle Ages the Norman Lords of Clare were among the leading nobles of England

The Belchamps

Belchamp Otten, Belchamp St Paul and Belchamp Walter are three small Essex villages which, along with the picturesquely named Foxearth, Gestingthorpe and Little Yeldham, lie in a quiet, rolling area of countryside between Sudbury and Haverhill, south and west of the Stour, which is the county boundary. Walter is the most attractive of them, with 18th-century Hall, 15th-century church, and fields running down to the Belchamp Brook. 'Belchamp' sounds like a Norman-French description of those fields, but apparently has an earlier, Anglo-Saxon meaning: house with 'roof made of beams'.

Castle Hedingham

One cannot but feel that the de Veres, to whom the Conqueror gave Hedingham in 1066 or soon after, had a sound sense of priorities. Within two years they had planted a vineyard, but it was 50 years before they got round to building the

castle – a square Norman keep with two 100ft (30.5m) corner towers still standing – which commanded the trade route along the Colne Valley a short distance to the west. The church is largely Tudor, within a fine west tower and hammerbeam roof; the triangular open space to its east was the site of the medieval market.

Cavendish

Although such perfection can sometimes seem eerie, a village like this nonetheless exerts a certain fascination. Thatched cottages cluster in the shadow of an ancient church, and there are several pubs, and the Cavendish Manor Vineyard, which offers tours and tastings.

Clare

Clare was once an important town, as shown by the remains here of the first Austin Friars priory in England, its Norman castle mound, with an impressive fragment of what must have been a massive keep, and its fine, largely 14th-century church. Clare is still recognisably a town, rather than a village, its harmonious townscape a feast for the eye, with buildings of substance that reflect its former commercial status. Note especially the pargeted 15th-century Ancient House adjoining the spacious churchyard.

Kentwell Hall

A fine Tudor house just to the north of Long Melford, Kentwell is the home of

A thatched cottage in the 'chocolate box' village of Cavendish, Suffolk

Built in the late 14th century, and afterward enlarged repeatedly, Little Hall in Lavenham was home to six families by the 1700s

J. Patrick Phillips QC and his family, and has a very 'lived in' feel to it. The Phillips have been undertaking a phased restoration project for both house, gardens and farm and have won several awards for their re-creations of Tudor domestic life on selected weekends in summer. There are also 1940s re-creations on several summer weekends. House and grounds are open Easter to October.

Lavenham

Even from the main road Lavenham looks old and interesting, but you need to stop and explore on foot. It is emphatically not a village, but a town which grew rich on wool and in Henry VIII's reign was reckoned to be the 14th wealthiest town in England. Standing in the hilltop marketplace, you are surrounded by signs of that past wealth – the beautiful, timber-framed, 15th-century Corpus Christi Guildhall, built for one of the town's four medieval guilds (now National Trust), and Little Hall, also timber-framed and appropriately headquarters of the lively and impressive Suffolk Preservation Society (SPS).

Round the corner in Barn Street is another fine timber-framed building, Molet House, then down Shilling Street, past a row of higgledy-piggledy but well-preserved weavers' cottages, comes yet another, Shilling Old Grange. And so it goes on. The SPS has published an excellent illustrated walk from the marketplace to the church and back, with drawings of the Tudor and later buildings, including the magnificent church of St Peter and St Paul, on the eastern edge of the village.

Long Melford

Living up to its name, this village is strung out along a main street of about a mile (1.6km). Melford means 'ford by the mill' – that mill being mentioned in the Domesday Book. At the south end of the main street stands the 18th-century Melford Place, followed by the 15th-century Cadges's House and a whole procession of timber-framed and Georgian houses, until you come to delicious Melford Green, with the late 15th-century Holy Trinity Church, which Pevsner called 'one of the most moving parish churches of England, large, proud and noble'. It, too, is long, with a splendid nave and clerestory.

Among other buildings round the green are the 16th-century Trinity Hospital and, from the same century, Melford Hall, turreted and mullioned in warm red brick. Queen Elizabeth I was a guest here in 1578 and, on the outside at least, the house is little altered since that time. It has an Elizabethan Long Gallery, a dramatic Georgian staircase, a Regency library and a Victorian bedroom, and there is a pretty two-storey Tudor pavilion, possibly a guardhouse, in the garden.

Interior of Kentwell Hall, Long Melford, Suffolk

Sudbury

A prosperous market town above the River Stour, Sudbury has its focus round St Peter's Church, a large church expressing the confidence and solidity of a rich wool town. Market Hill descends towards the bridge past a statue of the artist Thomas Gainsborough, who was born at 46 Gainsborough Street, a handsome early 18th century house, where, perhaps, his artistic achievement was stimulated by such a beautiful environment. His house is open to the public and displays a selection of his portraits and landscapes.

See Walk C, page 186
The Sound of Music at Thaxted

Tourist Information
Lavenham: Lady Street (seasonal) (tel: 01787 248207)
Sudbury: Town Hall, Market Hill (tel: 01787 881320)

ROMANS AND OYSTERS

Colchester was an important town even before the Roman invasion, mostly because it stood on a good, defensible hill above the Colne. This is just one of a series of rivers that divide up the country behind the coast and keep the land in something of a timewarp. Further inland you find gentle countryside, dotted with attractive, bustling market towns and villages.

Brightlingsea

A quiet little port and seaside resort islanded among marshes near the mouth of the River Colne, Brightlingsea may look faded and forgotten; but from time to time it comes unexpectedly awake as a port, as in 1984 during the coal strike and in 1995 with spirited demonstrations against live calf exports. It is, however, a town with enduring appeal for all who love the sea, boats and boatyards. Brightlingsea joined the Cinque Ports as a 'limb' or 'member' of Sandwich, to which it traditionally pays ten silver shillings each July, in a ceremony held in the belfry of All Saints' Church.

One of many merchants to make a fortune in the 15th-century wool trade, John Paycocke's home in Coggeshall, with its intricate woodwork, was designed to show off his wealth

Coggeshall

Coggeshall Grange Barn (National Trust) was originally part of a Cistercian monastery. Dating from 1140, it is the oldest surviving timber-framed barn in Europe, and exhibits a small collection of farm carts and wagons. In nearby West Street, Paycocke's is a wealthy wool merchant's house, built around 1500 by John Paycocke. The front is close-timbered with five oriel windows, while the interior has fine panelling, woodcarving and, in the Great Hall, a magnificent ceiling. There is also a display of Coggeshall lace. The attractive village has had its tranquillity restored by a bypass.

Colchester

Standing four-square on its hilltop site, Britain's 'oldest recorded town' is packed with history. It was the Romans' first *colonia* after they invaded Britain in AD43. Before they took it, it was already important as *Camulodunum*, the capital from which Cunobelin (Shakespeare's Cymbeline) ruled the whole of southeast Britain. In her last fling of defiance, Boudicca, Queen of the Iceni, sacked the city in AD60, then the Romans rebuilt it in the second century and the street pattern of the present town centre still shows their layout.

In its north-east corner, over the Roman temple, the Normans built a huge castle, but only its keep – the largest in Europe – remains. It houses the Colchester Castle Museum, with interesting Neolithic and Roman objects. Minutes from here are the Hollytrees Museum, documenting the social history of the town, the Natural History Museum in the old All Saints' Church, and the Minories Art Gallery, housed in two Georgian houses on the High Street. Redevelopment in the town centre has been generally sympathetic. The old Dutch Quarter, stretching from the High Street down to the River Colne, is worth exploring.

Colchester is traditionally renowned for its oysters, and still holds an annual oyster feast. Bourne Mill, a 16th-century fishing lodge converted into a cornmill, stands by a 4-acre (1.6ha) mill pond south of the centre. Three miles (4.6km) west of the town is one of England's finest zoos, with

Old timber-framed cottages on the riverside at Colchester, Britain's oldest recorded town

over 260 rare species and amusements, while to the east at Elmstead are the Beth Chatto Gardens, created from a wasteland over the last 50 years or so and featuring a dry, a shade and a wetland garden.

Halstead

One of those East Anglian market towns strung out along a main thoroughfare, Halstead gains visually from the steep descent of its bustling high street down to the River Colne. Here stands a handsome weatherboarded silk mill, built by Samuel Courtauld in 1826. Though reformist for his day, Courtauld opposed legislation that would protect children working in his mills. Higher up are a windmill and St Andrew's Church, with tombs of the Bourchiers, including Robert, who fought with the Black Prince at Crécy.

Layer Marney Tower

The Marney family were already in this part of Essex by the 12th century, but it was in 1520 that Lord Marney built his superb Layer Marney Tower. The tallest Tudor gatehouse in the country, and among the finest, it affords expansive views over the Essex countryside. The adjacent church, in the same mellow Tudor brickwork, contains Marney effigy tombs going back to 1414. The farm has a medieval barn, rare breeds of farm animals and deer.

Exterior of St Andrews' Church in Halstead

Boats on the Stour at Manningtree

Manningtree and Mistley

On the Essex bank of the Stour as it widens into its estuary, Manningtree was once an important port, but it is now a tranquil waterside village. Downstream, Mistley is the spa that never was – planned by Richard Rigby of Mistley Hall, whose fortune came from the South Sea Bubble. He became Paymaster General and poured his money into the spa at Mistley, even employing Robert Adam to design a new church, but when it was discovered that he had been embezzling the forces' pay, work on Mistley ceased. What is left is a green waterside with tall maltings buildings, gracious Georgian façades and swans. The twin towers of a demolished Mistley church have been kept as shipping landmarks.

Tourist Information

Colchester: 1 Queen Street (tel: 01206 282920)

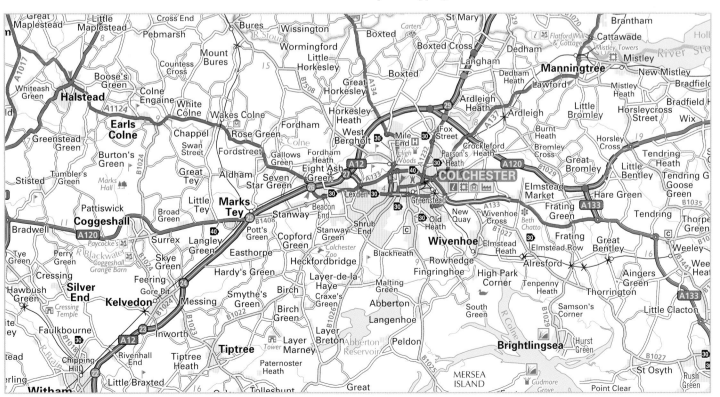

IPSWICH AND CONSTABLE COUNTRY

Suffolk is a delightfully rural county, forever associated with the painter John Constable, who immortalised many local scenes which remain unchanged to this day. The area he made famous extends into Essex. This county's recently acquired reputation for wide-boy excess is unfair on its rural reaches, which are as tranquil as you could wish for.

At Dedham's Boathouse Restaurant, summer visitors can rent a rowing boat for a leisurely trip down the Stour

Dedham

This handsome country town has a number of fine buildings and a particularly impressive church, built by wealthy cloth merchants in the late 15th century. If the church tower, completed in 1520, seems familiar it is because it has featured in paintings by Constable, who was born just over the border in Suffolk, but who went to school here.

The village has other artistic associations – Sir Alfred Munnings lived at Castle House, which remains as he would have known it. There is an interesting toy museum at the Arts and Crafts Centre in the old Congregational Church. From Dedham it is possible to walk (or drive) the 2 miles (3.2km) to Flatford Mill, owned by Constable's father and subject of one of the artist's most famous scenes.

Constable Country

The artist John Constable was born in East Bergholt, Suffolk, in 1776 and went to school across the Stour at Dedham in Essex. He wandered the fields and lanes of Dedham Vale, and later re-created what he saw in some of his best-known paintings. Flatford Mill, owned by his father, now serves as a field studies centre; Dedham Church, with its pinnacled tower still stands in a landscape which, thanks to the National Trust and the planners, is remarkably unchanged. From Dedham there is a pleasant walk along the Stour to Flatford Mill, where you can have tea by the riverside.

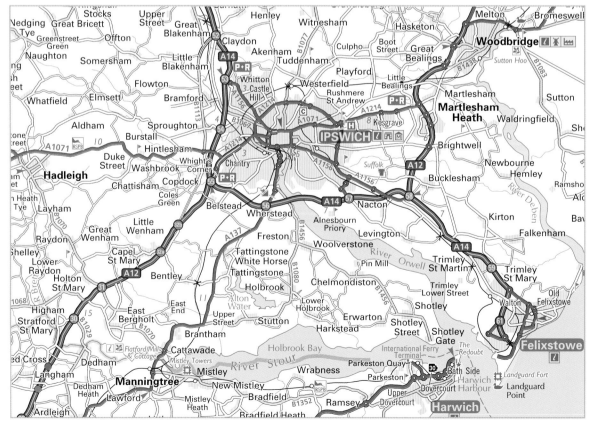

Harwich and the Redoubt

The principal passenger port for Essex has one or two oddities. The 17th-century treadmill crane preserved on the quay is probably the only one extant in the world and was originally used to service Royal Navy ships. Port life is commemorated in the Port of Harwich Maritime Museum, which is housed in the old Low Lighthouse and is devoted to the Navy, shipping and the lifeboat service. The old High Lighthouse contains a wireless museum. Harwich is also the (perhaps unlikely) home of one of Britain's oldest cinemas, the Electric Palace of 1911, which is still working.

The Redoubt on Tower Hill is a practically impregnable round fort with 18 rooms, built in 1808 as a defence against a possible Napoleonic invasion. The location for battle re-enactments during the summer, it houses a small military museum, and 11 guns can be seen on the battlements.

Erwarton

Legend states that the heart of Ann Boleyn is buried in the church of St Mary, in the handsome family vault of her uncle, Philip Calthorpe. Close to the church is the Calthorpe family home, Erwarton Hall, with its red-brick gatehouse, decorated in a distinctively Jacobean style.

Felixstowe

Suffolk's main port, situated on a peninsula across the Orwell Estuary from Harwich, is also an Edwardian seaside resort that still radiates a calm gentility. The beach is stony and in typical east-coast style, segmented by breakwaters, and behind it are avenues of sedate villas which once housed fashionable holidaymakers.

Its great days have, for the time being at least, gone, but it is a pleasant resort in which to take a restful stroll along the prom, or through the countryside beyond. There is a nature reserve at Landguard Point and close to it an 18th-century fort, while beyond Old Felixstowe is a pair of 19th-century Martello Towers.

Hadleigh

This is a rather beautiful Suffolk town, with a medieval bridge over the River Brett and an unusually long main street that is positively crammed with delightful buildings, many washed in those curiously fruity colours beloved of the region. St Mary's Church, with an interesting spire, stands close to Deanery Tower, a 15th-century gatehouse of some splendour. Hadleigh's most famous building is the Guildhall, which remains little altered since its construction in 1438.

Ipswich

An ancient town, founded in the sixth century, Ipswich became a prosperous inland port because of its location on the estuary of the Orwell. It was one of the first towns to be granted a charter and in the Middle Ages became a great trading centre, exporting East Anglian wool.

First impressions of the pedestrianised city centre are unpromising, but closer inspection reveals quite a lot of interest. Christchurch Mansion is a wonderful Tudor House with period furnished rooms and an art gallery, which is set in parkland and yet close to the heart of the town. Wolsey's Gateway was to be the portal of a college (never completed) in the town of his birth. In the vicinity of the new Buttermarket there is an extensive sprinkling of ornate medieval houses, most famously the Ancient House, with its added 17th-century pargeting – a decorative form of exterior plasterwork.

Ipswich's Victorian expansion is manifest in the Old Custom House at the Wet Dock, and in the Town Hall and Corn Exchange in the main square. Students of modern architecture will find much to enjoy, including Contship House at the Wet Dock, and Willis Corroon, by Sir Norman Foster. The Ipswich Museum contains replicas of the treasure found in the Saxon burial at Sutton Hoo. Boat cruises leave from the revamped historic waterfront, the Wet Dock, which is also a pleasant spot for a stroll.

Levington

This pretty Suffolk village overlooks the wider reaches of the River Orwell and has a charming little 12th-century red-brick church, conveniently located next to the pub. The church interior is delightfully rural and contains some unusual 17th-century Jacobean panelling around the chancel and a medieval font, complete with decoration which neither Puritan nor Victorian saw fit to despoil.

Woodbridge

This delightful town on the River Dene does not need to make a conscious effort to look good for visitors. Not only pretty, Woodbridge derives enormous charm from the fact that it goes about its business with unselfconscious zeal. There are handsome buildings to admire, especially on Market Hill, and on the quayside is the Woodbridge Tide Mill, rather Dutch in style, with a red gabled roof and brilliant white clapboard flanks. St Mary's Church is charmingly located amid a fan of gardens, and close by is the local museum. Not far away, and located in the Shire Hall, is the Suffolk Horse Museum.

The colourful gables of shops at Woodbridge, Suffolk

See Walk D, page 187
Stowmarket in the Heart of Suffolk

See Walk E, page 188
Benjamin Britten's Aldeburgh

Tourist Information
Felixstowe: 91 Undercliff Road West, Sea Front (tel: 01394 276770)
Harwich: Iconfield Park, Parkeston (tel: 01255 506139)
Ipswich: St Stephen's Church, St Stephen's Lane (tel: 01473 258070
Woodbridge: The Station (tel: 01394 382240)

With 550 berths, Suffolk Yacht Harbour in Levington ensures a steady supply of visitors to the village

ANCIENT SITES AND COUNTRY TOWNS

Where Suffolk meets Norfolk we find a great deal of variation and an indeterminate landscape which tends to produce the occasional curiosity. The route north from Bury St Edmunds is dominated by the vastness of Thetford Forest, contrasting with the small, mellow towns. In Ickworth House, the area has one of the great eccentricities of English architecture.

The Greene King Brewery is one of Bury St Edmunds' main employers and owns many of the local pubs, including the UK's smallest, The Nutshell, with space for a dozen customers

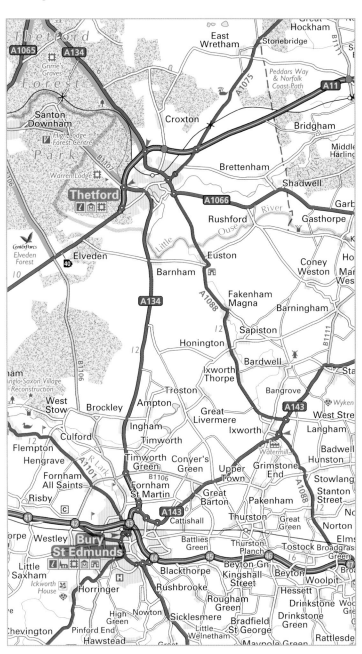

Bury St Edmunds

A very attractive rural town of 35,000 souls, Bury St Edmunds, attractively situated on the rivers Lark and Linnet, claims to be the birthplace of Magna Carta, and is replete with 18th-century architecture. St Edmund was the last Saxon king of East Anglia who, when asked to renounce his Christian faith by the Danes, refused and was then promptly executed. His martyrdom here meant that Bury Abbey became an important medieval place of pilgrimage. The abbey was, of course, dissolved by Henry VIII in the 16th century, but what remains, set in a wonderful garden, has some romantic charm, and the remaining Abbey Gate on Angel Hill is particularly impressive.

The largely 16th-century St Edmundsbury became a cathedral in 1914. A new Gothic-style lantern tower, bringing the height to 150ft (45m), chapel and cloisters were added in 2005.

The nearby St Mary's Church contains the tomb of Mary Tudor, sister of Henry VIII. The Moyses Hall Museum of local history and natural history is housed in one of the few Norman houses to survive in the country and is the oldest secular building in the region.

Thetford Forest is an ideal setting for a day out

Thetford Forest and Grimes Graves

In the 1920s, in an attempt to control the erosion of the Breckland, 80,000 acres (32,400ha) of woodland were planted, creating Britain's largest lowland pine forest and a scene more reminiscent of Scandinavia than of England. Under the auspices of the Forestry Commission, it has become an important source of timber as well as providing a habitat for wildlife, notably the treasured red squirrel. The area is now threaded by pleasant forest walks and provided with amenities of all types.

It is also the site of the ancient Grimes Graves, something of a misnomer, since these are nothing to do with burial chambers. Grimes Graves are, in fact, flint mines dug by Neolithic people between about 3000BC and 1900BC. Around 360 of these mines have been discovered here, consisting of shafts and underground galleries which present a memorable picture of the remarkable level of industry attained by people at this early stage of our civilisation.

The town is also home to a rare example of a Georgian provincial theatre, the Theatre Royal, recently restored. Across the road is the Greene King brewery, where (pre-booked) tours take in the historic brewhouse, museum and a tasting session.

Euston Hall

Overlooking a lake, and home to the Dukes of Grafton, Euston Hall was built in the 1660s by the Earl of Arlington, Secretary of State to Charles II. It subsequently came into the possession of Dukes of Grafton when Lord Arlington's daughter, Isabella, married a son of the king, Henry Fitzroy, who became the First Duke of Grafton. It contains a splendid art collection, including a number of portraits of Charles II (and Charles I) as well as works by Stubbs, Van Dyck and others.

Ickworth House

This extraordinary confection, now in the possession of the National Trust, was built by Frederick Hervey, the Fourth Earl of Bristol and Bishop of Derry. It is in that eccentric vein that was the hallmark of aristocratic architecture of the late 18th century and, though unfinished, it is one of Britain's great curiosities. The most pronounced feature is the huge rotunda, inspired by the Pantheon in Rome, among other places. Set in parkland landscaped by 'Capability' Brown, the house contains a magnificent collection of silver and paintings, including works by Gainsborough and Titian. Near the entrance to the park is Horringer Crafts, where demonstrations of traditional craftwork are given.

Thetford

In the heart of Breckland, an area that was once sparsely populated heathland, Thetford is a small, historic town. It was the birthplace of the great 18th-century philosopher, Thomas Paine, whose seminal work, *The Rights of Man*, was published in 1791. The place where he was born is in White Hart Street, close to the 15th-century Ancient House Museum, which is devoted to Paine and the history of the area. During the 11th century Thetford was the seat of the Bishops of East Anglia, and the ruined Cluniac priory is on the outskirts of the town.

Just outside Thetford is the village of Elveden, burial place of the last Sikh

Maharajah, Duleep Singh, who died in 1893. Having expropriated his Punjab state, the British Government lured him to England and presented him with a 17,000-acre (6,885ha) estate.

West Stow

Close to West Stow village is the West Stow Country Park and Anglo-Saxon Village, a 125-acre (51ha) country park that is a magnet for migrating birds as well as human visitors. The recreated Anglo-Saxon village has been built on the site of excavations made between 1965 and 1972 of a settlement dated AD420–650. Six buildings have been reconstructed, using the same techniques, tools and materials that would have been used in the original village. There is a visitor centre containing objects and displays telling the story of the settlement and the people who lived there.

Woolpit

A few miles to the southeast of Bury St Edmunds, Woolpit, close to some woodland, is the home of the Woolpit Bygones Museum which depicts traditional daily life in a Suffolk village. There are demonstrations of brick-making, an industry that thrived here during the 19th century – indeed ochre bricks from here were used in the construction of part of the Capitol in Washington, DC. The church ceiling is seemingly supported by an array of delicately carved angels.

The central rotunda at Ickworth House was designed by the Italian architect Mario Asprucci and built between 1795 and 1830 for the Fourth Earl of Bristol

Tourist Information

Bury St Edmunds: 6 Angel Hill (tel: 01284 764667)
Newmarket: Palace House, Palace Street (tel: 01638 667200)
Stowmarket: Museum of East Anglian Life (tel: 01449 676800)

The curious 'canopy of honour' in St Mary's Church, Woolpit, was once thought to be original, but is now known to have come from another church c1870

A SECLUDED CORNER OF EAST ANGLIA

There is perhaps nowhere as truly rural in Britain as this part of East Anglia. Not quite as flat as might be expected, although in places very flat indeed, this area abounds in interest. There are charming market towns and exquisite village churches with extraordinary carvings; great houses and ruined castles; few people and quiet roads. It all adds to the delight.

The ruins of Castle Acre Priory, Norfolk

Castle Acre

Situated on a steep slope overlooking the River Nar, the village of Castle Acre was once important because of its closeness to the pilgrim shrine at Walsingham. Its Cluniac priory was founded in 1090 by the son-in-law of William the Conqueror, William de Warenne. Although incomplete, it forms a series of extensive ruins, including a monastic herb garden and the great west front, with its sublimely beautiful Romanesque design. The charming little Saxon church of St Mary and All Saints has scarcely been altered.

Remains of the old castle earthworks are considerable, while the 13th-century Bailey Gate, at the edge of the town, is the only part of the medieval town to survive.

Castle Rising

Here you will find the 12th-century keep of a ruined Norman motte and bailey castle, but one which has retained much of its original decoration, including fine vaulted ceilings. Queen Isabella was confined here for 30 years from 1327 for her role in the murder of Edward II. In the village itself, which has a medieval atmosphere, is a row of handsome 17th-century almshouses, as well as a market cross.

Cockley Cley

A settlement of the Iceni tribe of the first century AD has been reconstructed here, on what is thought to be the actual site of the original village. It dates from the time of Queen Boudicca, who led the Iceni revolt against the Romans. Beautifully sited in the Breckland, close to the River Gadder, there is also a nature trail, a farming museum in a barn, an Elizabethan cottage and a Saxon church, which is thought to be one of the oldest in the country.

King's Lynn

A truly delightful, bustling and well cared-for town, King's Lynn was once England's greatest inland port, with many fine, ancient buildings. The old town is an integral part of an agricultural area, the sort where the bank is filled with farmers in wellington boots. The marvellous church of St Margaret is 12th century and overlooks the Saturday market and the early 15th-century Trinity Guildhall. King and Queen streets are lined with old merchants' houses, and St George's Guildhall is the largest surviving medieval guildhall in the country. The Tuesday Market is also surrounded by interesting buildings.

Sandringham

Norfolk's royal house was built in the late 19th century for the (then) Prince and Princess of Wales, later Edward VII and Queen Alexandra. The house is open in summer, except when the royal family is in residence, and most of the rooms they use are on show. The house contains some marvellous collections of firearms, jade and crystal. It is set in 60 acres (24ha) of informally landscaped grounds, within which is the Sandringham Museum, displaying royal memorabilia, from family photographs to vintage Daimlers. Visitors should make time for the parish church of St Mary Magdalene with its carved and painted angels and its many royal memorials. One of the finest carrstone buildings in existence, it dates back to the 16th century.

The Customs House in King's Lynn was designed by architect Henry Bell and built by Sir John Turner in 1685

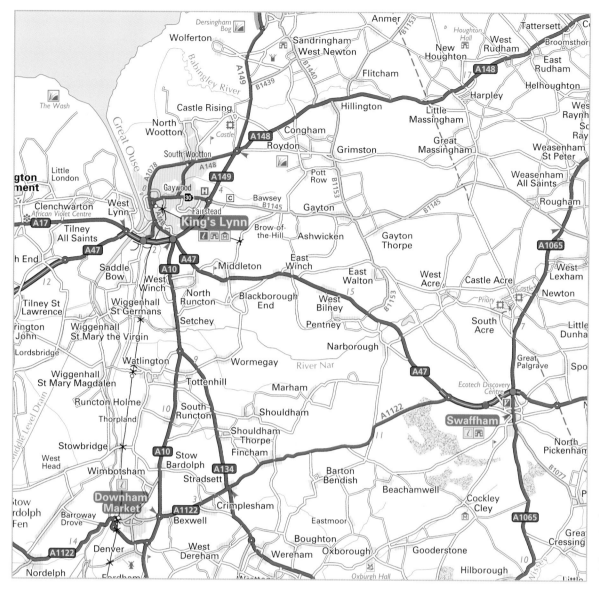

Oxburgh Hall, Norfolk

Oxburgh Hall

Built in 1482 by the Bedingfield family, this is a beautiful house with a water-filled moat and Tudor gatehouse. The gatehouse is particularly admirable in that it is completely original, unrestored by over zealous Victorians. The rooms within show the changes in style and comfort that evolved from the Tudor to Victorian periods. The chapel is noted for its altarpiece, while the formal gardens, which date from the 19th century, include an ornate knot garden in the French style.

There are many other delights to savour – the Custom House by the River Ouse, the Red Mount Chapel, Greyfriars Tower Gardens, the charming St Nicholas Chapel and the Jacobean Greenland Fisheries Building – and a number of museums, and you can watch the production of Caithness crystal on the Hardwick Industrial Estate.

The Massinghams

Little Massingham is a scattered village with a pretty church standing alone and containing memorials to the Mordaunt family, who were eminent in the area for some 300 years. However, it is Great Massingham that is the more impressive – a village of pretty houses built around several greens and duck ponds. St Mary's church, screened by chestnut trees, has an unusually complete 13th-century porch. The porch was once used as a schoolroom, and the young Robert Walpole was taught here.

Swaffham

A busy market town, situated 12 miles (20km) easy of King's Lynn with a huge market place, centred on a classical 18th-century market cross topped with the little statue of Ceres, Roman goddess of harvests. A fashionable focal point during the 18th century, the square is lined with handsome houses from the period, including Montpelier House, where Lady Nelson once stayed. The town sign features the 'Pedlar of Swaffham', who, it is said, went to London in a suicidal frame of mind, but was dissuaded from jumping into the Thames by a man who related a dream of finding treasure in a remote garden. The Pedlar recognised that garden as his own and went home to discover two pots of gold.

Discoveries of an environmental nature are on offer at the Ecotech Centre, which includes a huge wind turbine with a viewing platform.

See Walk H, page 191
It All Comes Out in the Wash

See Walk I, page 192
Blakeney Eye's Magical Marshes

Tourist Information

King's Lynn: The Custom House, Purfleet Quay (tel: 01553 763044)
Wisbech: 2–3 Bridge Street (tel: 01945 583263)

AROUND MEDIEVAL NORWICH

This is an area of almost surreal contrasts. From the noble medieval streets of Norwich, it is not very far to the saucy postcard world of the Norfolk resorts. Between them come a whole host of sleepy villages, the waterways of the Norfolk Broads and an astonishing variety of little churches with round towers and thatched roofs.

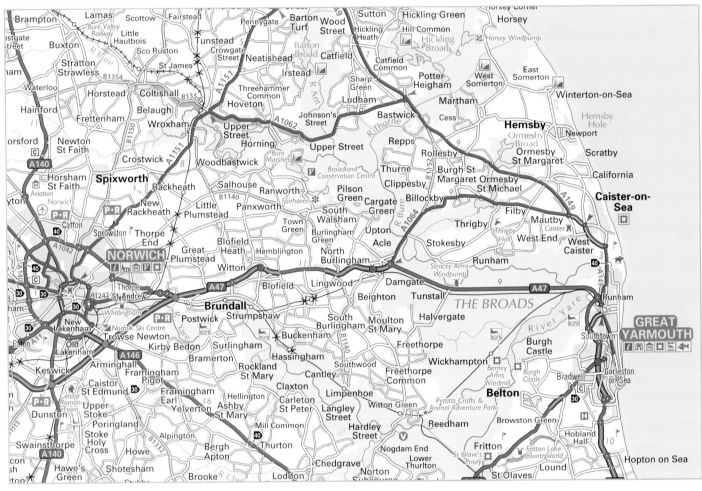

Burgh Castle

A summer evening at Great Yarmouth's North Beach. On the horizon is the Scroby Sands offshore wind farm

Burgh Castle, or *Gariannonum*, is a well-preserved Roman fort that formed part of the so-called Saxon Shore. It is in a secluded situation, close to the junction of the rivers Waveney and Yare.

Caister-on-Sea

Caister is an ancient Roman port and fishing village that has become a popular resort. The picturesque ruin of Caister Castle, built in the mid-15th century, now houses an excellent car museum. Nearby is Caister Hall, of similar date. The foundations of a Roman construction have been discovered on the edge of town and are open to the public.

Fritton

This village is noted for its exceptionally interesting church, mostly Norman, but with a Saxon apse which may have been the original wayside chapel. Fritton Lake is the largest in England outside the Lake District, and at Fritton Lake

Fairhaven Garden Trust

This area of woodland and water garden, extending to 131 acres (53ha), takes in the private Inner Broad and a bird sanctuary. The gardens, particularly good for primulas and rhododendrons, were laid out by the late Lord Fairhaven and include the 900-year-old King Oak. Daily boat trips between April and October take visitors out onto the water, to see kingfishers, swans and sometimes otters.

The cloister at Norwich Cathedral is the largest monastic cloister in England; it housed a community of about 100 monks

Bure Valley Railway

This narrow-gauge railway runs steam and diesel trains across 9 miles (14.5km) of attractive Broadland between Aylsham and the Broads 'capital' of Wroxham, with three intermedviate stops at Coltishall, Brampton and Buxton. Among the locomotives are two half-scale replicas of ZB class tender engines which were built for narrow-gauge railways in India, where the full-scale versions are still operating. Carrying 115,000 passengers a year, the construction of the railway was an initiative of the local district council, making use of an existing standard-gauge railbed. Steam driving courses are available, aimed both at the absolute beginner and more advanced levels.

Countryworld there is a falconry centre and stables with Shire and Suffolk Punch horses.

Great Yarmouth

An important seaside resort that is also a port, Great Yarmouth has a considerable history, its former herring industry now replaced with offshore gas, oil and wind. The Victorian seafront promenade has the typical resort trappings of pier, amusement arcades and fast-food outlets. The Sea Life Centre and Marina Leisure centre (complete with wave pool) keep families busy. On South Quay are the Elizabethan House (National Trust), with toys from the past and hands-on activities, and the Norfolk Nelson Museum. The Time and Tide Museum, in a preserved herring-curing works, tells the story of the town, while the Tollhouse museum in the old courthouse jail focuses on crime and punishment.

Parts of the old town centre remain and there are several stretches of medieval wall, as well as a number of the 'rows', narrow alleys linking the port with the river. In the marketplace is St Nicholas' Church, with the widest nave in the country, and nearby is the charming early 18th-century hospital for 'decayed fishermen'.

Horsey and Horsey Mere

Horsey is an attractively desolate expanse of dune and strand. A little way inland, standing between a narrow, undulating country lane and a Broad staith, is Horsey Windpump, acquired and restored by the National Trust in 1948.

Just beyond it stretches brackish Horsey Mere, part of a 2,000-acre (810ha) Site of Special Scientific Interest, where osprey and marsh harriers may flourish in comparative peace and where there are walks through the marshy landscape.

Norwich

Once an important *entrepôt* for the medieval weaving industry and one of the most prosperous centres outside London, Norwich went into decline for some time, although the establishment of a university and, in recent years, more industry, has made it prosperous once again. Those years of comparative isolation have contributed to what is probably the best-preserved medieval city in Britain.

Most notable perhaps is the cathedral, with the second highest spire in the country and a 13th-century cloister which is the only two-level example left in Britain. While the exterior is impressive, especially when viewed from the east, it is the airy interior that is of most interest, containing some excellent examples of medieval workmanship and artistry – look for the frescoes in the treasury and the carved misericords in the presbytery.

Southwest of the cathedral, in the heart of the town, are the remains of the 12th-century castle, now housing a museum of local history, and a fine collection of paintings, with special emphasis on the Norwich School of painters.

Linked to the castle is the Royal Norfolk Regimental Museum. Elsewhere in the heart of the city there are a large number of delightful corners, particularly in the picturesque area of Elm Hill, and several medieval halls. The Bridewell Museum, currently being redeveloped and due to reopen in 2011, focuses on the history of Norwich and its people, while the Mustard Shop tells the story of Colman's Mustard, still made here. The Sainsbury Centre for Visual Arts, situated on the university campus, includes works by Picasso, Bacon and Moore.

West Somerton

Sitting in the shadow of rows of sleek modern windmills, West Somerton's charming little church, with its round Norman tower built between 1000 and 1300, contains some fine wall paintings dating back to 1377.

The 15th-century pulpit has some tiny heads carved on it, while in the graveyard is the tomb of Robert Hales, the 'Norfolk Giant', who grew to 7ft 8in (2.3m) and was exhibited all over England and the United States along with his sister, a mere 7ft (2.1m) tall.

The Broads

Where the rivers Ant, Bure, Thurne, Waveney and Yare widen into small lakes, they become the Norfolk Broads. Long considered to be natural lakes, the Broads are, in fact, the result of peat extraction, creating pits that were filled with water following rising sea levels in the 13th and 14th centuries. The Broads are now protected as one of the most important wetland areas in Europe and are a haven for bird, plant and insect life.

Looking along river to Horsey Mill, which was built as a drainage windpump

See Walk J, page 193
Around the Mysterious Horsey Mere

Tourist Information
Great Yarmouth: Marine Parade (tel: 01493 846346)
Norwich: The Forum, Millennium Plain (tel: 01603 213999)

RARE BREEDS AND TRADITIONAL CROPS

Despite the Industrial Revolution and the proliferation of the great towns and cities that have become closely associated with the Midlands, England remains an essentially rural country. Gone, however, are the smallholdings that are still a significant feature of France and Italy; and gone, for the most part, are the meadows filled with orchids and other wild flowers that until recently seemed to fill summer horizons. England is one of the most advanced and efficient farming economies in the world, but has become so, it would seem, at the expense of a human dimension that has always seemed attractive to the romantically inclined outsider.

The truth is that changes in rural life have been taking place for centuries, and there have always been people who felt threatened by such change. Resistance sometimes took a peaceful form, with letters to newspapers or legislative disagreements, but often it erupted in riots and violence. The most famous example of this is the early 19th-century Luddite movement which is supposed to have been named after a Leicestershire worker, Ned Ludd, who destroyed his machinery in anger.

Changing the Landscape

Even as far back as the 17th century, the drainage scheme in the Norfolk fens instigated by the Duke of Bedford met with fierce opposition from local farmers who had previously made use of the marshes to rear geese, which were driven in their thousands as far away as London. Before the construction of the network of drainage ditches, the landscape of Norfolk had been essentially marshy with rivers flowing aimlessly and with fickle unpredictability across it, ideal for geese but hopeless for crops.

Yet, even the construction of drainage ditches proved inadequate for the successful leaching of the fields, particularly of the peaty, black soil which tended to subside. Thus a way had to be found to pump the water from field to ditch and then from ditch to main channel. The windpump made its entry to enhance the popular vision of the fenlands.

In the case of the fens, a farming landscape has been created deliberately and, although the sails of the windpumps no longer turn, modern pumps have taken their place. A flat landscape of hedgeless fields and farmsteads surrounded by dense, tall hedges as protection against the wind seems to have become permanent.

Norfolk and Leicestershire have both made several contributions to the changing aspect of English agriculture. The Norfolk Four Course Rotation is the foundation of modern farming. It is based on the principle of ploughing in compost instead of manure in sequence – roots, barley, seeds and wheat

Green-winged Orchid Anacamptis morio *plants in flower, North Lincolnshire*

Flax is one of the oldest fibre crops in the world

Selective breeding has resulted in two types of Lincoln red cattle: beef and dairy

The Lincoln was developed to produce heavy, long fleeces

– which is said to bring the best out of the soil. Leicestershire's contribution was the development of modern sheep farming.

Selective Breeding

There are around forty breeds of sheep still in existence in Britain, far more than in any other country in the world. Wool, after all, was the key to English prosperity in the Middle Ages, most notably in the Cotswolds and East Anglia. Yet, the breeds that provided the wool are no longer used and incredibly have come close to extinction. One reason for this is cross-breeding, which is not entirely a modern phenomenon. The man behind this was Robert Bakewell, a farmer born in 1725 in the hamlet of Dishley, near Loughborough. Before inheriting the family farm, Bakewell travelled extensively in England and the continent. By the time he started farming his own land, he had learned the science of selective breeding, but instead of selecting the best from other herds he concentrated on inbreeding. He used his ideas for cattle rearing but his greatest successes came with sheep, the result of a programme based on the Leicester breed, which were similar to the old Lincoln and Cotswold sheep that had been the foundation of the medieval wool trade. The result was that he was able to produce early maturing sheep for the butcher. His Leicesters, and his ideas, made vital contributions to sheep farming throughout the world.

Similarly, the Lincoln Long Wool breed was found all over the Midlands until it was later crossed with the ubiquitous Merino.

Other local breeds of sheep have been less successful and are hardly used – the Staffordshire Ryeland and the Norfolk Horn, although this latter is the ancestor of the Suffolk, which is still sometimes crossed for fat lamb. Most of these local breeds of sheep, however, have disappeared from commercial farms.

The same is true of cattle, though once again breeds from Lincolnshire and Suffolk have been important in producing modern strains. A good example of this is the pedigree Lincoln Red Shorthorn, which, along with all indigenous British breeds, suffered a sharp fall in popularity In the 1970s and 1980s. Although the native Lincoln Red is a rare sight today, the crossing of this breed with modern, European cattle has been a huge success.

As for pigs, local breeds such as the Essex Saddleback have lost out to fashion, leap-frogged by the popularity of the leaner Scandinavian varieties.

A certain monotony therefore grazes the landscape of our farms. But the developments that have led to this state of affairs are the fruition of centuries of striving as much as to the technocratic notions of our own time.

If the meadow flowers have gone, they have been replaced by the dazzle of yellow rape and the milky blue of flax; and no doubt the world will in due course regard them as much a part of the traditional rural panorama as were once upon a time poppies and cowslips.

Saddleback pigs are the most productive of the British rare breeds

The Bee Orchid is often found on sand dunes

RURAL PEACE AND RAILWAY HISTORY

Leicestershire is one of the 'shires', a word that epitomises Englishness and unchanging traditions. But don't expect it to be all country folk eating Stilton cheese and Melton Mowbray pork pies – amidst the timeless countryside there is a strong industrial heritage, including the preserved Great Central Railway at Loughborough and the Grand Union Canal at Leicester.

Blowing off steam, before leaving Rothley Station on the Great Central Railway. On the route, full-size steam engines can use a double set of tracks

Anstey

A large scattered village with some attractive houses, Anstey is often considered the home of the Luddite movement (workers against mechanisation in the Industrial Revolution), which was named after Ned Ludd, an Anstey man. On the road from Leicester, beside the modern bridge, look for the five-arched stone packhorse bridge, which is thought to date back to the early 16th century.

Bradgate Park, the largest country park in the county, is a mixture of heathland, woodland and rock outcrops. At its highest point is the well-known Leicestershire landmark, a folly called the 'Old John Tower'. The estate was owned by the Grey family, who attained their zenith when Lady Jane Grey was proclaimed Queen of England in 1553 after the death of her cousin Edward VI. The euphoria was short-lived – Jane was deposed after just nine days and beheaded the following year. The house has since fallen into ruin, but there is enough left to evoke its splendid past.

Burrough Hill

There are wonderful all-round views from this Iron-Age hillfort at 700ft (213.4m). The high earthen ramparts here indicate that this must have been a particularly important fort, and so effective were its defences that it appears to have been in continuous use from the Bronze Age to the last years of the Roman occupation. It is also the start and finishing point of the Leicestershire Round, a 100-mile (161km) waymarked path through the best of Leicestershire.

Leicester

The county town of Leicestershire suffered from war damage and industrial decline, but has forged ahead in more recent times thanks to the presence of its multicultural immigrant population. Today, Leicester has a revamped city centre and an exciting National Space Centre.

The past is by no means forgotten, though, with a positive glut of museums and historic places. In the High Street is the Jewry Wall Museum, where a remarkably tall piece of masonry wall from a Roman bathhouse complex has been preserved, together with some impressive mosaics and paintings. The Newark Houses Museum, in 16th-century buildings, is devoted to county history, with dedicated space given over to the Royal Leicestershire Regiment Collection. Others include the Leicestershire Museum and the Museum of Science and Technology, housed in the Abbey Pumping Station.

Leicester's early history can be further explored in its old churches, including the partly Saxon St Nicholas and the cathedral of St Martin. The area around the church of St Mary de Castro is the site of the old castle, but the only evidence that remains is in the Great Hall, which became part of the 17th-century Courthouse, and the Turret Gate. The nearby Trinity Hospital almshouses date from 1331.

One of the joys of a visit to Leicester is the chance to sample one of the city's famous Indian restaurants, many of which are to be found along Belgrave Road.

The Great Central Railway

In 1899 the line between Nottingham and London, formerly used for coal haulage, opened to passenger traffic. It was one of the later railway companies to come into being, and the last major line to open in this area, but in some ways it was too late. It was never able to compete seriously with the car, and by 1966 several sections of the line were closed. The M1 motorway actually covers part of the old line south of Leicester. Since 1969, however, enthusiasts have succeeded in reopening the section between Loughborough and Leicester, and several stations along the way have been restored, notably 1940s Quorn and Edwardian Rothley. Trains run every weekend, and daily in summer. Reconstruction events, bring to life the days when the railway was the heart of the community. Period and themed galas reflect more than a century of the Great Central Railway.

Fort and Fossils

Northwest of Leicester are 30 sq miles (77.6sq km) of heathland with some of the oldest crags and rock formations in the country. The area is known throughout the world for its fossils, some of which date back 700 million years and are the oldest evidence of anything more complex than seaweed. From the high points like Bardon Hill (912ft/278m), near Coalville, and Beacon Hill (818ft/249m), near Woodhouse Eaves, there are tremendous views.

Although Beacon Hill has not been excavated, there is evidence to show that it has been of interest to man since the early Bronze Age, and there is a line of defensive earthworks. The hill is also important geologically. The obtruding layered rocks are layers of volcanic ash formed on the seabed, each representing a different eruption around 700 million years ago.

The National Space Centre, Leicester, is the largest centre dedicated to space and space exploration in the UK

Loughborough

This Victorian town is perhaps best known for the sportspeople produced by its university, but it is also associated with the casting of bells, and a visit to the John Taylor Bellfoundry Museum is highly recommended. These workshops produced the carillon for Washington Cathedral in the United States and a 53-bell carillon for Canberra in Australia. In Queen's Park is the unmistakable 151ft (46m) Carillon Tower, a memorial to local men who were killed during the First World War. It has a 47-bell carillon, with recitals during the summer, and there is also a War Memorial Museum.

Melton Mowbray

In England Melton Mowbray is commonly associated with pork pies, and indeed they have been made here for at least 150 years, partly at least because the area was important for the raising of pigs. A Melton pork pie is distinguished by the fact that it is baked without hoops or moulds for support. They are still produced in the town by Dickinson and Morris.

Melton is responsible for the expression 'painting the town red', after the antics of an exuberant Marquis of Waterford, one of the hunting fraternity that regularly descended on Melton, who did just that in 1837. Visitors should seek out St Mary's medieval church, with its soaring tower and fine Perpendicular clerestory, and the Melton Carnegie Museum, which is devoted to local history, particularly to the production of pork pies and Stilton cheese.

Mountsorrel

There are good views from here over the River Soar, which forms part of the Grand Union Canal, and the part of the village on the canal is very pretty. The domed market cross dates back to 1793, and just off the main street is Stonehurst Family Farm, a working farm museum with forge, tractor rides and motor museum.

Tourist Information

Leicester: 7–9 Every Street, Town Hall Square (tel: 0844 888 5181)
Loughborough: Town Hall, Market Place (tel: 01509 218113)
Melton Mowbray: Windsor House, Windsor Street (tel: 01664 480992)

Pork pie shop, Melton Mowbray; Melton pork pies are made using uncured pork and have a high meat content

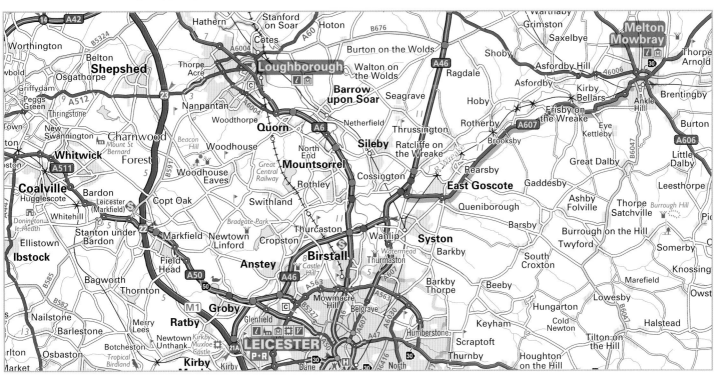

ENGLAND'S SMALLEST COUNTY

If Leicestershire can be seen as the heart of the 'shires', then Rutland is even more so, especially since it was reinstated as England's smallest county in 1997. Small it may be, but there is a surprising amount to see. Even so, we venture just across the border into Lincolnshire to visit the delightful town of Stamford and magnificent Burghley House.

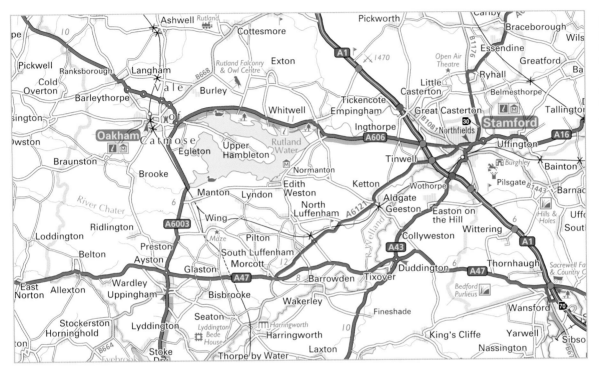

Rutland Reinstated

Only 17 miles (27.3km) wide, with an area of 150 sq miles (388.5sq km), England's smallest county has the motto *multum in parvo*, or 'much from little'. As an entity it has 1,000 years of history. In Saxon times it was a royal estate, the dower of the queens of England. As an historic county, however, 'Roteland', its name probably taken from the redness of its ironstone, goes back to the time of King John.

Because of its size Rutland fought against becoming part of Leicestershire in the 1960s and won, for which victory a special beer, 'Rutland Victory Ale', was brewed. That victory was short-lived, though, and subsequently they were overcome at the second attempt in 1974. However, the county of Rutland was never forgotten, and in April 1997 Rutland reclaimed its crown as Britain's smallest county.

Barnsdale Garden

This garden was created by the much-loved BBC *Gardeners' World* presenter, Geoff Hamilton, who died in 1996. Occupying the 8-acre (3.2ha) garden of his Victorian farmhouse at Exton, the gardens took shape, often on the air for the benefit of viewers, from 1984 onwards. They comprise a large number of different themed areas, including the First Time Garden, Ornamental Kitchen Garden, Town Garden, Japanese, Rose and Herb gardens, woodland walk, and many more. There is also a plant nursery with around 1,500 varieties for sale.

At Barnsdale Gardens, visitors can see more than 38 individual gardens

Burghley House

Just outside Stamford, Burghley House is a marvellous late Elizabethan mansion, built between 1565 and 1587 and surrounded by parkland. The house itself was rather fancifully designed with the help of William Cecil, whose descendants still live here, and who, in his political life as adviser to Elizabeth I, was better known for his caution and sobriety. The interior was considerably altered by later generations, especially by the fifth Lord Burghley, whose tour of Italy in the 17th century prompted the remarkable array of classical murals on the walls of the State Rooms. Burghley also houses a noted collection of 17th-century Italian paintings, as well as furniture and porcelain. The grounds are the venue for internationally famous horse trials and other events.

The lead roof of Burghley House extends across three-quarters of an acre

Harringworth Viaduct, which crosses the Welland Valley between Rutland and Northamptonshire

Cottesmore

Home to the famous hunt, which dates back to the early 18th century, Cottesmore is also associated with the iron horse. The Rutland Railway Museum has more than 30 locomotives, many of which are in working order, and one of the largest collections of goods rolling stock in the country. The village church has a chapel dedicated to the RAF and American Air Force personnel stationed here during the Second World War.

Lyddington

Strung prettily along the Gretton Road and village green are Lyddington's array of 17th- and 18th-century houses, and there is a 13th-century market cross. The church, in Perpendicular style, was probably built at the same time as Bede House, forming a fine range of 15th-century buildings which were originally intended to serve as a residence for the Bishops of Lincoln. The hall, with its 16th-century wooden ceiling, is particularly attractive.

Oakham

A small market town of stone terraces and Georgian villas, Rutland's county town has an attractive market place with a striking octagonal butter cross and stocks. Just off the square is a Norman fortified manor house known as Oakham Castle. Its interior walls are adorned with horseshoes; the earliest, which are 15th century, could stem from the ancient custom that all noblemen visiting Oakham were compelled by the lords of the manor, the de Ferrers, to present them with a shoe. Near the market place is Oakham School, a late 16th-century foundation. The 13th-century All Saints Church is near to the school and contains some fine medieval carving. The Rutland County Museum is housed in the former Riding School of the Rutland Fencible Cavalry.

Belvoir Castle

Looking for all the world like a fairy-tale medieval castle, with a plethora of turrets and towers, Belvoir's (pronounced 'Beever') current manifestation is actually of the 19th century. There has been a castle on the site since the 11th century. During the many political upheavals of the Middle Ages, it changed master many times, finally coming into the hands of the Dukes of Rutland. It was destroyed during the Civil War, and subsequently rebuilt, but the 5th Duchess decided that something more grand was required. Finished in 1830, Belvoir is still the home of the Dukes of Rutland, though it actually lies within Leicestershire, 10 miles (16.1km) from the county border. Inside are many lavishly decorated rooms with works by Poussin, Reynolds and Holbein.

Rutland Water

Much of the Vale of Catmose is now underwater – Rutland Water. One of the largest man-made lakes in Europe, this reservoir was created in the 1970s and, though controversial at the time, it has become an accepted part of the landscape. On its banks, like a docked ship, is Normanton Church, now a museum.

Stamford

This winsome town of ancient limestone buildings and narrow, sometimes cobbled streets, was once famous for its Stamford cloth and later became an important inland port. Stamford is one of those towns that is a delight to enjoy on foot.

There are some distinct places of interest. Brownes Hospital is a charming set of almshouses complete with chapel and 15th-century stained glass. St Martin's Church contains the extravagant Burghley tombs, including that of William Cecil, adviser to Elizabeth I.

In Stamford Museum there are exhibits devoted to the strange lives of the tiny 'General' Tom Thumb and, at the other extreme, the 53-stone (337kg) Daniel Lambert.

Wing

This village has a surviving medieval circular turf maze, some 40ft (12.2m) in diameter, the exact origins of which are unclear. One theory is that it provided a form of penance for sinners, who would crawl along its low passages on their hands and knees to shake off the devil, who cannot follow around curves. It may also have been associated with religious observances of pagan origin.

Welland Viaduct

This magnificent feat of Victorian engineering was built in 1876–8 to carry the Midland Railway line across the Welland Valley. It is one of the most spectacular viaducts left in Britain, with 82 arches looping across the vale for more than three-quarters of a mile (1.2km). In celebration of the completed work 'a grand banquet was given by Messrs. Lorden and Holmes ... in a large shed, tastefully decorated, near to Seaton Railway Station'.

See Walk G, page 190
A Rutland Waterside Walk

See Walk L, page 195
King of Belvoir Castle

Tourist Information
Rutland Water: Sykes Lane, Empingham (tel: 01572 653026)
Stamford: The Arts Centre, 27 St Mary Street (tel: 01780 755611)

The maze in Wing, Leicestershire

LINCOLNSHIRE'S CROWNING GLORY

Lincoln and its surrounding area is fascinating, and local people quite rightly point out that it tends to be overlooked. Clearly this is a shame, for Lincoln possesses one of the great cathedrals of the world, an impressive castle and narrow cobbled streets of ancient buildings. All of this stands on a high ridge above the flat Lincolnshire plain – a magical sight from afar.

Coates

Almost alone on the landscape, hidden among some trees, is the little church of St Edith's at Coates. A little church, with an interior which has been barely touched since the Middle Ages, the Norman font, Elizabethan brasses, early pews and, above all, the 15th-century rood screen, are charmingly evocative of Lincolnshire's rural past.

Looking down over the Knot Garden maze at Doddington Hall

Stephen Broadbent's sculpture Empowerment, *close to Brayford Pool in Lincoln*

Doddington

Close to Lincoln, this little village is noted above all for Doddington Hall, an Elizabethan house built for Thomas Taylor at the end of the 16th century by the architect of Longleat, Robert Smythson. Although the Hall has a Georgian interior, its exterior has hardly changed at all, and the formal gardens are among the finest in the county.

Not far from the village of Doddington is the Lincolnshire Road Transport Museum, which houses a display of an eclectic assortment of vehicles and early transport paraphernalia. The museum's vintage car society also hosts an annual vehicle rally in the grounds of Lincoln Castle.

Fossdyke Navigation

The Romans were quick to notice the strategic advantage of the place that was to become Lincoln, and this became the headquarters of the ninth Legion. The Romans were also responsible for the construction of the Fossdyke, which stretches for 11 miles (17.7km) between Torksey, on the Trent, and Brayford Pool, in Lincoln. More than 1,800 years old, this is the oldest working canal in England. Brayford Pool is in part responsible for Lincoln's name, which is derived from *Lindis Colonia*, meaning the 'colony by the water'.

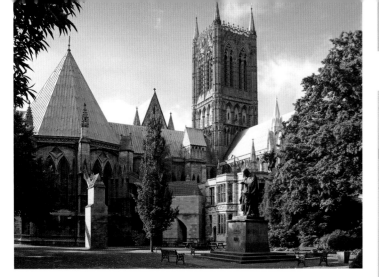

The library at Lincoln Cathedral contains a school book dating from 1410 with the first recorded rhyme about Robin Hood

The Delphs

The Delphs is an area of fenland to the southeast of Lincoln, where isolated farms sit on a flat, hedgeless landscape. This kind of featureless country is an acquired taste but it is not without interest. The Witham Valley, on the edge of this area of fen, was an important monastic area and there are several interesting churches in the area, notably at Nocton and Kirkstead. Of the villages, two are of specialised interest. Metheringham was the site of an important bomber airfield during the Second World War and photographs and memorabilia can be seen at the Metheringham Airfield Visitor Centre. At Timberland Delph, the old pumping station, which was built in 1839 to drain 2,500 acres (1,000ha) of the surrounding fenland, is open to visitors.

Gainsborough

A pretty town on the River Trent, spanned by a bridge built in 1791, Gainsborough boasts the only Georgian parish church in Lincolnshire, although its 90ft (27.4m) spire is Perpendicular. The most handsome building in the town is the Old Hall, parts of which date back to at least 1484, when Richard III stayed here. When in later years its owners, the Hickmans, built a new house, the Old Hall was put to various uses, including as a theatre, an inn and a Congregational chapel, until it was saved for posterity in 1952. It is one of the country's best-preserved manor houses – the Great Hall is magnificent. Gainsborough can also boast a fine building from the industrial age, the Britannia Works of 1850, formerly occupied by the firm of Marshalls, which manufactured steam engines and tractors.

Lincoln

Rising high above the gentle Lincolnshire wolds from the north bank of the River Witham, the ancient city of Lincoln is dominated by its magnificent cathedral, with a beautiful Romanesque west front, kaleidoscopic Bishop's Eye window and handsome cloister. It is the third largest medieval cathedral in the country, after St Paul's and York Minster, and towers majestically over the city and the surrounding countryside. It was begun in the 11th century, but most of the original is buried within later additions and alterations. Its famous library contains many treasures, including the best preserved of the four existing copies of Magna Carta, and first editions of *Paradise Lost*, *Don Quixote* and part of Spenser's *Faerie Queene*.

Many of Lincoln's other attractions are concentrated around the cathedral. The castle dates back to Norman times and substantial parts of it remain. There are many charming houses, medieval and Georgian, in the cathedral precincts and

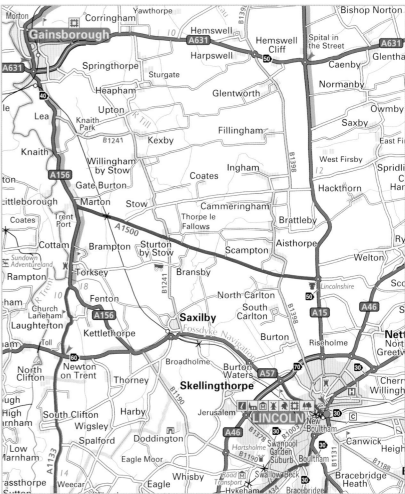

particularly along the well-named Steep Hill, which leads down to the High Street and the Norman vaulted High Bridge, still carrying timber-framed buildings. At the end of Bailgate is the Newport Arch, the only Roman arch in Britain still in everyday use; the 20ft (6.1m) Mint Wall is also Roman, all that remains of the Basilica.

Greyfriars is a beautiful 13th-century building and the oldest Franciscan church in the country. It is used as an exhibition centre with displays from the county's extensive historical collections. The Museum of Lincolnshire Life illustrates the social history of the county, and behind the museum is a working windmill, built in 1798, that still produces flour.

See Walk N, page 197
Churches of the Wolds

Tourist Information
Lincoln: 9 Castle Hill
(tel: 01522 873213)

Torksey

At the meeting point of the Trent and the Fossdyke, Torksey was a medieval town of some importance, with three churches, a monastery, a nunnery and a castle. One church remains, St Peter's, with an early English nave, as well as a fragment of the Elizabethan castle, destroyed during the Civil War, which stands forlornly on the banks of the Trent.

NEW TOWNS AND OLD TOWNS

Like many countries with long histories, Britain has had to adapt over the centuries to rapidly changing circumstances. Much that was taken for granted in the past has become redundant. Towns that were once prosperous have fallen on hard times as their once-famous products have become superfluous. New towns and communities have been planned and built, and their merits, or otherwise, continue to be debated.

Historically, with the exception of resort towns like Leamington Spa, towns have tended to grow organically. There was a moment of foundation in the sense that a family or a tribe settled at a particular place which sometimes attracted others as time passed. Industries in turn grew according to need. The 20th century in Britain saw the development of the 'new towns', not a result of serendipity but of philosophy.

Milton Keynes is a growth area for business

Unapologetically modern, Milton Keynes gave companies the utilitarian office and transport links they needed

Visions of Utopia

Although visions of Utopia have been expressed in England since the Elizabethan era, to a large extent the ideas behind 'new' towns have been based on post-Victorian philanthropic reactions to urban poverty. The functions of towns were rationalised and organised, sorted and graded and then new ones were designed and laid out. Public buildings, entertainments and shops were to be in the centre, around this would be residential areas, and then, at the perimeter, the factories. From this grew the 'garden' towns of the early 20th century.

After the Second World War, the New Towns Act of 1946 promoted the construction of new towns, the first generation including Corby and the second including Peterborough and Milton Keynes. Such towns were less genteel than their garden predecessors and made much more use of strictly modern materials and designs

and also made provision for traffic. Their express aim was to remove the poor from the slums of big cities, particularly London, to provide them with a more congenial and more humane environment. At the same time, it was hoped that they would divert potentially harmful pressure away from green belt areas.

In many ways the new towns appear to have been a surprising success, at least economically, and indeed there is still a lobby for the construction of more. Yet, curiously, there is still a tendency to sneer at them. The principal accusation levelled is that they are 'soulless', an accusation that

carries some weight when it is borne in mind that, although it has been reasonably easy to attract business and employees to Milton Keynes, for example, it has proved a great deal harder to get their bosses to buy homes for their families there.

The attraction of the leafy suburbs of old-fashioned cities or the traditional village green with pub is still very strong. In the case of Milton Keynes, founded in 1967, the business argument has been won – with a population in excess of 230,000, it has become one of the largest growth areas in the country. The challenge now is to find other reasons for people to move there.

View of the Mathematical Bridge, the popular name of a wooden bridge across the River Cam, between two parts of Queens' College. The bridge was built by James Essex in 1749. It has been rebuilt on two occasions (1866 and 1905) but has kept the same overall design

Marketing campaigns emphasise the mix of old and new, while its proximity to Cambridge, Oxford and Stratford is cited as an advantage for the visitor.

In Easy Reach

These days, perhaps, such arguments are almost superfluous. Milton Keynes, and others of the new towns, seem to be able to weather economic stagnation better than many of the older towns. One reason is location. The sites for the new towns were deliberately chosen with their relative position in mind and Milton Keynes is rated as being the best centre for distribution in the whole country. The older towns are, of course, stuck with their location and have to choose industries that suit them, not the other way around – although, should rail transport ever make a comeback, it could well be to the advantage of some of Britain's historic towns.

A good general location results in a town that will attract a broad range of companies. Coca-Cola was one of the first companies to choose Milton Keynes and since then at least another 10,000 businesses have followed, bringing with them more than 100,000 jobs.

If, however, the accent appears to be purely on financial gain, that is not an entirely accurate impression. Another advantage to 'newness' is that heritage legislation, for the time being at least, is meaningless. Experiments can be made, therefore, and not just visual ones. The National Energy Foundation, for example, resides in Milton Keynes and, as a result of the lessons learned in energy conservation there in the last 30 years, other towns are following its example. Another first for Britain was the move of Wimbledon Football Club to Milton Keynes, creating MK Dons FC. Soulless some of the new towns may be, but they are certainly not artless.

Shakespeare Hotel in Stratford-upon-Avon

Bridge of Sighs, Oxford
Left: Peterborough Cathedral was built in its present form between 1118 and 1238

THE POTTERIES

This area of the Midlands is often overlooked by visitors, probably because of a misplaced idea of what the industrial 'potteries' are really like. It is not all motorway and Alton Towers. There is some attractive countryside, threaded with canals, some wonderful historic houses and an industrial heritage that is well worth exploring, particularly in Stoke-on-Trent.

The Horn Dance at Abbots Bromley was first performed in 1226 and involves a walk of about 10 miles (16km)

Abbots Bromley

This attractive Staffordshire village is well known for its annual Horn Dance, which takes place in early September. One theory on its obscure origins is that the dance celebrates the establishment of ancient hunting rights; another, that it is derived from an ancient fertility rite. During the day the dance is performed at various places.

Cheddleton

See Walk F, page 189
Lichfield's Soaring Heaven on Earth

Tourist Information
Stafford: Eastgate Street
(tel: 01785 619619)
Stoke-on-Trent: Victoria Hall, Cultural Quarter
(tel: 01782 236000)

Cheddleton is situated where the Caldon Canal runs parallel with River Churnet. It was once important for the grinding of flint, used in the production of slip for the pottery industry. Its twin mills, with their picturesque water wheels, were last worked commercially in 1963, although they continue to turn through the dedication of volunteers. Also in Cheddleton is the Churnet Valley Railway, which offers a programme of special events and steam train rides.

The Shugborough Estate

The family home of the Earls of Lichfield, Shugborough House, now owned by the National Trust, dates back to 1693. It is beautifully furnished, but even more fascinating are the servants' quarters, with laundry, kitchens, brewhouse and coachhouse, all staffed by costumed guides who show what domestic life was like around 100 years ago. Within the estate is a Georgian farm with an agricultural museum, working corn mill and rare breeds centre.

Stafford

The county town of Staffordshire has few of its medieval buildings, but among those that have survived the Ancient High House, built in 1595 on Greengate Street, is the tallest half-timbered town house in England. It houses period room settings reflecting the history of the house. The Shire Hall Gallery and Craft Shop blends contemporary craftwork and changing art exhibitions, while the William Salt Library contains an important collection of books and drawings. Outside the town the extensive remains of Stafford Castle are brought to life through video, model reconstructions and hands-on equipment.

Stoke-on-Trent

Stoke-on-Trent, famous for its potteries, consists of the six towns of Burslem, Fenton, Hanley, Longton, Stoke and Tunstall, which were formally confederated in 1910. Stoke gives its visitors a real experience of Britain's industrial heritage through working museums and walks along canals and abandoned railway lines.

The heart of the modern town is Hanley, the largest of the old towns, where the Potteries Museum and Art Gallery houses one of the most magnificent collections of china and pottery in the world. In Longton the Gladstone Pottery Museum is housed in a working 19th-century pottery. Many of the famous china producers, including Royal Doulton, Coalport and Spode, offer tours. Just to the north at Smallthorne is Ford Green Hall, a 1624 timber-framed

Rear view of the Ancient High House in Stafford, the largest timber framed town house in England

Alton Towers

England's answer to Disneyland has more than 125 different attractions and rides of varying degrees of terror, but it is not all a 'white-knuckle' experience. There are gentler rides for younger children, cinema shows and sedate swan boats on the lake, as well as items that celebrate home-grown fictional characters such as Peter Rabbit. Among all these attractions it is easy to overlook the fact that the grounds were originally landscaped by 'Capability' Brown for the 15th Earl of Shrewsbury's great Gothic mansion, built in 1809 and now in ruins.

Caldon Canal

The Caldon Canal runs for 17.5 miles (28km) from the main line of the Trent and Mersey Canal at Etruria, near Stoke, to Froghall and passes through 17 locks. Completed in 1778, its main purpose was the carriage of limestone and horse-drawn tramways were built to link Froghall with the quarries. The Caldon was never officially closed down and indeed remained partly navigable until the 1960s. A canal of contrasts, it passes through some exquisite countryside. Parts of it, however, became impassable and it was only constant pressure from the Caldon Canal Society, and the work of volunteers, that finally led to its reopening in 1974.

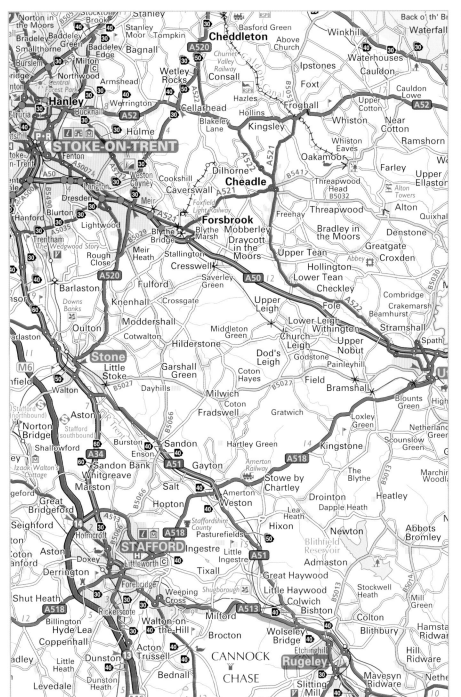

Old Oak trees in Cannock Chase, much of which is a Site of Special Scientific Interest

Cannock Chase

Officially designated an Area of Outstanding Natural Beauty, Cannock Chase is 20,000 acres (8,100ha) of heath and woodland. Once a Norman hunting ground, it still has fallow and red deer, which thrive in an environment that varies from oak and birch woodland to heather and gorse, and tracts of bracken. Vantage points, such as the Hednesford Hills, and Castle Hill and its Iron-Age hillfort, offer excellent views across the Chase and the countryside of the Trent Valley. Near Broadhurst is a surprising and poignant place – a German military cemetery where 5,000 German servicemen who died in Britain are buried. The Marquis Drive Visitor Centre provides detailed information and trail guides for walkers.

yeoman farmer's house showing what life was like before the Industrial Revolution.

Weston Park

Weston Park, the family home of the Earls of Bradford, was built in 1671 and is one of the finest examples of its kind. Set in over 1,000 acres (405ha) of landscaped park, the house contains a superb collection of art. Within the grounds are a miniature railway, playground and gardens.

Bridgewater Pottery is made from a mix that is a variant of Josiah Wedgwood's 18th-century recipe for creamware

NOTTINGHAM AND DERBY

The mention of Nottingham brings Robin Hood to mind, or perhaps D. H. Lawrence, who was born nearby. The Merry Men would not find much that is familiar today, and even Lawrence would notice a great many changes, but even though Sherwood Forest has largely disappeared, this area has lots of beautiful countryside, historic cities and unusual attractions.

The New Guildhall in Derby was built in 1828

🐾 **See Walk K, page 194**
Mackworth and Markeaton:
A Rural Idyll

🐾 **See Walk M, page 196**
A Merrie Tale of Sherwood Forest

Tourist Information
Derby: Assembly Rooms, Market Place (tel: 01332 255802)
Nottingham: 1–4 Smithy Row (tel: 08444 775678)

Castle Donington

This village is noted for its racetrack and the Donington Collection, the largest assembly of single-seater racing cars in the world. Many of the cars have been raced by the world's greatest drivers – Juan Fangio, Tazio Nuvolari, Stirling Moss and Ayrton Senna. There are more than 130 exhibits in five halls portraying the history of motorsport.

Denby

A name associated with pottery, although the modern pottery works are in fact some way from the village, closer to Ripley. Denby ware has been produced since 1809, based on local clay, the exceptional smoothness of which produces a flawless glaze when fired. Tours of the works are available. There is also a museum and a shop that sells slightly imperfect items as well as those of the highest quality.

Derby

Derby became a city only in 1977. Its growth began with the construction of silk mills, then came porcelain manufacture; but its essentially genteel character only changed with the coming of the railways, when Midland Railways established their headquarters here, and the motor car in the form of the Rolls Royce factory.

Much of the city centre has been rebuilt, not very kindly, but older Derby is well preserved in Friar's Gate and St Mary's Gate, with its County Hall dating back to 1660. There are fine houses in the Wardwick, as well as the church of St Werburgh, where Samuel Johnson was married. The cathedral has a magnificent 16th-century west tower, but its character is derived essentially from the clean lines of 18th-century architecture. The city also has several museums – the Derby Museum and Art Gallery, the Royal Crown Derby Visitor Centre devoted to the history of porcelain production, the Silk Mill, Derby's industrial and heritage museum and Pickford's House Museum, which focuses on the social history of the Georgian era.

Eastwood

The author D. H. Lawrence was born here in 1885 in a small terraced house at 8a Victoria Street, which is now a museum. The Lawrence family subsequently moved to 28 Garden Road, renamed 'Sons and Lovers House', since it featured in the novel. It can be visited by appointment.

Elvaston Castle

Formerly the home of the Earls of Harrington, Elvaston Castle is now a country park with woodland and play areas. The formal gardens were laid out in the 1830s for the Fourth Earl, as a gesture of love for his wife, and are especially notable for their topiary and evergreen bushes.

Holme Pierrepont

This village is noted for two establishments – Holme Pierrepont Hall and the Holme Pierrepont Country Park and National

Robin Hood

The archetypal English folk hero was first mentioned in 1377 in William Langland's *Piers Plowman.* According to legend he was a 12th-century gentleman robber who used his skill with the longbow to poach the land of Sherwood Forest in Nottingham and to rob the rich in order to help the poor. His driving ethos was one of English resistance to the Norman monarchy. Quests to substantiate these stories have failed, and what clues there are hint at a Yorkshire yeoman, nothing like the Robin Hood of legend. As for Maid Marian, Friar Tuck and so on, they appear to derive from a variety of sources, and when all is said and done Robin would seem to be a fabrication – an all-purpose English hero.

Kedleston Hall, where the great marble hall, topped by a high-coved cornice is designed to evoke the atrium of a Roman villa

Curzon family, whose most eminent member was Viceroy of India from 1898 to 1905 and about whom there is a display inside the house.

Nottingham

For centuries an important town, reaching its zenith with lace production in the 19th century, Nottinghamshire's capital has an imposing centre. The huge Old Market Square and surrounding streets have stately 19th and early 20th century buildings from its industrial heyday.

In a sense, the town is dominated by its historic castle, but in truth only the 13th-century gatehouse, sections of medieval wall and moat remain. Mostly it is a 17th-century Italianate palace, built by the Duke of Newcastle and now housing the Castle Museum, with a fine collection of British paintings, silver and ceramics. There are many other museums – Brewhouse Yard, the Lace Centre, the Costume and Textiles Museum – as well as a contender for the title of Britain's oldest pub, the Trip to Jerusalem. Wollaton Hall, a 16th-century mansion 3 miles (4.8km) outside the city, houses the Natural History Museum. As for Robin Hood, he and his lawless cohorts have been resurrected in tours of 'Robin Hood Country'.

The Trent and Mersey Canal

Much of this canal runs through Staffordshire, linking the River Trent near Derby with the Mersey at Runcorn, and is therefore largely rural. It was the most ambitious undertaking of the engineer James Brindley – a canal of enormous contrasts, varying in width to accommodate the largest commercial barges in some places and with room only for narrowboats in others. It was started in 1766, but such were the difficulties in construction that the 93 miles (149.6km) were completed only in 1777. It was a commercial success, many observers holding the opinion that its existence was entirely responsible for the growth of the Potteries. Regular commercial use came to an end only in the 1960s.

Watersports Centre. The latter offers facilities for, and tuition in all kinds of watersports and there is a nature reserve. The Hall dates from the 16th century. It contains period furnishings and in one of the bedrooms the ceiling has been removed to show the roof construction.

Ilkeston

A hilltop industrial town with fine views, Ilkeston's main attractions are the Erewash Museum, with displays of lacemaking and other crafts in a Georgian house with Victorian extensions.

Kedleston Hall

The finest Georgian house in Derbyshire was the work of three major architects, including Robert Adam, who also designed the park. The house belonged to the

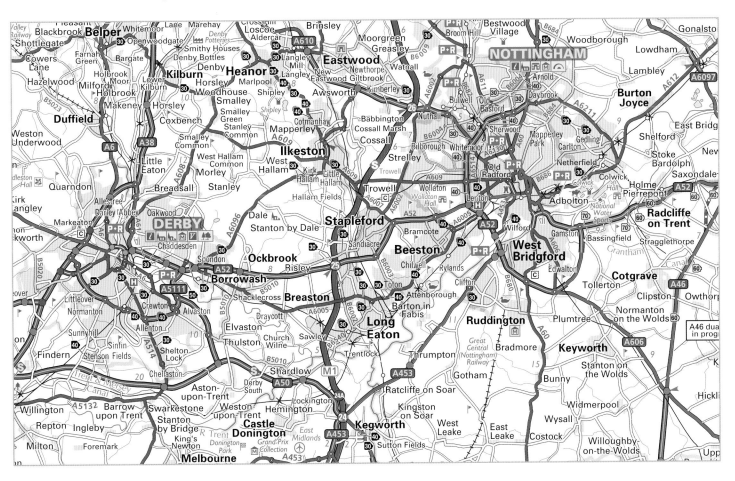

Walk
A

A VILLAGE TRAIL FROM BADBY

This route links three delightful villages west of Northampton.

The Windmill Pub at Badby

Distance: 6.75 miles (10.9km)
Minimum time: 3hrs 30min
Ascent/Gradient: 787ft (240m) ▲▲▲
Level of difficulty: +++
Paths: Mostly pasture, muddy where cows congregate, 11 stiles
Landscape: Undulating hills covered with fields, woods and parkland
Suggested map: OS Explorer 207 Newport Pagnell & Northampton South
Start/finish: Grid reference: SP 559589
Dog friendliness: Plenty of livestock, so strict control necessary, lots of stiles
Parking: On Main Street, Badby
Public toilets: None on route (nearest in Daventry)

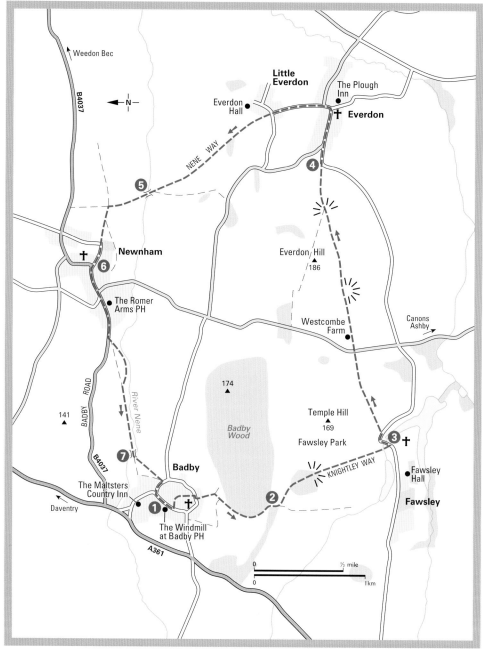

❶ With your back to the Windmill at Badby, walk up Vicarage Hill to reach Badby church. Take the alleyway path signposted 'Fawsley', opposite the south side of the church, then head right up a sloping field for a path around the western edge of Badby Wood, famous for its springtime bluebells.

❷ After about 0.25 mile (400m) take the right fork (upper path), and follow waymarks for the Knightley Way out across the open hilltop of Fawsley Park and down towards the lakes near the hall.

❸ Go ahead along the lane at the bottom to inspect the church, otherwise turn left, and in a few paces left again (before the cattle grid) for a footpath that heads up and across a large sloping field. Go through a gate and down a track to the road, then resume opposite climbing steadily through fields, passing Westcombe Farm on the left. Continue across Everdon Hill and down to the village of Everdon below, joining a lane via a stile to the right as you near the bottom of the hill.

❹ Walk through the village, following the road as it bends left past the church and Plough

Inn, and turn left for the lane to reach Little Everdon. When the road appears to split go ahead/left for a path to the left of the farm buildings. This continues out across open fields, with Everdon Hall to your right. On the far side, pass the end of a strip of trees and maintain your northwesterly direction to carry on through four more fields and reach the river (aim just to the right of Newnham's church spire when it comes into view).

❺ Cross the Nene via a footbridge and walk uphill through one field, then veer left in the second to cross a third, and drop down to pick up a farm drive which, beyond a gate, becomes Manor Lane. Walk on to join the main street.

❻ Turn left and drop down past the Romer Arms pub by The Green and continue along Badby Road out of the village. In 150 yards (137m) go left for field-edge paths alongside the infant River Nene.

❼ Go over the footbridge at the end and walk half-left through the field ahead, keeping left of the clump of trees in the middle and aiming for Badby church. At the far corner turn right into Chapel Lane to return to the centre of Badby.

FENLAND'S BIG SKIES

An enigmatic landscape links remote Manea with an historic drainage cut.

Welches Dam, near Manea

Distance: 6.25 miles (10.1km)
Minimum time: 3hrs
Ascent/Gradient: Negligible ▲▲▲
Level of difficulty: +++
Paths: Lanes and hard farm tracks, field-edge paths, 1 stile
Landscape: Wide, flat fields separated by ditches and drainage channels
Suggested map: OS Explorer 228 March & Ely
Start/finish: Grid reference: TL 478893
Dog friendliness: On lead at Ouse Washes Nature Reserve
Parking: Roadside parking in centre of Manea
Public toilets: Off Park Road, Manea, and at Ouse Washes Nature Reserve

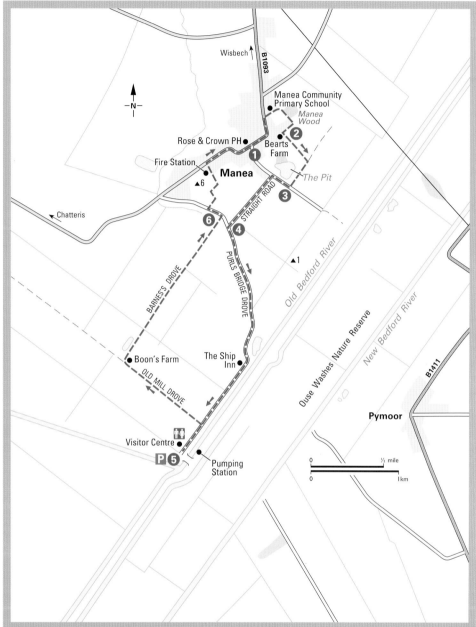

❶ With the Rose & Crown pub on your left, walk eastwards along Manea High Street and follow it round to the left as it becomes Station Road, then turn right for the public footpath alongside the primary school. At the football pitch at the far end, turn right and go past Manea Wood, planted in 1997 for the local community with ash, oak, white willow, birch and common alder. Continue along the path as it bears right and approaches Bearts Farm.

❷ Turn left by the old barns and sheds for the wide track out into the fields, and bear right at a junction of tracks to reach an attractive reedy lake known locally as 'The Pit'. This was originally dug for clay, which was then transported across the fields on a light railway

to shore up the banks of the nearby Old and New Bedford rivers. The Pit is now a popular place for fishermen and wildlife alike.

❸ At the end of the track, turn right on to a lane, with the lake still on your right, then, when you reach the junction at the corner of the road, turn left, on to Straight Road, and follow this through the fields to the end.

❹ Turn left on to Purls Bridge Drove, signposted 'Welches Dam' and 'RSPB reserve'. Follow this open lane all the way to Purls Bridge, by the Old Bedford River. Continue along the bank to reach the Ouse Washes Nature Reserve, where there's a visitor centre and public toilets.

❺ Return along the lane for 440 yards (402m) and turn left for the signposted public bridleway by some dark wooden sheds. Known as Old Mill Drove, this runs directly across the open fields as far as the rusting farm machinery and outbuildings of Boon's Farm. Turn right and walk along the dead-straight Barnes's Drove for 1.25 miles (2km) until you reach the road at the far end.

❻ Turn left, and after 150 yards (137m) turn off right through a gate for a public footpath across the fields back into Manea. The route zigzags between a series of paddocks – just follow the clear yellow waymarks and aim for the fire station tower. At the far side cross a stile and turn right, past the village stores, to follow the main road back to the centre.

THE SOUND OF MUSIC AT THAXTED

A glorious country walk following in the footsteps of composer Gustav Holst.

Thaxted Windmill, built in 1804

Distance: 3 miles (4.8km)
Minimum time: 1hr 30min
Ascent/Gradient: 92ft (28m) ▲▲▲
Level of difficulty: +++
Paths: Field-edge paths, bridleway prone to muddiness, riverbank and some town streets
Landscape: Arable fields, meadows and undulating farmland
Suggested map: OS Explorer 195 Braintree & Saffron Walden
Start/finish: Grid reference: TL 610311
Dog friendliness: Great for romping
Parking: Free car park at Margaret Street
Public toilets: Car park in Margaret Street

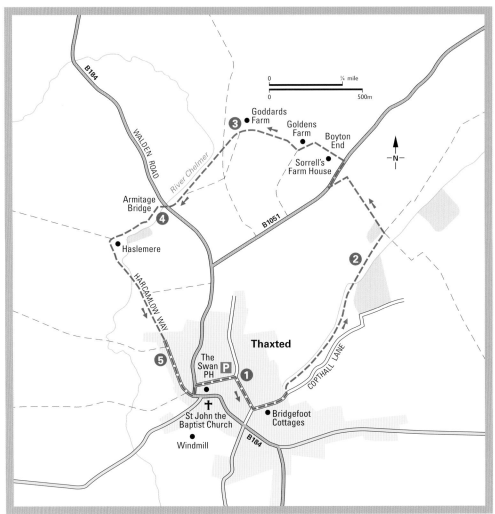

❶ From the car park turn left into Margaret Street, right into Weaverhead Lane and left into Copthall Lane, passing the row of cottages called Bridgefoot. After the houses on your left, pass through the gap between trees by the gate marked 'Walnut Tree Meadow'. Turn right along the grassy path and keep parallel with Copthall Lane on your right. After 400 yards (366m) bear left at the yellow waymark through trees, cross two footbridges at right angles, in quick succession, and turn right, keeping the stream and hedgerows on your right.

❷ Maintain direction along the field-edge path through two fields. After the spinney on your left, turn left at the waymark over the footbridge and follow another field-edge path, keeping the hedgerow on your left and crossing

another footbridge to the B1051, Sampford Road. In the distance, to your left is the spire of St John the Baptist Church. Turn right, cross the road with care, and take the first turning on the left along the farm track marked 'Boyton End'. The track zigzags left and right past Sorrell's Farm House and Goldens Farm. At Goldens Farm bear right on to the narrow canopied bridleway between buildings, and later bear right along a field-edge. Turn left outside Goddards Farm and follow the track downhill.

❸ Cross a road to the farm and the adjacent track to follow a fingerpost through the hedge. Turn half left across the field and follow the path with the River Chelmer on your right to Walden Road.

❹ At Walden Road turn right across Armitage Bridge and immediately left at the public footpath sign (now following Turpin's Trail). Follow the field-edge path with the river on your left passing conifers and, after 300 yards (274m), turn left at the waymark concealed in the hedgerows. You are now on the Harcamlow Way. Continue downhill along a driveway leading from the house called Haslemere, and go over concrete bridge across the river. Ignore paths left and right and continue along the tarmac road, past some elegant modern housing surrounded by rolling countryside.

❺ Continue along Watling Lane passing 17th-century cottages and Piggot's Mill until you emerge opposite The Swan. Turn left and right into Margaret Street and return to the car park.

STOWMARKET IN THE HEART OF SUFFOLK

Rural, urban and industrial landscapes all feature on this walk, together with a fascinating museum.

St. Peter and St. Mary church, Stowmarket

Distance: 6 miles (9.7km)
Minimum time: 2hrs 30min
Ascent/Gradient: 213ft (65m) ▲▲▲
Level of difficulty: +++
Paths: Town streets and footpaths, country lanes, field-edge and riverside paths
Landscape: Town, river, farmland and woodland
Suggested map: OS Explorer 211 Bury St Edmunds & Stowmarket
Start/finish: Grid reference: TM 046585
Dog friendliness: Dogs should be kept on lead
Parking: Meadow Centre pay-and-display car park, Stowmarket (follow signs to Museum of East Anglian Life)
Public toilets: At Meadow Centre

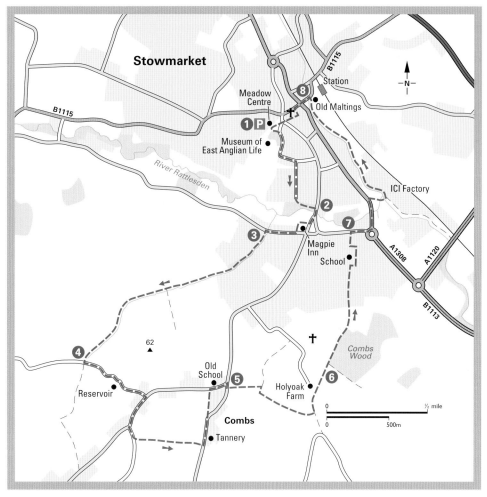

1 From the car park, take the path that runs past the museum and the gates of Abbot's Hall. When the path divides, fork right alongside a high brick wall, then turn right along a lane. At the end of the lane, turn left and look for a narrow path between the houses on the right, just before no. 19. Stay on this path as it drops down to the river, then turn left along a wide lane between houses and the River Rattlesden.

2 Reaching a road, turn right across the bridge and fork right when the road divides. Just before the Magpie Inn, turn right through the shopping precinct to reach Combs Lane. Cross the road and walk along the pavement until you cross a small stream just beyond Edgecomb Road.

3 Turn left at the stream by a telegraph pole with a 'Charcoal and Churches' circular walk sign. The path follows the stream, then heads through a wood and into open countryside. Cross a footbridge and turn right along a field-edge path.

4 At a metal barrier, turn left along a tarmac lane, past a mobile phone tower and reservoir. Turn right at the T-junction, then fork left along Mill Lane. After 70 yards (64m), turn left on a path that runs between parkland and fields. Turn left at the road to pass an old tannery, then head left on a tarmac path at Webb's Close to climb to the centre of Combs. Turn right at the road and walk past the old village school.

5 At the junction, turn right and immediately left, dropping down between the fields. Cross a footbridge and follow a field-edge path to the right. Go through a gate and bear diagonally across the field to reach a junction where you turn left, passing a thatched farmhouse on your way to Combs Wood.

6 Stay on this path as it runs alongside the wood and into a housing estate. Continue straight ahead on the paved path, crossing Lavenham Way and diverting around a school, turning left at the bottom, then right.

7 Turn right on Needham Road, then left along Gipping Way. Just before the paint factory, turn right, cross a bridge and go left on the signed 'Gipping Valley River Path'. Follow this path to the old maltings.

8 Climb the steps to the bridge and turn left along Station Road. Keep straight ahead at the crossroads, then go left through the churchyard. Narrow Buttermarket leads to the Market Place. Cross the square and walk through the Meadow Centre to the car park.

Walk E BENJAMIN BRITTEN'S ALDEBURGH

A walk in the footsteps of one of Britain's best-known 20th-century composers.

Aldeburgh beach, Suffolk

Distance: 5.75 miles (9.2km)
Minimum time: 2hrs 30min
Ascent/Gradient: Negligible ▲▲▲
Level of difficulty: +++
Paths: River and sea wall, meadows, old railway track
Landscape: Town, river, marshes and beach
Suggested map: OS Explorer 212 Woodbridge & Saxmundham
Start/finish: Grid reference: TM 463555
Dog friendliness: Off lead on river wall, on lead on permissive path – not allowed on beach between May and September
Parking: Slaughden Quay free car park
Public toilets: Slaughden Quay, Fort Green, Moot Hall

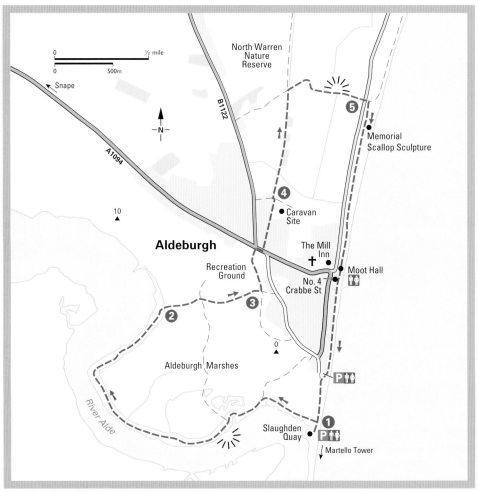

❶ Start at Slaughden Quay, once a thriving port, now a yacht club. Walk back briefly in the direction of Aldeburgh and turn left along the river wall on the north bank of the River Alde. There are good views to your left of the Martello Tower that marks the northern end of Orford Ness. Stay on the river wall for 2 miles (3.2km) as the river swings to the right towards Aldeburgh.

❷ When the river bends left, go down the wooden staircase to your right and keep straight ahead across a meadow with a water tower visible ahead. Go through a gate and bear half-left across the next meadow to cross over a footbridge. Next, follow the waymarks, bearing half-right, then keep straight ahead across the next field to come to another footbridge. After crossing a fifth footbridge, the path runs alongside allotments and goes through a gate to reach a lane.

❸ Turn left by a brick wall and cross the recreation ground. Continue past the fire station to reach a road. Turn right for 75 yards (69m), then go left on a signposted footpath almost opposite the hospital entrance. Follow this path between houses, cross a road and keep straight ahead with a caravan site on the right.

❹ When you see a footpath on the right, leading to a track across the caravan park, turn left and immediately right on a permissive path that follows the trackbed of an old railway. Stay on this path for 0.5 mile (800m) as it climbs steadily between farmland to the left and woodland and marshes to the right. Turn right at a junction of paths to reach the open meadows. Stay on this path, crossing the North Warren Nature Reserve with views of Sizewell power station to your left.

❺ Cross the road and turn right along a tarmac path that runs parallel to the beach. As you approach Aldeburgh, you pass a striking scallop sculpture on the shingle (erected in 2003 to celebrate Benjamin Britten's life in Aldeburgh), fishermen's huts and fishing boats that have been pulled up on to the shingle. Pass the timber-framed Moot Hall and continue along Crag Path, past a lifeboat station and a pair of 19th-century look out towers. At the end of Crag Path, bear right across a car park and walk around the old mill to return to Slaughden Quay.

Seagulls on an old fishing boat, Aldeburgh

LICHFIELD'S SOARING HEAVEN ON EARTH

A short and relatively simple town walk exploring the impact of the county's most magnificent cathedral.

Statue of Dr Johnson in Lichfield Market Square

Distance: 2.5 miles (4km)
Minimum time: 1hr
Ascent/Gradient: Negligible ▲▲▲
Level of difficulty: +++
Paths: Roads, surfaced paths and dirt trails
Landscape: Town centre and parkland
Suggested map: OS Explorers 232 Nuneaton & Tamworth; 244 Cannock Chase
Start/finish: Grid reference: SK 118095 (on Explorer 232)
Dog friendliness: Must be kept on lead near roads
Parking: Ample paid parking in Lichfield town centre
Public toilets: Town centre locations and Beacon Park

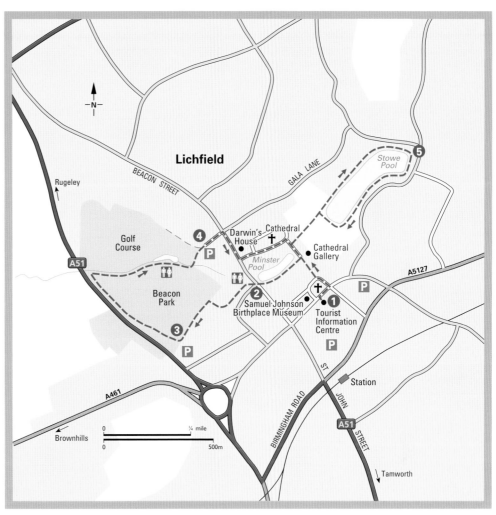

❶ From the tourist information centre, next to the Garrick theatre, go through Three Spires shopping arcade and turn left on to Conduit Street and ahead to Market Square. Carry straight along Dam Street, past a series of tea shops and cafés, until you get to Pool Walk. Go left here, keeping Minster Pool on your right-hand side, until you get to Beacon Street.

❷ Go diagonally right over Beacon Street to the public toilets and the entrance to the park. Skirt around the left-hand edge of the park, keeping first the bowling lawn and then the tennis courts to your right. After the tennis courts follow a path round to the right and, at the next path junction, walk left, continuing around the edge of the park.

❸ When you get to the car park bear slightly right, following the path to the far end of the playing fields. After the path has entered the narrow band of trees, and just before the A51, turn right along a narrow dirt trail and carry on to the golf course at the far end. Just before the footbridge on to the golf course, turn right and follow the small brook back along the edge of the playing fields until you reach a small lake. In the summer it's possible to hire boats here for a potter on the water. Continue on past the lake before crossing over a footbridge to the left to reach Shaw Lane.

❹ Follow Shaw Lane until you get to Beacon Street, then go right for 150 yards (137m) and then left along The Close to reach the cathedral. If you're not in any rush, it's worth doing a quick circuit of the cathedral inside and out, before continuing. There's an excellent shop with leaflets and guides and a free leaflet is also available, which describes the cathedral's highlights. Bear to the right of the cathedral and, at the end of The Close, just after Chapters Coffee Shop, go right down Dam Street and then immediately left down Reeve Lane to Stowe Pool. From the far end of Stowe Pool you can look back at the cathedral's towers and see right through the windows from one side to the other, giving the impression that they're lighter and more delicate than stone.

❺ Continue on the popular surfaced path all the way round the edge of Stowe Pool and return to Dam Street, before retracing your steps to the tourist information centre at the start.

Walk G
A RUTLAND WATERSIDE WALK

A short, but scenic, introduction to the aquatic charms of Rutland Water.

A view across Rutland Water to Hambleton Hall

Distance: 4.5 miles (7.2km)
Minimum time: 2hrs
Ascent/Gradient: 311ft (95m) ▲▲▲
Level of difficulty: +++
Paths: Wide and firm the whole distance, 3 stiles
Landscape: Low-lying peninsula of dipping fields and woodland
Suggested map: OS Explorer 234 Rutland Water
Start/finish: Grid reference: SK 900075
Dog friendliness: On lead in fields of stock and around nesting birds
Parking: Roadside parking in Hambleton
Public toilets: None on route (nearest in Oakham

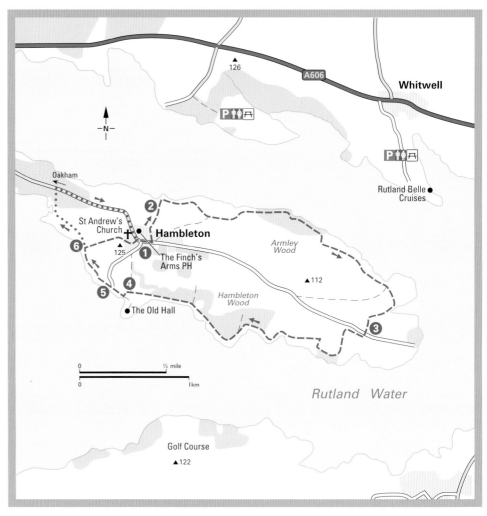

❶ From St Andrew's Church in the centre of Hambleton, walk eastwards on the long main street as far as the red pillar box. Turn left opposite the pillar box on a wide track indicated 'public footpath' that leads straight through a gate and down the middle of a sloping field.

❷ Go through the gate at the bottom of the field and turn right on to the wide track that runs just above the shore. This popular and peaceful route around the Hambleton peninsula is shared with cyclists, so enjoy the walk, but be alert. Follow it from field to field, and through Armley Wood, with ever-changing views across Rutland Water. As you gradually swing around the tip of the Hambleton peninsula with views towards the dam at the eastern end, you can begin to appreciate the sheer size of the reservoir, and how the birds, anglers, sailors and other users can all happily coexist.

❸ When you arrive at a tarmac lane (which is gated to traffic at this point, since it simply disappears into the water a little further on!), go straight across to continue on the same unmade track. It turns right and runs parallel with the road a short distance, before heading left and back towards the peaceful water's edge and a lovely section of mixed woodland. Continue along the lakeside for just over 1 mile (1.6km).

❹ Approaching The Old Hall, a handsome building perched just above the shore, turn left to reach its surfaced drive, then go right and walk along it for 160 yards (146m) to reach a cattle grid.

❺ At this point you can return directly to Hambleton by following the lane back uphill; otherwise veer left to continue along the open, waterside track, with views across to Egleton Bay and the corner of Rutland Water specially reserved for wildlife (it's out of bounds to sailing boats).

❻ After about 500 yards (460m) look for the easily missed stile in the hedge on your right, and the public footpath that heads straight up the field. (If you overshoot, or want to extend the walk by 0.5 mile (800m), simply carry on along the track to the very far end and return along the lane to the village.) Aim for the apex of the field, where successive stiles lead to a narrow passageway between a hedge and a fence that eventually brings you out in the churchyard in the centre of the village.

Looking across Rutland Water

IT ALL COMES OUT IN THE WASH

Choose between a wildlife wander or a spectacular aircraft display on the South Lincolnshire coast.

Irrigation channels at Melholme, Lincolnshire, similar to those found at Gedney Drove End

Distance: 5.75 miles (9.2km)

Minimum time: 2hrs 30min

Ascent/Gradient: Negligible ▲▲▲

Level of difficulty: +++

Paths: Field-edges, firm tracks and sea banks, 1 stile

Landscape: Open arable fields and bare marsh and mudflats

Suggested map: OS Explorer 249 Spalding & Holbeach

Start/finish: Grid reference: TF 463292

Dog friendliness: Overhead military planes on weekdays can be very loud

Parking: Roadside parking in centre of Gedney Drove End (off A17 east of Holbeach)

Public toilets: None on route

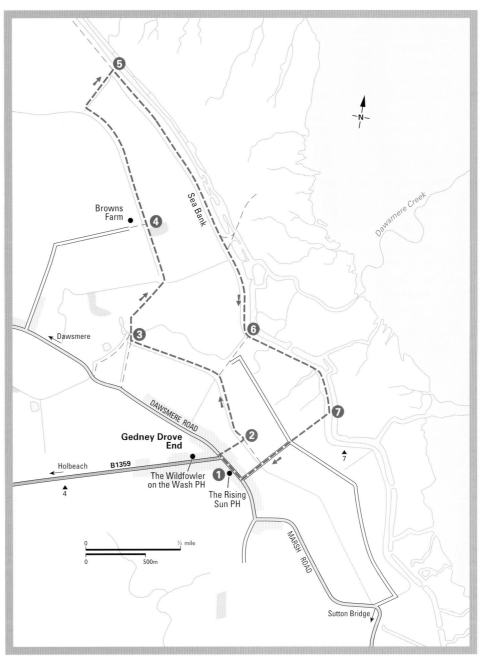

① With your back to The Rising Sun pub, turn left and walk along Dawsmere Road past the junction and take the signposted public footpath on the right, between bungalows, opposite the playground sign. At the far side of the field go across a small footbridge and up some steps in order to turn left into a wide field.

② For 1 mile (1.6km) walk along the edge of this field, which is in fact the line of the former sea wall, keeping more or less parallel with the present and much higher sea bank over to your right. And as a sign indicates, continue straight ahead at the point where the old sea bank veers invitingly away to the right.

③ When the field eventually ends near a strip of woodland turn right for 50 yards (46m), then, faced with a small thicket, drop down to join the wide farm track on your left. Turn right, and follow the main, higher route (ignore the lower track) alongside a narrow shelter-belt of woodland which includes apple, cherry,

hazel and birch. This wide, gravel track heads out towards the sea bank, then bends left and continues past Browns Farm.

④ Stay on the main track for about 0.75 mile (1.2km) beyond the farm, then go right by an old wartime pill box for a short path over to the sea wall.

⑤ Turn right and follow either the grassy top of the sea bank (a public right of way) or the surfaced lane just below it past a succession of military observation towers. The bombing range of nearby RAF Holbeach is spread out before you, with the low Norfolk coast over to your right and the Lincolnshire seaboard towards Boston and Skegness as you look leftwards.

⑥ After the third tower ignore the gated road that heads off inland (a short cut back to Gedney), but instead continue along the sea bank past one final watchtower until you reach a stile. Cross the stile and continue for another 400 yards (366m).

⑦ Turn right at a public footpath sign, down some steps, for a direct path along a field-edge to the junction of an open lane. Here continue straight ahead into Gedney, turning right at the end back on to Dawsmere Road. However, if you want to prolong your Wash-side wander continue beyond the stile for 1.25 miles (2km) until the sea bank divides. Bend right, on the inland arm, and join a small lane before turning right on to Marsh Road back into Gedney Drove End.

Walk

BLAKENEY EYE'S MAGICAL MARSHES

Walk along the sea defences to some of the finest bird reserves in the country.

Fishing boats in harbour at Blakeney

Distance: 4.5 miles (7.2km)
Minimum time: 2hrs
Ascent/Gradient: 98ft (30m) ▲▲▲
Level of difficulty: +++
Paths: Footpaths with some paved lanes, can flood in winter
Landscape: Salt marshes, scrubby meadows and farmland
Suggested map: OS Explorer 251 Norfolk Coast Central
Start/finish: Grid reference: TG 028442
Dog friendliness: Under control, as these are important refuges for birds
Parking: Carnser (pay) car park, on seafront opposite Blakeney Guildhall and Manor Hotel
Public toilets: Across road from Carnser car park

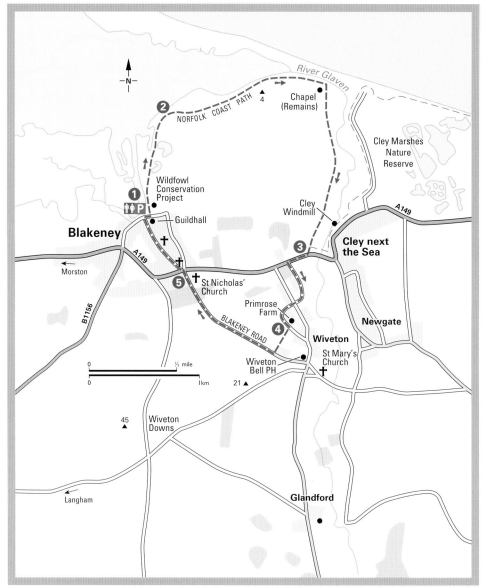

① From the car park head for the wildfowl Conservation Project, a fenced-off area teeming with ducks, geese and widgeon. A species list has been mounted on one side, so you can see how many you can spot. Take the path marked Norfolk Coast Path out towards the marshes. This raised bank is part of the sea defences, and is managed by the Environment Agency. Eventually, you have salt marshes on both sides.

② At the turning, head east. Carmelite friars once lived around here, although there is little to see of their chapel, the remains of which are located just after you turn by the wooden staithe (landing stage) to head south again. This part of the walk is excellent for spotting kittiwakes and terns in late summer. Also, look for Sabine's gull, manx and sooty shearwaters, godwits, turnstones and curlews. The path leads you past Cley Windmill, built in 1810 and which last operated in 1919. It is open to visitors and

you can climb to the top to enjoy the view across the marshes. Follow signs for the Norfolk Coast Path until you reach the A149.

③ Cross the A149 to the pavement opposite, then turn right. Take the first left after crossing the little creek. Eventually you reach the cobblestone houses of Wiveton and a crossroads; go straight ahead.

④ Take the grassy track opposite Primrose Farm, to a T-junction. This is Blakeney Road; turn right along it. However, if you want refreshments before the homeward stretch, turn left and walk a short way to the Wiveton Bell. The lane is wide and ahead you will see

St Nicholas' Church nestling among trees. This dates from the 13th century, but was extended in the 14th. Its two towers served as navigation beacons for sailors, and the east, narrower one is floodlit at night.

⑤ At the A149 there are two lanes opposite you. Take the High Street fork on the left to walk through the centre of Blakeney village. Many cottages are owned by the Blakeney Neighbourhood Housing Society, which rents homes to those locals unable to buy their own. Don't miss the 14th-century Guildhall undercroft at the bottom of Mariner's Hill. After you have explored the area, continue to the car park.

AROUND THE MYSTERIOUS HORSEY MERE

Explore whispering reed beds and silent windmills and finish at a National Trust-owned pub.

Sunset at Horsey Mere, Norfolk

Distance: 3.5 miles (5.7km)
Minimum time: 1hr 30min
Ascent/Gradient: Negligible ▲▲▲
Level of difficulty: +++
Paths: Marked trails along dykes (walk quietly to avoid disturbing nesting birds), 5 stiles
Landscape: Reed-fringed drainage channels, marshy lake and water-meadows
Suggested map: OS Explorer OL40 The Broads
Start/finish: Grid reference: TG 456223
Dog friendliness: On lead over farmland (livestock breeding area), avoid areas used by nesting water birds
Parking: National Trust pay-and-display at Horsey Drainage Mill
Public toilets: At car park

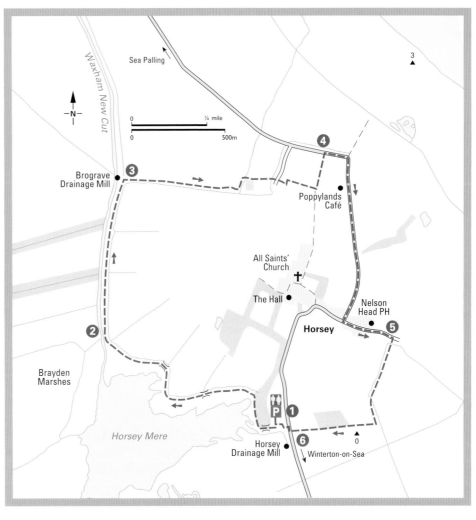

❶ From the National Trust car park, walk towards the toilets and take the footpath to the right of them. This leads to a footbridge. After crossing the bridge turn immediately right and follow the path along the side of Horsey Mere through reeds and alder copses. Cross a wooden bridge across a dyke and through a gate to enter a grassy water-meadow. Look for the white disc across the field. Go through a second gate and over a bridge.

❷ Turn right when the path meets a brown-watered dyke (Waxham New Cut). Eventually, you will see derelict Brograve Drainage Mill ahead. Herons and other birds often perch on its battered sails, so it's worth stopping to look.

❸ Turn right immediately adjacent to the mill and walk along the edge of a field. Reed beds give way to water meadow. Cross another plank bridge and continue straight ahead. The path bends left, then right, then crosses a small lane and continues through the field opposite. At the end of the field, make a sharp left, eventually coming to another lane.

❹ Go right at the lane, bearing right where it meets a track, and walk past Poppylands Café. When you reach a junction turn left, following the sign for the Nelson Head. Pass the pub on your left-hand side, then look for a well-defined footpath going off to your right.

❺ Walk past the gate and continue along the wide sward ahead, with a narrow dyke on either side. When the sward divides, bear left and head for a stile at the end of the footpath. Climb this and immediately turn right to walk along a spacious field. This area is used for

grazing breeding stock and you should look for signs warning about the presence of bulls. Since this part of the walk is permissive, and not a public footpath, the National Trust is within its rights to put bulls here, so it is important to check for warning signs before you venture forth. These are always prominently displayed. If this is the case, you will have to walk back to the lane and turn left. This will take you back to the car park at the start of the walk.

❻ Assuming there are no bulls to hinder your progress, climb the stile, between the field and the road, and then cross the road. The car park where the walk began is ahead of you and slightly to your right. This is a good time to explore the delights of restored Horsey Drainage Mill, which you will find just to your left.

MACKWORTH AND MARKEATON: A RURAL IDYLL

Very different from the Peak District, this slice of South Derbyshire belongs more to the Midlands than to the North.

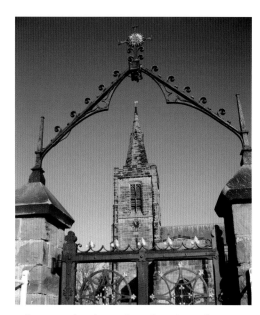

All Saints Church, Mackworth with Markeaton

Distance: 6 miles (9.7km)
Minimum time: 4hrs
Ascent/Gradient: 197ft (60m) ▲▲▲
Level of difficulty: +++
Paths: Farm tracks and field paths, can be muddy after rain, quite a few stiles
Landscape: Pastoral
Suggested map: OS Explorer 259 Derby Pagnell
Start/finish: Grid reference: SK 333379
Dog friendliness: Dogs can run free in the park away from the playgrounds and along early stretches of riverside path
Parking: Markeaton Park pay car park
Public toilets: Markeaton Park

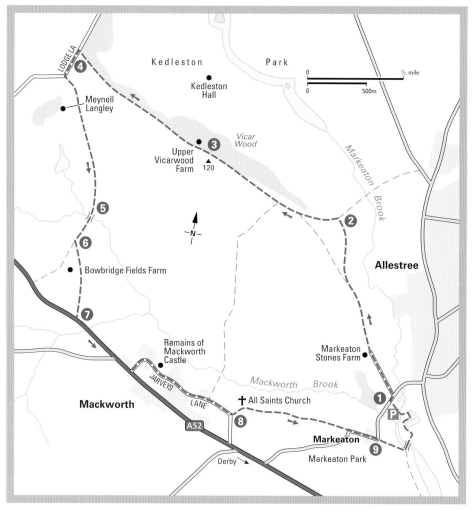

❶ Leave the car park at Markeaton Park and cross the road to follow a surfaced lane to Markeaton Stones Farm. When you're past the farm the track becomes a stony one, climbing gently around crop growing fields until you reach a T-junction.

❷ Here turn left and then follow a crumbling tarmac lane up past a stand of trees until you reach the buildings of Upper Vicarwood Farm.

❸ At the farm buildings, continue through a gate on the left-hand side of the stable block and follow a grassy hilltop track.

❹ Through a gate the track reaches Lodge Lane. Turn left along the lane to the gardens of Meynell Langley, then left again into a field next to the entrance to the drive. The path follows a hedge on the right. Through a small, wooded enclosure a lake appears in a hollow to the right. Beyond the next stile, the route enters a large field and the hedge wanders off to the right.

❺ Aim for a large lime tree at the far side of the field to find the next stile. Cross the footbridge spanning Mackworth Brook. The path now goes parallel to a hedge on the right, aiming for a large barn on the hillside ahead.

❻ On reaching a gateway the path divides. Take the one to the left, whose direction is highlighted by a waymarking arrow. Go through the next gate and follow the right field-edge, passing to the left of the fine red-brick Bowbridge Fields Farm. Now head south across fields following a hedge on the left.

❼ After going over a stile in a tall hedge, turn left along the pavement of the busy A52 (take care), passing a garage. After 600 yards (549m) go left along Jarveys Lane, passing through Mackworth village.

❽ Where the lane turns sharp right, leave it for a path passing in front of the church. Bonnie Prince Charlie waymarks show the well-defined route eastwards across fields to Markeaton.

❾ On reaching the road you can either turn left back to the car park or go straight ahead through Markeaton Park. For the latter go through the gateway, turn left over the twin-arched bridge spanning the lake, left by the children's playground, and left again past the boating lake.

KING OF BELVOIR CASTLE

Discover a fairy-tale castle and a lost canal on the Lincs–Leics border.

Belvoir Castle, near Grantham, Leicestershire

Distance: 4.75 miles (7.7km)
Minimum time: 2hrs
Ascent/Gradient: 230ft (70m) ▲▲▲
Level of difficulty: +++
Paths: Towpath, field and woodland tracks and country lane, 2 stiles
Landscape: Steep wooded hills and open arable land
Suggested map: OS Explorer 247 Grantham
Start/finish: Grid reference: SK 837342
Dog friendliness: Excellent, under close control near livestock
Parking: Main Street in Woolsthorpe by Belvoir
Public toilets: None on route (nearest in Grantham)

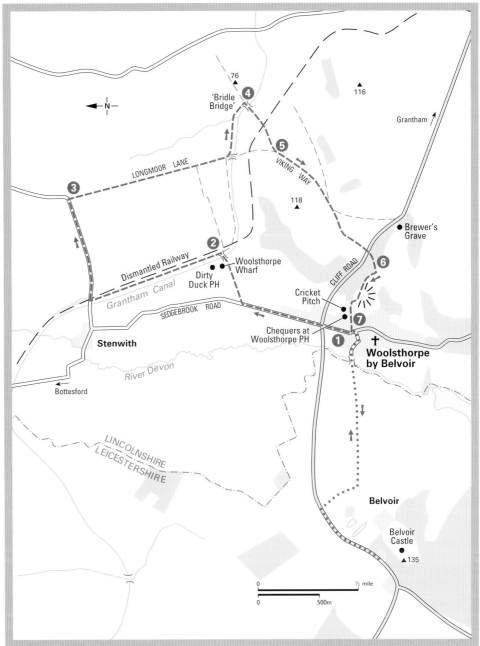

❶ Walk northwards out of the village of Woolsthorpe by Belvoir on the pavement of Sedgebrook Road, the continuation of Main Street, towards Bottesford. Turn right into the wide-verged lane for the Rutland Arms public house (signposted) and cross over the canal bridge at Woolsthorpe Wharf.

❷ Turn left and follow the straight, grassy bank along the Grantham Canal until Stenwith Bridge (No. 60). Climb the steps to your right, just before reaching the bridge, and turn right on to the road. Follow this over the old railway bridge and out along a lovely wide lane of oak trees. After 700 yards (640m) it bends left, and here turn right.

❸ Follow the initially hedged and unmade Longmoor Lane for just over 0.75 mile (1.2km). When you reach the far end turn left before the bridge, to join the gravel towpath, and walk along this as far as an elegant wooden arched bridge ('Bridle Bridge').

❹ Cross over the bridge and head out across the middle of a wide arable field. Go over the course of the old railway again and continue

up the left-hand side of a sloping field. At the top, turn left on to a well-walked track.

❺ Follow this pleasant route with lovely views out towards the hills surrounding Grantham. Where the track kinks left, after a fenced section, go straight on right across a wide field – follow the direction of the public footpath signpost and aim for the hedge opening at the very far side. Go across Cliff Road for a track into woodland.

❻ At the far side of the woods, cross the stile and turn right to follow the field-edge down the bumpy, grassy slope back to Woolsthorpe. There are excellent views across the head of the

Vale of Belvoir to Belvoir Castle opposite. At the bottom of the slope go over the stile behind the cricket scorebox, along the edge of the pitch (the football ground to your left), and down the drive of the pub to reach the village centre.

❼ If you want to extend the walk to visit Belvoir Castle, turn left into Main Street, then right into Belvoir Lane. At the end of this cul-de-sac go over a small bridge and continue ahead across fields towards the hilltop fortification. After the third stile, cross another stile to your right and follow this wide track uphill to the road, then turn left to reach the castle entrance.

A MERRIE TALE OF SHERWOOD FOREST

Enjoy a fascinating and enchanting walk among the age-old oaks of this legendary forest.

The oak tree is characteristic of Sherwood Forest's ancient woodland; a historic royal hunting forest

Distance: 5.5 miles (8.8km)
Minimum time: 2hrs 30min
Ascent/Gradient: 278ft (85m) ▲▲▲
Level of difficulty: +++
Paths: Easy woodland tracks and wide forest rides
Landscape: Beautiful mixed woodland, more open to north
Suggested map: OS Explorer 270 Sherwood Forest
Start/finish: Grid reference: SK 626676
Dog friendliness: On lead around Visitor Centre, otherwise excellent
Parking: Sherwood Forest Visitor Centre (pay-and-display)
Public toilets: Sherwood Forest Visitor Centre

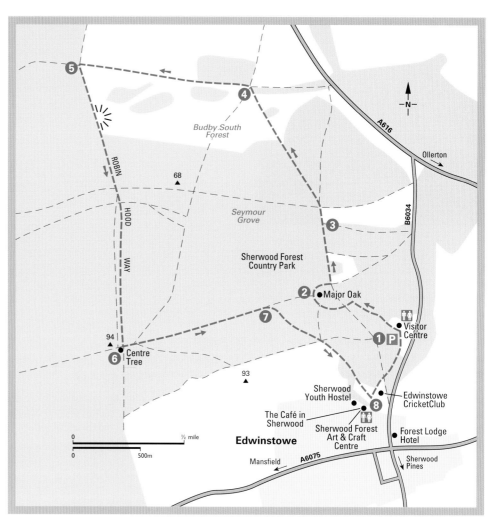

❶ Facing the main entrance to Sherwood Forest Visitor Centre from the car park, turn left and follow the well-signposted route to the Major Oak.

❷ Go along the curving path as it completes a semicircle around the impressive old tree and continue as far as the junction with a public bridleway (signposted). Turn left here, then walk this straight and uncomplicated route for 0.25 mile (400m), ignoring all paths off.

❸ At a green noticeboard, warning of a nearby military training area, the main path bears left. Instead go straight ahead, past the metal bar gate, for a path that continues over a crossroads to become a wide, fenced track through pleasant open country of heather and bracken known as Budby South Forest.

❹ At the very far side go through a gate and turn left on to an unmade lane, and walk this undulating route for 0.75 mile (1.2km).

❺ At the major junction just before the plantation begins, turn left, indicated 'Centre Tree'. With the rows of conifers on your right, and good views across Budby South Forest on your left, keep to this straight and obvious track. Where the track divides into two parallel trails, the gravelly track on the right is technically the cycle route, while the more leafy and grassy ride to the left is the bridleway, but either can be used.

❻ When you reach the Centre Tree – a huge spreading oak – the two routes converge to continue past a bench down a wide avenue among the trees. Don't go down this, but instead turn left and, ignoring paths off right and left, carry straight on along the main track back into the heart of the forest.

❼ After almost 0.75 mile (1.2km) you pass a metal bar gate on the right and then meet a bridleway coming in from the left. Ignoring the inviting path straight ahead (which returns to the Major Oak) bear right on the main track, past some bare holes and dips hollowed out by children's bikes. At a large junction of criss-crossing routes go straight on (signposted 'Fairground') so that an open field and distant housing becomes visible to your right. This wide sandy track descends to a field by Edwinstowe cricket ground. The Art and Craft Centre and Sherwood Youth Hostel are on the far side, and the village centre beyond.

❽ To return to the visitor centre and car park, follow the well-walked, signposted track back up past the cricket ground.

CHURCHES OF THE WOLDS

Explore two beautiful Lincolnshire villages through their contrasting churches on this quiet circular ramble.

*Ramblers and Christ stained glass window,
All Saints Church, Walesby, Lincolnshire*

Distance: 4.25 miles (6.8km)

Minimum time: 2hrs

Ascent/Gradient: 721ft (220m) ▲▲▲

Level of difficulty: +++

Paths: Field paths, some steep and others muddy

Landscape: Undulating chalk hills, deep valleys and woodland

Suggested map: OS Explorer 282 Lincolnshire Wolds North

Start/finish: Grid reference: TF 157907

Dog friendliness: On lead near livestock, fine on hedged tracks and lanes

Parking: Front Street, Tealby, near tea rooms

Public toilets: None on route (nearest in Market Rasen)

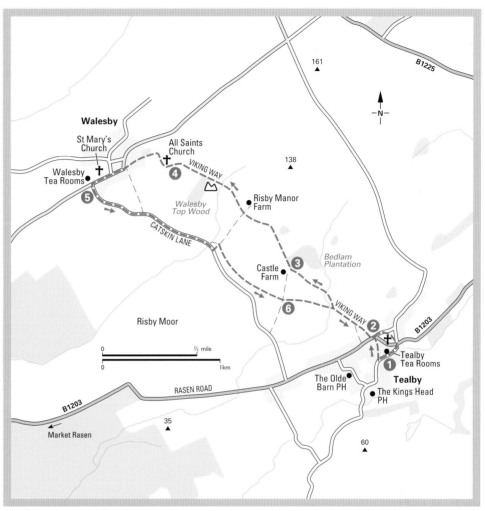

❶ From the Tealby Tea Rooms walk down Front Street as far as B. Leaning & Sons, a butcher and maker of traditional Lincolnshire sausages established in 1860. Turn right into Church Lane, which soon becomes a walkway. At the top, turn left and cross over Rasen Road to follow the public footpath that runs between houses on the opposite side. As far as Walesby you will be following the Norse helmet waymarks of the Viking Way.

❷ Pass through a gate and cross open pasture, aiming for another gate in the far bottom corner. Go through this and along the path ahead, ignoring a footbridge to the left. Walk up the open hillside ahead to reach the corner of Bedlam Plantation which is above Castle Farm.

❸ Turn right and go through a gate for a fenced path beside the woods. At the far end head diagonally left down an undulating grassy field to pass below Risby Manor Farm. Cross the lane leading up to the farmhouse and continue ahead, crossing a deep valley and climbing steeply towards Walesby Top Wood. Pass through a gate and keep straight ahead across a field of crops to reach All Saints Church.

❹ Walk through the churchyard and continue along the Viking Way as it drops down a wide track into the village. When you reach Rasen Road at the bottom go straight on, past the 'new' parish church of St Mary until you reach the junction with Catskin Lane.

❺ If you need refreshment, cross the road to visit Walesby Tea Rooms. Otherwise turn left and walk along Catskin Lane for 0.75 mile

(1.2km). Just past a right-hand curve, turn left at the entrance of a farm drive and go over a cattle grid. This is in fact a public bridleway that leads back up to the hilltop, but you should turn right in a few paces and join a footpath across rough pasture, initially parallel with the road. Stay on this path as it runs along the left-hand side of a field to arrive at the drive to Castle Farm.

❻ The public footpath now continues almost due east across the vast sloping field beyond. When you reach the far side of the field, pass through a gate and drop down to cross a wooden footbridge. Turn right on the far side of the bridge to re-join the earlier route back into Tealby, this time turning left up Rasen Road to visit All Saints Church. Drop down through the churchyard and follow Beck Hill to the memorial hall, then turn right along Front Street to return to the start of the walk.

WALES & THE BORDERS

WALES & THE BORDERS

The quayside, Fishguard Old Harbour

Of all parts of Britain, the last western outpost of Wales has always maintained its fierce historical independence and individuality. Nowhere else in Britain is the ancient Celtic mother tongue so vigorously defended and promoted, and nowhere else retains its spirit of separateness and that almost indefinable feeling of longing and nostalgia known in Welsh as *hiraeth*. It is communicated through the fierce nationalism of its people, and in the elements of earth, water, fire and air (*daear, dwr, tan* and *awyr*) in its landscape. The land of Wales includes some of the oldest rocks on earth and the highest ground south of the Scottish border.

But Wales is much more than mountains and sheep. It has a coastline which, because it is the first part of Britain to receive the balmy influence of the Gulf Stream, can at times seem positively Mediterranean. Crystal-clear Welsh water has played an important part in the creation of the spectacular landscapes of Snowdonia, the Cambrian Mountains and the Brecon Beacons. And it is still in demand today, filling the many reservoirs of mid- and South Wales which slake the thirst of a large part of industrial Britain, just as the blue slate from Snowdonia's hills roofed the Empire a century ago.

Today, about half the population of Wales live in the industrial towns and cities such as Cardiff, Swansea, Newport and Wrexham which circle its mountainous interior. And, although the traditional industrial base in the South Wales valleys of coal mining and steel making has long gone, the Welsh people still manage to exert a disproportionate influence on the world through its famous choral music, its brass bands and its fervent love of sport, particularly rugby football. But perhaps the true spirit of Wales can only be found in its sparsely populated interior, on the hill farms where Welsh is still the first language and where the people are still close to the land and the elements which made the country what it is today.

Although the principality of Wales officially became part of the Union as long ago as 1536, any visitor passing through the Marches – as the beautiful border country with England is still known – can have no doubt that they are entering a proudly different country. But despite that long, and at times bloody, history of conflict between nations, the visitor is assured that the true Welsh *croeso* (welcome) will be as warm as ever.

*Previous page: View from Snowdon to Crib Goch (on the left) and Moel Siabod
(in the distance), Snowdonia National Park*

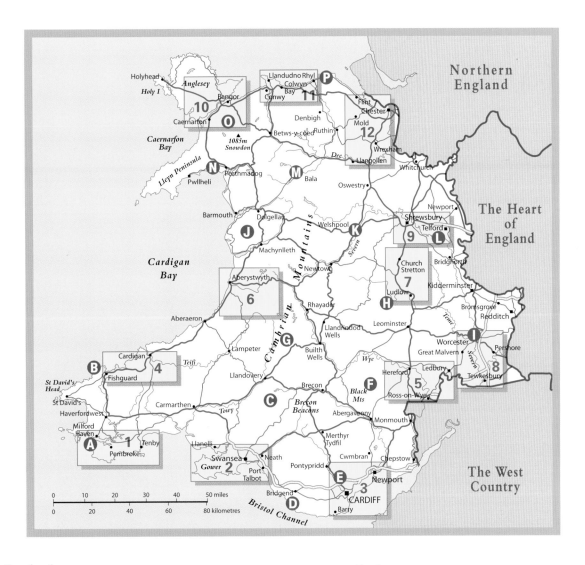

Section Contents

1	Little England beyond Wales	202–203
2	Swansea and the Gower	204–205
3	Cardiff and the Coastal Plain	206–207
4	Cardigan Bay	208–209
5	Cider Country and the Wye Valley	210–211
6	Aberystwyth and the Vale of Rheidol	214–215
7	Shropshire's Hill Country	216–217
8	Worcester and the Malvern Hills	218–219
9	Shrewsbury and Ironbridge	220–221
10	Both sides of the Menai Strait	222–223
11	The North Wales Resorts	226–227
12	Chester and the River Dee	228–229

Features

| The Welsh Marches – A Frontier Land | 212–213 |
| The National Parks of Wales | 224–225 |

Walks

A	Two Faces of the Haven	230
B	An Invigorating Trundle around Strumble	231
C	The Escarpments of the Carmarthen Fan	232
D	An Easy Stroll along the Heritage Coast	233
E	Castell Coch and the New South Wales	234
F	Llanthony and its Hills	235
G	Take a Walk on the Wild Side	236
H	Picturesque Downton Castle	237
I	The Sights of Worcester City	238
J	The Dysynni Valley and Castell y Bere	239
K	Powis Castle and the Montgomery Canal	240
L	Revolution at Coalbrookdale	241
M	A View of Bala's Lake – Llyn Tegid	242
N	In the Country of Lloyd George	243
O	Snowdon the Long Way	244
P	Where the Mountains Meet the Sea	245

LITTLE ENGLAND BEYOND WALES

Giraldus Cambrensis, the 12th-century Welsh cleric and scholar who was born at Manorbier Castle, described Pembrokeshire as 'the most beautiful part of Wales'. The thousands who flock to the resorts on the lovely craggy coastline of Wales's most westerly county, seem to agree. This area has history, wildlife, wonderful scenery and a coastline that is all National Park.

Holidaymakers gathered on Tenby's south beach on a summer's afternoon

A 20-minute boat trip to Caldey Island offers the chance to see grey seals and seabirds, and to visit the Cistercian monastery

Bosherston

The Norman church of St Michael's at Bosherston has a fine medieval cross in the churchyard, but this picturesque village is most famous for its lily ponds. These were formed by the Stackpole Estate in three narrow limestone valleys in the late 18th and early 19th centuries, and are now nationally important examples of calcareous marl lakes, protected as a National Nature Reserve. They are reached by raised causeways, which take the path across the water. Southeast of Bosherston is a wonderful secluded beach at Barafundle Bay, which is well worth the walk.

Caldey Island

Regular boat trips from Tenby take visitors to Caldey Island, the only Pembrokeshire island which is permanently occupied. The inhabitants are the monks of the modern Cistercian priory, who make sweet-smelling perfume here. There are also the remains of a 12th-century Benedictine monastery, and the ancient priory church contains a stone with inscriptions in Latin and fifth century Ogham script.

Carew Castle

This 13th-century castle standing on the Carew estuary was modified with mullioned and oriel windows in Tudor times, giving it the appearance of a romantic ruined country house. Now owned by the Pembrokeshire Coast National Park Authority, it is the scene of regular 'living history' events. Downstream is the restored Carew tidal cornmill, also owned by the Park and open to the public. Guarding the entrance to the castle is the 11th-century Carew Cross, a royal memorial inlaid with a pattern of intricate Celtic knotwork.

Carew Castle at low tide in the Pembrokeshire Coast National Park

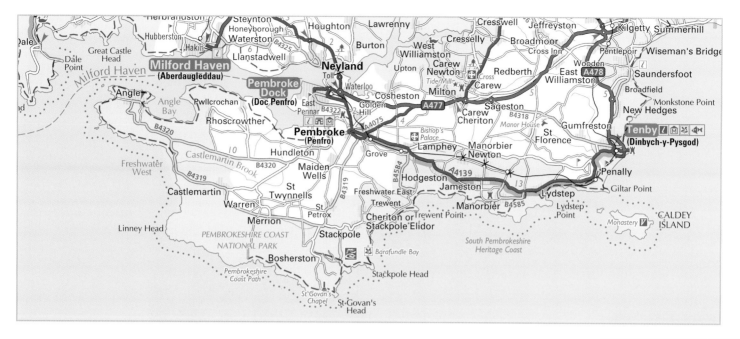

Birds of Dyfed

One of the great joys of walking the 186-mile (299km) Pembroke-shire Coast Path National Trail, which runs from St Dogmael's to Amroth, is the variety of birdlife. The steep cliffs and sea stacks, such as those found around Govan's Head and Castlemartin, are home to the rare red-beaked chough, surely the most acrobatic of the crow family, as well as kittiwake, guillemot and razorbill, the plump, penguin-like emblem of the National Park. Comical puffins and the rare Manx shearwaters nest in burrows on the islands of Skomer, a National Nature Reserve, and Skokholm, while Grassholm, an RSPB Reserve, is the site of the largest gannetry in England and Wales.

Manorbier

Giraldus Cambrensis, born here around 1146, described Manorbier as 'the most delectable spot in Wales'. The mighty walls of Manorbier Castle have been compared to the great crusader castles of the Middle East, and its grey walls dominate the delightful sandy beach from its low headland overlooking the bay. The parish church of St James, entered down crypt-like steps, contains a memorial to a member of the de Barri family, of whom Giraldus was a member.

Pembroke

The ancient county town of Pembroke lies on a low ridge of limestone, where the impressive castle was built in the late 11th century. The circular vaulted keep is 75ft (22.9m) high with walls 7ft (2.1m) thick, and a subterranean cavern known as the Wogan leads out to the harbour. Henry VII was born in the castle in 1457.

Pembroke has a pleasing High Street with some Tudor façades, and retains parts of its original town wall and water defences, including the attractive Mill Pond to the north. Pembroke Dock is a creation of the 19th century where about 240 men-of-war were built, and was an important flying-boat base during the Second World War.

St Govan's Chapel

This is one of the real gems of the Pembrokeshire Coast. Approached by a steep flight of steps down through the cliffs near Bosherston, this tiny 13th-century chapel is only accessible when firing is not taking place on the nearby Castlemartin military ranges.

West along the Coast Path are the Huntsman's Leap, a giddy gash in the cliffs, the equally spectacular Elegug Stacks, two massive pillars of limestone standing out from the cliffs, and the huge natural arch known as the Green Bridge of Wales.

Saundersfoot

This is a small town whose popularity as a holiday resort is strangely due to its development as a harbour to export high-quality anthracite in the early 19th century. Today its golden beaches and fine little harbour reflect nothing of its industrial past, and it has become one of the most popular resorts on this coast.

Tenby

The largest town (pop. 5,000) within the National Park, Tenby retains its medieval charm and character despite the annual influx of thousands of tourists.

The sailboat-dotted harbour and narrow, winding streets between what remains of the medieval town walls give Tenby the air of a Cornish resort. Notable Tudor buildings are the Merchant's House and Plantagenet House on Quay Hill, both now in the care of the National Trust.

There is a very good town museum and art gallery, incorporating part of Tenby Castle, built to defend the natural harbour in the 13th century. The parish church of St Mary, also 13th century, is one of the largest and most splendid in Wales, and contrasts with the tiny fishermen's chapel of St Julian, which overlooks the Harbour Sands.

St Govan's Chapel is reputedly named after St Govan, a sixth century Irish Monk who spent his last years in Pembrokeshire

See Walk A, page 230
Two Faces of the Haven

Tourist Information
Milford Haven: 94 Charles Street (tel: 01646 690866) Pembroke: Commons Road (tel: 01437 776499) Tenby: Unit 2, Upper Park Road (tel: 01834 842402)

SWANSEA AND THE GOWER

Between the industrial towns of Swansea Bay and the great sweep of Carmarthen Bay are startling contrasts. The long finger of the Gower Peninsula pokes out into the Bristol Channel like a delightful cameo of the best of the English West Country, while on either side the industry-ravaged towns of the valleys are slowly recovering from generations of dereliction and decay.

Built in 1794, the Mumbles Head Lighthouse is now unmanned, but still warns shipping away from the treacherous Mixon Shoal sandbanks in Swansea Bay

Near Neath, the Aberdulais Falls (National Trust) have been powering industry since 1584. Visitors can see the working waterwheel (a replica of the original), now used to generate electricity

Aberdulais

The River Neath emerges from its

lovely valley here in a series of beautiful waterfalls. The recently excavated ironworks and the carefully restored sections of the Neath and Tennant Canal make this small village on the outskirts of Neath of great interest to the industrial archaeologist. Two miles (3.2km) north of the village is the Penscynor Wildlife Park.

Mumbles

The southernmost headland of Swansea Bay is known as The Mumbles, and there are fine views from the summit of Mumbles Head. The modern resort of Mumbles owes its existence to the first and one of the longest-running railway passenger services in the world, opened in 1807 between here and Swansea, using horses as the motive power. The railway closed in 1960.

Mumbles has now swallowed up the fishing village of Oystermouth, whose All Saints Church has bells from Santiago Cathedral. The ruins of 13th-century Oystermouth Castle are on a small hill overlooking the bay.

Neath

Guarding the entrance to the narrow Vale of Neath, this busy market and industrial town boasts the remains of a 12th-century

Benedictine abbey and a Norman castle. Nearby Briton Ferry, with its small dockyard, is now part of the borough and is overshadowed by the massive viaduct which carries the M4 motorway round the South Wales coast.

Port Talbot

Famous for its massive steelworks on Margam Burrows, Port Talbot is a relatively modern creation, owing its existence to the plentiful supplies of coal from the Welsh valleys and to its easy access to the sea. In contrast to the industrial landscape to seaward, Margam Country Park, covering 850 acres (344ha) is in the grounds of Margam Castle, home of the Talbot family which gave the town its name, and includes abbey ruins, the orangery gardens, a fine herd of deer, a sculpture trail and children's attractions.

Reynoldston

At the very centre of Gower, Reynoldston stands on the west flank of the central Cefn Bryn ridge, on which visitors can enjoy fine walks with views across the entire peninsula. Around 1 mile (1.6km) to the northwest of the village, on the next rise, lies King Arthur's Stone, or Maen Ceti, an unusually large Neolithic chambered tomb consisting of ten uprights and a massive, 30-ton capstone.

The Gower Peninsula

'Golden Gower' is often dubbed the 'lung' of Swansea, but this 15-mile by 8-mile (24km by 12.9km) peninsula is really a place apart from the rest of South Wales. It is also a place of great scenic beauty and contrast. Gower's south coast is more akin to southwestern Dyfed, with superb beetling cliffs of limestone where many ships have foundered on the rocks, which terminate at weird Worms Head. The northern coast consists of broad sand and mudflats leading down to the Burry Inlet, while the interior is pastoral and scattered with pretty little villages.

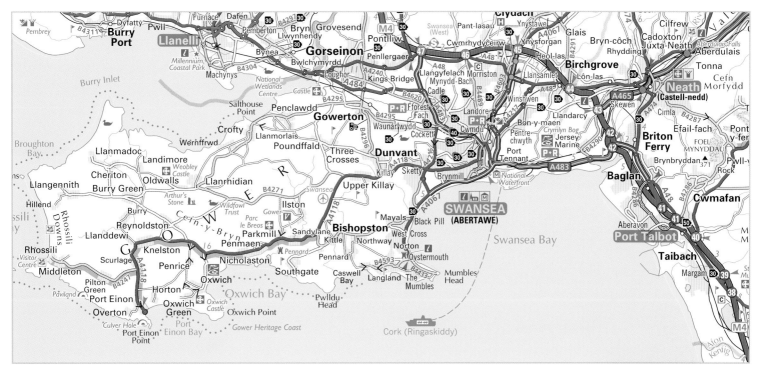

Oxwich

Situated at the western end of the sweeping sands of Oxwich Bay, this charming little village, with its Devon-like thatched and whitewashed cottages, has been important since a castle was built here by the Norman de la Mare family. Their tombs can still be seen in the lovely church of St Illtyd, which stands deep in woodland at the edge of the bay, some way from the village. Oxwich Burrows is an important National Nature Reserve.

Rhossili

Rhossili stands at the southern end of the superb beach of Rhossili Bay, one of the finest stretches of flat sand in Wales. The church contains a memorial to Edgar Evans, who went with Scott to the South Pole. The village is backed by the open downland of Rhossili Downs, a veritable treasurehouse of prehistory which rises to The Beacon at 632ft (192.6m). The bracing downs contain 14 Bronze-Age burial mounds and at Sweyne's Howes, just north of the Beacon, there are a pair of Neolithic burial chambers. Rhossili Downs are very popular with the hang-gliding fraternity, and are now owned by the National Trust.

The westernmost extremity of Gower is the spectacular headland of Worm's Head, which takes its name from the Old English *orme* meaning 'dragon' or 'serpent'. The long ridge of the Inner Head is joined to the conical Outer Head by a treacherous route across slippery rocks, which should only be attempted by the sure-footed, and then only at low tide (more information is available from the National Trust Visitor Centre at Rhossili).

Swansea

Many of the finest prehistoric remains from the caves and burial mounds of Gower are to be found in the Royal Institution of South Wales in Swansea, which was made a city, Wales' second largest, in 1969. The Swansea Museum has local exhibits, echoing Swansea's industrial past, and the Guildhall is worth a visit if only to admire the magnificent Empire Murals of artist Frank Brangwyn. The dockland areas have been extensively redeveloped as a leisure centre and marina.

Anchor and rope outside red-brick flats at Swansea Marina

The sands of Rhossili beach, viewed from the National Trust Visitor Centre, which contains an exhibition on the area

See Walk C, page 232
The Escarpments of the Carmarthen Fan

See Walk D, page 233
An Easy Stroll along the Heritage Coast

Tourist Information
Swansea: Plymouth Street (tel: 01792 468321)

205

CARDIFF AND THE COASTAL PLAIN

The great city of Cardiff, capital of Wales, dominates the mouth of the Severn and the famous valleys of South Wales, which lead up to the mountains beyond. It is the natural focal point of the coastal plain, important as the gateway to Wales ever since the Romans and Normans built their fortifications at places like Caerleon, Cardiff and Caerphilly.

The Chapel

A feature of almost every Welsh village is the Nonconformist chapel, and these stern, functional buildings, usually well over 100 years old, are still the focal point for many. Following the advent of Methodism in the second quarter of the 18th century and the Calvinist preaching of John Wesley, the Welsh people turned almost exclusively against the Anglican Church. By 1851 a survey showed that there were nearly 3,000 dissenting chapels in Wales, compared with just over 1,000 Anglican churches. From the chapels came the wonderful Welsh male voice choirs and strongly nonconformist Liberal politicians like David Lloyd George.

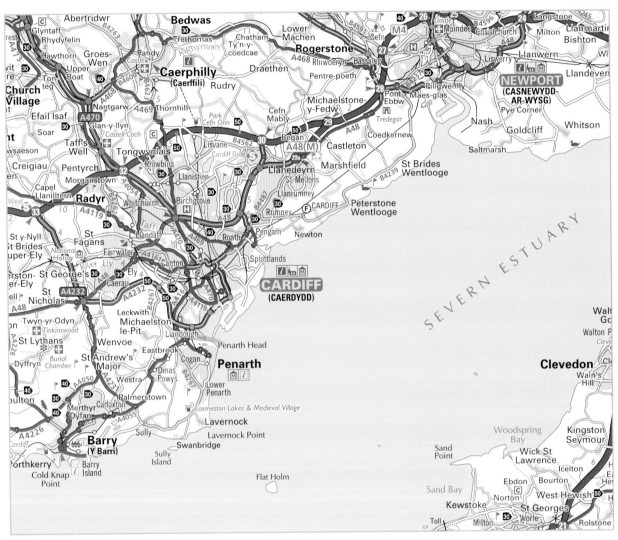

Barry

Barry was once one of the biggest ports in the world, established specifically to serve the nearby coalfield. Its development as a holiday resort for the mining towns coincided with the development of its dockyards in the 19th century, and the population exploded.

Today holidaymakers flock to the enormous amusement park, the beaches at Whitmore Bay and the Porthkerry Country Park. The Welsh Hawking Centre is another popular attraction, which has more than 200 birds of prey.

View over the remains of the Roman army Barracks at Caerleon

Caerleon

Home of the second Augustan Legion for 300 years, the Roman fort of *Isca Silurum*, as Caerleon was known, was one of their most important fortresses in Wales, and is the most complete survivor. Most impressive is the great amphitheatre built around AD80, which could seat 6,000 people – the most complete excavated Roman amphitheatre in Britain. Other remains include barracks blocks and cook-houses, and there is a very good small museum by the church, which stands in the middle of the 50-acre (20ha) complex.

Caerphilly Castle was built in the late 13th-century

Caerphilly

Best known for its white, crumbly cheese, Caerphilly also boasts one of the largest and best-preserved castles in Britain, second only in size to Windsor. The site incorporates magnificent remains of its original water defences and most of the inner, middle and outer walls. The castle was started in 1268 by Richard de Clare, Earl of Gloucester and Hereford, to defend his lands against the Welsh. This it did until the Civil War, when exposives used by besieging Parliamentary forces gave the southeast tower its precarious lean.

Cardiff

Cardiff has only been the capital of Wales since 1955, but is now a truly international city of culture and commerce, and, since 1998, the seat of the Welsh Assembly. The city grew mainly due to the efforts of successive Marquesses of Bute, who were also responsible for restoring the castle. During the 1898 restorations the walls of an extensive Roman fort were discovered and restored, and its history had to be rewritten. The remains of the handsome circular Norman keep stand beside the ornate 19th-century Gothick living quarters.

Buildings of note include the splendid City Hall and Law Courts, the National Museum of Wales in Cathays Park, the University College and the Welsh Assembly building on the redeveloped Cardiff Bay. Cardiff Arms Park is the Welsh 'home' of rugby football, and the splendid Millennium Stadium hosts national and international games as well as concerts. The Wales Millennium Centre is another architectural standout, and is a popular venue for musicals, opera and dance.

North of the city centre is the leafy suburb of Llandaff, where the city's cathedral, Bishop's House and Deanery are dominated by Joseph Epstein's soaring central arch depicting Christ in Majesty.

Penarth

Just 2 miles (3.2km) from Cardiff, this is a popular seaside resort which came to prominence in Victorian times. The old harbour retains its charm, although sailing and waterskiing are now the most common activities. The Turner House Art Gallery, part of the National Museum of Wales, is one of the best in the country, containing works by Turner, Cox and Cotman. Further south along the coast, beyond Lower Penarth, is Lavernock and the Cosmeston Lake Country Park and Medieval Village.

St Fagans

This small village of thatched cottages is most famous for the National History Museum, housed in the grounds of St Fagans Castle, an Elizabethan manor house which is also open to the public. Within the 100-acre site, more than 40 different types of traditional Welsh buildings have been reconstructed, ranging from a Unitarian chapel to cottages, farmhouses, a smithy, a tannery and a working woollen mill. A museum at the entrance houses agricultural and costume collections.

Thatched house in St Fagans

Wales Millennium Centre, Cardiff Bay, panoramic view showing inscription, which says 'In these stones horizons sing'

Newport

Newport is a busy industrial town, standing where the River Usk flows into the Bristol Channel. There is a good museum and art gallery, and St Woolos Cathedral has Norman arches and a medieval tower. Nearby is the fine 18th-century mansion of Tredegar House, its grounds now a country park.

See Walk E, page 234
Castell Coch and the New South Wales

Tourist Information

Barry Island: The Triangle, The Promenade (tel: 01446 747171)
Caerleon: 5 High Street (tel: 01633 422656)
Caerphilly: Lower Twyn Square (tel: 029 2088 0011)
Cardiff: 16 Wood Street (tel: 029 2087 3573)
Newport: John Frost Square (tel: 01633 842962)
Penarth: Penarth Pier, The Esplanade (tel: 029 2070 8849)

CARDIGAN BAY

The heather-clad heights of the Preseli Hills look down across a neatly hedged landscape to the blue waters of Cardigan Bay. This delectable corner of Dyfed is something of a backwater on the normal tourist trail, and is all the more delightful because of it. The ancient market towns of Cardigan and Newcastle Emlyn remain charmingly unspoilt.

Castell Henllys Iron-Age Fort in the Pembrokeshire Coast National Park

Cardigan

Coracles, the ancient handmade small Welsh craft, can still be seen plying for salmon and sea trout on the River Teifi at Cardigan. In medieval days before the harbour silted up, this was an important seaport, giving its name to the whole sweep of Cardigan Bay. There are few reminders of its former glory, but chief among them are the remains of the Norman castle, overlooking the 17th-century, six-arched bridge over the Teifi.

A weekly market is still held beneath the arches of the 19th-century Guildhall. Just off the modern resort of Gwbert-on-Sea is Cardigan Island, which is now a nature reserve.

Castell Henllys

Near Felindre Farchog, this is an award-winning reconstruction of an Iron-Age village, owned and run by the Pembrokeshire Coast National Park Authority. It is an imaginative and exciting project which enables visitors to step inside a heather-thatched dwelling and experience just how people lived 2,000 years ago.

5,000-year-old megalithic long barrow, Pentre Ifan, Pembrokeshire Coast National Park

Cilgerran

Romantic Cilgerran Castle, perched high on a crag overlooking the River Teifi, makes a splendid backdrop to the annual coracle 'regatta' where local fishermen compete against each other in various contests of skill. The pretty village of Cilgerran is dominated by the early 13th-century castle. It was built by William Marshall, Earl of Pembroke, shortly after he captured this strategic site, on a promontory between the Teifi and the Plysgog, from the Welsh. The gatehouse and the two great circular towers are the most impressive remaining features.

Fishguard

The old fishing village of Fishguard in the picturesque bay between Carregwastad Point and Dinas Head was the scene of the pathetic conclusion of the last invasion of Britain, by a drunken rabble of Frenchmen, in 1797. They were, apparently, frightened off by the sight of a group of local women in Welsh traditional costume, the headgear of which is somewhat reminiscent of soldiers' helmets.

The Old or Lower Town is particularly attractive, while the Upper Town has a fine Square, complete with Market Hall. Nearby Goodwick is the terminus for ferries crossing the Irish Sea to Rosslare. A few miles to the east is the lovely village of Dinas Cross, sheltering behind the great 500ft (152.4m) cliffs of Dinas Head, from where basking seals can often be seen.

Mynydd Preseli

Famous as the source of the Stonehenge bluestones which were somehow transported to far-off Wiltshire by Neolithic man, the Preseli Hills include the highest point of the Pembrokeshire Coast National Park, reaching 1,759ft (536m) at Foel Cwm Cerwyn.

The views from these rugged summits of Ordovician rock are truly panoramic, extending as far south as Dunkery Beacon on Exmoor and to Cadair Idris

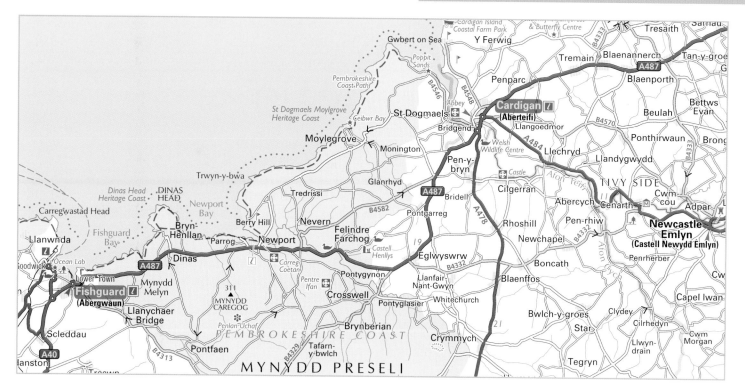

The Pembrokeshire Coast Path

Officially opened in 1970, the Pembrokeshire Coast Path has its northern terminus at St Dogmaels. It runs its roller-coaster route for 186 miles (299.3km) around the rugged coastline of Pembrokeshire, with only a slight hiatus at Milford Haven, to Amroth, beyond Tenby.

It was surveyed by the distinguished local naturalist Ronald Lockley in the early 1950s, so it is appropriate that among its greatest attractions are the wildlife that the walker can see along the way, from the wheeling seabird colonies on the cliffs to the carpet of wildflowers, especially glorious in the early months of summer.

in Snowdonia to the north. Sometimes even the Wicklow Mountains of Ireland are visible across the Irish Sea.

Nevern

A firm candidate for the title of most beautiful village in Wales, Nevern's cottages are set on a slope overlooking the River Nyfer, which is crossed by a medieval bridge. Nevern is famous for its wonderful, intricately carved Celtic cross of St Brynach, which dates from around AD1000 and stands more than 12ft (3.6m) high in the churchyard. There are other carved stones nearby, and the churchyard also has a famous 'bleeding' yew which secretes blood-red sap. The church of St Brynach is of cruciform construction with a low battlemented tower, and dates mainly from the 15th century.

Newcastle Emlyn

This bustling little market town on the Teifi gets its name from the castle, which was 'new' in the 15th century – its builders wanted to distinguish it from the older Cilgerran Castle downstream. The town was the site of the first printing press in Wales, set up in 1718, and was also a centre of the 'Rebecca Riots' of the mid-19th century, in which men dressed as women were protesting against road tolls.

Pentre Ifan

Probably the best-known and most-photographed prehistoric monument in

Wales, and certainly one of the finest megalithic monuments in Britain, this Neolithic chambered long barrow occupies a spectacular site on the northern slopes of the Preseli Hills. Originally covered by earth and stones, the massive capstone, thought to weigh about 17 tons, is still delicately balanced on the three pointed uprights that have supported it for the last 5,000 years.

St Dogmaels

St Dogmael, a descendant of Ceredig, after whom Ceredigion was named, founded a hermitage here in the sixth century. The Benedictine abbey was founded by Robert Fitz-Martin in 1115, but the remaining ruins mainly date from the 14th to 16th centuries. Among the most important remains that can be seen in the adjoining 19th-century parish church is the Sagranus Stone, a 7ft (2.1m) pillar inscribed in both Latin and Ogham lettering, which helped scholars to decipher this mysterious, Dark-Ages script.

Just beyond the village are the beautiful and extensive Poppit Sands, which lead up to the wild cliffscape of Cemaes Head.

See Walk B, page 231
An Invigorating Trundle around Strumble

Tourist Information

Cardigan: Theatr Mwldan, Bath House Road
(tel: 01239 613230)
Fishguard: Town Hall, Market Square
(tel: 01437 776636)
Fishguard Harbour: Ocean Lab, Goodwick
(tel: 01348 872037)

Sunset at Poppit Sands on the River Teifi estuary, looking towards Cemaes Head

CIDER COUNTRY AND THE WYE VALLEY

The meandering River Wye coils down through green pastureland as it makes its way south from the cathedral city of Hereford to the Forest of Dean. This is prime agricultural land, where the dusty red soil matches the sandstone of the rocks and the hides of the famous Hereford cattle, whose white faces are now to be found all over the world.

Hereford Cathedral's 'new' west front was built to celebrate Queen Victoria's diamond jubilee

In Herefordshire celebrations surround apple harvests in local parishes

Abbey Dore

This quiet village lies at the heart of the apple orchards at the southern end of the long valley of the River Dore, on the eastern shoulder of the Black Mountains. The valley is known as the Golden Valley, though it is a vision of pink blossom in the spring. Abbey Dore takes its name from the fact that its magnificent parish church was once part of a Cistercian abbey, founded in 1147.

Dorstone

Richard de Brito, one of the knights who murdered Thomas à Becket, founded the church here at the northern end of the Golden Valley. When it was restored, his tomb was opened and a chalice which was found inside is now on display.

Not far to the north, near Pen-y-Moor Farm, is the Neolithic chambered long barrow known as Arthur's Stone – one of many alleged burial sites of that legendary monarch. It has nine uprights and a massive capstone which weighs about 25 tonnes. The ruined passageway still survives.

Hereford

The small Norman cathedral of Hereford, with its great forest of pink sandstone columns lining the nave, is one of the finest in England. The massive central tower of around 1325 adds distinction to every view of the building, which underwent extensive restoration after the collapse of the 14th-century west tower in 1786.

One of the cathedral's greatest treasures, saved for the nation by public outcry and subscription, is the *Mappa Mundi*, drawn on vellum around 1290, making it one of the earliest maps of the world in existence. The cathedral's famous chained library, containing 1,500 books, is the largest in the world.

Formerly the Saxon capital of West Mercia, Hereford reflects its place in history, and its fascinating Art Gallery and Museum in Broad Street has many exhibits from its ancient past. High Town is the nucleus of Old Hereford, while the River Wye, with its 15th-century bridge, just upstream from the cathedral, is a constant artery.

Kilpeck Church

Kilpeck is a tiny hamlet 8 miles (12.9km) southwest of Hereford, usually overlooked by travellers on the A465. But it is worth stopping for a while to visit the tiny 12th-century parish church, which contains some of the finest examples of Romanesque carvings in Britain. The richness of the carvings, especially around the south doorway, is overpowering, with mythical beasts, warriors, angels and devils competing for space. Nearby are the remains of Kilpeck Castle and the 6-acre (2ha) site of a deserted medieval village.

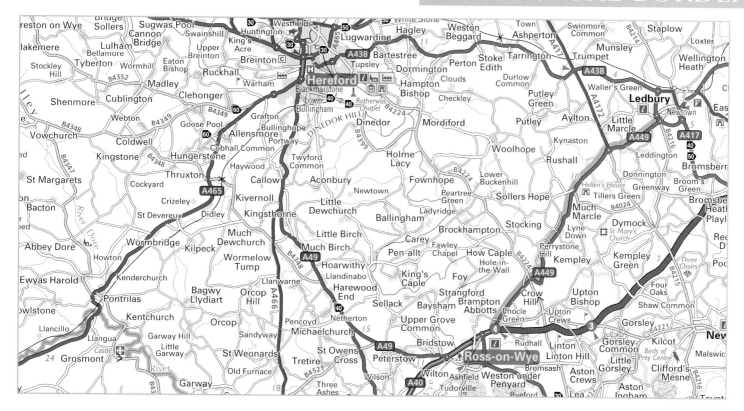

Hereford Cattle

One of the finest sights in British agriculture is that of a curly, white-faced Hereford bull being led to receive the prized winner's rosette in the superb setting of the Three Counties Show at Malvern.

Renowned for their fine lean beef, hardiness and early maturity, the red and white Hereford cattle have transported the name of their county of origin around the world. Their distinctive white faces can often be seen in Western films, and their hardiness makes them suitable for conditions ranging from the Arctic to the Equator.

Major improvements to the breed were made by the local Tompkins family in the 18th century, and it was not until the 19th century that the red and white colour that we know so well predominated.

Ledbury

Historic Ledbury, with its leaning, half-timbered cottages and narrow winding alleyways, is for many people the quintessential small English market town. Gathered around the soaring, detached Georgian spire of the mainly early 14th-century parish church of St Michael and All Angels, Ledbury continues in its role as the commercial centre for the surrounding Herefordshire villages.

John Masefield was born here, and Ledbury has long been a favourite place for poets and painters, from Wordsworth to the Brownings. The October Hiring Fair no longer hires farm labourers, but continues as a festival. Nearby is Eastnor Castle, a magnificent Georgian pile in a fairytale setting, with Italianate and Gothic interiors which have been splendidly restored. The grounds include a deer park, nature trails, an arboretum and a lake.

Much Marcle

The centre of the Herefordshire cider country, Much Marcle is the place where local farmer Henry Weston set up one of the first specialist cider-making factories in the 19th century. However, local farmers have been selling surplus supplies of the clear, strong, golden beverage since the 17th century.

Much Marcle's church dates mainly from the 13th century and contains a fine collection of carved effigies, one of which, dating from about 1350, is sculpted from a solid block of local oak.

Pembridge

Pembridge is a compact village of ancient timber-framed houses, and its 600-year-old parish church of St Mary recalls the days when Welsh raids across Offa's Dyke were frequent. The detached timber-framed belfry tower – one of seven in Herefordshire – was used as a place of refuge for villagers in times of trouble, like the peel towers of Northumberland. Arrows could be shot from the embrasures, or slits in the stone base of the tower.

Ross-on-Wye

Another fine little Herefordshire market town, Ross-on-Wye stands on a bluff overlooking a sweeping meander of the River Wye, with marvellous views across to the Welsh hills to the west.

At the top of the hill in Ross, just beyond the half-timbered and arcaded 17th-century Market Hall is the elegant 14th-century spire of the parish church of St Mary. There are splendid views of the Wye Valley from the Prospect, near the churchyard, and many reminders of John Kyrle, the local philanthropist made famous as Alexander Pope's *Man of Ross*.

Ross is now one of the main visitor hubs for exploring the Wye Valley and Symonds Yat, but it retains its peaceful market town atmosphere with good shops and a lively community spirit.

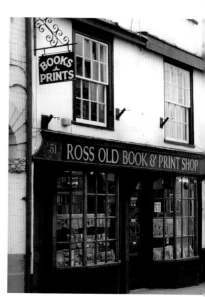

The first illustrated tour guide to be published in Britain was William Gilpin's Observations on the River Wye *in 1782 – Ross-on-Wye was established as a centre for visitors by 1850*

See Walk F, page 235
Llanthony and its Hills

Tourist Information

Hereford: 1 King Street (tel: 01432 268430)
Ledbury: The Masters House, St Katherines (tel: 01531 636147)
Ross-on-Wye: Swan House, Edde Cross Street (tel: 01989 562768)

THE WELSH MARCHES – A FRONTIER LAND

A glance at Sheet 137 of the Ordnance Survey's 1:50,000 Landranger series, covering Church Stretton and Ludlow and the western edge of Shropshire, shows a landscape shaped by conflict and war. Here in the heart of the troubled borderland of the Welsh Marches, many examples of defensive structures are still visible.

Ludlow's great red sandstone keep, built by Roger Montgomery, Earl of Shrewsbury, in the 11th century to repel Welsh raiders, was succeeded by many smaller 'motte and bailey' castles, such as those scattered along Offa's Dyke. A classic example can be found at New Radnor. Later, the fortified manors of Stokesay Castle, Bromfield, and Richard's Castle tell of more settled times, while the manors of Wilderhope and Croft Castle show the gradual trend away from defence towards the country houses found in more peaceful areas.

Built by Edward I, Harlech Castle looks over Cardigan Bay and the Snowdonia mountain range. It stands on a 200ft (61km) crag and was completed in 1290

Early Times

In prehistoric times, the slopes of every major hill formed their own frontier with everything below, and settlers fortified their summits with banks, ditches and palisades, within which they enjoyed the best possible coigns of vantage. One of the most striking features of the above-mentioned map is the number of these 'Forts,' 'Camps' and 'Earthworks' – more than 20 of them – marked in the Gothic typeface which the OS uses, rather imprecisely, to indicate a 'Non-Roman antiquity.'

The better-known examples include Croft Ambrey, southwest of Ludlow, where hundreds of regularly placed huts have been traced; and Caer Caradoc, overlooking the Church Stretton valley, where Caractacus is alleged to have made his last stand against the Romans. But there are many other lesser-known examples. Some, like Burfa Camp, Bury Ditches and Bagbury, are now hidden under blanket forestry plantations, but many others command the same sweeping views over the countryside which first attracted their builders more than 2,000 years ago.

Radiocarbon dating shows that most British hillforts were built between 750 and 500BC, though many were still in use up to the Roman invasion in the first century AD. The name 'hillfort' can be misleading, although many must have had a defensive purpose. But the idea that they were all the last outposts of the native Britons who fled there in the face of the invading Romans is one which is no longer in favour with modern archaeologists. Some believe that hillforts were the spiritual or religious centres of the Iron Age, and temples have been found in some of them. But there is no doubt that many others were settlements which were perhaps used only in the summer to watch over grazing stock, or as administrative or market centres.

After the Romans

Winding up from south to north through the western side of Sheet 137 is the ancient earthwork known as Offa's Dyke – now followed by the 177-mile (285km) Offa's Dyke Path, which opened in 1971. Built in the last quarter of the eighth century by King Offa of Mercia to mark the western edge of his kingdom and to control Welsh incursions, Offa's Dyke is the longest continuous earthwork in Britain, and links the Severn and Dee estuaries.

There can be little doubt from its method of construction that Offa's Dyke was primarily defensive in nature, and there is some evidence that it may once have had a permanently manned stockade along its crest. It was said to have been instigated by Offa in AD782, but the first reference to this monumental earthwork is not recorded until a century later, when Bishop Asser notes that Offa ordered the dyke to be built between Wales and Mercia 'from sea to sea'.

Following the decline of Mercia, the usually bickering Welsh princes united under Gruffydd ap Llywelyn and began serious incursions across the Dyke into England. These were eventually thwarted by Harold, who was later to become the short-lived king of England, in a vicious campaign of retaliation in 1063.

Ludlow Castle became Crown property in 1461 and remained a royal castle for 350 years

The 13th-century Conwy Castle's eight grey-stone towers overlook the town of Conwy and the River Conwy

Norman Barons and Welsh Princes

The next chapter in the trouble-torn history of the Marches begins with the Norman conquest of 1066. William set about subduing his new nation by making grants of land to favoured 'Marcher' barons, who ruled by right of conquest and claimed special rights, not subject to the usual restraint of the law. It was these autocratic barons who built the string of earth mounds and wooden forts known as 'motte and bailey' castles, such as that still visible at New Radnor. The word 'Marches' has the same origin as 'mark', meaning a boundary.

The great stone castles of the Marches, such as Ludlow, Monmouth, Chepstow, Rhuddlan and Shrewsbury, came later, as the English overlords tried to stamp their authority over an unwilling populace. A double, and sometimes triple, line of castles was erected along the border, such as Grosmont, Skenfrith and White castles in Monmouthshire.

But the Welsh princes like Gruffydd, now known as Llywelyn the Last, were still unwilling to bow under the English yoke, and after he evaded taking the oath of loyalty to Edward I, he was soon in open conflict with the king's army, commanded by Roger de Mortimer, Earl of Shrewsbury. Mortimer was just one of the immensely powerful Marcher Lords. Others included Roger de Lacy of Ludlow and Robert de Say of Clun.

Llywelyn was eventually defeated by Edward in 1282, and to confirm his conquest he built a series of massive fortresses throughout Wales. These castles, such as Conwy, Caernarfon, Harlech and Beaumaris, were at the forefront of medieval military architecture and even today stand as impressive ruins.

By 1472, in an attempt as much to subdue the powerful Marcher Lords as the still-warring Welsh, Edward IV set up a Lord President and Council of the Marches, who were to supervise the affairs of Wales and the border for the next two centuries. The Council usually sat at Ludlow or Shrewsbury Castles, but Welsh opposition was not finally stamped out until the defeat of Owain Glyndwr, another great hero of Welsh nationalism, in 1410.

After the Tudors

It was not until the reign of Henry VIII that the boundary between England and Wales was finally settled, and today's visitor can still hear strong echoes of the troubled history of the Welsh Marches. One of the most impressive is Roger Montgomery's still-formidable red sandstone castle towering above the River Teme at Ludlow. Started in 1085 during the first wave of castle-building, in its chequered history it has been the prison for Edward IV's sons – 'the Princes in the Tower' – and the place where Arthur, elder brother of Henry VIII, died. On a more cultural note, it was the scene in 1634 of the first production of John Milton's masque, *Comus*, and is still the regular venue for open-air Shakespearean productions.

Monmouth, with its rare portcullised gatehouse over the River Monnow, still boasts the ruins of its 11th-century castle, where Henry V was born in 1387. Chepstow's great Norman castle still dominates the town's medieval streets, and across the border at Goodrich an almost perfectly preserved 13th-century castle still frowns down over the River Wye. At Rhuddlan, near Rhyl on the coast of north Wales, Edward I is said to have made his famous sacrificial move to win over the Welsh by proclaiming his infant son as the first Prince of Wales, later presenting him to his people at Caernarfon in 1284.

Thomas Telford's suspension bridge of 1822, leading to Conwy Castle

ABERYSTWYTH AND THE VALE OF RHEIDOL

Aberystwyth looks out on to the broad expanse of Cardigan Bay and has as its backdrop the mountains of Central Wales. These rise to 2,467ft (752m) at Plynlimon Fawr, the great mountain mass which gives rise to the mighty border rivers of the Severn and the Wye and to the Rheidol, which dashes down over wild waterfalls at Devil's Bridge to enter the Irish Sea at Aberystwyth.

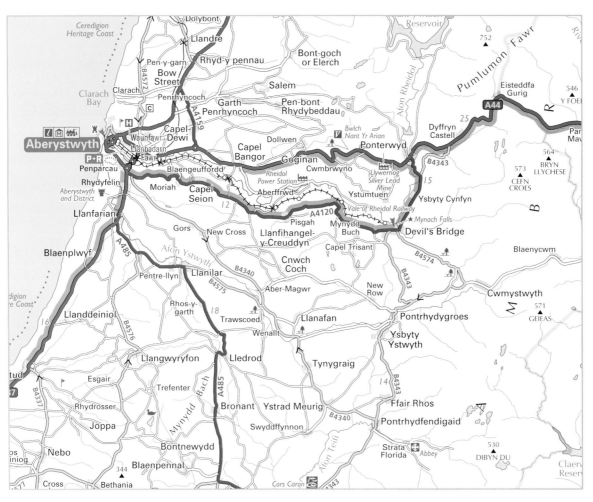

Borrow's Wild Wales

When George Borrow, Norfolk-born linguist and traveller, reached Devil's Bridge in his classic travelogue *Wild Wales* (published in 1862), he was harangued by the natives, who were terrified by his appearance and could not understand his earnest though bombastic attempts at the Welsh language.

Wild Wales remains one of the most entertaining and amusing of the early guidebooks to Wales, and Borrow's description of Pumlunion Fawr, where he symbolically drinks in turn from the sources of the Rheidol, Severn and Wye, 'all three ... contained within the compass of a mile', sees the author at his descriptive best.

Aberystwyth is the main holiday resort and administrative centre on the west coast of Wales

Aberystwyth

This pleasant seaside town has a good claim to be the Oxbridge of Wales. 'The college by the sea' – University College of Wales – occupies a splendid position in a former hotel on the seafront near the pier; the rest of the campus is on the hills behind at Penglais, where the National Library of Wales houses some of the great literary treasures of the Principality.

The largest resort on Cardigan Bay, Aberystwyth combines seaside attractions with a history that goes back to the Iron Age. The hillfort of Pen Dinas overlooks The Bar to the south of the town, and the ruins of one of many castles built in Wales by Edward I is perched on a headland just south of the pier. There is a small harbour and a beach of shingle and sand.

A Victorian funicular railway operates on Constitution Hill at the north end of the promenade, and the views from the 430ft (131m) summit extend to Snowdonia in the north and the Preseli Hills to the south.

Devil's Bridge

Three bridges, built on top of one another in a sequence covering seven centuries, make this dramatic wooded gorge of the River Mynach one of the great scenic highlights of Wales. The first (lowest) bridge was built in the 12th century by the monks of nearby Strata Florida Abbey, and was succeeded by another stone bridge and lastly by a modern steel structure. The Mynach meets the Rheidol here in a series of spectacular waterfalls, the highest of which is 300ft (90m) high.

Pumlumon Fawr

One of the three great mountains of Wales, Pumlumon Fawr (2,467ft/752m) lacks the imposing appearance of Snowdon and Cadair Idris only because it rises from almost uniformly high ground. But, as the source of the rivers Severn, Wye and Rheidol, its significance as a physical feature cannot be denied. Its boggy and mainly featureless slopes show signs of previous industry in the remains of lead and silver mines, and the easiest approach to the undistinguished summit is from Eisteddfa Gurig Farm on the A44 between Ponterwyd and Llangurig.

Strata Florida Abbey

Now reduced to romantic, though sparse, ruins, the Abbey was once one of the major cultural centres of Wales and governed a large part of mid-Wales. The community of Cistercian monks, founded by Prince Rhys ap Gruffydd in 1184, administered huge sheep ranches over the surrounding Cambrian Mountains. All that remains now is a soaring western doorway, some foundations laid out in the grass, and some lovely medieval floor tiles.

Nearby in the upper reaches of the River Teifi near Tregaron is the Cors Caron National Nature Reserve, the largest peat bog in Wales, covering around 1,900 acres (770ha). There is a nature trail along which visitors can spot rare wetland birds such as the golden plover and the curlew.

Vale of Rheidol Railway

Running for 12 sylvan miles (19.3km) through the valley of the Rheidol between Aberystwyth and Devil's Bridge, the Vale of Rheidol Railway was the last narrow-gauge steam railway owned by British Rail before privatisation in 1989.

Originally opened in 1902 to carry lead ore to the coast from the mines in the mountains, the railway is now exclusively used for tourist passenger traffic. It is a popular and attractive way to reach the honeypots of the waterfalls of Mynach and Devil's Bridge from Aberystwyth and the coastal resorts of Cardigan Bay.

Rheidol Railway opened in 1902. It was originally built to serve the lead mines in the Rheidol Valley

The Welsh Lake District

The insatiable thirst of the booming industrial cities of the West Midlands in the late 19th and early 20th centuries turned the attentions of the water engineers to the isolated, steep-sided valleys of the River Elan and its tributaries in mid-Wales.

Its clean, unpolluted water and the comparative ease of providing gravity-fed pipelines to the Midlands made it an ideal choice, and the Craig Goch, Penygarreg, Garreg-ddu, Caban-coch and, finally, Caerwen reservoirs followed. They now supply Birmingham and the surrounding district with more than 80 million gallons of Welsh water every day. The sheer scale of the engineering and the imposing architecture of the dams make a visit to the area worthwhile.

Garreg Ddu Dam is part of a scheme opened by King Edward VII and Queen Alexandra in 1904

See Walk G, page 236
Take a Walk on the Wild Side

Tourist Information
Aberystwyth: Lisburn House, Terrace Road (tel: 01970 612125)

SHROPSHIRE'S HILL COUNTRY

Shropshire's 'blue remembered hills' are dominated by the northeast southwest ridges of the Stiperstones, the Long Mynd, Caer Caradoc, Wenlock Edge and the Clee Hills to the east. It is a surprisingly wild part of the Midlands, where heather-covered hills rise dramatically from steep-sided valleys and where fortified houses tell of a troubled past.

Shire Horses work the fields of Acton Scott Farm, location for the BBC television series Victorian Farm

Acton Scott

Acton Scott Historic Working Farm near Little Stretton is a marvellous place for both children and adults to experience farming in the Shropshire hills before the days of tractors and combine harvesters. Shire horses are used for most of the heavy work, such as ploughing and the pulling of carts, and there is a varied range of demonstrations in a lovely setting, transporting the visitor back to when craftsmen created the countryside.

Church Stretton

Capital of Shropshire's hill country, Church Stretton nestles at the eastern end of the Carding Mill Valley, one of the most beautiful of the approaches to the Long Mynd, which dominates the town. Cheerful tearooms and a range of other shops are a feature of this pleasant little village, which was granted its market charter by King John in 1214. The parish church features an unusual blocked-up Corpse Door on its north side.

The Clee Hills

At 1,791ft (546m), Brown Clee Hill near Abdon is the highest point in Shropshire, with Titterstone Clee Hill at 1,749ft (533m), a close second. These bleak hills

Legends of the Hills

Myths and legends abound in the isolated hill country of Shropshire, where tales of mysterious happenings have been retold over the generations. Perhaps the earliest is the legend of the giant Ippikin, who can be recalled by chanting his name near his rock on Wenlock Edge. The Devil himself is supposed to be sitting on the highest point of The Stiperstones, still known as the Devil's Chair, when the frequent clouds and mists envelop the quartzite summit.

Another giant, known as Wild Edric – a Saxon lord who was deprived of his lands by the Normans – is supposed to be imprisoned in the lead mines below the Stiperstones, while Caer Caradoc, the fort-topped hill opposite Church Stretton, is alleged to be where Caractacus made his last stand against Roman troops.

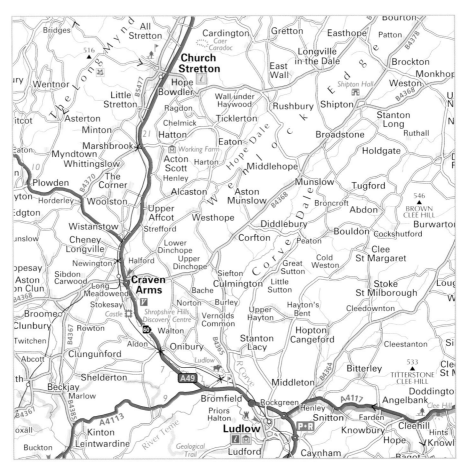

Ludlow's timber-framed Feathers Hotel, with its carved façade and first-floor balcony, was built in 1603 and stands in Corve Street

Wilderhope Manor

Tucked away in a fold of the hills beyond Wenlock Edge is Wilderhope Manor, a beautifully gabled Tudor manor house which is now surely one of the most romantic youth hostels in Britain. Built in 1586 by the Smallman family, it was the home of Major Thomas Smallman, who escaped a party of raiding Roundheads during the Civil War by leaping off Wenlock Edge on his horse. He landed in a crab-apple tree, which broke his fall and saved his life.

of Carboniferous limestone, later covered by volcanic basalts, have been extensively exploited by man over the centuries. There are many remains of coal mines on Brown Clee, and iron ore, copper and limestone have also been extracted. Even today, black basalt is still extracted for roadstone from Titterstone Clee Hill, where a massive quarry blights the hillside.

The highest points of the hills were settled by Iron-Age people, who built a series of hillforts – at Abdon Burf, Clee Burf, Nordy Bank and on the quarry-ravaged Titterstone Clee, the largest fort of all.

Craven Arms

Craven Arms, a bustling little market town on the busy A49 Shrewsbury to Ludlow road, takes its name from its Georgian coaching inn. It is famous for its autumn sheep sales, when farmers from the surrounding hills come to buy and sell their livestock, including the local brown-faced Clun Forest breed.

The Long Mynd

This 10-mile (16.1km) whaleback is the most massive physical feature in Shropshire, although its summit at Pole Bank (1,693ft/516m) is not the county's highest point. Crossed by the prehistoric track known as the Portway, the Long Mynd is the most southerly grouse moor in England, with plentiful heather on the broad plateau. It is split by coombs and steep-sided valleys, especially on the eastern side of the ridge. The most famous of these is the Carding Mill Valley, which runs west from Church Stretton, and is now owned by the National Trust. Among the plentiful wildlife on the Long Mynd, which is a site of special scientific interest, are red grouse, buzzards and wheatears, with ring ouzels and dippers in the batches.

Ludlow

One of Britain's best-preserved medieval towns, Ludlow has a wealth of the black and white, half-timbered box-framed houses which are such a feature of Shropshire. Perhaps the most famous of these is the much-photographed 17th-century Feathers Hotel in the Bull Ring, where bulls were baited in the Middle Ages. But Ludlow is dominated by the massive red sandstone castle, built by Roger Montgomery, Earl of Shrewsbury, shortly after the Conquest to repel Welsh incursions. The castle has been the home of kings and princes ever since, and today plays host to regular Shakespearean performances in its ancient courtyard.

Stokesay Castle

This perfect and romantic example of a 13th-century fortified manor house stands frozen in time at the end of a lane, just off the A49. Its North Tower is uniquely topped with a half-timbered construction, the earliest part of the house, begun about 1240. It has a massive polygonal South Tower of 1291 and an Elizabethan gatehouse, and was the home of the Say and Ludlow families, before passing to the Cravens (of Craven Arms) and the Baldwyns from nearby Diddlebury.

Wenlock Edge

Wenlock Edge is a well-wooded 18-mile (29km) escarpment of Silurian limestone to the south of Much Wenlock, bounded in the northwest by Hope Dale and in the southeast by Corve Dale.

Now owned by the National Trust, the Edge is a fine viewpoint for the Shropshire Hills, with Caer Caradoc and the Long Mynd across Ape Dale, and the Wrekin to the north.

👣 **See Walk H, page 237**
Picturesque Downton Castle

Tourist Information
Ludlow: Castle Street
(tel: 01584 875053)

The great South Tower of Stokesay Castle, which was not called a castle before the sixteenth century

The hills of Wenlock Edge contain ancient quarries and lime kilns, fossils, wildlife, woods and rare flowers

WORCESTER AND THE MALVERN HILLS

The mighty River Severn is the silver thread which binds together these lush fields, bordered by the whaleback spine of the Malvern Hills to the west and Bredon Hill and the Cotswolds to the east. The cathedral of Worcester, the abbey of Tewkesbury and the priory of Malvern dominate their streets, while in the villages, many half-timbered houses still survive.

Great and Little Comberton

The villages of Great and Little Comberton are home to many timber-framed thatched cottages

Of the Bredon Hill villages, the Combertons are among the most attractive. Great Comberton lies on the northern slopes of the hill, clustered around the Norman Church of St Michael. Little Comberton, despite its name, is bigger and busier, and boasts a good medieval church and early 18th-century manor house, complete with dovecote and 16th-century barn.

Great Malvern

The composer Edward Elgar was born near Worcester, and is buried next to his wife in Little Malvern

The hillside town of Great Malvern was a spa in the mid-19th century, although it had been attracting people who believed in the curative powers of its pure spring water since the 17th century. With its great rambling houses and steeply climbing streets, the town retains an air of faded gentility. The 15th-century priory is famous for its outstanding medieval glass, tiles and choir stalls, perhaps the most complete in the country.

Its neighbours of Malvern Wells, where the composer Edward Elgar is buried, and Little Malvern, which climbs up the hills to the pass of Wynds Point, contain many villas built at the height of its health spa heyday. The annual Three Counties Show, on one of the best showgrounds in the country, is held near Malvern Wells.

Pershore

Pershore is in the heart of Worcestershire's orchard country, and is renowned for the delicious Pershore plums, celebrated in the month-long Plum Festival, each August. The parish church is the only remaining part of the abbey. The magnificent lantern tower, built in about 1330, was the central tower of the abbey, which John Betjeman claimed must have been finer than Worcester Cathedral.

A path towards North Hill, Malvern Hills

Tewkesbury

The view of the magnificent Norman tower of Tewkesbury Abbey, peeping over the black and white half-timbered buildings of Mill Street from the Abbey Mills, is one of the most famous sights in the Midlands. Dominated by the massive Norman abbey, Tewkesbury has a strategic position at the confluence of the rivers Severn and Avon. A crucial battle in the Wars of the Roses was fought in the water meadows near here in 1471.

Upton upon Severn

The soaring iron bridge over the Severn here is a well-known landmark, as is the sandstone church tower, topped by an eight-sided cupola, locally known as 'The Pepperpot'. This is now a heritage centre which tells the story of the town, including an account of the Civil War battle of Upton Bridge.

Worcester

Watched over by the soaring spires of the 14th-century tower of the cathedral, Worcestershire's Severnside cricket ground is surely one of the most beautiful in the country. The city is rich in ancient buildings, such as City Art Gallery and

The Malverns

This impressive miniature mountain range has long had the ability to inspire. From the medieval author of *The Vision of Piers Plowman* to that most supremely English of composers, Edward Elgar, born in their shadow at Lower Broadheath, the Malverns have exerted their influence. They were historically important and the Herefordshire Beacon is the site of an impressive Iron-Age hillfort.

The Malverns stand between upland and lowland Britain, and the views from their 5-mile (8km) ridge are stunning. Formed from Precambrian rocks, their name echoes their frontier role, coming from the Welsh, *Moel Bryn* or 'bald hill'.

Saxon Church and Chapel

The isolated little priory church of St Mary at Deerhurst is one of the earliest surviving Saxon churches in England, originally built in the seventh century. Look for the tiny, triangular-headed windows, the superb font and the animal heads in the porch.

The nearby Saxon Chapel was only discovered in 1885, when repairs were being carried out to a medieval farmhouse. Its Saxon antecedents were proved by the discovery of the so-called Odda's Stone, now in the Ashmolean Museum, Oxford.

Bredon Hill

In summertime on Bredon
The bells they sound
so clear

The Worcestershire poet A. E. Houseman could have heard the bells of 10 churches from Bredon Hill, and this prominent Jurassic limestone outlier of the Cotswolds dominates many of the views east of the Severn Plain. Its 958ft (292m) summit was pushed to more than 1,000ft (304.8m) by the addition of a summerhouse by a Mr Parsons of Kemerton in the early 19th century.

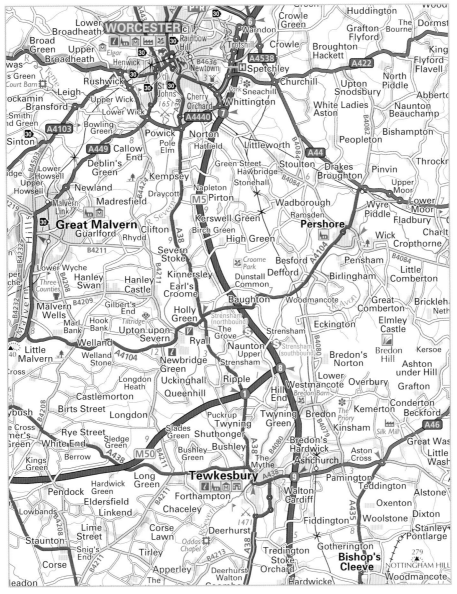

See Walk I, page 238
The Sights of Worcester City

See Walk J, page 239
The Dysynni Valley and Castell y Bere

Tourist Information

Malvern: 21 Church Street (tel: 01684 892289)
Pershore: 19 High Street (tel: 01386 556591)
Tewkesbury: 64 Barton Street (tel: 01684 855040)
Worcester: The Guildhall, High Street (tel: 01905 726311/722480)

Museum, the Guildhall and the Tudor House Museum. The Commandery is a splendid 15th-century timber-framed building which was the headquarters of Charles II's army during the Battle of Worcester in 1651. Now England's only Civil War Centre, it has spectacular audio-visual displays, including the trial of Charles I. The world's largest collection of Worcester's famous porcelain is displayed at the Worcester Porcelain Museum on Severn Street.

Luckless King John is buried in the cathedral, and there is an effigy of him in the chancel. Henry VIII's elder brother, Prince Arthur, is also buried here. The cathedral was started in the 11th century, and the crypt is a fine example of Norman architecture. The Chapter House and Cloisters, dating from the 12th century, are reminders of the cathedral's monastic past.

Just 3 miles (4.8km) west of Worcester, at Lower Broadheath, is the cottage in which Sir Edward Elgar, the composer, was born in 1857. The house museum and adjacent Elgar Centre contain musical scores, photographs and memorabilia.

St Mary the Virgin Abbey Church overlooks the town of Tewkesbury, by the banks of the River Severn

SHREWSBURY AND IRONBRIDGE

The River Severn and the Roman Watling Street, still followed by the modern A5, are the main arteries of this corner of Shropshire, both watched over by the Wrekin. Shrewsbury is one of the most pleasant English towns; Telford is one of the most modern, but it includes the 'suburb' of Ironbridge, where the Industrial Revolution first sparked into life.

Iron bridge spanning the River Severn gorge at Ironbridge

grounds, landscaped by Humphry Repton, have a fine herd of deer and afford sweeping views towards the Wrekin.

Buildwas Abbey

Overshadowed now by the massive cooling towers of the Buildwas Power Station, the noble remains of this 12th-century abbey were once one of the most important in Shropshire. Founded in 1135 as a Savignac monastery, it was later merged into the Cistercian order, but was razed by Thomas Cromwell. The Norman arches are among the finest in Britain.

Atcham and Attingham Park

The pretty little village of Atcham has two fine bridges over the Severn, one classical, built in 1771, and a more modern road bridge. The Palladian mansion of Attingham Park, built in 1785 by Lord Berwick to designs by John Nash, is now owned by the National Trust. The

Coalbrookdale and Ironbridge

Generally held to be the birthplace of the Industrial Revolution, it was here in 1709 that Abraham Darby first used coke to fire an iron furnace. The incredible, lace-like iron bridge, the first in the world, which spans the Severn here, was built by Darby's son in 1777 and gave the town both its fame and its name.

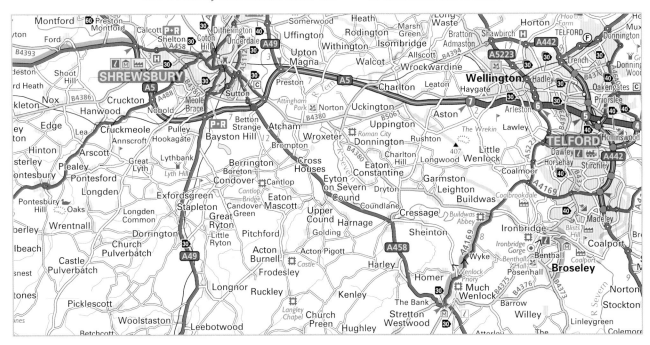

The earliest mention of the Wrekin is in a charter of 855. For several centuries it was known as Mount Gilbert, after a hermit who lived there

The Wrekin

'All friends around the Wrekin' is still a favourite Shropshire toast, and this modest 1,335ft (407m) summit, which is such a prominent feature for travellers on the M65 motorway, exerts a powerful influence on the surrounding countryside.

There are many legends associated with this isolated hill, which is crowned by a hillfort of the Iron-Age Cornovii people. The best known is that of a malevolent Welsh giant, who had a grudge against the people of Shrewsbury and was on his way to drop a great load of earth to dam the Severn and flood the town. Getting weary from his load, he stopped to ask a cobbler carrying a sack of boots and shoes for repair how far it was to Shrewsbury. The quick-thinking cobbler said he had worn out his sack of boots just walking from the town. The giant groaned and dumped his load of earth where he stood, forming the Wrekin.

Now these twin settlements are the home of the Ironbridge Gorge Museum complex covering 6sq miles (15.5sq km). You will need a full day to explore the various sites, which include the original hearths used by the Darby family in their revolutionary methods of smelting, the houses where their workers lived and the incredible inclined plane which took materials down from the Shropshire Canal to a wharf on the Severn. The main attraction is the Blists Hill Open-Air Museum, a recreated town of the 1890s covering 42 acres (17ha), where visitors can really step back in time and experience how people lived and worked. Two miles (3.2km) downstream at Coalport there is a museum on the site of the original Coalport China Works.

Much Wenlock

Shropshire's 'magpie' villages reach their black-and-white crescendo at Much Wenlock, a pretty settlement at the northern end of Wenlock Edge. Among the half-timbered gems are The Goal, Raynald's Mansion and the Guildhall, built on sturdy wooden pillars. The little town was granted its market charter in 1468, but by then its splendid priory, founded in the seventh century by King Merewald of Mercia, was already ancient. It was later converted to a Cluniac priory by Roger of Montgomery. The Early English tracery work in the chapter house wall is particularly fine.

Shrewsbury

Shrewsbury stands on an enormous loop of the River Severn, which is crossed by two splendid bridges – the English and the Welsh – reflecting its role as a border town. It is full of romantic old half-timbered houses, leaning together as if whispering secrets in intriguingly named streets such as Grope Lane, Frankwell and Butcher Row. There is an equal wealth of fine Georgian buildings, notably the town's library, art gallery and museum which are housed in the 17th-century buildings of Shrewsbury's famous public

school. Circular St Chad's Church, also dating from the 17th century, is topped by a dome and overlooks the River Severn.

Much of the rich red sandstone for the town's buildings came from the Quarry, now the centrepiece of the beautiful park gardens known as The Dingle. It was created by one of Britain's best-known gardeners – the late Percy Thrower. Shrewsbury Castle, which stands above the railway station, was severely restored by Thomas Telford when he was appointed surveyor of public works for the county in 1788. It was from here that Henry IV conquered the Welsh rebels in 1403 at the Battle of Shrewsbury, fought 3 miles (4.8km) north of the town.

Telford

One of the latest of Britain's post-war new towns, Telford takes its name from Thomas Telford, the county surveyor from 1788 who was famed for his pioneering work on canals, aqueducts, bridges and turnpike roads.

The town was built in the early 1970s on land which had been scarred by 19th-century industrialisation, to house overspill populations from Birmingham and the Black Country. Today it is bisected by the M54 motorway and watched over by the conical hill of the Wrekin.

Wroxeter

The Roman columns at the gate to the church of St Andrew in the small village of Wroxeter give a small clue to the historical importance of the place. The tribal home of the Cornovii was taken over by the Romans and made their provincial capital of *Vironconium Cornoviorum*, headquarters of the XIV Legion in their campaign against the Ordovices of North Wales.

Partly discovered and protected by Thomas Telford, the most impressive remaining feature of the Roman town is the enormous wall which formed part of the entrance to the baths, the foundations of which can be seen. There is a good museum which explains the significance of this remarkably well-preserved site.

👣 See Walk K, page 240
Powis Castle and the Montgomery Canal

👣 See Walk L, page 241
Revolution at Coalbrookdale

Tourist Information

Ironbridge: The Toll House (tel: 01952 884391)
Much Wenlock: The Museum, High Street (tel: 01952 727679)
Shrewsbury: Rowley's House, Barker Street (tel: 01743 281200)
Telford: Telford Shopping Centre (tel: 01952 230032)

Wroxeter's Roman City, home to 5,000 people, was unearthed in 1859. Among the first Victorians to see the site was the author Charles Dickens

BOTH SIDES OF THE MENAI STRAIT

The Menai Strait, between the castle-crowned towns of Beaumaris and Caernarfon, has always made ancient Anglesey a place set apart from the rest of Wales. Its dolmen-scattered interior is fringed by a beautiful coastline of steep cliffs and sandy bays. Over on the mainland, the narrow coastal plain rears up to the Llanberis Pass and the cloud-capped foothills of Snowdonia.

Llanfair PG

This small, otherwise undistinguished village has traded on its name (the full version, that is) to become quite a tourist attraction. Few visitors can resist turning their cameras on the famous railway sign of: Llanfairpwllgwyngyllgogerychwyrndrobwyllllantysiliogogogoch. Llanfair PG's other, and perhaps most abiding, claim to fame is that the first UK branch of the Women's Institute was founded here in 1915.

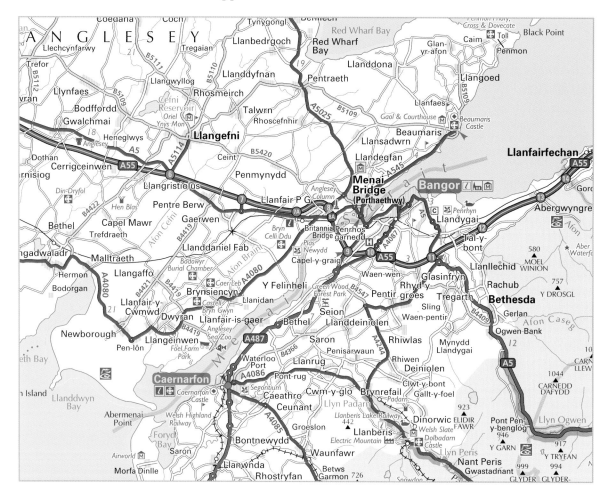

Beaumaris Castle was begun in 1295 and was the last and largest of the castles to be built by Edward I in Wales

Bangor

Bangor is a university and cathedral city which boasts the oldest bishopric in Britain. Bangor is part of the collegiate system of the University of Wales, founded in 1893. Old Bangor is a delightful maze of streets leading down to the sea, and on Ffordd Gwynedd is an art gallery and museum of Welsh antiquities.

Three miles (4.8km) east is the splendid Penrhyn Castle, which has all the appearance of an authentic Norman fortress, with a cavernous great hall and enormous stone staircase, but it was actually built in the early 19th century as a sumptuous family home. There is an industrial railway museum in the stables.

Prehistoric Anglesey

The distinguished archaeologist Jacquetta Hawkes commented that there was no better place than Anglesey to combine a seaside holiday with painless archaeology. Certainly, this small, ancient island, known to the Romans as *Mona* and to the Welsh as *Ynys Môn*, is a treasurehouse of prehistoric remains, and the fabled home of the mysterious priesthood known as the Druids, who caused Julius Caesar so much anguish.

Among the most impressive sites are the Neolithic chambered barrows of Barclodiad y Gawres near Llangwfan and Bryncelli Ddu near Llanddaniel Fab, both unequalled outside Ireland, along with the various 'dolmens' at Lligwy, near Amlwch and Trefignath, just south of Holyhead. These are now known to be the exposed remains of other Neolithic tombs and barrows.

Beaumaris

One of the most beautiful of Edward I's castles, moated Beaumaris Castle was built in the late 13th century to guard the approaches to the Menai Straits. The concentric walls with their circular towers were never completed to their full height, and the castle never saw military action. The Great Hall and chapel in the central tower are particularly memorable. The town itself is interesting, with such attractions as the former Gaol and Courthouse, where visitors can see the treadmill, grim cells and foreboding 19th-century courtroom.

Caernarfon

Dominated by the most imposing and complete of Edward I's castles, with its banded walls and angled towers on the sea front, Caernarfon does have deliberate echoes of Constantine's city. The castle was built over 44 years and completed to its present unequalled magnificence in 1327. The old town is still ringed by the almost intact town walls built on the order of Edward I, and the even earlier foundations of the Roman fort of *Segontium* can still be seen on the eastern edge of the town.

Holyhead

Holyhead Mountain (719ft/219m) is one of the best viewpoints in Anglesey, taking in the distant coast of Ireland to the west, the Isle of Man to the north, and the jagged peaks of Snowdonia to the southeast. Nearer to hand are a wealth of prehistoric remains and the rocky little island of South Stack, with its gleaming white lighthouse serving as a beacon to the Ireland-bound ferries which scuttle in and out of this busy port. Holyhead is the biggest town on Anglesey, and its 13th-century church of St Cybi is built on the site of a Roman fort.

Llanberis

Slate predominates in this grey little town at the foot of the Llanberis Pass, and just across the waters of Llyn Padarn are the terraced shelves of the Dinorwig Slate Quarry, in its time one of the biggest in the world. It is now the location of the National Slate Museum and an underground hydro-electric scheme, also open to visitors.

Today, Llanberis is a popular visitor hub and the starting point for two of the

The Pass of Llanberis wends its way through the mountainous Snowdonia National Park

easiest ways to the summit of Snowdon. One is the Llanberis Path, which winds up the southern slopes, and the other is the famous Snowdon Mountain Railway, operating since 1896. Between the lakes of Llyn Padarn and Llyn Peris is the circular 13th-century keep of Dolbadarn Castle, a rarity in that it was built by Welsh princes before the English conquest.

Menai Bridge

Two feats of civil engineering dominate this Victorian town, which grew up as a result of them. Thomas Telford's graceful suspension bridge of 1826 originally took mail coaches across the Menai Strait. Today, the busy A5 crosses the Britannia Bridge, originally a tubular structure constructed by Stephenson in 1850 to carry the railway, but substantially rebuilt in 1970 to carry both road and rail traffic.

Newborough Warren

A National Nature Reserve and Site of Special Scientific Interest covering 1,500 acres (608ha) of shifting sand dunes and forest plantations, Newborough Warren has waymarked nature trails enabling visitors to enjoy the famous birdlife of the reserve.

Plas Newydd

Plas Newydd, now in the care of the National Trust, was designed by James Wyatt for the Marquess of Anglesey in the late 18th century, and contains a military museum with a collection of uniforms and relics of the Battle of Waterloo, where the First Marquess lost his leg. There are magnificent views across the Menai Strait to Snowdonia from the park, which also contains two fine prehistoric dolmens.

🐾 See Walk M, page 242
A View of Bala's Lake – Llyn Tegid

🐾 See Walk L, page 243
In the Country of Lloyd George

🐾 See Walk O, page 244
Snowdon the Long Way

Tourist Information
Bangor: Town Hall, Deiniol Road (tel: 01248 352786)
Caernarfon: Oriel Pendeitsh, Castle Street (tel: 01286 672232)
Holyhead: Penrhos Beach Road (tel: 01407 762622)
Llanberis: 41A High Street (tel: 01286 870765)
Llanfair PG: Station Site (tel: 01248 713177)

Newborough Warren Reserve is an important haven for pintails and cormorants

THE NATIONAL PARKS OF WALES

The three National Parks of Wales – Snowdonia, the Brecon Beacons and the Pembrokeshire Coast – could hardly offer greater scenic contrasts. From the jagged volcanic peaks of Snowdonia, which includes the highest British ground south of Scotland, to the sweeping sandstone escarpments of the Brecon Beacons and the dramatic cliffs and bays of the Pembrokeshire Coast, the variety is breathtaking. In their tightly controlled protected areas, they encapsulate the very best of the landscapes in the Principality.

A proposal for a fourth Welsh National Park in the Cambrian Mountains of mid-Wales, centred on Plynlimon and the source of the rivers Severn and Wye, was thwarted as a result of local opposition, mainly from farmers and landowners, in the mid-1970s.

Snowdon reflected in Llynnau Mymbyr in Snowdonia National Park

Snowdonia

Snowdonia, at 827sq miles (2,142sq km), is the second largest National Park in Britain after the Lake District, and was the first of the three to be designated (in 1951). Outdoor campaigners such as Sir Clough Williams Ellis, who built the Italianate fantasy village of Portmeirion, had long pressed for the proper protection of this unique landscape.

It was medieval English sailors crossing the Irish Sea who gave Snowdon and Snowdonia its name – the wild, rocky landscape beyond Anglesey always seemed to be brushed with snow. To the Welsh, though, this mountainous region had always been known as *Eryri*, the 'abode of eagles', and it was the place where their leaders, from the legendary Arthur through to the historical figures of Llywelyn the Great and Owain Glyndwr, traditionally sought refuge from the invading English.

There is still an indefinable air of nostalgia and 'Welshness' in these sometimes savage hills, where Welsh speakers are still in the majority.

The physical shape of the National Park is best described as a large diamond split into three by valleys which run northeast to southwest. These deep gashes neatly separate the main mountain groups of Snowdon, the Glynders and Carneddau in the north; the rugged Rhinogs and Arenig in the centre; Cadair Idris and the Arans to the south. Most visitors gravitate to the area around Snowdon, which at 3,560ft (1,085m) is a natural magnet to the peak-bagger. There are several well-established routes to the summit, some of which have had to be extensively restored because of overuse. If the climb is too much, there is always the rack-and-pinion railway which winds up from Llanberis to the summit, where there is a visitor centre.

Slate and forestry have been the traditional industries in Snowdonia, but tourism is now as important in the slate-built villages of Llanberis, Capel Curig, Betws-y-Coed and Blaenau Ffestiniog.

The Brecon Beacons

The Brecon Beacons National Park, straddling the borders of Powys, Dyfed, Gwent and Mid Glamorgan, takes its name from, and is centred on the triple peaks of the Beacons themselves, which dominate the lush valley of the River Usk. These old red sandstone mountains, the highest of which is Pen-y-Fan at 2,907ft (886m), stand like a petrified wave about to break over the ancient county town of Brecon, where the Romans had a fort at Y Gaer. The ascent of Pen-y-Fan is most easily achieved from the Storey Arms on the A470; the climb is rewarded with spectacular views.

Cefn Cyff ridge, with the Black Mountains in the distance in the Brecon Beacons National Park

240sq miles (620sq km) one of the smallest of Britain's National Parks – is the only one which is largely coastal, and it is not difficult to understand why. Its main glory is its superb 230-mile (370km) coastline, which is followed for most of its way by the 186-mile (299km) Pembrokeshire Coast Path, a wonderful roller-coaster of a walk with rugged cliffs, secluded sandy bays and the ever-changing seascapes.

The 186 miles (299km) of the Pembrokeshire Coast Path also offer a crash course in geology, for the route shows at a glance the story of the formation of the earth from the earliest pre-Cambrian rocks around the tiny cathedral city of St David's to the Ordovician volcanic structure that underpins the the northern area.

There is much more to the 522sq mile (1,352sq km) park, established in 1957, than the Beacons. Two other distinct mountain masses make up the area, both of which confusingly carry the name 'Black'. The Black Mountains (plural) are a range of sandstone hills running north–south between Hay-on-Wye and Abergavenny. Offa's Dyke, the eighth century boundary embankment and ditch which separated England and Wales, runs along its crest and makes a fine walk. The Black Mountain (singular) is a wilder, less-visited area to the west of the A406 Sennybridge to Ystradgynlais road. It is centred on the sweeping crest of Carmarthen Van, at 2,631ft (802 m) the highest point in the Black Mountain, which has the mysterious little glacial lake of Llyn y Fan Fach at its feet. Further west, near the boundary of the National Park, remote Carreg Cennen Castle has one of the most spectacular situations of any castle in Wales.

There is another, altogether different landscape which dominates the south of the park. The area of Carboniferous rocks which stretches across the southern boundary has created a landscape of tumbling waterfalls, huge caves and potholes and beautiful woodlands – a major attraction to visitors, and easily accessible from the valleys of South Wales. A pleasant way to view the scenery is on the Brecon Mountain Railway. North of Merthyr Tydfil, it runs from Pant to the Pontsticill reservoir and dam.

The Mellte and Hepste valleys, between Ystradfellte and Pont Nedd-Fechan, are the centre of the Beacons caving country. Dan-yr-Ogof Showcaves system, north of Abercraf, has the largest chamber in any

British showcave, and in Bone Cave evidence was found of human occupation 3,000 years ago. The caves are now part of a tourist complex with a number of attractions.

The Pembrokeshire Coast

This area of Dyfed is sometimes known as 'Little England beyond Wales' and the popularity of resorts such as Tenby and St David's is undeniable. But the epithet has its basis in history, since a string of castles were erected by the Norman invaders, along a line from Newgale in the west to Amroth in the east, to subdue the native Welsh. The line – known by the Norse word *landsker* meaning frontier – can still be traced through the area's place names. South of the line, there is a predominance of places with anglicised names and English is still the most common language, but north of the *landsker* Welsh is more commonly spoken and it is Welsh place names that abound.

The only real uplands in this mainly coastal park are the Preseli Hills in the north, a self-contained moorland block of Ordovician rocks rising to 1,759ft (536m) at Foel Cwm Cerwym south of Bryberian. The Preseli Hills are famous as the source of the Bluestones which were transported to far-off Wiltshire for the inner circle of Stonehenge, either by man or glacial movement.

The main attraction of Pembrokeshire will always be its coastline, and there are few more invigorating walking experiences in Britain than to stride along these cliffs in early spring, on a carpet of wild flowers, accompanied by the cries of the seabirds and the salty tang of the sea.

St Brides Haven looking out to St Brides Bay in the Pembrokeshire Coast National Park

THE NORTH WALES RESORTS

One of the most pleasant and refined of the North Wales coastal resorts, Llandudno shelters between the great twin limestone headlands of the Great Orme and Little Orme, west of Colwyn Bay. Further east, the candy floss and kiss-me-quick attractions of Rhyl and Prestatyn beckon. To the west lies Conwy, guarded by its splendid medieval castle, one of the finest in Wales.

The Croquet Terrace at Bodnant Garden overlooks the lily pond, with the mountains of Snowdonia in the distance

Edward I's Castles

The 35-year reign of Edward I saw an unprecedented period of castle-building in North Wales, of which Conwy and Rhuddlan are just two. Most of these superb examples of medieval military architecture were supervised by Master James of St George, the outstanding military engineer of his day. But the craftsmen who built them were nearly all conscripted from English counties by the king. All the major castles – Flint, Rhuddlan, Conwy, Caernarfon, Beaumaris, Criccieth and Harlech – were built so that they could be supplied from the sea, because of the threat to land-borne supplies by the constantly warring Welsh princes.

Abergele

This ancient market town is now also a busy resort, with the caravan-besieged suburb of Pensarn on the coast at the centre of 5 miles (8km) of sand and shingle beaches. A short distance down the A55 is the famous 'white marble' and lavishly ornate church at Bodelwyddan, its shining white limestone spire a landmark for miles.

Bodnant Garden

One of the finest gardens in the UK. Bodnant consists of 80 acres (40ha) of formal terraces, a pinetum and a wild garden, all laid out in 1875. It shelters in the valley of the River Hiraethlyn, a tributary of the Conwy. Bodnant is especially famous for its rhododendrons, azaleas and camellias, and for its magnificent laburnum arch.

Colwyn Bay

A charming traditional Victorian resort, Colwyn Bay has some fine architecture and a wonderful promenade, unfortunately shared by the parallel railway line. Colwyn stretches round its east-facing bay from Old Colwyn to Rhos-on-Sea. Among the attractions is the interesting Welsh Mountain Zoo, which has a fine collection of mountain birds of prey and the fascinating Chapel of St Trillo, thought to be the smallest church in Britain, with space for just six worshippers. A little way south on the A470 is Felin Isaf, a working flour mill on the River Conwy.

Conwy

The eight drum towers of Edward I's superb 13th-century castle dominate this pleasant little town at the mouth of the River Conwy. The massive 15ft (4.6m) thick castle walls are matched by the virtually complete town walls with gates and their barbicans still intact.

Three bridges span the river beside the castle – a modern road bridge, Stephenson's tubular railway bridge of 1848 and Thomas Telford's pioneering road suspension bridge of 1826, which has 'medieval' towers to match those of the castle. This bridge is now in the care of the National Trust.

Another National Trust property in Conwy is the fascinating 14th-century Aberconwy House, the only medieval merchant's house to survive in this once-thriving seaport. It now contains a heritage centre telling the story of the town. Visitors, though only a few at a time, can also see Britain's smallest

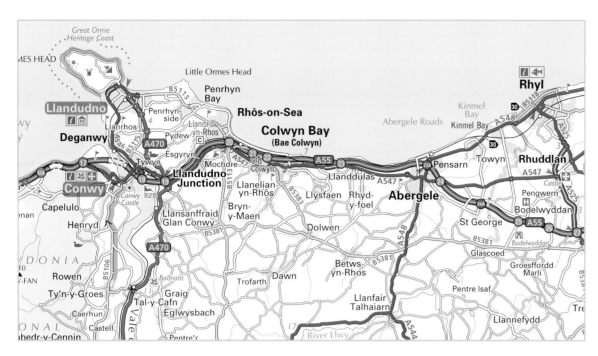

See Walk P, page 245
Where the Mountains meet the Sea

Tourist Information
Colwyn Bay: Imperial Buildings, Princes Drive (tel: 01492 530478)
Conwy: Castle Buildings, Castle Street (tel: 01492 592248)
Llandudno: Library Building, Mostyn Street (tel: 01492 577577)
Prestatyn: Offa's Dyke Centre, Central Beach (tel: 01745 889092)
Rhyl: The Village, West Promenade (tel: 01745 344515)

house (verified by the Guinness Book of Records) – just 6ft (1.8m) wide by 10ft (3m) high.

Llandudno

A century ago, Llandudno was just a sleepy little fishing village, but today it is the largest resort on this coast and is justly popular with holidaymakers. The architect of this transformation was the Liverpudlian surveyor, Owen Williams, who laid out the sweeping Promenade, the Marine Drive and the spacious streets. Modern Llandudno includes a conference centre and many good shops. The Mostyn Art Gallery and the Llandudno Museum are well worth a visit.

Dominating the town is the great limestone bulk of the Great Orme, which can be reached by the quaint Victorian tramway, or in the modern cable car. Whichever route you take, the views from the 676-ft (206-m) summit are stunning.

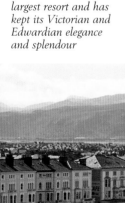

Llandudno is Wales's largest resort and has kept its Victorian and Edwardian elegance and splendour

Rhuddlan Castle

Rhuddlan Castle, guarding the mouth of the River Clwyd and the coastal route into North Wales, is a good example of how a castle develops over the centuries. Just to the southeast are the earthworks of a much earlier motte-and-bailey castle, built in 1073 in the first phase of the English invasion. The present castle dates back to the 13th century, its massive West Gatehouse being particularly impressive, and was one of the first to be built in the concentric style. The River Clwyd was re-channelled by the castle builders to enable it to be supplied from the sea 2.5 miles (4km) away.

The castle is also historically important – the Statute of Rhuddlan was signed here in 1284, confirming Edward I's sovereignty over Wales. The castle was badly damaged by Parliamentary forces in 1646.

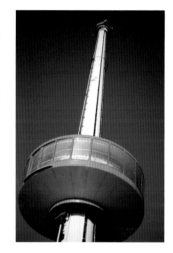

The Sky Tower is a 240ft observation gyro tower which has been operating since 1993

Rhyl

Rhyl was developed into a successful resort in Victorian days. 'Sunny Rhyl' now offers the holidaymaker all the entertainments that a modern seaside town should. The sandy beach seems to go on for ever when the tide is out, while the Sun Centre provides year-round water rides, slides and amusements, protected from the unpredictable Welsh weather. The town's miniature railway is Britian's oldest, operating since 1911.

CHESTER AND THE RIVER DEE

Inland from its estuary, the River Dee passes through the beautiful cathedral city of Chester, then loops around Wrexham to the south-east before reaching the eisteddfod town of Llangollen. The first hills of Wales rise up to the north, and snaking up between the Llantysilio and Cyrn-y-Brain ranges is the hairpin Horseshoe Pass, with its fine views over the Vale of Clwyd.

The Llangollen Railway takes visitors on a 7.5 mile (12km) steam train ride along the banks of the River Dee

Tourist Information

Chester: Town Hall, Northgate Street (tel: 01244 402111) Llangollen: Y Capel, Castle Street (tel: 01978 860828) Wrexham: Lambpit Street (tel: 01978 292015)

Chester

County town of Cheshire, and famous for its fine red sandstone cathedral and two-storey galleried medieval shops known as The Rows, Chester is a bustling, thriving place. The Romans were the first to realise the strategic importance of the first crossing point on the Dee and set up their fortress of *Deva*. There are fine Roman exhibits in the Grosvenor Museum, and a Roman amphitheatre east of Newgate.

The cathedral started as a Benedictine abbey, but what can be seen today is mainly restored 14th-century work. It is especially noted for its unusual Early English rectangular chapter house.

A fine way to explore Chester is to take the 2-mile (3.2km) walk around its city walls, some parts of which are the Roman original, but which are embellished by mainly medieval towers and gates. King Charles's Tower is so named because Charles I is said to have watched the defeat of his forces at the Battle of Rowton Moor from here in 1645. Chester's Heritage Centre, visitor centre and the Grosvenor Museum offer an excellent introduction to the city. Chester Zoo has 7,000 animals in 110 acres (45ha) of enclosures and landscaped gardens.

Flint

Once the county town for this part of Wales, Flint has always occupied a strategic position on the western shore of the Dee Estuary. Flint Castle was the first of Edward I's chain of castles to control the Welsh, built between 1277 and 1284 at the huge cost (in those days) of £7,000. Richard II surrendered to Henry Bolingbroke at Flint Castle in 1399.

Llangollen

Llangollen, sheltered in its green vale, is famous as the annual venue, since 1947, for the International Musical Eisteddfod. During that summertime festival of song and dance, the streets of this pretty Dee-side town are colourful with folk costumes and music from all over the world.

But Llangollen has other attractions, including the 14th-century bridge over the Dee – one of the 'Wonders of Wales' – and Plas Newydd, a stunning black and white, timber-framed house on the edge of the town which was the home of the hospitable 'Ladies of Llangollen' in the 18th century.

Mold

Mold is a busy little market town which was once the 'capital' of the old county of Flintshire. The splendid parish church of St Mary, with its 16th-century aisled nave and magnificent 18th-century tower, dominates the lovely High Street and, indeed, the whole of the Alun Valley. Look out for the unusual art deco flooring in the War Memorial chapel.

Pontcysyllte Aqueduct

This 'canal in the clouds' was one of the wonders of Britain when it was built by Thomas Telford as a revolutionary solution to the question of how he could carry the Ellesmere Canal across the valley of the River Dee. The aqueduct takes the canal on 19 arches in an iron trough more than 1,000ft (305m) long, 120ft (37m)

The Horseshoe Pass

Motorists using the precipitous 1,299ft (396m) Horseshoe Pass between Llangollen and Ruthin in the Vale of Clwyd get an intimate view of the Llangollen Hills. Passing Eliseg's Pillar, a ninth-century monument to a Welsh prince, and the lovely ruins of Valle Crucis Abbey, the A542 heads towards Pentredwr with tremendous views of the sweeping limestone escarpments of the Eglwyseg Rocks to the north, where the northern summit is known somewhat prophetically as World's End (1,614ft/492m). These terraced hills of white limestone scars and scree are said to take their alternative name of Church Rocks from the abbey which lies in the valley below.

From Pentredwr, the road climbs relentlessly between Llantysilio and the Cyrn-y-Brain Mountains, with a bird's-eye view of the Vale of Clwyd below, before dropping back down to the valley.

above the valley of the Dee. Technology may have come a long way, but this is still a breathtaking piece of engineering.

Valle Crucis Abbey

The name of this romantic, tree-framed ruin, one of the most beautiful in Wales, is the 'Vale of the Cross' and is thought to come from the nearby Eliseg's Pillar, on the hill to the north. Founded in 1202, this Cistercian house fits perfectly the monks' vow to 'glory in their poverty'. The slender, Early English windows of the western end are particularly beautiful.

Wrexham

Although the collieries and steelworks on which Wrexham prospered are largely things of the past, this bustling town is still the largest in North Wales. The church of St Giles is the chief architectural attraction, with its elegant 135ft (41m) steeple, dating from the 14th century. A copy of the church tower was built on the campus of Yale University in the 1920s in memory of Elihu Yale, the Pilgrim Father who is buried in the churchyard here, and who gave his name to the distinguished American university.

Offa's Dyke Path, at the summit of Hay bluff, with views over the Wye Valley and west towards the Brecon Beacons

Offa's Dyke Path

The Offa's Dyke long-distance footpath winds under the limestone terraces of Eglwyseg Mountain and across the moorland of Cyrn-y-Brain on one of the last stages of its 177-mile (285km) journey from Chepstow on the Severn Estuary to Prestatyn on the North Wales coast.

The creation of the path, which follows fairly faithfully the line of King Offa of Mercia's defensive western boundary of his kingdom, was the brainchild of the Offa's Dyke Association and the Ramblers' Association. Years of patient campaigning came to fruition in July 1971, when the path was officially opened by Lord Hunt at Knighton.

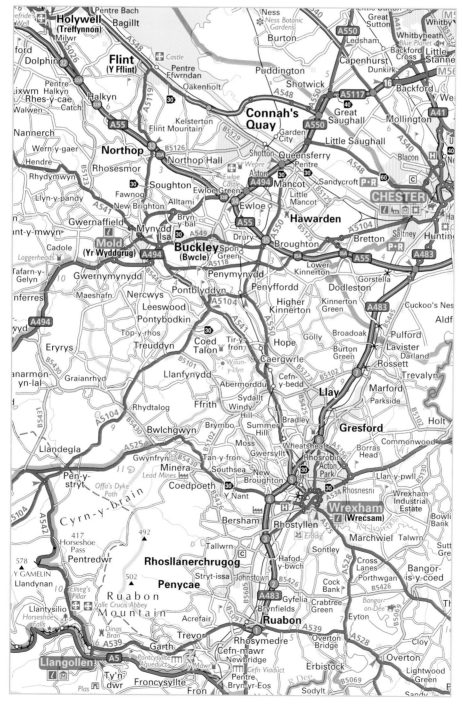

One of the few remaining towers of the ruined Flint Castle, dating from the 13th century

Walk A

TWO FACES OF THE HAVEN

The waters of Milford Haven and the coastline that forms its entrance.

Boats at Milford Haven marina, including a lightship named Haven

Distance: 9 miles (14.5km)

Minimum time: 4hrs

Ascent/Gradient: 1,017ft (310m) ▲▲▲

Level of difficulty: +++

Paths: Coast path and easy tracks over agricultural land, short road section, 9 stiles

Landscape: Rugged coastline, magnificent beach and sheltered harbour

Suggested map: OS Explorer OL36 South Pembrokeshire

Start/finish: Grid reference: SM 854031

Dog friendliness: Care needed on cliff tops and near livestock

Parking: Car park at West Angle Bay

Public toilets: At start and just off route in Angle village

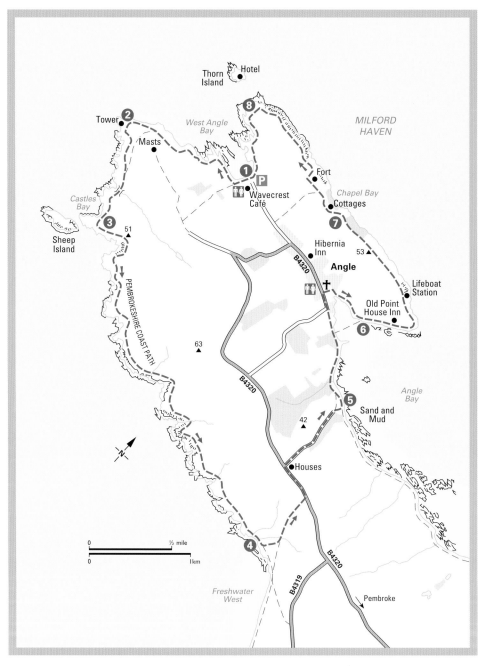

❶ Facing the sea, walk left out of the car park and pass between the café and the public conveniences to a waymarked gate. Follow the field-edge along, passing through further gates, and eventually leading out on to the coast, where a right fork drops to a ruined tower on a slender headland.

❷ Continue back up from this, pass through further gates and then go down to a footbridge. Climb up from this and pass Sheep Island on your right.

❸ Continue along the coast, dropping steeply into a succession of valleys and climbing back up each time. As you reach the northern end of Freshwater West, keep your eye open for a footpath waymarker to the left.

❹ Cross a stile and walk up the floor of the valley, swinging left to a stile at the top. Cross the next field, and another stile, and continue to the road (B4320). Turn left on to the road

and walk past a cluster of houses to a right-hand turn. Follow this all the way down to the coast and turn left on to the coast path to merge on to a drive.

❺ Take the drive to a bridleway sign on the right. If the tide is low, you can cross the estuary here and continue along the bank of pebbles to the road on the other side. If it's not, carry on along the drive to join a road that leads into Angle village and bear right by the church to follow a dirt track over a bridge and around to the right.

❻ Continue around, pass the Old Point House Inn on your left and follow field-edges to the

gravel turning point above the Lifeboat Station on your right. Keep straight ahead, through a gate, and continue through a succession of fields into a wooded area.

❼ You'll join a broad track that runs around Chapel Bay cottages and fort. Keep straight ahead to follow the narrow path back above the coast. This eventually rounds the headland by Thorn Island.

❽ As you descend into West Angle Bay, the path diverts briefly into a field to avoid a landslide. Continue downwards and bear right on to a drive that drops you back to the car park.

AN INVIGORATING TRUNDLE AROUND STRUMBLE

A walk in some of the wildest countryside of the Pembrokeshire coast.

Strumble Head and Lighthouse, Pembrokeshire

Distance: 8 miles (12.9km)
Minimum time: 3hrs 30min
Ascent/Gradient: 920ft (280m) ▲▲▲
Level of difficulty: ++﹢
Paths: Coast path, grassy, sometimes muddy tracks, rocky paths, 13 stiles
Landscape: Rugged headland, secluded coves and rocky tor
Suggested map: OS Explorer OL35 North Pembrokeshire
Start/finish: Grid reference: SM 894411
Dog friendliness: Care needed near cliff tops and livestock
Parking: Car park by Strumble Head Lighthouse
Public toilets: None on route

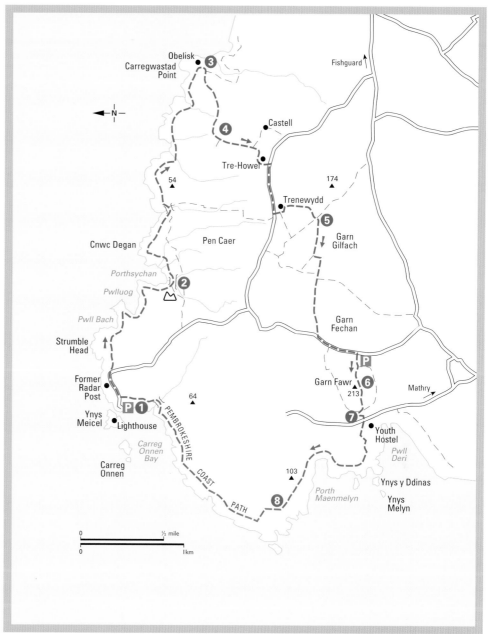

❶ Walk back up the road and cross a gate on the left on to the coast path. Pass above the bays of Pwll Bach and Pwlluog, then drop steeply to a footbridge behind the pebble beach of Porthsychan.

❷ Follow the coast path waymarkers around Cnwc Degan and down to another bridge, where a couple of footpaths lead away from the coast. Continue along the coast, passing a cottage on the right and climbing and dropping a couple of times, before you reach the obelisk at Carregwastad Point.

❸ Follow the main path inland and cross a stile on to a farm track, where you turn right, away from the coast path. Continue with this path, which is vague in places, up through the gorse to a wall, then turn right on to a good track. Take this through a succession of gates and around a left-hand bend.

❹ Ignore a track to the right and continue up the cattle track, eventually bearing right into the farmyard where you follow a walkway past livestock pens before swinging left, after the buildings, to the road. Turn right and follow the road past a large house to a waymarked bridleway on the left. Pass Trenewydd and go

through a gate on to a green lane. Follow this up to another gate and on to open ground.

❺ Turn right here and follow the wall to yet another gate. This leads to a walled track, which you follow to the road. Turn left and climb up to the car park beneath Garn Fawr. Turn right, on to a hedged track, and follow this up, through a gap in the wall, and over rocks to the trig point.

❻ Climb down and cross the saddle between this tor and the other, slightly lower, one to the south. From here head west towards an even lower outcrop and pass it on the left. This

becomes a clear path that leads down to a stile. Cross this and turn left, then right on to a drive that leads to the road.

❼ Walk straight across and on to the coast path. Bear right and cross a stile to drop down towards Ynys y Ddinas, the small island ahead. Navigation is easy as you follow the coast path north, over Porth Maenmelyn and up to a cairn.

❽ Continue along the coast, towards the lighthouse, until you drop to a footbridge above Carreg Onnen Bay. Cross a stile into a field, then another back on to the coast path and return to the car park.

Walk C

THE ESCARPMENTS OF THE CARMARTHEN FAN

An exacting expedition through the Brecon Beacons National Park's most spectacular and remote scenery.

The Black Mountain on a sunny day in Carmarthenshire

Distance: 7.5 miles (12.1km)
Minimum time: 4hrs 30min
Ascent/Gradient: 2,000ft (610m) ▲▲▲
Level of difficulty: +++
Paths: Faint paths, trackless sections over open moorland, no stiles
Landscape: Imposing mountains, hidden lakes, wild and remote moorland
Suggested map: OS Explorer OL12 Brecon Beacons National Park Western & Central areas
Start/finish: Grid reference: SN 798238
Dog friendliness: Care needed near livestock and steep drops
Parking: At end of small unclassified road, southeast of Llanddeusant
Public toilets: At end of small unclassified road, southeast of Llanddeusant
Note: Best not undertaken in poor visibility

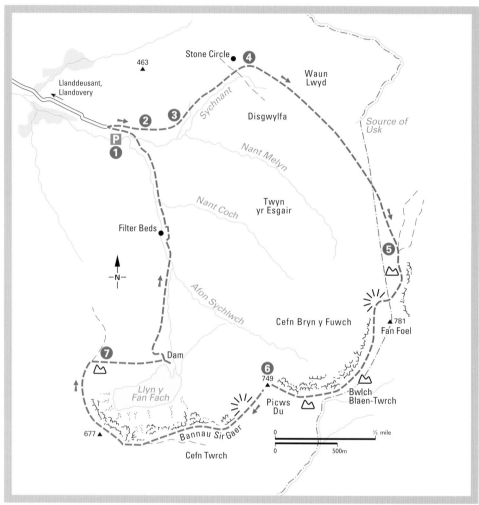

❶ From the car park at the end of the unclassified road, head back towards Llanddeusant, and after about 100 yards (91m) turn sharp right, almost doubling back on yourself, to continue on a faint track that contours eastwards around the hillside. Follow this track as it then veers northeast into the small valley carved out over the centuries by the Sychnant brook.

❷ The track becomes clear for a short period, but don't be drawn uphill to the north, instead remain true to the course of the stream, keeping left at the confluence with another distinct valley, this one belonging to the Nant Melyn.

❸ The track is faint but the going reasonably easy as you continue up the valley, crossing a small tributary and following the bank above the Sychnant. Numerous paths and sheep tracks cross your way, but continue unhindered upwards, aiming for the shallow saddle on the blunt ridge above. The stream eventually swings to the right and peters out. At this stage, bear right and head along the ridge.

❹ You're now aiming for the steep and obvious spur of Fan Foel, which lies southeast of you, approximately 1.5 miles (2.4km) away. Follow whatever tracks you can find over Waun Lwyd and, as the ridge starts to narrow, keep to the crest, where you'll meet a path coming up from the northeast.

❺ Climb steeply up the narrow path on to the escarpment and keep right to follow the escarpment along. The path becomes clearer as it drops steeply into Bwlch Blaen-Twrch. From here, climb up on to Bannau Sir Gaer and continue to the summit cairn.

❻ Stay with the main footpath and follow the edge of the escarpment above the precipitous cliffs into a small saddle or col and up again above Llyn y Fan Fach. Continue around the lake, with the steep drop to your right and you'll see a good path dropping down a grassy spur to the outflow of the lake.

❼ Follow this obvious footpath and then, when you reach the dam, pick up the well-surfaced track that heads back downhill. This will lead you to the right of the waterworks filter beds and back to the car park.

AN EASY STROLL ALONG THE HERITAGE COAST

A foray through rolling sand dunes, returning along the impressive and little-known South Wales coast.

The coast at Ogmore, part of the Glamorgan Heritage Coast

Distance: 6 miles (9.7km)

Minimum time: 2hrs 30min

Ascent/Gradient: 460ft (140m) ▲▲▲

Level of difficulty: +++

Paths: Easy-to-follow across farmland and coastline, 5 stiles

Landscape: Deciduous woodland, farmland, bracken-covered sand dunes and rocky coastline

Suggested map: OS Explorer 151 Cardiff & Bridgend

Start/finish: Grid reference: SS 885731

Dog friendliness: Some difficult stiles; total ban on beach at Dunraven in summer

Parking: Large car park at Heritage Centre above Dunraven Beach

Public toilets: Heritage Centre, also at Ogmore

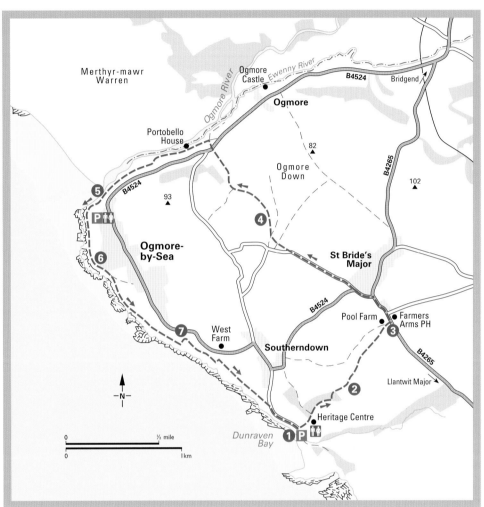

❶ From the car park, head up the lane at the back of the car park and pass the Heritage Centre on the right. Keep walking straight ahead as the track swings left, and go through a gate to duck into woodland. Continue to a fork, where you keep left to reach a stile. Cross this stile and walk along the edge of the field to reach a gate on your left. Go through the gate, then cross a stone stile on your right to keep ahead with hedge to your right.

❷ Cross into another field and keep to the left-hand side, following the hedgerow, which is now on your left. When you reach the next stile, continue ahead, go past a gate on the left, to reach another stone stile on the left. Cross this stile and head right over another stile, next to a gate, to another stone stile between the house and the farmyard.

❸ Turn left on to the road and walk into the village. Keep left into Southerndown Road, then fork right into Heol-y-slough. Follow this road for 0.75 mile (1.2km), then, as the road bends left, continue across the common. Keep ahead where a bridleway crosses the track. As you join another track, maintain your direction along the valley floor.

❹ The path winds its way down through sand dunes, passing a tributary valley on the left, and eventually emerges on the B4524. Cross the road and continue towards the river until you locate one of the many paths that lead left, parallel to the river, towards Portobello House. Keep left on the drive, then, once above the house, bear left to follow a clear path through the bracken, again parallel to the Ogmore River.

❺ Make sure you stay above the small cliffs as you approach the mouth of the estuary and you'll eventually arrive at a car parking area above the beach. From here, follow the obvious track along the coast around to the left.

❻ You'll come to a dry-stone wall, which will funnel you through a gate marked 'Coast Path'. Continue along the coast path until, 1.25 miles (2km) from the gate, you meet with a very steep-sided valley. Turn left into this valley, then turn immediately right, on to a footpath that climbs steeply up the grassy hillside.

❼ Stay with the footpath as it follows the line of a dry-stone wall around to West Farm. Keep the wall to the left to continue to the upper car park. A gap in the wall, at the back of this, leads you to a grassy track that follows the road down into Dunraven.

Walk E

CASTELL COCH AND THE NEW SOUTH WALES

From a fairy-tale castle to a wild, windswept hillside the new-look valleys at their scenic best.

Castell Coch was rebuilt in 1890 for the third Marquess of Bute

Distance: 5.5 miles (8.8km)

Minimum time: 2hrs 30min

Ascent/Gradient: 920ft (280m) ▲▲▲

Level of difficulty: +++

Paths: Forest tracks, disused railway line and clear paths, short section of tarmac, 2 stiles

Landscape: Mixed woodland and open hillside with views over residential and industrial developments

Suggested map: OS Explorer 151 Cardiff & Bridgend

Start/finish: Grid reference: ST 131826

Dog friendliness: Care needed near livestock; not allowed in castle

Parking: Castell Coch

Public toilets: In castle and nearby Countryside Visitor Centre

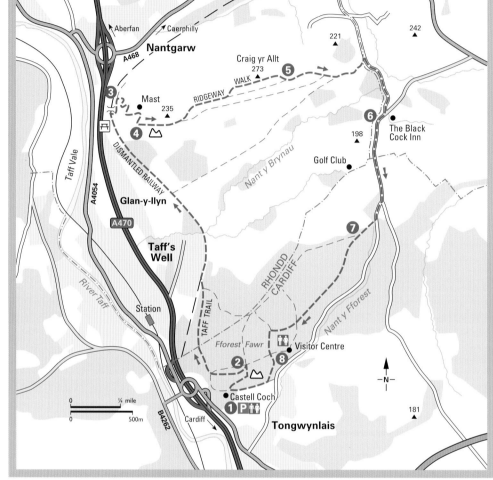

❶ From the car park, walk up to the castle entrance and turn to the right to walk to a stone information plaque. Take the path next to this and climb steeply on a good path past a waymark post and through a gap in a fence to a junction of tracks.

❷ Turn sharp left, signposted 'The Taff Trail', by a picture of a viaduct, and follow this broad forest track around the hillside and then down, where it meets the disused railway line close to some houses. Pass through the barrier on the right and follow the clear track for more than a mile (1.6km) until you pass a picnic area and come to another barrier.

❸ Go through the barrier, then, as you come to a disused bridge, turn right over a stile, signposted 'Ridgeway Walk'. Take this and follow it up for a few paces and then around to the right. Ignore one turn left and then turn

sharp left to zigzag back across the hillside, where you turn right again. Follow this around to the left again, aiming at the mast and then, as you reach the field-edge, bear right once more. This leads up to a post on a narrow ridge where you turn left.

❹ Climb steeply up the ridge and continue, with high ground to your left, until you reach a clear path that leads left, up to the ridge top. Follow this and bear right at the top to walk easily along, with great views. Keep ahead to drop slightly and then bear left on to a broad track.

❺ Follow it down through the bracken to a stile. Cross this and take the track down to a gate that leads on to a tarmac drive. Turn left and continue past some houses on the right-hand side to a junction. Turn right and climb up to another junction, where you bear right.

❻ Carry on past the golf club, then fork right on to a narrow lane that drops and bears around to the left. Turn right here to walk past the Forestry Commission sign and then turn immediately left, on to a clear footpath marked by a post.

❼ Follow this path, ignoring tracks on both the right and left, until the posts become blue and you come to a T-junction by a sign forbidding horse-riding. Cross the small brook and turn left to continue steeply downhill, past a turning on the left to the Countryside Visitor Centre.

❽ The track eventually swings around to the right and descends to meet the drive. Turn right to climb up the drive and back to the castle.

LLANTHONY AND ITS HILLS

A demanding trek along the ridges of the southern end of the Vale of Ewyas.

Distance: 9.5 miles (15.3km)

Minimum time: 5hrs 30min

Ascent/Gradient: 2,460ft (750m) ▲▲▲

Level of difficulty: +++

Paths: Easy-to-follow paths, steep slopes, open moorland, muddy lowland trails, 10 stiles

Landscape: Classic U-shaped valleys topped with broad heather-strewn moorland

Suggested map: OS Explorer OL13 Brecon Beacons National Park Eastern area

Start/finish: Grid reference: SO 255314

Dog friendliness: Some difficult stiles, care needed near livestock. No dogs in grounds of priory

Parking: Narrow pull-in at southern edge of Capel-y-ffin, close to bridge

Public toilets: Next to Llanthony Priory

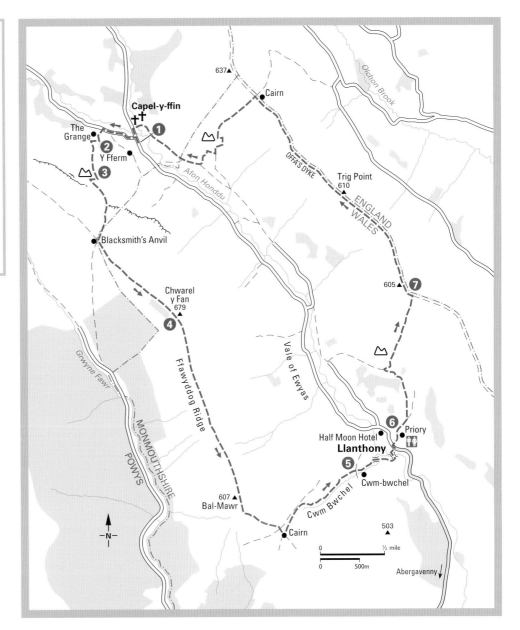

1 Walk towards the bridge, but before you cross it bear left up a narrow lane, signposted to The Grange Pony Trekking Centre. Follow this along the side of the stream and past a footpath on the left, marked by a stone archway. Continue to a drive on the left, again leading to the trekking centre, and follow this up to a cluster of barns.

2 Keep right here and continue uphill to a large house on the right, with a gate blocking your progress ahead. Bear around to the left and climb on a loose rocky track that leads up to another gate. Pass through this and follow a rough, eroded track as it zigzags up on to easier ground. Cross the source of a small stream, and continue to the foot of a steep zigzag track that climbs steeply up the escarpment.

3 Follow this, bearing both right and left and then, as the gradient eases, continue ahead on a broad and often boggy track. Take this past a few small cairns to a large one, the Blacksmith's Anvil, that sits on top of the ridge. Turn left here and continue to follow the track south over Chwarel y Fan.

4 Walk straight on, along the line of the Ffawyddog Ridge, to reach the summit of Bal-Mawr. Go down to the left and pass a good track on your left-hand side. Keep ahead to a cairn and then descend to the left. Drop to a fork where you keep right to follow the brook to a crossroads of paths. Maintain your direction (signposted 'Cwm Bwchel').

5 Continue through two fields, down past a house, and over another stile. Ignore another stile on the right and continue down to another

at the bottom of the field. Cross this and bear right to cross another and a footbridge. Keep walking straight ahead to another stile and then continue to a gate. Follow the stream down through another gate to another footbridge. Cross this and take the lane to the road. Turn left here, then turn right to visit the Priory.

6 Go through a gate on the left, in front of the Priory (signposted to Hatterrall Hill), and follow the main track to a stream, where you turn left to a gate. Continue through a succession of fields and through a small copse to reach an interpretation board. Follow the path up on to the ridge and continue to a crossroads; Offa's Dyke is where you turn left.

7 Walk along Offa's Dyke, pass the trig point and continue for another mile (1.6km) to a cairn and a marker stone at a crossroads of paths. Turn left and follow the path down around a sharp left-right zigzag to a wall. Turn right here, then turn left over a stile. Walk down, over another stile to a hedge at the bottom of the next field, then turn right to continue to another stile on the left. This leads on to a tarmac lane. Turn right and follow this through a yard, where it becomes a rough track. Keep ahead to a sharp left-hand bend and keep straight ahead, up steps and over a stile. Continue straight ahead through more fields to join another lane and follow this down, past two chapels to the road. Turn left to return to your car.

Walk G

TAKE A WALK ON THE WILD SIDE

A tough walk that really explores the more austere side of the Welsh uplands.

Distance: 9.5 miles (15.3km)
Minimum time: 6hrs
Ascent/Gradient: 2,000ft (610m) ▲▲▲
Level of difficulty: +++
Paths: Riverside path, faint or non-existent paths over moorland, some good tracks, some awkward stream crossings, no stiles
Landscape: Stunning valley, remote moorland, some forestry
Suggested map: OS Explorer 200 Llandrindod Wells & Elan Valley
Start/finish: Grid reference: SN 860530
Dog friendliness: Care needed near livestock
Parking: Car park northeast of Abergwesyn
Public toilets: At start
Notes: Difficult navigation, avoid in poor visibility

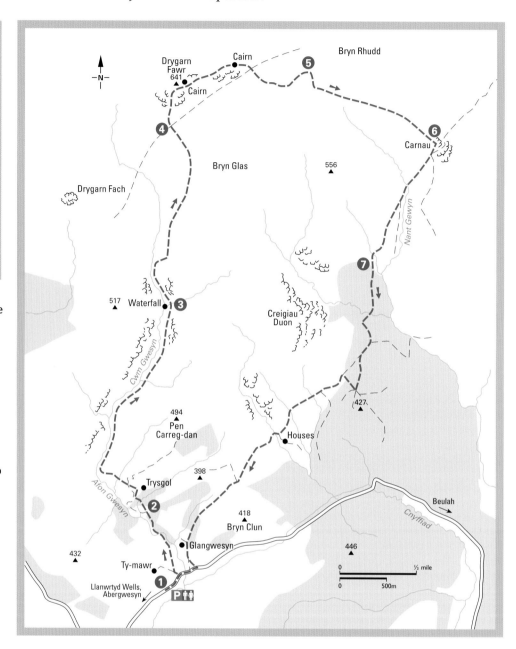

❶ Turn right on to the road and walk up to the bridge, where a gravel track heads up left. Take this and turn almost immediately right, through a gate. Follow the track across fields and down to the Afon Gwesyn, which you ford. Continue to a gate and up towards a wood where the track splits. Choose the top option and then, as this bends around to the left and heads downhill, fork right, to traverse the clearing to a gap in the wood.

❷ Follow the path down to a ford. Climb on to open ground and bear right to a farm track by some buildings. Turn left on to this and follow it through a gate, where you fork left to walk beneath some crags. Ignore another fork to the left and continue to open ground. Follow the east side of the valley for more than 1.5 miles (2.4km) to a waterfall.

❸ Pass this on the right, then continue until the path almost disappears. Follow the line of the stream until you reach a distinctive small ridge coming in from the right. Take this uphill for 100 yards (91m) and then bear left on to a narrow path, which leads you around a number of boggy patches until the cairned summit of Drygarn Fawr becomes visible.

❹ Climb the grassy slope to the trig point, then follow the ridge east past both cairns. A close scan of the hillsides to the southeast should reveal two grassy tops, 1.5 miles (2.4km) away, one with a large cairn on top – this is Carnau, your next objective. A clear grassy track descends east from the cairn. Follow this until it levels completely and rounds a left-hand bend, where you'll make out a faint path forking right. This is the start of the careful navigation, and if you're in any doubt about visibility you'll be better off turning around and retracing your tracks.

❺ Follow the track, which links a number of boundary stones for 200yds (183m), until you see one stone offset to the right of the path. Turn sharp right here (south), away from the path, and cross wet ground to climb slightly on to a very broad rounded ridge. You'll make out the head of a small valley ahead and, as you drop into this, bear slightly left to follow the high ground with the valley to your right. Continue on sheep tracks to cross a couple of hollows, until you reach a grassy hilltop. From here, you should be able to see the cairn ahead. Take the clear path that leads to it.

❻ From Carnau you'll see the start of a clear gorge away to the southwest. Walk towards this, on a visible path, and you'll pick up a good track as you cross the river. Continue downstream on the far bank and then stay with the path as it bears away right and crosses open hillsides before dropping into the bottom of the valley, where you need to ford the stream to go through a gate.

❼ Climb on a good track that eventually drops to cross another stream and then continue up to a five-way junction. Turn sharp right here, go through a gate and then another on the left. Drop down through the field on to an enclosed track and follow this to a junction above some houses on your left. Keep right, cross a stream and then take the track across a field to a path junction. Keep straight ahead and descend through the yard of Glangwesyn to the road. Turn right on to the road to return back to your car.

PICTURESQUE DOWNTON CASTLE

A long stretch in a landscape designed to please the eye.

Wysteria vines can climb as high as 20m

Distance: 10 miles (16.1km)

Minimum time: 5hrs

Ascent/Gradient: 1,200ft (366m) ▲▲▲

Level of difficulty: +++

Paths: Pastures, leafy paths, grass tracks, dirt tracks, tarmac lanes, one steep, earthy bank, 13 stiles

Landscape: Rolling country, wooded and farmed, above River Teme

Suggested map: OS Explorer 203 Ludlow

Start/finish: Grid reference: SO 403741

Dog friendliness: Mostly on lead, lots of game birds

Parking: Community centre and village hall car park, Leintwardine

Public toilets: At start (not always open)

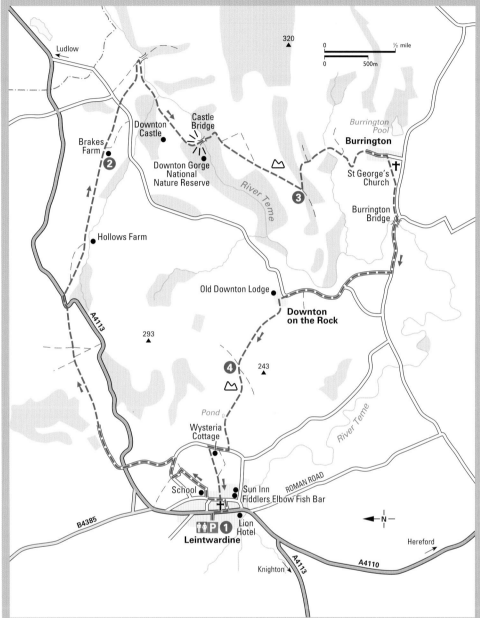

❶ Begin downhill, very soon taking the first left, Church Street. Turn left. As you reach the primary school, turn right. Aim for a brick, brown-and-white house but, after a two-plank footbridge, go left to a tarmac road. Turn right. In 300 yards (274m) turn left, to the A4113. Cross, turning immediately right up a lane. Ascend for a short mile (1.6km). Soon after a skew junction go forward, taking the left of two gates. Just beyond a corrugated shelter, take a stile on the right. Go three-quarters left, across two more fields, to replanted woodland. At the A4113 turn left but soon right, beside a wire fence. At the end follow the field-edge round to the left for 40 yards (37m). Go down an earthy bank in trees to pass stables on your right, then along a good dirt road, dead straight for 0.5 mile (800m) to Brakes Farm.

❷ Go straight ahead (waymarker). Cross a minor road diagonally, then cross fields to a minor lane beside houses Nos. 20 and 19. Turn left. Soon turn right, downhill. Turn right, along the river, just before a bridge over the River Teme. Skirt two unnamed houses. Up a bank, join a dirt road. Follow this to Castle Bridge. Ascend, but within 110 yards (100m) of leaving woodland go half-right, across a field, re-joining

the dirt road into forest for perhaps 60 yards (55m). (If the footpath is not established, it would make sense to go round the road, not trample the crop.) Scramble up a bank (waymarker). Traverse the steep meadow to a gate in the top, among oaks. Keep this line to go down a wide meadow, locating a stile on the left into harvested trees.

❸ Turn left and descend. When you reach open meadow, curve round a dry valley. At a left bend, go through a gate on the right. Go left of a specimen oak to a hidden stile in the bottom corner. Cross over a footbridge and turn right. Cross meadow to a gate, and soon reach a minor road. Turn right. Descend easily through Burrington, to St George's Church. Behind the church, cross meadows

to Burrington Bridge. Cross the River Teme. After 650 yards (594m) take the right turn. When you reach Downton, head towards Old Downton Lodge, but then turn left. Beyond a wall take the rightmost gate (waymarker), along an old lane. Shortly move right to ascend a right-hand field-edge, soon following a beech-lined avenue to reach a junction with a dirt track.

❹ Over a stile into an expansive field, swing left to descend, initially steeply. Past a small (possibly dry) pond, veer left along a right-hand field-edge to a road. Turn right. Within 275 yards (251m), at Wysteria Cottage, take a kissing gate. Cross three fields to soon emerge on Watling Street. Turn right to Church Street and back to the start.

THE SIGHTS OF WORCESTER CITY

Walk 1

An enjoyable trail through the city of Worcester.

Edward Elgar was born near Worcester

Distance: 2.5 miles (4km)
Minimum time: 1hr 30min
Ascent/Gradient: Negligible ▲▲▲
Level of difficulty: +++
Paths: City streets and tarmac riverside path
Landscape: Urban with riverside
Suggested map: OS Explorer 204 Worcester & Droitwich Spa
Start/finish: Grid reference: SO 846548
Dog friendliness: Not dog friendly (except short stretch by river)
Parking: Long-stay pay-and-display car parks at New Road, Tybridge Street and Croft Road (and elsewhere)
Public toilets: Near start at Croft Road and bus station; several elsewhere

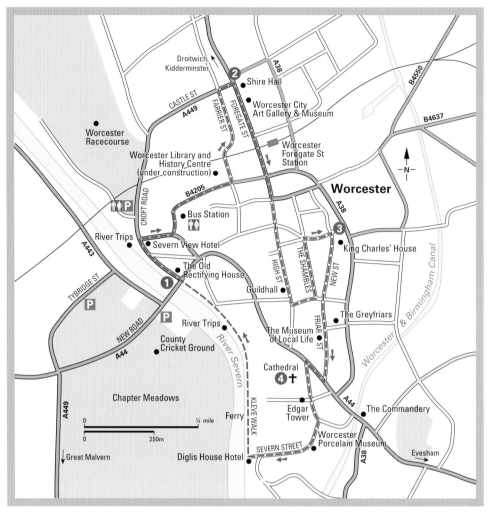

❶ The described route begins at the city side of the road bridge, but you can pick it up anywhere – at The Commandery or the Guildhall, for example – depending on where you have parked. Turn left, passing The Old Rectifying House (wine bar). Turn right after the Severn View Hotel, then left, in front of the bus station, following the road round to pass The Butts Dig (archaeological site). Turn left along Farrier Street, right into Castle Street, reaching the northern extremity of the route at its junction with Foregate Street.

❷ Go right along Foregate Street, passing the Shire Hall and the Worcester City Art Gallery & Museum. Continue along The Cross and into the pedestrianised area called High Street. Turn left into Pump Street. (Elgar's statue stands close to his father's piano shop, at the southern end of High Street.) Turn left again, into The Shambles. At a junction turn right into Mealcheapen Street. Another right turn and you're in New Street (which later becomes Friar Street).

❸ Head down this partial timewarp as slowly as you can, admiring The Greyfriars (a National Trust property) in particular, for a dual carriageway awaits you at the end. Turn right, then cross over carefully, to visit the cathedral.

❹ Leave the cathedral along College Precincts to the fortified gateway known as Edgar Tower. (It is named after the 10th-century King Edgar, but was actually built in the 14th century. Go through this gateway to see College Green.) Continue along what is now Severn Street which, unsurprisingly, leads to the River Severn. Turn right, to complete your circuit, by following Kleve Walk, a leafy waterside avenue; this section floods frequently, as does the county cricket ground opposite at great cost to the club's revenue.

Worcester Cathedral by the River Severn

THE DYSYNNI VALLEY AND CASTELL Y BERE

Explore the valleys where the princes of Wales once held out against Edward I.

The Talyllyn railway was built to carry slates

Distance: 5 miles (8km)
Minimum time: 3hrs
Ascent/Gradient: 656ft (200m) ▲▲▲
Level of difficulty: +++
Paths: Field paths and tracks, 14 stiles
Landscape: Pastured hills and valleys
Suggested map: OS Explorer OL23 Cadair Idris & Llyn Tegid
Start/finish: Grid reference: SH 677069
Dog friendliness: Dogs should be on leads at all times
Parking: Car park by community centre in Abergynolwyn
Public toilets: At community centre

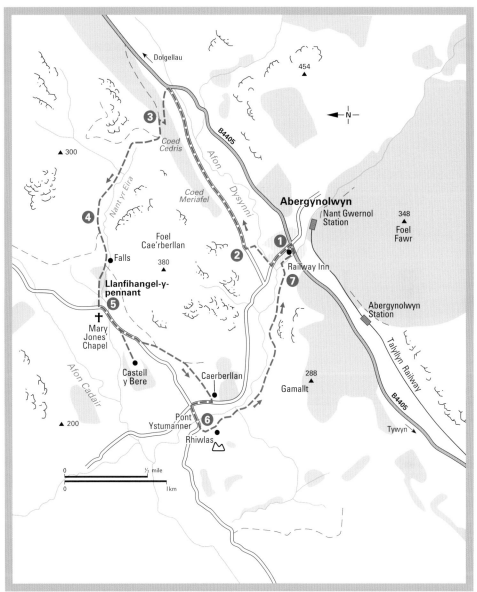

❶ Cross the road to the Railway Inn and take the lane signposted to Llanegryn. At the far side of the bridge spanning the Dysynni River, turn right through a kissing gate and trace above the north banks. At a second step stile the path turns left before climbing some steps alongside some tall leylandii to reach a country lane.

❷ Turn right along the lane which heads east through the Dysynni Valley and beneath the woodlands of Coed Meriafel. At the junction with the B4405, turn left, over a stile and climb northwest across a field. Continue over two more stiles to a woodland path. Follow this path to reach a forestry track near the top of the woods.

❸ Turn left along the track which climbs out of the woods before veering right to a gate and adjacent stile, giving entry into a large field. Go straight ahead to pick up a ruined overgrown wall. Where this ends, bear left to descend a high grassy cwm with a stream developing just to your left. Ford another stream, which joins from the right near a ruin.

❹ The green path develops a flinted surface. Leave it where it starts to climb and re-join a streamside path on the left. This descends into the woods and stays close to the stream. After passing several cascades it comes out of the woods to reach a track, which in turn leads to the road at Llanfihangel-y-pennant just opposite the chapel.

❺ Turn left past the chapel and Castell y Bere (detour through gates on the right for a closer look). Just beyond the castle, take a path on the left that climbs to the gate at the top right-hand corner of the field. Turn right along a green track which passes Caerberllan farm to come to the road. Turn right, go left at the

crossroads and cross Pont Ystumanner (a bridge).

❻ On the other side, a footpath signpost highlights a track on the left, which passes below Rhiwlas farm and continues as a green path above the river. The path eases across the slopes of Gamallt and swings left with the valley.

❼ Beyond a river gorge, the path approaches the back of Abergynolwyn village and turns left to cross an old iron bridge across the river. Turn right along an unsurfaced street to return to the village centre.

Walk K

POWIS CASTLE AND THE MONTGOMERY CANAL

See how the Earls of Powis lived as you walk through their deer park and past their huge red palace on the hill.

Powis Castle remained a private home until 1988

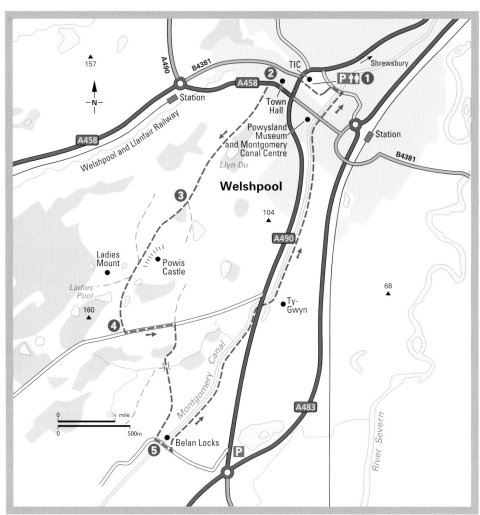

Distance: 4 miles (6.4km)
Minimum time: 2hrs
Ascent/Gradient: 328ft (100m) ▲▲▲
Level of difficulty: +++
Paths: Tarmac drive, field path, canal towpath, 3 stiles
Landscape: Country town, parkland and canal
Suggested map: OS Explorer 216 Welshpool & Montgomery
Start/finish: Grid reference: SJ 226075
Dog friendliness: Dogs not allowed on the Powis Castle estate
Parking: Large pay car park off Church Street, Welshpool
Public toilets: By information centre in car park

1 From the main car park go past the tourist information centre, then go left along Church Street. At the crossroads in the centre of town, turn right to head up Broad Street, which later becomes High Street.

2 When you get to a point just beyond the town hall, turn left past a small car parking area and pass through the impressive wrought-iron gates of the Powis Castle Estate. Now follow the tarmac drive through the park grounds and past Llyn Du (which means 'the black lake' in English).

3 Take the right fork, the high road, which leads to the north side of the castle. You can detour from the walk here to visit the world-famous gardens and the castle with its fine paintings and furniture and works of Indian art collected by Robert Clive. Continue on the walk on the high road and follow it past two more pools on the left and the Ladies Pool on the right to reach a country lane.

4 Turn left along the country lane. Opposite the next estate entrance leave the lane over a stile beside a gate on the right, from which a grass track winds down to a bridge. Climb away beside the right-hand fence. Continue over another stile in the corner along an old way, which gently falls to a lane beside the Montgomery Canal. This canal, which runs for 33 miles (53km) from Welsh Frankton in Shropshire to Newtown in Powys, is gradually being restored. You may see a number of narrowboats cruising along this section.

5 Turn over the bridge at Belan Locks, immediately dropping left to the canal towpath. Head north along the canal, later passing beneath the main road. Entering Welshpool, remain on the towpath, passing the Powysland Museum and Montgomery Canal Centre (on the opposite bank), with its exhibits of local agriculture, crafts and the canal and railway systems. Beyond a short aqueduct and former railway bridge, climb out to the road and turn left back to the car park.

REVOLUTION AT COALBROOKDALE

An absorbing walk in the wooded hills and valleys where the Industrial Revolution began.

The nearby Iron Bridge spanning the River Severn gorge at Ironbridge

Distance: 5 miles (8km)
Minimum time: 2hrs
Ascent/Gradient: 770ft (235m) ▲▲▲
Level of difficulty: +++
Paths: Woodland paths, lots of steps (mostly descending), may be fallen trees at Strethill, 2 stiles, some paths very overgrown
Landscape: Wooded hills of Severn Gorge
Suggested map: OS Explorer 242 Telford, Ironbridge & The Wrekin
Start/finish: Grid reference: SJ 664037
Dog friendliness: Excellent, but keep under strict control at Strethill (sheep)
Parking: Dale End Riverside Park, just west of Museum of the Gorge
Public toilets: In Museum of the Gorge car park

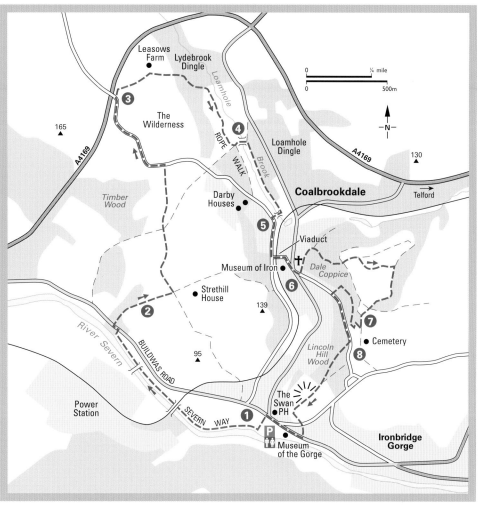

❶ Follow the River Severn upstream, using the Severn Way. Take care as the path is narrow and there's a big drop to the river in places. Pass under two bridges. After the second one, bear away from the river towards Buildwas Road. At the road, turn left for a few paces, then cross to a footpath that ascends through woodland. Keep close to the edge until a waymarker directs you obliquely to the right.

❷ Cross a stile and continue in the same direction over pastureland. Pass under a pylon, then join a farm track climbing to a gate. Turn right and follow the hawthorn hedge to a junction. Turn left and follow three field-edges, then go up through the middle of a meadow to a lane. Turn left and continue on the lane.

❸ Leave the lane just before it bridges a road, turning right on a farm access track (Shropshire Way). Just before Leasows Farm, go through a gate on the right, then downfield to enter Lydebrook Dingle at a stile. A path descends through the wood, with numerous steps. Continue along a path called Rope Walk.

❹ Descend some steps on the left into Loamhole Dingle. Cross Loamhole Brook at a footbridge and climb 41 steps on the other side. Turn right and follow the undulating boardwalk to Upper Furnace Pool. Cross its far end on the first of two footbridges to meet the road.

❺ Your onward route is to the left, but a short detour right leads to the Darby Houses, Tea Kettle Row and the Quaker Burial Ground. Resuming the walk, go down to Darby Road and turn right beside the Viaduct and the Museum of Iron. Turn left under the viaduct at a junction with Coach Road. Follow the road past the museum and Coalbrookdale Works to a junction.

❻ Cross into Church Road. Immediately after the Wesleyan chapel, turn left then go up steps to enter Dale Coppice. Follow signs for Church Road at two junctions, then keep following the steps, bearing left up through the woods. Leave the wood to enter grassland and go forward a few paces to meet a track. Turn left, then

shortly fork right, staying on the track. Bear left at another junction, then bear right at the next two. Dale Coppice is on your right, a cemetery on your left.

❼ Partway along the cemetery, a small wooden gate accesses Dale Coppice. Turn right, then soon left, going downhill to a junction marked by a bench. Turn right, then left when a sign indicates Church Road, then left again down the road.

❽ Turn right into Lincoln Hill Wood and follow signs to the Rotunda, presently arriving at a viewpoint where the Rotunda formerly stood. Descend a very steep flight of steps to a junction. Turn right, then left down more steps and left again, signposted to Lincoln Hill Road. Cross the road to a footpath opposite, that descends to the Wharfage. Turn right past Lincoln Hill lime kilns and The Swan to Dale End Riverside Park.

Walk M — A VIEW OF BALA'S LAKE – LLYN TEGID

Climbing above Bala to get the best view of Wales' largest natural lake.

Sailing boats on Bala Lake (Llyn Tegid)

Distance: 5 miles (8km)
Minimum time: 3hrs
Ascent/Gradient: 656ft (200m) ▲▲▲
Level of difficulty: +++
Paths: Woodland and field paths, 7 stiles
Landscape: Woods and upland pasture
Suggested map: OS Explorer OL23 Cadair Idris & Llyn Tegid, or OS Explorer OL18 Harlech, Porthmadog & Bala
Start & finish: Grid reference: SH 929361
Dog friendliness: Dogs should be on lead at all times
Parking: Car park at entrance to Bala town from east
Public toilets: At car park

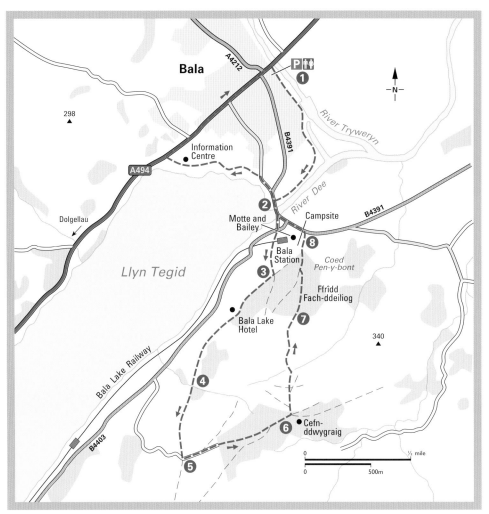

❶ Go to the north corner of the car park in Bala to access the riverside path. Turn right to follow a raised embankment along the west bank of the Tryweryn. After a dog-leg to the right, passing through two kissing gates, the footpath continues, first by the banks of the Tryweryn, then by the north banks of the Dee.

❷ On reaching the road, cross the bridge over the River Dee, then a smaller, older bridge. Go through a kissing gate to cross a small field to Bala Station on Bala Lake Railway. A footbridge allows you to cross the track before traversing two small fields.

❸ Turn right along a cart track, and continue to pass behind the Bala Lake Hotel. A waymarker points the direction up a grassy bank on the left, and the path continues to a stile and then follows a fence on the right.

❹ Descend slightly to cross a stream beside a small cottage, go up again then along a level fence to a stile. Bear left up through some bracken and wind up steeply at first, then continue more easily to a tarmac lane.

❺ Turn left along the lane to a cattle grid from where you continue on a stony track, passing through felled plantations.

❻ Just before the isolated house of Cefn-ddwygraig, turn left off the track to a ladder stile. Follow a grooved grass track across gorse-covered slopes. Keep left at a fork and then drop down to a stile. The well-waymarked path continues north, with Bala town ahead.

❼ Go over a partially hidden step stile into the commercial forestry plantations of Coed Pen-y-bont. A narrow footpath descends to the bottom edge of the woods (ignore the forestry track you meet on the way down).

❽ At the bottom of the woods turn right along a track that reaches the road by the Pen-y-bont Campsite. Turn left along the road, cross the Dee again, bear left and then follow the lakeside footpath past the information centre. When you reach the main road, turn right to explore the fascinating town centre.

IN THE COUNTRY OF LLOYD GEORGE

Explore the countryside and coastal haunts of the last Liberal Prime Minister.

Criccieth castle is still dominated by the twin-towered gatehouse built by Prince Llywelyn ab Iorwerth ('the Great')

Distance: 6 miles (9.7km)

Minimum time: 4hrs

Ascent/Gradient: 300ft (91m) ▲▲▲

Level of difficulty: +++

Paths: Generally well-defined paths and tracks, 4 stiles

Landscape: Riverside woodland, fields, town streets, coastline

Suggested map: OS Explorer 254 Lleyn Peninsula East

Start/finish: Grid reference: SH 476383

Dog friendliness: Dogs can run free in riverside woods and on coast

Parking: Large car park at east end of village

Public toilets: Near museum at Llanystumdwy and at Criccieth

Note: Small section of coast path engulfed by highest tides. Make sure you know times of tides before setting off

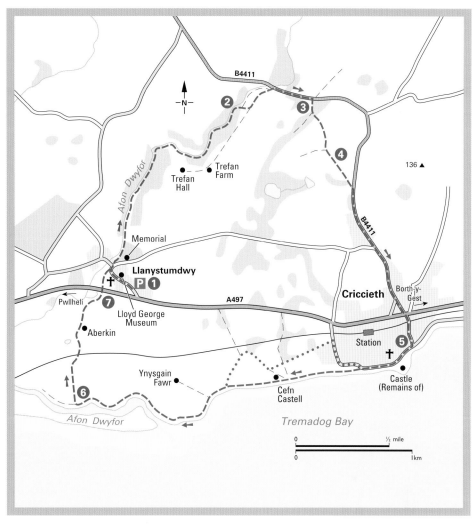

❶ Turn right out of the car park and go through Llanystumdwy village, past the museum to the bridge over the Afon Dwyfor. Turn right along the lane, then follow the footpath on the left past the memorial and down to the wooded riverbanks.

❷ After 1.5 miles (2.4km), the path turns right, then goes under a stone archway to meet a tarred drive. Turn left along this, carry on to the B4411 and turn right.

❸ After about 500 yards (457m), turn right down an enclosed drive. As another drive merges from the left, turn half-left along a path shaded by rhododendrons. After a few paces, go though the kissing gate, then cross the field guided by a fence on the left. Through another kissing gate the path veers half-right, following a fence which is now on the right.

❹ Beyond another gate the now sketchy route cuts diagonally (southeast) across two fields to rejoin the B4411, a mile (1.6km) or so north of Criccieth. Follow the B4411 into town. Keep straight on at the crossroads, and bear left after the level crossing to reach the promenade.

❺ Follow the coast road past the castle and continue until it turns firmly inland. From here, tide permitting, simply follow the coast path or walk along the sands. Otherwise, follow the road to a bridleway on the left. Go past Muriau and then to the right of Ty Cerrig. Cross a track and a field then turn right on a green track, nearly to the railway. Head left, back to the coast east of Ynysgain Fawr. Follow the coast path west through coastal grasslands and gorse scrub to the estuary of the Dwyfor and some crumbled concrete sea defences.

❻ At a metal kissing gate, waymarks point inland. Follow these, with the fence on your right. The route becomes a farm track that cuts under the railway and passes through the yard of Aberkin farm before reaching the main road.

❼ Cross the main road with care and go through the gate on the opposite side. A short path leads to an unsurfaced lane, which in turn leads to the village centre. Turn right for the car park.

Walk
0

SNOWDON THE LONG WAY

A route that takes its time on one of Snowdon's seldom-trod ridges.

Distance: 10 miles (16.1km)
Minimum time: 6hrs 30min
Ascent/Gradient: 3,839ft (1,170m) ▲▲▲
Level of difficulty: +++
Paths: Well-defined paths and tracks, 1 stile
Landscape: High mountain cwms and tarns
Suggested map: OS Explorer OL17 Snowdon
Start/finish: Grid reference: SH 577604
Dog friendliness: Sheep, trains and crags: best on lead throughout
Parking: Several car parks throughout Llanberis
Public toilets: Just off High Street, south of tourist information centre

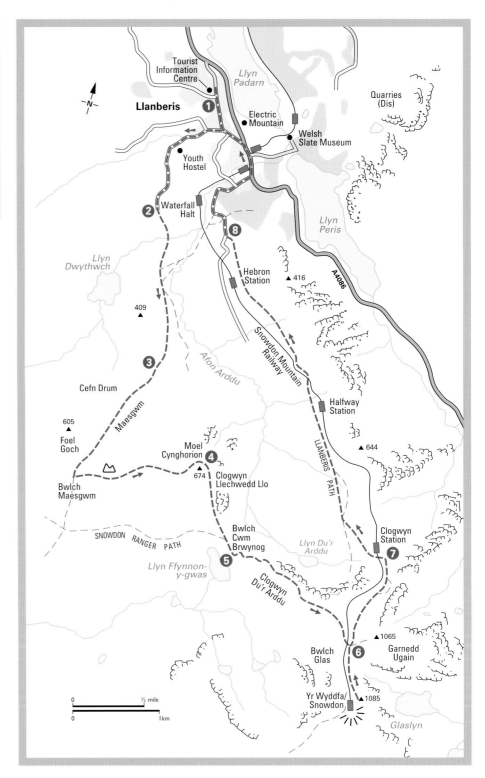

❶ From the tourist information centre in the heart of Llanberis, head south along the High Street (Stryd Fawr) before turning right up Capel Coch Road. Go straight ahead at a junction, where the road changes its name to Stryd Ceunant, and follow the road past the youth hostel. The road winds and climbs towards Braich y Foel, the northeast spur of Moel Eilio.

❷ Where the tarmac ends at the foot of Moel Eilio, continue along the track, which swings left (south-east) into the wild cwm of the Afon Arddu. On the other side of the cwm you'll see the trains of the Snowdon Mountain Railway, puffing up and down the line.

❸ On reaching the base of Foel Goch's northern spur, Cefn Drum, the track swings right into Maesgwm and climbs to a pass, Bwlch Maesgwm, between Foel Goch and Moel Cynghorion. Go through the gate here, then turn left and follow the route for the steep climb by the fence and up the latter-mentioned peak.

❹ From Cynghorion's summit the route descends along the top of the cliffs of Clogwyn Llechwedd Llo to another pass, Bwlch Cwm Brwynog, which overlooks the small reservoir of Llyn Ffynnon-y-gwas. Here you join the Snowdon Ranger Path.

❺ Follow the zigzag route up Clogwyn Du'r Arddu, whose cliffs, on the left, plummet to a little tarn, Llyn Du'r Arddu, which sits uneasily in a dark stony cwm. Near the top the wide path veers right, away from the edge, meets the Snowdon Mountain Railway, and follows the line to the monolith at Bwlch Glas. Here you are met by both the Llanberis Path and the Pyg Track and look down on the huge cwms of Glaslyn and Llyn Llydaw.

❻ The path now follows the line of the railway to the summit. Retrace your steps to Bwlch Glas, but this time follow the wide Llanberis Path traversing the western slopes of Garnedd Ugain and above the railway. (Make sure you don't mistake this for the higher ridge path to Garnedd Ugain's summit.)

❼ Near Clogwyn Station you come to Cwm Hetiau, where cliffs fall away into the chasm of the Pass of Llanberis. The path goes under the railway and below Clogwyn Station before re-crossing the line near Halfway Station.

❽ The path meets a lane beyond Hebron, and this descends back into Llanberis near the Royal Victoria Hotel. Turn left along the main road, then take the left fork, High Street, to get back to the car.

WHERE THE MOUNTAINS MEET THE SEA

A nature walk through wooded hillsides and limestone knolls, with a coastal panorama from Prestatyn to Llandudno's Great Orme.

Rhuddlan Castle dates from the 13th century

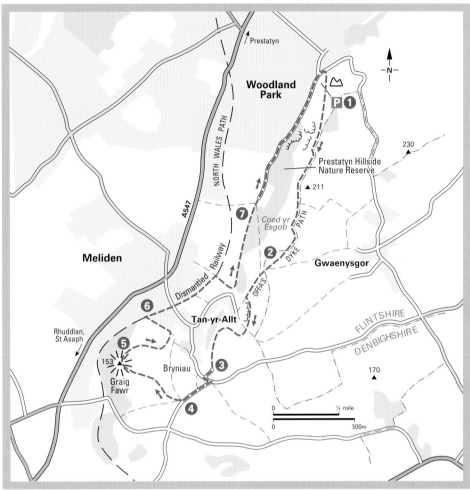

Distance: 3.5 miles (5.6km)

Minimum time: 2hrs

Ascent/Gradient: 820ft (250m) ▲▲▲

Level of difficulty: +++

Paths: Well-defined woodland paths and tracks

Landscape: Limestone hillside and mixed woodland

Suggested map: OS Explorer 264 Vale of Clwyd or 265 Clwydian Range

Start/finish: Grid reference: SJ 071821

Dog friendliness: Dogs should be on leads

Parking: Picnic site at foot of hill

Public toilets: None on route

❶ Turn right, out of the car park and climb a few paces up the steep lane. Turn right along the public footpath marked with the Offa's Dyke National Trail acorn sign. This enters an area of scrubby woodland with a wire fence to the right, before climbing above some quarry workings. As the footpath reaches high fields, ignore all the paths off to the left.

❷ Continue along the top edge of the woods towards Tan-yr-Allt, eventually dropping to a junction. Go left, passing above another quarry and then around a wooded cove. Ignore a path off left there, and later, at a waymark, keep ahead towards Bryniau.

❸ Go through a kissing gate on to a metalled lane by Red Roofs. Turn left at the next junction, then right a few paces further on, to follow a lane rounding the south side of Graig Fawr.

❹ Turn right through a gate on to the Graig Fawr Estate and follow a footpath leading to the trig point on the summit.

❺ Descend eastwards along a grassy path that weaves through bracken to pass beneath an overhead power cable at the edge of a wood. Now stepped, the onward way drops beside a fence into the trees, emerging through a kissing gate at the bottom.

❻ Turn right along a disused railway track, before taking the second footpath on the right, that crosses a field back towards Prestatyn Hillside. Turn left and follow a footpath into Coed yr Esgob, the woods at the foot of Prestatyn Hillside.

❼ Where the path divides, take the upper fork that joins Bishopwood Lane. Follow this back to a junction near the car park at the start of the walk.

The hillside above Prestatyn is a designated Area of Outstanding Beauty

NORTHERN ENGLAND

NORTHERN ENGLAND

Norman Bamburgh Castle standing beside the sea in Northumberland

The North of England is often referred to as a single entity, but it is by no means a homogeneous region. Topographically, culturally and historically there are great differences – the barren emptiness of the Cumbrian fells is totally different from that of the rolling hills of Northumberland; the west coast has golden sands and a mild climate, while the east is famous for its rugged cliffs and bracing weather; there is gentle pastoral scenery in the limestone Dales, in contrast with the dramatic Lake District.

The Industrial Revolution changed the face of the North of England more than any other part of the country, with great conurbations developing around the coalfields and the ports. Though these areas may not immediately suggest themselves as tourist attractions, many have been revitalised in recent years and have much to offer – proud museums to their industrial heritage, imaginative new uses for redundant sites, lively arts and entertainments, and superb sporting venues. Even shopping attains new heights at Gateshead's MetroCentre, at Meadowhall in Sheffield and at Manchester's Trafford Centre.

Even in the North's great cities, you are never far from peaceful landscapes, pretty villages and stunning scenery, and in spite of the conurbations of Tyneside, South and West Yorkshire, Manchester and Merseyside, this is one of the most sparsely populated parts of the country. This sense of isolation, combined with the constant struggle against a hostile landscape and inclement weather and a history of aggressive neighbours, has created a common spirit of independence and self-reliance in the North, which is as obvious in the Dalesman as it is in the Cumbrian. Famed for their taciturnity, their sense of humour and their apparent refusal to compromise, the people of the North also pride themselves on their hospitality – visitors are warmly welcomed and, in all probability, fed to bursting point.

Whether travelling by train on the scenic Settle to Carlisle or Pickering to Grosmont lines, by car along narrow roads that climb and twist before reaching some breathtaking summit, or on foot along the Pennine and Cleveland ways, the Lyke Wake Walk or the Three Peaks, the natural beauty of the landscape is enhanced by its history. Bronze-Age stone circles on remote mountains or moorlands; Roman roads, walls and forts; medieval abbeys in lush valleys and castles presiding over the hills and rivers; higgledy-piggledy cottages in small fishing villages and splendidly grand crescents in fashionable Victorian and Edwardian seaside resorts.

Modern times have brought the excitement of theme parks at Morecambe, Southport and Lightwater Valley near Ripon, equally matched by the famous Pleasure Beach in Britain's premier resort, Blackpool.

Previous page: A barn in the Manifold Valley, Peak District National Park

Section Contents

1	Around the River Mersey	250–251
2	Manchester	252–253
3	Steel City on the Fringe of the Peaks	254–255
4	Lancashire's Holiday Playground	258–259
5	Leeds and Bradford	260–261
6	Around Morecambe Bay	264–265
7	The Yorkshire Dales	266–267
8	Between Dales and Moors	268–269
9	In and Around York	270–271
10	The Isle of Man	274–275
11	The Lakeland of the Poets	276–277
12	Carlisle and the Western Wall	278–279
13	The City above the Wear	280–281
14	Alnwick	282–283

Features

The Peak District		256–257
The Abbeys of the North		262–263
The North York Moors		272–273

Walks

Ⓐ	Following in the Steps of Mr Darcy	284
Ⓑ	Linacre's Peaceful Retreat from Chesterfield	285
Ⓒ	High Ackworth and East Hardwick	286
Ⓓ	Haworth's Brontë Moors	287
Ⓔ	The Bottom and the Top: Around Beacon Fell	288
Ⓕ	Spectacular Landscapes in Limestone Country	289
Ⓖ	Hidden York	290
Ⓗ	Around Buttermere	291
Ⓘ	Brant Fell above Bowness-on-Windermere	292
Ⓙ	A Riverside Circuit High in the Dales	293
Ⓚ	Roseberry Topping and Captain Cook Country	294
Ⓛ	Historic Hexham	295
Ⓜ	Kirknewton and Ancient Yeavering Bell	296
Ⓝ	Berwick Town Walls	297

AROUND THE RIVER MERSEY

The Beatles have hijacked Liverpool's more recent history – long after the world's most famous group split up, they attract ever more visitors to the city. But Liverpool has a long and fascinating history as one of the world's great ports, and the revitalisation of once-derelict dockland areas is helping to bring that history alive once again.

Port Sunlight

The Wirral peninsula lies only a short ferry ride across the River Mersey. Late in the 19th century Lord Leverhulme built a 'model' village for the workers at his soap factory. Port Sunlight (named after the company's most famous brand of soap) offered tree-lined roads, open spaces and good housing – a fine example of social engineering at a time when not all employers gave much thought to their employees' well-being. A heritage centre tells how the garden village, now a conservation area, was planned (a total of 30 architects were employed) and built, and you can explore it by following the village trail. Visitors are also welcome at the splendid Lady Lever Art Gallery, dedicated by Lord Leverhulme to his wife, and built to house his extensive collection of art treasures. These include a world-famous collection of Pre-Raphaelite paintings and Wedgwood.

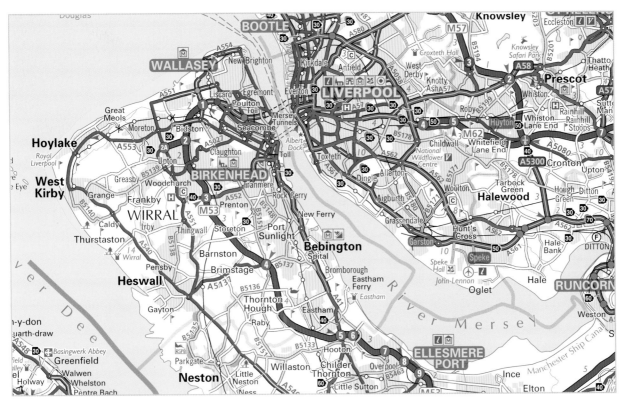

In the 1850s, Birkenhead's East Float Mill was the embarkation point for emigrant ships bound for Australia

Birkenhead

Only the width of the River Mersey separates Liverpool and Birkenhead, just a hamlet until the shipbuilding boom of the 19th century. The town contains the oldest building on Merseyside – Birkenhead Priory, where interpretative displays describe the daily routine of the monks. They were granted a charter by King Edward III in 1150 to run the first ferry across the river. Don't miss the view across the river from the adjacent tower, all that remains of St Mary's Church.

Birkenhead's other main attraction is the Williamson Art Gallery, which is renowned for its collection of English watercolours and works by the Liverpool school of artists. At Birkenhead's Woodside ferry terminal, the 'U-boat Story' showcases the Second World War German submarine, U-534, one of only four remaining U-boats in the world. Visitors can view sections of the boat through glass panels, and learn about its history through interactive displays.

Ferries depart hourly from Woodside in Birkenhead and Liverpool's Pier Head, to Spaceport at Seacombe on the River Mersey. The multi-million-pound attraction features walk-through galleries about space and space travel.

Croxteth Hall and Country Park

On the outskirts of Liverpool, near the junction of the M57 and A580, this fine historic mansion and its 500-acre (203ha) park was once the home of the Earls of Sefton. The rooms of the hall are now a wonderful re-creation of its Edwardian heyday, furnished in style and populated by figures in appropriate garb. Outside, visitors can step back a little further in time in the Victorian walled garden and visit the collection of rare breeds of farm animals. Other attractions include a miniature railway and a playground, and there is a full programme of special events.

The River Mersey crossing is served by a fleet of three ferries named Snowdrop *(pictured),* Royal Daffodil *and* Royal Iris of the Mersey

Ferry across the Mersey

Celebrated in song, film and folklore, the ferry from Liverpool to Birkenhead has acquired almost legendary status. The first ferry across the Mersey was operated by the monks of Birkenhead Priory as early as the 12th century, when Liverpool itself was a mere village. The ferries now run from Liverpool's Pier Head, where splendid Victorian buildings create a skyline that is as readily identifiable as Manhattan's. There is no better way to view the city's waterfront and architectural heritage.

Liverpool

Liverpool, a city with two cathedrals, gazes out across the River Mersey to the sea, as it has done for centuries. In its long history as a port Liverpool has unloaded cargoes such as tobacco, cotton and cane sugar from across the Atlantic. Until the practice was outlawed in 1807, many of those same ships would continue on to West Africa, taking wretched human cargoes back to the Americas to be sold into slavery.

Albert Dock, built in 1846 to accommodate sailing ships, proved too shallow for steamships, and by the end of the 19th century it had become largely obsolete. Comprising the largest collection of Grade I listed buildings in the country, Albert Dock has been sensitively restored in recent years to become the city's recreational centrepiece. Around the dock are a fascinating array of attractions, including the acclaimed Merseyside Maritime Museum, the northern outpost of the Tate Gallery and the Museum of Liverpool. Also at Albert Dock is the 11,000-seat Echo Arena, built for Liverpool's 2008 stint as European Capital of Culture.

Albert Dock's greatest attraction is 'The Beatles Story'. Forty years after they broke up, The Beatles are a bigger tourist attraction than ever, and The Beatles Story (open 'eight days a week...') tells the remarkable story of the four local lads who conquered the world with their music. The Cavern Club, which became synonymous with the Liverpool sound in the 1960s, still stands on Mathew Street at the heart of the 'Cavern Quarter'. The current club is a reconstruction of the original, which closed in 1973. A few miles away in Allerton, the National Trust has restored Paul McCartney's former family home, 20 Forthlin Road – a 1950s terraced house where The Beatles met and wrote many of their early songs.

Liverpool Football Club has supporters all over the world and they will be drawn to Anfield, not just for fixtures but also for the club's visitor centre and museum.

Prescot

On a road map, Prescot seems to be lost amidst a network of motorway and road junctions to the east of Liverpool, but it is well worth a visit, particularly if you are interested in horology. In an attractive 18th-century town house in Church Street you will find a museum of clock- and watchmaking, which illustrates the main industry of the area. It includes a reconstruction of part of a traditional watchmaker's workshop and displays of the equipment used to make the intricate parts of clock and watch movements.

Just to the north of the town is Knowsley Safari Park, with a 5-mile (8km) drive through reserves containing lions, tigers, elephants, rhinos, monkeys and many other animals. Children will also enjoy the pets' corner, the reptile house and the amusement park.

Speke Hall

Speke Hall seems to shrug off its uninspiring surroundings, and it is remarkable that this delightful and unpretentious house, with parts dating from as early as 1490, has survived at all. Built around a courtyard, and enclosed by a dry moat, this 'black and white' house is one of the most richly timbered houses in England; the vast Tudor Great Hall is particularly impressive. There is also some fine plasterwork, and the kitchen and servants' hall offers fascinating glimpses into domestic life below stairs in days gone by. There is a 16th-century priest hole, where persecuted Catholics could be hidden when danger threatened, together with examples of William Morris wallpaper and Mortlake tapestries.

Consecrated in 1967, Liverpool's Roman Catholic Metropolitan Cathedral is in stark contrast to the Gothic Revival design of its Anglican counterpart

Tourist Information

Liverpool: 08 Place, Whitechapel
(tel: 0844 870 0123)

Speke Hall, near Liverpool, dates mainly from the 16th century with gardens developed from the mid-nineteenth century

MANCHESTER

Manchester has a reputation for its damp climate, but this was a positive asset as cotton brought prosperity to the city, and it is easier to spin in a damp atmosphere. Great names of the Industrial Revolution – Arkwright, Hargreaves, Crompton – made the mass production of cloth possible, and a network of canals and railways set the seal on the city's lasting importance.

The Lowry art gallery in Salford Quay is named after the artist who captured scenes of the industrial northwest in the early 20th century

Dunham Massey Hall

This beautiful country house is set in parkland and gardens near Altrincham. It contains fine 18th-century furniture and magnificent silverware, and no less than 30 rooms of the house are on show, including a fully equipped kitchen, butler's pantry and laundry. The formal landscaping was the handiwork, 300 years ago, of George Booth, 2nd Earl of Warrington. The gardens have been restored by the National Trust, and include an 18th-century orangery and a well-house, which once supplied the Hall with fresh water.

Manchester

There is quite a buzz to this cosmopolitan city today, with a huge variety of restaurants and nightclubs. The colourful Chinatown district (the second largest in Britain) is announced by the Imperial Chinese Archway, which overlooks the pavilions of the Chinese Garden.

In building on its industrial heritage – two centuries at the forefront of cotton manufacture – the city now attracts large numbers of visitors each year. The legacy of handsome Victorian buildings is much in evidence.

Manchester boasts a clutch of exceptionally good museums, particularly the Museum of Science and Industry, the Museum of Transport and the Gallery of English Costume. There is also a centre dedicated to Emmeline Pankhurst and the Women's Suffrage Movement, and the People's History Museum, which records the day-to-day struggles of ordinary working people through the ages. The city is known throughout the world for sporting excellence. It boasts some of the best cycling facilities in Britain at the Velodrome, while at Old Trafford visitors can revel in the footballing glory surrounding one of the world's richest soccer clubs. The Manchester United museum and megastore is open all week, not just on match days.

Nearby Salford was immortalised by the artist L. S. Lowry and the largest collection of his unique works is now displayed in the Lowry arts complex next to the Salford Quays waterfront development. Salford is also home to the Lancashire Mining Museum, and a few miles further west, the Trafford Centre is the largest purpose-built shopping and entertainment destination in the northwest of England. East of the centre of the old town of Ashton-under-Lyne is the Museum of the Manchester Regiment and the Portland Basin Museum, an industrial and social history museum located at the junction of three canals.

Quarry Bank Mill

Founded in 1784 by Samuel Greg, Quarry Bank Mill at Styal was one of the very first factories to use water power to drive its textile machinery. It is now owned by the National Trust and fully restored as a working museum of the cotton industry. The centrepiece is England's biggest working waterwheel (weighing 50 tonnes and 24ft/7.3m high) that transforms the quiet waters of the River Bollin into a powerful driving force. The museum tells the story of the industry and emphasises the contrasting lives of the Greg family, the mill's workforce and the children who helped to tend the machines.

Saddleworth Moor

Just a few minutes' drive from industrial Oldham brings you to one of the wildest landscapes in the North. Saddleworth Moor extends mile after lonely mile – perfect for those hardy walkers who want to swap the din of the town for the bubbling call of the curlew. The Saddleworth district incorporates a number of intriguing little gritstone villages, former centres of woollen industries, where traditions such as rushbearing and morris dancing are very much alive. Uppermill is the home of the Saddleworth Museum and Art Gallery, in an old mill building by the Huddersfield Narrow Canal. Displays include a reconstruction of an 18th-century weaver's cottage and working machinery from a woollen mill.

The 76m (249ft) Lovell radio telescope at Jodrell Bank

Jodrell Bank

A name synonymous with the study of distant stars and galaxies, the Jodrell Bank Centre for Astrophysics brings the interplanetary world down to earth in its visitor centre, which stands at the foot of one of the largest fully steerable radio telescopes in the world – the famous Lovell telescope. As well as its exhibitions on space, astronomy and satellites, it has 'hands-on' exhibits and a 3-D theatre. More down to earth, literally, is the Environmental Discovery Centre and a the 35-acre (14ha) arboretum, with more than 2,000 species of trees and shrubs.

Tatton Park

At the end of a long, tree-lined drive, Tatton Park is a great country estate and one of the National Trust's most popular properties. It has Japanese gardens, a 1,000-acre (400ha) deer park, orangery, outdoor and sailing centre based around Tatton Mere, playground and a 1930s working farm, echoing to the rumble of vintage machinery. The rooms of the Old Hall offer a glimpse into various periods from the Middle Ages to the 1950s. The mansion is Georgian, and is a storehouse of fine furniture, paintings and family treasures.

Urban Heritage

Designated as Britain's first Urban Heritage Park, the Castlefield area of Manchester has been transformed into a major recreational amenity for locals and visitors alike. The original castle, dating from the Roman occupation, made way, during the late 18th century, for the building of the country's first modern canal. The Bridgewater Canal helped to transform Manchester into a major industrial city, exemplified by the wharves and warehouses that line the canal.

Castlefield gradually slipped into dereliction, a decline halted in recent years by a massive restoration scheme. Now there are festivals, carnivals and exhibitions throughout the year to supplement permanent attractions such as the Museum of Science and Industry.

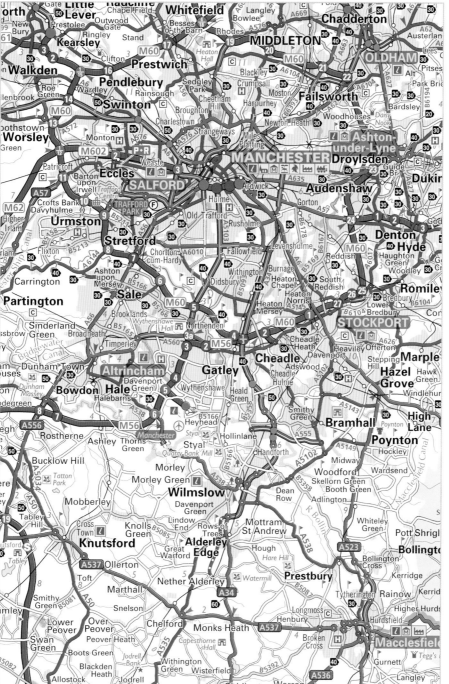

Canals recall the old Manchester, while the 47-storey Beetham Tower, with its luxury hotel and apartments, is unapologetically new

See Walk A, page 284
Following in the Steps of Mr Darcy

Tourist Information

Bury: Fusilier Museum, Moss Street (tel: 0161 253 5111)
Knutsford: Council Offices, Toft Road (tel: 01565 632611)
Manchester: Town Hall Extension, Lloyd Street (tel: 0871 222 8223)

The Dovestones reservoir in Saddleworth Moor

STEEL CITY ON THE FRINGE OF THE PEAKS

Now the fourth largest city in the country, Sheffield rose to prominence during the 19th century to become the steel capital of the world. The legend 'Made in Sheffield', engraved on tools and cutlery, has long been a byword for quality. Yet industrial Sheffield lies on the fringe of the Peak National Park, very close to some of the finest scenery in the north.

Castle ruins, Sheffield; Mary, Queen of Scotts was held prisoner here by the sixth Earl of Shrewsbury

Abbeydale Industrial Hamlet

This open-air museum, in a leafy waterside suburb of Sheffield, occupies one of the oldest industrial sites around the city. In its workshops, some dating back to the 18th century, agricultural tools were made. The motive power came from the waters of the River Sheaf, diverted over a huge waterwheel, which is still in working order. Today visitors can see the forges, water-driven forge hammers, grindstones and the only surviving crucible steel furnace in the world. Some of the workshops are occupied once again by craftsmen, carrying on Sheffield's tradition of working in metal. Visitors can also look round the Victorian manager's house and a workman's cottage.

Conisbrough

The 12th-century castle at Conisbrough, towering over the River Don, is now owned by English Heritage and visitors to the heritage centre will discover much about the castle's history. The keep, still standing to its original height of 90ft (27.4m), was probably built by Hamelin Plantagenet, the bastard half-brother of Henry II. Readers of Sir Walter Scott's books will probably recognise Conisbrough Castle from his novel *Ivanhoe*.

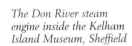

The Don River steam engine inside the Kelham Island Museum, Sheffield

Rotherham

Northeast of Sheffield, at the meeting of the rivers Rother and Don, is Rotherham – much the older of the two communities, with an entry for its church in the Domesday Book. Earlier relics, from Roman times, can be seen at the Clifton Park Museum, a mansion house of 1783. Heavy industry put Rotherham on the map – the cannons that decided the outcome of the Battle of Trafalgar were made here. In the cavernous former Templeborough Steelworks is Magna, Britain's first science adventure centre.

Rother Valley Country Park

Sheffield is one of the 'greenest' cities in Europe, with more than 50 public parks and gardens. Indeed, more than a third of the city falls within the borders of the Peak National Park. The 750 acre (304ha) Rother Valley Country Park has excellent facilities for watersports, such as sailing, windsurfing and canoeing (equipment can be rented). Less energetic visitors can enjoy peaceful woodland walks, and visit the craft centre. A visitor centre has been created in the restored 17th-century Bedgreave Mill.

Sheffield

Sheffield is trying very hard to shake off its rather dour image; today the city is being revitalised as a centre for leisure activities, conferences and sporting excellence. The Sheffield Arena is major entertainment venue, while, nearby, the 25,000-seat Don Valley Stadium for athletics emphasises Sheffield's ambition to be the sporting capital of the north, an aim helped by the healthy competition between local rivals the 'Blades' and 'Owls'. Sheffield is also home to the Crucible Theatre, home of the World Snooker Championship, and the Ponds Forge International Sports

Sheffield Ski Village

This is one of the largest artificial ski resorts in Europe, which occupies a splendid setting, looking over the City of Sheffield and the Peak District beyond. Eight ski runs cater for all levels of skill – nursery runs for the novice and testing descents and moguls for the more experienced. All the other elements of a ski resort are here too, including a café, a restaurant and a fitness suite. Everything, indeed, except the likelihood of snow.

The Cutting Edge is a 90m (295ft) long sculpture made from Sheffield steel that defines the area between Midland Railway Station and Sheaf Street. At night, flowing water is illuminated along its entire length with blue light

These sculptures by Colin Rose entitled Rain, *sited outside the Winter Gardens, are a distinctive feature of Millennium Square*

Centre, which boasts Olympic-standard swimming facilities.

This diversification does not consign Sheffield's steelmaking to the history books and the heritage industries. The city is still a hive of industry. In fact, more steel and cutlery is made today than ever before, though production is streamlined. At the lively Kelham Island Museum, on Alma Street, visitors can trace the history of Sheffield's industrial development over the last 400 years, with displays of working machinery and some of the products that have made Sheffield famous, particularly iron, steel and silverware. One curiosity is a penknife with no fewer than 365 retractable blades! The massive and mighty River Don steam engine – the largest in the world – once powered a steel-rolling mill and it can still be seen 'in steam'. Skilled cutlers, using traditional methods, can be seen at work in the 'Little Mesters' workshops.

Sheffield's Supertram system is an enviable public transport system that is quiet, quick and comfortable. The trams offer the most convenient way to get to both the Don Valley Stadium and the Meadowhall Shopping Centre. This huge complex has risen, phoenix-like, from the ashes of the industrial wasteland that was one of the city's largest steelworks.

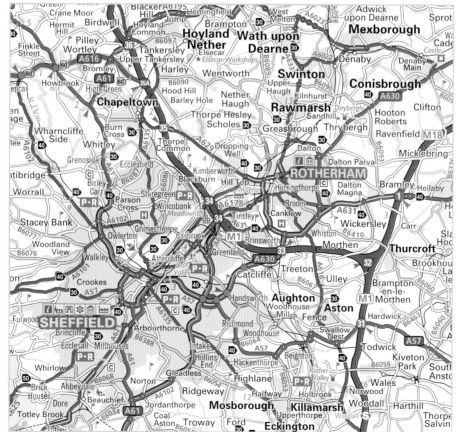

See Walk B, page 285
Linacre's Peaceful Retreat from Chesterfield

See Walk C, page 286
High Ackworth and East Hardwick

Tourist Information
Rotherham:
40 Bridgegate
(tel: 01709 835904)
Sheffield: 14 Norfolk Row
(tel: 0114 2211900)

THE PEAK DISTRICT

The Peak District stands at the crossroads of Britain – a beautiful link between the hard, uncompromising landscapes of the north and the lush greenness of the lowland south. As the southernmost extremity of the Pennine Chain, the Peak is the last knobbly vertebra in the backbone of England, and the first real hill country to be met by the traveller from the south and east. The change is quite sudden, and is perhaps best described by the remembrances of an early 18th-century traveller leaving Ashbourne to enter the Peak. 'At the summit of the hill,' he reflected, 'it was a top coat colder.'

The landscape changes, too, as you climb on to the limestone plateau in the south and centre, which is known as the White Peak. Gone are the neatly hedged fields of the Midlands, replaced by tumble down drystone walls spreading up hill and down dale, seemingly oblivious to the swelling contours.

Cloudberry flowers

Early Settlers

The Peak District, like any upland region, is the creation of its underlying geology, and the high and dry plateaux of the Peak were particularly attractive to the first settlers, who made their way across the land bridge from Europe. The remoteness of the region has resulted in the survival of a surprising number of remains of these first hunter-gatherers, including perhaps the most spectacular – the stone circles of Arbor Low, near Youlgreave and the Nine Ladies on Stanton Moors. Almost every hilltop in the Peak seems to be marked by a burial mound or barrow, most dating from the Bronze Age and known by the local name of 'low'. Complete Bronze-Age landscapes, including huts, stone circles, fields and barrows, have been identified on the moorlands to the east.

The Iron Age saw the construction of a number of apparently defensive hillforts, such as Mam Tor, commanding the upper

Wild Flowers of the Peak

To the botanist, the Peak represents the best of both worlds. Here can be found southern types, like the nettle-leaved bell-flower, at their northern limit, and northern types, like the cloudberry, at their southernmost extent. But to see the delicate white flowers of the cloudberry, the visitor has to travel north, leaving the limestone of the White Peak behind. Enclosing the limestone plateau to the north, east and west is a mantle of bleak and sometimes forbidding, peat-covered moorland known, in contrast, as the Dark Peak. This is the home of hardy species such as the cloudberry which, as its name suggests, is frequently to be found in the clouds, and of the blue or mountain hare, which changes the colour of its coat to match the winter snows.

The Rocks Beneath

The predominant rock in the Dark Peak is millstone grit, a coarse sandstone which takes its name from the fact that it was once much in demand for mill and grindstones. Abandoned millstone quarries can be found beneath many gritstone edges, with piles of finished but now unwanted stones. The Peak District National Park, which encompasses 555sq miles (1,437.4sq km) and was the first in Britain to be set up, in 1951, took the millstone symbol as its boundary marker and logo.

Both limestone and gritstone were laid down under tropical seas during the Carboniferous period, about 330 million years ago; if you look carefully at a limestone wall or gatepost, you may be able to see the remains of the sea lilies and shells which created the rock. The grit was laid down later over the limestone under deltaic conditions not unlike those found in the Mississippi or Nile today.

Late afternoon sun reflects off a boulder on Stanage Edge, a millstone grit face cliff edge and a highly popular location for rock climbing in the Peak District

The white weathered limestone blocks of the prehistoric Arbor Low stone circle near Youlgreave

Hope Valley near Castleton, and Fin Cop above Monsal Dale. Whether these defensive positions were ever the last resort of native Brigantians against the invading Romans will probably never be known, but the Imperial legions' chief interest in the Peak was in its abundant supplies of lead ore.

Wealth from the Land

The Romans were the first to exploit the mineral wealth of the Peak District, and mining and quarrying has been a major local source of employment ever since. In the 18th and 19th centuries, lead production was a major source of Peak District wealth and more than 10,000 miners were at work in the limestone area. Evidence of their passing can still be seen in White Peak meadows, where more than 50,000 shafts lie hidden beneath the surface.

The wealth won from lead and from the wool of their sheep gave landowners like the dukes of Devonshire and Rutland the confidence to build their magnificent houses of Chatsworth and Haddon Hall, both near Bakewell and superb but contrasting examples of the English country house. Haddon Hall, the older and more intimate of the two, was abandoned for 200 years and therefore not significantly 'improved' since the late Middle Ages. It stands on a prominent bluff overlooking the River Wyel. Just over the hill in the Derwent Valley is Chatsworth, the palatial, Palladian-style seat of the Dukes of Devonshire, largely rebuilt in the 17th century and now a treasurehouse of works of art. A working farm and extensive parkland complete the picture.

A much earlier seat of power in the Peak is the romantic ruin of Peveril Castle, high

Chatsworth House, built by the first Duke of Devonshire (1687–1707) and extended by the sixth Duke. The bridge over the River Derwent was added when Capability Brown landscaped the grounds in 1761

above the tiny township of Castleton in the Hope Valley. It was built by William Peveril shortly after the Conquest as the administrative centre for the Royal Forest of the Peak – a hunting preserve for medieval kings and princes.

Most-Visited National Park

Today, Castleton is a popular centre for the millions of visitors who throng to Britain's most-visited National Park, many coming to visit the four famous caverns. Treak Cliff and the Blue John Cavern and Mine are where the rare semi-precious stone, Blue John, is found. Peak Cavern is the most spectacular, while Speedwell's flooded passages are explored by boat.

Matlock and Matlock Bath have family attractions such as Gulliver's Kingdom, the Heights of Abraham, with its cable cars, caverns, maze and water gardens. Matlock Bath is also home to Temple Mine and the Peak District Mining Museum.

The 'capital' of the Peak is Bakewell, famous for the pudding (never known as a 'tart' here). The friendly little town is the natural centre and has the biggest local livestock and street market every Monday.

Most of today's 22 million annual visitors come from the surrounding towns and cities. Half the population of England live within day-trip distance of this precious island of scenery. To them, the Peak District is a vital lung and breathing space – right on their doorstep.

It is generally accepted that Bakewell Puddings were first made by accident, in 1820, when a cook in the White Horse Inn (now the Rutland Arms) was asked to make jam tarts but, instead of stirring eggs and almond paste into the pastry, spread it on top of the jam

LANCASHIRE'S HOLIDAY PLAYGROUND

The resorts of Lancashire are where the North of England has traditionally gone on holiday; whole mill-towns would once decamp here during 'Wakes Week'. Despite the lure of foreign climes, Blackpool and Lytham St Anne's still attract millions, and yet away from the resorts much of the coastline has sandy beaches where yours may be the only footprints.

Blackpool's beach and brightly lit seafront. The town's ambitions as a holiday resort were confirmed in 1894, when Blackpool Tower was built

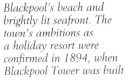

Blackpool

A late starter as a resort, Blackpool soon made up for lost time. In the 1840s it was just a village, but the arrival of a railway branchline provided the impetus for creating a major resort along this strand of sandy beach. Ever since then the town's main concern has been to find more and more ways of entertaining visitors, who number more than 1 million per year. It was in Blackpool, for example, that the first sticks of seaside rock were made, their success assured by having 'Blackpool' written all the way through.

Brash, brazen and bustling, Blackpool wears its heart on its sleeve; there is nothing subtle about the attractions of the Pleasure Beach and the celebrated Golden Mile. It is noted, as Stanley Holloway used to sing, 'for fresh air and fun', and those who want their pleasures to involve 'white knuckles' will not be disappointed. When the sky turns leaden there are as many amusements under cover, including the attractions at the base of the famous tower and the fascinating Sea Life Centre. Here visitors can view marine life at close quarters, including a walk through one of the largest shark displays in Europe.

In autumn, when most other resorts are putting up the shutters, Blackpool gears up for a major influx of visitors. The famous illuminations, along 7 miles (11.3km) of seafront, bring a touch of Las Vegas to the country's biggest holiday resort.

Blackpool Tower

There can be few better-known landmarks in the country than Blackpool Tower. It is a convincing 519ft (158.2m) replica of the Eiffel Tower in Paris. Blackpool's version is more than just a tower: It rises out of a building large enough to accommodate the famous circus and the vast Tower Ballroom, with its mighty Wurlitzer organ. There are lifts to the top of the tower, from where there are magnificent views over the resort and miles of coastline.

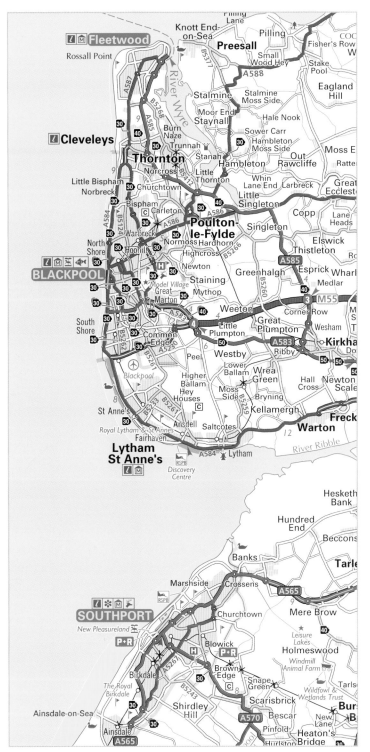

Rarities such as the East African Crowned Crane fill the Wildlife and Wetlands Trust Centre at Martin Mere

St Anne's was a Victorian creation, built on sand dunes by entrepreneurs who took note of the prevailing fashion for sea-bathing. They created a health resort that would be a little more elegant than some of its more boisterous neighbours; the resort's name was found in the chapel, which is dedicated to St Anne.

Martin Mere

This Wildlife and Wetlands Trust Centre near Ormskirk was established in 1976 and has birds from all over the world, including ducks, geese, swans and flamingos, which can be observed from hides overlooking the floodwaters.

In winter the bird population is swelled by the arrival of huge numbers of pink-footed geese (up to one tenth of the world population) and migrating whooper and Bewick's swans which can be viewed at close quarters from the many hides or watched from the comfort of the heated Raines observatory.

The centre has a fascinating beaver enclosure, a waterfront garden with more than 100 species of rare birds and a children's playground.

See Walk E, page 288
The Bottom and the Top: Around Beacon Fell

Tourist Information
Blackpool: Clifton Street (tel: 01253 478222)
Fleetwood: Old Ferry Office, The Esplanade (tel: 01253 773953)
Lytham St Anne's: Town Hall (tel: 01253 725610)
Southport: 112 Lord Street (tel: 01704 533333)

Marine Way Bridge links Southport's town centre to the seafront

Lytham St Anne's

At Lytham St Anne's you get two resorts in one. Until 1923 Lytham and neighbouring St Anne's were two distinct communities. Lytham, mentioned as a port in the Domesday Book, is kept at arm's length from the shore by the expanse of the Green. Here you will see the town's most distinctive landmark – a beautifully restored windmill dating back to 1805; at one time there were many such mills on the flatlands of the Fylde peninsular.

Southport

In the early 19th century, the place where Southport now stands was nothing but sand dunes. A passion for sea-bathing prompted a local man, Duke Sutton, to build the South Port Hotel at the best beach. Though he ended his days in a debtors' prison, he inspired the town's creation and his hotel gave it a name. By 1860 this was the largest seaside resort in the north, when Blackpool was just being developed. Lord Street is the main thoroughfare: wide, elegant and lined with fine Victorian buildings, their elaborate canopies extending over the pavement.

LEEDS AND BRADFORD

Brick-built Leeds and stone-built Bradford are the closest of neighbours. Once vital cogs in the engine room of the Industrial Revolution, these twin cities are being revitalised to meet the expectations of the 21st century. Harrogate, to the north, is content to offer echoes of a more leisurely age, and in between are some delightful villages in surprisingly rural settings.

Harewood House was built in the 1760s for Lord Harewood and in 1994 became the first stately home to be granted museum status in Britain

Bradford

Cosmopolitan Bradford is a bustling city with fine Victorian architecture. The Wool Exchange, textile mills and the warehouse district are evocative reminders of a time when Bradford was the woollen capital of the world. The story is vividly told at the Industrial and Horses at Work Museum, in a former spinning mill in Eccleshill, which includes working machinery, horse-drawn rides, textile workers' cottages and the mill-owner's house to visit.

The National Media Museum and Television portrays the history and future of the media using special effects, interactive devices and a massive IMAX cinema screen. There are extensive cinematography, photography and television collections, and a rolling programme of changing exhibitions.

Harrogate

The discovery of spring waters – and their restorative powers – transformed Harrogate from a sleepy village into a bustling spa town. By the 16th century it was well known as an inland resort, where well-heeled visitors would socialise and 'take the waters'. In more recent times Harrogate has successfully reinvented itself as a venue for conventions and trade shows. The old Royal Pump Room, now a museum, still stands in the town centre, and adventurous visitors can still taste the water. The Valley Gardens are nearby; further out are the impressive Harlow Carr Botanical Gardens.

Knaresborough

This idiosyncratic and historic little town has a castle which gazes down into the steep gorge of the River Nidd, a cobbled marketplace which boasts the oldest chemist's shop in the country and a Petrifying Well that turns to 'stone' any objects hung in its flow. Nearby is the cave in which Old Mother Shipton lived 500 years ago and foretold the future.

Harewood House

Halfway between Leeds and Harrogate lies one of Yorkshire's finest and stateliest homes. Harewood House was designed by John Carr and Robert Adam, and the 1,000 acres (405ha) of parkland was created by that doyen of landscaping, 'Capability' Brown. The house contains many treasures, including an unrivalled collection of 18th-century furniture made especially for Harewood by Thomas Chippendale, who was born in Otley.

Harewood House stages a variety of exhibitions and events, and the bird garden brings visitors face to face with rare and exotic species from around the world.

Some of her prophecies strike resonant chords. Could these four lines perhaps refer to the M25 and the internet?...

'Carriages without horses shall go, and accidents fill the world with woe. Around the world thoughts shall fly in the twinkling of an eye.'

Leeds

Its reputation built on the textile and tailoring trades, Leeds is rapidly changing to meet new challenges. Smoke-blackened mills are giving way to new developments overlooking the River Aire and the Leeds–Liverpool Canal, creating riverside walks and, at Granary Wharf, a labyrinth of speciality shops. Other buildings, such as the splendid, domed Corn Exchange, have a new lease of life, filled with shops, and the city's arcades have been restored to their original Victorian splendour.

Bobbins and shuttles still fly at Armley Mills Industrial Museum, evoking memories of its heyday and showing all the stages of production, from sheep to clothing. Along the waterfront from

Establishments such as Betty's Café Tea Rooms illustrate Harrogate's genteel spa-town history

Kirkstall

On the outskirts of Leeds, on the banks of the River Aire, is Kirkstall Abbey, founded in 1152 and one of the finest monastic sites in the country. After the Dissolution of the Monasteries, the building fared better than many and still stands substantially to its full height. Nearby is the Abbey House Museum, a major folk museum with full-size Victorian shops, workshops and cottages.

Tetley's Brewery Wharf development you'll find the superb Royal Armouries – a purpose-built museum displaying more than 8,000 exhibits from 3,000 years of conflict.

Otley

John Wesley, on a preaching visit in 1759, found 'such noise, hurry, drunkenness, rioting and confusion I know not when I have met with before'. It is hard to believe he was speaking of Otley, a delightful little market town straddling the River Wharfe. This was the birthplace, in 1718, of cabinet maker Thomas Chippendale. The artist, J. M. W. Turner, was a regular visitor to Farnley Hall, as guest of the Horton-Fawkes family (whose most notorious relative was Guy Fawkes), and the landscapes of the Yorkshire Dales provided the inspiration for many of Turner's paintings.

View inside one of the two arcades that form a part of the Victoria Quarter in Leeds, often described as one of the UK's most beautiful shopping centres

Temple Newsam House

This fine house, dubbed 'The Hampton Court of the North' and dating from the 16th and 17th centuries, was the birthplace of Lord Darnley. Just 4 miles (6.4km) from Leeds city centre, the house enjoys views over parkland designed by 'Capability' Brown. The walled gardens are a riot of colour in the rhododendron season, while the house itself boasts a fine collection of Chippendale furniture and Leeds pottery.

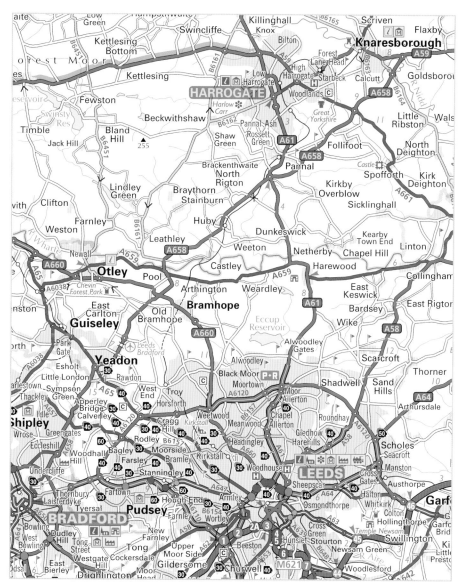

See Walk D, page 287
Haworth's Brontë Moors

Tourist Information

Bradford: City Hall (tel: 01274 433678)
Harrogate: Royal Baths Assembly Rooms, Crescent Road (tel: 0845 389 3223)
Knaresborough: 9 Castle Courtyard (seasonal) (tel: 0845 389 0177)
Leeds: Leeds City Train Station (tel: 0113 242 5242)
Otley: Nelson Street (tel: 01943 462485)

The Chapter House at Kirkstall Abbey, where Benedictine monks would have met to discuss daily business and read a chapter of The Rules of Saint Benedict

ABBEYS OF THE NORTH

From the very earliest days of Christianity, the remoteness and wildness of the northern English landscape attracted hermits and monastic communities alike, offering opportunities for retreat from the civilised world and the adoption of a life of self-sufficiency and poverty. It is ironic, then, that the success of these establishments resulted not only in the building of some of the finest and richest abbeys in the kingdom, but also in a transformation of their surroundings. The Cistercian brotherhood, in particular, by a combination of sheer hard work and technical expertise, turned unproductive land into fertile, well-drained fields which supported vast numbers of sheep. Though their grandiose abbeys are now reduced to ruins, the achievement of these medieval pioneers lives on in the oases of lush pasture which they created in the midst of moorland and fells.

Stained glass window depicting the Venerable Bede (AD673–735) at Bede's World in Jarrow, Tyne and Wear

Early Christianity

St Paulinus (d. AD644) was the first successful Christian missionary in the North, converting King Edwin, who made him Archbishop of York. Paulinus preached, baptised and encouraged the setting up of churches throughout the North, but when his patron was killed in battle, he returned to Kent and the North reverted to paganism. The second wave of missionaries came from the Irish, rather than Roman, tradition and were spearheaded by St Columba (AD521–97), who founded the monastery on Iona. His monks established churches throughout the north and one of them, St Aidan (d. AD651), became the first Bishop of Lindisfarne (Holy Island), off the coast of Northumberland. The clash between the Celtic and Roman monasticism was finally resolved at the great Synod of Whitby, held at Whitby Abbey on the North Yorkshire coast, where it was decided to adopt Roman, Papal observances.

The most famous chronicler of these events was the Venerable Bede (AD673–735), whose reputation has stood longer than the great abbey at Jarrow, where he lived and

Furness Abbey, near Barrow-in-Furness, was one of the richest Cistercian monasteries in England

died. Bede was born into a Saxon family who sent him, at the age of seven, to be brought up as a monk at Wearmouth Abbey; he soon moved on to Jarrow, where he spent the rest of his life. He learned Latin, Greek and Hebrew and wrote treatises on theology, natural phenomena and orthography, but his most famous work was his *Ecclesiastical History of the English People*. Full of vividly told anecdotes, the work is also scholarly and accurate. Its extraordinary qualities were immediately recognised and it has remained the standard textbook on the early English Church for more than 1,200 years.

Cistercian Pioneers

It was the Cistercians who left the greatest legacy of monastic architecture. The oldest foundation, Rievaulx, was, as its name suggests, established by French monks from Clairvaux, where the abbot, St Bernard (1091–1153), was one of the most influential of all medieval Christians. Rievaulx was founded in 1131 and by the end of the century there were said to be more than 140 monks and 500 lay brothers living there. Its evocative ruins are set in a wooded valley in the Hambleton Hills of North Yorkshire. They are best seen from the vantage point of Rievaulx Terrace, which, with its Tuscan and Ionic temples, was built specifically for that purpose in the middle of the 18th century.

On an even grander scale are the ruins of Fountains Abbey, founded a year after Rievaulx, but reconstructed in the second half of the century after a disastrous fire.

Built on a site once described as 'fit more for the dens of wild beasts than for the uses of man', the abbey became the wealthiest Cistercian house in England, a pre-eminence which is still evident from the sheer size of the remaining buildings and the rich beauty of their setting. Approached through the delightful water gardens of Studley Royal, the sight is breathtaking.

Between Rievaulx and Fountains are the ruins of Byland Abbey, founded in 1134, which boasts the longest Cistercian church in England. Its daughter house, Jervaulx, was, according to tradition, founded by a group of monks from Byland who lost their way on the banks of the River Yore and were guided to safety by a vision of the Virgin and Child, who declared 'Ye are late of Byland but now of Yorevale.'

The distinctive red sandstone remains of Furness Abbey in Cumbria, which was founded in 1123 but taken over by the Cistercians in 1147, testify to the fact that it came second only to Fountains in terms of wealth, owning extensive properties in northern England and the Isle of Man. In terms of size, it belittled even Fountains, having a dormitory twice as long.

The Cistercians were not the only monks to settle in this area. Two 12th-century Augustinian foundations were preserved to a degree. Brinkburn Priory, despite its pretty setting by the River Coquet, was always impoverished, but its church survived the Reformation because it served the parish; it was completely restored in the 19th century and is regarded as Northumberland's finest example of early Gothic architecture. Newburgh Priory in North Yorkshire lives on only because it was incorporated into the mansion built by Henry VIII's

chaplain; the house boasts possession of the tomb of that other destroyer of churches, Oliver Cromwell. The most unusual of all, however, is Mount Grace Priory, founded in 1398, the best-preserved Carthusian charterhouse in England. Living in individual two-storey cells, each with its own garden, the Carthusians lived the life of hermits within the Priory precincts, reviving the Irish ideal which had inspired the very first monastic foundations in the area.

The Dissolution

Picturesque and tranquil though their ruins may be now, the great abbeys were once at the centre of religious, social and commercial life. This might have continued, had Henry VIII not divorced Katherine of Aragon so that he could marry Anne Boleyn. Because the Pope refused to approve of the arrangement, Henry VIII made himself Supreme Head of the Church in England, and the Dissolution of the Monasteries began in 1536, with around 800 monasteries suppressed. In the south of England there was little resistance, but in the north up to 40,000 men rallied to join the Pilgrimage of Grace, a peaceful protest which soon became an armed revolt, with finance, and even physical support, from the monks of Byland, Furness, Rievaulx and Whitby. With typical guile, Henry VIII persuaded the rebels to disband by promising that the monasteries would be saved, but then reneged and exacted a terrible revenge on all who had taken part. Monks were among the leaders whom he had executed, and every religious house was forcibly disbanded, its wealth seized and its lands sold.

Rievaulx Abbey, North Yorkshire was founded in 1131

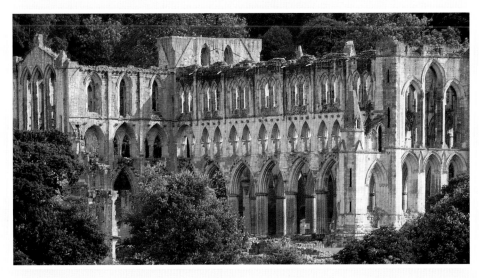

AROUND MORECAMBE BAY

A mild climate and seemingly endless sands have made Morecambe Bay popular with generations of holidaymakers, who enjoy the genteel pleasures of its seaside towns. In sharp contrast are the bleaker beauties of the surrounding hills, the Lake District, visible to the north across the bay, and the Pennines to the east, with their tumult of moors and stormy skies.

The stone-built façade of 18th-century Leighton Hall overlooks its grounds and a lake

Leighton Moss Reserve

The Royal Society for the Protection of Birds has turned this man-made fen, which was drained in about 1920, into a birdwatcher's paradise. Open water, reed beds, marshes and woodland offer a variety of habitats to attract abundant birdlife, which can be observed from a network of footpaths and hides. Escorted wildlife events, such as otter and deer watches, allow visitors to see some of the other rare inhabitants of the reserve.

Carnforth

Once a busy steelworking town, Carnforth has unlikely romantic associations. Its station, at the junction of railway lines linking the scenic Settle to Carlisle, the West Cumbria and the main London to Glasgow routes, was the setting for the classic 1940s film *Brief Encounter*, starring Celia Johnson and Trevor Howard. There are splendid views across Morecambe Bay from Warton Crag, a hill remarkable for its limestone pavements and cliffs, which is now a nature reserve; park in Warton Crag Quarry and walk along the trails, one of which is suitable for wheelchairs.

The ruins of the 14th-century Old Rectory at Warton suggest that it was like a small medieval manor house, built of stone, with the remains of the hall, buttery, kitchen and chambers still visible. The village of Warton has other historic links, including the ancestors of George Washington, in whose honour the Stars and Stripes are flown from the church tower on Independence Day.

In the 19th century Warton was a favoured holiday destination of Mrs Gaskell, the novelist, who wrote part of her *Life of Charlotte Brontë* at Lindeth Tower.

Grange-over-Sands

Taking its name from the grange or granary once built here by the Augustinian monks of Cartmel Priory, the town became a popular holiday resort in the 19th century. Sheltered by the Lakeland fells, its mild climate has made it a gardener's paradise: Grange is renowned for its ornamental gardens, and the Lakeland Rose Show is held each July at nearby Cark-in-Cartmel. Holker Hall is close by, a charming house which dates from the 16th century and contains a delightful mix of fine furniture and woodcarving, alongside family photographs and personal possessions. There are formal and woodland gardens, a 120-acre (49ha) deer park and the Lakeland Motor Museum.

The beautiful 12th-century monastic church of Cartmel Priory at Cartmel, 3 miles (4.8km) from Grange, is one of only a handful to have survived the Reformation and should not be missed. Among its treasures is a first edition of Spenser's *Faerie Queene*. At Lindale-in-Cartmel, 2 miles (3.2km) north of Grange, there is an unusual iron monument to John Wilkinson, the 18th-century forgemaster, who grew up in the area and cast the pieces for the world's first iron bridge at Ironbridge in Shropshire.

Lancaster

The county town of Lancashire, Lancaster goes back to Roman times, when a fort (*castrum*) was built to guard the crossing over the River Lune of the road from Chester to Hadrian's Wall. A medieval castle, which is owned by the Queen as 'Duke of Lancaster', still dominates the city today. Since the 18th century the castle has housed the county courts and prison; the notorious Pendle witches, convicted and hanged in 1612, were also held there while awaiting trial.

Exploring the network of streets below the castle offers more pleasant reminders of Lancaster's wealth in Georgian times. The Old Town Hall in the Market Square houses the excellent City Museum, which illustrates aspects of local life from the Neolithic age all the way up to the present day. It is also home to the Museum of

Forest of Bowland

The Forest of Bowland is one of the most dramatic natural features of the Lancashire landscape. A vast plateau of rolling hills and moors rising to more than 1,800ft (550m) above sea level, it is dissected by deep valleys, such as the Trough of Bowland, once notorious as the haunt of smugglers from Yorkshire, and highwaymen. Drive from Quernmore, near Lancaster, to Dursop Bridge, 12 miles (19.3km) to the southeast, to get a taste of this lonely, rugged hill country. Better still, discover its waterfalls, sweeping views and wildlife on foot. For leaflets and information about guided walks, contact Lancaster Tourist Information Centre.

Beyond the spire of Lancaster's Cathedral of St Peter lies Williamson Park and the Ashton Memorial

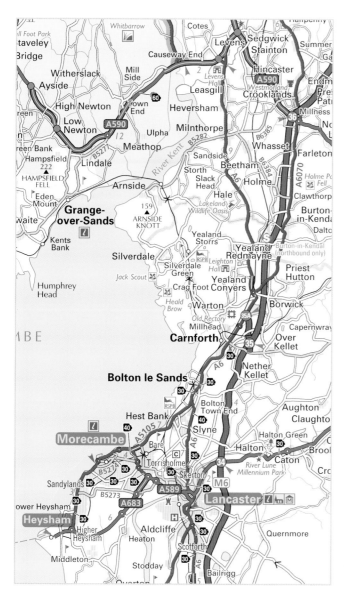

The Forest of Bowland is not filled with trees as you might expect because 'forest' described a royal hunting ground

cabinet-making business, based in Lancaster, is well represented throughout the house. A replica of a Maryland mansion, built in the 1870s and containing 1,200 antique fittings, is just one of its many treasures.

Morecambe

Morecambe is famous for its seaside promenade, which is 4 miles (6.4km) long and provides every holiday amusement you could imagine, from theatres, funfairs and amusement arcades to a modern leisure park and entertainment complex. The town's seafront renaissance has included public projects such as the Platform arts centre and the Stone Jetty, a breathtaking place to sit and watch the famous Morecambe Bay sunset. There is a statue of the town's favourite son, too – Eric Morecambe, who took his stage name from his boyhood home.

All this is a long way from Morecambe's humble origins as the little fishing village of Poulton-le-Sands, though the boats still fish locally for whitebait, cockles and shrimps. The sands are vast and flat and, though it is possible to walk across the bay to Grange, treacherous currents, quicksands and the speed of the incoming tide make this extremely dangerous without an official guide. The walk takes three hours and is subject to the weather.

Tourist Information

Grange-over-Sands: Victoria Hall, Main Street (seasonal) (tel: 015395 34026)
Lancaster: The Storey, Meeting House Lane (tel: 01524 582394)
Morecambe: Old Station Buildings, Marine Road Central (tel: 01524 582808)

Strolling on Morecambe's beach at low tide

the King's Own Royal Regiment; the Judges' Lodgings on Castle Hill houses the Gillow Furniture Museum and a Museum of Childhood. A Maritime Museum, occupying the former Custom House on St George's Quay, tells the fascinating story of Lancaster's trading past and the fishing communities of Morecambe Bay. For panoramic views of the city and beyond, head for the Ashton Memorial in Williamson Park, a folly built in 1909.

Leighton Hall

Three miles (4.8km) north of Carnforth, set against a dramatic backdrop of Lakeland fells, is Leighton Hall, an Adam-style house with a splendid neo-Gothic façade. A fortified manor was first built on this site in 1246, but during the 1715 rebellion it was sacked and burned by Government troops. Rebuilt in 1763 by George Townley, it then passed into the hands of the Gillow family, whose

THE YORKSHIRE DALES

The landscape of the Yorkshire Dales National Park was formed by water and ice wearing deep into the limestone and creating gorges and waterfalls, wide valleys and gentle rivers, strange rock formations, potholes and hundreds of miles of caves and underground passages. Lush valley pastures give way to crags, grassland and moors on the hilltops.

Clapham Beck meanders through the village of Clapham

Clapham

Clapham is idyllically situated at the foot of Ingleborough, one of the three highest peaks in the Dales. Stone cottages line the beck which flows through the village, having tumbled spectacularly down Gaping Gill pothole in a 340ft (104m) waterfall. Half an hour's walk away is Ingleborough Cave – not for the faint-hearted, but its limestone formations are worth seeing. Clapham has claims to fame. Michael Faraday, discoverer of electromagnetism, was the son of the village blacksmith and Reginald Farrer, often regarded as one of the founding fathers of English gardening, lived at Ingleborough Hall, where his rock gardens incorporated rare and exotic plants from all over the world.

The Pennine Way and Three Peaks

Britain's first long-distance footpath, the Pennine Way covers 256 miles (412km) from Derbyshire to the Scottish Border, taking in some of the wildest and most beautiful parts of the Dales. From Malham it climbs via the Cove and Tarn to the peak of Pen-y-Ghent, the 'hill of the winds', which is 2,274ft (693m) high. It then crosses Dodd Fell to Hawes, with another dramatic section on Great Shunner Fell, overlooking the unique and treacherous Buttertubs Pass, where a series of long fluted columns of limestone separate apparently bottomless holes. There are magnificent views over wild and lonely Swaledale as the walk descends to Muker before following the river up to Tan Hill, the highest inn in England. Equally strenuous is the Three Peaks challenge, which takes in 5,000ft (1,524m) of climbing and 25 miles (40.2km) of walking over the three highest mountains in the Dales, Pen-y-Ghent, Whernside and Ingleborough. The hardiest of mortals can compete on foot or bicycle in the two annual Three Peaks races.

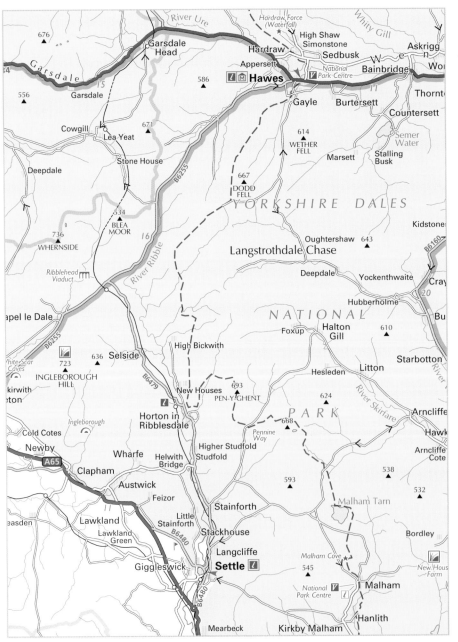

Gordale Scar, near Malham in the Yorkshire Dales National Park

Gordale Scar

A deep funnel-shaped gorge, Gordale Scar was carved out of the limestone by melting glaciers. Following the river from Gordale Bridge, the crags close in, until, passing through a narrow entrance to the left, they open out again and the path is barred by a waterfall gushing from the rock face. The dramatic effect of the high cliffs, only 30ft (9m) apart at their base, is heightened by the tremendous overhang, beneath which you get the best view of the waterfall. Wordsworth's friend, the artist George Beaumont, rightly described it as 'beyond the range of art'.

Hardraw Force

One of England's highest waterfalls, tumbling 98ft (30m) in a single drop over a limestone crag, is a spectacular sight. It is situated behind the Green Dragon Inn at Hardraw, via a pleasant walk through a narrow wooded valley. So sheer is the drop from the overhanging rock that it is possible to walk behind the waterfall without getting wet. A challenge of a more bizarre kind was undertaken by Blondin, who crossed the gorge on a tightrope, stopping halfway to cook an omelette!

Hawes

One of the highest market towns in England, Hawes occupies a prime position in upper Wensleydale at the junction of three major valleys and is a natural tourist centre. The Dales Countryside Centre, in the Station Yard, has an extensive collection of bygones, which offer an insight into the changing landscapes and the Dales communities.

Kettlewell

This charming village, with its grey stone cottages and three inns crammed into its narrow streets, enjoys an incomparable position at the heart of Upper Wharfedale. It looks down over rich valley pastures, divided by mile upon mile of drystone walls. Behind the village soar the steep slopes of Buckden Pike and Great Whernside, over which a winding road climbs, with spectacular views, leading to the bleaker beauty of Coverdale. The pretty church contains its original Norman font, and the grave of local novelist, C. J. Cutcliffe Hyne, is in the churchyard.

Malham

Centred round a single stone-arched bridge across Malham Beck, this is a lovely village with inns, cafés and shops. Park here to walk 1 mile (1.6km) upstream to Malham Cove, a spectacular natural amphi-theatre of limestone crag, 330ft (100m) high and more than 1,000ft (304.8m) wide, it was formed when the rocks fractured, slipped and dropped vertically. The pavement at the top is completely flat bare rock, riddled with fissures. Just north

Curious rock formations look out over the Pennine Way at Malham Cove

is Malham Tarn, one of only two natural lakes in the Dales; of particular scientific importance, it is now a bird sanctuary and nature reserve. The National Park Centre in the village has interesting displays on the area's history.

Settle

The start of the scenic Settle to Carlisle railway line, this small market town is an attractive tourist destination and a busy working town. It has many 17th-century buildings, including The Folly on Kirkgate, with its unusual corner windows. For a glimpse of the past, visit the town's Museum of North Craven Life; for good contemporary art, visit the Linton Court Art Gallery.

See Walk F, page 289
Spectacular Landscapes in Limestone County

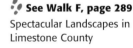
See Walk J, page 293
A Riverside Circuit High in the Dales

Tourist Information
Hawes: Dales Countryside Museum, Station Yard (seasonal) (tel: 01969 666210) Settle: Town Hall, Cheapside (tel: 01729 825192)

The waterfall at Hardraw Force was once visited by William Wordsworth

BETWEEN DALES AND MOORS

Between the Yorkshire Dales and the Great North Road (A1) are two of Yorkshire's most ancient settlements – Ripon and Richmond. Ripon is dominated by its beautiful cathedral, while Richmond's marketplace is overlooked by the keep of its castle. Around both of them are fascinating villages, delightful countryside and, at Fountains Abbey, one of the best-preserved monasteries in Europe.

The 200-tonne Idol, at the Brimham Rocks; the rocks are formed from a tough sandstone, Millstone Grit

Brimham Rocks

This delightfully eccentric group of weathered rocks has long been a popular playground and picnic site. The formations were created over millions of years, as wind and rain transformed these outcrops of millstone grit into fantastic shapes – faces, figures and animals, which have inevitably been named. Look out for the Dancing Bear, the Sphinx and the Anvil. The Idol is a huge boulder perched incongruously on the tiniest of pedestals.

Tourist Information
Richmond: Friary Gardens, Victoria Road (tel: 01748 828742)
Ripon: Minster Road (seasonal) (tel: 01765 604625)

Fountains Abbey

One of the country's few World Heritage Sites, Fountains Abbey is arguably the best-preserved Cistercian abbey in Europe. Finding the Benedictine order too lax, a group of 12th-century monks broke away to found the Cistercian order. They completed the building of Fountains Abbey between 1150 and 1250. Ironically, for a community dedicated to poverty and obedience, the order went on to be very prosperous, owning farms throughout Yorkshire.

The splendidly austere ruins of the abbey, on the banks of the River Skell, were incorporated, in the early 18th century, into the Studley Royal estate. The abbey became the centrepiece of an elaborate water garden. With its lakes, temples, formal hedges, deer park and artfully contrived vistas, it epitomised the Romantic ideal.

Jervaulx Abbey

Cistercian monks came from France in the 12th century to found a monastic community here, in the valley of the River Ure (the name 'Jervaulx' is simply a literal translation into French of 'Yoredale'). Though it is no match for Fountains Abbey in terms of size or setting, Jervaulx Abbey is well worth a visit. The ruins, surrounded by wooded parkland and ablaze with floral colour, exert a feeling of tranquillity that is almost tangible.

Masham

Masham (pronounce it 'Massam') is best known for a formidably strong ale from Theakston's called Old Peculier. The name refers to the Peculiar Court of Masham, first convened in the 12th century to combat outbreaks of lawlessness. Theakston's has a brewery museum, where the art of coopering (barrel-making) is demonstrated. The town has a huge market square where, every September, a two-day sheep fair is held.

Richmond

One of the few English towns to have kept its original medieval layout, Richmond is the 'capital' of beautiful Swaledale. The huge, sloping marketplace is overlooked

Pateley Bridge and Nidderdale

When the boundaries of the Yorkshire Dales National Park were drawn up in 1954, Nidderdale found itself on the outside. Yet the valley loses nothing in comparison with better-known dales – it is a delight all the way from bustling Pateley Bridge to the head of the dale, where a trio of reservoirs – Angram, Gouthwaite and Scar House – were built to quench the thirst of industrial Bradford.

With its craft shops and riverside walks, Pateley Bridge is a popular destination with visitors. But it was the mining of lead – in one of the bleakest landscapes in Yorkshire – that brought prosperity to the town. Until the industry collapsed around the end of the 19th century, miners laboured in elaborate tunnels (known as 'levels') driven deep into the hillsides.

Stream flowing over rocks at How Stean Gorge in Nidderdale near Lofthouse in the Yorkshire Dales

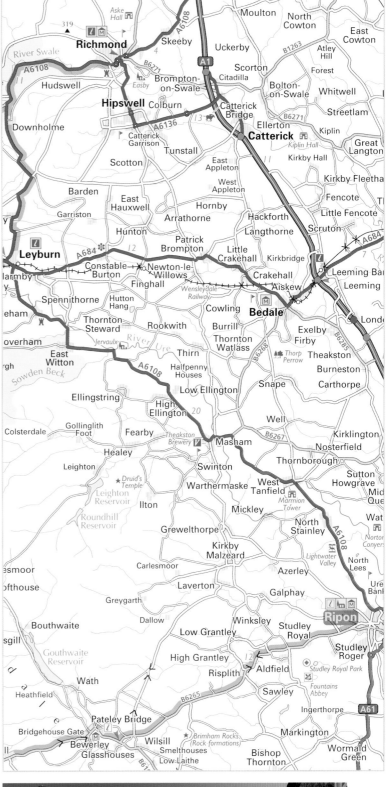

The chapel that was once part of County Bridge is long gone, washed away by the great floods of 1661

Barnard Castle

The 'Gateway to Teesdale', Barnard Castle is a market town set in some splendidly rugged countryside. The castle, built by Bernard Baliol in the 12th century, sits on an exposed site overlooking the River Tees and County Bridge, once the site of illicit weddings. The Bowes Museum, a 'French château' in an English setting, houses an extensive collection of furniture and artworks from the second Napoleonic Empire period – collected by Francophiles John and Josephine Bowes prior to the museum's opening in 1892.

by the castle, built by Earl Alan Rufus shortly after the Norman invasion; it was roofed with lead from the productive Swaledale mines. From the top of the tall keep, you can see the little alleyways (known as 'wynds') leading off from the marketplace and some of the features that are worth a visit, including the delightful and diminutive Georgian Theatre and the Green Howards Regimental Museum.

Ripon

It was Alfred the Great who granted Ripon its charter more than 1,000 years ago, and markets are still held on Thursdays and Saturdays in the shadow of a tall obelisk. Ripon maintains much of its medieval layout, though most of the finer buildings are Georgian and Victorian. An unusual attraction is the early 19th-century prison, which is now the Prison and Police Museum.

A short walk from the market square, along Kirkgate, offers a surprise, as the splendid west front of the cathedral suddenly comes into view. With some parts dating from as early as AD672, the cathedral features almost every architectural style, and contains what is believed to be the oldest Anglo-Saxon crypt in England.

Ripon is ringed by places which are well worth a visit, including Fountains Abbey to the southwest, and the splendid 17th-century Newby Hall and Gardens to the southeast. Norton Conyers, to the north, is a late medieval house with later additions, and is believed to have been the inspiration for Thornfield Hall in Charlotte Brontë's *Jane Eyre* (a family legend of a mad woman in the attic would seem to bear more than a coincidental similarity to the mad Mrs Rochester).

Also to the north is the Lightwater Valley Theme Park and Village, which includes the world's longest roller-coaster and similar thrills, along with gentler rides for the more faint-hearted. It is set in 175 acres (71ha) of country park and there is an adjacent shopping area.

The 13th-century west front of Ripon Cathedral

IN AND AROUND YORK

To stroll around York is to feel history beneath your feet. With fascinating buildings and features from so many important periods of history, it is no surprise that the city is pencilled in on so many visitors' itineraries. To the north of York the landscape changes, from flat, arable farmland to the heather moorland and green valleys that typify the North York Moors National Park.

A sloping street in the village of Coxwold, leading up to the 15th-century St Michael's Church

Boroughbridge

Stagecoach passengers would have heaved a sigh of relief as Boroughbridge hove into view, for this little town's main distinction was being the halfway point on the Great North Road between London and Edinburgh. Just outside the town are the Devil's Arrows, a trio of standing stones that may date from the Bronze Age.

At the nearby village of Aldborough there are the remains of *Isurium*, the most northerly of the Romans' settlements to have been built without military purpose.

Coxwold

This picturesque village of honey-coloured stone houses became the home of the Rev Laurence Sterne, best known as the author of the comic classic, *The Life and Opinions of Tristram Shandy, Gentleman*. Without false modesty he renamed his house Shandy Hall (open to the public).

Nearby Newburgh Priory was built in 1145 as an Augustinian priory; after the Dissolution of the Monasteries Henry VIII presented the building to his chaplain, who converted it into a splendid country residence. Later Oliver Cromwell's daughter lived here for a time; it is said that she secretly took his body down from the gallows and buried it in the grounds of Newburgh Priory. The house is open during early summer and Cromwellian relics are among the items on display.

All Saints Church dominates Helmsley, but the village's four former coaching inns offer more historic interest

Helmsley

Though it is the size of a village, Helmsley has the purposeful air of a county town – especially on Friday, market day. This is the starting point for the Cleveland Way, a long-distance walk that takes 'the long way round' the moors, ending up at Filey. Those with less energy can explore the 12th-century castle, its Norman keep still dominating the town.

Just outside Helmsley is Duncombe Park, standing in 300 acres (122ha) of parkland, which includes a spectacular early 18th century landscaped garden of

30 acres (12ha). The house, much altered since it was built in 1713, was in use as a school until the 1980s, since when it has been restored as a family home.

Rievaulx

When Walter Espec dispatched a band of French monks to create a new community, they found the area 'fit only

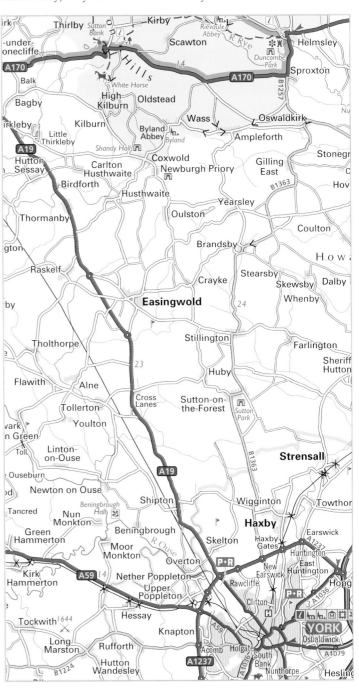

A glider soars above Sutton Bank in the North York Moors National Park

A Fine Country House

The severely symmetrical brick façade of Beningbrough Hall looks out over spreading parkland and delightful walled gardens. This early Georgian country house, now looked after by the National Trust, reveals much about life here, both upstairs and down, during the 18th century. A hundred contemporary paintings, on loan from the National Portrait Galley, enhance the room settings.

The Shambles in York

This short, narrow street of almost perfectly preserved medieval buildings was where the city's butchers once plied their trade and displayed their cuts of meat. The buildings huddle so close together that two attic-dwellers could shake hands across the street. The narrowness kept direct sunlight away from the meat – a wise precaution in the days before refrigeration. The butchers' shops are all gone, though many of the shopfronts still incorporate the wooden ledges on which meat used to be displayed.

for wild beasts and robbers'. No matter; the monks' asceticism thrived on such challenges, and in the year 1131 they began to build what many people consider to be the finest Cistercian abbey in the country.

Rievaulx Abbey occupies a splendid wooded setting in the valley of the River Rye ('Rievaulx' is a French rendering of 'Rye Vale'). Enough remains of the Norman nave to show how the abbey would have looked all those centuries ago.

Overlooking the abbey is Rievaulx Terrace, a 0.5 mile (0.8km) curved grassy terrace with two mock-Greek temples, which was created entirely for the views of the abbey, of Ryedale and of the Hambleton Hills beyond.

Sutton Bank

From the top of Sutton Bank you can enjoy one of the finest views in Yorkshire – on a clear day you can even see the Three Peaks of the Yorkshire Dales. This vantage point provides a sharp distinction between the flat Vale of Mowbray to the west and the Hambleton Hills to the north and east.

A delightful walk hugs the edge of Sutton Bank, passing a flying club where pencil-slim gliders are towed off the edge to exploit the thermals, and soon arriving at a much-loved landmark. The White Horse of Kilburn is a hill-figure cut into the slope by Thomas Hodgson in 1857 – his imagination having been fired by visiting the famous White Horse of Uffington in Oxfordshire.

York

The main problem for York is how to find time to see all that this remarkable city has to offer. Two historical periods – first Roman, then Viking – helped to create the York of today, leaving an astonishingly rich legacy of architectural gems, with the glory of the Minster at its heart. The Roman settlement – known as *Eboracum* – was vital to the Empire right up to the

time when the legions left Britain and went back to Italy.

The city is still skirted by its medieval wall, interrupted by the impressive battlements of the four gates, known as 'bars', on which the heads of traitors were once displayed. Clifford's Tower still sits on its prominent mound; here, 900 years ago, the Jews of York were slaughtered.

York boasts a remarkable collection of medieval churches, any one of which would be the architectural highlight of most other cities. But York's treasures form a long list: the Castle Museum, with artfully reconstructed streets and shops of the past, the Museum Gardens, King's Manor, the Treasurer's House, Merchant Adventurer's Hall and St William's College ... all these and many, many more.

The National Railway Museum chronicles our rich railway heritage, and visitors queue around the block to climb aboard the 'time capsules' of the Jorvik Viking Centre, which transport them back in time into a Viking settlement, where the sights, sounds – and even the smells – of village life have been recreated.

See Walk G, page 290
Hidden York

See Walk K, page 294
Roseberry Topping and Captain Cook Country

Tourist Information
Helmsley: Helmsley Castle (seasonal) (tel: 01439 770173)
York: De Grey Rooms, Exhibition Square (tel: 01904 550099)

A visit to the Shambles in York evokes images of Elizabethan England

THE NORTH YORK MOORS

The most extensive area of moorland in England or Wales, the North York Moors cover 554sq miles (892sq km) of glorious scenery. Rolling hills are ablaze with purple heather in late summer and there are pretty green valleys, with rock-strewn streams, and acres of forest. Apart from the busy seaside resorts, there are only a scattering of small market towns. Most settlements are villages, usually centred on a bridge over a river; the cottages are built of stone with distinctive red pantiled roofs. In the more remote dales and on the moortops, there are isolated farms and shooting lodges, reminders of the great estates which still own much of the land.

Ruins of Whitby's Benedictine abbey; the abbey was founded in AD657 and was the site of the Synod of Whitby in AD664

The Norman remains of Scarborough Castle; the site includes the remains of a Roman signal station

Saints and Poets

Whitby holds a significant place in the history of early Christianity. The abbey, perched on the cliff top, was founded in AD657 by St Hilda, and seven years later it hosted the Synod of Whitby, at which it was decided to adopt Roman, rather than Celtic practice in England. Caedmon, the first English Christian poet, appropriately had his home at the abbey. The dramatic ruins which command the coastline today are those of a much later, 13th-century foundation – on a dark night it is easy to see why Bram Stoker used it as the setting for his novel *Dracula*. St Mary's Church, reached by 199 steps from the harbour below, is a rare survivor from the 18th century, with its double-decker pulpit, galleries and box pews.

The Middle Ages

Originally a Celtic settlement founded in 270BC, Pickering continued to thrive because it lay on the crossroads of the Malton to Whitby and Helmsley to Scarborough roads. The parish church

Early Days

The earliest man-made features on the North York Moors date from the Bronze Age and are appropriately mysterious. The 40 bridestones at Nab Ridge in Bilsdale are the remains of a stone circle, 40ft (12.2m) in diameter, which may once have formed the retaining wall of a burial chamber. Above Grosmont, at High and Low Bridestones, there are remains of stone circles and some standing stones. The most dramatic group is on Bridestones Moor, on the western edge of Dalby Forest, where the huge rocks have been weathered into fantastic shapes by the elements.

The Romans also left their mark. South of Goathland, stretching across Wheeldale Moor, is one of the best-preserved examples of a Roman road in Britain, built to connect the Roman fortress of Malton with Whitby on the coast. Its culverts, kerbstones and foundations, 16ft (4.9m) wide, are visible for 16 miles (25.7km) over this remote moor. The road gave access to Roman forts, dating from AD100, and their remains can be visited at Cawthorn Camps, to the north of Pickering. A Roman signal station, built on the cliffs at Scarborough in about AD370, is the only one of five on the coast to have been excavated.

Narrow, steeply-sloping streets in Robin Hoods Bay, once a smuggler's paradise

Scarborough's Victorian Spa complex looks out over the sands, while just to the north (top left) stands the Grade 2 listed Grand Hotel

is deservedly famous for its unusually complete set of medieval wall paintings, but it is the ruins of its motte-and-bailey castle which dominate this busy market town. Dating from the 12th century, the castle was reputedly used as a hunting lodge by every king from 1100 to 1400. Parts of the old Royal Forest of Pickering are still Crown Land, and there are forest drives, nature trails and picnic sites in nearby Dalby Forest.

The Normans built an even more impressive castle at Scarborough, with a curtain wall which envelops the headland; its massive square keep, rising 80ft (24.4m) high, is a landmark for miles around, though the rest of the castle was almost completely destroyed during the Civil War.

Seafarers and Smugglers

The coastal towns of the North York Moors enjoyed their heyday in the 18th century. Whitby was then the base for a hugely successful whaling fleet, commemorated in Pannett Park Museum (there is a massive whalebone arch on the north cliff), and for colliers plying the North Sea. The Rev William Scoresby (1789–1857), son of a local whaling captain and explorer, unusually combined a career in the church with Arctic explorations, and became a leading authority on magnetism. Captain James Cook (1728–1779), the explorer and map-maker, also learned his trade in Whitby. Though the town still has a fishing fleet and is famous for its shellfish, its importance as a port and harbour has declined.

Further down the coast, at Robin Hood's Bay, a more notorious trade was carried on. This town, its cobbled streets and tiny cottages crammed into the small gap between the sea and steep cliffs, was a haven for smugglers. The only access is on foot down a long, narrow and precipitous road, though there are plenty of cafés and inns in which to break the journey.

Victorian Seaside Spas

It was in the 19th century that the greatest changes came to the seaside towns of Scarborough and Whitby. Scarborough had claimed healing properties for its waters, taken from the stream flowing across the South Sands, for almost 200 years. They were said to cure asthma, skin diseases and melancholy as well as to cleanse the blood and stomach.

The town also lays claim to the invention of the bathing machine which enabled bathers to maintain their modesty. The craze for sea-bathing, another highly regarded cure for all manner of ills, swept the whole of the country. Anne Brontë (1820–1849), was one of many invalids who came to Scarborough for the sea cure. She died in here in 1849 and is buried in St Mary's churchyard.

Scarborough and Whitby were immensely fashionable in Victorian and Edwardian times, and many elegant buildings date from that time. Whitby's jet industry also thrived. The coal-black mineral was cut, polished and turned into mourning jewellery; it became an essential fashion item when adopted by the widowed Queen Victoria.

The Moors Today

The enduring popularity of the east coast owes much to the long sandy beaches, while the lure of the wild moorland and its communities never fades. Some of its spectacular views can be enjoyed from the steam trains of the North York Moors Railway, running 18 miles (28.9km) from Pickering to Grosmont; others can be seen along the 93 miles (149.6km) of the Cleveland Way footpath, which skirts the northern and western edges of the moors and then follows the coast towards Scarborough.

One major attraction of the moors is the Ryedale Folk Museum in pretty Hutton-le-Hole, illustrating more than 2,000 years of local history with an array of fascinating bygones. This is one of Britain's most remarkable open-air museums, with a reconstructed cruck house, Elizabethan manor and cottages from three different centuries. The museum also contains the oldest daylight photographic studio in England and a small glassmaking furnace of 1590 from Rosedale Abbey.

The North York Moors Railway; the line runs between the market town of Pickering and the village of Grosmont

THE ISLE OF MAN

The Isle of Man is Britain in miniature, encompassing rocky cliffs, long sandy beaches, moorland and forest glens. The gulf stream warms the south and the Atlantic winds blow over the mountains of the north. Celtic and Viking civilisations have left a permanent legacy, including Tynwald (the Manx Parliament) the Manx Gaelic language and a lasting spirit of independence.

Manx Railways

One of the best ways of seeing the Isle of Man, if the Raad ny Foillan (Road of the Gulls) around the coastline is too arduous for your taste, is to use the railways. Sixteen steam engines, mostly built in Manchester, pull trains from Douglas to Port Erin during the summer months; this scenic route, notable for its absence of platforms, travels by the sea and passes through Castletown. A more dramatic route is taken by the Manx Electric Railway, which clings precariously to the sheer cliffs of Maughold Head and Dhoon Bay as it wends its way from Douglas to Ramsey via Laxey. Best of all is the Snaefell Mountain Railway, which opened in 1895 and runs from Laxey to the summit of Snaefell, 2,000ft (609.6m) above. From this vantage point, on a clear day, you can see England, Scotland, Wales and Ireland.

Castletown

A gem of a town, still bustling with ordinary working life despite its venerable history, Castletown is built around a picturesque harbour at the mouth of the Silverburn. Narrow winding streets and stone cottages huddle close to the massive bulk of 600-year-old Castle Rushen, the centre of Manx government until 1874. It has also housed the island prison, lunatic asylum and barracks, as well as being the home of the Stanley family, Earls of Derby and Lords of Man. The Manx Nautical Museum includes the armed yacht *Peggy*, last in a line of locally built clippers.

Horse-drawn trams in Douglas, the island's capital

Colourful blooms of thrift on the Calf of Man, looking across the Irish Sea to the Isle of Man

The Calf of Man

A mile (1.6km) square and rising 400ft (121.9m) from the sea, the Calf of Man is the largest of three uninhabited islands off the southern tip of Man. Owned by the Manx Museum and National Trust since 1937, it is now a nature reserve for large colonies of puffins, kittiwakes, razorbills, guillemots and grey seals. Access for walkers, during the summer and in good weather only, is by boat from Port Erin or Port St Mary; remember to ensure that they return to pick you up! If the walk is too strenuous, boat trips round the Calf are a delightful alternative, bringing you close to the seabirds nesting on the cliffs and seal colonies on the shores; basking sharks can often be seen in the bay.

Cregneash Village Folk Museum

A unique survivor of the traditional Manx way of life, this small crofting hamlet of single-storey thatched cottages, restored by the Manx Museum, overlooks the beautiful Calf Sound. The cottages contain typical furniture and everyday equipment, and demonstrations of traditional crafts take place in summer. The Meayl stone circle nearby is one of several Bronze-Age sites on the island.

Douglas

The largest town on the island, spreading for 2 miles (3.2km) along the sandy curve of Douglas Bay's natural harbour, Douglas is the modern capital of Man and an internationally important finance centre. Thanks to its superb beach, mild climate and hundreds of Victorian and Edwardian hotels and guesthouses, tourism has flourished in Douglas since the mid-19th century. Ferries from Britain and Ireland still dock in the harbour at the southern end of the town and horse-drawn trams carry passengers the length of the promenade in a service that began in 1876. The Manx Museum houses the treasures of the island's ancient history, while modern shops and restaurants, specialising in locally caught seafood, make this the busiest of all its towns.

Laxey

One of the island's most striking sights is the Lady Isabella, the world's largest working waterwheel, built in 1854 to drain the Laxey lead mines. Dominating the narrow valley, it can be seen from many miles around, and there are fine views over the lower slopes of Snaefell and the sea from the top of the wheel. The village of Laxey consists of rows of miners' cottages, and a small section of the mine is open to the public in summer. Remnants of the old tramways which carried ore from the mines can still be seen, but Laxey station is also the starting point for the spectacular Snaefell Mountain Railway. Another traditional industry is in operation at the Laxey Woollen Mills on Glen Road, where Manx tweed is woven on handlooms.

Peel

Boasting the only cathedral on the Isle of Man, Peel is a small but busy fishing town on the west coast. A jumble of narrow streets and cottages leads from the Market Square, with its unusual raised churchyard, down to the harbour where seals greet the fishing boats.

The dramatic ruins of Peel Castle command the coastline. Built on St Patrick's Isle and joined to the mainland by a short causeway, the castle seems part of the natural fortress of rock which gave sanctuary to monks fleeing Viking raids. A 10th-century tower, the medieval ruins of St Germain's Cathedral and burial sites within the castle precincts have provided exciting new archaeological evidence of Norse and pre-Norse Celtic settlements. *Odin's Raven*, a replica Viking ship which sailed from Norway to the Isle of Man to celebrate the island's millennium in 1979, can be seen on the quayside.

St John's

Though little more than a straggling village, St John's is physically and historically central to Manx history. Lying at the heart of the island, at the junction of all four major routes, it was the natural meeting place for Viking settlers who established their Tynwald, the independent Manx Parliament, there. Now, as then, the curious grassy mound, rising in tiers, is the centrepiece of the annual opening ceremonies, where the elected members of the House of Keys meet. Hidden in the trees behind Tynwald Green, former woollen mills are now a huge craft centre, specialising in locally produced goods.

Mummers (folk dramatists) in the Manx Tynwald annual celebration, St John's

Tourist Information
Douglas: Sea Terminal
(tel: 01624 686801)

Peel Castle on St Patrick's Isle, where one archaeological dig revealed a treasure trove of 11th-century coins, and the grave of the 'Pagan Lady' with her Viking necklace

THE LAKELAND OF THE POETS

Despite its popularity, most of this beautiful northwest corner of England retains its air of emptiness and remoteness. Narrow passes, soaring mountains, plunging waterfalls and lakes of every shape and size create a landscape which has inspired poets, writers and artists for 200 years. And in countless towns and villages you can discover the real life of Cumbria.

Ambleside, dwarfed by the surrounding mountains, is a good northern base from which to explore Lake Windermere

Ambleside

Picturesquely situated at the head of Windermere, with mountains on three sides, this attractive Victorian town was celebrated by the Lakeland Poets. Wordsworth, Coleridge, De Quincey and Southey all lived in or near the town, making Ambleside a fashionable place to visit. A little way to the north is Rydal Mount, the home of William Wordsworth from 1813 until his death in 1850. In a wonderful setting, the house contains many of the poet's possessions and first editions of his work.

Grasmere

William Wordsworth lived at Grasmere with his sister, wife and young family from 1799 to 1808, writing some of his finest poetry in what he described as 'the loveliest spot that man hath ever found'. His home, Dove Cottage, is open to the public and an exhibition centre next door displays his manuscripts and memorabilia. Before Wordsworth arrived, the cottage was an inn called The Dove and Olive. In the village is the churchyard where the Wordsworths and Samuel Taylor Coleridge are buried; the studio of the Lakeland artist, W. Heaton Cooper, is also worth a visit. And you can fortify yourself on the way home with some of Sarah Nelson's Original Celebrated Grasmere Gingerbread, baked to a traditional local recipe in the old village school.

Hawkshead

Hawkshead has a delightful network of narrow streets, with alleyways and arches, leading to the square. In Main Street is the Beatrix Potter Gallery, with a changing exhibition of illustrations from her children's books and a display about her work and life in the Lake District.

To the southeast at Near Sawrey is Hill Top, an unpretentious 17th-century farmhouse with a delightful cottage garden, where Beatrix Potter wrote and illustrated many of her books between 1905 and 1913. Hill Top has been preserved unaltered, and its particular delight is that so much is recognisable from the stories – the dolls that were the models for Lucinda and Jane, the grandfather clock in the Tailor of Gloucester's kitchen, the garden explored

The lake at Grasmere, central Cumbria

Coniston and Grizedale Forest Park

The steam yacht *Gondola,* first launched in 1859 and later restored by the National Trust, runs a daily service during the summer from Coniston pier to Brantwood. It crosses the lake where Donald Campbell was killed in 1967, trying to break the speed record in his jet-powered *Bluebird,* and the whole scene is dominated by the brooding mass of the mountain known as Coniston Old Man.

On the hills above Brantwood the Forestry Commission has created Grizedale Forest, the first of their enterprises which actively encouraged visitors by providing special facilities. A visitor centre illustrates the story of the forest and offers information on walks and wildlife. Grizedale has some of the best nature trails in the country (red squirrels, roe and red deer can all be seen), with forest walks, picnic areas, a tree nursery and a wildlife museum. At the heart of the woodland is the Theatre in the Forest, which hosts a variety of community events. Nearby is the Gallery in the Forest, which has art, sculpture and craft exhibitions. There is also outdoor art in the form of a unique Sculpture Trail through the forest.

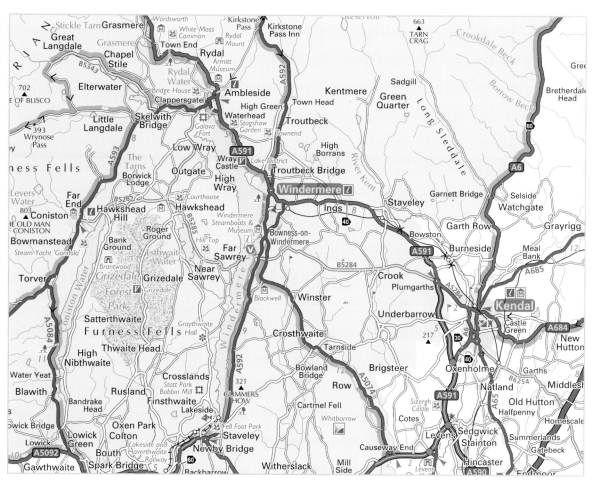

See Walk H, page 291
Around Buttermere

See Walk I, page 292
Brant Fell above Bowness-on-Windermere

Tourist Information

Ambleside: Central Buildings, Market Cross (seasonal) (tel: 015394 32582)
Coniston: Ruskin Avenue (seasonal), (tel: 015394 41533)
Hawkshead: Main Street (seasonal), (tel: 015394 36946)
Kendal: Town Hall, Highgate (tel: 01539 797516)
Windermere: Victoria Street (tel: 015394 46499)

by Tom Kitten and even the rhubarb patch favoured by Jemima Puddleduck.

The Poets

The Lake District was an unregarded corner of England until the poets of the early 19th century Romantic movement began to celebrate its beauties. Most famous of this group of friends was William Wordsworth (1770–1850), who was appointed Poet Laureate in 1843. Settling first at Dove Cottage, Grasmere, he then moved to Rydal Mount, just outside Ambleside, where he spent the rest of his life. Samuel Taylor Coleridge (1772–1834) collaborated with him in *Lyrical Ballads* and spent four years at Keswick. Robert Southey (1774–1843), Wordsworth's predecessor as Poet Laureate and renowned as both a poet and biographer, lived at Greta Hall, Keswick.

Kendal

Once famous for its cloth and snuff, Kendal is now better known for its Mint Cake, the essential standby of hillwalkers and explorers. The steep streets of the town are dominated by the hill-top ruins of the castle where Catherine Parr, sixth and last wife of Henry VIII, was born. Narrow enclosed yards, where the weavers lived and worked, survive behind the shop fronts of Stricklandgate and Highgate. Down by the river are the grounds of Abbot Hall, now an Art Gallery with a museum of local life and industry. Kendal has remained unspoilt by tourism and is a busy working town with a weekly market.

Troutbeck

A typical Lakeland hillside village, spread out along a narrow lane, Troutbeck consists of a series of groups of farms and cottages. At the southern end is Townend, a modest farmhouse built by a yeoman farmer on his marriage in 1625. Home to the same family for more than 300 years, it remained virtually untouched by the passing years. Visiting times are limited to daylight hours, as there is no electricity.

Windermere

Windermere is the largest natural freshwater lake in England, more than 10 miles (16.1km) long, 1 mile (1.6km) wide and 200ft (61m) deep. Boating and watersport facilities here are excellent. A good place to start your visit is at the Lake District National Park Visitor Centre at Brockhole, which stands in 32 acres (13ha) of landscaped gardens on the eastern shore of the lake. As well as information about the park, there are various exhibitions, lake cruises an adventure playground and special events.

The town of Windermere grew up around the railway station, and gradually spread along the lakeside into Bowness. Dedicated to visitors, the town has a huge range of accommodation. Sight-seeing launches depart from piers at Bowness-on-Windermere and Waterhead every half hour, and trips are also available on a Victorian steam launch from the Windermere Steamboat Museum at Bowness. Here, a historic collection of Victorian and Edwardian craft are on show, including the world's oldest steamboat.

Bowness-on-Windermere, where boats of all sizes set sail out onto the lake

CARLISLE AND THE WESTERN WALL

On the border between England and Scotland, where warfare was endemic until the mid-18th century, this beautiful landscape and its sparse settlements bear the marks of continual violence. Most striking of all is Hadrian's Wall, 73 miles (117.5km) long and almost 2,000 years old, marking the northern boundary of the Roman Empire.

An intact section of Hadrian's Wall. The wall was the most heavily fortified border in the Roman Empire

Black cannon at the battlements of Carlisle Castle

Gilsland

Hadrian's Wall passes through this small village, the most westerly in Northumberland, and a section of it is in the vicarage garden. One of the best preserved milecastles on the wall, with remains of north and south gates, walls and two small barrack blocks, can be found near the railway bridge. The River Irthing flows just north of the village through a delightful wooded gorge with romantic associations – Sir Walter Scott proposed to Charlotte Carpenter at the Popping Stone.

Carlisle

Known as *Luguvalium* in Roman times, Carlisle is the only historic English town or city not mentioned in the Domesday Book, because it was in Scotland at the time, on the other side of a border which has moved a number of times during the course of history. Its castle and city walls were begun by William Rufus, who recaptured it from the Scots in 1092, but for the next 700 years it was a garrison town and scene of many battles between the English and the Scots. The castle hosted parliaments under Edward I, the 'Hammer of the Scots', and medieval prisoners of war, who scratched their marks on the cell walls, were incarcerated there. In later years, another temporary lodger was Mary, Queen of Scots; Queen Mary's Tower now houses the King's Own Royal Border Regiment Museum.

After the 1745 rebellion, peace and prosperity, based on the textile trade, descended on the town. Many elegant streets and the attractive Town Hall in the Market Square date from this time. Medieval Carlisle is portrayed in the Guildhall Museum in Green Market, while the Tullie House Museum and Art Gallary houses an imaginative interpretation of Border history, with a stroll through Roman Carlisle, a climb on part of Hadrian's turf wall and other displays.

Greenhead

There has been a river crossing at Greenhead since at least Roman times. The A69 is the latest of a series of important routes crossing the Tipalt Burn, following both the Maiden Way and the Stanegate Roman road, which served Hadrian's Wall. The village lies in a small hollow beside the burn, and to the north are the picturesque ruins of medieval Thirlwell Castle, where Edward I is reputed to have stayed on one of his many brutal campaigns against the Scots. Around 0.5 mile (0.8km) further east, next to one of the highest standing sections of Hadrian's Wall, is the unexcavated Roman fort of *Carvoran*, where a Roman Army Museum, with excellent access for disabled visitors, depicts the life and times of the Roman soldier.

Haltwhistle

A small market town serving the South Tyne valley, Haltwhistle suffered badly during the Border raids of the Middle Ages. Suggestions of its violent past are to be seen everywhere. The Red Lion Inn incorporates a medieval peel tower, as does the nearby Jacobean mansion, Featherstone Castle. The Holy Cross Church is one of the most important in

The River Irthing near Gilsland

Hadrian's Wall

When the Emperor Hadrian visited Britain in AD122 he decided to solve the problem of the troublesome northern tribes by building a wall from coast to coast. Taking advantage of a prominent natural ridge, a massive fortification around 73 miles (117km) long was built from a million cubic yards of stone, strengthened at key points by forts, milecastles and turrets. The project took about five years to complete, but succeeded in holding back the Picts for more than 200 years. Now a World Heritage Site, the Romans' tremendous achievement can still be appreciated; substantial portions of both the stone section, running from Newcastle to Gilsland, and the turf rampart from Gilsland to Bowness, can be seen and excavations, most notably at Housesteads, have revealed the forts and living quarters of the garrisons. Other Roman sites worth visiting are Birdoswald, near Gilsland, Chesters Fort and Museum at Walwick, Corbridge, Carrawburgh and Vindolanda at Bardon Mill, where a new gallery is under construction.

Northumberland. Originally built in Saxon times, on a site associated with St Aidan and St Paulinus, the present church was sensitively restored in Victorian times, but dates principally from the 13th century.

Lanercost Priory

There has been continuous worship at Lanercost Priory since the 12th century, despite Henry VIII's Dissolution of the Monasteries. Though some of the monks were executed, the nave of the old Priory of Augustinian canons is now the local parish church, and many of the other original buildings are remarkably well preserved. Red sandstone blocks taken from Hadrian's Wall by the monks can still be seen in the Priory remains, together with a fine collection of Roman altar stones in the undercroft.

Talkin Tarn

A 65-acre (26ha) lake, ideal for boating, fishing and swimming, lies just north of Talkin at the heart of Talkin Tarn Country Park. There are sandy bays around the tarn and a signposted nature trail leads through attractive woodland. From the top of the wooded rise behind the Victorian boathouse are some lovely views over the surrounding countryside.

Arched window and ceilings of Lanercost Priory, founded by Robert de Veaux during the reign of Henry II in 1166 to house Augustinian canons

Wetheral

At the centre of Wetheral is a large triangular green, edged with gracious houses built from the distinctive local red sandstone. Two buildings stand out from the rest – Eden Bank, a grandiose mock château of the 19th century, which has millstones set in its garden wall, and the elegant Crown Hotel, with a columned porch. An early five-arched railway bridge spans the wide River Eden, and from the footpaths in Wetheral woods, to the south of the village, there are charming views of the picturesque ruins of Corby Castle on the opposite bank. Nearby, a 15th-century gatehouse is all that survives of the local Benedictine priory. Also overlooking the river is Holy Trinity Church, with an unusual octagonal tower and some splendid effigies.

Wetheral Train viaduct was begun in 1830 and finished in 1834; it is a memorial to Henry Howard, Esq. of Corby Castle

Tourist Information
Brampton: Moot Hall, Market Place (seasonal) (tel: 016977 3433)
Carlisle: Carlisle Visitor Centre, Old Town Hall, Green Market, (tel: 01228 625600)
Haltwhistle: Church Hall, Main Street (tel: 01434 322002)

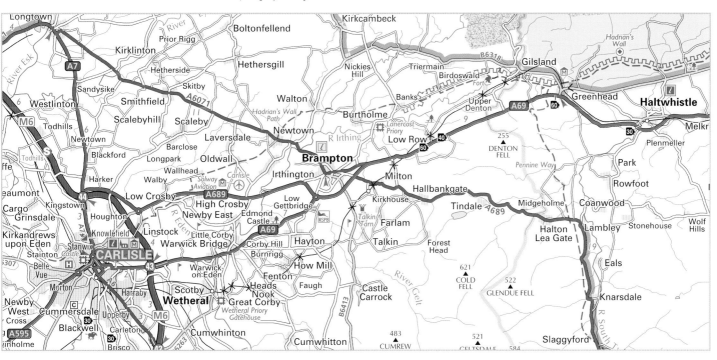

THE CITY ABOVE THE WEAR

Once at the heart of the ancient kingdom of Northumbria, Durham's importance is reflected in the fact that its cathedral and castle have been declared a World Heritage Site. Ruined abbeys and ancient churches testify to the region's role in spreading Christianity, while Roman remains and medieval castles tell the story of its often violent past.

Converted from a banqueting hall, the chapel at Auckland Castle ranks among the largest private chapels in Britain

Auckland Castle

An 18th-century gatehouse leads from the market square of Bishop Auckland into the 800 acres (324ha) of woodland and lawn of Bishop's Park. A Gothic-style cloister in the park is an unusual deer shelter of the same period. Home of the Bishops of Durham since 1183, the present 13th-century castle (also known as the palace) is separated from the park by a screen of stone arches. Its Great Hall, state apartments and exceptional chapel, converted from a banqueting hall in 1660, are periodically open to the public. The park is open all year round.

Brancepeth

Dominated by its castle, the origins of which go back to Saxon times, Brancepeth is a delight to explore, particularly on foot.

👣 **See Walk L, page 295**
Historic Hexham

Tourist Information

Durham: Millennium Place (tel: 0191 384 3720)
Newcastle upon Tyne: The Guildhall, Quayside, and 8–9 Central Arcade (tel: 0191 277 8000)
Peterlee: 20 The Upper Chare (tel: 0191 586 4450)

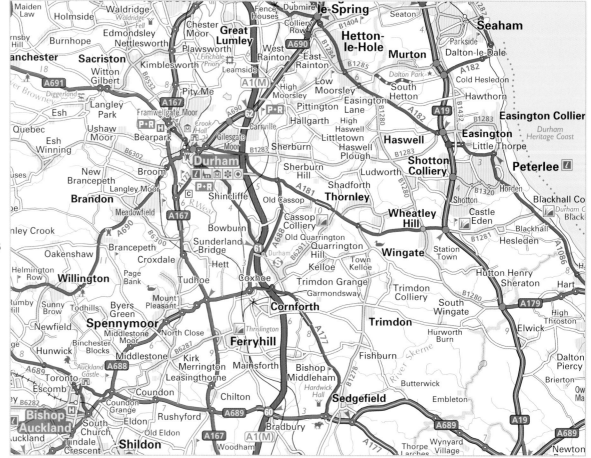

Pinnacled west towers and central crossing tower of Durham's Norman cathedral are visible through the trees towering over the stone buildings of Fuller Mill, The Mill is on the banks of the River Tyne adjacent to a weir

Rows of pretty Georgian cottages line the village streets, but the 12th-century church of St Brandon stands apart, in its own wooded grounds within the castle curtilage. Although badly damaged by fire in 1998, the building was meticulously restored and still contains the tombs of the Neville family who once owned the castle. The castle itself, which is now in private hands, was virtually rebuilt in 1837 by Matthew Patterton, son of a wealthy mine owner who had purchased the property. Its distinctive 'chessmen' watchtowers are the work of his architect, John Patterson of Edinburgh.

Durham

Built within a loop of the River Wear, on a high sandstone outcrop, Durham has one of the most dramatic skylines of any city. The cathedral and nearby castle, towering high on a bluff above the river, are an unforgettable composition of Norman splendour. The site was chosen by monks in AD995 as a sanctuary from Viking raids for the bones of St Cuthbert, one of the founders of English Christianity. Its present cathedral, rebuilt in stone in 1093, was the seat of the wealthy Prince Bishops who enjoyed a unique position of secular and ecclesiastical power. Close by is the Norman castle which, together with most of the buildings round Palace Green and in the North and South Bailey, is now part of the famous university, England's third oldest, after Oxford and Cambridge. It contains a fascinating Oriental Museum. Predominantly a Georgian and Victorian city, Durham has many good shops, hotels and museums, and there are pleasant riverside walks and picnic places.

Binchester Blocks

Fine views of Auckland Castle are seen from Binchester Blocks, less than 1 mile (1.6km) to the north. Excavations here have uncovered a Roman fort, *Vinovia*, built on Dere Street, the main route from York to Hadrian's Wall, in AD80 to guard one or possibly two bridges over the River Wear. A number of buildings have been identified, the most important being a bath suite attached to the commanding officer's house, the finest of its kind in Britain.

Finchale Priory

A reformed pirate, St Godric, founded a wooden hermitage at Finchale on the banks of the River Wear in 1110. After his death, tales of his sanctity and reports of miracles at his tomb, which is marked by a cross on the floor, brought monks from Durham Priory to found a monastery on the site in 1180. The present ruins date from the rebuilding of 1237, which proved to be too grandiose for its community to support. By the 14th century the Priory had become a holiday retreat for monks from Durham, who abandoned the refectory and greatly reduced the size of the church, keeping up only the prior's lodgings and domestic residence. Henry VIII's Dissolution of the Monasteries in 1536 ended all monastic life here.

Millennium Bridge in Newcastle upon Tyne, the Sage Gateshead music venue (centre) and the Baltic Centre for Contemporary Art (left)

Peterlee

Named after Peter Lee (1864–1935), who began work underground at the age of 10 and rose to be President of the International Federation of Miners, this town was built in 1950 to serve as a dormitory for the local coalfields and a centre for the surrounding villages. It claims to be the most attractive of the northeast's new towns. Lying amidst gently rolling countryside 2 miles (3.2km) from the sea, the characteristics of the site were fully exploited by the planners, who created attractively grouped housing which is well segregated from the industrial areas. Peterlee quickly established its own character and, despite the decline in mining, has succeeded in attracting new industry.

Seaham

A late Saxon church, with Roman stones in its walls and a 12th-century font, stands on the top of the limestone cliffs of Seaham. There are stunning views over the privately operated harbour built by Lord Londonderry in 1828 for the shipment of coal from his mines in the locality. Seaham, like so much of the northeast, has suffered from the decline of the Durham coalfields and no pits now work here. The seafront has been cleaned up and new 'natural' landscapes created. To the north of the town is Seaham Hall, a white mansion, now a hospital, where Lord Byron stayed after his marriage to the heiress, Anne Millbanke, in 1815. As he separated from her the following year and left England for ever, this may account for his jaundiced comment that the coast here was dreary.

Newcastle upon Tyne

The commercial and industrial capital of the northeast is a grandiose city which, at the dawn of the 21st century, had reinvented itself to keep pace with the region's economic changes. Ten bridges cross the River Tyne here, linking the city with the borough of Gateshead, the newest being the Millennium Bridge, which opened in 2001. George Stephenson's high-level, two-tier bridge is one of the most remarkable feats of Victorian engineering. Built in 1849, it carries both the railway and a road. Stephenson, the great railway pioneer, was born 8 miles (12.9km) west of the city at Wylam, the son of a colliery fireman. He taught himself to read and write, and went on to build the world's first public railway line and the *Rocket* locomotive. His home now belongs to the National Trust.

Fishing boats moored in Seaham, County Durham

ALNWICK

Described as the last great wilderness in England, Northumberland encompasses the remote and empty Cheviot hills, mile upon mile of sandy beaches and rugged islands which were once the bastions of early Christianity. Hadrian's Wall, pele towers and castles bear abundant and stern witness to the centuries of violence this border country has endured. While they were once an essential means of survival, now they simply add further romance to a landscape of contrasts.

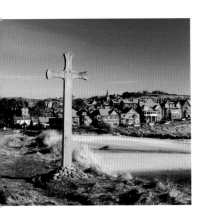

A large cross on Church Hill, Alnmouth, marks the spot where a Norman church dedicated to St Waleric once stood

Alnmouth

The quiet, pretty seaside town of Alnmouth sits where the River Aln meets the North Sea. Once a busy centre of shipbuilding and a grain port, the great storm of 1806 changed the course of the river, destroyed the Norman church and closed the harbour. Now all that remains of that industrial past are the 18th-century granaries, converted into houses which jostle for room with the shops and ancient inns in the narrow streets. The sands stretch as far as the eye can see, part of the 56-mile (90km) Northumbrian Heritage Coast.

Alnwick

Still home to the Percy family, whose ancestors ruled much of northern England for 200 years as Earls of Northumberland, Alnwick is dominated by its superb castle. A massive keep and curtain wall reflect its importance as a medieval military stronghold but the interiors, restored in the 18th and 19th centuries by Robert Adam and Anthony Salvin, are Italian Renaissance on a monumental scale. The only surviving gateway to the original walls of the town is the Hotspur Tower, built in 1450 by the son of Harry Hotspur, who was immortalised by Shakespeare in *Henry IV*. His rebellion cost the family dear, as did their participation in Catholic uprisings from the Pilgrimage of Grace to the Gunpowder Plot, but no king could afford to ignore the powerful Percys, who were always restored to favour.

Bamburgh

One of Britain's most impressive castles, built on a huge outcrop of rock rising dramatically above the flat sandy beach, Bamburgh has a venerable history going back to at least AD547, when it was a stronghold of Northumbrian royalty. St Aidan, a monk from Iona, first established a wooden church in Bamburgh in AD635; its successor dates mainly from

🐾 **See Walk M, page 296**
Kirknewton and Ancient Yeavering Bell

🐾 **See Walk N, page 297**
Berwick Town Walls

Tourist Information
Alnwick: 2 The Shambles (tel: 01665 510333)
Berwick-upon-Tweed: 106 Marygate (tel: 01289 330733)
Craster: Craster Car Park (seasonal)
(tel: 01665 576007)

Bamburgh Castle is an impressive sight from the sands that lie to the north

the 13th century. Grace Darling, daughter of the lighthouse keeper and heroine of the rescue of the shipwrecked *Forfarshire*, is buried in the churchyard. The cottage in which she was born is opposite the church and a Grace Darling Museum commemorates her valour.

Craster

This fishing village centres round a tiny harbour built by the Craster family in memory of a soldier brother who was killed in 1906 fighting in the Tibetan campaign. The small local fleet fishes mainly for crabs, lobster and salmon. The kippers for which the town is famous are smoked in a building on the harbour, but the herrings are now purchased from Scotland. The Craster family, after whom the village is named, still own Craster Tower, which was their home for more than 700 years. A dramatic but not too strenuous walk from the village leads to the ruins of Dunstanburgh Castle. Built

Holy Island and Chillingham Castle

Just outside the area are two very different places which are both well worth a visit. Holy Island (Lindisfarne), perhaps the most famous of all religious retreats, lies to the north of the Farne Islands. It has a ruined 11th-century priory, built on the site of St Aidan's seventh-century monastery, which was destroyed by Vikings, and a Tudor castle, restored by Sir Edward Lutyens with gardens designed by Gertrude Jekyll. Accessible only at low tides via a narrow causeway from Beal, no crossing should be attempted in the two hours before and three hours after high tide.

The ancestral home of the Earl of Tankarville, medieval Chillingham Castle is privately owned but is open to the public in summer. Here you might catch a glimpse of the unique herd of wild cattle which have roamed the estate for 700 years. With their distinctive white colouring and large horns, they are believed to be similar to the oxen used by the ancient Britons. The prehistoric remains of Ross Castle, an earthwork with a double rampart, can be seen to the east of the village where the ground rises 1,000ft (304.8m), giving wonderful views all around.

The Farne Islands' peaty soil is perfect for Puffins, with close to 50,000 pairs regularly nesting in excavated burrows there

Berwick-upon-Tweed

Fought over by English and Scots, the border town of Berwick-upon-Tweed changed hands 14 times between 1147 and 1482. The town is a product of its violent past, with fortified walls dating back to the 14th century and a ruined castle – ironically demolished not by military action but by the Victorians, who wanted to build a railway station. Fine views of the harbour and town, with its cobbled streets and jumble of houses, can be seen from the walls. The museum of the King's Own Scottish Borderers is housed in the 18th-century Berwick Barracks at Ravensdowne, the oldest purpose-built barracks in the country. The town museum and art gallery are also housed in the barracks.

in 1316 on a rocky promontory, which rises sheer from the sea, it has superb coastal views.

Farne Islands

Seventeen different species of seabird and a large colony of grey seals have made these treeless islands a remarkable wildlife sanctuary. Depending on the height of the tide, there are between 15 and 28 islands, of which only Inner Farne and Staple are open to visitors. Each island has rocky cliffs in the south and west and slopes gently to the sea in the north and east. Inner Farne was a favoured retreat for hermits; most famously, St Cuthbert lived there for six years and, after he became Bishop of Lindisfarne, returned to the islands to die in AD687. A chapel to his memory is one of the few remaining buildings.

Warkworth

A horseshoe-shaped loop in the River Coquet almost encircles this pretty village, and its main street leads straight up the hill to the striking ruins of Warkworth Castle, birthplace of Harry Hotspur. The castle was owned by the Percy family for over 600 years and has a huge, cruciform keep, 12th-century Great Hall and vaulted gatehouse. The medieval stone-cobbled bridge, which carried traffic over the Coquet until 1965, provided an outer defence to the village and castle and is a rare example of a fortified bridge.

Beside the river, and only accessible by boat, are a small 14th-century hermitage and chapel, hewn out of the rockface by Sir Bertram of Bothal as a penance for accidentally killing the woman he loved. A Norman church replaced the eighth-century Saxon one, built by King Ceolwulf of Northumbria, which was destroyed by the Danes; it has the longest nave in the county and was the site of a massacre by the Scots of 300 villagers in 1174.

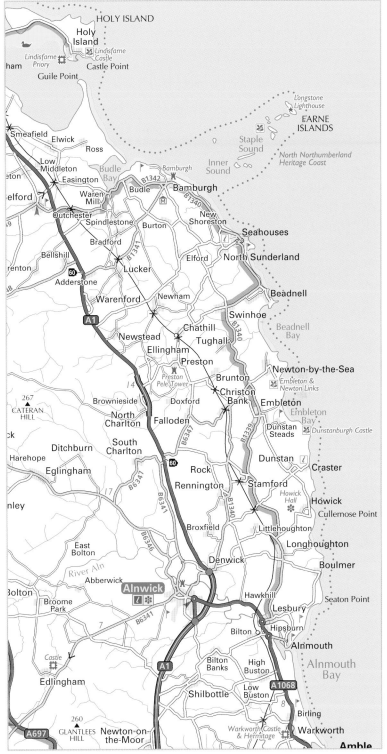

Craster's famous oak-smoked kippers

Walk A
FOLLOWING IN THE STEPS OF MR DARCY

A circuit of the attractive grounds of Lyme Park, used in the well-known TV adaptation of Pride and Prejudice.

National Trust gardens, Disley

Distance: 5.5 miles (8.8km)
Minimum time: 3hrs 30min
Ascent/Gradient: 950ft (290m) ▲▲▲
Level of difficulty: +++
Paths: Generally firm, field tracks can be slippery if wet, a few stiles
Landscape: Rolling parkland and fields, some moorland
Suggested map: OS Explorer OL1 Dark Peak
Start/finish: Grid reference: SJ 964823
Dog friendliness: On lead in deer sanctuary and around livestock
Parking: Lyme Park, off A6 (free to National Trust members)
Public toilets: By Old Workshop Coffee Shop, near main car park

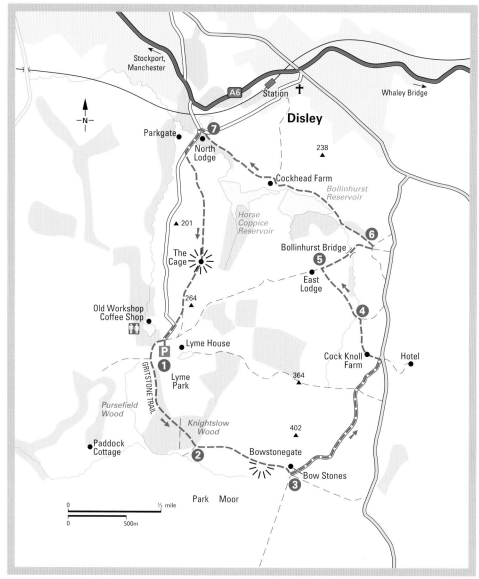

❶ With the lake on your right-hand side and the house on your left, leave the car park by the drive and, as it begins to bend to the right, turn left for a wide track to go through a gate signposted 'Gritstone Trail'. Follow this through Knightslow Wood, through several gates, until you emerge on moorland.

❷ Go straight ahead/left on the main track as it climbs the moorland, aiming for the small TV masts on the skyline. At the top, cross a stile and a short field to emerge at the end of a surfaced lane by the Bow Stones.

❸ Turn left and follow the lane downhill until you reach its junction with another road, opposite the driveway to a hotel. Turn left and walk up the drive of Cock Knoll Farm. When you get to the buildings head right, across the

farmyard, as indicated by footpath signs. At the far side, go through a gate and down the left-hand side of a field.

❹ As you draw level with a small thicket in the shallow valley on the left, go over a stile and through the trees. Out on the other side head right, across the bottom of a field. Clear waymarks now point you through several rough fields to a walled lane on the far side.

❺ Once you're on the lane, turn right and continue over Bollinhurst Bridge. (If you turn left you can take a short cut back to the house via East Lodge.) Beyond Macclesfield Borough's newly planted Millennium Wood, you reach a junction of tracks. Go through the gate on the left and take a grassy track, half left, signed to North Lodge.

❻ Descend the right-hand side of a rough field to the woodlands at the bottom. The path now goes over several stiles as it skirts round Bollinhurst Reservoir – keep close to the wall on your left. A newly waymarked, gated path takes you around the side of Cockhead Farm, and then continues across another field and down a shaded gravel lane. At the end of the lane turn right, on to a surfaced drive, to reach North Lodge.

❼ Go through the pedestrian gate at the lodge, then turn left and walk along the main drive for about 250 yards (229m). Take the obvious footpath up the hillside on your left, between a short avenue of trees, to reach the top of the open, grassy ridge. Head for the hilltop folly, The Cage, then continue straight on to return to the house and car park.

LINACRE'S PEACEFUL RETREAT FROM CHESTERFIELD

Three reservoirs secreted between the Chatsworth moors and Chesterfield.

Bluebells on the woodland floor

Distance: 5 miles (8km)
Minimum time: 3hrs
Ascent/Gradient: 820ft (250m) ▲▲▲
Level of difficulty: +++
Paths: Generally good paths and farm lanes, field paths can be muddy at times of high rainfall
Landscape: Wooded valley and pastured hillsides
Suggested map: OS Explorer OL24 White Peak
Start/finish: Grid reference: SK 336727
Dog friendliness: Farmland, dogs should be kept under close control
Parking: Linacre Wood car park
Public toilets: Near car park by Ranger's office

❶ From the bottom of the lowest car park, go down the steps into the woods. After about 100 yards (91m) turn right along a waymarked bridleway heading westwards, high above the lower reservoir. Ignore the path going off to the left, which goes to the dam of the middle reservoir, but continue on the wide bridleway along the north shore of the middle reservoir.

❷ Take the right fork on a footpath raking up to the top end of the woods, high above the upper reservoir's dam. The path continues westwards, dipping to one of the reservoir's inlets. Cross over the lower of two bridges and then follow a well-defined concessionary footpath along the lovely shoreline.

❸ On reaching the end of the reservoir, ignore the left turn over the Birley Brook footbridge, but head west on the waymarked footpath. This soon leaves the woods via a ladder stile and goes straight on through scrub woodland and along the foot of an open slope.

❹ Go left over a wooden footbridge and then cross a stone slab over the brook, and go straight on. A muddy path now climbs through more woods before emerging in fields north of Wigley Hall Farm. It passes to the right of the farm to a tarmac lane in the small hamlet of Wigley. Follow the lane to a crossroads.

❺ Turn left towards Old Brampton. Just beyond the Royal Oak pub turn right down a tarmac bridleway, Bagthorpe Lane, following it past Bagthorpe Farm. The lane, now unsurfaced, descends into the valley of the River Hipper, passing through the farmyard of Frith Hall, down to the river bridge. A winding surfaced track climbs to Westwick Lane, where you should turn left.

❻ Just before Broomhall Farm, descend left on another track down to the river, then continue up the other side of the valley into Old Brampton.

❼ Turn left along the lane, passing the George and Dragon pub and the church, before turning right by a telephone kiosk. The cart track descends to the top edge of Linacre Wood, then swings to the right.

❽ At a junction of paths, turn left and descend to the dam. At the far side of the dam, turn left on the metalled lane, passing the public conveniences and ranger's office and climb back to the car park.

Wild garlic may be found in the woods

HIGH ACKWORTH AND EAST HARDWICK

An undemanding stroll through history in rolling, pastoral countryside to the east of Wakefield.

A grass path near High Ackworth

Distance: 5.5 miles (8.9km)
Minimum time: 2hrs 30min
Ascent/Gradient: 180ft (55m) ▲▲▲
Level of difficulty: +++
Paths: Mostly field paths, 12 stiles
Landscape: Gently rolling, arable country
Suggested map: OS Explorer 278 Sheffield & Barnsley
Start/finish: Grid reference: SE 440180
Dog friendliness: Dogs on leads in villages and through farmyards
Parking: A few parking places in middle of High Ackworth, near church and village green
Public toilets: None en route

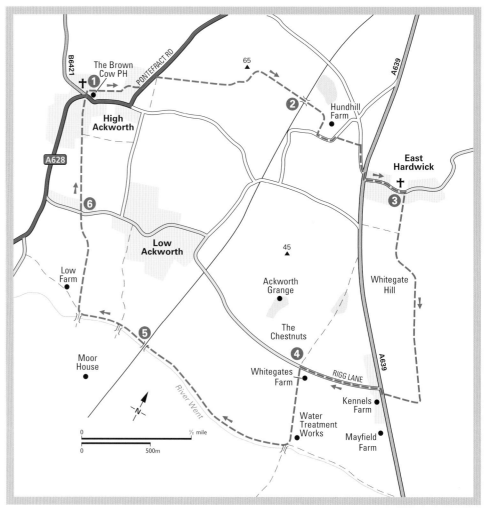

❶ From the top of the village green, take a narrow ginnel immediately to the right of Manor House. Beyond a stile made of stone slabs (not the last you'll see today), keep to the right-hand edge of a small field, to another stile. A ginnel brings you out into Woodland Grove; go left here, then first right, to meet the A628, Pontefract Road. Go left, but for just 100 yards (91m). Look out on the right for a gap in the hedgerow and a footpath sign (opposite a house called Tall Trees). Walk straight across a field (follow the direction of the sign), to a tiny footbridge over a beck. Continue along the right-hand edge of the next two fields. In the third, dog-leg left and right to continue beside the hedge, which then curves left. After 150 yards (137m), watch for an unmarked road striking right, due east across the open field. Continue across a second field to a bridge spanning a railway.

❷ Maintain your direction between fields towards Hundhill Farm. By the farm, turn within the field corner along its bottom edge to a stile. Emerging on to a lane, go left, walking 100 yards (91m) to round a bend. Immediately after, go over a stile on the right to follow an enclosed path. Beyond the next stile, turn right along a minor road that soon meets the A639.

Cross to Darrington Road opposite, passing the old village pump, and walk into the village of East Hardwick. Where the road swings left, look out for a sign ('Public Bridleway') on your right, just before a house called Bridleways.

❸ Go right here, along a track between hedgerows. After 0.25 mile (400m), it bends sharply left. Continue for a further 100 yards (91m) and turn through a wide gap into the field on your right. Leaving the top of this narrow field, go right and then left on a footpath between fields to meet a crossing track. Go right here, to reach the A639 again at a junction. Take the road almost opposite (Rigg Lane) and, at Whitegates Farm, go left, between farm buildings, on to a concrete track.

❹ Follow this track past a water treatment works, to a concrete bridge over the River Went (notice the old packhorse bridge next to it). Without crossing either bridge, turn right, on a field-edge path, to accompany the river. A little plank bridge takes you across a side-beck. Now walk beneath a six-arched railway viaduct.

❺ Continue by the riverside, passing one bridge to reach a second, 0.25 mile (400m) further on. Turn right here, crossing the field to a stile beside a gate, to the right of the barns of Low Farm. Walk away, first at the edge of a large field and then beside a playing field. Leave at the far side over a stile on to the road in Low Ackworth.

❻ Cross the road and take a ginnel between houses. Beyond a stile at the far end, bear half-left across a field to a stile and across another field. A stile gives access to another ginnel. Continue along Hill Drive, and then turn right into a cul-de-sac. At the bottom, take a narrow ginnel on the left, to arrive back in High Ackworth near the village green.

HAWORTH'S BRONTË MOORS

Across the wild Pennine moors to the romantic ruin of Top Withins.

Distance: 7.5 miles (12.1km)
Minimum time: 3hrs 30min
Ascent/Gradient: 968ft (295m) ▲▲▲
Level of difficulty: +++
Paths: Well-signed and easy to follow, 1 stile
Landscape: Open moorland
Suggested map: OS Explorer OL21 South Pennines
Start/finish: Grid reference: SE 029372
Dog friendliness: Under control near sheep on open moorland
Parking: Pay-and-display car park, near Brontë Parsonage
Public toilets: Central Park, Haworth

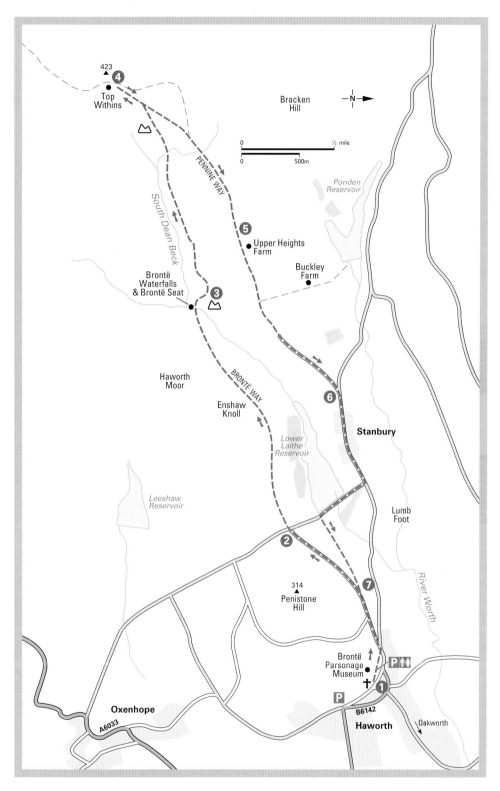

❶ Take the cobbled lane beside the King's Arms, signed to the Brontë Parsonage Museum. The lane soon becomes a paved field path that leads to the Haworth–Stanbury road. Walk left along the road and, after just 75 yards (69m), take a left fork, signed to Penistone Hill. Continue along this quiet road to a T-junction.

❷ Take the track straight ahead, soon signed 'Brontë Way and Top Withins', gradually descending to South Dean Beck where, within a few paces of the stone bridge, you'll find the Brontë Waterfalls and Brontë Seat (a stone that resembles a chair). Cross the bridge and climb steeply uphill to a three-way sign.

❸ Keep left, uphill, on a paved path signed 'Top Withins'. The path levels out to accompany a wall. Cross a beck on stepping stones; a steep uphill climb brings you to a signpost by a ruined building. Walk a short distance left, uphill, to visit the ruin of Top Withins, possibly the inspiration for *Wuthering Heights*.

❹ Retrace your steps to the signpost, but now keep ahead on a paved path, downhill, signed to Stanbury and Haworth and the Pennine Way. Follow a broad, clear track across the wide expanse of wild Pennine moorland.

❺ Pass a white farmhouse – Upper Heights Farm – then bear immediately left at a fork of tracks (still signed here as the Pennine Way). Walk past another building, Lower Heights Farm. After 500 yards (457m), you come to a crossing path: where the Pennine Way veers off to the left, you should continue on the track straight ahead, signed to Stanbury and Haworth. Follow the track to meet a road near the village of Stanbury.

❻ Bear right along the road through Stanbury, then take the first road on the right, signed to Oxenhope, and cross the dam of Lower Laithe Reservoir. Immediately beyond the dam, turn

left on a road that is soon reduced to a track uphill, to meet a road by Haworth Cemetery.

❼ From here you retrace your outward route: walk left along the road, soon taking a gap stile on the right, to follow the paved field path back into Haworth.

THE BOTTOM AND THE TOP: AROUND BEACON FELL

A very popular slice of upland Lancashire countryside, by turns both expansive and intimate.

Distance: 6 miles (9.7km)
Minimum time: 2hrs
Ascent/Gradient: 689ft (210m) ▲▲▲
Level of difficulty: +++
Paths: Field paths, in places indistinct, clear tracks, 19 stiles
Landscape: Forest, heathland, farmland, woodland, riverside
Suggested map: OS Explorer OL41 Forest of Bowland & Ribblesdale
Start/finish: Grid reference: SD 565426
Dog friendliness: Dogs should be under close control throughout
Parking: By Beacon Fell Visitor Centre
Public toilets: At Visitor Centre

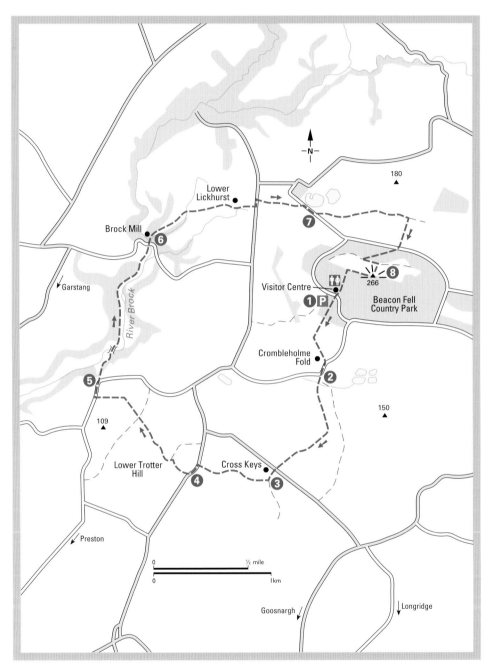

❶ Look for a public footpath sign in the left-hand corner of the lower car park by the visitor centre. Go down the broad, shady track, then through a field. Bear left towards Crombleholme Fold and walk through the farmyard. Turn right on to a lane to a bend.

❷ Go left, cross a stream, then up a track swinging right. After 50 yards (46m) go left, slanting gently down to a stile just before the field ends. Make for a gate at the far end of the field, then angle right to reach a low bridge and up the track beyond.

❸ Go through the Cross Keys car park, through a farmyard and into a field. Go right to a stile, then straight on to the corner of a hedge. Follow it to a tree, then angle left to a stile. Go right, then straight ahead to a lane and go left.

❹ Go right to Lower Trotter Hill. Cross a cattle grid, go left, then round to the right and past a house. Go through the left-hand gate and up to a stile. Follow the field-edge, eventually bending left. Go down a stony track and then turn right on a road.

❺ As the road bends to the right, keep walking straight ahead. Descend on a sunken track through woods and cross a footbridge. Go up a few paces, then right, and follow obvious paths near the river to reach Brock Mill picnic area.

❻ Cross the bridge, then go through a gateway on the left. Bear right up a track, then go right, through rhododendrons. Follow the edge of a wood, then go right, crossing the stream. Go up a field-edge and straight on towards Lower Lickhurst. Go round into the drive and up to the road. Go left for just a few paces, then go right, up a drive. Keep straight on as it bends left, up fields to a lane. Continue right for 140 yards (128m).

❼ Go left over a stile and diagonally to an isolated thorn tree. Continue almost level to a gateway and then to a stile and footbridge. Follow an old boundary, now a muddy depression, then bear left to power lines. Follow these to a marker post. Go right, directly uphill. Cross the road to a track rising through forest. At a junction go left for 200 yards (183m) then right up a narrow path to the summit trig point.

❽ Go left. Bear right along the edge of the forest, then left across a boardwalk. Keep ahead to return directly to the visitor centre.

SPECTACULAR LANDSCAPES IN LIMESTONE COUNTRY

The noble Malham Cove is the majestic highlight of this quintessential limestone Dales walk.

Limestone scenery at Malham Cove

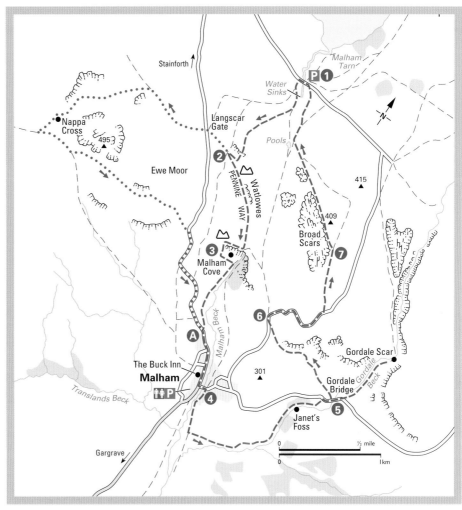

Distance: 6.25 miles (10.1km)
Minimum time: 3hrs
Ascent/Gradient: 1,148ft (350m) ▲▲▲
Level of difficulty: +++
Paths: Well-marked field and moorland paths, more than 400 steps in descent from Malham Cove, 5 stiles
Landscape: Spectacular limestone country, including Malham Cove
Suggested map: OS Explorer OL2 Yorkshire Dales – Southern & Western
Start/finish: Grid reference: SD 894658
Dog friendliness: Mostly off lead, except where sheep are present or signs indicate otherwise
Parking: At Water Sinks, near gateway across road and in Malham village
Public toilets: Car park in Malham village

❶ From the car parking space, walk through the gate, then turn left through the kissing gate at the Malham Cove sign. Keep left at the next signpost, following the Pennine Way down the dry valley until the path bends sharp right, overlooking another dry valley.

❷ Turn left, cross a stile and descend steeply into the lower valley. Walk down the level valley to a stile at the end. Just beyond this is the limestone pavement at the top of Malham Cove. Turn right and walk along the pavement. Take great care here, both of the sheer drop down to your left and the gaps in the limestone pavement (known as grikes). Turn left to descend beside a stone wall; go through a gate, then descend more than 400 steps to the foot of the Cove.

❸ At the bottom, fork left to visit the very base of the cliff, then follow the obvious track beside the river. On reaching the road, turn left and follow it into the centre of Malham village. Turn left to cross the bridge.

❹ Turn immediately right on a track past some houses, then continue along a gravelled path. Follow it left at a sign to Janet's Foss. Eventually the footpath enters woodland, then climbs beside a waterfall (Janet's Foss) to a kissing gate. Turn right along the road, towards Gordale Scar.

❺ At Gordale Bridge (actually two bridges), go through a gate to the left. (To visit Gordale Scar, continue straight ahead here. Take a signed gate to the left and follow the path through a field into the gorge. Continue as far as the waterfall and then follow the same route back to the bridge.) On the main route, follow the signed public footpath uphill through three gates. Climb alongside a lane before emerging on to it.

❻ Turn right and follow the lane uphill for 600 yards (549m), to a ladder stile on the left. Follow a track to a footpath fingerpost.

❼ Bear left and walk over a broad open moor before descending to some small pools. Turn right at a sign for Malham Tarn, go over a ladder stile, take the left-hand path and follow it back to the car park.

Extending the walk
You can avoid the steep descent by Malham Cove by taking a scenic extension to this walk, across the limestone uplands to Nappa Cross and descending to Malham along an old drove road which joins a minor road to re-join the main route at point ❹.

Walk G

HIDDEN YORK

Through streets and alleys of the historic walled city.

The Rose Window in York Minster was fully restored in the 1980s

Distance: 3.25 miles (5.3km)
Minimum time: 1hr 30min
Ascent/Gradient: 82ft (25m) ▲▲▲
Level of difficulty: +++
Paths: City pavements
Landscape: Historic city
Suggested map: AA Street by Street York Page 2 C3
Start/finish: Grid reference: SE 598523
Dog friendliness: City streets, so dogs on lead
Parking: Marygate Car Park, off Bootham
Public toilets: Museum Gardens and Bootham Bar

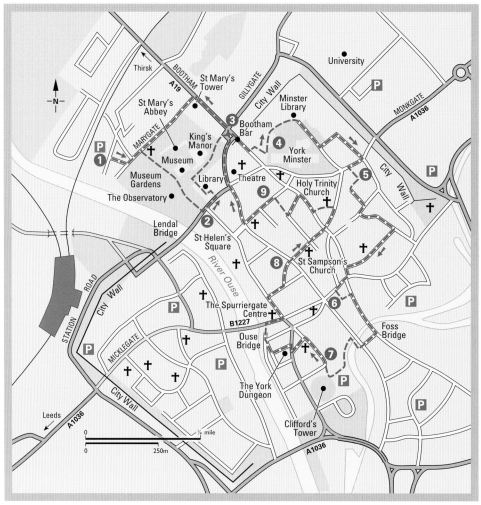

❶ Walk back into Marygate, turn left, cross the road and enter Museum Gardens through the archway. Follow the path straight ahead, passing the Observatory, and leave the gardens by the lodge.

❷ Turn left, then left again towards the library. Go left through a gate, and along the side of the library. Go up the steps, and through a gate in the wall. At the bottom of the slope, turn right and follow Abbey Wall into Exhibition Square.

❸ Cross at the traffic lights and go through Bootham Bar. A few paces on your left, take a passageway beside The Hole in the Wall pub and turn right down Precentor's Court. By the Minster, go left through the gate, signed 'York Minster Dean's Park'.

❹ Follow the path left to the Minster Library building. Bend right through the gate and along

the cobbled road. Turn left by the postbox down Chapter House Street, bending right into Ogleforth. At the crossroads turn right, then go left through an archway opposite the National Trust Café.

❺ Bear right into Bartle Garth, which bends left. At the T-junction turn right, and then go left down Spen Lane. Opposite Hilary House, go right along St Saviourgate. At the T-junction turn left, then right at the crossroads. Next to Jones's shoe shop on the left, take a passage, Lady Peckitt's Yard.

❻ Go under the buildings, then turn left to Fossgate. Turn right, go over the bridge and then turn right along Merchantgate. At the T-junction, cross the road and take the glazed walkway beside the bridge, signed 'Castle Area', into the car park by Clifford's Tower.

❼ Bend right and go to the left of the Hilton Hotel. Just after the church on the right, go left

down Friargate, right along Clifford Street, and left by the York Dungeon. At the riverside turn right, ascend the steps by Ouse Bridge and turn right. At the traffic lights, turn left by The Spurriergate Centre. By the NatWest Bank, go right, forking left into Feasegate.

❽ Go ahead to cross Parliament Street and pass St Sampson's Church. Go straight on at the next crossroads into Goodramgate. After 50 yards (46m), go left through a gateway into Holy Trinity churchyard, and leave by a passage to the left of the tower, to reach Low Petergate. Turn right, then take the next left into Grape Lane. Where it bends left, turn right down the narrow Coffee Yard into Stonegate.

❾ Go left to St Helen's Square and turn right by LloydsTSB. Go straight on at the next crossroads back to Exhibition Square. At the traffic lights, turn left up Bootham. Turn left down Marygate by the circular tower to return to the car park.

AROUND BUTTERMERE

A relaxing walk in one of Lakeland's most attractive valleys.

Buttermere, Lake District

Distance: 4.5 miles (7.2km)
Minimum time: 2hrs
Ascent/Gradient: 35ft (11m) ▲▲▲
Level of difficulty: +++
Paths: Good path, some road-walking, 2 stiles
Landscape: Lake, fells, woodland and farmland
Suggested map: OS Explorer OL4 The English Lakes (NW)
Start/finish: Grid reference: NY 173169
Dog friendliness: On lead near farms and open fells where sheep are grazing
Parking: National Park car park beyond Fish Hotel (fee)
Public toilets: At start

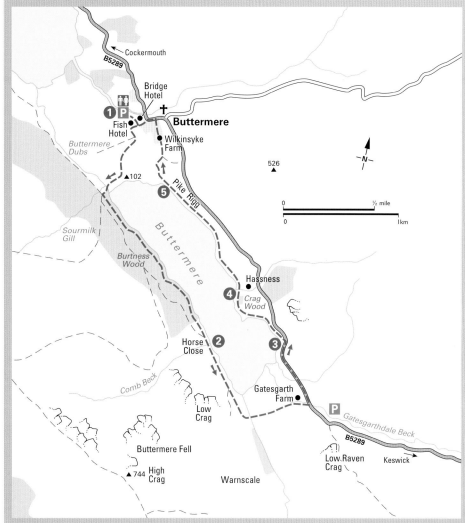

❶ Leave the car park and turn right, passing the Fish Hotel to follow a broad track through gates. Ignore the signposted route to Scale Force and continue along the track towards the edge of the lake. Then follow the line of a hedgerow to a bridge at Buttermere Dubs. Cross a small footbridge and go through a nearby gate in a wall at the foot of Burtness Wood and the cascade of Sourmilk Gill. Turn left on a track through the woodland that roughly parallels the lakeshore, finally emerging from the woodland near Horse Close, where a bridge spans Comb Beck.

❷ Keep on along the path to reach a wall leading to a sheepfold and a gate. This is Point A, where Walk 44 branches off. Go left through the gate, cross Warnscale Beck and walk out to Gatesgarth Farm. At the farm, follow the signs to reach the valley road. This is Point B, where Walk 44 re-joins. A short stretch of road-walking, left on the B5289, now follows, along which there are no pathways. Take care against approaching traffic.

❸ As the road bears left, leave it for a lakeside footpath on the left. The path leads into a field, beyond which it never strays far from the shoreline and continues to a stand of Scots pine, near Crag Wood.

❹ Beyond Hassnesshow Beck bridge, the path enters the grounds of Hassness, where a rocky path, enclosed by trees, leads to a gate. Here a path has been cut across a crag where it plunges into the lake below, and shortly disappears into a brief, low and damp tunnel, the only one of its kind in the Lake District. The tunnel was cut by employees of George Benson, a 19th-century mill owner who owned the Hassness Estate, so that he could walk around the lake without straying far from its shore. After you emerge from the tunnel a gate gives access to a gravel path across the wooded pasture of Pike Rigg. A path leads through a series of gates beyond the foot of the lake to a bridge of slate slabs.

❺ A short way on, through another gate, the path leads on to Wilkinsyke Farm, and an easy walk out to the road, just a short way above the Bridge Hotel. Turn left to return to the car park.

Autumn view through the trees of Buttermere

Walk 1

BRANT FELL ABOVE BOWNESS-ON-WINDERMERE

The woods, open spaces and breathtaking views over Windermere contrast markedly with the bustle below.

Sightseeing boat at Bowness-on-Windermere

Distance: 3.5 miles (5.7km)

Minimum time: 1hr 15min

Ascent/Gradient: 525ft (160m) ▲▲▲

Level of difficulty: +++

Paths: Pavement, road, stony tracks, grassy paths, 2 stiles

Landscape: Town, mixed woodland, open fell, lake and fell views

Suggested map: OS Explorer OL7 The English Lakes (SE)

Start/finish: Grid reference: SD 398966

Dog friendliness: Popular route for dogs; busy roads and sheep grazing, so must be under control

Parking: Fee car park on Glebe Road above Windermere lake

Public toilets: At car park and above information centre

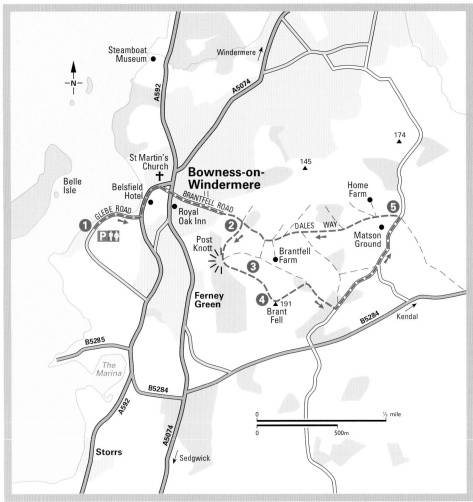

❶ Take Glebe Road into Bowness town. Swing left and, opposite the steamer pier, go right over the main Windermere road and then turn left. Opposite the impressive St Martin's Church turn right to ascend the little street of St Martin's Hill. Cross the Kendal road to climb Brantfell Road directly above. At the head of the road a little iron gate leads on to the Dales Way, a grassy and stony path which climbs directly up the hillside. Continue to a kissing gate by the wood, leading on to a lane.

❷ Pass through the kissing gate and turn right, signposted 'Post Knott', to follow the stony lane. Continue on the lane rising through the woods until it crests a height near the flat circular top of Post Knott. Bear left and make the short ascent to the summit. The view from

here was once exceptional but is now obscured by trees. Retrace a few steps back to the track then bear right to find a kissing gate leading out of the wood on to the open hillside.

❸ Beyond the kissing gate, take the grassy path, rising to a rocky shoulder. Cross the shoulder and first descend, then ascend, to a ladder stile in the top corner of the field by some fir trees. Cross the stile, then bear right to ascend directly up the open grassy flanks of Brant Fell to its rocky summit.

❹ Go left (northeast) from the top of the fell, following a line of cairns down to a kissing gate. Descend through a young plantation to a second gate and a track. Turn right and follow the track to a stile and gate leading out to a road. Turn left along the road and continue left at the junction, to pass Matson Ground. Immediately beyond is a kissing gate on the left, waymarked for the Dales Way.

❺ Go through the kissing gate and continue down the path to cross a track and pass through a kissing gate into another field. Keep along the track beneath the trees and beside a new pond, until the path swings left to emerge through a kissing gate on to a surfaced drive. Go right along the drive for 30 yards (27m) until the path veers off left through the trees to follow the fence. An iron gate leads into a field. Follow the grassy path, first descending and then rising to an iron gate in the corner of the field. Continue to join a grassy track and go through the kissing gate. Cross the surfaced drive of Brantfell Farm and keep straight on to another kissing gate leading into a field. Follow the path, parallel to the wall, descending the hill to intercept a track, via a kissing gate, and regain Point ❷. Retrace your steps back to Glebe Road.

A RIVERSIDE CIRCUIT HIGH IN THE DALES

A classic walk in Upper Swaledale from Keld to Muker along Kisdon Side, and back by the river.

Stone barn and walls at Keld, Swaledale

Distance: 6 miles (9.7km)

Minimum time: 2hrs 30min

Ascent/Gradient: 820ft (250m) ▲▲▲

Level of difficulty: +++

Paths: Field and riverside paths and tracks, 5 stiles

Landscape: Hillside and valley, hay meadows, riverside and waterfalls

Suggested map: OS Explorer OL30 Yorkshire Dales – Northern & Central

Start/finish: Grid reference: NY 892012

Dog friendliness: Dogs on lead (there are lots of sheep)

Parking: Signed car park at west end of Keld near Park Lodge

Public toilets: Keld and Muker

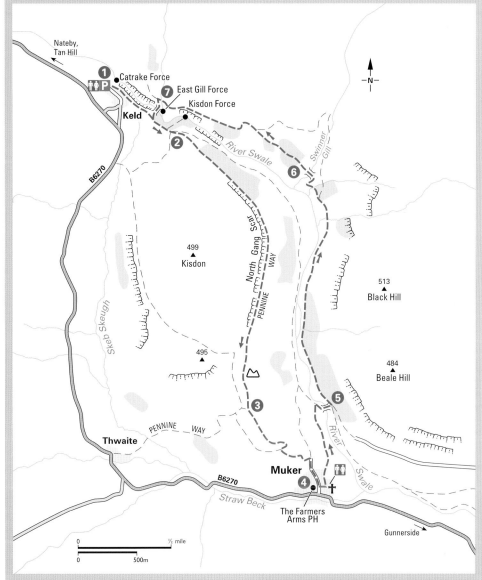

❶ Walk back down the car park entrance road, and straight ahead down a gravel track, signed 'Muker'. Continue along at the upper level, ignoring a path downhill to the left. Go through a gate, pass a sign to Kisdon Upper Force, and continue along the path below crags to a signpost.

❷ Turn right, following the Pennine Way, and go up to a gap in a wall and another signpost. Go left and follow a rough but mostly level path along Kisdon Side, first above woodland, then across more open slopes. Cross a ladder stile as the path starts to descend. Go down to a signpost and bear right to another signpost, where the Pennine Way goes right.

❸ Bear left down a walled track, marked 'Muker'. The track becomes gravelled and then metalled, finally descending into a walled lane on the edge of the village. Continue to a T-junction.

❹ Turn left and in a few paces left again by a sign to Gunnerside and Keld. Follow the paved path through six gates to the river. Turn sharp right and walk downstream to a footbridge.

❺ Ascend steps beyond the footbridge and turn left, signed 'Keld'. Follow a clear track up along the valley, until it curves right into Swinner Gill. Cross a footbridge by the remains of lead workings, and go up to a wooden gate.

❻ Go straight ahead up the hill and through woodland. The track levels out, then starts to descend, winding left round a barn, then swinging back right. Continue steadily downhill to reach a gate above East Gill Force.

❼ Fork left by a wooden seat, at a sign to Keld. Follow the path down to a footbridge then bear right, uphill, to a T-junction, where you turn right and follow the track back to the car.

Kisdon Force waterfall at Keld, Swaledale

Walk K

ROSEBERRY TOPPING AND CAPTAIN COOK COUNTRY

An ascent of Roseberry Topping for fine views and reminders of one of Britain's great explorers.

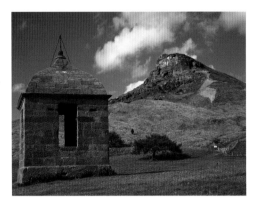

The Ancient Shooting Lodge near Roseberry Topping hill

Distance: 5.5 miles (8.8km)

Minimum time: 2hrs 30min

Ascent/Gradient: 1,214ft (370m) ▲▲▲

Level of difficulty: +++

Paths: Hillside climb, then tracks and field paths, 5 stiles

Landscape: One of the best 360-degree views in Yorkshire

Suggested map: OS Explorer OL26 North York Moors – Western

Start/finish: Grid reference: NZ 570128

Dog friendliness: Off lead, except in farmland

Parking: Car park on A173 just south of Newton under Roseberry

Public toilets: In car park at foot of Roseberry Topping

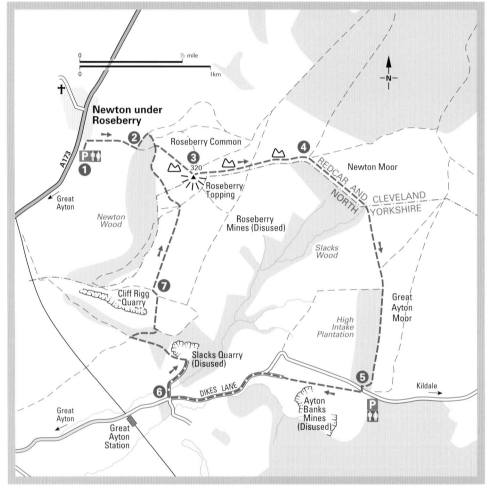

❶ Take the rough lane beside the car park towards Roseberry Topping. The path goes through a gateway then rises to a second gate at the beginning of the woodland.

❷ Go through the gate into National Trust land and turn left. There is a well-worn, mostly paved, path to the summit. It is a stiff climb to the trig point on the top of the hill.

❸ From the summit, walk east from the trig point, past two iron poles set into rock, and straight on along the paved way. Go steeply downhill. At the bottom, bear right to go up a track that bends right around the corner of woodland to a gate.

❹ Go through the gate and take the path alongside the wood, following yellow waymarkers. Continue on the path until it eventually follows a wall and descends the hillside to reach a road.

❺ Turn right, cross the cattle grid and bear left between two benches, then go right, along the fence line, at first parallel with the road. Go down the field, through a gate and then over a stile and out into a lane. Walk past the cottages to reach a road, where you go straight ahead.

❻ At a crossroads go right, down Aireyholme Lane. Follow the lane as it winds past houses, then take a signed footpath left over a stile. Follow the fence to two gates into woodland. After 0.5 mile (800m), go right at a National Trust sign, up a path ascending through the woods to a signposted stile. Over it, turn left to another stile, then after it, go right along the edge of the woodland. Bend left to a gate near a house.

❼ Walk across two fields to a stile, then continue uphill to the tower. Beyond it, take a grassy path left down a gully, to a gate into woodland. Follow the path downhill through the woods to return to the gate at the top of the lane leading back to the car park.

Wheat growing beside Roseberry Topping hill from Newton

HISTORIC HEXHAM

A walk round and about the abbey and market town of Hexham.

Hexham Abbey

Distance: 3.75 miles (6km)

Minimum time: 2hrs

Ascent/Gradient: 590ft (180m) ▲▲▲

Level of difficulty: +++

Paths: Town streets, lanes and woodland paths, 4 stiles

Landscape: Market town and small wooded valleys

Suggested map: OS Explorer OL43 Hadrian's Wall

Start/finish: Grid reference: NY 939641

Dog friendliness: Can run free in woods of Cowgarth Dene and Wydon Burn

Parking: Pay-and-display car park, next to supermarket

Public toilets: At car park, by tourist information centre

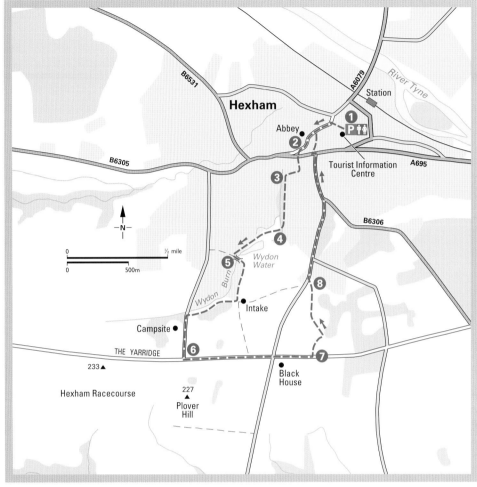

❶ From the car park (not the supermarket end), take the exit between the tourist information centre and the café to follow a narrow street past the Old Gaol. Go under the arches of the Moot Hall and enter the Market Place. Take a tour of The Sele, the park grounds surrounding Hexham Abbey, before aiming roughly southwest across them to the Queen Hall on Beaumont Street.

❷ Turn right along here to reach Benson's Monument, then continue straight ahead on an unnamed street. After taking the first turning on the right, ignore Elvaston Road on the left, but instead go straight ahead on a tarred lane that leads to the foot of Cowgarth Dene.

❸ When you get to a bridge, turn off into the woodland where the now unsurfaced track crosses a footbridge and climbs out to a little park at the edge of a modern housing estate. Follow the woodland edge, then a track past a water treatment works and some new houses.

❹ Turn left through a gate before you reach the estate proper into the Wydon Water car park. Turn right along a grassy ride, dipping left through the hedgerow after 100m (110 yards) to round the head of the reservoir. When you reach a lane, turn left, following it up the hill, where it becomes unsurfaced, past a house.

❺ Emerging on a road, turn left then, at Intake farm, turn right along a path that leads into the thick woodland of Wydon Burn's upper reaches. A narrow path continues through the woods to reach the lane at Causey Hill, where you turn left past the campsite to a junction with a road known as The Yarridge. The modern building here is part of the Hexham Racecourse.

❻ Turn left along the road and go straight ahead at the crossroads.

❼ Beyond Black House, a stile on the left marks the start of a downhill, cross-field path into Hexham. Beyond a step stile the path veers right to round some gorse bushes before resuming its course alongside the left field-edge.

❽ Just before reaching a whitewashed cottage, go over the stile on the left and follow the road down into the town. Turn left along the shopping street at the bottom, then right along St Mary's Chare, back to the Market Place.

Panels in Hexham Abbey by Edward Burne-Jones

KIRKNEWTON AND ANCIENT YEAVERING BELL

Views of the Cheviot Hills and the sea are the reward for climbing up to this hilltop fort.

Walk M

The Cheviots mountains from Yeavering Bell

Distance: 5 miles (8km)

Minimum time: 2hrs 15min

Ascent/Gradient: 1,115ft (340m) ▲▲▲

Level of difficulty: +++

Paths: Tracks, field paths and moorland, steep ascent and descent

Landscape: Farmland and hillside, wide views from Yeavering Bell

Suggested map: OS Explorer OL16 The Cheviot Hills

Start/finish: Grid reference: NT 914302

Dog friendliness: Dogs on leads

Parking: In Kirknewton village, in wide area of road beyond school and church, off B6351

Public toilets: None en route

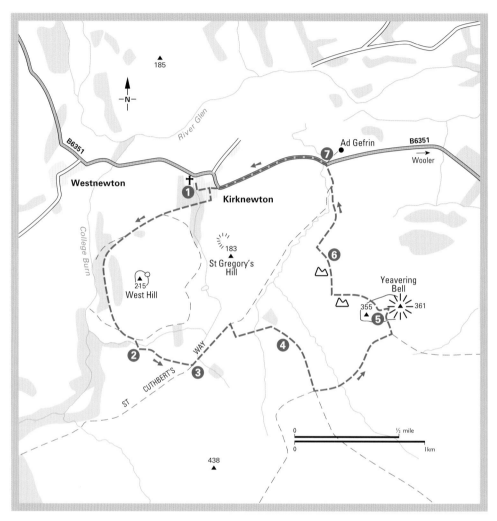

❶ From the parking place, walk ahead towards the village centre, then turn left. Just before a gate, bend right along the lane, following the 'Hillforts Trail' sign. The metalled lane bends right again and becomes a grassy track. Go through a metal gate and straight on at the next waymarker. Go through two more metal gates and a gateway. At the next marker post, bear right, signed 'Permissive Path', and go over a stream and a ladder stile.

❷ Turn left after the stile, then go over another stile. Bear half-right across the field to a hand gate in a crossing wall. Go through the gate, and bear right to reach a waymarked post beside the track. This track is part of St Cuthbert's Way.

❸ Turn left along the track and follow it through a wooden waymarked gate, past a farmhouse and over a cattle grid. Just before the next cattle grid, turn right off the track, following the 'St Cuthbert's Way' sign. Bend left through a gate and continue along the grassy track uphill to a ladder stile in the wall on your left.

❹ Go over the stile and turn right to follow the footpath uphill. At a low-level signpost, turn left, signed 'Yeavering Bell'. Follow the waymarks down into the valley, across the stream, then uphill. The path eventually passes through the fort wall. Bend right to reach the summit of Yeavering Bell.

❺ After enjoying the view, go downhill to the valley between the two peaks. Bear right and head downhill, on the opposite side of the hill to that which you came up. Go through the

wall and follow the waymark just beyond. The path is waymarked all the way down the steep hill, until you reach a stile.

❻ Go over the stile, then over a ladder stile on your right on to a track. Follow the track past a marker post and, just after it, bend left towards another track, which leads towards the farm buildings in the valley bottom. Go over a ladder stile by the buildings and turn right along the track. Go through a metal gate and past the cottages to reach the road. The site of the Ad Gefrin palace can be visited from an access path here.

❼ Turn left along the road and follow it back to Kirknewton. At the 'Yetholm' sign at the entrance to the village, go straight ahead, through the gate, then turn right back to the car parking.

BERWICK TOWN WALLS

Explore old Berwick, then take a longer ramble beside the Tweed.

Royal Border Bridge takes trains across the border between England and Scotland

Distance: 6.5 miles (10.4km)
Minimum time: 2hrs 15min
Ascent/Gradient: 98ft (30m) ▲▲▲
Level of difficulty: +++
Paths: Paved pathways and field paths; flood-meadows may be wet and muddy, particularly around high tide, 4 stiles
Landscape: Town, riverside and woodland
Suggested map: OS Explorer 346 Berwick-upon-Tweed
Start/finish: Grid reference: NT 998529
Dog friendliness: On leads in town and near livestock
Parking: Below ramparts outside Scots Gate
Public toilets: At car park, below ramparts
Note: Sheer, unguarded drop from outer edge of town walls and bastions, keep to marked pathways

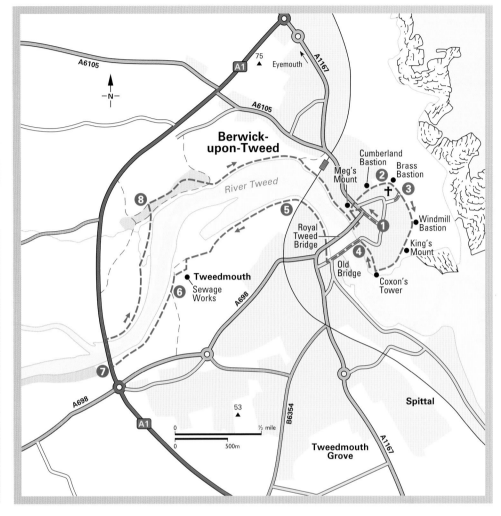

❶ You can climb on to the walls by Meg's Mount. Follow the wall back over Scots Gate and on past the Cumberland Bastion.

❷ The next battery, Brass Bastion, lies at the northern corner of the town. Some 100 yards (91m) beyond, a path descends inside the wall to meet the Parade by the corner of the parish church graveyard. Turn right past the barracks to the church, both of which are well worth visiting.

❸ Return to the walls and continue around, passing Windmill Bastion and the site of the earlier Edward VI fort. Beyond King's Mount, the walls rise above the Tweed Estuary before turning upriver at Coxon's Tower, past elegant Georgian terraces and on above the old quay.

❹ Leave the walls at Bridge End and cross the Old Bridge. Turn right past the war memorial, go beneath the modern Royal Tweed Bridge and remain by the river beyond, shortly passing below Stephenson's railway viaduct.

❺ The way continues upstream along an often muddy path. Where the bank widens to a rough meadow, pick up a track on the left, leading through a series of kissing gates to an open hide. A further gate leads out on to the next section of riverbank. Eventually, beyond another gate, a contained path skirts a water treatment plant. Turning left through a second gate, it emerges on to a tarmac track, where you should turn right.

❻ At a bend 40 yards (37m) on, bear off right along a field-edge above the steep riverbank. Continue in the next field but, towards its far end, look for a stepped path descending the bank to a stream. Rising to a stile beyond, bear right to the main road.

❼ Cross the Tweed and drop right on to a path, signed 'Berwick via Plantation', which crosses a couple of stiles to a riverside pasture. Walk away beside the left boundary for about 0.5 mile (800m). After crossing the head of a stream, move away from the hedge, aiming to meet the river below a wooded bank. Over a side-bridge, bear right to a stile and continue through the trees beyond to a path at the top of the bank.

❽ Go right, eventually dropping from the wood by a cottage, where a riverside promenade leads back to Berwick. Just beyond the Royal Tweed Bridge, turn sharp left, climbing back beneath it and continue beside the town walls to return to Meg's Mount.

Berwick Castle was once one of the most important of border castles

SCOTLAND

SCOTLAND

The silhouette of Castle Stalker and hills beyond Loch Linnhe at sunset, Argyll

The Emperor Hadrian had his men build a wall from coast to coast across the top of England to keep out, or at least to regulate the passage of, the barbarians to the north. This was one in a series of border struggles which were only brought to an official end in 1706, when Scotland united with England and Wales. The arguments still rumble on, for the Scottish identity is a strong one, though the establishment of an autonomous Scottish Parliament at the devolution of 1999 went some way to fulfilling the Scots' desire for independence.

The border today is further north than Hadrian's crumbled wall, but tall peel towers hidden among the trees and fierce traditions of common riding upheld in the wool towns of the Tweed Valley are reminders of later skirmishes in the eastern Lowlands. To the west, tales of raiders and pirates still colour the Galloway coastline, immortalised in the novels of S. R. Crockett and Sir Walter Scott. In fact, Scott, with his stirring stories of Highland heroes (and heroines), and dramatic tales of Scottish history in a romantic landscape, is frequently credited with single-handedly popularising the attractions of his native land. Certainly visitors are drawn here by the wide-open spaces and magnificent landscapes, infused with a turbulent history.

Scotland's story is of a nation constantly divided against itself, for political or religious reasons. The land, scored through by the sweeping fault line of the Great Glen, lends itself to division – but this is more apparent in the people than in the landscape. The Highlanders of the northwest were Celts, eking a subsistence from their crofts and living under a system of extended family, or clanship. Those of the east and south farmed a more fertile land, and were of mixed blood that stemmed from trading with the Norse, Picts and English.

Today, of course, the Scots are largely urban, but divisions remain just below the surface. The New Town of Edinburgh has gracious Georgian buildings growing around the twin landmarks of Arthur's Seat and the old castle which still dominate the city today. Less than 50 miles (80km) away across the pinched waistline of Scotland, the industrial sprawl of Glasgow contains a contrasting and very splendid Victorian heart (along with a healthy disrespect for fancy Edinburgh 'airs'). Scotland's other great cities include St Andrews, seat of learning since 1412 and the queen of golfing resorts, and Aberdeen, capital of the northeast, a trading and fishing port which took new life from the offshore oil industry. Between and beyond these great cities lies some of Britain's most spectacular scenery, which includes its highest mountain, deepest lake, largest trees and most remote area of wilderness. Scotland is a country of superlatives which, sadly, the Emperor Hadrian failed to appreciate.

Previous page: Ben Macdui (Beinn MacDuidh) viewed from Glen Lui near Braemar, Cairngorms National Park

Section Contents

1	The Western Borderlands	302–303
2	The Isle of Arran	304–305
3	The Land of Robert Burns	306–307
4	The 'Dear, Dirty City' on the Clyde	308–309
5	Scotland's Historic Capital	310–311
6	Stirling and the Trossachs	314–315
7	The Fair City	316–317
8	Both Sides of the Tay	318–319
9	In the Perthshire Highlands	320–321
10	From Ben Nevis to Glen Coe	324–325
11	Around the Granite City	326–327
12	The Capital of the Highlands	328–329

Features

The Wildlife of Scotland	312–313
Scotland's Strongholds	322–323
The Scottish Highlands and Islands	330–333

Walks

A	Caerlaverock Castle and the Solway Merses	334
B	Discover Dunaskin Ironworks	335
C	The Thirty-Nine Steps in Broughton	336
D	Edinburgh's Old Town	337
E	The Romance of Roslin Glen	338
F	Exploring Glasgow's Heritage	339
G	Stirling's Braveheart, William Wallace	340
H	Climbing to the Castle of Cups	341
I	Into the Lost Valley	342
J	The Inspirational Landscape of Auchenblae	343
K	Loch An Eilein's Castle and Ord Ban	344
L	Seeing Sea Eagles at Portree Bay	345
M	Strathpeffer and the Rogie Falls	346
N	Into Scotland's Great Wilderness	347

THE WESTERN BORDERLANDS

A land that was once in the midst of border warfare between the Scots and the English is now a haven of peace and tranquillity, with quiet roads, lush pastures, hills and woodlands. Robert Burns wrote more than 100 of his poems here, Robert the Bruce began Scotland's quest for nationhood here in 1306, and countless couples plighted their troth at Gretna Green.

13th-century Caerlaverock Castle is a popular attraction and wedding venue

Amelia Paton Hill's statue of Robert Burns, commissioned in 1877, graces the town centre in Dumfries

Caerlaverock

Caerlaverock Castle was built in 1290 for the Maxwells and has the unique shape of a triangular shield, fronted by a twin-towered gatehouse and surrounded by a moat. In 1301 the castle was captured by Edward I, then retaken by Maxwell's forces in 1312. Its final battle was in 1640, when it fell to the Covenanters following a 13-week siege.

The Wildfowl and Wetlands Trust's Reserve on the north Solway shore encompasses 1,350 acres (527ha) of salt-water marsh. It has outstanding hide and observation facilities, giving impressive views of the huge numbers of wildfowl that over-winter here, including thousands of barnacle geese. There are also pink-footed and greylag geese, waders, whooper swans and many varieties of duck. The rare natterjack toad is another inhabitant.

Dumfries

In 1306, in what was then Greyfriars Abbey, Robert the Bruce stabbed Sir John Comyn, representative of Edward I, and began Scotland's quest for nationhood. Eight miles (12.9km) from the sea, this former seaport straddles the River Nith, and beside the 15th-century bridge the Old Bridge House Museum illustrates everyday life in the town.

Whitesands is a pleasant river-front area on the east bank, while on the west bank is the 18th-century watermill which now houses the Robert Burns Centre, commemorating the poet's association with the town. He spent the last three years of his life here, and his house, his mausoleum in St Michael's churchyard and the centre are all on a heritage trail.

The Dumfries Museum is the largest museum in southwest Scotland and portrays the region's history; the Camera Obscura of 1836 on the top floor gives a panoramic view of the town and surrounding countryside.

Ecclefechan

Thomas Carlyle, the essayist and historian, was born at Ecclefechan in 1795 and his grave is in the churchyard of Hoddom Castle, 2 miles (3.2km) away to the southwest. His house is now a museum with a collection of letters and other memorabilia. The Burnsward to the north of the town has a complex of early earthwork fortresses, which, as in so many other places, were later adapted to their needs by the Romans.

Gretna Green

This village in Dumfries and Galloway owes its fame to the fact that, after marriage by declaration was banned in England in 1754, Gretna was the nearest point for runaway couples to secure a legitimate marriage under the laxer statutes of Scottish law.

The blacksmith, popularly known as 'the anvil priest', would, in front of witnesses, hear the declaration of elopers' willingness to marry. After 1856 it became necessary for one of the parties to have been resident in Scotland for 21 days prior to the ceremony, but marriage by declaration was not prohibited until 1940. Exhibitions at the Old Blacksmith's Shop Centre tell Gretna's story.

Scots Wha Hae

Robert Burns, Scotland's national poet, now enjoys world acclaim. His birthday on 25 January is celebrated worldwide as Burns' Night. Although he was born in Alloway, much of his important writing life was spent in Dumfries. From his farm at Ellisland, 6 miles (9.7km) north of the town, he wrote *Tam O'Shanter* and re-penned *Auld Lang Syne*.

For those prepared to penetrate the Scottish dialect, they will find a man ahead of his time. Despite a rakish reputation, his writing reflects a champion of noble causes and an advocate for a compassionate society.

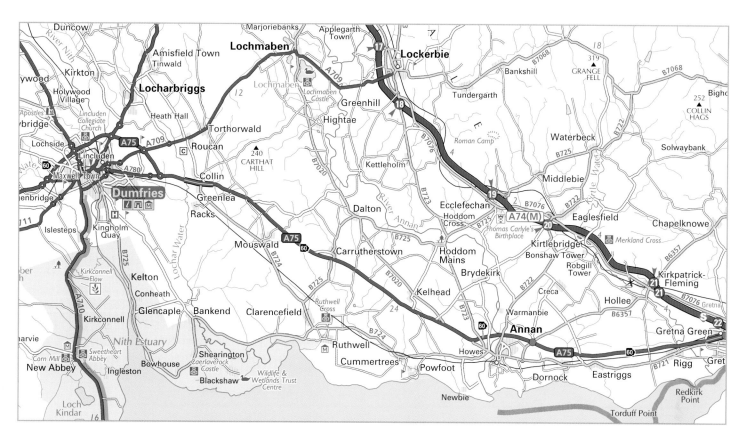

Kirkpatrick-Fleming

This is where Robert the Bruce is said to have spent three months in a cave and been inspired by the unrelenting efforts of a spider. The cave, on an open cliff face, is thought to have megalithic origins. Until recently it could only be reached by a rope descent, but there is now a footpath.

Britain's worst rail disaster, in which over 200 people died, occurred at nearby Quintinshill signal box in 1915. The Station Inn contains sad reminders of the event, along with other items of railway memorabilia.

Lochmaben

This was the birthplace of the victor of Bannockburn, and the Latin inscription on the statue of Robert the Bruce at the head of main street reads 'From us is sprung the liberator king.' As a former headquarters for English forces, the town was a focal point in frequent border skirmishes and wars. As if that wasn't trouble enough, the town also had to endure the constant feuding between the Johnstone and Maxwell clans. In 1593, this culminated in a defining conflict beside the River Dryfe at which the Maxwells were routed. Of Lochmaben's two castles, the first, belonging to the Brus family, is now just a mound and the second is a ruin beside the loch.

New Abbey

This graceful village is dominated by the beautiful ruins of Sweetheart Abbey. It was founded in 1273 by Devorgilla Balliol to the romantic memory of her husband, John, whose embalmed heart she carried in a casket until her own death, when it was buried with her. She commemorated his name by founding Balliol College, part of Oxford University.

Close by is Shambellie House, a Victorian mansion housing a Museum of Costume. The New Abbey Corn Mill, dating from the 18th century, has been restored and still grinds oatmeal on traditional stone.

Ruthwell

In an apse in Ruthwell's church stands one of Europe's finest early Christian stone crosses, dating from the seventh century. Standing 18ft (5.5m) high, it is carved with runic and Latin inscriptions around biblical scenes. It was badly damaged in 1642, but restored by the Revd Dr Henry Duncan, the parish minister. He also founded the world's first savings bank in his cottage. It succeeded, even though it was managed on draconian lines, with depositors fined for any default. The Savings Banks Museum in the reverend's former house focuses on the growth of savings banks from 1810 to the present day.

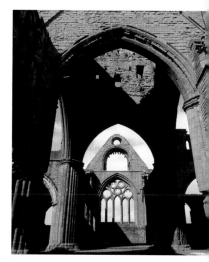

Sweetheart Abbey in New Abbey; the central tower was 92ft (30m) high and the church was 203ft (67m) long

👣 See Walk A, page 334
Caerlaverock Castle and the Solway Merses

Tourist Information
Castle Douglas: Markethill Car Park (seasonal) (tel: 01556 502611)
Dumfries: 64 Whitesands (tel: 01387 253862)
Gatehouse of Fleet: Mill on the Fleet, High Street (seasonal) (tel: 01557 814212)
Kirkcudbright: Harbour Square (seasonal) (tel: 01557 330494)

THE ISLE OF ARRAN

Arran is sometimes described as 'Scotland in miniature'. It is also one of Scotland's best-kept secrets. Because it lies off the Ayrshire coast, it is easy to suppose that the island must share the gentle lowland landscape of that region. What a surprise, then, when the sharp Arran peaks come into view across the water!

More than 10 miles (16km) of way-marked wildlife trails surround the castle buildings and garden in Brodick

Brodick

The setting of Brodick in its wide bay, backed by high peaks, with Brodick Castle rising from the trees on the lower slopes, is remarkably beautiful. The castle, formerly owned by the Dukes of Hamilton, was taken over by the National Trust for Scotland in 1957. Retaining the warm and surprisingly intimate air of a family home, its garden is one of the most charming on the west coast, with semi-tropical plants and trees and a delightful water garden.

The interesting Arran Heritage Museum is housed in an attractive cluster of low white buildings. It was founded by local people to show every aspect of island life in the past. Three rooms in one of the cottages are furnished as they would have been in the early 20th century and there is a forge, a dairy and an extensive archive. The original village of Brodick was on the north side of the bay, below the castle, and the remains of this earlier settlement can be seen at Cladach.

Corrie

Lying below the peaks of the north, Corrie was once the source of sandstone for building in the area. Seen from the sea, backed by the granite peaks and with the White Water burn flowing down to the shore, the Corrie was deservedly called one of the prettiest villages in Europe by Prime Minister Herbert Asquith.

Above the village is High Corrie, an older settlement built on an earlier shoreline – the 'raised beach' which circles much of the island. This idyllic clachan, in a natural garden of short springy turf with outcrops of rock, enjoys a delightful situation between mountain and sea.

The Glens

The Arran glens, some small and mysterious, others grand and dramatic, attract climbers, walkers and picnickers. Glen Rosa, running inland from Brodick, is a wide and peaceful valley, ideal for a gentle walk. Glen Sannox is sharper, and awe-inspiring in stormy weather. Each glen has its particular character, and the burns flowing through them are a constant pleasure; some steep as a staircase with many waterfalls, others a quiet flow of water with deep pools. A trek up the wild and lonely Catacol Glen leads to Loch Tanna.

Lochranza

Lochranza is dominated by its ruined castle, which stands on a promontory running out into the sea loch. The castle probably dates from the 13th or 14th century and was once a royal hunting lodge. In stark contrast is the newly built distillery.

A rewarding walk from Lochranza to the Cock of Arran starts on a track, well signed, on the far side of the Chalmadale Burn. A slow, but not too steep climb above the village leads to a moorland plateau, finally dropping down to a marvellous viewpoint overlooking the Sound of Bute. The ruins of the Cock Farm are far below – in summer almost submerged in bracken – and on the lower level are the remains of the coal mines which provided fuel for the salt production in this area. This route can be

Prehistoric stones

Of all prehistoric sites on Arran the most impressive are those on Machrie Moor – visible even from the distant String Road in their isolated moorland setting.

The site is signposted just south of Machrie on the A841, from where the standing stones are reached via an ancient track which passes through the derelict Moss Farm. The Auchgallon stone circle, dating from the Bronze Age, is the most accessible and is well preserved in an attractive situation.

Unfortunately many of the ancient sites are engulfed in forestry plantations, robbing them of their former wild and open aspect. Carn Ban, probably the highest prehistoric site in Arran, is surrounded by conifer plantations, though because it stands high there are views over some of the trees. It is reached by a long and sometimes muddy walk of about 3.75 miles (6km) from the A841.

One very large stone circle is Kilpatrick Dun, thought to have been a defended farmstead around 1,800 years ago. The quiet and open position and the beautiful view north to the cliffs and fort of Drumadoon combine to make this great ring of stones and turf dyke a magical place. It is reached by a rough cart-track which starts just outside the farmyard at Kilpatrick Farm.

Lochranza is clustered around an inlet on the northern tip of Arran

Golden Eagles have a wingspan of over 7ft (2m) and can dive upon their prey at over 150 miles (241km) per hour

Arran Wildlife

In summer birdwatching tours can be arranged and offer the chance to see a golden eagle soaring above the granite cliffs. Arran's birdlife is extensive and it is only necessary to pause by the shore to see a great variety of seabirds. The coast road between Brodick and Corrie runs near the water, and shelduck, eider, mallard, shags, cormorants and herons are a common sight here. A group of diving gannets, wings streamlined as they plummet from a great height into the water for fish, is a thrilling spectacle, and not unusual along the Corrie, Catacol and Pirnmill shores.

A virus took its toll of the seal population in the late 1980s, but these delightful creatures are again numerous and can be seen basking on the rocks just to the north of Brodick below the castle. Porpoises, which could once be seen rolling and leaping in the water quite near the shoreline, are now uncommon; but the immense (and harmless) basking shark patrols the inshore waters from time to time. Its great dorsal fin, sailing along smoothly with only an occasional movement in the water to indicate the shark's length, is an astonishing sight.

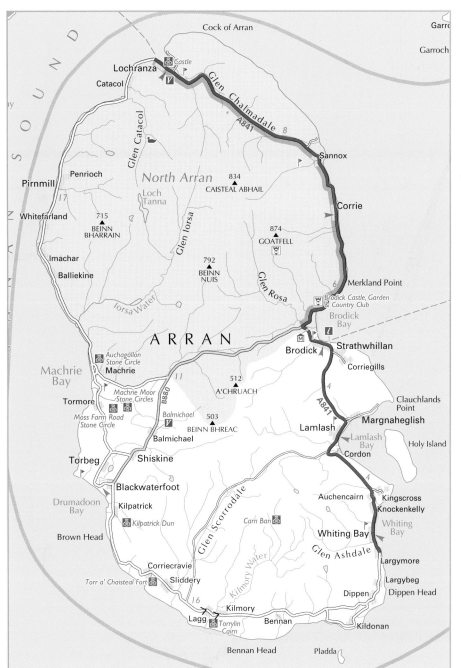

The mallard duck is the ancestor of most domestic ducks

retraced, or you can turn left at sea level and return to Lochranza by the coast – something of a scramble on the rocky foreshore, which can be wet and muddy approaching the village, but on a fine sunny day the views are unsurpassed and the absolute silence of this inaccessible part of the coast is truly memorable.

Mid Thundergay and Coire Fhionn Lochan

Mid Thundergay, between Lochranza and Pirnmill, is the starting point for a walk which should not be missed by anyone able to tackle a moderately steep hillside. A signpost on the A841 points to Coire Fhionn Lochan, the most picturesque of

the inland lochs. Follow the burn uphill for nearly 2 miles (3km) and the lochan comes suddenly into view – clear, clean and blue in a bowl of surrounding hills. It is fringed by a narrow white gravel beach. The views are splendid, taking in the peaks of Jura and the softer hills of Islay, seen over the Mull of Kintyre.

Common seals, feeding on fish, crabs and squid are a common sight around Arran's coast

THE LAND OF ROBERT BURNS

This stretch of coastline is the playground for Glasgow and industrial southwest Scotland, with sandy beaches, first-class golf links and the promise of lively nightlife in the vibrant resort of Ayr. The undulating landscape of rich farmland is peppered with noble castles, while to the east of Kilmarnock are the deeper clefts of the Irvine Valley.

Once frequented by Robert Burns himself, this inn in Ayr is the very one described in Tam o' Shanter

Ayr

With a seafront esplanade stretching for 2.5 miles (4km), Ayr is famed as the favourite resort of the Clyde towns. As well as its broad beach, the town is blessed with lovely gardens and parks, and Belleisle has an aviary and two golf courses. Family outdoor recreation is

The 15th-century Brig o' Doon was made famous by Robert Burns in Tam o' Shanter

its forte, but history and culture are not entirely lacking. Ayr's charter dates back to 1202, and south harbour is overlooked by the ruins of Cromwell's citadel and St John's Tower. And there is the inevitable Burns Heritage Trail. During the summer the *Waverley*, the last seagoing paddle steamer, offers popular excursions to Arran. Caledonian MacBrayne offer regular sailings year round. Ayr is Scotland's leading horse-racing venue, with both flat and national hunt meetings.

Irvine

At first glance Irvine has all the appearance of a 1960s town, but at its heart there is an old burgh with an interesting past. Until the Clyde was dredged, this was the port for Glasgow, and it is also noted for the Treaty of Irvine, signed in 1297 by William Wallace's deserters. It was also a place of inspiration – the little cobbled street where Robert Burns once worked and lodged, known as the Glasgow Vennel, has been lovingly restored. Nearby is the Irvine Burns Club where a small museum contains many manuscripts and first editions.

Down at the harbour in the Scottish Maritime Museum, preserved and restored craft are on display beside their (often tragic) stories. Children can test their own boat designs in the indoor model tank. Outside is the fascinating ASR-10 rescue craft from the Second World War, and moored quayside are the museum's larger vessels, including a steam yacht and Clyde 'puffer'. The Magnum Leisure Centre, with pools and water slides, ice rink and theatre is a good wet-weather option.

Kilmarnock

This industrial town was once famous as the home of Johnny Walker whisky. It is also the place where John Wilson published the famous 'Kilmarnock' first edition of the poetry of Robert Burns,

Auld Lang Syne

This is probably one of the most sung songs, after 'Happy Birthday to You', but few could get past the first verse and a chorus, and fewer still could tell you what 'auld lang syne' means. Even through the dialect, the complete song portrays a sentimental celebration of enduring friendship.

Should auld acquaintance
be forgot,
And never brought to
mind?
Should auld acquaintance
be forgot,
And days o' lang syne?

For auld lang syne, my jo,
For auld lang syne,
We'll tak a cup o'
kindness yet
For auld lang syne.

And surely ye'll be your
pint-stowp
And surely I'll be mine!
And we'll tak a cup o'
kindness yet
For auld lang syne.

We twa hae run about
the braes,
And pu'd the gowans
fine
But we've wander'd mony
a weary foot
Sin auld lang syne.

We twa hae paidl'd i' the
burn
Frae mornin sun till dine,
But seas between us braid
hae roar'd
Sin auld lang syne.

And there's a han' my
trusty fiere!
And gie's a hand o' thine.
And we'll tak a right gude
willy-waug\ht
For auld lang syne.

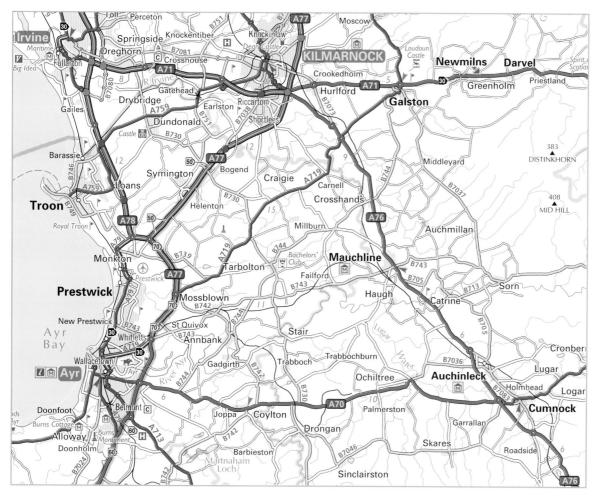

The Auld Kirk in Alloway, burial place of the Bard's parents, and setting for drunken apparitions in Tam o' Shanter

Burns Cottage, Alloway

Tourist Information

Ayr: 22 Sandgate
(tel: 01292 290330)
Girvan: Bridge Street
(tel: 01465 713389)
Irvine: New Street
(01294) 313886
Largs: Railway Station,
Main Street (tel: 01475
689962)

who is now commemorated with a statue, which forms the centrepiece of the Burns Monument Centre. The leading museum is the Dick Institute, specialising in local archaeology, geology and natural history, which also has an art gallery with an important collection of paintings.

Dean Castle, the focal point of a 200-acre (81ha) country park with nature trails, started out as a 14th-century stronghold, but later developed into a palace. It contains a renowned collection of medieval ephemera, from armour and tapestries to musical instruments. The ruined Louden Castle, the place where the Act of Union was signed in 1707, is now a park.

Mauchline

Located on a rise some 8 miles (12.9km) south of Kilmarnock, this small town overlooks Mossgiel Farm, once farmed by Robert Burns. Many of his most significant works were written here, and some of the characters he wrote about now lie in the village churchyard, which was the setting for *Holy Fair*. At first glance signposts for the Burns Heritage Trail seem to outnumber the houses. They point out the Burns Museum in Castle Street, in the house he took when he married Jean Armour in 1788, the Burns Memorial Tower of 1896, Mauchline Castle and Poosie Nansie's Tavern, which is still a pub. Mauchline is also renowned for the manufacture of curling stones.

Five miles (8km) west in Tarbolton is the thatched cottage where Burns founded a debating society, the Bachelors' Club. Four miles (6.4km) to the east lies Sorn, a delightful riverside village with a 14th-century castle.

Troon

This dignified town has moved on from its fishing port origins to become a place for golf and yachting. Troon is almost surrounded by its five golf courses, the Royal Troon being the most prestigious, with its famous Postage Stamp, a par 3 short hole.

The Marine Highland Hotel is a landmark for miles around, and Troon's distinctive stalwart homes are embellished with turrets and towers. Three miles (4.8km) to the northeast are the impressive ruins of Dundonald Castle, where the Stuart dynasty was founded.

The Birthplace of Burns

The leafy suburb of Alloway at the southern edge of Ayr is where Robert Burns was born on 25 January 1759, and it attracts visitors by the coachload. The Birthplace Museum is adjacent to the white thatched cottage, built by his father, where Burns lived until he was seven years old. Nearby are a cluster of Burns 'sites', including real-life landmarks from *Tam o'Shanter*, such as the Auld Brig o' Doon, over which Tam escaped the witches. The story is brought to life in the *Tam o'Shanter* Experience. Devotees can also seek out the Burns Monument, with its Corinthian pillars and the Auld Kirk.

See Walk B, page 335
Discover Dunaskin Ironworks

THE 'DEAR, DIRTY CITY' ON THE CLYDE

This sprawling metropolis, famed for leading the Industrial Revolution, has undergone a self-imposed renaissance. Shipbuilding, steam locomotive works and other heavy engineering have given way to an image of art and culture. Set amongst some of the finest Victorian architecture in Britain, the reborn Glasgow offers a totally new experience in city sightseeing.

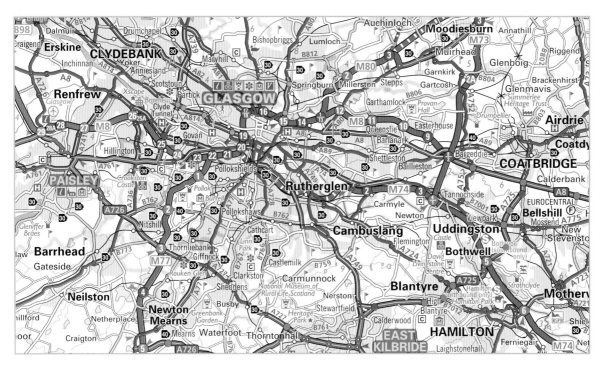

Blantyre

A tram and conductor at Summerlee Heritage Park, Coatbridge

The great explorer, David Livingstone, was born in Blantyre and at the age of 10 worked in the local mill. The David Livingstone Centre, situated in the tenement block of his birth, traces his life in Africa and recalls his battle against slavers, his search for the source of the Nile and his famous meeting with Stanley.

To the north, standing above the Clyde, lies the breathtaking red sandstone ruin of Bothwell Castle, which saw much action during the 13th and 14th centuries. The immense circular tower tested the ingenuity of its attackers, including Edward I who, in 1301, stormed it with a siege tower taller than the battlements.

Coatbridge

Coatbridge is one of the great ironwork towns that sprang up with the Industrial Revolution. The Summerlee Heritage Trust, one of Scotland's most interesting and certainly noisiest museums, recreates the sights and sounds of 200 years of industrial and social history. Set in the old Summerlees ironworks of 1835, it has clattering working machinery, re-enactments, an electric tramway, a shallow mine and miners' cottages.

Glasgow

One of the most remarkable cities in Britain, Glasgow transformed its public image during the 1980s, throwing off its sometimes exaggerated reputation as a run-down, post-industrial city and becoming known for its friendliness, vibrant arts and entertainment scene, first-class shopping and superb museums and galleries.

Though Glasgow began to develop in the 18th century, through trading tobacco, cotton and sugar from America, it was the Industrial Revolution that really started its economic boom, and many of the city-centre buildings are bold

The Coat of Arms

The Glasgow crest features a salmon with a ring in its mouth – a curious image, until you hear the legend regarding Queen Languoreth, who, attracted by a knight, gave him a ring. The King, while resting during a hunting party, noticed the ring on the knight's finger and, suspecting an intrigue, took the ring off the sleeping knight's finger and threw it into the Clyde. He later questioned the Queen as to the whereabouts of the ring, and threatened her with death if she couldn't produce it. She pleaded with St Mungo, who sent a monk to fish the river. The first caught salmon was landed with the ring in its mouth.

The interior of the music room in the House for an Art Lover, designed by Charles Rennie Mackintosh in 1901, and built 90 years later in Glasgow

Charles Rennie Mackintosh

Scotland's most famous architect, artist and designer was born in 1868. He spent most of his working life in Glasgow and was most active between 1897 and 1912. Many buildings feature his work including houses, schools and even a church. He is internationally acclaimed for transforming the Victorian influence into innovative art nouveau styles, applied to exteriors, interiors and furnishings. The Glasgow School of Art and the Willow Tearooms in Sauchiehall Street are noted achievements. A reconstruction of the interior of his own home can be viewed at the Hunterian Art Gallery.

statements in brick and stone of Glasgow's 19th-century prosperity and pride. In recent years the grime has been wiped away, displaying these fine buildings in all their glory, set off by exciting new architectural developments. Buildings range from the medieval splendours of the city's cathedral, founded in the sixth century by St Kentigern (St Mungo) and the most complete medieval cathedral in mainland Scotland, to the charms of the Willow Tearooms in Sauchiehall Street. These were designed by Charles Rennie Mackintosh, Glasgow's major architectural force of the early 20th century – don't miss his buildings such as the Glasgow School of Art or the House for an Art Lover in Bellahouston Park.

Bellahouston is only one of Glasgow's lovely parks and gardens; others include the Botanic Gardens, Greenbank and Pollok Country Park. The latter houses not only Pollok House, home to the Stirling Maxwell collection of fine and decorative arts, but also the magnificent Burrell Collection, in its purpose-built gallery. The 8,000 items were amassed by Sir William Burrell, who presented them to the city in 1944. Highlights include fine art, ceramics and superb examples of stained glass and tapestries. Other fine pictures, and much more, are found at the Kelvingrove Art Gallery and Museum, the city's main museum, the Hunterian Art Gallery and the Gallery of Modern Art.

The Centre for Contemporary Arts has changing exhibitions, performance arts and film events. Social history is related at the People's Palace, while Clydebuilt, in Braehead, offers interactive experiences such as piloting a virtual ship. The Glasgow Science Centre celebrates science and innovation with numerous exhibits and an IMAX cinema.

Hamilton

Bordering the Strathclyde Country Park, Hamilton has a history stretching back to the sixth century, but its 19th-century prosperity was firmly based on the mining industry. The hugely rich Dukes of Hamilton were its lairds; they built the bizarre hunting lodge of Chatelherault overlooking the Clyde Valley, while the 10th Duke was buried in an Egyptian sarcophagus within the extraordinary Hamilton Mausoleum. The Low Parks Museum, occupying a fine 17th-century house, tells the story of the Dukes and the town.

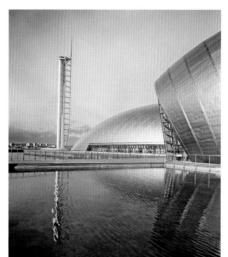

At 417ft (127m) high, the rotating Glasgow Tower dominates the Glasgow Science Centre

Motherwell

Motherwell (its name comes from a healing well) was once a proud industrial centre, which saw its last days of steel with the closure of the Ravenscraig works. The town stands on the edge of Strathclyde Country Park, part of which is home to M & D's Theme Park, complete with thrill rides and a range of other attractions.

Paisley

This pleasing industrial town is the place where the handkerchief was invented, but more famously it has given its name to the Kashmiri teardrop design on fabrics. The Museum and Art Gallery contains some 500 shawls, reflecting the town's days as a weaving centre, and the Sma' Shot Cottages are now a museum illustrating the life of weavers and mill workers. Later the town became the world's largest manufacturer of cotton thread. The 12th-century Abbey, restored by Sir Robert Lorimer in 1897, is noted for its depictions of the life of St Mirren.

See Walk F, page 339
Exploring Glasgow's Heritage

Tourist Information
Glasgow: 11 George Square (tel: 0141 204 4400)
Paisley: 9a Gilmour Street (tel: 0141 889 0711)

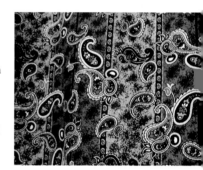

The patterned shawls brought back from Kashmir so impressed Victorian ladies that Paisley's weavers were inundated with order for imitations, and the pattern was given the town's name

Decorative lawn and gatehouse forming part of Chatelherault Country Park, designed in the mid-18th century for James, fifth Duke of Hamilton

SCOTLAND'S HISTORIC CAPITAL

This is a city built on hills, and from its high crests and ridges are views which overlook its steeples, twisting medieval wynds and the neat symmetry of its delightful Georgian crescents and squares – and the freshness of the surrounding hills is ever present. From the famous castle, the boom of the 'one o'clock' gun reverberates across the city, signalling the exact time to shipping on the Firth of Forth.

Edinburgh Castle is perched on an extinct volcano; there is evidence of settlement on the site from 900BC

Leisure craft on the River Almond, near Cramond

Cramond

A pleasant village of white cottages and narrow alleys, Cramond is set above the anchorage where the River Almond flows into the Forth, with the uninhabited Cramond Island just offshore. The Romans established a substantial fortress at Cramond, with a small settlement including a bath house, and the ruins and outlines can be seen behind the church. To the southeast is Lauriston Castle.

Edinburgh

Scotland's capital has everything a capital city should have – a castle, a royal palace, national collections of art, splendid museums, excellent shopping, fine architecture and lovely parks. It is compact enough to explore on foot, but it's hilly, so start out on high ground, enjoy the wonderful views to the surrounding hills and the Firth of Forth, then explore downhill.

The city centre has two distinct parts. The New Town, to the north, is an architectural setpiece of Georgian town houses lining gracious streets, squares and crescents. Princes Street, overlooked by the Castle, is the main thoroughfare, a busy street with high-street stores, while parallel George Street offers more up-market shopping. Charlotte Square is the jewel of the New Town, and No. 7 has been restored to its late 18th-century style.

The Old Town, south and east of the Castle ridge, brims with curiosity and history. Tall tenements and public buildings set in cobbled streets are the keynotes here, with atmospheric wynds and alleys to explore. It is dominated by the Castle, strategically set on an extinct volcanic plug and guarded by sentries in Scottish regimental uniform. The buildings have served various purposes over the past 900 years, with the oldest – tiny St Margaret's Chapel – dating from the 11th century. The Great Hall, with its hammerbeam ceiling, was where the Scottish Parliament met until 1639. The adjacent palace, where Mary, Queen of Scots gave birth to James VI and I, also houses Scotland's crown jewels and regalia and the Stone of Destiny, returned from Westminster Abbey in 1998.

Edinburgh Castle is connected to the Palace of Holyroodhouse, and now the Scottish Parliament, by the Royal Mile. Along its length, visitors can learn about the city and its citizens at the Museum of Children, at People's Story, at the Museum of Edinburgh, at the Writers' Museum – devoted to Burns, Scott and Stevenson – and at Gladstone's Land, a restored 17th-century tenement.

There's more history at the National Museum of Scotland, and fine art at the National Gallery of Scotland and the Scottish National Gallery of Modern Art. Near the Scottish Parliament, Our Dynamic Earth is a state-of-the art attraction which tells the story of the planet, while at the port of Leith, the Royal Yacht *Britannia* is now a perfectly preserved floating museum.

The Forth Bridges

Opened in 1890 at a cost of more than £3 million, the Forth Railway Bridge was considered the 'Eighth Wonder of the World'. Construction began in 1882 under Sir John Fowler and Benjamin Baker, and at its height it employed 4,600 men. The viaduct, standing 157ft (47.8m) above the water, is 8,296ft (2,528.7m) long, comprising 53,000 tons of steel that require 7,000 gallons of paint. The 1½ mile (2.4km) long suspension bridge for motor traffic was opened in 1964.

Tourist Information

All telephone enquiries (tel: 08452 255121)
Bo'ness: Bo'ness Station, Union Street
Edinburgh: 3 Princes Street and Edinburgh Airport

The entire cast assemble at the finale of the Military tattoo at Edinburgh Castle

The Edinburgh Festival

Founded in 1947, the three-week festival for the visual and performing arts, which takes place every August and September, is now the world's premier cultural event. There are two distinct sides: the 'official', with set programmes for opera, ballet, dance and theatre; and the 'fringe', which of late has almost dominated the 'official'. However, each complements the other. Attendees are advised to book early, especially their accommodation.

Prestonpans

Eight miles (12.9km) to the east of Edinburgh, Prestonpans takes its name from its medieval salt pans, and it has many houses dating from the 17th century. Preston Tower is a fortified tower house with an interesting stone dovecote that could roost nearly 1,000 birds. The Mercat Cross is considered the finest of its kind in Scotland.

This was the site of the Jacobite victory of Preston Pans in 1745 (over in minutes). More recent history is on show at the Scottish Mining Museum at nearby Newtongrange, in the oldest documented coal-mining site in Britain, which has been worked for some 800 years.

South Queensferry

This delightful village, on the shore of the Forth, has the best view of the bridges, and of Inchcolm Island, with its 12th-century abbey. As its name suggests, this was the ferry point from 1169 until the opening of the road bridge in 1964. Just outside the nearby village of Dalmeny, Dalmeny House contains the Rosebery Collections of paintings, furniture, tapestries and porcelain, while 2 miles (3.2km) west is Hopetoun House, Scotland's finest Adam mansion, with beautiful furniture and a notable collection of paintings.

Advanced paints mean workers can finally take a break from painting the Forth Railway Bridge

See Walk C, page 336
The Thirty-Nine Steps in Broughton

See Walk D, page 337
Edinburgh's Old Town

See Walk E, page 338
The Romance of Rosslyn Glen

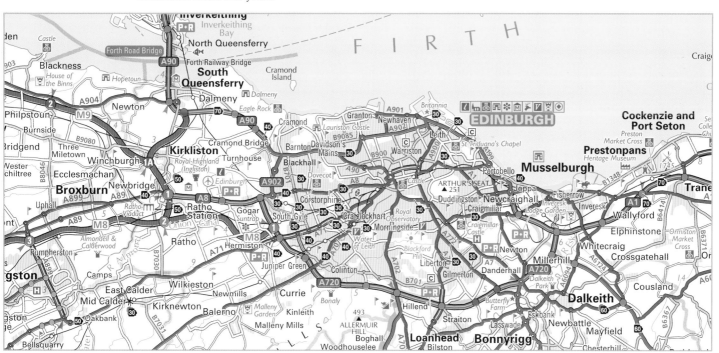

THE WILDLIFE OF SCOTLAND

From soaring crags to misty marshland, from mountain top to coastline, from lowland plain to high moorland, the habitats of Scotland are immensely varied. Sub-tropical trees flourish less than 50 miles (80km) from the north coast in Inverewe gardens, warmed by the Gulf Stream. On the Cairngorm plateau genuine Arctic conditions, more typical of regions 1,000 miles (1,609km) north, prevail. Between these two extremes lie the high moorland, the lush glens, the rock-bound coasts and the gentle rivers that are home to many distinctive species.

It is now possible to see Scotland's most precious treasures – the golden eagle, the osprey or the red squirrel. However, the fierce wild cats are not easy to spot in moorland and forest. Otters, too, are seldom seen, though they hunt beside the seashore of the west coast and among the islands as well as by inland burns. Despite their rarity, however, such species seem unlikely to go the way of others – wild reindeer died out here in the 12th century, the beaver probably in the 15th (though there are plans to reintroduce it), and the last wolf in Scotland was killed in 1743.

A new dawn rises behind pine trees in the Rothiemurchus forest, in the Cairngorms National Park

There are ancient oak woods, too, especially in the Argyll glens towards the Atlantic coast, where gnarled trees are hung with lichens and the forest floor is home to an amazing multitude of ferns and flowers. In places, too, are survivors of ancient birch forests – among the most accessible of them is the Birks of Aberfeldy.

A Record Dozen

The climate of Scotland is excellent for trees of all types – which may be why 12 of Britain's 30 tallest trees are here, among them a dead heat of two Douglas firs at the Hermitage in Perthshire and Dunans in Argyll, both of which measure 212ft (64.5m). Tayside also has the tallest holly and beech – both 150ft (46m) – at Hallyburton House, as well as a Sitka spruce measuring 200ft (61m) at Strathearn. Other giants are the 206ft (63m) grand fir at Strone in Argyll and a western hemlock 167ft (51m) nearby at Benmore; and – a pigmy by comparison – the 98ft (30m) silver birch at Ballogie in Grampian. Scotland holds two sequoia records – for the tallest in Britain, 174ft (53m) at Strathpeffer, and for the largest, at Clunie Gardens in Tayside, with a diameter of 11ft 4in (3.5m). And, as for age, the UK's oldest known tree still survives near Aberfeldy – the Fortingall Yew. It is thought to be around 1,500 years old.

At the other extreme are the miniature willow forests that clothe some Scottish mountains, high above the normal treeline. Cold and infertile, often covered with snow which may linger into the summer, these are inhospitable climates for vegetation. But still plants survive, often clustered in hollows or forming dense mats of green, which may suddenly burst into colourful flower in favourable conditions. Ben Lawers

Forests Old and New

Many of the lost animals of Scotland needed the huge stretches of native pine forest which once covered much of Scotland. Now only 1 per cent of the Caledonian Forest survives, having fallen victim to man's greed for timber.

Eighteenth-century iron smelting accounted for the loss of many trees, which were felled and floated down the rivers to be burned for charcoal to fuel the furnaces. Others produced valuable timber, while deliberate clearance of forest (as well as of inhabitants) to introduce vast sheep runs accounted for much more. The bare, open, rocky landscape of much of the Highlands, although admired by visitors, is to a large extent the result of these predations. Where there is forest today, much of it

is the result of planting since the two world wars and, although in recent years the ruler-straight edges have given way to more sensitive planting, the denseness, uniformity and blanketing effect of the trees have been much criticised. There has also been controversy over the commercial afforestation of large areas of open land, such as the unique bogland environment known as the Flow Country.

Where pockets of native pinewood survive – at the Black Wood of Rannoch and Rothiemurchus Forest by the Cairngorms, for example – they are magical places, with mosses, blaeberries and junipers plentiful amid the trees, and wild flowers such as wintergreens and lady's tresses.

The name Ptarmigan is derived from the gaelic 'tàrmachan', the silent 'p' was added in the 17th century

Foula in Shetland has vast numbers of great skuas, and in the friable mountainsides of Rum in the Inner Hebrides thousands of Manx sheerwaters have their burrows. On the mainland, the cliffs of Sutherland are thronged with colonies of fulmars, kittiwakes and guillemots, the mouth of the Tay with eider duck and the Solway Estuary with barnacle geese.

The leaping salmon, on its journey upstream to its spawning grounds, is king of Scottish fish, but the claims of the more prosaic sea trout and mountain trout cannot be disregarded. In deep mountain lochs the ferox trout – golden and spotted with black – keeps company with its red and black relative, the char. In the deepest of all – Loch Ness – may lurk the most mysterious of all Scotland's wildlife. If it does, it will add another aspect to the rich diversity of the country's treasures.

in Perthshire is particularly famous for the variety of its mountain flowers, including such rarities as the vivid blue alpine gentian and the drooping saxifrage.

Animals and birds, too, need to be hardy to survive the high mountain tops. The ptarmigan is one, often seen by skiers; its mottled brown plumage turns white in winter. A summer visitor, the dotterel, is much rarer; it breeds regularly in the eastern Highlands. Snow buntings also visit from their Arctic homes in the summer, but few stay to breed. The only butterfly regularly breeding here is the mountain ringlet. Mountain hares and stoats survive on the rocky slopes; they, too, go white in the winter.

colours in the landscape, from the brightest greens to stabbing orange and yellow. Where the bogs are wettest, plants like the cranberry gain a foothold, as well as the insect-eating sundew. Glittering dragonflies are often seen flittering over bogland.

In extreme contrast are the flower-rich sea-meadows – the machair – which lie behind many Highland beaches, and are particularly spectacular on the shores of the Outer Hebrides, where the shell sand tempers the acidity of the peat soil. Here buttercups, orchids and gentians grow in colourful profusion. The primrose banks of Barra are especially wonderful.

Birds, too, congregate on the islands. Remote St Kilda has its own species of wren, while

After years in the feeding grounds of Greenland, the Atlantic salmon struggles past weirs and waterfalls to spawn at its birthplace

Moors and Shores

On lower moorland two game species come into their own – the red deer and the grouse. Britain's largest wild animal, the red deer was encouraged by Victorian landowners for sport, and stalking is still important in some areas. The sight of a magnificently antlered stag in a misty valley has been a favourite image of Scotland since before Landseer painted *The Monarch of the Glen*. The managed heather moors, where regular burning helps regenerate the plants, provide the habitat for many grouse – the red is the main target for sportsmen. Larger is the black grouse; each male has its territory – called a lek – where pinewoods meet moorland. The capercaillie, hunted to extinction in Scotland by 1800, was reintroduced in 1837 and is now found deep in the woodlands of the east of the country. Where bogland predominates – in the Flow Country, for example, and on Rannoch Moor – domes of bog moss can provide striking

Native red deer, like this roaring stag, are found in many of Scotland's National Parks

STIRLING AND THE TROSSACHS

So wond'ous wild, the whole night might seem, the scenery of a feary dream.' So wrote Sir Walter Scott, who set two of his greatest works, *Rob Roy* and *The Lady of the Lake* in the Trossachs around Loch Katrine. Poets and writers have long been inspired by the scenery of hills and lochs. Coleridge, the Wordsworths, Ruskin and Hogg all succumbed to its spell.

The lochs of the Trossachs offer watersports for all ages and tastes

Aberfoyle

Tucked below the slopes of the Trossachs, Aberfoyle is a popular tourist centre and the 'gateway to the Trossachs'. At the Scottish Wool Centre you can learn about wool production. The town is handy for the spectacular 67sq mile (173.5sq km) Queen Elizabeth Forest Park, which includes trails, picnic areas and wildlife lookouts. A scenic route into the Trossachs takes you over Duke's Pass, between Lochs Achray and Katrine. The Achray Forest Drive to Brig o'Turk and to the lochs of Ard and Chon is also beautiful.

Bannockburn

This suburb of Stirling was, in 1314, the site of the decisive defeat by Robert the Bruce of Edward II's English army, 10 times larger than the Scots force. The Bannockburn Heritage Centre includes an exhibition and audiovisual on the battle, outlining the confusion in the English army in the marshlands. The victory resulted in the surrender of Stirling Castle and recognition by the Pope of Robert the Bruce's kingship, culminating in Scottish independence. Though the Heritage Centre stands close to the Borderstone site, said to be Robert the Bruce's command post, the exact whereabouts of the battleground is still disputed after all these years.

Tourist Information

Aberfoyle: Main Street, (seasonal) (tel: 01877 382352)
Callander: Ancaster Square (tel: 01877 330342)
Dunfermline: 1 High Street (tel: 01383 720999)
Stirling: 41 Dumbarton Road (tel: 01786 475019)

Callander

Set against a Highland backdrop, this neat market town and tourist centre was developed in the 18th century on forfeited Jacobite lands. The legends of its local

Statue of Robert the Bruce at Bannockburn

hero, Rob Roy MacGregor, are retold in an audiovisual in the old kirk in the town centre.

Children love the Hamilton Toy Collection, while the whole family can escape the crowds on the scenic footpath to the lovely Bracklinn Falls.

Doune

The awe-inspiring 14th- to 15th-century castle, built for the Duke of Albany, regent of Scotland from 1388 until 1420, with its fine tower and gatehouse, is strategically situated between the rivers Teith and Ardoch. Red kites can be seen at Argaty, which is signposted from the centre of the village. Two miles (3.2km) south is Blair Drummond Safari and Adventure Park, where visitors can drive through the wild animal reserves, or leave the car and take to the water in pedal boats.

Dunblane

Though it is only a small place, Dunblane is actually a city because of its cathedral. The cathedral was restored in the late 19th century, and its origins go back to 1240, with foundations laid on the site of the church established by St Blane in AD602.

Until the Reformation, Dunblane was a city of power and influence. Today it is remembered for the song, *Jessie, the Flower of Dunblane*, composed by a local weaver, and a complex tartan comprising 14 colours. Leighton Library holds 4,000 rare books, including Johnson's first dictionaries. The caves on the riverside walk to the Bridge of Allan are said to be where Robert Louis Stevenson often sought inspiration for his books. To the east lies the battlefield of Sheriffmuir, which, though an indecisive event, ended the 1715 Jacobite rebellion.

Lake of Menteith

Scotland's only inland water not called a loch is noted for fishing in the summer. The largest of the three islands on this

The 1922 'Wallace window' in St Margaret's chapel, Edinburgh Castle, depicts William Wallace astride his mount with sword in hand

Wallace and Bruce

Two of Scotland's fabled warrior heroes, who achieved their fame within sight of Stirling Castle. William Wallace, son of a Renfrewshire knight, was a resistance fighter and appointed Guardian of Scotland. His great victory in the Battle of Stirling Bridge in 1297 was short-lived. He was later captured and executed in London in 1305.

Robert the Bruce, born in 1274 of Norman ancestry, with lands in England, declared himself for Scotland and was crowned king in 1306. Even though defeated, excommunicated and outlawed, his guerrilla warfare campaign over many years culminated in victory at Bannockburn, which led to Scotland's independence in 1328. He died in Cardross Castle, possibly of leprosy, in 1329.

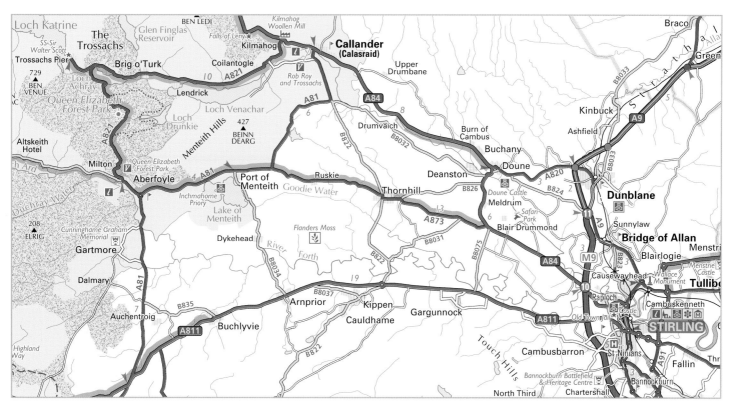

Loch Katrine

This spectacular 10 mile (16km) loch is evocative of Sir Walter Scott's ballad, *The Lady of the Lake* and his novel *Rob Roy*, based on the legendary rebel. Best approached via Dukes Pass from Aberfoyle, this inspiring loch can be cruised in summer aboard the *Sir Walter Scott*, a steamer built in 1900. At the northwest end of the loch in Stronachlar is the graveyard of Clan MacGregor. Further on is Glengyle House, the birthplace of Rob Roy.

serene loch is Inchmahome, with the ruins of an Augustinian priory. It was the hideout in 1547 of Mary, Queen of Scots, aged five, before her flight to France. The summer ferry will take you across.

Stirling

For centuries the lowest bridging point on the River Forth, Stirling, dominated by its castle, occupies the slopes of a volcanic outcrop above reclaimed marshland. A royal burgh since 1124, the city and its castle became a favourite with the Stuart monarchs, and Mary, Queen of Scots, was crowned here in 1543. Stirling is well endowed with splendid Scottish Renaissance buildings, notably Argyll's Lodgings, near the castle, and Mar's Wark, the ornate but incomplete palace of the Earl of Mar. Other landmarks include the Church of the Holy Rude, scene of James VI's coronation in 1567, Cowane's Hospital and the Tolbooth.

Stirling Castle overlooks the cemetery at the Church of the Holy Rude

Visitors can learn more of Stirling's history at the excellent Stirling Visitor Centre, while other attractions include the Old Town Jail, complete with living history performances, and the Smith Art Gallery and Museum.

To the northeast stands the National Wallace Monument, built in 1860 on an outcrop overlooking the scene of William Wallace's 1297 victory at Stirling Bridge. From the top of the 220ft (67m) tower there are panoramic views over the Ochil Hills and the Stirling plains, while the interior houses a Hall of Scottish heroes and gives an insight into Wallace's life.

The steamship Sir Walter Scott *on the waters of Loch Katrine. Its boilers have been converted to run on biodiesel*

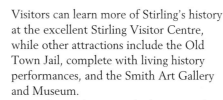**See Walk G, page 340**
Stirling's Braveheart, William Wallace

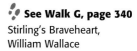**See Walk H, page 341**
Climbing to the Castle of Cups

THE FAIR CITY

This area encompasses the long-gone seat of the Scottish kings, which is now the 'Fair City' of Perth, and the pepperpot towers of Falkland Palace, a favourite of the Stuart dynasty. This is a historic 'royal' region of Scotland, where rich rolling farmlands, elegant fortified mansions and great country estates bask in the shelter of the Highlands.

Begun in 1500, Falkland Palace is an outstanding example of French-influenced Renaissance architecture

Falkland

Tucked beneath the Lomond Hills, this tiny Royal Burgh has more than 100 listed buildings, with twisting wynds and courtyards between the cottages and sandstone town houses of the 17th to 19th centuries. Its fame and influence was at its height in the 16th and 17th centuries, when the turreted, Renaissance-style Falkland Palace, now owned by Her Majesty the Queen, was the favourite hunting lodge of the Stuart monarchs, particularly Mary, Queen of Scots. Royal monograms decorate the King's Bedchamber, while fine Flemish tapestries hang in the chapel, and a prime feature is the tennis court of 1539, the oldest in Britain. The castle was sacked by Cromwell's forces, but restored by John Crichton Stuart in 1889, whose family still act as guardians for the Queen.

Kinross

This peaceful town on the banks of Loch Leven is surrounded by rich farmland, with the Cleish Hills in the south, the Ochills in the north and the Lomonds in the east.

The area is rich in historical sites and popular for country pursuits – the 4,000-acre (1,620ha) Loch Leven is world renowned for its fishing. The RSPB reserve at Vane Farm on the south side of the loch has hides for observing migrant geese and duck, together with a bumblebee sanctuary.

Close to the centre of the town, Kinross House is a Palladian-style mansion built in 1690 and noted for its formal gardens and yew hedges. Out in the loch, Castle Island, with its 14th-century fortress, is where in 1567 Mary, Queen of Scots was imprisoned until her romantic boat escape organised by Willie Douglas.

Perth

Once the capital of Scotland, this commercial centre, with its working port and fine Georgian buildings, maintains the

Elcho Castle

This fortified mansion on the south bank of the Tay, complete with towers, turrets and crow-stepped gables, was built for the Earl of Wemyss in the late 16th century. Across the river lies 17th-century Megginch Castle, home of the Drummonds since soon after it was a built. First laid out in the 17th century, its formal gardens contain some superb and ancient holly and yew trees, a beautiful rose garden and an 18th-century physic garden incorporating astrological planting.

The River Devon, near Kinross, 'rumbles' through a deep gorge

atmosphere of a county town. Straddling the River Tay, it rose to eminence in AD838, when Kenneth MacAlpin, the first king of United Scotland, brought the legendary Stone of Destiny to nearby Scone. Kinnoull Hill, overlooking the 'Fair City', offers spectacular views to the Highlands, and across the two green parks beside the river, the North and South Inches. The North Inch was the site of the Battle of the Clane in 1396. Close by is the Black Watch Museum illustrating the proud history of this regiment, and the Fair Maid's House, one of the oldest buildings, associated with Sir Walter Scott's novel *The Fair Maid of Perth*. The well-marked Old Perth Trail in this compact city leads through former trading streets, such as Ropemakers Close and Cow Vennel, and to the historic Church of St John (1126).

Flowers are very much part of Perth's heritage. It has been winner of the Britain

Rumbling Bridge

This wayside site, some 7 miles (11.3km) west of Kinross, is a long-time favourite, especially after heavy rains. The River Devon dashes over waterfalls through a deep cleft beneath the bridge, which curiously has been built over an earlier crossing, and there are footpaths and walkways along the side of the ravine. The heaviest 'rumbles' are heard to emanate from Devils Mill.

Caithness Glass

Since it was founded in 1961 in Wick, the world has taken to the hand-made paperweights of Caithness Glass and the company now has a second factory and visitor centre 2 miles (3.2km) north of the centre of Perth. It incorporates a popular viewing gallery, from where the hand-making of their famous paperweights in abstract and modern designs, based on millefiori, can be seen. The visitor centre, with its audiovisual show, tells the story of the coloured and engraved glassware, including jewellery made from intricate multicoloured glass canes.

The Stone of Scone

Legend has it that the Stone of Destiny was the pillow upon which Jacob had his dream. Thought to have come from the Middle East, it was brought to Scone by Kenneth MacAlpin, Scotland's first king. In 1296, Edward I seized the Stone. A myth exists that the monks were forewarned, made an imitation and buried the original. The 458lb (208kg) block of hewn sandstone was taken to Westminster Abbey in London, and installed in the Coronation Chair. Since the crowning of Edward II in 1308, all monarchs have been seated above the Stone for the ceremony. In 1998 it was formally returned to Scotland and can now be seen in Edinburgh Castle.

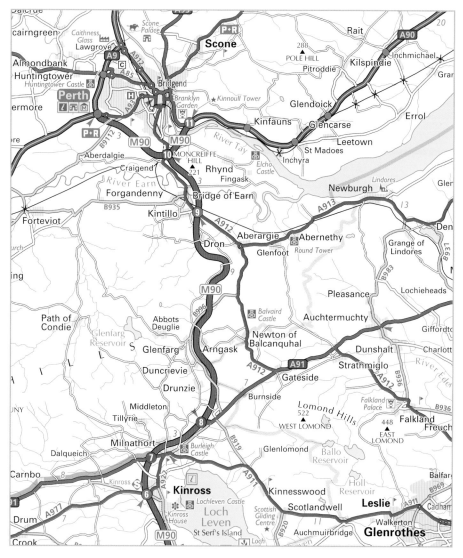

Tourist Information
Auchterarder: Glen Sherup and Glen Quay (tel: 01764 663450)
Crieff: Town Hall, High Street (tel: 01764 652578)
Perth: Lower City Mills, West Mill Street (tel: 01738 450600)

Riches of The Tay

Rising in the Hills of Breadalbane, this river is Britain's largest in terms of volume, moving more water than the Severn and Thames combined. It is world famous for salmon and the coveted wild pearls from the freshwater mussel, *Unio Margaretifera*. Still fished in the traditional manner, the most exquisite pearl, known as the 'Abernethy', weighs 44 grains. The pearls vary in colour and lustre, from matt black to pink-white and white.

in Bloom contest on more than one occasion. Bells Cherrybank Gardens, covering 18 acres (7ha), incorporates the National Heather Collection, whilst Branklyn Garden, on the eastern side of the town, is noted for its rhododendrons and alpines, and is reputed to be one of the finest small private gardens in Britain.

Scone Palace

Standing proud, just 2 miles (3.2km) north of Perth, is this imposing neo-Gothic fortified palace, built in 1803 for the Earl of Mansfield. The current structure incorporates many features from its ruined predecessor. Of great historical significance is Moot Hill, adjacent to the site of Scone Abbey, of which little can be seen today. This is where the Scottish kings were crowned under the Stone of Scone from the 9th century until its removal to London for 700 years by Edward I. The palace is splendidly furnished and has some exquisite collections, which include porcelain, china, ivory, clocks and

needlework. The well-laid-out gardens have a children's playground, picnic area, maze and nature trails.

Scone Palace

BOTH SIDES OF THE TAY

Over the last 1,000 years, St Andrews has led the country in 'mind, body and soul'. Throughout the Middle Ages, St Andrews was the spiritual capital and soon became the first seat of learning, with the nation's first university. It is best known today for golf, fulfilling the 'body' element. North of the river is Dundee, known for marmalade, fruit cake and the *Beano*.

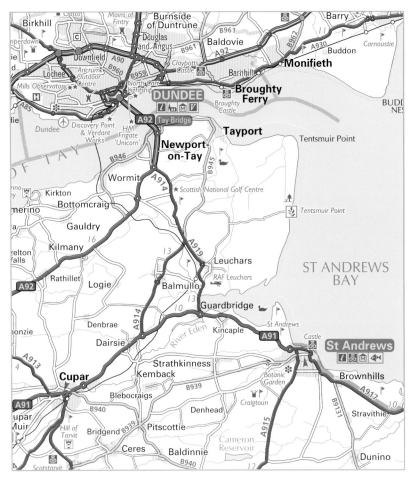

A statue of the god, Pan, in the rose garden at Hill of Tarvit Mansionhouse, near Cupar

atmospheric 17th- and 18th-century wynds to explore. The 1683 Mercat Cross marks the town centre; other landmarks include the 1785 parish church, whose spire dates from 1620. The graveyard contains the heads of two Covenanters involved in the murder of the Archbishop of St Andrews in 1679. Just outside town the Scottish Deer Centre fascinates wildlife enthusiasts, while devotees of country houses will enjoy Hill of Tarvit, an Edwardian mansion with fine furniture, pictures and porcelain.

Ceres

Ceres is an attractive old village with 18th-century pantiled cottages and a Folk Museum in the 17th-century weigh-house, giving an insight into agricultural life in earlier times. Every June the village bursts with life when it stages the oldest Highland Games in Scotland, an event which was granted to honour the villagers, who fought at Bannockburn. At the crossroads sits a benign statue, 'The Provost', which also commemorates them.

Dundee

Dundee stands on the slopes of the northern shore of the estuary of the River Tay, a port and industrial city that has experienced economic ups and downs over the centuries, but has always been quick to adapt. Founded in the 12th century, the city grew rich on jute and linen manufacture and whaling, then diversified into confectionery and jam production, light industry and, today, an increasing amount of modern industry. Despite its fine Victorian buildings, this a predominantly modern-looking city, with sweeping roadways and malls.

Visitors should head for Discovery Point to see RRS *Discovery*, Captain Scott's Antarctic ship, built here in 1901, before learning all about jute at the Verdant

Tourist Information
Dundee: Discovery Quay, Discovery Point (tel: 01382 527527)
St Andrews: 70 Market Street (tel: 01334 472021)

Cupar

Set amongst a patchwork of fertile farmlands in the Lomond Hills, Cupar is crossroads for many routes. Chartered in 1382, this market town is one of Scotland's oldest burghs, with some

The RRS (Royal Research Ship) Discovery *carried Scott to the Antarctic and is now one of Dundee's star attractions*

Golf is a huge money-spinner for St Andrews

Golf

The world pays homage to St Andrews as the home of golf, although the game's origins may lie in the low countries. The Royal and Ancient Golf Club, founded in 1754, is the ruling body for the sport worldwide, except in the US and Mexico. Visitors can trace golf's fascinating history at the British Golf Museum at St Andrews, while players can tee off one of its five courses. The famous Old Course, founded in the mid-15th century, is unique in that it evolved from 'natural' play and was never designed. The others include the New Course, over a century old, the Eden, Jubilee, Strathtyrunn and the nine-hole Balgove. All the links are open to club golfers, but should be booked well in advance.

Works, a stunning industrial museum. Elsewhere in the city, Sensation features interactive exhibits themed around the senses, while the Dundee Sweet Factory tells the story of confectionary – with plenty of free samples. East lies Broughty Ferry, a residential suburb with a good beach, picturesque castle and museum.

Leuchars

Leuchars is known mainly for its airbase, and Tornado jets thunder in the airspace above this once marshland village. The 12th-century Church of St Athernase, overlooking the village, is one of the finest examples of Norman architecture in the British Isles.

To the north, between the Tay and Eden estuaries, is the Tentsmuir Forest, covering some 15sq miles (38.8sq km) and fringed by the wide sandy Kishalfy beach. These woodlands have trails that offer plenty of opportunity for spotting a variety of wildlife, including deer.

St Andrews

The city of St Andrews attributes its founding to St Regulus (or St Rule), whose ship foundered in the fourth century while carrying the relics of St Andrew, the patron saint of Scotland.

Best explored on foot, the town runs almost east to west. In the east is the harbour, which in the Middle Ages thrived on trade with the low countries. Nearby are the ruins of the Church of St Mary on the Rock, close to St Rule's Tower, adjacent

The Tay Rail Bridge stretching into the distance over the Firth of Tay

to the cathedral ruins. The cathedral was consecrated in 1318 and was the largest in Scotland (measuring some 355ft by 160ft/108.1m by 48.7m), confirming St Andrews as the nation's spiritual centre.

The ruined castle became the Bishop's Palace, notorious for its rule of terror – from the early 15th through to the mid-16th century, many martyrs to the cause of the Reformation were burned at the stake.

John Knox, in his challenge to the old faith, brought the fight right to the archbishop. He was captured by a French squadron in 1547 defending the castle and taken to the galleys in Nantes.

The university became the first to take a female student in 1862 and is the oldest in Scotland, having been founded in 1412. At the west end of St Andrews, amongst the dunes, golf evolved. The clubhouse of the world-famous Royal and Ancient overlooks the Old Course, which, like several others here, is available to the public.

Tay Bridges

Two fine bridges straddle the Tay. The road bridge, started in 1963 and completed in 1966, is over 1 mile (1.6km) in length, and has 42 spans, with a high point of 120ft (36m) to allow passage of ships.

The rail bridge, 2 miles (3.2km) west of the road bridge, is 2 miles (3.2km) long and is built on 73 piers. It was constructed between 1883 and 1888 and is only a few yards from the site of the original cast-iron bridge, which collapsed within a year of its opening during the stormy night of 28 December 1879.

The ruins of St Andrews Cathedral, seen from St Rule's tower, which predates the cathedral. There are 156 steps to the top of the tower

IN THE PERTHSHIRE HIGHLANDS

The Black Watch, Killiecrankie, Loch Tay, the Road to the Isles, the Grampian Mountains – all of these are names that evoke the history and beauty of Scotland and all have their links with the Perthshire Highlands, long renowned for wonderful scenery, a sense of history and Highland hospitality.

General Wade's Bridge at Aberfeldy was built as part of a military road network in the Scottish Highlands

Loch Tummel

The Road to the Isles winds along the north side of Loch Tummel. At Queen's View, visited by Victoria, the vista down the tree-lined loch is, justifiably, famous. The fine conical peak of Schiehallion, towards the southwest, has a place in scientific history – a determination of its mass in the 18th century led to calculations of the earth's density.

The entrance hall at Blair Castle, filled with armour and weaponry

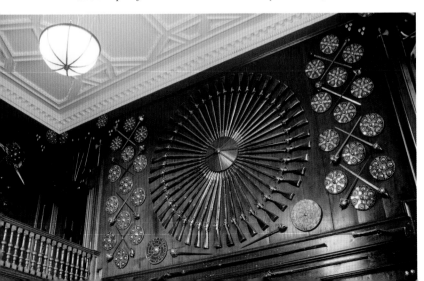

Aberfeldy

The River Tay at Aberfeldy is crossed by the handsome Wade's Bridge, designed by Willam Adam for General Wade in 1733. Beside it stands a tall cairn, topped by a kilted figure of a Higland soldier, which commemorates the raising of the Black Watch. On the town's eastern approach, visitors can tour a working distillery at Dewar's World of Whisky, while the town centre houses a traditional working watermill with demonstrations of oatmeal milling. Walkers can stroll through the native birchwood of the Birks of Aberfeldy, celebrated in a poem by Robert Burns, to the enchanting Falls of Moness on the Urlar Burn.

Blair Atholl

The stone-built village of Blair Atholl clusters around the gates of Blair Castle, home to the Duke of Atholl and his Atholl Highlanders, Britain's only private army. Founded as a single fortified tower in 1269, the castle was the last British castle to be besieged – by its owner, Lord George Murray, after he forfeited it for supporting the Young Pretender. It owes its present look to a restoration of 1869, which changed Georgian additions into something resembling the castle's medieval appearance. A succession of impressive rooms, from the entrance hall hung with weapons, to the drawing room, with its 18th-century decoration and the 19th-century ballroom, reflect the wealth and prestige of the Dukes, and there is fine china, furniture, portraits and costumes.

Dunkeld

Many of the small, white-painted houses around Dunkeld's attractive square owe their good repair to the National Trust for Scotland's 'Little Houses Scheme'. From beside one, the Ell House, which houses a Trust shop, a lane leads to the cathedral, invisible from most of the town. Beautifully sited beside the Tay, it dates mostly from the 14th and 15th centuries. The nave and aisles have been roofless since 1560, but the choir is now the parish church; an exhibition in the Chapter House outlines the history of the town and the cathedral. Behind the nave is the Parent Larch, sole survivor of the first group to be planted in Scotland.

Kenmore

The pretty, planned village of Kenmore, at the eastern end of lovely Loch Tay, was built at the gateway of Taymouth Castle, the former seat of the Earls of Breadalbane. The estate village houses one of Scotland's oldest inns and is the scene on 15 January of the opening of the Tay salmon-fishing season. Nearby, time rolls back at the Scottish Crannog Centre, which shows how, in prehistoric times, people built dwellings out in the centre of the lochs.

Killiecrankie

The narrow, heavily wooded Pass of Killiecrankie was the site of the last victory of the Jacobites before their final defeat at Dunkeld during the first uprising of 1689. Under the leadership of Bonnie Dundee, they routed the English, leaving the pass a bloody and terrifying scene. One Highlander escaped pursuing Redcoats in a spectacular jump from Soldiers Leap. The visitor centre describes the battle and introduces the varied wildlife of the pass.

Pictish Stones

Dunfallandry Stone, 2 miles (3.2km) south of Pitlochry, is an impressive example of the more than 200 Pictish stones of Scotland. The Picti – painted people – fought against the Romans, and by the sixth century Pictland occupied much of what later became Scotland. The standing stones are their most enduring legacy. They seem to have been put up between AD550 and 850; by the mid-ninth century the Picts had been overrun by the Scots and, in the north, by the Vikings. The early stones are rough slabs, simply carved, but they became more elaborate, with relief sculpture. After conversion to Christianity in the late sixth century, the Picts used their mysterious symbols alongside the cross and biblical scenes. What the symbols mean remains a mystery – they include animals, like the fine boar of Knocknagael (see Inverness, page 329) and the odd 'swimming elephant', as well as tools (hammers and anvils are quite common), mirrors, combs and Z- and V-shaped rods. Were the stones boundary markers, gravestones or monuments to alliances? No one knows.

Ossian's Hall

The romantic imagination of the 18th century was gripped by translations of Gaelic poetry from the supposed third-century bard Ossian – though most of it was written by James Macpherson, a farmer's son from Kingussie. In wooded country near Dunkeld, beside the River Braan, the fourth Duke of Atholl converted a folly – then called The Hermitage – into Ossian's Hall, complete with now-vanished paintings of the bard's life. Restored by the National Trust for Scotland in 1952, it is now the focal point of woodland walks. Nearby is Ossian's Cave, another Atholl folly, and, guaranteed natural, one of Scotland's two tallest Douglas firs.

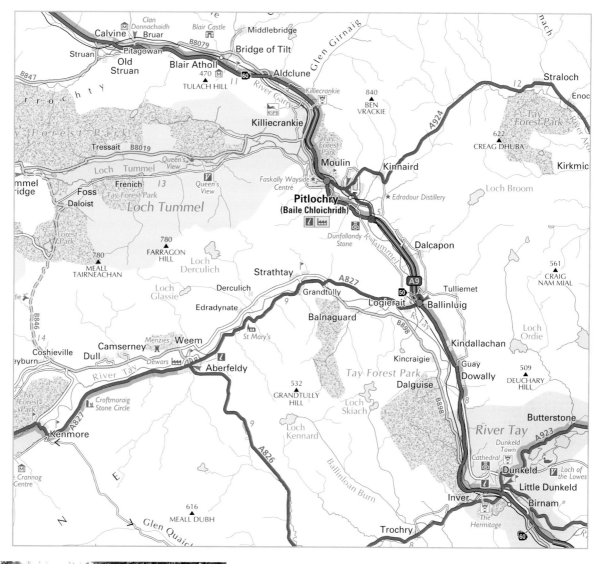

An 18th-century stone bridge near Ossian's Hall, Dunkeld

Pitlochry

Beautifully set on the wooded banks of the Tummel, Victorian Pitlochry is dignified and varied. Fine tweeds and woollens draw many visitors, as does the summer festival of drama and concerts. Beside the dam just upstream is a fish-ladder, installed to help migrating salmon reach their spawning grounds. Visitors can watch their progress by means of an underwater viewing chamber. The pure waters of the area have attracted two distilleries to Pitlochry, both of which welcome visitors.

Weem

Castle Menzies, west of the village of Weem, is a 16th-century tower house, complete with turrets and gables, which gives a vivid impression of the spartan conditions the family must have endured for most of its occupation. Among the important possessions in the house are the death mask of the Young Pretender and a fearsome claymore used at Bannockburn.

Tourist Information

Aberfeldy: The Square (tel: 01887 820276)
Blairgowrie: 26 Wellmeadow (tel: 01250 872960)
Dunkeld: The Cross (tel: 01350 727688)
Pitlochry: 22 Atholl Road (tel: 01796 472215)

Eradour, Scotland's smallest distillery produces a fine Highland Malt in the hills above Pitlochry

SCOTLAND'S STRONGHOLDS

Alone piper on the ramparts of Edinburgh Castle during the Military Tattoo is for many an enduring image of the Scottish castle – massively set on an impregnable rock, battlemented and guarded with cannon, manned by fierce Highlanders urged to deeds of heroism by the call of the pipes. For others, Eilean Donan on the road to Skye is the Scottish castle *par excellence*, an island-held fairytale reflected in ruffled waters of a loch and backed by dramatic mountains. Or it may be the pepperpot turrets and crow-stepped gables of towering Craigievar in the gentler country of Scotland's northeast. Such is the variety of Scottish castles, reflecting the troubled history of this determinedly independent country.

The Castle is Edinburgh's crowning glory

Royal Fortresses

The story of the Scottish castle really starts in the 13th century. Motte-and-bailey castles had been built to the Norman plan by the kings Alexander I and David I, who were brought up in Norman England, and these were gradually replaced by stone fortresses. Edinburgh was an early example. Continually fought over by the Scots and English, little other than the chapel survives from its earliest days. It last saw action in 1745, when the Young Pretender failed to take it but was incarcerated there instead.

Another royal castle, Stirling, 'the key to Scotland', has an equally formidable setting, and many great battles, including Bannockburn in 1314, were fought nearby. Most of the present buildings are late medieval, and Mary, Queen of Scots was crowned here as an infant in 1543. But it was not just monarchs who built great fortresses. Wherever a suitable site was available, and circumstances demanded, the great landowners of Scotland would build.

Clan Castles

The MacLeods at Dunvegan in the west of the Isle of Skye still live in their ancestral castle beside a tongue of the sea. Enlarged and made more comfortable over the centuries, it still tells of a lawless past. The family has additional protection from the Fairy Flag, possibly from the seventh century, which legend says will save the MacLeods from destruction on three occasions – it has already worked twice.

On the opposite side of the country St Andrews Castle was the stronghold for the powerful bishops, who were as involved in worldly politics as in prayer. As Scotland fought to retain (or recapture) its independence from England, the castle frequently changed hands before being all but destroyed during the Reformation, as its battered walls overlooking the sea testify.

One of the best of the early castles is set in wooded, rather undramatic country down on the Solway Firth, south of Dumfries. Caerlaverock is a wonderful triangular castle still surrounded by the waters of its moat – the very latest in military thinking when it was built in around 1280. Captured by the English King Edward I, 'the Hammer of the Scots', in 1300, it was constantly dismantled and besieged in the Middle Ages, yet managed to retain its splendour, which was later enhanced by a splendid Renaissance façade.

Not far away to the west is a much sterner castle – the massive 14th-century tower and walls of Threave. It sits on an island in the River Dee, and was built by the appropriately named Archibald the Grim, a bastard son of Sir James Douglas. A later member of the Douglas family surrendered the castle to James II in 1455 after the king had bombarded it with the huge gun 'Mons Meg', one of the world's oldest cannons, now in Edinburgh Castle. The Douglases also held the now-ruined Tantallon Castle on the southeast corner of the Firth of Forth near North Berwick.

Some of the most impressive of Scottish castles are the result of careful restoration. Duart, on the Isle of Mull overlooking Loch Linnhe, retains 13th-century fragments, and was restored by Sir Fitzroy Maclean from 1911 onwards. It is now the home of the Clan Chief. The smaller Eilean Donan on Loch Duich was in utter ruin after bombardment from an English warship in 1719 until it was restored in 1932.

Eilean Donan Castle, sitting romantically on Loch Duich is one of the most visited and photographed attractions in the Highlands and has appeared in several films, including Highlander *(1984)*

Built early in the 17th century, Craigievar Castle is a fine example of original Scottish Baronial architecture

The Castles of Mar

Once the crowns of England and Scotland had been united by King James VI and I, a new type of castle developed – the tower house. Increasing political stability demanded increasing comfort, without altogether abandoning a defensive role. These new towers are characterised by a plain lower storey – sometimes square, but more often L- or Z-shaped. On the upper floors they burst into a riot of corbelled-out towers and gables to increase the amount of accommodation, though access is still usually by spiral stairways.

There are examples elsewhere, mostly found to the west of Aberdeen, between the Don and the Dee valleys – the former province of Mar. Among the best of the Castles of Mar is Craigievar, unaltered since it was completed in 1626. Significantly, it was built not for a monarch or a clan chief, but for one of the Jacobean nouveau riche, the Aberdeen merchant William Forbes. The largest of the Castles of Mar were Castle Fraser, Crathes and the extended Drum Castle. Glamis Castle, childhood home of Queen Elizabeth, the Queen Mother, has one of the most prickly rooflines of all, stiff with cone-topped towerlets.

At Drumlanrig, built in the 1680s, the Douglas Dukes of Queensberry built themselves a huge square palace, which manages to combine the appearance of a medieval stronghold with an early 17th-century mansion. Like many of the inhabited Scottish castles, its interiors are a luxurious contrast to its outward appearance.

Scottish Baronial

It was not long before the style established by the Castles of Mar began to influence architects. Inveraray Castle, designed in the mid-18th century, uses the same vocabulary

Balmoral Castle, summer residence of the Royal Family and constructed in local granite, features a tall tower that dominates the Scottish Baronial mansion

of turrets and battlements, though regulated with classical order, which also underpins superb cliff-top Culzean on the Ayrshire coast, where Robert Adam's skills blend a castellated façade with wonderful Italianate interiors.

By the mid-19th century, Scottish Baronial architecture was very fashionable among the landed gentry. Blair Castle was reconstructed in the style, and so was Dunrobin. Most famous of all is Queen Victoria's Balmoral, where Prince Albert (with professional help, it must be said) provided a huge square keep with a more comfortable country house attached, tricked out in tartan in all its main apartments – the apotheosis of the Scottish castle.

FROM BEN NEVIS TO GLEN COE

Sparkling lochs and some of Scotland's highest mountains, including the towering Ben Nevis; the stunning beauty of the road to Kinlochleven; the grim story of the massacre at Glen Coe – all of these combine to make the Fort William area one of the country's most popular tourist spots. The winter sports boom has brought benefits to summertime visitors, with cable-car access to some of the mountains.

North and South Ballachulish are separated by the still waters of Loch Leven, which empties out into Loch Linnhe

Ballachulish

From 1693 until 1955 the slate quarries of Ballachulish produced millions of tonnes of roof slates. Today, grassy slopes have replaced the quarries besides the shores of Loch Leven and families will enjoy a visit to the Highland Mystery World, a visitor attraction complete with monsters, bogles and live performance. In South Ballachulish, near the bridge across the neck of Loch Leven, is a monument to James of the Glen, whose story inspired Robert Louis Stevenson's *Kidnapped*. Visitors can indulge themselves with a tasting tour of the confectionery factory across the bridge in North Ballachulish.

Corpach

The Caledonian Canal has its basin at Corpach, and there are stunning views along Loch Eil to Ben Nevis from the village. The Treasures of the Earth exhibition displays gems and crystals from throughout the world, including huge amethysts and emeralds, as well as prehistoric fossils and petrified trees.

Fort William

A busy tourist hub, Fort William hugs the narrow lochside strip and straggles up the hillside between Ben Nevis and Loch Linnhe. General Monk's 1655 earthwork fort and its stone replacement were sacrificed in the 19th century for the railway, which still brings visitors to the heart of the Highlands. From here you can take the scenic West Highland Railway to Mallaig.

Fort William held out against the Jacobites in both 1715 and 1745, but the West Highland Museum in Cameron Square makes much of the Pretenders' cause. Fort William is a pleasant place to stroll around – although most visitors head for the mountains, either on foot or, more easily, by the cable cars that climb the Nevis range to the north of the town.

Neptune's Staircase

The Caledonian Canal, linking Inverness with the west coast, faced its biggest challenge at Banavie, where a rise of 70ft (21.3m) in only 500 yards (457.2m) had to be negotiated. Thomas Telford designed a magnificent series of eight linked locks, dubbed 'Neptune's Staircase' by the navvies who built them – they were paid 1/6d (about 7p) a day. Work began in 1807 and lasted more than three years, but it was not until 1822 that the canal opened, with a regular steamboat service between Fort William and Inverness.

Ben Nevis, snow-covered for much of the year, looks down over Loch Linnhe, Scotland's longest sea loch

Glen Coe

Since 6 February 1692, when the Campbells, acting for the government, slew some 40 MacDonalds, the name of Glencoe has been a byword for treachery. Slow to accept William and Mary as monarchs, MacIain of Glencoe's oath of loyalty papers arrived late in Edinburgh, providing a pretext for government intervention to set an example to other recalcitrant clans. Campbell of Glenlyon and his troops were billetted on the Glencoe MacDonalds, with secret orders to 'fall upon the rebels ... and put all to the sword'. Five days later, MacIain, his wife and 36 others were slaughtered in a night-time frenzy. The Glencoe Visitor Centre tells the story, and visitors can walk to Signal Rock, the MacDonalds lookout point.

Glencoe also attracts hill walkers, climbers and mountaineers all year. The great peaks of Buchaille Etive Mhor (Great Shepherd) and Bidean nam Bean (Three Sisters) dominate the glen, providing an awe-inspiring backdrop for one of Scotland's most scenic glens.

Inverlochy Castle

West of Fort William, ruined Inverlochy Castle, built in the 13th century by John Comyn, Lord of Badenoch and Lochaber,

Ben Nevis

Of all 277 'munros' (Scottish mountains more than 3,000ft/914.4m), Ben Nevis is the highest. Indeed, it is the UK's highest mountain and, though it is not the most difficult to climb, it should never be attempted without making thorough preparation and wearing the right footwear and clothing. From its 4,409ft (1,344m) summit are spectacular views – the line of the Great Glen, the distant Cuillins on Skye and, very occasionally, the coast of Ireland. An observatory, now ruined, was built here in 1823 to study sun spots. For the less energetic, a drive into Glen Nevis will provide views of the mountain and ends by a water slide. From here you can follow a rocky path through a dramatic ravine to a secret valley, closed by a waterfall, and the brave can cross the minimalist suspension bridge to the foot of Coire Dubh an Steill.

Glen Coe, a steep-sided valley, climbs steadily from the village of Glencoe to emerge on Rannoch Moor

stands on the banks of the River Lochy. There's a fine view of the castle from nearby Primmy Hill, once used as a place of execution. Visitors can glimpse both from the comfort of the Jacobite Steam Train which covers the route from Fort William to Mallaig, one of the world's most scenic rail journeys.

Kinlochleven

The roads along the banks of Loch Leven provide some of the area's finest views of water and rugged hills, so Kinlochleven comes as a surprise. For nearly 100 years the aluminium industry provided employment here, where hydroelectricity could run the smelters cheaply. An exhibition and audiovisual display in the visitor centre tell about aluminium production. Not far away is the spectacular Grey Mare's Tail waterfall, and the West Highland Way long-distance trail passes close to the village.

Loch Linnhe

Loch Linnhe stretches from Fort William to Oban, more than 30 miles (48.3km), and for most of its length is backed by some of Scotland's highest mountains. A drive from Fort William down the A82 has spectacular views, but the best way to enjoy the stunning scenery is to take a cruise from Fort William. The journey takes in fish farms and islands dotted with basking seals, and offers superb views of Ben Nevis.

The West Highland Way

From the outskirts of Glasgow, the West Highland Way threads 95 miles (152.9km) through Lowland and then Highland scenery to Fort William. It passes Loch Lomond and Glen Coe, following ancient routes for much of its length – drove roads (including the famous Devil's Staircase out of Glen Coe), military ways built to help suppress the clans, old coaching roads and, occasionally, disused railway lines. It is possible to walk short and spectacular sections, with the chance of seeing deer and golden eagles. To tackle the whole walk, it is best to go south to north, thus starting easy and working up to the more rugged terrain.

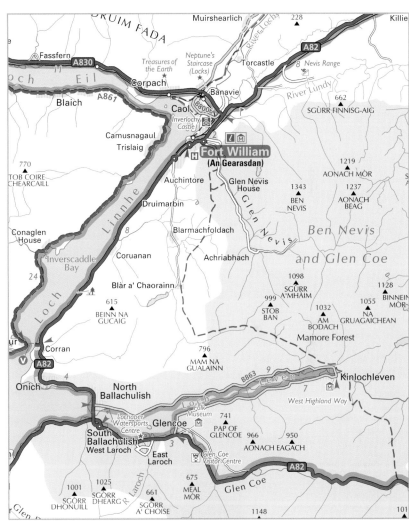

During summer, the Jacobite Steam Train, immortalised in Harry Potter *as the Hogwarts Express, crosses over the spectacular, 21-arch Glenfinnan Viaduct*

See Walk I, page 342
Into the Lost Valley

Tourist Information
Ballachulish: (tel: 01855 811866)
Fort William: 15 High Street (tel: 0845 2255121)

AROUND THE GRANITE CITY

Scotland's northeast focuses on Aberdeen, the country's third largest city, but away from the bright lights and glittering granite buildings is mellow countryside bristling with monuments to the past – stone circles, castles and industrial landmarks – as well as the lure of fine whisky.

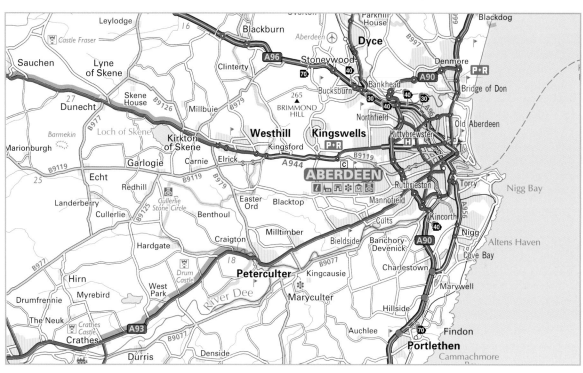

Traditional oak barrels have been made at Speyside Cooperage since 1947

Aberdeen Art Gallery is housed in a building that was purpose-built in 1884 and includes good examples of 19th, 20th and 21st-century works

Aberdeen

Fish, granite and oil are, for many, words that sum up Aberdeen. Although the fishing industry has declined dramatically in recent years, a visit to the fish market is well worth the early start. Oil, too, makes its presence felt, not just in the lights winking far out to sea in the dusk, but in the prosperity of the city. Just a stone's throw away are the grey granite buildings that dominate the city centre – most spectacular are the early 20th-century spiky towers of the ancient Marischal College, founded in 1593.

On Union Street a colonnade heralds the Kirk of St Nicholas. There are no fewer than three cathedrals — St Mary's Roman Catholic, the Episcopal St Andrew's, where the first bishop in the United States was consecrated in 1784, and the oldest, the granite St Machar's, with its splendid heraldic ceiling, in Old Aberdeen.

Nearby is King's College, founded in 1495 and, like Marischal College, now part of Aberdeen University. Its chapel, topped with an open crown, dates from around 1500. The Chanonry is the traditional home of the university's professors.

The Whisky Trail

Even more than for tartan, Scotland is known worldwide for its superb single malt whiskies. There are distilleries throughout Scotland, but the majority are found on the northern edge of the Grampian Mountains, in the valley of the River Spey and its tributaries. The pure Highland water of the region is the basic ingredient of whisky, together with malted barley – as well as much time and care. Eight distilleries – and a cooperage, where barrels are prepared – are open to visitors and linked by The Whisky Trail, a signed route of around 70 miles (112.7km). You can see the great copper stills and learn about whisky production from start to finish, often with the help of an audiovisual programme, in the visitor centre. And nearly all offer you a 'wee dram' of their product, so make sure you have a teetotal driver handy!

Castle Fraser, which includes a fortified tower house, is one of the grandest of the Castles of Mar

Roses all the Way

For a city so much associated with its grey granite buildings, the flowers of Aberdeen come as a surprise. The city blazes with colour everywhere; main roads are bordered with blooms, roundabouts become luxurious gardens and streets are festooned with tubs and baskets. Most prominent of all are the roses – there are said to be 2.5 million of them. Duthie Park boasts a 'Mountain of Roses' as well as Europe's largest indoor garden. Not surprisingly, Aberdeen has won the 'Britain in Bloom' contest so often that it had to retire to give others a chance.

Cullerlie Stone Circle

Atmospherically set in remote countryside and approached through an avenue of pines, the eight boulders of the circle, the tallest around 5ft (1.5m), surround eight burial cairns. The circle, which dates from the Bronze Age, between 1500 and 1200BC, may mark the tomb of a chief and his descendants.

The Mercat Cross in Castlegate, at the heart of the city, has medallion portraits of the 10 Stuart monarchs of Scotland. The homes of two 16th-century Provosts of Aberdeen still survive – Provost Skene's, in Broad Street, which illustrates city life in a series of period rooms, and Provost Ross's in Shiprow, housing the fascinating Maritime Museum.

To complete Aberdeen's attractions, 2 miles (3.2km) of sandy beach stretch northward from the pier, backed by a wide promenade. Aberdeen has a wide choice of sporting and leisure activities, too, including large amusement parks and leisure centres on Beach Boulevard.

Castle Fraser

Like Crathes, one of the famous Castles of Mar which are special to this part of Scotland, Castle Fraser is a Z-plan tower house begun in 1575 and finished in 1636 for the Fraser family. Much remains to remind visitors of the castle's early history – such as the 'Laird's Lug', a tiny room high above the impressive Great Hall with its massive fireplace, from where the Fraser family could listen to their guests' conversations. The former chapel has its masons' calculations on the stonework.

The wooden leg of an early Victorian Fraser, as well as the lead bullet that injured him, is on show in the library, one of the rooms redecorated in the 1830s. From the roof of the castle's tallest tower are views of attractive wooded hills and, nearer at hand, the walled garden with its fine borders.

Crathes Castle

Vibrant colour is a dominant feature both inside and outside Crathes Castle. Built on land given by Robert the Bruce to Alexander Burnett in 1323, Crathes is a romantic L-shaped tower house of gables and turrets, winding stairs and

polished wood. It is famous for its painted ceilings, where elongated figures stand proudly between decorated beams swirling with leaves and flowers. This lively riot is echoed in the walled garden with its massive yews, where a succession of beautifully planned spaces offer tranquil corners and wonderful contrasts of shape and colour.

Drum Castle

Drum presents two faces to the visitor – a gaunt, battlemented tower, one of the oldest tower houses in Scotland, built in 1296, and beside it a Jacobean mansion of 1619. Oddly, the two were only joined in the 19th century when the castle was refurbished. The home of the Irvine family, it is full of solid 18th- and 19th-century furniture, as well as family portraits – don't miss the artist Hugh Irvine's Byronic self-portrait as the Angel Gabriel. The walled gardens hold a collection of historic roses, planted in period settings, while north of the castle is the Old Wood of Drum, ancient oak woodland from the Royal Hunting Forest given to the Irvines by Robert the Bruce.

Garlogie

Garlogie, which stands in the gentle rolling landscape to the west of Aberdeen, was once the centre for a thriving wool-spinning industry. The 19th-century mills have now mostly been demolished, but the village still retains its old beam engine, the only one of its type still in situ in Scotland. Built around 1830 to supplement the original water power, the engine has been restored to working order, and an audio visual presentation gives the story of this local industry.

The extensive gardens at Crathes Castle are sheltered by stately yew hedges, planted in 1702

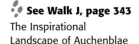

See Walk J, page 343
The Inspirational
Landscape of Auchenblae

Tourist Information
Aberdeen: 23 Union Street (tel: 01224 288828)
Banchory: Bridge Street (tel: 01330 822000)
Inverurie: 18 High Street (tel: 01467 625800)
Stonehaven: 66 Allardice Street (seasonal) (tel: 01569 762806)

Drum Castle, dating from between the 13th and 17th centuries, with a 13th-century keep, near Peterculter

THE CAPITAL OF THE HIGHLANDS

Southwest from Inverness the dark waters of Loch Ness refuse to yield up their secrets; to the east, the desolation of Culloden tells of the crushing of the clans; to the west, Beauly has links with Mary, Queen of Scots. This is quintessential Scotland – the sea, the lochs and the mountains – all converging on a congenial city.

Beauly Priory, founded in 1230

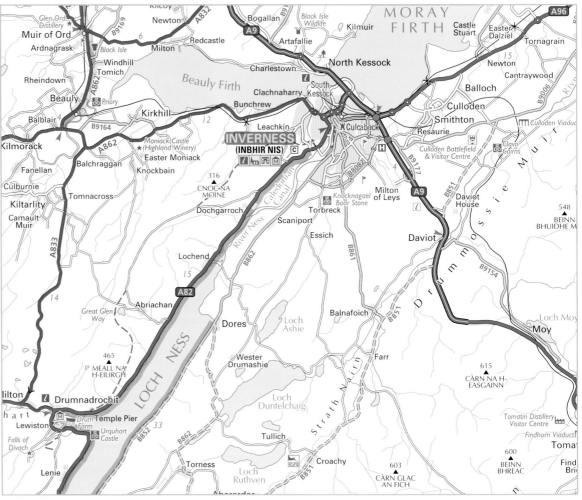

Beauly

West of Inverness the Moray Firth becomes the Beauly Firth, fed by the River Beauly, one of Scotland's best salmon rivers, which flows through a lovely wooded strath. At the head of the Firth is the little town of Beauly – where the austere Valliscaulain monks built their priory. Only the ruins of the church, with its lovely 13th-century windows, remain. The town was laid out in 1840 by Lord Lovat; the wide central square contains a monument to the raising of the Lovat Scouts in 1905. Visitors can learn more at the Beauly Firth and Glens Trust, with its traditional, early 20th-century Village Store, kilt maker and the Clan Fraser Exhibition.

Kirkhill

The little village of Kirkhill lies south of the Beauly Firth, and is a good starting point for cycling or walking in this pretty wooded landscape – there are lots of waymarked trails in the area to cater for both activities.

The village is home to Highland Aromatics, where visitors can see the production of naturally based soaps and creams. Nearby is the 17th-century L-plan Moniack Castle, once a Lovat stronghold, now home to the Highlands' only winery, specialising in traditional herb and fruit wines. There are tours and tastings, and an audiovisual to explain the production process.

Tourist Information

Fort Augustus: car park (seasonal) (tel: 01320 366367)
Inverness: Castle Wynd (tel: 01463 234353)
North Kessock: picnic site (tel: 01463 731701)

Christianity has played an important role in the life of Inverness since St Columba converted the King of the Picts, Brude, at his fortress near the River Ness in AD565

In Search of The Monster

St Columba is the first person reported to have met a monster in Loch Ness – he supposedly prevented it from eating his servant by making the sign of the cross. Quiescent for more than a millennium thereafter, 'Nessie' attracted public attention again while the main A82 road along the north side of the loch was being constructed in the 1930s. Photographs of varying authenticity, as well as inconclusive scientific research, have added to its fame – two exhibitions in Drumnadrochit, as well as millions of plastic models in souvenir shops, indicate the worldwide interest. Yet still the loch keeps its secret, aided by its 24 mile (33.8km) length and a depth in places of 900ft (274.3m).

The irregular shape of Urquhart Castle appears to have emerged naturally from the rock on which it stands

Clava Cairns

Clava should not be missed in the excitement of nearby Culloden. Set amongst trees, this fascinating site of major archaeological importance has three principal cairns – large stone burial mounds, each surrounded by a circle of standing stones, built between about 2000 and 1500BC. The two outer ones have stone-lined passages to the centre. The central cairn has no passage, but is unique in having odd, rough pavements radiating from it. This group is the most important of a whole series of such cairns found only in the region of the Moray Firth.

Culloden

Culloden, despite its summer crowds, remains a sad and moving place. On this bleak moorland the hopes of Charles Edward Stuart to regain the throne met their end 16 April 1746 in the last major battle fought on British soil. His 5,000 Highlanders, used to savage skirmishing among the hills, faced 9,000 trained and disciplined troops under the Duke of Cumberland and, despite courageous fighting, were swiftly defeated. The number of dead was greatly increased by 'Butcher' Cumberland's order that no prisoners should be taken. The clansmen who died are buried around the site, their graves marked with small stones. The 76 English who died lie in the Field of the English. Flags mark the disposition of the armies, and the large memorial cairn was built during the 19th century. Next to the visitor centre is Old Leonach Cottage, scene of a battle atrocity, restored to its 18th-century condition.

Inverness

Inverness, 'the Capital of the Highlands' and a royal burgh since the 12th century, stands on the Moray Firth. The mainly modern city centre is dominated by the castle, built and restored over the centuries. Mary, Queen of Scots hung its governor from the walls in 1562 for refusing her entry, and Bonnie Prince Charlie's troops blew it up shortly before Culloden in 1746; it was rebuilt by General Wade. The present structure is 19th century, as is the statue of Flora MacDonald in the forecourt. Below here, the Inverness Museum and Art Gallery gives an insight into the history, art and culture of both Inverness and the Highlands. The old part of town also contains Abertarff House, a rare surviving 16th-century town house.

Across the river are the twin towers of St Andrew's Cathedral, consecrated in 1869 and the first cathedral to be built in Britain after the Reformation. The riverbanks and islands are laid out with attractive gardens, and near here is the departure point for cruises down the Caledonian Canal to Loch Ness. Dolphin and wildlife cruises also operate from Inverness harbour into the Moray Firth.

Standing 20ft (6m) high, the Memorial Cairn is the largest monument to be found on Culloden Battlefield

Urquhart Castle

From the promontory that Urquhart Castle occupies, it is possible to see almost the full length of Loch Ness – which accounts for its popularity with monster-spotters. Ruined since it was blown up in 1692 so that it could not be used by the Jacobites, most of the visible buildings date from after 1509, when Urquhart was given by James IV to the Grant family. The medieval castle, once Scotland's largest, was captured by Edward I and then held by Robert the Bruce against Edward III. Floodlighting makes it a fine spectacle at night.

Building the Caledonian Canal

The north coast of Scotland has often proved hazardous to small boats, so the idea of avoiding that journey by constructing a canal to link the string of lochs along the Great Glen, as it slices through the Highlands from Inverness to Fort William, appealed to late 18th century minds. Surveyed in 1773, the Caledonian Canal was finally begun by Thomas Telford in 1803. The work raised the level of Loch Ness by 6ft (1.8m). When it opened in 1822 it was not deep enough, so completion was only achieved in 1847. Between the natural lochs on the 60-mile (96.6km) route from Loch Linnhe to the Moray Firth are 22 miles (35.4km) of canal, rising through 29 locks – most spectacularly at Neptune's Staircase. The canal is mainly used by pleasure boats today, a relaxing way of seeing spectacular scenery.

See Walk K, page 344
Loch An Eilein's Castle and Ord Ban

See Walk L, page 345
Seeing Sea Eagles at Portree Bay

See Walk M, page 346
Strathpeffer and the Rogie Falls

See Walk N, page 347
Into Scotland's Great Wilderness

THE SCOTTISH HIGHLANDS AND ISLANDS

From space, Scotland north of the Forth and Clyde looks like a loosely woven cloth – an ancient tartan, perhaps – ragged at its western edge and crumpled in a series of irregular folds. Patches of smoother fabric to the north and northeast contrast with the agitation of the rest, while loose scraps and threads lie around its fringes. These are the Highlands and the Islands, where high mountains and deep glens, tumbling seas and shimmering lochs, open moorland and spreading forests lure the visitor to one of the most fascinating areas in Europe.

The Highland Line – the divide between the smooth Lowlands and the sudden lifting of the mountains, and between the former Gaelic speakers and others – runs northeast from the south end of Loch Lomond to a little inland from Aberdeen, then curves around to Inverness. Across it you are in what many people regard as 'real' Scotland. Here, narrow roads twist through mountain passes or beside the lochs, and towering summits rear overhead. The result of millions of years of sometimes tumultuous geological activity, the Highland landscape can be rugged and uncompromising, but never fails to impress.

Above left: The Cairngorms National Park, a spectacular expanse of wilderness, seen from Glenmore Forest Park
Above: The remarkably well-preserved Stone-Age dwellings of Skara Brae, Orkney, were hidden for centuries under shifting sand

The Role of the Rocks

It would be wrong to think of the area as uniformly mountainous, or that all the mountains are the same. Although large tracts both north and south of the Great Glen, a fault line, are similar in their geological formation, there are outcrops of other rock. Granite forms the most jagged peaks, like the Cairngorms, and there are basalts, chiefly in Argyll and on Skye, Mull and, most famously, at Fingal's Cave on Staffa. From the Mull of Kintyre to Aberdeen and the northeast coast, the basic rocks of the Grampians are normally smoother, rounder peaks mellowing into gentler hills in the east.

Around Inverness, north along the coast to Caithness, and out to the Orkney Islands, is easily weathered sandstone, giving the landscape a softer grain, while the deeply indented coastline from Skye northwards is mostly of heavily scarred sedimentary rocks. The Outer Hebrides are mostly low-lying. Only in Harris does the granite show through again as mountains. The backbone of Shetland is rock like the Grampians, varied with sandstones and granite.

In the Northern Sea

These distinctive landscapes give the Highlands and Islands their fascination. From the most northerly of the Shetland Islands (Muckle Flugga) southwards, history and tradition are interwoven with the sometimes unforgiving land.

The 100 or so islands of Shetland are distinctively different from the rest of Scotland. Slashed by the sea into thousands of inlets, the rocky land is backed by huge, ever-changing skies. Birdwatchers are in their element here, and there are reminders of early settlement, like the broch on Mousa and the settlement at Jarlshof. Norse place names – *voe* and *wick* – abound, and the winter highlight of the islands is Up-Helly-Aa, a 24-hour Viking ritual in which a longboat is burned in an avalanche of flaming torches.

Fair Isle, between Shetland and Orkney, is another magnet for bird watchers – and for those determined to buy its brightly patterned knitwear straight from the needles of traditional knitters.

Fishing boats in Thurso, where Vikings established themselves in AD900, and whose name means 'Thor's River' in Norse

Orkney is a green and fertile contrast to Shetland, and the ideal place for the study of early history, including the 60-stone Ring of Brodgar, the huge chambered tomb at Maes Howe, and the complex Skara Brae site, where ancient homes, occupied from 3100 to 2450BC and then buried by sand, show how our remote ancestors lived. Perhaps most surprising of all is the magnificence of Kirkwall's St Magnus Cathedral, built for the Norse earls.

The huge natural harbour of Scapa Flow, where the German fleet was scuttled after its surrender in 1918, is defended by the Second World War Churchill Barriers. On Lamb Holm at its eastern edge Italian prisoners of war built an emotive chapel from Nissen huts, and decorated the inside like a Mediterranean shrine. A visit to rocky Hoy provides a contrast to the rest of Orkney – the Old Man of Hoy, a rock stack in the sea, offers spectacular climbing for the really experienced. You can reach Orkney from Scrabster on the mainland.

The Far North

On the mainland of Scotland, treeless and often windswept Caithness is the northern extremity. Its main towns, Wick and Thurso, are good bases for exploration. The undoubted attraction here, for its name, not its beauty, is John o' Groats, traditionally the top of Scotland (though Dunnet Head projects further north). The name derives from Jan de Groot, a Dutch ferryman who

plied the Pentland Firth from here to Orkney.

Westwards is the Flow Country, Europe's most important and fragile area of blanket bog, home to unique plants, animals and insects, and recently under threat from large areas of commercial forestry. Northwards, the coast is quiet and largely unvisited, with wonderful beaches and rocky inlets. Reaching Cape Wrath, the northwesterly tip of mainland Britain, involves a ferry trip and a bumpy 10-mile (16.1km) ride in a small bus, but the feeling of remoteness is worth the effort.

Turning south, the area becomes more mountainous, as the road wanders beside sea or across boggy land towards Ullapool. It passes the Inverpolly Nature Reserve, wild moorland and lochs punctuated by magnificent peaks like Suilven. Ullapool is an 18th-century planned fishing village, with a real working harbour that attracts commercial vessels and leisure craft, including cruise ships, from around the world.

Golf and Whisky

On the opposite coast, the land swings southwest down from Wick to the Dornoch Firth. Helmsdale, where the Strath of Kildonan joins the coast, was built to house displaced crofters from the valley. The Dukes of Sutherland, responsible for much rural depopulation during the Clearances of

the 19th century, have their ancestral home at Dunrobin Castle near Golspie. Their wealth is evident in the sumptuous rooms and spreading Victorian gardens.

Dornoch's world-class golf course has stunning views of the Dornoch Firth. West and south is Easter Ross, a quiet, mild landscape, though the heights of Ben Wyvis tell of the nearness of the main Highland mountains. The Black Isle, between the Cromarty and Beauly firths, is actually a peninsula of fertile farmland; its name comes from its mild, frost-free climate that lets the winter ploughland remain dark. It is worth making the journey to Cromarty at its tip, an 18th-century seaport that has been preserved intact.

From Inverness the coast road passes through prosperous towns, with branches plunging off to fishing villages, on its way to Peterhead and Aberdeen. Southeast is Strathspey, distillery country, where the magical names – including Glenlivet, Cardhu and Glenfiddich – roll smoothly off the tongue. From Grantown-on-Spey, cross the Grampian Mountains on the road through Tomintoul and Cockbridge, down into Royal Deeside. Queen Victoria first came here in 1848, and the royal family still spend summers on their Balmoral estate. Up the valley is Braemar, where the Highland Games, complete with the traditional sports like tossing the caber as well as the rather gentler pursuits of Highland dancing, have royal patronage each September. The Old Man of Lochnagar, of the Prince of Wales' children's story, lived on the nearby mountain.

The whiskies found on the Malt Whisky Trail around Strathspey are wonderfully warming

Loch Lomond, in the Loch Lomond and The Trossachs National Park, is the biggest expanse of fresh water in the UK

Serious Scenery

West of Braemar is serious Highland scenery, in the shape of the Cairngorms, Britain's highest mountain mass, with six peaks more than 4,000ft (1,220m). At their heart is the Cairngorms National Nature Reserve, with its sub-Arctic plateau and rare plants and wildlife. Aviemore is regarded as the heart of the Cairngorms, a useful rather than an attractive centre, stepping-off point for numerous mountain activities, including excellent winter skiing. The chair-lifts make it easy for summer visitors to ascend the mountains too.

Only the A9 road disturbs the peace. Otherwise it is wilderness, where the waters rush foaming down the mountainsides, the peaks beckon the skilled climber and birdwatchers can be content from the soft light of dawn to the gathering of dusk. These mountains can be dark, brooding and very wet and cold at times, too, and it is not just nature that has threatened the peace and

tranquillity. The Perthshire Highlands remind us that, amidst all this beauty, politics have never been far away from Scottish minds. The Pass of Killiecrankie, north of Pitlochry, was the scene of bitter fighting in the 1690s in the aftermath of the abdication of King James VII and II, and at nearby Aberfeldy the Black Watch, first of the Highland Regiments, was raised to help keep the rebellious country under control.

'By Loch Tummel and Loch Rannoch and Lochaber I will go', says the song 'The Road to the Isles', but beyond Loch Rannoch, west of Pitlochry, the road disappears today in the wastes of Rannoch Moor. Better to head southeast first, alongside Loch Tay and down the Tay Valley, through Killin and Crianlarich down to Tarbet at the head of Loch Lomond. The 'bonny, bonny banks', overshadowed by Ben Lomond, are for many their first introduction to the Highlands.

Saints and Stuarts

Oban on the west coast is a popular departure point both for tours on the mainland and boats to further afield. An attractive town, overlooked by the Romanesque coliseum of McCaig's Folly, it is the starting point for ferries to Colonsay, Lismore and Mull, to Coll and Tiree; if you want to visit Jura or sample whisky on Islay you will need to go to Kennacraig for the ferry. Mull has an amazingly wild coast, though it takes effort to reach it from most of the island. The central part is rather bleak, but many visitors make straight for the holy island of Iona off Mull's western tip. It was from this magical place that St Columba spread the light of civilisation in the sixth century. It still retains its feeling of sanctity, despite the large numbers of visitors who come to see the Abbey and the burial place of Scottish kings, including Duncan and Macbeth.

North of Mull, the mainland breaks down into a succession of sea-girt promontories – the Morvern, Ardnamurchan and Moidart peninsulas – each with its own character and secrets. At the top of Loch Shiel, dividing Moidart from Sunart, is Glenfinnan, where Bonnie Prince Charlie raised his standard to mark the start of his attempt to regain the crown for the Stuarts in 1745; it ended tragically in the bloody rout of Culloden the following year. After that, everything that we recognise as typically Highland was banned – the kilt and all forms of tartan, the clan system, even the bagpipes. They returned only in the following century, after the novels of Sir Walter Scott had inspired George IV to venture north of the border in 1822, clad in a fancy-dress version of Highland costume.

In the cloisters of Iona Abbey, the carvings of local birds, flowers and plants, as well as biblical images, were created between 1967 and 1997

Snow settles on the peaks of the Cairngorms National Park

The dramatic Cuillin Hills appear to rise out of the sea at the furthest most reaches of Loch Scavaig's rocky shore

Over the Sea

Since the completion of the toll bridge, the prosaic way to Skye is along the A87 and over the straits towards Broadford. But romantics still prefer to head for Mallaig, where both road and railway end at the ferry terminal. From here other islands of the Inner Hebrides can be reached, too. Knoydart, across Loch Nevis, is accessible only by sea, and provides wonderful walking country. Another way to reach Skye is via the tiny six-car ferry across the Sound of Sleat from Glenelg, where Gavin Maxwell's *Ring of Bright Water* trilogy was set. It is reached by the hairpin road through the Ratagain pass, with views of the Five Sisters of Kintail above Loch Duich, rivalled in scenic splendour only by the Bealach na Ba from Kishorn to Applecross, 15 miles (24.1km) north.

However you arrive, Skye is quickly captivating. South of Broadford is Sleat, green and gentle, from which the island's mountains stand out clearly. Closer to them is Elgol, with its ferry to Loch Coruisk, isolated among the jagged Cuillins. Northward, Waternish juts towards the Outer Hebrides, sheltering Dunvegan Castle, home of the MacLeods, while Trotternish is an extraordinary landscape around the Quirang and the Old Man of Storr.

Britain's Edge

Beyond Skye, across the sometimes treacherous waters of the Little Minch, lie the Western Isles (Outer Hebrides). From Barra to the Butt of Lewis is more than 120 miles (192km), and, although the three central islands are joined by causeways, travelling the full length needs expert juggling with ferry timetables. Barra sums up the whole chain, with empty silver beaches backed by flower meadows, stretches of peat bog and small crofts.

South Uist is dotted with lochans, many of them home to a wide variety of birds. Flora Macdonald was from South Uist, and from the next island north, Benbecula, she sailed across the Minch to Skye with Bonnie Prince Charlie disguised as her maid to aid his escape after Culloden. Most of North Uist is shattered into fragments by lochs and inlets. From the west it is sometimes possible to glimpse precipitous St Kilda, 45 miles (72km) out in the Atlantic. The population was dramatically evacuated in 1933, when life became insupportable.

Largest of the Outer Hebrides is the island that comprises Harris and Lewis. Though joined, they are very different in character. Harris is mountainous, with long empty beaches and wonderful views. Lewis is flat and bare, mostly peat bogs and outcrops of rock. The capital, Stornoway, is a lively town, and the centre of the prestigious Harris Tweed industry.

Away to the west is one of Scotland's most enduring and important monuments, Callanish Stone Circle, a dramatic ring of 13 tall, thin stones, some up to 15ft (4.6m) high, approached along avenues of similar stones. It is a moving sight, very far removed from the tartan tam o'shanters and model monsters that sometimes represent the Highlands and Islands. Here, amid the bleakness of the Western Isles with only the sea and the wind for company, visitors may truly experience the reality of Scotland.

Remote Huisinis Bay, on the Isle of Harris overlooking the uninhabited Isle of Scarp, is the start of a number of excellent walks through coastal landscapes

The central ring of the Callanish standing stones which have both astronomical and religious significance, dates back to between 2900 and 2600BC, from which rows of stones form a Cruciform pattern

Walk A

CAERLAVEROCK CASTLE AND THE SOLWAY MERSES

A ramble taking in an ancient fortress and a National Nature Reserve.

13th-century Caerlaverock Castle, with its unique triangular moat

Distance: 5.25 miles (8.4km)
Minimum time: 2hrs 30min
Ascent/Gradient: 82ft (25m) ▲▲▲
Level of difficulty: +++
Paths: Country lanes, farm tracks and salt marsh, 1 stile
Landscape: Pastures, salt marsh, riverside and gentle hills
Suggested map: OS Explorer 314 Solway Firth
Start/finish: Grid reference: NY 051656
Dog friendliness: Keep on lead on reserve
Parking: Car park at Wildfowl and Wetlands Trust Reserve
Public toilets: At Wildfowl and Wetlands Trust Reserve Visitor Centre

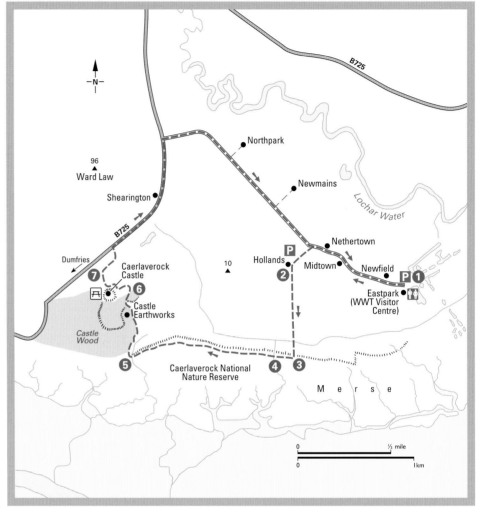

❶ Exit the car park and turn right on to a farm road. Follow this past the farms of Newfield and Midtown, then turn left and go past a bungalow and some houses. Just before you reach the farm of Hollands, there is a waymarker pointing to a car park, on the right, and straight ahead for walks. Go straight ahead and continue to the farm steading, then turn left.

❷ Go through a gate and on to a farm track. This stretches away into the distance and has high hedges on both sides. Continue along this track between the hedges and on, over an overgrown section, until you reach the end. Then turn right at the signpost that indicates Caerlaverock.

❸ A sign here informs visitors that regulated wildfowling (shooting) takes place between 1 September and 20 February. Follow the rough track through the grass along the edge of the merse in the direction of the arrow on the footpath waymarker post. The path can be very boggy at all times and the grass will be high in the summer.

❹ The path through the nature reserve varies from faint to non-existent; wellington boots are recommended. It splits at several points and then meanders back and forth, but all the lines of the path re-join and you'll end up at the same place whichever one you decide to take.

❺ Eventually some cottages can be seen in the field to the right. Bear right, through a gate and into the field. Walk to the left around the field perimeter, past some cottages, then turn left through a gate to emerge on to a farm track, passing a sign for Caerlaverock Castle and into the castle grounds.

❻ Follow the road past the old castle, which has been excavated and has information boards to explain the ruins, and go through a wood with nature trail information boards to Caerlaverock Castle. There is a children's playground, a siege machine and picnic tables around the ramparts of the castle.

❼ At the far end go through an arch and continue to the T-junction with a country lane. Turn right and continue for about 1 mile (1.6km), then turn right on to another lane signposted 'Wildfowl and Wetlands Reserve'. Continue on this road past the farms of Northpark, Newmains and Nethertown and then back to the car park at Eastpark.

DISCOVER DUNASKIN IRONWORKS

*A hill walk from a 19th-century industrial monument to a deserted,
but not forgotten, village.*

There are many marked walks in forests in Scotland

Distance: 4 miles (6.4km)
Minimum time: 3hrs
Ascent/Gradient: 492ft (150m) ▲▲▲
Level of difficulty: +++
Paths: Old rail and tram beds and
rough hillside
Landscape: Hills, moorland and industrial
buildings
Suggested map: OS Explorer 327 Cumnock
& Dalmellington
Start/finish: Grid reference: NX 440084
Dog friendliness: Keep on lead near sheep
and at lambing time
Parking: Dunaskin Open Air Museum
Public toilets: At visitor centre

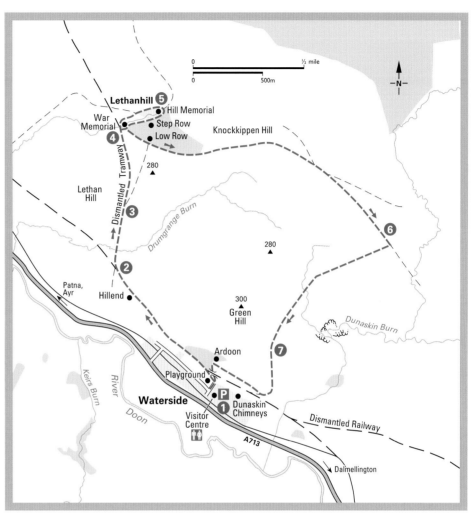

❶ Turn right in front of the visitor centre
and follow the road towards the adventure
playground. Go uphill on a track to the right
of the playground and through a kissing gate
into woodland. Emerge at a T-junction opposite
a railway bridge and then turn left here onto
a grassy trail.

❷ When you reach a metal gate across the
trail, go through a small wooden one at its side.
Climb over the next gate, turn right and head
uphill following the line of a disused tramway,
between the ends of an old bridge. This is the
trackbed of the former horse-drawn tramway,
which was used in order to bring the iron ore
down from the plateau.

❸ At the top of the hill, when the path divides,
keep left and follow the path as it goes through
two short sections of wall. The ground to your
right in front of the conifer plantation was
once the village football field. Where the path
is blocked by a fence, turn right and then go
left to walk through a gate and right on to a
metalled lane.

❹ Head along here, past the remains of the
miners' houses of Step Row, which are clearly
visible amongst the trees. A stone memorial
to the 'hill' stands near the site of the former
village store. To the right of this, and now
within the wood, is the former village square
and the remains of more houses.

❺ From the stone memorial, turn back
towards the war memorial, then return to the
gate at the corner of the wood and continue
along the track beside the wood. In the trees
are the remains of Low Row. Go through
another gate and continue along the former
railway. When it forks, keep right.

❻ Continue until the route ahead is blocked
by sheets of corrugated iron. Cross the wall and
turn right, heading downhill to pick up a faint
path. Continue on this to reach a cluster of
trees beside a ruined building.

❼ Head down from here towards the right of
a row of cottages. Go through a gate, turn right
then right again at a fork to reach Ardoon. Go
past the house, turn left on to a footpath and
follow it downhill and under a small, disused
railway bridge. Cross the track and carry on,
heading back downhill on the footpath which
leads back to the visitor centre.

Walking in hillside forests can be very atmospheric

THE THIRTY-NINE STEPS IN BROUGHTON

A lovely walk through landscapes immortalised by John Buchan.

Broughton Place was built in 1938, in the style of a 17th century Scottish tower house

Distance: 5 miles (8km)
Minimum time: 2hrs 30min
Ascent/Gradient: 1,575ft (480m) ▲▲▲
Level of difficulty: +++
Paths: Hill tracks and grassy paths, 1 stile
Landscape: Rolling hills and exposed ridge
Suggested map: OS Explorer 336 Biggar & Broughton
Start/finish: Grid reference: NT 119374
Dog friendliness: Good, but keep on lead because of sheep
Parking: Parking in front of cottage past Broughton Place and art gallery
Public toilets: None en route

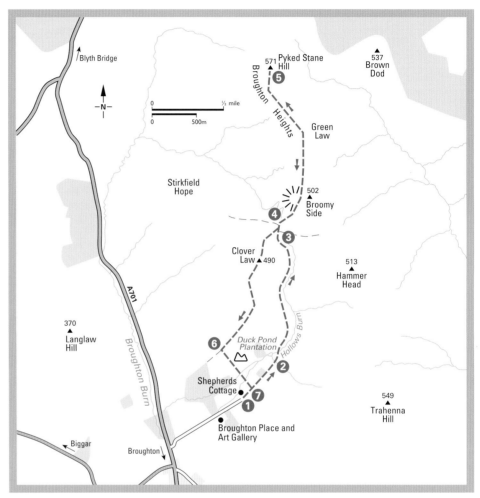

❶ From the parking place, go through the gate and follow the obvious, grassy track that runs in front of the cottage. You'll soon pass a copse on the left-hand side, then pass the attractively named Duck Pond Plantation, also on the left-hand side. The track becomes slightly rougher, and you cross a small footbridge over a burn.

❷ Your track continues ahead past feathery carpets of heather and bracken – listen for the skylarks in the summer. Continue walking and the path will soon level out and lead you past a gully on the right-hand side. Follow the track until it bends, after which you come to a meeting of tracks.

❸ Take the track that bears left and head for the dip that lies between the two hills – Clover Law on the left and Broomy Side in front. You should just be able to spot the fence 100 yards (91m) on the skyline. Make for that fence and, as you near it, you'll eventually spot a gate, next to which is a wooden stile.

❹ Cross the stile, then turn right and follow the fence line. You soon get superb views to the left – well, you do on a clear day. Continue following the fence and walk up the track until you reach the trig point on Broughton Heights – the final ascent's a bit of a puff – but it's thankfully not too long.

❺ Now retrace your steps to reach the stile again, nip over it, but this time turn right and follow the narrow track that climbs Clover Law. Continue walking in the same direction, following the fence line as it runs along the top of the ridge. When you near the end of the ridge, keep your eyes peeled for a path to the left, down an old earth boundary bank.

❻ Follow the track as it runs down roughly in the direction of the cottage – it's quite a steep descent. At the bottom you'll come to an old wall and a burn, which you cross, then continue ahead to cross over another burn and across a field to reach the main track.

❼ Turn right here and walk past the little cottage again, through the gate and back to your car. If you want to visit Broughton Place and its art gallery, just continue walking down the track to reach the house on your left.

A stone house in Broughton

EDINBURGH'S OLD TOWN

A stroll through the streets of Edinburgh.

The view across Edinburgh from Arthur's seat

Distance: 2 miles (3.2km)	
Minimum time: 1hr	
Ascent/Gradient: 197ft (60m) ▲▲▲	
Level of difficulty: +++	
Paths: City streets, some hill tracks	
Landscape: Atmospheric ancient city and brooding castle	
Suggested map: AA Street by Street Edinburgh	
Start/finish: Grid reference: NT 256739	
Dog friendliness: Keep on lead, watch paws don't get trodden on by crowds	
Parking: Several NCP car parks in Edinburgh	
Public toilets: At Waverley Station	

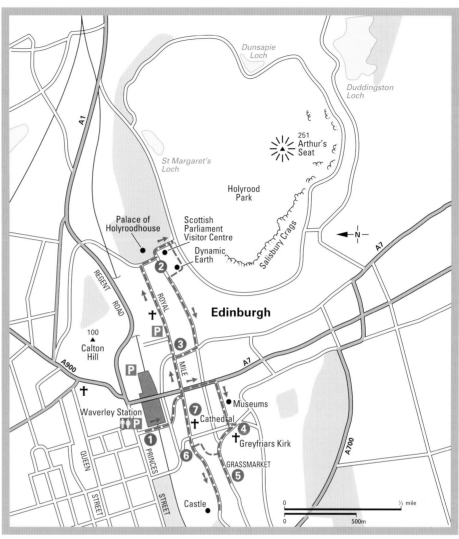

❶ From the main entrance to Waverley Station, turn left, go to the end of the street, then cross over and walk up Cockburn Street to the Royal Mile, where you turn left and walk downhill. Continue to the black gates of Holyroodhouse. Turn right and walk to face the new Scottish Parliament Visitor Centre.

❷ Turn left and follow the road to the right, then turn right again past Dynamic Earth (the building looks like a huge white woodlouse) and walk up into Holyrood Road. Turn left, walk past the new buildings of *The Scotsman* newspaper, and walk up to St Mary's Street, where you turn right and re-join the Royal Mile. Were you to continue ahead you would join the Cowgate, some parts of which were devastated by fire in December 2002.

❸ Turn left, to the main road, then turn left along South Bridge. At Chambers Street turn right and walk past the museums. At the end of the road, cross and then turn left to see the little statue of Greyfriars Bobby, the dog that refused to leave this spot after his master died.

❹ You can now cross the road and make the short detour into Greyfriars Kirk to see where Greyfriars Bobby is buried close to his master. Or simply turn right and walk down Candlemaker Row. At the bottom, turn left and wander into the atmospheric Grassmarket – once the haunt of Burke and Hare, it's now filled with shops and lively restaurants.

❺ When you've explored the Grassmarket, walk up winding Victoria Street (it says 'West Bow' at the bottom). About two-thirds of the way up, look out for a flight of steps hidden away on the left. Climb them and, when you emerge at the top, walk ahead to join the Royal Mile again.

❻ Turn left to walk up and visit the castle. Then walk down the Royal Mile again, taking a peek into the dark and secretive wynds (alleyways) that lead off it. You eventually pass St Giles' Cathedral on your right, which is well worth a visit if you have time.

❼ Next on your left you pass the City Chambers (under which lies mysterious Mary King's Close). Continue until you reach the junction with Cockburn Street. Turn left and walk back down this winding street. At the bottom, cross the road and return to the entrance to Waverley Station.

Detail from the gates of Holyrood Palace

THE ROMANCE OF ROSLIN GLEN

Tree-lined paths take you beside a river to a very special ancient.
chapel in this glorious glen.

Rosslyn Chapel was founded in 1446

Distance: 5 miles (8km)
Minimum time: 2hrs 30min
Ascent/Gradient: 279ft (85m) ▲▲▲
Level of difficulty: +++
Paths: Generally good, but can be muddy and slippery
Landscape: Woodland and fields, short sections of road
Suggested map: OS Explorer 344 Pentland Hills
Start/finish: Grid reference: NT 272627
Dog friendliness: Can mostly run free, steps and climbs might not suit some
Parking: Roslin Glen Country Park car park
Public toilets: None en route; nearest at Rosslyn Chapel Visitor Centre

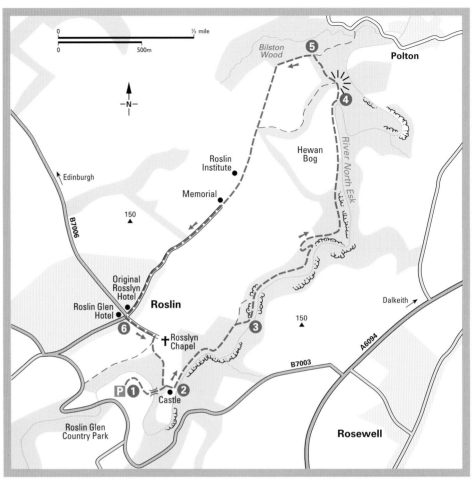

❶ From the country park car park, walk northeast with the sound of the river through the trees to your left. Go up the metal stairs, cross the footbridge, then walk ahead, following the path uphill. In summer, the smell of wild garlic will soon waft over you. At the bottom of a flight of steps, turn right, walk under the old castle arch, down some stone steps, then turn to your left.

❷ Follow the path through scrub and up some steps into dense woodland. Just by a muddy burn, bear left, keeping to the main path with the gorge to your right. Beyond a line of yew trees growing from an old stone wall, turn right and follow the path that winds steeply downhill until you reach the water's edge.

❸ Walk to your left, then follow the path as it climbs again. At a crossing of paths turn right, following the direction of the river. Your way now takes you high above the river, and you continue ahead to cross a stile. After you cross another stile the view opens out to fields on your left, then takes you closer to the river again, until you reach a kissing gate.

❹ Turn left and follow the path up steps with fields to your left. When you reach the top of the ridge, there are good views to your right. Continue until you go through a kissing gate.

❺ Turn left and follow the wide path. You eventually walk past buildings of the Roslin Institute, where Dolly the sheep was cloned, then pass a memorial to the Battle of Rosslyn on your right-hand side. Keep walking straight ahead, through the outskirts of Roslin and up to the crossroads at the village centre.

❻ Turn left here and walk ahead. After a short distance you see Rosslyn Chapel on the right-hand side. If you don't intend to visit the chapel, take the path that bears downhill to the right, just in front of it. When you reach the cemetery turn left, following the signpost for Polton, and walk between the cemeteries to the metal gate for Rosslyn Castle. Go down the steps on the right-hand side, over the bridge again and return to the car park at the start.

The interior of Rosslyn Chapel

EXPLORING GLASGOW'S HERITAGE

Discover the architectural delights of a Victorian city.

Kelvingrove Art Gallery

Distance: 6.5 miles (10.4km)
Minimum time: 3hrs 30min
Ascent/Gradient: 98ft (30m) ▲▲▲
Level of difficulty: +++
Paths: Pavements
Landscape: City streets
Suggested map: OS Explorer 342 Glasgow;
AA Street by Street Glasgow
Start/finish: Grid reference: NS 587653
Dog friendliness: Not great walk for dogs
Parking: Sauchiehall Street multi-storey or
on-street parking
Public toilets: At Central Station

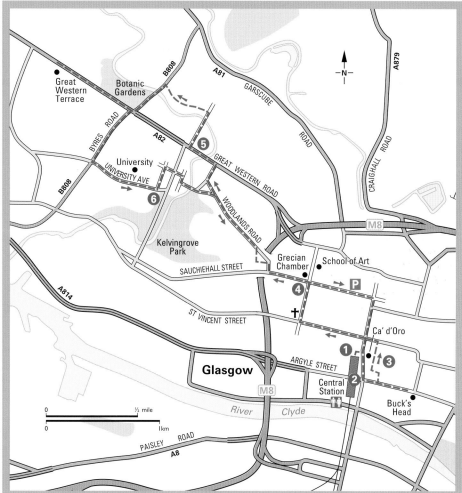

❶ Exit Central Station and turn right. At the junction with Union Street turn right. The building on the opposite corner is the Ca' d'Oro building, a late 19th-century Italianate warehouse by John Honeyman, based on the Golden House in Venice. The upper storeys are made of cast iron. A little way down Union Street from here on the same side as the Ca' d'Oro is Thomson's Egyptian Halls, sadly in need of some renovation.

❷ Cross over, then head down Union Street, turning left into Argyle Street at the next junction. Cross Argyle Street, then walk along to the junction with Dunlop Street where you will find the Buck's Head building, named after an inn that previously stood on this spot. Cross Argyle Street again, retrace your steps, turning right into Buchanan Street. Turn left into Mitchell Lane, pass the Lighthouse, then turn right.

❸ Walk up Mitchell Street, continue along West Nile Street, then turn left into St Vincent Street. Continue on this for just under 0.5 mile (800m), going uphill to the junction with Pitt Street. You are now standing in front of 'Greek' Thomson's St Vincent Street church, one of his greatest achievements. Cross St Vincent Street here, then head up Pitt Street to Sauchiehall Street.

❹ On the opposite corner is Thomson's Grecian Chamber (1865) and to the right along Scott Street is Rennie Mackintosh's Glasgow School of Art. From the front of the Grecian Chamber turn left, head down Sauchiehall Street to Charing Cross, then take the pedestrian bridge over the motorway to Woodlands Road. Go along here until it ends at Park Road, turn right, then left again into Great Western Road.

❺ Go right on Belmont Street, left at Doune Gardens, continue along Doune Quadrant, then left again at Queen Margaret Drive. Cross the road and head down past the Botanic Gardens to turn right, back into Great Western Road. Cross the road and continue to Great Western Terrace, another Thomson masterpiece. Retrace your steps back from here to the top of Byres Road and turn right then, near the bottom, turn left into University Avenue.

❻ Go left into Oakfield Avenue, pass Eton Terrace on the corner with Great George Street. Turn right into Great George Street, right at Otago Street, left into Gibson Street and keep going when it becomes Eldon Street. Turn right into Woodlands Road and return to Sauchiehall Street. Follow this to the junction with Renfield Street, then turn right and head downhill to Central Station.

Walk G STIRLING'S BRAVEHEART, WILLIAM WALLACE

Follow this town trail and learn more about a Scottish hero.

Old Stirling Bridge with the Wallace Monument in the background

Distance: 5 miles (8km)

Minimum time: 2hrs 30 min

Ascent/Gradient: 279ft (85m) ▲▲▲

Level of difficulty: +++

Paths: Ancient city streets and some rough tracks

Landscape: Bustling little city topped with magnificent castle

Suggested map: OS Explorer 366 Stirling & Ochil Hills West

Start/finish: Grid reference: NS 795933

Dog friendliness: Mostly on lead, not good for those that dislike crowds

Parking: In multi-storey car parks in town centre, or use Castleview Park and Ride (signposted from M9) which has stop opposite tourist information centre

Public toilets: At visitor centre by the castle

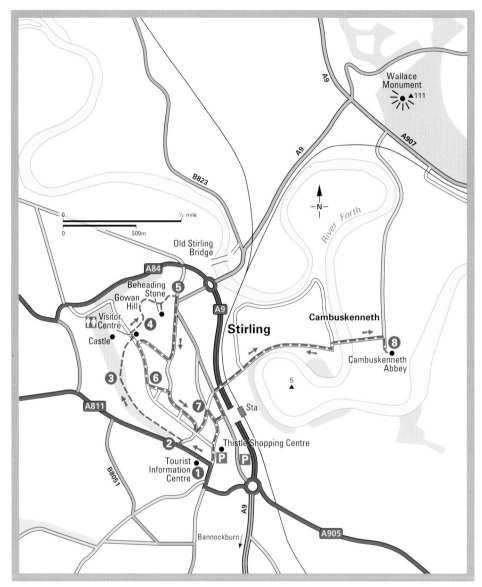

1 From the tourist information centre on Dumbarton Road, cross the road and turn left. Walk past the statue of Robert Burns then, just before the Albert Halls, turn right and walk back on yourself. Just past the statue of Rob Roy, turn left and take the path along the Back Wall.

2 Almost immediately (20 yards/18m) turn right up the flight of steps that takes you on to the Upper Back Wall. It's a steady climb now, up past the Church of the Holy Rude, where James VI was crowned in 1567 and on past Ladies' Rock – where the ladies of the castle sat to watch tournaments.

3 Continue following the path uphill to reach Stirling Castle. Cross the car park to take the path running downhill just to the side of the visitor centre, so that the castle is on your left. At the cemetery, turn right along the footpath signposted to Moto Hill. Continue up steps and across the cemetery to the gap in the wall.

4 Follow the track downhill on to Gowan Hill. There are several branching tracks, but you should continue on the main path – heading for the cannons on the hill ahead. At a junction turn right down a track signposted to Lower Bridge Street. Turn on to a grassy slope to the right to see the Beheading Stone. Retrace your steps to the wide track and then follow it to reach the road.

5 Turn right along Lower Bridge Street, then fork right into Upper Bridge Street. Continue ahead, then 50 yards (46m) beyond Settle Inn, turn right up a cobbled lane – it looks a bit like the access to a house. Follow it uphill, then go left at the top. Eventually you'll pass the Castle Esplanade, followed by Argyll's Lodging, and will reach a junction.

6 Turn left, passing Hermann's Restaurant and the Mercat Cross. Turn right at the bottom down Bow Street, then left along Baker Street. When you reach Friars Street (pedestrianised), turn left and walk down to the end.

7 Turn right now, then first left to reach the station. Turn left, then right over the bridge, then bear left in front of a new development to reach the riverside. Maintain direction and join Abbey Road. Bear left at the end, go right over the footbridge and continue along South Street, turning right at the end to visit the remains of Cambuskenneth Abbey.

8 Retrace your steps back to the station. Turn right, then left, then right again at the Thistle Shopping Centre. Go along Port Street, then turn right along Dumbarton Road to the start.

CLIMBING TO THE CASTLE OF CUPS

Dun na Cuaiche offers a fine view of Inveraray, Campbell capital of Argyll.

Inveraray was built on the site of an earlier fishing village in the mid 1700s by the third Duke of Argyll

Distance: 4 miles (6.4km)
Minimum time: 2hrs 15min
Ascent/Gradient: 900ft (274m) ▲▲▲
Level of difficulty: +++
Paths: Clear, mostly waymarked paths, no stiles
Landscape: Steep, wooded hill, some rocky outcrops
Suggested map: OS Explorer 363 Cowal East
Start/finish: Grid reference: NN 096085
Dog friendliness: Must be under control, not necessarily on lead
Parking: Pay-and-display, Inveraray Pier
Public toilets: Inveraray Pier and Castle

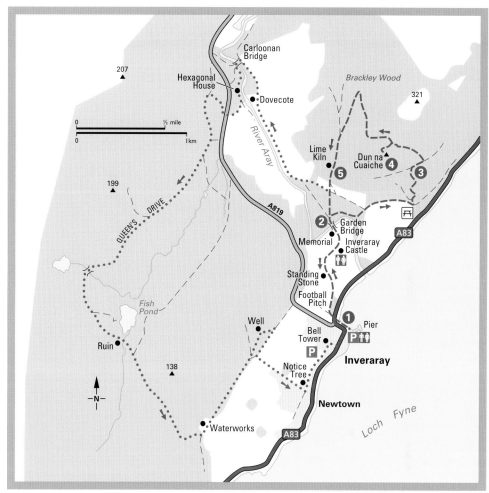

❶ Follow the seafront past the Argyll Hotel and bear left towards Inveraray Castle. At the first junction, turn right past a football pitch with a standing stone. After the coach park on the left and the end wall of the castle on the right, the estate road on the left is signed 'Dun na Cuaiche Woodland Walks'. It passes a memorial to clansmen who were killed for religious reasons in 1685. Cross the stone-arched Garden Bridge to a junction.

❷ Half-right now is the uphill path with coloured waymarkers that will be the return leg of the walk. During the coming summers this may be affected by timber lorries, in which case there will be a notice closing this path. If you should see such a notice, it is fine to continue with the route described below up to Dun na Cuaiche, Point ❹, before returning by the way you came up, via Point ❸. Turn right on a riverside track and follow it to a picnic table with a view back to the castle. A rough track runs up left, but turn off instead on to a small path just to the right of this, beside a stone gatepost. It climbs quite steeply through an area where attempts have failed to eradicate rhododendron plants.

❸ At a green track above, turn right, slightly uphill, for 100 yards (91m) to a turning circle. Turn left up a muddy path which passes under

trees. This improves, bending left and slanting uphill across a stream. The path continues directly uphill under birch trees, with a stream nearby on its left through woods. As the slope eases, the path crosses a grassy clearing to meet a wider one. Turn left, in zigzags, to reach the summit of Dun na Cuaiche. The tower offers outstanding views on a fine day.

❹ Return down the path to the clearing, but this time keep ahead. The path, rather muddy, bends left then enters the plantation and becomes a clear track. This track passes between two dry-stone pillars where a wall crosses. It then turns back sharp left, and passes between two more pillars lower down the same wall. Continue down the track, ignoring side-tracks on the left, to a lime kiln on the right.

❺ Past the lime kiln, a gate leads into a field. Fork right off the track, re-crossing it below to a gate beyond. This leads into a wood. The path runs down to the track junction before the Garden Bridge (Point ❷). Return along the castle driveway to Inveraray.

Extending the walk
From Point ❺, you could take the track on the right, to head upstream to the right of River Aray, past a white dovecote and through Carloonan farm. Cross Carloonan Bridge and head back downstream on a track that bends right to the A819. Turn right on an old road opposite to a path on the left. At a T-junction, turn left over a stream. With the track about to rejoin A819, turn right and keep right at the next fork to follow Queen's Drive through Coille-bhraghad Wood. It passes to the right of a large fishpond. In 440 yards (402m) keep ahead on a smaller track, down a pretty wooded glen to a waterworks. Turn left along the wooded footpath. With a metal turnpike gate on the right, fork up left to visit the ornamental well. Return to the turnpike gate, which leads out towards Newtown. At the Notice Tree turn left to Inveraray.

INTO THE LOST VALLEY

A rugged waterfall walk into the hidden hollow where the MacDonalds hid their stolen cows.

The scenery of Glen Coe is breathtaking

Distance: 2.75 miles (4.4km)
Minimum time: 2hrs 15min
Ascent/Gradient: 1,050ft (320m) ▲▲▲
Level of difficulty: +++
Paths: Rugged and stony, stream to wade through
Landscape: Crags and mountains
Suggested map: OS Explorer 384 Glen Coe & Glen Etive
Start/finish: Grid reference: NN 168569
Dog friendliness: Dogs must be reasonably fit and agile
Parking: Lower of two roadside parking places opposite Gearr Aonach (middle one of the Three Sisters)
Public toilets: Glencoe village

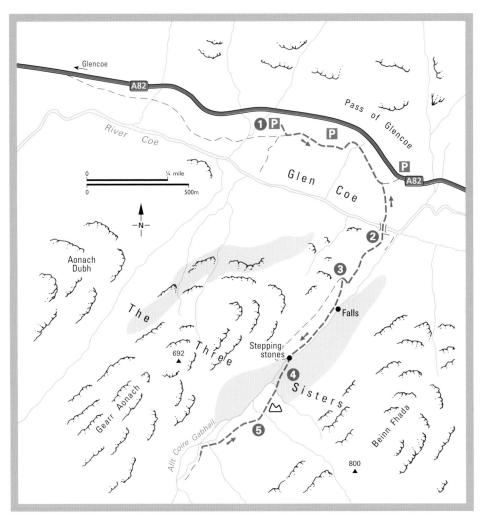

❶ From the uphill corner of the car park, a faint path slants down to the old road, which is now a well-used wide path. Head up the valley for about 650 yards (594m). With the old road continuing as a green track ahead, your path now bends down to the right. It has been rebuilt, with the bog problem solved by scraping down to the bedrock. The path reaches the gorge where the River Coe runs in a geological dyke of softer rock. Descend here on a steep wooden step ladder, to cross a spectacular footbridge.

❷ The ascent out of the gorge is on a bare rock staircase. Above, the path runs through regenerating birch wood, which can be very wet on the legs; sheep and deer have been excluded from the wood with a temporary fence. Emerge from this through a high gate. The path, rebuilt in places, runs uphill for around 60 yards (55m). Here it bends left; an inconspicuous alternative path continues uphill, which can be used to bypass the narrow path of the main route.

❸ The main route contours into the gorge of the Allt Coire Gabhail. It is narrow with steep drops below. Where there is an alternative of rock slabs and a narrow path just below, the slabs are more secure. You will hear waterfalls, then two fine ones come into view ahead. After passing these, continue between boulders to where the main path bends left to cross the stream below a boulder the size of a small house. (A small path runs on up to the right of the stream, but leads nowhere useful.) The river here is wide and fairly shallow. Five or six stepping stones usually allow dry crossing. If the water is above the stones, then it's safer to wade alongside them; if, however, the water is more than knee-deep, the crossing should not be attempted.

❹ A well-built path continues uphill, now with the stream on its right. After 100 yards (91m), a lump of rock blocks the way. The path follows a slanting ramp up its right-hand side. It continues uphill, still rebuilt in places, passing above the boulder pile that blocks the valley, the result of two large rockfalls from under Gearr Aonach opposite. At the top of the rockpile the path levels, giving a good view into the Lost Valley.

❺ Drop gently to the valley's gravel floor. The stream vanishes into the gravel, to reappear below the boulder pile on the other side. Note where the path arrives at the gravel, as it becomes invisible at that point. Wander up the valley to where the stream vanishes, 0.25 mile (400m) ahead. Anywhere beyond this point is more serious hillwalking than you have done up to now on this walk. Return to the path and follow it back to the start of the walk.

THE INSPIRATIONAL LANDSCAPE OF AUCHENBLAE

Walk through the fields and woods of the Howe of Mearns, that inspired the writer James Leslie Mitchell.

Drumtochty Castle was built in the 19th century

Distance: 6.75 miles (10.9km)
Minimum time: 3hrs 30min
Ascent/Gradient: 459ft (140m) ▲▲▲
Level of difficulty: +++
Paths: Established footpaths, overgrown woodland tracks
Landscape: Acres of arable fields and cool forests
Suggested map: OS Explorer 396 Stonehaven, Inverbervie & Lawrencekirk
Start/finish: Grid reference: NO 727787
Dog friendliness: Fallen trees make it unsuitable except for fit dogs
Parking: On street in Auchenblae
Public toilets: Off main street in Auchenblae and at Drumtochty Castle car park

❶ Halfway up the steep High Street, turn left, signed 'Woodland Walks'. The lane runs steeply downhill and crosses Pamphil Burn beside a play area, then runs uphill to a T-junction.

❷ Turn right to walk past a cemetery and then take a grassy track on the left. The track runs up between arable fields to reach the plantation above. Scramble over or past a rusty gate (take care here) and then walk through long grass to reach a track.

❸ Turn right and follow the thickly vegetated track along the bottom edge of the forest. There are a couple of fallen trees to clamber over or walk around. At a wider gravel track, turn right and then continue with fields still visible through the trees below. Above where these fields end, ignore a side-track up to the left. In another 220 yards (200m), fork left on a fainter track.

❹ The track runs level then gently uphill. Where a pylon rises on the right-hand side of the track, strike downhill through the cleared ground under the electric wires – this is awkward going, with brushwood underfoot.

❺ At the bottom left corner of the cleared ground, a small path strikes left, taking you into the forest. The path becomes clearer as it slants gradually down to join the valley road below. Turn sharp right along the road, passing a huge Sitka spruce tree, to Drumtochty car park on the left.

❻ Take the track through the car park, bending up left past some toilets. After a stiff climb on tarmac, turn right (red waymarker) down a zigzag path to a mill lade. Turn left along this, to a footbridge above a weir. A little way upstream, the path climbs out of the steep valley, and contours upstream to pass above a small reservoir.

❼ At the track beyond, turn left and return to Drumtochty car park. Turn left along the road until a path forks up right past a vehicle barrier. This leads to a forest track, which joins a larger one. Keep ahead, now level, until the track descends left to re-join the road below.

❽ Turn right and walk along the road, to a junction where you turn left, signed 'Auchenblae', and cross Pamphil Burn. At the following junction bear right, to reach the top end of Auchenblae's High Street.

The Church of Scotland St Palladius Church near Auchenblae, Angus, Scotland

Walk K

LOCH AN EILEIN'S CASTLE AND ORD BAN

The castle on the island in the loch is the heart of Rothiemurchus Forest.

Loch an Eilein is set within one of the largest remaining ancient Caledonian Forests

Distance: 4.25 miles (6.8km)
Minimum time: 1hr 45min
Ascent/Gradient: 100ft (30m) ▲▲▲
Level of difficulty: +++
Paths: Wide smooth paths, optional steep hill with high ladder stile
Landscape: Ancient pine forest around loch
Suggested map: OS Explorer 403 Cairn Gorm & Aviemore
Start/finish: Grid reference: NH 897084
Dog friendliness: Keep on lead on Rothiemurchus Estate
Parking: Estate car park near Loch an Eilein, charges apply
Public toilets: Visitor centre

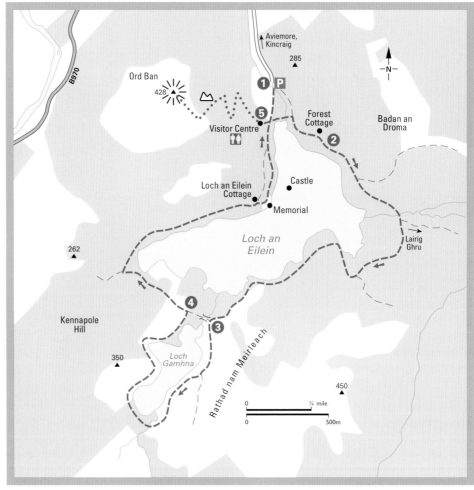

① From the end of the car park at the beginning of the walk, a made-up path leads to the visitor centre. Turn left to cross the end of Loch an Eilein, then turn right on a smooth sandy track. The loch shore is nearby on the right. There are small paths leading down to it if you wish to visit. Just past a red-roofed house, a deer fence runs across, with a gate.

② The track now becomes a wide, smooth path, which runs close to the loch side. After a bridge, the main track forks right to pass a bench backed by a flat boulder. The smaller path on the left leads high into the hills and through the famous pass of the Lairig Ghru, and eventually to Braemar. After crossing a stream at a low concrete footbridge, the path bends right for 120 yards (110m) to a junction. Just beyond you'll find a footbridge with wooden handrails.

③ To shorten the walk, cross this footbridge and continue along the main track, passing Point **④** in another 170 yards (155m). For a

longer walk, turn left before the footbridge on to a narrower path that will pass around Loch Gamhna. This second loch soon appears on your right-hand side. Where the path forks, keep right to pass along the loch side, across its head (rather boggy) and back along its further side, to re-join the wider path around Loch an Eilein. Turn left here.

④ Continue around Loch an Eilein, with the water on your right, to a reedy corner of the loch and a bench. About 55 yards (50m) further, the path turns sharply right, signposted 'footpath'. After a gate, turn right to the loch side and a memorial to Major General Brook Rice, who drowned here while skating. Follow the shore to the point opposite the castle, then back up to the wide track above. A deer fence on the left leads back to the visitor centre.

⑤ From here, a stiff climb (500ft/152m) can be made on to the rocky little hill of Ord Ban, a superb viewpoint. Cross a ladder stile

immediately to the right of the toilet block and follow the deer fence to the right for 150 yards (137m), to a point behind the car park. Just behind one of the lowest birches on the slope, a small indistinct path zigzags up the steep slope. It slants to the left to avoid crags, then crosses a small rock slab (take care if wet) and continues on to the summit. Descend by the same path.

Ruined castle on Loch an Eilean or Eilein

SEEING SEA EAGLES AT PORTREE BAY

A coastal walk to a raised beach called The Bile, then returning by way of Ben Chracaig.

Portree Bay

Distance: 3.5 miles (5.7km)

Minimum time: 1hr 15min

Ascent/Gradient: 459ft (140m) ▲▲▲

Level of difficulty: +++

Paths: Smooth, well-made paths, farm track, 3 stiles

Landscape: Views across Minch from wooded coast and hill above

Suggested map: OS Explorer 409 Raasay, Rona & Scalpay or 410 Skye – Portree & Bracadale

Start/finish: Grid reference: NG 485436

Dog friendliness: Dogs on lead through farmland, scoop poop on shore path

Parking: On A855 (Staffin Road) above Portree Bay. Another small parking area near slipway

Public toilets: Town centre, just off main square

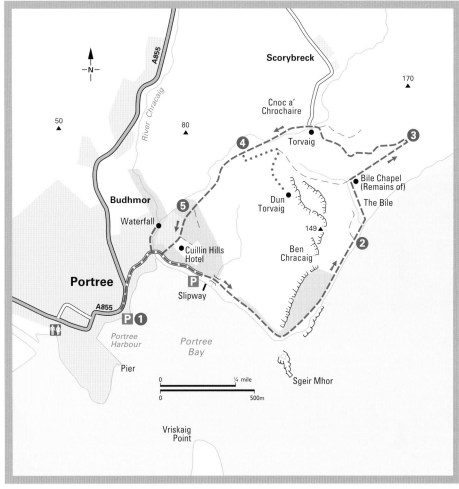

❶ Turn off the main A855 on to a lane signed 'Budh Mor', to walk down to the shoreline and then continue to a small parking area. A tarred path continues along the shore past a slipway. After a footbridge, it passes under hazels which show the typical ground-branching habit of bushes formerly coppiced, cut back every seven years for firewood. The path passes below a viewpoint with flagpoles and then rounds the headland to reach the edge of a level green field called The Bile.

❷ A wall runs up the edge of The Bile. A sign points up left for Scorybreck, but ignore it and go through a small gate ahead. A rough path leads into the corner of The Bile field. Go up its left edge and turn across its top, to a stile just above a field gate. Cross the top of the next field on an old green path, to a stile at its corner. You will see a track just beyond.

❸ Turn sharp left, up the track. At the top it passes through two gates to reach a stony road just to the right of Torvaig. Turn left past the house and cross the foot of a tarred road into a gently descending track. It runs down between two large corrugated sheds and then through to a gate with a stile.

❹ The grassy path ahead leads down into Portree, but you can take a short, rather rough, diversion to Dun Torvaig (an ancient fortified hilltop) above. For the dun, turn left along the fence, and left again on a well-made path above. It leads to a kissing gate above the two sheds. Turn sharp right along the fence for a few steps, then bear left around the base of a small outcrop and head straight up on a tiny path to the dun. Remnants of drystone walling can be seen around the summit. Return to the well-made path, passing above Point ❹ to join the wall on the right. The path leads down under goat willows into a wood where it splits; stay close to the wall.

❺ At the first houses (The Parks Bungalow 5), keep downhill on a tarred street. On the left is the entrance to the Cuillin Hills Hotel. A few steps later, fork right on to a stony path. At the shore road, turn right across a stream and at once right again on a path that runs up for 60 yards (55m) to a craggy little waterfall. Return to the shore road and turn right to the walk start.

White-tailed sea eagles are tracked by the RSPB

Walk M
STRATHPEFFER AND THE ROGIE FALLS

From a Victorian spa to a salmon-leaping waterfall.

Strathpeffer developed as a spa town in the 1800s

Distance: 10 miles (16.1km)
Minimum time: 5hrs
Ascent/Gradient: 1,200ft (366m) ▲▲▲
Level of difficulty: +++
Paths: Waymarked paths and tracks, no stiles
Landscape: Plantation, wild forest and riverside
Suggested map: OS Explorer 437 Ben Wyvis & Strathpeffer
Start/finish: Grid reference: NH 483582
Dog friendliness: Keep on lead for section past Loch Kinellan
Parking: Main square, Strathpeffer
Public toilets: At start, Contin (Point ④) and Rogie Falls car parks

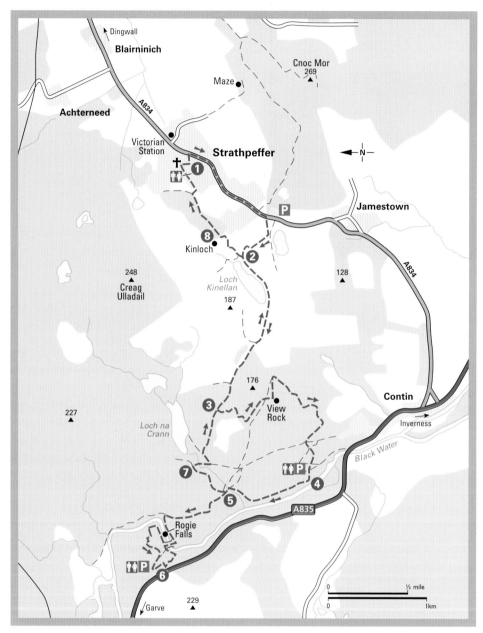

① Head along the main road towards Contin. When you reach the edge of the town, turn right at a metal signpost for Garve, then, on reaching a bend in the lane, turn left, following another signpost.

② Follow track to the left of Loch Kinellan. As it bends right, keep ahead up a path beside tall broom bushes to the corner of a plantation. Here you join a larger track leading into the forest. Continue for 0.5 mile (800m) until it reaches a signpost.

③ Turn left for View Rock on a good path with green waymarkers. At View Rock, a side-path diverts to the right for the viewpoint, then re-joins. After a long descent, ignore a green path off to the left and follow green waymarkers downhill. At a forest road, go straight over beside a signpost. The path crosses two more forest roads to Contin Forest car park.

④ At the end of the car park, pick up a wide path, 'River Walk'. Where red waymarkers turn back right, keep ahead on a rougher path with deer-head markers. It bends up right beside a stream to a forest road. Turn left, signed 'Garve', and in 80 yards (73m) bear left, heading slightly downhill.

⑤ Go on for 600 yards (549m), when a small track on the left is signed 'Rogie Falls Bridge'. At its foot, cross a spectacular footbridge below the falls and turn right, upstream. The path has green waymarkers and after 0.25 mile (400m) bends left, away from the river. It crosses rocky ground to a junction. Turn up right, to Rogie Falls car park.

⑥ Leave the car park through a wooden arch and follow the green waymarkers back to the bridge. Retrace the outward route to Point ⑤ and turn sharp left up another forest road. It leads uphill to where a much fainter track crosses.

⑦ Turn right down the smaller track to pass between obstructing boulders, to a

signpost. Turn left, signed 'Strathpeffer'. After 600 yards (549m) it reaches the signpost at Point ③. Keep ahead and retrace the outward route to Point ②. Turn left on the tarred lane, which becomes a track. At Kinloch house bear right, then turn left through a kissing gate, with a second one beyond leading into a plantation with a signpost for Strathpeffer.

⑧ Follow the main path ahead until you see Strathpeffer down on the right. At the next junction, bear right down the wood edge and turn right into town. The street on the left leads past a church with a square steeple, where you turn down right to the main square.

INTO SCOTLAND'S GREAT WILDERNESS

A pleasant walk around Loch Kernsary and down the Ewe.

Inverewe Gardens, Poolewe

Distance: 6.5 miles (10.4km)
Minimum time: 2hrs 45min
Ascent/Gradient: 250ft (76m) ▲▲▲
Level of difficulty: +++
Paths: Mostly good, but one short rough, wet section, 3 stiles
Landscape: Moorland and loch side
Suggested map: OS Explorer 434 Gairloch & Loch Ewe
Start/finish: Grid reference: NG 857808
Dog friendliness: Close control on moorland and tracks carrying estate traffic
Parking: In Poolewe, just up B8057 side street
Public toilets: At start

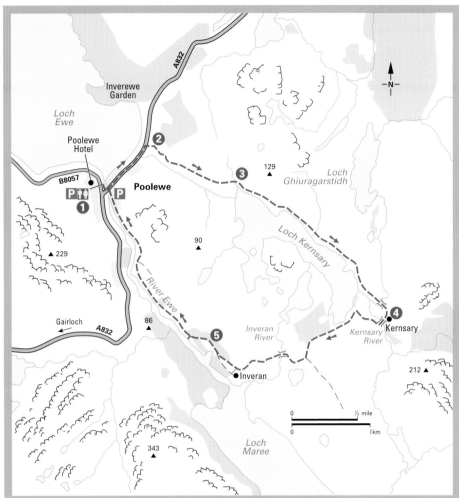

❶ A kissing gate beside the public toilets leads to a path that crosses the Marie Curie Field of Hope to the main road. Turn left to cross the bridge over the River Ewe and then head all the way through the village. At the 40mph de-restriction sign, there's a white cottage on the right. Beside it, look for a tarred trackway that has a Scottish Rights of Way Society signpost for Kernsary.

❷ Follow the track over a cattle grid to a new track that forks off to the left. After 50 yards (46m), keep ahead on a path with a wall on its left. It passes through a kissing gate into Cnoc na Lise, the Garden Hill. This has been replanted as a community wood with oak and birch trees. Another kissing gate leads out of the young wood. The good, reconstructed path runs through gorse and then under a low-voltage power line. It crosses a low spur to a fine view of Loch Kernsary and the remote, steep-sided hills of the Great Wilderness, then goes over a stream to the loch side.

❸ The path follows the left-hand shore of the loch, passing through patches of birch scrub. After a stile, near the loch head, it suddenly deteriorates, becoming a braided trod of boulder and bog. Once past the loch head, slant to the left down a meadow to find a footbridge under an oak tree. Head up, with a fence on your right, to join a track beside Kernsary farm.

❹ Turn right, through a gate. Follow the track past the farm, to a culvert crossing of the Kernsary River. This becomes a ford only after heavy rain. If needed, you will find a footbridge 70 yards (64m) upstream. After crossing, turn right on a smooth track. The new track bears left, away from Loch Kernsary towards the hollow containing Loch Maree. After the bridge over the Inveran River is a gate with a ladder stile. Signs welcoming responsible walkers (and even cyclists) reflect the principles of the Letterewe Accord. Soon come the first views of Loch Maree. The driveway of Inveran house joins from the left and the track from here is tarred.

❺ At a sign, 'Blind Corners', a green track on the left leads down to the point where the narrow loch imperceptibly becomes a wide river. Return to the main track and follow it above and then beside the River Ewe. It reaches Poolewe just beside the bridge.

The view towards Loch Maree, Poolewe

INDEX

A

Abbeydale Industrial Hamlet 254
Abbey Dore 210
Abbots Bromley 180
Abbotsbury 34
Aberdeen 326–7
Aberdulais 204
Aberfeldy 320
Aberfoyle 314
Abergele 226
Abernethy pearl 317
Aberystwyth 214–15
Abingdon 110, 137
Abinger Hammer 100
Ackworth 286
Acton Scott 216
Alcester 146
Aldeburgh 188
Aldershot 100
Alfriston 84
Alnmouth 282
Alnwick 282–3
Alresford 98
Alton 98
Alton Towers 180
Alum Bay 74
Amberley 78
Ambleside 276
Amesbury 44
Ampfield 96
Andover 96
Anglesey 223
Anglesey Abbey 154
Anstey 172
Appledore 26
Appuldurcombe 75
Arboretum 96
Arundel 78–9, 129
Ascot 108
Ashdown Forest 135
Atcham 220
Attingham Park 220
Auchenblae 343
Auckland Castle 280, 281
Auld Lang Syne 306
Avebury 48, 68
Avon Canal 106
Axbridge 38, 39
Axminster 32
Ayot St Lawrence 112
Ayr 306

B

Badby 184
Bala's Lake 242
Ballachulish 324
Bamburgh 282

Bangor 222
Bannockburn 314
Barnard Castle 269
Barnsdale Garden 174
Barnstaple 26
Barry 206
Basildon Park 106
Basingstoke 98
Bath 46–7
Battle 86, 131
Beachy Head 84, 85
Beacon Fell 288
Beauly 328
Beaumaris 223
Beer 32, 33
Belchamps 158
Belvoir Castle 175, 195
Beninbrough Hall 271
Ben Nevis 324
Berkeley Castle 50
Berkshire 108–9
Berkswell 148
Berwick 297
Berwick-upon-Tweed 283
Bexhill 86
Bideford 26, 27
Binchester Blocks 281
Birkenhead 250
Birmingham 150
Bishop's Waltham 76
Blackpool 258
Blair Atholl 320
Blakeney 192
Blantyre 308
Blenheim 110, 111
Bloomsbury 84
Bodmin 20
Bodmin Moor 24
Bodnant Garden 226
Boroughbridge 270
Boscastle 24
Bosherston 202
Bournemouth 36
Bournville 150
Bowness-on-Windermere 277, 292
Bradford 260
Bradford-on-Avon 67
Brading 74
Brancepeth 280–1
Brecon Beacons National Park 224–5, 232
Bredon Hill 219
Bridport 33
Brightlingsea 160
Brighton 80
Brimham Rocks 268
Bristol 46, 47
Broads 169
Brodick 304

Brontë Moors 287
Broughton 336
Budleigh Salterton 30
Buildwas Abbey 220
Bure Valley Railway 169
Burgh Castle 168
Burgh Island 57
Burghley House 174
Burnham 108
Burrough Hill 172
Bury St Edmunds 164–5
Buttermere 291

C

Cadburys 40
Caerlaverock 302
Caerlaverock Castle 334
Caerleon 206
Caernarfon 223
Caerphilly 207
Caister-on-Sea 168
Caithness Glass 317
Caldey Island 202
Caldon Canal 181
Caledonian Canal 329
Calf of Man 275
Callander 314
Calstock 22
Cambridge 154–5
Cannock Chase 181
Canterbury 92
Cape Cornwall 16
Cardiff 206, 207
Cardigan 208
Cardigan Bay 208–9
Carew Castle 202
Carisbrooke 74, 75
Carlisle 278
Carnforth 264
Castell Coch 234
Castell Henllys 208
Castell Y Bere 239
Castle Acre 166
Castle Donington 182
Castle Fraser 327
Castle Hedingham 158
Castle Rising 166
Castletown 274
Cathedral Close 133
Cavendish 158
Ceres 318
Cerne Abbas 34, 65
Charlecote Park 146
Chartwell 88
Cheddar 38
Cheddleton 180
cheeses 38–9
Cheltenham 50
Chesil Beach 34

Chester 228–9
Chesterfield 285
Chew Magna 47
Chichester 79
Chilham 92–3, 136
Chillingham Castle 282
Christchurch 36
Church Stretton 216
Cilgerran 208
Cinque Ports 90
Cirencester 50–1
Cistercians 263
Clapham 266
Clare 158
Claremont 102
Clava Cairns 329
Clee Hills 216–17
Clent Hills 150
Clifton 47
Cliveden 108
Coalbrookdale 220–1, 241
Coatbridge 308
Coates 176
Cockley Cley 166
Coggeshall 160
Coire Fhionn Lochan 305
Colchester 160–1
Coleford 52
Colwyn Bay 226
Colyton 33
Combe Martin 26
Comberton 218
Conisbrough 254
Coniston 276
Conwy 226–7
Cookham 108
Corby 152
Corfe Castle 36
Cornwall 16, 18–19
Corpach 324
Corrie 304
Cottesmore 175
Country Park 250
Coventry 148–9
Cowes 74
Coxwold 270
Cramond 310
Craster 282–3
Crathes Castle 327
Craven Arms 217
Cregneash Village Folk Museum 275
Criccieth Castle 243
Cricklade 69
Croxteth Hall 250
Croyde 26–7
Cullerlie Stone Circle 327
Culloden 329
Cumbria 276
Cupar 318

D

Dales 266–7, 293
Danebury 97
Dartmoor 22–3, 58
Dawlish resort 30
Deal 90
Dean Forest 52–3
Dedham 162
Delphs 177
Denby 182
Denman's Garden 79
Derby 182
Devil's Bridge 215
Devil's Dyke 130
Devizes 48, 49
Devon 59
Ditchling 80–1
Doddington 176
Dodman Point 18
Doone Valley 60
Dorchester 34–5
Dorset 32–3, 63, 66
Dorstone 210
Douglas 275
Doune 314
Dover 90
The Downs 78–9, 85
Downton Castle 237
Drum Castle 327
Dudley 150–1
Dumfries 302
Dunaskin 335
Dunblane 314
Dundee 318–19
Dunham Massey Hall 252
Dunkeld 320
Durham 280, 281
Duxford 155
Dyfed 203
Dyrham 47
Dysynni Valley 239

E

Eastbourne 85
Eastwood 182
Ecclefechan 302
Edenbridge 88
Eden Project 21
Edinburgh 310–11, 317, 337
Egdon Heath 64
Elcho Castle 316
Eleanor Crosses 153
Elvaston Castle 182
Ely 154
Emsworth 79
English Riviera 31
Erwarton 163
Eton 108

Euston Hall 165
Evesham 146
Exeter 30
Exmoor 27
Exmouth 30–1

F

Fairhaven Garden Trust 168
Falkland 316
Falmouth 18
Fareham 76
Farne Islands 283
Farnham 100–1
Faversham 93
Felixstowe 163
Fenlands 154–5, 185
Finchale Priory 281
Fishbourne 79
Fishguard 208
fishing 19
Flint 228, 229
Folkestone 90
Forest of Bowland 264, 265
Forest of Dean 52–3
Forth Bridges 310
Fort William 324
Fossdyke 176
fossils 33, 173
Fountains Abbey 268
Fowey 20–1
free trade 32
Freshwater 128
Fritton 168–9

G

Gainsborough 177
Garlogie 327
Gilsland 278
Glasgow 308–9, 339
Glastonbury 39
Glen Coe 324, 325, 342
Glens 304
Gloucester 50–1
Glynde 81
golf 319, 331
Goodrich Castle 52
Goodwood 79
Gordale Scar 267
Goring 106
Gosport 77
Gower Peninsula 204
Grange-over-Sands 264
Grasmere 276
Great Comberton 218
Great Malvern 218
Great Torrington 27
Great Yarmouth 168, 169
Greenhead 278

Gretna Green 302
Grimes Graves 165
Grizedale Forest Park 276
Guildford 101

H

Hadleigh 163
Hadrian's Wall 278
Halstead 161
Haltwhistle 278–9
Hambledon 77
Ham Hill 41
Ham House 102
Hamilton 309
Hampshire 76–7, 96–7, 98–9, 105
Hampton Court 103
Hampton Lucy 149
Hardraw Force 267
Hardwick 286
Harewood House 260
Harrogate 260
Harwich 163
Haslemere 101
Hastings 86
Hatfield 112
Hawes 267
Hawkshead 276–7
Headbourne Worthy 97
Heale Garden 44
Helford Estuary 18
Helmsley 270
Hemingford Grey 154
Henley-on-Thames 108
Hereford 210, 211
Herstmonceux 85
Hever 88
Hexham 295
Hidcote Manor Garden 146
Highclere Castle 106
Hillier Gardens 96
Hindhead 101
Holdenby House 152
Holme Pierrepont 182–3
Holyhead 223
Holy Island 282
Honiton 31
Horseshoe Pass 228
Horsey 169
Horsey Mere 169, 193
Hove 80

I

Ickworth House 165
Ide Hill 88
Ightham 89
Ilfracombe 27
Ilkeston 183

Ilmington 146
Inveraray 341
Inverlochy Castle 324–5
Inverness 329
Ipswich 162, 163
Ironbridge 220–1
Irvine 306
Isle of Arran 304–5
Isle of Man 274–5
Isle of Wight 74–5, 105
Isles of Scilly 16
Itchen Valley 133

J

Jervaulx Abbey 268
Jodrell Bank Centre 252

K

Kedleston Hall 183
Kelmarsh Hall 152
Kendal 277
Kenilworth 149
Kenmore 320
Kennet Canal 106–7
Kent 92–3, 104–5, 136
Kentwell Hall 158–9
Kettering 152
Kettlewell 267
Kew 103
Kifsgate Court Gardens 146
Killiecrankie 320
Kilmarnock 306–7
Kilpeck Church 210
King's Lynn 166–7
Kingston Lacy 36
Kingston upon Thames 103
Kinlochleven 325
Kinross 316
Kinver Edge 151
Kirkhill 328
Kirknewton 296
Kirkpatrick-Fleming 303
Kirkstall Abbey 260
Knaresborough 260
Knebworth 112
Knole 89

L

Lake District 215, 276–7
Lake of Menteith 314–15
Lamport Hall 152
Lancashire 258–9
Lancaster 264–5
Land's End 17
Lanercost Priory 279
Launceston 24
Lavenham 159
Laxey 275

Layer Marney Tower 161
Leamington Spa 149
Ledbury 211
Leeds 260–1
Leeds Castle 88
Leicester 172–3
Leighton Hall 265
Leighton Moss Reserve 264
Leuchars 319
Levington 163
Lewes 81
Lichfield 189
limestone 289
Lincoln 177
Lincolnshire 176–7, 191, 197
Little Comberton 218
Liverpool 251
Lizard Peninsula 18
Llanberis 223
Llandudno 227
Llanfair PG 222
Llangollen 228
Llanthony 235
Llyn Tegid 242
Loch an Eilein 344
Loche Linnhe 325
Loch Ewe 347
Loch Katrine 315
Loch Kernsary 347
Lochmaben 303
Loch Ness 328–9
Lochranza 304–5
Loch Tummel 320
London 114–27, 139, 172
Long Melford 159
Long Mynd 217
Looe 21
Lostwithiel 21
Loughborough 173
Ludlow 217
Lulworth Cove 37
Luton 112–13
Lyddington 175
Lydford 22
Lydney 52–3
Lyme Park 284
Lyme Regis 33
Lytham St Anne's 259

M

Mackworth 194
Madingley 154–5
Maiden Castle 36
Malham 267
Malham Cove 289
malt whiskies 326, 331
Malvern Hills 218–19
Manchester 252–3
Manningtree 161

Manorbier 203
Manx Railways 274
Mapledurham 106–7
Marble Hill 102
Margate 91
Markeaton 194
Marlborough 48
Martin Mere 259
Masham 268
Massinghams 167
Mauchline 307
Medway Towns 93
Melton Mowbray 173
Menai Bridge 223
Menai Strait 222–3
Mendip Hills 38
Mevagissey 18
Mid Thundergay 305
Milford Haven 230
Milton Keynes 141
Minions 21
Ministry of Defence 77
Minster Lovell 111
Mistley 161
Mold 228
Montacute 40
Montgomery Canal 240
Morecambe 265
Morecambe Bay 264–5
Motherwell 309
Mottisfont 97
Mount Gilbert 221
Mountsorrel 173
Mousehole 17
Muchelney 40
Much Marcle 211
Much Wenlock 221
Mumbles 204
Mylor 18
Mynydd Preseli 208–9

N

Naseby 152
National Parks of Wales 224–5
Neath 204
Needles 74
Neptune's Staircase 324
Nevern 209
New Abbey 303
Newborough Warren 223
Newbury 107
Newcastle Emlyn 209
Newcastle upon Tyne 281
New Forest 94–5, 132
Newport 74, 207
Nidderdale 268
Northampton 152–3
North Devon 59
Northington Grange 98–9

North York Moors 272–3
Norwich 168–9
Noss Mayo 22
Nottingham 172, 182–3

O

Oakham 175
Odiham 99
Offa's Dyke 229
Old Basing 99
Old Sarum 44
Ord Ban 344
Orleans House 102
Osborne estate 74
Ossian's Hall 321
Otley 261
Ottery St Mary 31
Oxburgh Hall 167
Oxford 111
Oxwich 205

P

Padstow 24, 25
Painshill 102
Painswick 51
Paisley 309
Pateley Bridge 268
Peak District 256–7
Peel 275
Pembridge 211
Pembroke 203
Pembrokeshire 209, 225
Penarth 207
Pennine Way 266, 267
Penshurst 89
Pentire Point 24
Pentre Ifan 209
Penzance 17
Pershore 218
Perth 316–17
Perthshire Highlands 320–1
Peterlee 281
Pevensey 85
Pictish stones 320
Pilgrims' Way 92
Pitlochry 321
Plas Newydd 223
Plymouth 22
Polperro 21
Pontcysyllte Aqueduct 228–9
Poole 37
Poolewe 347
Portchester 77
Porthcurno 17, 54
Port Isaac 25
Portland 35
Portreath 55
Portree Bay 345
Portsmouth 77

Port Sunlight 250
Port Talbot 204
Potteries 180–1
Powis Castle 240
prehistoric stones 304
Prescot 251
Prestonpans 311
Prinknash 51
Pumlumon Fawr 215
Purbeck Stone 36–7

Q

Quantocks 27, 62
Quarry Bank Mill 252
Queen Elizabeth Country
    Park 77
Queensferry 311

R

Rame Peninsula 23
Reading 107
Reynoldston 204
Rhossili 205
Rhuddlan Castle 227, 245
Rhyl 227
Richmond 103, 268–9
Ridgeway 48
Rievaulx 270–1
Ripon 269
River Dee 228–9
River Devon 316
River Irthing 278
River Mersey 250–1
River Wye 53
Rochester 140
Rogie Falls 346
Romsey 96, 97
Roseberry Topping 294
Roseland Peninsula 18–19
Roslin Glen 338
Ross-on-Wye 211
Rotherham 254
Rother Valley Country Park
    254
Rothiemurchus Forest 344
Rousham House 110
Royal Shakespeare Company
    146
Rumps 24
Ruthwell 303
Rutland 174
Rutland Water 175, 190
Rye 87

S

Saddleworth Moor 252
St Albans 113
St Andrews 318, 319

St Anthony's 56
St Austell 21
St Dogmaels 209
St Fagans 207
St Govan's Chapel 203
St Ives 17
St John's 275
St Mawes 18
Salisbury 44–5
Sandown 74–5
Sandringham 166
Sandwich 91
Saundersfoot 203
Saxon Church 219
Scilly Isles 16
Scone Palace 317
Seaham 281
Seaton 33
Selborne 98, 99
Settle 267
Sevenoaks 89
Seven Sisters 84
Shambles 271
Shanklin 74–5
Shaugh Prior 23
Sheffield 254–5
Shepton Mallet 39
Sherborne 40, 41
Sherwood Forest 182, 196
Shipston on Stour 147
Shrewsbury 220, 221
Shropshire 216–17
Shugborough Estate 180
Sidmouth 31
Silbury Hill 49
Silchester 107
Sissinghurst Castle Gardens 89
ski villages 254
Slimbridge 51
Snowdon 244
Snowdonia 224
Solway Merses 334
Somerset 66
Somerton 41, 169
Soudley 53
South Downs 85
Southport 259
South Queensferry 311
Speech House 53
Speke Hall 251
Stafford 180
Stamford 175
Standsted Park 79
Stanton St John 111
Stirling 315, 340
Stoke-on-Trent 180–1
Stokesay Castle 217
Stonehenge 44, 45
Stone of Scone 317
Stourbridge 151

Strata Florida Abbey 215
Stratfield Saye 107
Stratford 146–7
Stratford-upon-Avon 147
Strathpeffer 346
Streatley 106
Street 39
Strumble 231
Sudbury 159
Sudeley Castle 50
Surrey 100–1
Sussex 80–1, 84–5, 105
Sutton Bank 271
Swaffham 167
Swansea 204, 205
Swindon 49
Symonds Yat 53

T

Talkin Tarn 279
Tarr Steps 61
Tatton Park 253
Tavistock 23
The Tay 317, 318–19
Tehidy 55
Telford 221
Temple Newsam House 261
Tenby 203
Tenterden 87
Tewkesbury 218, 219
Thames River 69, 102–3,
   108–9, 110–11, 124–5, 126–7
Thames Valley 106–7
Thanet Resorts 91
Thaxted 186
tin mining 16
Tintagel 25
Tintern Abbey 53
Torksey 177
Toy's Hill 88
Trelissick 19
Trent and Mersey Canal 183
Triangular Lodge 153
Troon 307
Troutbeck 277
Truro 19
Tunbridge Wells 89
Turville 138

U

Ufton Fields 149
Upton upon Severn 218
Urban Heritage Park 253
Urquhart Castle 329

V

Vale of Evesham 146–7
Vale of Rheidol 214–15

Vale of the White Horse 111
Valle Crucis Abbey 229
Veryan 19
The Vyne 99

W

Wallops 97
Wandlebury 155
Wareham 37
Warkworth 283
Warwick 149
Waterperry 111
Waverley 134
Weald and Downland Museum
   79
Weem 321
Welland Valley 175
Wellesbourne 147
Wellingborough 153
Wells 39
Welsh Marches 212–213
Welwyn Garden City 113
Wenlock Edge 217
Westdean 85
Westerham 89
West Highland Way 325
West Kennet Long Barrow 49
Weston Park 181
West Stow 165
Wetheral 279
Weymouth 35
Whipsnade Zoo 113
whiskies 326, 331
white chalk horses 49
Whitstable 93
Wicken Fen 155
Wilderhope Manor 217
Wilton 45
Wiltshire 66
Wimborne Minster 37
Winchelsea 87
Winchester 97, 133
Windermere 277, 292
Windsor 109
wines 38–9
Wing 175
Wolds 197
Wolverhampton 151
Woodbridge 163
Woodhenge 44
Woodstock 111
Wookey Hole 39
Woolpit 165
Worcester 218–19
Worcester City 238
Wrekin (Mount Gilbert) 221
Wrexham 229
Wroxall 75
Wroxeter 221
Wye Valley 210–11

Y

Yarmouth 75, 168, 169
Yeavering Bell 296
Yeovil 41
York 270–1, 290
Yorkshire Dales 266–7

ACKNOWLEDGEMENTS

The Automobile Association would like to thank the following photographers, companies and picture libraries for their assistance in the preparation of this book.

Abbreviations for the picture credits are as follows – (t) top; (b) bottom; (c) centre; (l) left; (r) right; (AA) AA World Travel Library.

2/3 AA/S Watkins; 10/11 AA/D Hall; 12/13 AA/J Wood; 14 AA/J Wood; 16 AA/P Baker; 17t AA/C Jones; 17c AA/J Wood; 17b AA/J Wood; 18l AA/R Tenison; 18r AA/R Moss; 19 AA/C Jones; 20 AA/J Wood; 21t AA/J Wood; 21b AA/R Tenison; 22 AA/G Edwardes; 23 AA/J Wood; 24 AA/J Wood; 25l AA/J Wood; 25r AA/R Tenison; 26l Photolibrary.com; 26r Photolibrary.com; 27 David Hughes/Robert Harding; 28l Mary Evans Picture Library; 28c Mary Evans Picture Library; 28r © Illustrated London News Ltd/Mary Evans Picture Library; 29t AA/C Jones; 29c AA/H Williams; 29b AA/R Ireland; 30l AA/N Hicks; 30r AA/N Hicks; 31 AA/N Hicks; 32 AA/N Hicks; 33l Photolibrary.com; 33r Ken Wilson/Robert Harding; 33b AA/A Lawson; 34 AA/R Newton; 35l AA/P Baker; 35r AA/M Jourdan; 36t AA/A Burton; 36b AA/A Burton; 37 AA/M Jourdan; 38 AA/J Tims; 39l AA/J Tims; 39r AA/J Tims; 39b AA/J Tims; 40 AA/S Day; 41t AA/J Tims; 41b Photolibrary.com; 42l AA/R Moss; 42r AA/A Baker; 43t AA/J Tims; 43b Photolibrary.com; 44t AA/M Moody; 44b AA/J Tims; 45t AA/J Tims; 45b AA/J Tims; 46l AA/C Jones; 46r AA/M Birkitt; 47t AA/S Day; 47b AA/S Day; 48 AA/M Moody; 49t AA/M Moody; 49b AA/M Moody; 50t AA/S Lund; 50b AA/F Stephenson; 51 AA/J Wyand; 52 AA/H Williams; 53l AA/A J Hopkins; 53r Photolibrary.com; 54 AA/R Moss; 56 AA/H Williams; 58t AA/A Lawson; 60 Photolibrary.com; 61 AA/W Voysey; 62 AA/J Tims; 63 AA/M Jourdan; 64 AA/R Ireland; 65 AA/C Jones; 66 AA/M Moody; 67 AA/M Moody; 68t AA/M Moody; 68b AA/M Moody; 69 AA/D Hall; 70/71 AA/J Miller; 72 AA/M Moody; 74 AA/S McBride; 75c AA/A Burton; 75b AA/A Burton; 76l AA/S Day; 76r Photolibrary.com; 77l AA/A Burton; 77r AA/D Croucher; 78 AA/J Miller; 79l AA/J Miller; 79r AA/J Miller; 80t AA/J Miller; 80b AA/J Miller; 81t AA/J Miller; 81b AA/M Busselle; 82 Photolibrary.com; 83t Photolibrary.com; 83b Photolibrary.com; 84t AA/M Busselle; 84b Photolibrary.com; 85t AA/C Coe; 85b AA/D Forss; 86t AA/J Miller; 86b AA/J Miller; 87t AA/C Sawyer; 87b AA/D Noble; 88t AA/M Busselle; 88b AA/M Busselle; 89t AA/N Setchfield; 89b AA/N Setchfield; 90t AA/N Setchfield; 90b AA/M Busselle; 91t AA/M Busselle; 91b AA/M Busselle; 92l AA/M Busselle; 92r AA/N Setchfield; 93 Jean Brooks/Robert Harding; 94l AA/P Baker; 94r AA/A J Hopkins; 95t AA/A Burton; 95b AA/A Burton; 96l AA/M Moody; 96r AA/M Moody; 97 AA/M Moody; 98 AA/M Moody; 99t AA/M Moody; 99c AA/M Moody; 99b AA/M Moody; 100 AA/J Tims; 101t AA/D Forss; 101c AA/J Tims; 101b AA/J Tims; 102t The National Trust Photolibrary/Alamy; 102b AA/R Turpin; 103t AA/N Setchfield; 103b AA/N Setchfield; 104 AA/D Forss; 105t AA/D Forss; 105b AA/M Moody; 106t Photolibrary.com; 106b AA/M Moody; 107 AA/V P Otter; 108l AA/J Tims; 108r AA/J Tims; 108b AA/D Forss; 109 AA/J Tims; 110 AA/A Lawson; 111l AA/C Jones; 111r Photolibrary.com; 112l AA/M Birkitt; 112r AA/M Moody; 113l AA/M Birkitt; 113r Photolibrary.com; 114 AA/R Mort; 115l AA/J Tims; 115c AA/J Tims; 115r AA/J Tims; 116 AA/J Tims; 117tl AA/R Turpin; 117tc AA/J Tims; 117tr AA/M Jourdan; 117bl AA/M Jourdan; 117bc AA/M Jourdan; 117br AA/C Sawyer; 118l Photolibrary.com; 118r AA/J Tims; 119tl AA/J Tims; 119tr AA/J Tims; 119bl AA/J Tims; 119br AA/J Tims; 120c AA/C Sawyer; 120bl AA/N Setchfield; 120br AA/J Tims; 121tl AA/J Tims; 121tr AA/J Tims; 121b AA/J Tims; 122tl AA/N Setchfield; 122tr AA/N Setchfield; 122bl AA/J Tims; 122br AA/J Tims; 123tl AA/R Turpin; 123cl AA/N Setchfield; 123cr AA/J Tims; 123b AA/S Montgomery; 124t AA/N Setchfield; 124b AA/J Tims; 125tl AA/N Setchfield; 125tr AA/P Kenward; 125bl AA/J Tims; 125br AA/J Tims; 126t AA/P Baker; 126b AA/J Miller; 127tl AA/S & O Mathews; 127tr AA/R Strange; 127c AA/N Setchfield; 127b AA/D Forss; 129 AA/D Forss; 130t AA/J Miller; 130b AA/J Miller; 132 AA/A Burton; 133 AA/S Day; 134t AA/J Tims; 134b AA/J Tims; 136t Photolibrary.com; 136b AA/D Noble; 137 Photolibrary.com; 138t Photolibrary.com; 138b G R Richardson/Robert Harding; 139 AA/N Setchfield; 140 AA/N Setchfield; 141 AA/M Moody; 142/143 AA/C Jones; 144 AA/C Jones; 146tl AA/C Jones; 146tr AA/C Jones; 146b AA/S Day; 147 AA/D Hall; 148l AA/C Jones; 148r AA/C Jones; 149t AA/C Jones; 149b AA/C Jones; 150t AA/C Jones; 150b Illustrated London News; 151l AA/C Jones; 151r AA/C Jones; 152t Angela Hampton Picture Library/Alamy; 152b charistoone-stock/Alamy; 153t Colin Underhill/Alamy; 153b Graham Oliver/Alamy; 154t AA/T Mackie; 154c AA/C Coe; 155 AA/T Mackie; 156l Keystone/Getty Images; 156r Popperfoto/Getty Images; 157t AA/M Moody; 157b AA/J Tims; 158l Angela Hampton Picture Library/Alamy; 158r Tom Mackie/Alamy; 159l AA/T Mackie; 159r Mike Booth/Alamy; 160l ©NTPL/D M Nicholson; 160r Rodger Tamblyn/Alamy; 161l AA/N Setchfield; 161r Quentin Bargate/Alamy; 162 AA/T Mackie; 163t AA/T Mackie; 163b AA/T Mackie; 164 Robert Estall photo agency/Alamy; 165tl AA/T Mackie; 165tr ©NTPL/Robert Morris; 165b Sid Frisby/Alamy; 166l Mike Booth/Alamy; 166r Tom Mackie/Alamy; 167 The National Trust Photolibrary/Alamy; 168 jon gibbs/Alamy; 169l Mike Booth/Alamy; 169r AA/T Mackie; 170l Susan & Allan Parker/Alamy; 170r Alistair Dick/Alamy; 171tl Agripicture Images/Alamy; 171tr Sylvia Cordaiy Photo Library Ltd/Alamy; 171c David Chapman/Alamy; 171b Chris Mattison/FLPA; 172 Graham Oliver/Alamy; 173t Howard Harrison/Alamy; 173b geogphotos/Alamy; 174l Robert Bird/Alamy; 174r AA/M Birkitt; 175t Dave Porter/Alamy; 175b AA/R Newton; 176l AA/T Mackie; 176r Tommy (Louth)/Alamy; 177 AA/T Mackie; 178l Elmtree Images/Alamy; 178r AA/M Moody; 179t AA/M Moody; 179cr nagelestock.com/Alamy; 179cb David Ball/Alamy; 179b AA/M Birkitt; 180l Paul Gapper/Alamy; 180r John Keates/Alamy; 181t The Fine Art Picture Library/Alamy; 181b AA/C Jones; 182l AKP Photos/Alamy; 182r AA/P Baker; 183 The National Trust Photolibrary/Alamy; 184 AA/N Channer; 185 Photolibrary.com; 186 AA/M Birkitt; 187 Jeremy Hoare/Alamy; 188t AA/T Mackie; 188b AA/T Mackie; 189 AA/J Beazley; 190t Photolibrary.com; 190b Photolibrary.com; 191 AA/D Forss; 192 AA/T Mackie; 193 AA/T Mackie; 194 UK City Images/Alamy; 195 Tom Mackie/Alamy; 196 AA/R Newton; 197 Photolibrary.com; 198/199 AA/S Lewis; 200 AA/I Burgum; 202t AA/M Moody; 202c AA/C Warren; 202b AA/M Moody; 203 AA/C Warren; 204t AA/C Jones; 204c AA/C Jones; 205t AA/C Jones; 205b AA/I Burgum; 206 AA/N Jenkins; 207tl AA/I Burgum; 207tr Photolibrary.com; 207b AA/I Burgum; 208t AA/C Warren; 208b AA/I Burgum; 209 AA/I Burgum; 210t AA/C Jones; 210b AA/C Jones; 211 AA/C Jones; 212 AA/T D Timms; 213tl AA/C Jones; 213tr AA/R Newton; 213b AA/C Jones; 214 AA/C Molyneux; 215t AA/N Jenkins; 215c AA/N Jenkins; 216 Pilchards/Alamy; 217t AA/I Burgum; 217c AA/C Jones; 217b AA/M Short; 218tl AA/M Moody; 218tr AA/C Jones; 218c AA/M Moody; 219 AA/C Jones; 220 AA/M Hayward; 221t AA/C Jones; 221b Loraine Wilson/Robert Harding; 222 AA/I Burgum; 223t AA/R Weir; 223b AA/H Williams; 224 AA/C Jones; 225t AA/I Burgum; 225b AA/C Warren; 226 AA/N Jenkins; 227r Steve Unsworth/Alamy; 227b AA/C Jones; 228 AA/C Jones; 229t AA/D Santillo; 229b AA/N Jenkins; 230 AA/I Burgum; 231 AA/N Jenkins; 232 Photolibrary.com; 233 Photolibrary.com; 234 AA/H Williams; 237 AA/N Hicks; 238t AA/C Jones; 238b AA/M Moody; 239 AA/M Allwood-Coppin; 240 AA/N Jenkins; 241 AA/J Welsh; 242 AA/N Jenkins; 243 AA/P Aithie; 245t AA/R Eames; 245b © Paul Hobson/naturepl.com; 246/247 AA/T Mackie; 248 AA/J Beazley; 250 AA/S Day; 251tl Photolibrary.com; 251tr AA/S Day; 251b Photolibrary.com; 252l Photolibrary.com; 252r Photolibrary.com; 253t Peter Richardson/Robert Harding; 253b Photolibrary.com; 254t AA/T Woodcock; 254b AA/S Day; 255tl Photolibrary.com; 255tr Photolibrary.com; 256l Photolibrary.com; 256r Photolibrary.com; 257t AA/T Mackie; 257c AA/J Beazley; 257b AA/R Newton; 258l AA/C Jones; 258r AA/C Jones; 259t AA/C Jones; 259b AA/C Jones; 260l AA/L Whitwam; 260r Photolibrary.com; 261t Photolibrary.com; 261b Photolibrary.com; 262 Photolibrary.com; 263t AA/E A Bowness; 263b AA/M Kipling; 264t AA/R Czaja; 264b AA/S Day; 265t AA/J Beazley; 265b Photolibrary.com; 266 AA/A Baker; 266tl AA/T Mackie; 266tr AA/H Williams; 266b AA/S & O Mathews; 268l AA/T Mackie; 268r AA/T Mackie; 269t AA/C Lees; 269b AA/T Mackie; 270t AA/M Moody; 270b AA/M Kipling; 271t AA/M Kipling; 271b AA/C Jones; 272tl AA/M Kipling; 272tr AA/C Molyneux; 272b AA/M Kipling; 273t AA/P Wilson; 273b AA/R Newton; 274 Photolibrary.com; 275tl Photolibrary.com; 275tr Photolibrary.com; 275b Photolibrary.com; 276l AA/T Mackie; 276r AA/S Day; 277 AA/A Mockford & N Bonetti; 278tl AA/R Coulam; 278tr AA/R Coulam; 278b AA/R Coulam; 279l AA/R Coulam; 279r AA/R Coulam; 280 AA/R Coulam; 281tl AA/C Lees; 281tr AA/R Coulam; 281b Photolibrary.com; 282l AA/R Coulam; 282r AA/A J Hopkins; 283t AA/R Coulam; 283b AA/R Coulam; 284 AA/J Mottershaw; 285t AA/D Hall; 285b AA/J Wood; 286 AA/J Morrison; 289 AA/T Mackie; 290 AA/L Whitwam; 291t AA/T Mackie; 291b AA/E A Bowness; 292 AA/A Mockford & N Bonetti; 293t AA/T Mackie; 293b AA/T Mackie; 294t AA/M Kipling; 294b AA/M Kipling; 295t AA/R Coulam; 295b AA/C Lees; 296 AA/R Coulam; 297t AA/J Beazley; 297b AA/J Beazley; 298/299 AA/M Hamblin; 300 AA/S Anderson; 302t AA/M Alexander; 302b AA/S Anderson; 303 AA/D Hardley; 304t AA/K Paterson; 304b Photolibrary.com; 305t © Pete Cairns/naturepl.com; 305c © Steve Knell/naturepl.com; 305b © Simon King/naturepl.com; 306t AA/S Anderson; 306b AA/K Paterson; 307t AA/K Paterson; 307c AA/S Anderson; 308 Photolibrary.com; 309tl AA/S Whitehorne; 309tr AA/S Whitehorne; 309c Plinthpics/Alamy; 309b AA/K Paterson; 310t AA/J Smith; 310b AA/K Paterson; 311tl AA/J Smith; 311tr AA/J Smith; 312 AA/M Hamblin; 313t AA/M Hamblin; 313c © Ian McCarthy/naturepl.com; 313b AA/M Hamblin; 314l AA/D W Robertson; 314r AA/J Smith; 314b AA/S Day; 315c AA/S Day; 315b AA/D W Robertson; 316l AA/S Whitehorne; 316r AA/S Day; 317t Antiques & Collectables/Alamy; 317b AA/J Smith; 318t AA/S Day; 318b AA/K Paterson; 319tl AA/A Baker; 319tr AA/M Taylor; 319b AA/R Weir; 320t AA/S Day; 320b AA/J Smith; 321bl AA/S Day; 321br Photolibrary.com; 322l AA/A Baker; 322r AA/S Whitehorne; 333l AA/R Weir; 333r AA/J Beazley; 324l AA/S Anderson; 324r AA/S Day; 325t AA/S Anderson; 325b AA/J Carney; 326l Photolibrary.com; 326r AA/E Ellington; 327tl AA; 327tr AA/R Weir; 327b Patrick Dieudonne/Robert Harding; 328 Phil Crean/Alamy; 329tl AA/J Smith; 329tr AA/S Whitehorne; 329c AA/R Weir; 329b AA/J Smith; 330l AA/J Smith; 330r AA/S Whitehorne; 331t AA/J Henderson; 331b AA/S Anderson; 332t AA/S Anderson; 332bl AA; 332br AA/R Elliott; 333t AA/S Whitehorne; 333c AA/S Whitehorne; 333b AA/S Whitehorne; 334 AA/M Adelman; 335t AA/A Burton; 335b AA/A Burton; 336t AA/C Lees; 336b AA/C Lees; 337t AA/D Corrance; 337b AA; 338t AA/M Alexander; 338b AA/R Elliott; 339 Photolibrary.com; 340 AA/S Whitehorne; 341t AA/S Whitehorne; 342 AA/J Henderson; 343t Simon Price/Alamy; 343b © Simon Price/Alamy; 344t AA/J Smith; 344b AA/J Smith; 345t AA/K Paterson; 345b © David Kjaer/naturepl.com; 346 AA/J Smith; 347t AA/S Whitehorne; 347b AA/J Henderson

Every effort has been made to trace the copyright holders, and we apologise in advance for any accidental errors. We would be happy to apply any corrections in the following edition of this publication.